MYSTE
MARVELS
MIRACLES

HEART TOUCHED BY THE PASSION. The Augustinian mystic, St. Clare of Montefalco, was graced by an apparition of Our Lord in which He said to her, "I have sought a place in the world where I might plant My Cross, and have found no better site than your heart." The Saint's heart, removed after her death, revealed clearly distinguishable symbols of Our Lord's Passion.

MYSTERIES MARVELS MIRACLES

IN THE LIVES OF THE SAINTS

By

Joan Carroll Cruz

"I will show wonders in the heaven above and signs on the earth beneath."—Acts 2:19

TAN Books
Charlotte, North Carolina

OTHER BOOKS BY THE AUTHOR

Miraculous Images of Our Lord
Miraculous Images of Our Lady
Secular Saints
Prayers and Heavenly Promises
The Incorruptibles
Eucharistic Miracles
Relics
Desires of Thy Heart

Nihil Obstat: Rev. Stanley P. Klores, S.T.D.
                  Censor Librorum

Imprimatur: ✠ Most Rev. Francis B. Schulte
                  Archbishop of New Orleans
                  June 21, 1996

The Nihil Obstat and Imprimatur are the Church's declarations that a work is free from error in matters of faith and morals. It in no way implies that the Church endorses the contents of the work.

Cover Picture: *The Mystical Marriage of St. Catherine of Siena*, by A. Franchi. Used by arrangement with B. N. Marconi, Genoa, Italy.

Library of Congress Catalog Card No.: 96-60581

ISBN: 978-0-89555-541-0

Printed and bound in the United States of America.

TAN Books
Charlotte, North Carolina
www.TANBooks.com
2013

"He that believeth in me, the works that I do, he also shall do; and greater than these shall he do."

—*John* 14:12

CONTENTS

Author's Note ix

Introduction xi

—Part I—

THE MIRACULOUS IN THE LIVES OF THE SAINTS

1. Bilocation 1
2. Levitation 19
3. The Odor of Sanctity 49
4. The Odor of Sin 62
5. Mystical Hearts 66
6. Miraculous Transport 87
7. Money Mysteriously Provided 104
8. Multiplication of Food 116
9. Mystical Marriage and Heavenly Jewelry 141
10. Miraculous Protection 156
11. Lights and Rays of Love 159
12. Fire and Heat of Love 173
13. Prophecy 186
14. Invisibility 206
15. Saints Who Knew the Date of Their Death 210
16. The Stigmata 216
17. The Gift of Tongues 239
18. Mystical Fasts 246
19. Mystical Knowledge 258

—Part II—

THE MIRACULOUS BODIES OF THE
SAINTS AFTER DEATH

20. The Incorruptibles 283
21. Saints' Bodies Transformed, Moved or
    Weighted After Death 298
22. Lights about the Bodies of Saints 318
23. Blood Miracles 321
24. Voices of the Dead 343

25. Death Warnings and Other Signals from the Dead 352
26. Manna.. 358
27. Perfume from the Sainted Bodies of the Dead 382

—Part III—
THE SAINTS AND THEIR INFLUENCE OVER NATURE

28. Earth, Sea and Sky 399
29. Rain, Snow and Ice.. 405
30. Plants, Fruit and Flowers 420
31. Birds, Bees and Bugs 433
32. Animals, Reptiles and Creatures of the Sea 472
33. Wells, Springs and Holy Water... 496
34. The Saints and Fire.. 517

—Part IV—
MARVELS OF EVERY SORT

35. Marvels of Every Sort... 527

Notes 555
Index 573
Bibliography 577

AUTHOR'S NOTE

Since the very beginning of my work I seem to have had a great interest in the wonders related in the lives of the Saints. This interest is revealed in the many marvels mentioned in my first non-fiction book, *The Incorruptibles*. The subject of phenomena also found its way, in a large part, into my other works: *Relics, Eucharistic Miracles, Miraculous Images of Our Lady* and *Miraculous Images of Our Lord*. This present volume, therefore, is a culmination of my interest in this subject of phenomena.

From the outset it should be noted that this is not a textbook study or a detailed analysis of phenomena. An introduction is given for each chapter, followed by interesting examples of the phenomenon. Once again I serve as a reporter—telling of many wonders, but leaving all to the judgment and opinion of the reader.

Because of the interesting cases mentioned here, my work has been a pleasure and a most interesting occupation. I pray it will prove to be as interesting to the reader.

It is also my prayer that the reader will derive a greater appreciation of the wonders of God, who has proved by so many miracles His love for His children, His concern for their welfare and His ever-abiding willingness to provide aid in times of distress.

A line from Scripture reads: "I will show wonders in the heaven above and signs on the earth beneath." (*Acts* 2:19). Through His sainted children, God indeed has worked a great variety of signs and wonders which can be characterized as mysteries, marvels and miracles.

—Joan Carroll Cruz

INTRODUCTION

A phenomenon can be defined as something extraordinary; out of the course of nature, a marvel, a wonder; or even as something abnormal. Webster explains it as an instance or deed that is extraordinary in bulk, quantity or degree.

How else can one explain levitation, bilocation, the odor of sanctity and so many other supernatural events mentioned so often in the lives of the Saints?

In introducing this subject we should first look back to Apostolic times following the coming of the Holy Ghost upon the Apostles when St. Paul speaks to the Corinthians of various gifts:

> To one, indeed, by the Spirit, is given the word of wisdom: and to another, the word of knowledge, according to the same Spirit; to another, faith in the same spirit; to another, the grace of healing in one Spirit: to another, the working of miracles; to another, prophecy; to another, the discerning of spirits; to another, diverse kinds of tongues; to another, interpretation of speeches. But all these things one and the same Spirit worketh, dividing to every one according as he will. (*1 Cor.* 12: 8-11).

St. Paul goes on to report his own experience with the phenomenal when he tells:

> I know a man in Christ above fourteen years ago (whether in the body, I know not; God knoweth) . . . that he was caught up into paradise, and heard secret words, which it is not granted to man to utter. For such a one I will glory; but for myself I will glory nothing, but in my infirmities. (*2 Cor.* 12:2-5).

One wonders what St. Paul would think if he knew of the many other gifts that would be given in future generations to God's chosen, such as the stigmata, the ability to subsist on the Holy Eucharist alone, the many events involving mystical hearts, etc.

Who can explain why one soul is given an extraordinary gift and not another? How can it be that many souls who have had a great compassion for Our Lord's sufferings have not received the stigmata, while others, who never suspected they would be so graced, received the wounds of the Crucifixion? Certainly, St. Teresa of Jesus did not want to levitate, fought against it at times, but nevertheless levitated in the presence of her sisters and even once in tandem with St. John of the Cross.

But many of the gifts were welcomed, such as those of mystical espousal and marriage, and those gifts that helped the people with whom the Saints came in contact, such as the multiplication of food, the mystical knowledge of a confessor in knowing the sins of a penitent, the quieting of storms, the providing of rain during droughts, or the gift of tongues.

It should be considered that the gift of tongues mentioned in this work is not that described by St. Paul in which one person speaks in an unknown tongue and another interprets the message, but the gift of one of God's Saints speaking or preaching in his own language—but understood by those who knew a different language. In other words, no interpreter was needed.

As a by-product of these miracles and phenomena there was a certain awe and respect for the Saint which could only strengthen faith and increase reverence for the One who actually worked the marvel through the instrument of the holy mortal. Of course, the wonders worked by the Saint were also significant in their being introduced to the beatification and canonization processes.

To understand how phenomena were regarded when holy persons were being considered for beatification and canonization, we should briefly consider the canonization process throughout the history of the Church.

Since the earliest days, martyrs for the Faith incurred immediate recognition, their tombs being decorated and piously visited and even the anniversaries of their death being celebrated. This veneration was approved by ecclesiastical authorities who were not blind to the errors and abuses that might occur.

According to Rev. Thomas F. Macken in his work, *The Canonisation of Saints*, the Church was most prudent in testing the cultus to be paid to martyrs. He gives as an example St. Cyprian (d. 258), who recommended that utmost diligence should be exercised in investigating the claims of those who were said to have died for the Faith. St. Cyprian indicated that the circumstances accompanying the martyrdom were to be investigated; the faith of those who suffered was to be considered, and the motives that animated them were to be rigorously studied. Rev. Macken stated that the utmost caution was employed to prevent the recognition of undeserving persons—this gathered from St. Cyprian's letters.

In the fourth century St. Optatus wrote a history of the Donatist heresy. It was at this time that religious honor was not to be rendered to a martyr unless it was declared legitimate by the Church. In the fifth century St. Augustine (d. 430) wrote about the procedures employed in his day for the recognition of a martyr and cites the bishops who organized a Canonical Process.

Following the age of the martyrs, at the end of the Roman era, confessors were then considered for Church recognition. These were the persons who had suffered imprisonment or torture for the Faith, but who had not attained the crown of martyrdom. Later the word "confessor" was given to those men who did not belong to a special class such as martyr, apostle or evangelist.

During the age of the Fathers of the Desert, mystical gifts were often those that had an influence over nature, such as related of St. Hilarion and St. Didymus, when serpents and ferocious animals became docile in their presence.

Msgr. Albert Farges, in his *Mystical Phenomena,* reports:

> Although some parts of the wonders related in the lives of the Fathers of the Desert may be legendary, the foundation of a great part of these accounts is certainly authentic: it is confirmed by so great a mass of evidence that it cannot be doubted.

When the solitaries began the transition to monastic orders as organized by ST. BENEDICT (d. 543), records of events were carefully recorded.

By the seventh century public veneration of deceased servants of God was approved or disapproved by the local bishop, but there were examples of veneration being sanctioned by provincial and national councils. The bishops notified the Holy See of their recommendations, which were generally accepted by the Church. At this time we are assured that mystical and phenomenal gifts were carefully considered.

During the tenth century the more solemn issues were referred to the Holy See, the central authority of the Church. The first example of a solemn canonization took place in the year 993 when Pope John XV decreed canonization to St. Udalric, Bishop of Augsburg. Some authorities, however, maintain that the first solemn canonization was that of St. Swibert by Pope Leo III in the year 804.

Gradually the process became more organized, with candidates for canonization, their miracles and phenomenal gifts being studied, rejected or approved by bishops. But then papal interventions in the making of Saints became more pronounced—especially under Pope Urban II (1088-1099) and Pope Alexander III (1159-1181), both of whom required proof of sanctity and eyewitness accounts of miracles and phenomena worked by the subjects before they could be considered for canonization. Since the year 1234, when Pope Gregory IX published his *Decretals,* absolute jurisdiction in the matter of canonizations was given to the Pope.

From then on phenomena and the matter of sanctity were placed under increasing scrutiny and strict investigation until, during the fourteenth century, the procedures took the form of official trials with the Promoter of the Faith arguing for canonization, while the Devil's Advocate argued against it.

Kenneth L. Woodward, in his book, *Making Saints,* reports on the trial conducted for the Augustinian hermit St. Nicholas of Tolentino. He tells that testimony was heard from 371 witnesses from July 7 to September 28, 1325 during a full-blown trial to determine his sanctity.

Despite these formal procedures, various holy persons were honored by their villages or towns. The papacy then conceded that the title "Saint" would be given only to those declared as such by the Vatican, while those honored locally or in religious orders could be given the title of "Beati" or "Blessed." But soon even the granting of the title Beati or Blessed was reserved to the Holy See.

To finally settle the matter of papal authority came Pope Benedict XIV, Prospero Lambertini, who reigned from 1740 to 1758. As a nineteen-year-old student he took doctorates in law and theology. As archbishop he proved to be a great spiritual leader; as cardinal he became a trusted adviser of popes; as pope he "stands out among modern popes as a great legislator." His gift of scholarship aided him when writing four hundred pages of instructions to settle the matter of phenomena, miracles and sanctity. His work entitled *On the Beatification and Canonization of the Servants of God* gives directives for the proper investigation of cases involving every facet of mystical phenomena and miracles.

The Pope makes fundamental distinctions among the gifts. There are those phenomena which render the recipient more pleasing or closer to God such as mystical marriage and the transverberation of the heart, among other gifts. Then there are other gifts which were given for the benefit of others, such as prophecy and the reading of hearts.

Pope Benedict XIV also set forth a fundamental principle: heroic virtue must be established before mystical phenomena and miracles may be presumed to be of divine origin. And, in fact, even when mystical phenomena are judged authentic, they have no influence on the candidate's claim to sanctity.

Pope Benedict's work also gives directives for determining if the marvels and miracles are the result of diabolical influences, whether the holy person is of sane mind, and whether all surrounding elements were scrutinized that might reflect on the phenomenon, as, for instance, whether flowers or perfumed ointments were near the person from whom the odor of sanctity was detected.

The outlined directives were observed until recent times when Pope Paul VI altered a few of the steps toward beatification and canonization, as, for instance, the previous requirement that 50 years should elapse before beatifying. This was to insure that the claim of sanctity was secure. A lesser time lapse is now acceptable.

The bishop of the Saint's diocese still has great input in the process, as does the Postulator of the Cause who is assigned to each candidate and sees the process to its conclusion.

So it is that early on, a holy person could be declared a Saint by a local bishop after studying the phenomena and miracles, as well as scrutinizing the sanctity of the candidate. Many of the histories of the early Saints were given us by the most reputable scribes, such as the Venerable Bede (d. 735) and St. Gregory the Great (d. about 604), whose writings are quoted in this work.

For other reports of mystical experiences we can look to St. Augustine in the fifth century and St. Peter Damian in the eleventh. Their works were regarded as authoritative by mystical theologians.

It is to be noted that the greater majority of Saints mentioned in this book were from the thirteenth century to modern times—that is, during the time when the Causes were given the most attention, with phenomena and miracles being studied and accepted under structured procedures.

Msgr. Farges notes that there are three conclusions to be deduced during the centuries from the early days of the Church to modern times.

> The first is that mysticism and phenomena are certainly an historical fact, at least for all those who do not wilfully close their eyes . . . For, indeed, what man of good faith could accuse such masters of critical history as the Bollandists of ignorance or imposture in their monumental researches? Who would dare to speak lightly of the processes of canonization, at which these same facts have been set forth at length, before such honest and competent judges, and then severely scrutinized and discussed . . .?

The second conclusion is the fact that mysticism and phenomena have existed throughout the ages. This is incontestable and appears as one of the greatest sources of the life of the Church, reaching from the bloody persecutions of the first three centuries, through the various heresies and difficulties in the Church.

The third conclusion is that the phenomena and mystical elements should be studied. Msgr. Farges gives as his reason:

> If the wonders of the visible heavens proclaim and sing the glory of the Creator, as the Psalmist has well said, what shall we say of the hidden marvels of souls raised to the highest states of holiness.

It is hoped that readers will find this book to be an interesting recital of mystical gifts and phenomena for their study and consideration as suggested by Msgr. Farges, and that, as a result, they will acclaim that God is truly wonderful in His Saints.

MYSTERIES
MARVELS
MIRACLES

—Part I—

THE MIRACULOUS
IN THE LIVES OF THE SAINTS

BILOCATION

Bilocation is the phenomenon in which a Servant of God is in one place at a given time, and at the same moment, by a mysterious presence, is in another place a distance away, where impartial witnesses hear him speak and see him move in a normal fashion.

One writer explains: "That bilocation is physically impossible, that is, contrary to all the conditions of matter at present known to us, is the practically unanimous teaching of Catholic philosophers in accordance with universal experience and natural science." It is also noted that some of these great thinkers believe that "the instances of bilocation narrated in the lives of the Saints can be explained by phantasmal replications or by aerial materializations."

No matter how it is explained, or whether or not it is believed, the subject of bilocation has been mentioned in the lives of numerous Saints—their instances of bilocation have been witnessed by trustworthy persons at both the places where they appeared, even at times being acknowledged by the Saint who performed such a wonder through the grace of God. Additionally, numerous instances of bilocation have been so well-documented, witnessed and investigated that they are accepted facts in the history of the Church and in hagiography.

It is understood that the mystical gift is not given for the convenience of the recipient, but to aid him in helping his fellow man or in performing a function some distance away that had been forgotten. Often the recipient of this gift employs it to attend the dying, to comfort, to instruct and for many other reasons which we will now explore.

Credible witnesses on a number of occasions attested to the fact that ST. ALPHONSUS MARY DE LIGUORI (d. 1787) was seen at two different locations at the same time, once being seen in the pulpit preaching a sermon and at the same time being in the confessional. Another time he was known to be in Naples preaching to university students when a poor woman called at Pagani to receive the alms usually given to her by the Saint. A lay brother, on answering the door, told her of the Saint's presence in another city and sent the poor woman away. Suddenly St. Alphonsus appeared and gave her the usual amount of money.[1]

The most extraordinary incident of this Saint's ability to bilocate took place when Pope Clement XIV was dying. The Rev. Tannoia, a companion of the Saint, relates:

> During the morning of September 21, 1774, Alphonsus, after saying Mass, threw himself in his armchair, as he was not wont to do. He appeared prostrate and absorbed in thought, making no movement, speaking no word and asking no one for anything. He remained in that state for all that day and the night that followed, and all the while took no food and made no sign that he would undress. The servants who saw him in this position, wondering what was to happen, stood by the door of his room, unwilling to go in. On the morning of the 22nd he had not changed his attitude and the household did not know what to think. The fact is that he was in a prolonged ecstasy. Later on in the morning, however, he rang the bell to announce that he wished to say Mass. At that signal, it was not only Brother Romito who came as usual, but everybody in the house ran to the bishop's room. On seeing so many people, the Saint asked in surprised tones what was the matter. "What is the matter?" they answered, "this is the second day that you have not spoken, eaten, nor given any sign of life." "You are right," said Alphonsus, "but you do not know that I have been assisting the Pope, who has just died."

Shortly afterwards it became known that Clement XIV had died on September 22 at seven o'clock in the morning, at the very time that the ecstasy of St. Alphonsus came to an end.[2]

ST. GERARD MAJELLA (d. 1755), a member of the Redemptorist Order, which was founded by St. Alphonsus, also experienced the phenomenon of bilocation on a number of occasions. One day when he had received no answer from Muro about a pressing affair, he said to his companion, "I must go there." The next day he was seen at Muro while, on the other hand, his companions declared that he had not left the monastery.

Another time, Fr. Margotta revealed to Dr. Santorelli that St. Gerard, although in his room, had nevertheless spent the night in ecstasy before the Most Blessed Sacrament in the choir of the Franciscans.

The Rev. Nicholo Fiore of Teora, impressed by the Saint's reputation, spoke to Dr. Santorelli about his desire to meet him. Dr. Santorelli replied that he would arrange a meeting. A few days later the Rev. Nicholo arrived at the monastery to conduct business and informed Dr. Santorelli that an introduction was unnecessary since Gerard had visited with him at his home some days earlier. Dr. Santorelli, who knew that the Saint had not left the monastery, took the Rev. Nicholo to a place where Gerard and the community had gathered and asked the Rev. Nicholo to identify him. Rev. Nicholo pointed him out without hesitation.[3]

After conducting a mission at Piombino, ST. PAUL OF THE CROSS (d. 1775) was accompanied to his ship by a great number of people. Among them was Dr. Gherardini, who remained on the pier until the ship was out of sight. On returning to the city and going into a friend's house, Dr. Gherardini saw St. Paul of the Cross coming out of a room. Not believing his own eyes, he went to the Saint and said, "How now, Fr. Paul, are you here? I have been with you down to the pier, I have watched you to a distance out at sea, and now I find you here?" The Saint replied, "Be still. I came here for an act of charity." He then disappeared.[4]

There lived at Cupertino an elderly gentleman, Octavius Piccinno, who was affectionately called "Father." He had asked ST. JOSEPH OF CUPERTINO (d. 1663) if he would kindly assist him at the hour of death. The Saint promised to do so and added, "I shall assist you, even though I should be in Rome." This proved to be a prophecy, since the Saint was in Rome when the old gentleman became sick. When the last hour of the man's life approached, those who were tending him saw St. Joseph of Cupertino speaking with him. Among the many witnesses was Sr. Teresa Fatali of the Third Order, who spoke to the Saint and in amazement asked, "Fr. Joseph, how did you come?" He replied, "I came to assist the soul of 'Father,'" and then suddenly disappeared.

During the time that the Saint lived at Assisi, he was seen at Cupertino assisting his mother during her last hour of life. Realizing that she would be denied her son's presence, she cried out, "Alas, my dear Joseph, I shall not see you again." To the amazement of all who were in the room, a bright light filled the place. Presently St. Joseph was standing beside the dying woman, who exclaimed, "O Father Joseph! O my son!" At that same moment Fr. Custos at Assisi met the Saint, who was crying as he entered the church. When Fr. Custos inquired about his sadness, Joseph replied, "My poor mother has just died." A letter, arriving a few days later, verified the Saint's statement, as did several persons who lived with the Saint's mother. They solemnly testified that the Saint had assisted his mother on her deathbed.[5]

ST. LYDWINE OF SCHIEDAM (d. 1433), a victim soul who endured numerous afflictions that kept her perpetually bedridden, was once visited by the prior of the monastery of St. Elizabeth, which is situated near Brielle on the Island of Doorne. The Saint gave him a description so detailed of the cells, the chapel, the chapter house, the refectory and the porters' lodge that the prior was astounded. "But how can you know all this?" he asked in amazement, knowing that she could not leave her bed. "My Father," she replied with a smile, "I have been there frequently when I was in ecstasy . . ."[6]

It is a certainty that ST. MARTIN DE PORRES (d. 1639) spent all his religious life at the Monastery of the Holy Rosary in Lima, Peru; yet, according to reliable witnesses, he was seen at different times in Mexico, China, Japan, Africa, the Philippine Islands and perhaps even in France. The accounts of these bilocations are well-authenticated, especially that which took place in Mexico City.

A merchant who had resided in Lima and was a good friend of the Saint went on business to Mexico City, but before leaving he visited his friend to implore his prayers for a safe journey and success in his business undertakings. Upon his arrival in Mexico he became desperately ill. At the height of his sufferings he asked, "O my God! Why isn't my good friend Brother Martin here to take care of me when I am so desperately ill?"

Immediately the Saint was beside him. The sick man, full of questions about the Saint's providential arrival, was told, "I just arrived." After ministering to the merchant, setting the room in order and prescribing a medicinal draught, the Saint reassured the merchant that he would soon recover. The saintly Dominican then disappeared as mysteriously as he had arrived.

The merchant promptly returned to health, and hoping to thank his benefactor, whom he thought was visiting Mexico City, he tried to locate him. He first visited the Dominican friars at their monastery, but learned that they had not been visited by anyone from Lima. He went to the residence of the Archbishop of Mexico, but without success. After inquiring at hostels and inns he learned that no one could give him information about his friend. It was not until the merchant returned to Lima that he understood what had taken place. After telling his story to the priests of the Saint's monastery, he learned that Br. Martin had never left Peru. The merchant then understood that Martin had not only prayed for the success of his Mexican trip, but had also extended his promise by supernaturally ministering to his needs.[7]

A native of Peru returned to Peru after spending many years in China and listened with astonishment as St. Martin conversed with him on the customs of the Chinese Empire. The Saint also gave him a minute and accurate description of a holy Dominican lay brother of extraordinary virtue who resided in Manila, whom St. Martin had met in the Philippines in some mysterious way.[8]

The Saint himself alluded to his gift of bilocation when he was tending to a patient who was suffering agonies from erysipelas. The Saint advised that the blood of a fowl be applied, but the patient objected, expressing a repugnance to the treatment. The Saint persisted, saying, "I do assure you it is an efficacious means of relieving your sufferings—for I saw it used successfully in the hospital at Bayonne, in France."[9]

What is regarded as the most substantiated case of St. Martin de Porres' bilocations was vouched for under oath by a man named Francisco de Vega Montoya and concerns the Saint's miraculous visits to northern Africa. A man whom Francisco knew well had been held captive in Barbary. Many times he saw the Saint carrying out his mission of mercy among the captives: caring for the sick, comforting the afflicted, clothing the naked and encouraging the prisoners to remain steadfast in their faith. After regaining his liberty the man travelled to Spain, and after a time journeyed to the city of Lima. One day, while visiting the monastery of the Dominican friars, he spied Brother Martin. Rushing up to him, he thanked the Saint for all his acts of kindness in Africa, but the Saint merely motioned for him to be quiet. When they were alone, the Saint begged the man not to mention his presence in Africa to anyone. The man later learned from one of the Saint's companions the supernatural nature of the Saint's visits. With enthusiasm he went about telling everyone of the supernatural grace afforded the humble lay brother.[10]

ST. CATHERINE DEI RICCI (d. 1590) was born of a distinguished Florentine family. She became prioress of St. Vincent's convent at Prato and was outstanding among mystics for the intensity of her gifts and ecstasies. A stigmatic who suffered the agony of the Passion twenty-eight hours every week beginning at midday on Thursday and ending at four o'clock on Friday, Catherine also had the gift of bilocation. She is known to have had frequent conversations with St. Philip Neri while he was in Rome and she in her convent at Prato. Although they had exchanged a number of letters, they never met, except through their mystical visits, which St. Philip Neri readily admitted had occurred and which five reputable persons swore they had witnessed.[11]

Perhaps the most extraordinary case of bilocation is that recorded in the life of VEN. MARY OF AGREDA (d. 1665), a humble nun who spent forty-six years in the Convent of the Conception in Agreda, Spain. Not only did the Venerable travel mystically across Spain and Portugal, but she also crossed an ocean to visit another continent that was known as America. Her final destination was New Mexico and the Indians of an isolated tribe. The event took place in the following manner.

One day in the year 1620, while rapt in ecstasy, Maria was transported to New Mexico, where she was commanded by Jesus to teach the Indians. She spoke in her native Spanish, but was nevertheless understood; she, in turn, understood the language of the Indians. Because they did not know her name, the Indians called her the "Lady in Blue" because of the blue mantle she wore over her habit. When she awoke from her ecstasy she found herself in the convent in Agreda.

Two reports of a nun teaching the Indians reached Don Francisco Manzo y Zuniga, Archbishop of Mexico. One report was from

Mary of Agreda's own confessor, Fray Sebastian Marcilla, who contacted the Archbishop to learn if Mary of Agreda's report to him that she had bilocated to the Indian territory was correct. The other report came from missionaries who related how the Indians sought them out under the direction of a Lady in Blue. To determine the truth of these reports the Archbishop assigned Fray Alonzo de Benavides of the Franciscan Order to investigate. Fray Benavides was then the director of the missionaries who labored from Texas to the Pacific.

One day in the year 1629 Fray Benavides was sitting outside the Isleta Mission when a group of fifty Indians from an unknown tribe approached him and asked that he send missionaries to their territory. In his letters to both Pope Urban VIII and King Philip IV of Spain, Fray Benavides revealed that the Indians had travelled a great distance from a place called Titlas, or Texas, and that they knew where to find the friars from the directions given them by a Lady in Blue who had taught them the religion of Jesus Christ. Two missionaries were sent back with the Indians. These holy men found the Indians well instructed in the Faith and baptized the entire tribe.

After searching for eleven years, Fray Benavides finally found the mysterious nun, not in America, but in Spain. On his return to Spain in 1630, he visited the Superior General of his order, Fr. Bernardine of Siena. It was he who told Fray Benavides that the Lady in Blue was Sr. Maria of the convent in Agreda. Realizing that the nun, out of humility, would not reveal her secret to him, the holy nun was placed under obedience to tell all she knew about the visits to America. In the presence of her confessor, Fray Benavides questioned her in regard to the various peculiarities of the province in New Mexico. She described the customs of the different tribes of Indians, the nature of the climate and other details. Fray Benavides later wrote that "she convinced me absolutely by describing to me all the things in New Mexico as I have seen them myself, as well as by other details which I shall keep within my soul."

Fray Benavides was later installed as the Auxiliary Bishop of Goa, India. He was ordered by His Holiness Pope Urban VIII in 1634 to write an account of his personal investigations. Of Sr. Mary of Agreda, Fray Benavides once wrote, "I call God to witness that my esteem for her holiness has been increased more by the noble qualities which I discern in her than by all the miracles which she has wrought in America."

The Provincial of Burgos, Fr. Anthony da Villacre, submitted Mary of Agreda to a rigorous ecclesiastical examination. In the end he declared her mystical favors to be authentic.

Abbe J. A. Boullan, a Doctor in Theology, wrote of Sr. Mary, "In the highest rank among the mystics of past ages, who have been endowed with signal graces and singular privileges . . . must be placed, without hesitation, the Venerable Mary of Jesus, called of Agreda . . ."[12]

Ven. Mary of Agreda bilocated to America during an eleven-year period from 1620 to 1631. She experienced more than five hundred "flights," sometimes making as many as four visits in one day. Mary of Agreda is also the author, with the help of the Blessed Virgin, of *The Mystical City of God,* which is regarded as the autobiography of the Mother of Jesus.

ST. FRANCIS OF PAOLA (d. 1507), known as "God's Miracle Worker Supreme," was also given this mystical gift of bilocation. It is recorded that once, while serving at the altar in the chapel, he was also seen by some of his monks working simultaneously at his chores in the kitchen.[13]

Another time, while the Saint was in Paterno, his biographers report that:

> . . . people who wanted to see him approached the chapel and found him so deep in prayer that they decided not to disturb him. When they returned to the street, they were surprised to see him talking to some people. They hurried back into the chapel and saw him still lost in prayer.[14]

Before ST. DROGO (d. 1186) was born, his father died and at his birth his mother also died, leaving him an orphan. When he was old enough to understand, he learned that his mother's life had been sacrificed for his own, a revelation that distressed him greatly.

Around the age of eighteen he decided to follow Our Lord in strict poverty and embarked on a penitential life as a pilgrim, visiting churches and shrines in several lands. After a time he settled at Sebourg, near Valenciennes, where he was hired as a shepherd by Elizabeth de la Haire. In this humble position he grew even deeper in prayer and virtue and was regarded as a Saint by the people of the district. It is known that he tended the sheep every day, yet he was often seen assisting at the offering of the Holy Sacrifice in distant churches. So many of these bilocations were noted that a local saying became widely known: "Not being St. Drogo, I cannot be in two places at the same time."[15]

After six years the holy man resumed his pilgrimages. St. Drogo died at the age of eighty-four after suffering for many years from a repulsive and painful hernia, which could not be hidden. He is the patron of shepherds.

ST. ANTHONY OF PADUA (d. 1231) has been given a number of impressive titles, some of which are "The Wonder-Worker of Padua," "Evangelical Doctor" and "The Hammer of Heretics." He is regarded as the first theologian of the Franciscan Order and has been numbered among the Doctors of the Church since 1946. Renowned as a worker of miracles, he was also acclaimed as a preacher. It is said that St. Anthony ". . . possessed in an eminent degree all the good qualities that characterized an eloquent preacher: a loud and clear voice, a winning countenance, wonderful memory, and profound learning, to which were added from on high the spirit of prophecy and an extraordinary gift of miracles."

About the many miracles performed by the Saint before and after his death, one authority states that most of the miracles ". . . come to us on such high authority that it is impossible either to eliminate them or explain them away without doing violence to the facts of history."

Among his many mystical gifts was that of bilocation. One account tells us that he was preaching one Easter Sunday in the Cathedral of Montpellier in the presence of the clergy and a vast multitude. Suddenly he remembered that he was expected to sing at the same time at the Solemn High Mass in the choir of a neighboring convent monastery. Distressed that he had forgotten this appointment, he drew the cowl of his habit over his face, sank back in the pulpit and remained silent for a long time. His biographer continues:

> At the moment when he ceased speaking in the cathedral, though all the while visible to the congregation, he appeared in the monastery choir among his brethren and sang his office. At the close of the service he recovered himself in the pulpit of the cathedral and,

as his chronicler says, finished his sermon with incomparable eloquence.[16]

The Spanish Franciscan ST. PETER REGALADO (d. 1456) entered the Order at the age of thirteen and practiced all the austerities and virtues of a perfect religious. After his ordination he was made superior, and then, soon afterwards, was appointed head of all the monasteries of the reformed movement in Spain. He is known to have kept an almost continuous silence and to have spent the greater part of the night in prayer. God rewarded his faithful service with extraordinary graces: he was often seen raised above the ground with flames radiating from his body and he possessed an agility and ease which our glorified bodies will one day experience. Strangest of all, it was also established that he was often found at the same hour at monasteries far distant from one another, transacting business for the Order.[17]

ST. FRANCIS XAVIER (d. 1552) is regarded as one of the Church's most illustrious missionaries. He was born of noble parents and was by nature refined, aristocratic and ambitious. He was for a time professor of philosophy at the University of Paris, where he met St. Ignatius Loyola and became one of that Saint's original seven followers. His missionary career began in 1540, when he journeyed to the East Indies. Within ten years he had made successful visits to Ceylon, India, Malaya and Japan. He performed many miracles and exercised many mystical gifts, including that of bilocation. He is reported to have been at several places at the same time preaching to the natives. So carefully witnessed were these bilocations and so numerous were they that one biographer admits that the "bilocations which are related in the story of St. Francis Xavier would seem to be of quite ordinary occurrence."

ST. VINCENT PALLOTTI (d. 1850) was born in Rome, spent all his life there, and even died in his native city. He is the founder of the Society of the Catholic Apostolate, which is also known as the Pallottines. Founded in 1835, there are now several houses of the Order in the United States that are active in educational, parochial and mission work. An order of women known as Pallottine Sisters of the Catholic Apostolate was founded by St. Vincent Pallotti in 1843.

Many of the Saint's mystical experiences are mentioned elsewhere in this book, but we will consider here the time he was in the confessional and suddenly fell into a deep trance. He could not be awakened, but later it became known that at the same time he was present at a deathbed in a distant part of the city. Many other times he was known to have bilocated to deathbeds where his presence resulted in conversions and the saving of a sinner's soul.

JOHN EDWARD LAMY (d. 1931), known simply and lovingly as Père Lamy, was the founder of the Congregation of the Servants of Jesus and Mary. He had frequent visions of Our Lady, Our Lord and the Angels—yet, while experiencing many mystical favors, he was a parish priest who devoted himself at Troyes to the downtrodden rag-pickers and poor delinquent boys. One of his gifts was that of bilocation.

On one occasion in February of 1930, while travelling with a friend, he reached the village of Chambourg, where there was a small property for sale which he wanted to purchase for his order. Because he was scheduled to return home by train, and there were only a few minutes to spare, he hurriedly looked at the property. There was only time to glance at the courtyard and the ground floor of the house. Due to the press of time he could not visit the rest of the house or the garden. Four days after arriving home the friend who had accompanied Père Lamy paid him a visit. The holy priest surprised his guest by relating that he was praying in the garden of the infirmary after the journey, when he somehow visited the house in Chambourg, which he had hurriedly viewed days before. He then related how he had inspected the drawing room, the bathroom and garden.

> I had gone in by the kitchen door which faces the street . . . I went up the first staircase and came down the other . . . there are apple trees. I saw a big row of apple trees. I saw the old clock tower and the press house with its big screw press. I devoted myself to the garden and went across country, cutting across the walk which runs diagonally . . .

After a few minutes he turned to his guest and solemnly warned, "Say nothing of this to anyone."[18]

Among the many mystical gifts lavished on FR. PAUL OF MOLL (d. 1896), a Flemish Benedictine who is regarded as "The Wonder-Worker of the Nineteenth Century," was the ability to bilocate. Many such instances have been recorded in his biographies. One of these took place on February 4, 1896, when he was confined to his cell suffering from dropsy, from which he died twenty days later.

The wife of an innkeeper in Oostacker who was acquainted with Fr. Paul reports that at eleven o'clock in the morning Fr. Paul suddenly appeared at the inn. He seemed healthy and refused a glass of wine, saying that he had to make other visits—especially to a beguinage, which is a community of lay women. He added solemnly, "You will never see me again; carefully note the day and hour of my visit. I came because you still require this." He gave the woman a scapular of rough wool, seven inches by five, to which a medal was attached. Taking her old scapular from her, he threw it into the fire. He also gave her a handful of medals to distribute "among those who would make good use of them." After forbidding her to assist at his funeral, saying that she would not be able to overcome her emotions, he told her, "Go now to the kitchen and put your potatoes on the fire." As the woman relates, "The potatoes were, as a matter of fact, peeled and ready for boiling. I went to the kitchen and came back to the room after a few minutes, but to my great astonishment Fr. Paul had disappeared." The innkeeper and his wife soon afterwards went to the beguinage to inquire about the good Father's visit. The members of the community remembered the visit, saying that they had offered him a glass of wine, but he would not accept it, saying, "I shall not return here anymore." After a few minutes he walked off hurriedly. The innkeeper and his wife then wrote to the priest's doctor, who replied that he had visited his holy patient on January 31, 1896.

> I found Fr. Paul in such a state of health as absolutely to preclude the possibility of his leaving the monastery on that day, or on the 4th of February following. February 13th I found the patient considerably weaker than on my previous visit, that is January 31st, and this weakness constantly increased until the day of his death which took place February 24, 1896. Such are the details as I find in my notebook and of which my

memory, which is good for dates, has kept until now a faithful remembrance. [The letter was signed] Dr. Cyr. Planquaert.[19]

The following few lines were extracted from a letter written by the holy priest at Termonde, August 30, 1894, which again indicates Fr. Paul's gift of bilocation: "I arrived home safe, without seeing or hearing anything on the way. While you were still looking at me, I was already at home."[20]

ST. JOHN BOSCO (d. 1888) was the founder of the Salesians, an order named in honor of St. Francis de Sales, whom Don Bosco admired. St. John Bosco also founded an order for women called the Daughters of Mary, Help of Christians. Both orders were dedicated to helping young people learn trades, and in the case of those who had seemed destined to take the wrong path in life, to convert and become respectable citizens.

One of the Saint's most impressive demonstrations of bilocation took place in 1886 when he was in Turin, Italy and Fr. Branda was at the Salesian College of Sarria in Spain. The college, unfortunately, contained some dangerous and scandalous boys who were hypocritically pretending to be upright students. They were, in reality, plotting a serious crime. The bilocations took place in the following manner:

> In the first instance, during the night of January 28-29, Fr. Branda was sound asleep when he heard the voice of Don Bosco calling him by name and instructing him to get up and follow him. Fr. Branda went back to sleep after he decided it must have been a dream, since he knew Don Bosco was in Italy. A week later, during the night of February 5-6, he again heard the voice of Don Bosco and saw him standing at the foot of his bed. Fr. Branda got up quickly, dressed, approached the Saint and kissed his hand as a sign of respect. The Saint then said, "Your house is going on well. I am pleased with you, but there is one dark spot." Suddenly Fr. Branda saw an apparition of four young men, two of whom he recognized as boarders of the house and two as pupils. With a look of anger and

severity, Don Bosco pointed at one of the apparitions
and said, "Tell this one to be more prudent. As for the
others, they must be expelled. Show them no pity, and
do it as soon as possible."[21]

After this, Don Bosco and Fr. Branda walked through two dormitories. Fr. Branda recorded, "I did not see Don Bosco use any key
to unlock the rooms, the doors opened of themselves before him
and a luminous halo appeared to surround him on his way, lighting
up everything on his path." When they returned to Fr. Branda's
room, Don Bosco again repeated the order of expulsion and disappeared. It was four o'clock. Fr. Branda, now plunged into darkness
by the absence of the apparition, wondered about the vision and the
order to expel three boys when there was no proof of their guilt. He
decided to wait, but within a few days he received a letter from
Turin written by Fr. Rua which stated: "As I was walking with Don
Bosco today under the porticoes of the Oratory he bade me ask you
whether you had carried out the order he had himself intimated to
you a short time ago."

In spite of this, Fr. Branda decided to wait a day or two, but then
one morning, when he was about to start Holy Mass, he reported:
"While I was reciting the *Introibo* at the foot of the altar, I felt in
my innermost being an imperious voice murmuring: 'If you fail to
carry out the order, this is your last Mass.'"

After Holy Mass, Fr. Branda called for the boys. "Strange to say
during the interrogation, each of them unwittingly assumed the attitude in which he had appeared as an apparition on the night of February 6." The three were summarily expelled.[22]

PADRE PIO (d. 1968), the only priest to bear the Wounds of Our
Lord, experienced many mystical favors, not the least of which was
bilocation, which he first experienced while he was still a divinity
student at San'Elia a Pianisi. The archives of the friary of Santa
Maria delle Grazie at San Giovanni Rotondo preserve the original
handwritten pages in which the holy student explains what happened.

Several days ago I had an extraordinary experience.
Around 11:00 p.m. on January 18, 1905, Fra Anastasio
and I were in the choir when suddenly I found myself far

away in a wealthy home where the father was dying while a child was being born. Then there appeared to me the Most Blessed Virgin Mary who said to me: "I am entrusting this child to you . . . I want you to work with her because one day I wish to adorn myself with her."

I answered, "How is this possible, since I am still a mere divinity student and do not yet know whether I will one day have the fortune and joy of being a priest? And even if I become a priest, how can I take care of this child, since I am so far away?"

The Madonna said, "Do not doubt. She will come to you, but first you will meet her at St. Peter's in Rome."

After that, I found myself again in the choir.[23]

The dying man was Giovanni Battista Rizzani, a fervent Mason who refused to be baptized. At the same time that his wife, Leonilde Rizzani, was praying at his bedside, Padre Pio was having "the extraordinary experience" at San' Elia a Pianisi. Leonilde looked up and saw a young man wearing a Capuchin habit. As soon as she saw him, the young monk turned and left the room, but when she went to look for him he was nowhere to be found.

She soon went into labor pains, gave birth to a baby girl and later returned to her husband's bedside. A priest soon arrived, and over the objections of his Masonic friends who did not want a priest to minister to him, the dying man looked at the priest and said, "My God, my God. Forgive me!" and died within a few hours. This took place in 1905.

After her husband's death, Leonilde moved to Rome with her children. Seventeen years later, Giovanna, who was named for her father and was born the night of her father's death, was in St. Peter's Basilica with a friend when they encountered a young Capuchin who agreed to hear Giovanna's confession. After confessing, Giovanna and her friend stood close by to speak again with the Capuchin priest, but a guard insisted they leave since the basilica was closed. He also added that no priest was in the basilica to hear confessions. An examination of the confessional by the guard left the two young women confused, since the Capuchin was not there and they had stood there waiting for him to leave and had not seen him.

Later that year Giovanna was shown a picture of Padre Pio, whom she promptly recognized as the priest who had heard her confession. This prompted her to visit San Giovanni Rotondo to see Padre Pio, and she did so with an aunt and several friends. When the Padre saw Giovanna, he smiled and exclaimed, "Why, Giovanna, I know you. You were born the night your father died." He then revealed that her father had been saved because of her mother's prayers and his intercession, that he was the priest who had heard her confession in St. Peter's Basilica, and then told her about his strange experience when he had visited the room of her dying father. He also told her about the vision of Our Lady, who placed her in his charge. Padre Pio then invited her to come often to see him for spiritual direction.

Giovanna told her mother all that had taken place, and by comparing Giovanna's experience to those of her mother, both were convinced that Padre Pio had bilocated twice on their account, once to the death chamber and another time to the confessional.

Padre Pio had told Giovanna that it was not in God's plan for her to enter religious life. She later married and became the Marchioness Boschi of Cesena. She remained a devoted disciple of the holy Padre and gave a detailed deposition before the Archiepiscopal Curia of Manfredonia for the cause of beatification. The Curia compared her document to that written by Padre Pio in 1905 and noted the similarities. The document of Padre Pio was never read by Giovanna and the priest's bilocations were known up to that time only by his superiors.[24]

But there were many other times when Padre Pio was seen at two places during the same time period, sometimes speaking, sometimes not. There were other times when only his presence was detected, or at other times there was the perfume of his stigmata which indicated his presence. A number of these bilocations are mentioned in the many biographies of this holy priest, which prove to be of great wonder and edification to those who study them.

TEACHING THE INDIANS. Ven. Mary of Agreda, a Spanish nun, bilocated to America more than 500 times between 1620 and 1631. Our Lord had commanded that she go there to teach the natives.

HERE *AND* THERE. While remaining in his cell in the monastery, St. Gerard Majella often used his gift of bilocation to spend the night in prayer before the Blessed Sacrament.

— 2 —

LEVITATION

In his book, *The Spiritual Life*, the Very Rev. Adolphe Tanquerey writes that rationalists have attempted to explain this phenomenon by natural causes such as by air drawn into the lungs, by an unknown physical force, the intervention of spirits, etc., "which amounts to saying that they have no sufficient explanation to offer." Pope Benedict XIV explains that a well-authenticated levitation cannot be explained on natural grounds and that with the Saints it is a sort of anticipation of a prerogative of glorified bodies.

Who can better tell us about this phenomenon of having one's body raised in the air by supernatural means, than someone who experienced it? We therefore turn to ST. TERESA OF AVILA (d. 1582), who not only experienced this mystical phenomenon but also wrote about the happenings—and her reactions to them—in Chapter XX of her *Autobiography*. Countless Saints have also experienced levitations, but she is one of the few, if not the only one, who has described the experience in detail. Her reactions to this phenomenon may very well be the same as the others who likewise were raised spirit and body in a loving transport.

The Saint tells us that the rapture comes "like a strong, swift impulse, before your thought can forewarn you of it or you can do anything to help yourself; you see and feel this cloud, or this powerful eagle, rising and bearing you up with it on its wings."

The Saint did not want others to witness these raptures, nor did she want to appear singular or to be thought of as holy ("Lord . . . do not permit a creature so vile as I am to be taken for a holy woman.") As a result she tried many times to resist this phenomenon, but she tells us,

> . . . when I tried to resist these raptures, it seemed that I was being lifted up by a force beneath my feet so powerful that I know nothing to which I can compare it, for it came with a much greater vehemence than any other spiritual experience and I felt as if I were being ground

to powder. It is a terrible struggle, and to continue against the Lord's will avails very little, for no power can do anything against His.[1]

In his biography of the Saint, Fr. Diego de Yepes, who was a contemporary, wrote that once when Bishop Alvaro de Mendoza was giving Communion to the nuns at their *comulgatorio* (an opening in the wall of the chapel) the Saint was suddenly rapt in ecstasy and, being irresistibly lifted up from the ground above the height of the opening, she was in consequence unable to communicate.

With regard to these incidents, the Saint wrote in her *Autobiography* that:

> It seemed to me a most extraordinary thing and I thought there would be a great deal of talk about it, so I ordered the nuns (for it happened after I was appointed Prioress) not to speak of it. On other occasions, when I have felt that the Lord was going to enrapture me (once it happened during a sermon, on our patronal festival, when some great ladies were present), I threw myself on the ground; then the nuns came round to hold me; but still the rapture was observed.[2]

How does one feel in this state? The Saint writes that it produces a great humility but also, she confesses,

> In me it produced great fear—at first a terrible fear. One sees one's body being lifted up from the ground; and although the spirit draws it after itself, and if no resistance is offered does so very gently. One does not lose consciousness—at least, I myself have had sufficient to enable me to realize that I was being lifted up. The majesty of Him who can do this is manifested in such a way that the hair stands on end, and there is produced a great fear of offending so great a God.[3]

At the Segovia monastery, Sr. Anne of the Incarnation stated in her deposition taken under oath that on one occasion,

>   . . . between one and two o'clock in the daytime I was

in the choir waiting for the bell to ring when our holy Mother Teresa entered and knelt down for perhaps the half of a quarter of an hour. As I was looking on, she was raised about half a yard from the ground without her feet touching it. At this I was terrified and she, for her part, was trembling all over. So I moved to where she was and I put my hands under her feet, over which I remained weeping for something like half an hour while the ecstasy lasted. Then suddenly she sank down and rested on her feet, and turning her head round to me she asked me who I was and whether I had been there all the while. I said yes, and then she ordered me under obedience to say nothing of what I had seen, and I have in fact said nothing until the present moment.[4]

Fr. Yepes recorded that on another occasion when a rapture suddenly came upon her in choir, she clutched at the mats on the floor and was raised up into the air with them still in her hands. Another contemporary, Marie de San Jose, declares in certain manuscript notes that Mother Maria Baptista had on two different occasions seen her beloved superior raised from the ground.[5]

Another Saint who experienced this phenomenon and wrote about it was VEN. MARIA VILLANI, a Dominican nun (d. 1670). In documenting the experience for her confessor she wrote:

On one occasion I was conscious of a new experience. I felt myself seized and ravished out of my senses, and that so powerfully that I found myself lifted up completely by the very soles of my feet, just as the magnet draws up a fragment of iron, but with a gentleness that was marvelous and most delightful. At first I felt much fear, but afterwards I remained in the greatest possible contentment and joy of spirit. Though I was quite beside myself, still, in spite of that, I knew that I was raised some distance above the earth, my whole body being suspended for a considerable space of time. Down to last Christmas Eve (1618) this happened to me on five different occasions.[6]

Another case that is well documented is that of ST. BERNARDINO REALINO, S.J. who died at Lecce in 1616. In preparing an application for his beatification in 1621, Signor Tobias da Ponte, a gentleman of rank and high character, was asked to testify to an incident which he had witnessed. Signor Tobias deposed on oath that in the year 1608 he came to Lecce to ask the spiritual help of the holy priest. Since the door to the father's cell seemed to be closed to visitors, Signor Tobias took a seat in a lobby which was just outside the Saint's room. As he sat watching the door, he noticed that it was completely shut and that a certain radiance of light was streaming through. The intensity of the light piqued his curiosity so that he drew near the door and pushed it open. Through the brightness he saw the Saint in a kneeling position before his prie-dieu, his face uplifted, his eyes closed and his body raised about two and a half feet above the floor. All the while, the Saint kept repeating: *"Gesu Maria state in mia compagnia."*

After telling this, Signor Tobias was asked to think well if it was an hallucination or a fancy of the mind and whether the light he had seen was not a reflection of the sun's rays or an optical illusion. Signor Tobias replied:

> The thing was so clear, unmistakable and real, that not only do I seem to see it still but I am as certain of it as I am of speaking now, or of seeing the things around me . . . I noticed the light coming through the doorway not only once, but twice, thrice and four times before the shadow of any such idea (the levitation) occurred to me. And so I began to debate with myself how there could be any fire in the room, since the rays which issued from it could only be caused by a great fire . . . and so I stood up on purpose and pushing open the door I saw with my own eyes Father Bernardino raised from the ground as unmistakably as I now see your Illustrious Lordship . . .

After being cautioned not to exaggerate the matter and being questioned as to whether he wanted to modify any of the statements, Signor Tobias replied: "What I have deposed is the whole, pure truth, without fiction or exaggeration . . ."[7]

The number of Saints who have experienced this phenomenon is so numerous that a whole book could be devoted to naming them and telling of their experiences. Here we will mention some of them and briefly relate the incidents which have been recorded for us.

ST. GERARD MAJELLA (d. 1755) was at Melfi in the company of several priests and lay people, visiting the picture gallery of the Canon Capucci, when suddenly his eyes became fixed on a painting of the Blessed Virgin. At the same instant he was elevated to the height of the picture and, seizing it in transport, he covered it with pious kisses, exclaiming, "How beautiful she is! How beautiful she is!" The witnesses of this scene were not only amazed, but were also moved to tears.[8]

Another time, when St. Gerard had just arrived at Oliveto, he retired to his room to pray and fell into a profound rapture. At the dinner hour the archpriest went to the Saint's room to invite him to dinner and discovered, to his great amazement, that St. Gerard was raised about three feet from the floor. The archpriest left, but soon returned to find the Saint in the same position. To preserve the memory of this rapture, the archpriest marked on the wall of the room the height to which he had seen the Saint elevated.[9]

On Good Friday in the year 1753, when a portrait of the crucified Saviour was carried into the church during a procession, St. Gerard was already in the church, deeply engaged in prayer. As soon as he saw the sacred image, and before the eyes of the congregation, he was elevated to a considerable height from the ground, his eyes fixed on the portrait.[10]

And again, Gerard was returning one day to Iliceto with two young companions. As they were passing before a chapel dedicated to the Blessed Virgin, the Saint took a pencil and wrote on a scrap of paper before tossing the paper in the air, as if it were a letter. At the same time his two companions saw him rise in the air and fly rapidly to a distance of over a quarter of a mile. The Saint's biographer tells that "They never ceased in after life to recount this prodigious fact, of which they had been witnesses."[11]

ST. ALPHONSUS MARY DE LIGUORI (d. 1787) was preaching a mission with fourteen companions in Foggia when the Heavenly Father gave the people an extraordinary sign that the founder of the Redemptorist Order was a Saint. It was at Foggia that the Saint had witnessed an apparition of the Blessed Mother fourteen

years earlier in the collegiate church. In this same church at Christ-
mastime in the year 1745 he was preaching on the patronage of
Mary when, as before, the same picture of the Virgin Mary became
animated. As she moved within the frame of her portrait the faithful in the pews gazed in wonder and were startled when a ray of
heavenly light left the Virgin's face and rested on that of Alphonsus, giving it a marvelous glow. At the words, "My Lady, is it your
pleasure to play with me?" the Saint fell into an ecstasy and was
raised bodily in the air several inches from the floor. This not only
convinced the witnesses that Alphonsus was a Saint, but it also
produced countless conversions, and created in sinners a deep sorrow for sin.[12]

FR. PAUL OF MOLL, called "The Wonder-Worker of the Nineteenth Century" (d. 1896), was offering Holy Mass and was about
to give the Holy Eucharist to one of his penitents when, as the penitent describes the incident:

> I saw Father Paul standing before me in ecstasy,
> raised a considerable distance above the floor, holding
> the Sacred Host. I cannot tell exactly how long he con-
> tinued in this attitude, but I think it was at least five min-
> utes. It would be impossible for me to describe how
> attractive the countenance and attitude of the Rev. Father
> appeared, and the atmosphere was scented with the most
> delicious perfume of roses and other flowers, such as I
> had never before experienced.[13]

While visiting a religious community at Bruges, the Sisters
noticed that Fr. Paul, while passing from one room to another,
hardly moved his feet but seemed to glide over the floor rather than
step upon it. A lady from Ghent reported that she saw Fr. Paul
raised a foot above the ground absorbed in an ecstasy which lasted
about ten minutes. Another lady from Ghent, while visiting Fr. Paul
in 1889, heard him exclaim, "For the love of Jesus!" and saw him
fall into an ecstasy and levitate three feet above his chair. He
remained in this attitude for eight or ten minues before descending
upon his chair and continuing the conversation.[14]

One of the levitations of ST. ANTHONY MARY CLARET

(d. 1870) was witnessed by Fr. Fernando de Agullana, who left a record of what took place:

> Father Claret went to preach a Mission. The people were very indifferent in religious matters.
>
> As was our custom, the two of us made an hour of prayer together in the morning before beginning our apostolic task. His presence alone abstracted me from worldly thoughts. What fortune to make an hour's prayer near the holy missionary. It seems as though a heat of great devotion emanated from his body. This time, above all others, I noticed an extraordinary fervor in Fr. Claret. He was on his knees, with his hands joined. His shining eyes were turned toward heaven; his face seemed to be on fire; his lips whispered ejaculatory prayers. I looked upon him in silence and absorption.
>
> Soon I saw that little by little, he was leaving the earth and rising in ecstasy; more than two meters in height had been reached in slow ascension.
>
> I feared that he would rise higher and that he would run the risk of injuring himself and fall to the floor when coming out of his ecstasy. I declare frankly, that I tried to make all the noise possible to awaken him from his rapture.
>
> It lasted a long time. Then, with the same suavity with which he was raised, he descended again to earth and continued his prayer normally until the accustomed hour.[15]

ST. MARTIN DE PORRES (d. 1645) had nursed a young Spaniard named Juan Vasquez, who was to witness many of the supernatural gifts which St. Martin experienced. One day when Juan Vasquez was walking past the Saint's cell he saw the Saint kneeling before a crucifix, his arms extended in the form of a cross, his eyes fixed intently on the figure of the Crucified. What caused Juan great concern was that the Saint was raised three feet above the floor.[16]

One evening a Dominican at the monastery of the Saint went to Martin's cell to speak with him about an important matter and found the cell apparently empty. As he was leaving the darkened cell, the hood of his habit caught on something. Reaching up to free the hood, he found to his amazement that it was caught on the Saint's foot. St. Martin was suspended in the air, rapt in a profound ecstasy.[17]

Another time, Fr. Pedro de Mendoze was leaving church after praying before the Rosary altar when he saw St. Martin elevated in the air before the statue of St. Dominic. Fr. Pedro stood in amazement while he studied the face of the Saint, which was glowing with a heavenly light. He noticed, too, that the image of St. Dominic appeared animated, reverently turning and inclining in adoration towards the main altar. Fr. Pedro then understood that the holy founder of the Order of Preachers and the saintly Negro were praying in unison. The priest estimated that the ecstasy lasted an hour.[18]

One night a gentleman who was residing at the convent struck a light in the chapter room and was terrified to see St. Martin elevated in the air. He ran immediately to call the surgeon Don Marcelo Rivera, who happened to be in the monastery at the time. Joining them were Fr. Antonio Arce, a master in sacred theology, and Fr. Pedro Loayza. They saw the Saint raised almost four feet from the floor. A peculiar feature of this ecstasy, which all four men carefully observed, was that the Saint's body had been diminished in proportion to the size of the sacred image hanging on the cross. After a while, the Saint calmly descended and went out of the chapter room to his cell.[19]

Still another time, when one of the priests was dying, Br. Martin Cabezas went looking for St. Martin and found him raised above the ground with his lips pressed to the pierced side of the large image of Christ on the cross. The Brother notified priests of the order, and they also witnessed the prodigy. St. Martin soon descended and went straight to the infirmary, where he knew by supernatural means that he was needed.

The instances of the Saint being raised from the ground before a crucifix were numerous. Several priests who had witnessed these levitations gave depositions for the Process of beatification that they had seen Martin miraculously raised above the ground. They also testified to various other prodigies which they had witnessed that are reported elsewhere in the Saint's biographies.[20]

Another Saint who was discovered levitated with lips against a crucifix is ST. GEMMA GALGANI (d. 1903). In the dining room of her home was a large crucifix that was highly venerated by the whole family—particularly by Gemma, who visited it often during the day. It happened at least once that she found herself raised from the floor with her arms around the crucifix while kissing the sacred wound on the side of the Crucified.[21]

ST. PAUL OF THE CROSS (d. 1775) was in the town of Latera, in the diocese of Montefiascone, and was in the sacristy of a church speaking with other priests when he became so inflamed with the love of God that he rose in the air, to the complete astonishment of his witnesses. Another time he was in a town on the isle of Elba giving a mission when, at the most fervent part of his sermon, he walked off the platform, through the air and over the heads of the people and then returned as though nothing unusual had taken place. One can only imagine the emotions felt by those who had witnessed such an unexpected display of the supernatural.

During the last years of his life the Saint was sitting in the sacristy of St. John and Paul Church in holy conversation with a number of people when, as the deposition states:

> He began, according to his custom, to have his countenance lighted up, brilliant rays flashing from his face; then his whole body began to tremble; then, as I believe, he perceived that he was losing the control of his senses, he clung with both his hands to the arms of the chair, and leaned his shoulders on the back of it; as soon as he had done this, he began to rise, together with the chair, and that to such a height, that I think he must have risen at least to the height of five or six feet . . . in this state he continued a very long time in most sublime contemplation. Finally he returned to himself, and, as the rapture passed away, a slight tremor took place all over his body, and gradually the servant of God, with the chair, descended and rested on the ground.[22]

VEN. DOMINIC OF JESU MARIA (d. 1630), a Discalced Carmelite, levitated in the state of ecstasy while in the presence of King Philip II of Spain. On another occasion, while Ven. Dominic was rising in the air, he was grabbed by a skeptic who thought the levitation to be a trick. The skeptic was carried up with the Saint, but when he became frightened he let go, fell to the ground and suffered serious injury.[23]

BL. THOMAS OF CORI, O.S.F. (d. 1729) fell into an ecstasy while distributing Holy Communion in the church at Civitella. He rose to the roof so swiftly that the congregation thought he must have fractured his head against the rafters. After a short time he sank gently to the floor, still holding the ciborium in one hand and a particle between the thumb and forefinger of the other. The Life of this Saint, which was based upon the Process for his beatification, also relates that he was raised up horizontally from his bed into the air during his last sickness.[24]

Bishop Ximenes Samaniego was a close friend of VEN. MARY OF AGREDA (d. 1665), the author of *The Mystical City of God*. In his biography of Ven. Mary of Agreda, the Bishop describes her ecstasies in this manner:

> The body was entirely bereft of the use of the senses, as if it were dead, and it was without feeling if violence was done to it; it was raised a little above the ground and as light as if it had no weight of its own, so much so that like a feather, it could be moved by a puff of breath even from a distance. The face was more beautiful than it normally appeared; a certain pallor replaced the naturally swarthy hue. The whole attitude was so modest and so devout that she seemed a seraph in human form. She frequently remained in this state of ecstasy for two or even three hours.[25]

In a biography published in Venice in 1682, a number of levitations are recorded of PASSITEA CROGI, a Sienese Capuchin nun (d. 1615) whose Process for beatification was submitted in 1711. Her biographer writes:

> According to the violence of the ecstasy she was lifted more or less from the ground. Sister Felice deposed that she had seen her raised three *braccia* (arm lengths), Sister Maria Francesca more than four *braccia* and at the same time that Passitea was completely sur-

rounded with an immense effulgence of light. This lasted for two or three hours. On one occasion at Santa Fiora in the house of the Duchess Sforza, when she was present with a crowd of other people, Passitea was surprised by a rapture, under the influence of which she remained raised from the ground at the height of a man. The Duchess, who was a witness of the occurrence, caused an attestation of the fact to be drawn up, which was signed by all present.[26]

BL. MARY OF JESUS CRUCIFIED (d. 1878), a Discalced Carmelite nun of Pau, is said to have soared in the air to the top of a lime tree until she was commanded by her superior to come down. In her haste to obey, she left one of her sandals in the top branches, where it was discovered the next day.[27]

Closer to our time is the case of SR. MARIA OF THE PASSION (d. 1912), whose Cause was introduced in 1928. One of her fellow religious wrote in a letter dated June 3, 1913 that,

> I was still a novice and on those last occasions when Sr. Maria of the Passion was able to come down to the choir to receive Holy Communion, the Rev. Mother Superior bade me take her back to her cell because, as she was so ill, she had to return to bed almost immediately. Well, no sooner had we left the choir together than I noticed that the servant of God, though she was in a most suffering state, mounted the stairs in an instant, as if she flew on wings, while I, though I was in perfect health, could not keep pace with her; so much so that it seemed to me that she never touched the ground but that she really flew up the flight of stairs which led to her cell.[28]

When ST. FRANCIS OF PAOLA (d. 1507) visited the kingdom of Naples in 1483 with three members of his order, he was met by the King of Naples, various nobles and so many townspeople who wanted to see the miracle-worker of Calabria that the militia was needed to maintain order. He reluctantly accepted the King's invitation to stay at the palace, but the King had another reason for the invitation besides that of mere hospitality. He wanted to see for himself if the hermits really observed strict self-denial and prayer. In order to spy on them, the King arranged with his servants to cut peep-holes in the door to the Saint's room. During the night the King approached the door and saw that the three companions were asleep on the floor beside the luxurious beds that had been prepared for them. As for the Saint, he was seen floating in mid-air, his whole body glowing with light, his hands clasped while in a profound ecstasy. The monarch was stunned and watched for some time in amazement. This incident was recorded in the Acts of his canonization.[29]

Bl. Raymond of Capua, in writing the biography of ST. AGNES OF MONTEPULCIANO (d. 1317) fifty years after her death, relates that even at the early age of fifteen, St. Agnes was often lifted five feet or more from the ground in the ecstasy of prayer. After she joined the Dominican Order the levitations were witnessed by the sisters of the Convent del Sacco, some of whom testified to what they had seen when Bl. Raymond was gathering information for the biography.[30]

According to the Bollandists, BL. CLARA OF RIMINI (d. 1346) was travelling one day from Assisi to the church of the Portiuncula about a mile away when her companions noticed that her feet never once touched the ground. According to them, "angels carried her to the church of their queen."[31]

ST. FRANCIS OF POSADAS (d. 1713), a Dominican, was often lifted without support during his offering of the Holy Mass. He once said after returning to the floor that, "I cannot tell whether I left the earth or the earth withdrew from me." Once, after reciting the words of Consecration, his body rose in the air and remained suspended. When he finally descended, the congregation saw that he was encompassed with a great light and that his face was transformed: his wrinkles had disappeared, his skin was as transparent as crystal and his cheeks were a deep red.[32]

While ST. JOHN JOSEPH OF THE CROSS (d. 1734) was building his monastery he often assisted the workmen by carrying materials, such as bricks, mortar or timber. On one occasion when he was missed, he was found in the chapel in deep prayer, lifted so high off the ground that his head touched the ceiling. [33]

The *Acta Sanctorum* records that ST. JOHN OF ST. FACOND (d. 1479) was also seen suspended in the air many feet above the ground and that he sometimes remained thus throughout the night.[34]

Sometime during the canonization of ST. FRANCIS XAVIER (d. 1552), on January 19, 1622, Cardinal de Monte, in speaking before Pope Gregory XV, related that many a time the Saint was lifted above the earth during prayer. Unable to contain his joy, the Saint would exclaim, "It is enough, O Lord; it is enough!"[35]

The Saint who is best known for levitating during prayer, ST. JOSEPH OF CUPERTINO (d. 1663), experienced so many levitations that were witnessed by his brothers in the Franciscan Order that he is regarded as the patron saint of passengers who fly on planes. In Fr. Angelo Pastrovicchi's "official biography" of the Saint, which was first published in 1767, the author states that:

> Not only during the sixteen years of the Saint's stay at Grottella, but during his whole life, these ecstasies and flights were so frequent, as attested in the acts of the Process of beatification, that for more than thirty-five years his superiors would not permit him to take part in the exercises in the choir and the refectory or in processions, lest he disturb the community.[36]

To report on a few of the Saint's levitations we will start with his return to Assisi when he was led into the church. Seeing a picture of Our Lady on the ceiling, he cried, "Ah, my dear Mother, you have followed me," and was lifted about eighteen paces into the air, as if to embrace the holy image.[37]

One Christmas Eve the Saint invited some shepherds to join in celebrating the birth of the Saviour. When they started to play bagpipes and flutes, the Saint began to dance and with a loud cry flew a considerable distance through the air to the high altar. He remained in his rapture about a quarter of an hour. Although he was in the air leaning over several lighted candles, his garments were not affected. The shepherds, it is said, marvelled exceedingly.[38]

During a profession ceremony at Cupertino, the Saint, dressed in a surplice, suddenly rose to the height of the pulpit and remained for some time with outstretched arms and bent knees. One can only imagine the amazement of the religious and the congregation. One Holy Thursday, while praying before a representation of the holy sepulchre which was situated above the high altar and lit with many candles and lamps, the Saint rose in the air and flew to the altar. Without touching any of the decorations, he remained for a time until the superior ordered his return.

Another time on hearing a priest say, "Father Joseph, how beautiful God has made Heaven," the Saint flew up and "rested" on the top branches of an olive tree. He remained there in a kneeling position for half an hour while the branch which "supported" him swayed as lightly as if a small bird had perched on it.[39] Once while passing through Monopoli on his way to Naples, he was led by his fellow religious to the church of the monastery to see a new statue of St. Anthony of Padua. After spying it from a distance, he suddenly flew to the statue and then returned to his former place. After the Inquisition heard of these marvels, they felt the need to investigate and commanded that the Saint say Mass in their presence at the Church of St. Gregory of Armenia, which belonged to the nuns of St. Ligorio. Suddenly the Saint rose with a loud cry from a corner and while praying, flew to the altar. He remained standing in the air, bending over the flowers and lighted candles with his arms spread in the form of a cross. The nuns cried in alarm that he would catch fire, but he returned to the floor unharmed.[40]

One of the most illustrious witnesses to the Saint's levitations was Pope Urban VIII. During the Saint's first stay in Rome he went with the Father General to visit the Pope. While bending over the feet of the Pontiff the Saint became enraptured and rose in the air until the Father General commanded that he return. The Pope marvelled at the phenomenon and told the Father General that he himself would bear witness to the occurrence should the Saint die during his pontificate.[41]

To satisfy the curiosity of the Spanish Ambassador to the Papal Court and his wife who went to Assisi on purpose to see St. Joseph, the Saint was told by Fr. Custos to go into the church and visit Our Lady's statue. Upon entering the church he looked toward the statue of the Immaculate Conception on an altar, and flew over the heads of those present, and remained in the air at the feet of the statue. After a few moments he flew back and then retired to his cell.[42]

Occasionally the Saint's raptures lasted six or seven hours. A peculiar aspect was that, when a rapture overtook him at Holy Mass, he always resumed where he had left off. Another unusual aspect is that his garments were never disturbed during his many flights whether he travelled forward or backward, up or down.

Herbert Thurston counted more than seventy levitations that took place in the Saint's early life at Grotella. The raptures and levitations took place so often, especially at Holy Mass, that the total number of his flights in Cupertino, Naples, Rome and Assisi cannot be estimated.

J. Gorres reported that Daumer, a one-time enemy of Christianity, accepted these miraculous facts as being well established by reason of the "mistrust and suspicion to which St. Joseph was subject during life . . . and the severity with which the ecclesiastical enquiry concerning him was conducted." It has also been observed that the spectators to these levitations were men of rank, credibility and intelligence, as were those who testified to the marvels for the Process of beatification.

One of her first biographers, Thomas of Cantimpré, tells of the levitation of ST. LUTGARDE OF AYWIERES (d. 1246). He first tells that some nuns came upon her when she was alone at prayer in the middle of the night and found her "filled with a vivid radiance that poured from her body and not only dazzled their eyes but filled their souls with a sweet and sensible grace." Thomas of Cantimpré also tells that on the Feast of Pentecost, "when the *Veni Creator Spiritus* was intoned in choir, Lutgarde was suddenly lifted two cubits from the floor and left floating in the air on the wings of some unseen spiritual power." The thirteenth-century biographer explains that "her body had thus been granted a momentary share in the privileges of her spirit, because of the fact that her soul had already arrived at a high degree of purity and union with God."[43]

BL. MARGARET OF METOLA AND CASTELLO (d. 1320) was dwarfed, blind, hunchbacked and lame. Unfortunately, she was deserted by her parents when a cure at a miraculous shrine was not received. Cared for by various families of the city, she devoted her life to prayer and endeared herself to everyone. She became a Dominican tertiary and cared for the sick and dying, but she showed special solicitude toward prisoners and frequently visited them. One special prisoner, Alonzo, came to her attention.

Alonzo, it is reported, was imprisoned on a false charge, leaving his wife and young son destitute. Tortured by guards who were attempting to learn of the crime he did not commit, Alonzo was permanently crippled. Later, his despair was uncontrollable when he learned that his little son had died of starvation. In his despair, he became known for his blasphemous language and uncontrollable rages.

One day when Margaret was visiting Alonzo with two of her companions, she detected the man's distress and stood beside him in prayer. In a moment there were loud gasps and cries of astonishment. Margaret had levitated 20 inches from the ground. With her hands joined in prayer and her head thrown back as though she were looking toward the heavens, her typically unattractive face was transformed by a glorious radiance.

When Margaret finally descended she spoke of God's mercy and encouraged Alonzo to repent. The desperate man tried to blaspheme, as was his custom, but he could not. Instead he pleaded, "Little Margaret, please pray for me."[44]

Margaret performed many other miracles, which are mentioned elsewhere in this book. She is one of the Incorruptibles and was beatified in 1609.

We read in the life of ST. DOMINIC (d. 1221) that he was once approached by a distraught man who told the Saint that a young man named Napoleon, the nephew of a Cardinal, had just been thrown from a horse and was horribly mangled and apparently dead. The Saint at once ordered that Holy Mass be offered, and together with a number of cardinals, friars, an abbess and several nuns, he repaired to the altar. With many tears St. Dominic began the Holy Sacrifice, but when he came to the elevation of Our Lord's Body and held the Host high, ". . . he himself was raised a palm above the ground, all beholding the same and being filled with great wonder at the sight."[45]

After the Holy Sacrifice, the Saint and his companions journeyed to where the body of the dead youth lay on the ground. One of the witnesses, Sr. Cecilia, tells what happened:

> The saint arranged the limbs one after another with his holy hands, then prostrated himself on the ground, praying and weeping. Thrice he touched the face and limbs of the deceased to put them in their place, and

thrice he prostrated himself. When he was risen for the third time, standing on the side where the head was, he made the Sign of the Cross; then, with his hands extended towards heaven, and his body raised more than a palm above the ground, he cried with a loud voice, saying, "O young man, Napoleon, in the name of our Lord Jesus Christ, I say unto thee, arise." Immediately in the sight of all those who had been drawn together by so marvellous a spectacle, the young man arose alive and unhurt . . ."

St. Dominic's biographer reports, "Never, perhaps, was any miracle better attested, or more accurately described."[46]

ST. PHILIP NERI (d. 1595), known as "The Apostle of the City of Rome," became very ill with fever and was in great pain during the month of April, 1594. When his pulse became very weak the doctors agreed that he was near death and closed the curtains around his bed. In a few moments they heard the patient cry out in a loud voice: "He who desires aught else but God deceives himself utterly. Ah, my most holy Madonna, my beautiful Madonna, my blessed Madonna!"

The curtains were pulled back, and all those who had gathered to pray for the dying Saint saw that his body was raised in the air about a foot above the bed, his arms being stretched out as though embracing someone with great affection. After he returned from his ecstasy, St. Philip answered the questions of the doctors by stating that the Madonna had come to free him from his pain and had restored him to health.

When Cardinals Cusano and Borromeo heard what had happened they went at once to see Philip and persuaded him to tell them of his vision, which they, in turn, repeated to the Pope. We are told that all the rest of that evening, Philip did nothing but recommend devotion to Our Lady as a means of obtaining graces from God. And we can assume that he continued to recommend this devotion for the rest of his life.[47]

We read in *The Little Flowers of St. Francis* that the Saint and his companions once entered a forest where they decided to spend the night. St. Francis, wanting to pray by himself, walked a little distance away from the others. During the night his companions heard the Saint's voice and wondered about him. Approaching the secluded spot they "saw him praying with his arms crossed on his chest, raised up above the ground and suspended in the air for a long time, surrounded by a bright cloud."[48]

This, however, was not the only time St. Francis of Assisi levitated. We are also told in the same work that "Brother Leo, with great innocence and good intention, began carefully to observe and meditate on the life of St. Francis and quietly tried as much as he could to see what the Saint was doing." Because of his innocence he was permitted to see the Saint raised above the ground on many occasions.

> He found St. Francis outside the cell raised up into the air sometimes as high as three feet, sometimes four, at other times halfway up or at the top of the beech trees—and some of those trees were very high. At other times he found the Saint raised so high in the air and surrounded by such radiance that he could hardly see him.[49]

BL. FLORA OF BEAULIEU (d. 1347) was a member of the Hospitalieres Nuns of the Order of St. John of Jerusalem. She was so overwhelmed by every kind of spiritual trial that her condition became a source of irritation to the other nuns who, unfortunately, ridiculed her. Under the guidance of a holy spiritual director she advanced quickly in virtue and was granted many mystical favors. We are told that one Sunday morning during Holy Mass, ". . . while meditating on the Holy Ghost, Bl. Flora was raised some four feet from the ground, and [was seen] to have hung suspended in the air for some time while all were looking on." She died at the age of thirty-eight and was regarded as a Saint by those who obtained extraordinary favors at her tomb.[50]

About the year 1269 ST. THOMAS AQUINAS (d. 1274), the great Dominican theologian and teacher, wrote a definitive document regarding the Real Presence of Jesus in the Holy Eucharist which settled a dispute that had been dividing certain teachers at the university. His treatise, which is still extant, was accepted by the university and then by the whole Church. About this time we learn of an apparition of Our Lord in which the Saviour said to the Saint,

"Thou hast written well of the Sacrament of My Body." We are told that the Saint went into ecstasy and remained a long time raised from the ground. In fact the levitation was of such duration there was time to call many of the brethren to witness it.[51]

St. Thomas has been called "The Angelic Doctor" and "Universal Teacher." At the time of his canonization Pope John XXII called the Saint's doctrine "miraculous," and continued: "He has enlightened the Church more than all the others." He was declared a Doctor of the Church by Pope St. Pius V.

The phenomenon of levitation was also experienced by ST. JEAN MARIE BAPTISTE VIANNEY, the Curé of Ars (d. 1859), the holy parish priest who is known for having spent long hours in the confessional and for having been tormented by the devil on numerous occasions. One of the Saint's levitations was witnessed by Canon Gardette, chaplain to the Carmelites of Chalon-sur-Saone who testified to the fact under oath. The brother who accompanied Canon Gardette on this occasion tells in another document:

> One day my brother (Canon Gardette) came with me to Ars. In the evening, while the servant of God (the Curé of Ars) recited night prayers, we took up a position facing the pulpit. About the middle of the exercise, when M. Vianney was saying the act of charity, my brother, whose eyesight is excellent, saw him rise into the air, little by little, until his feet were above the ledge of the pulpit. His countenance was transfigured and encircled by an aureole. My brother looked round, but witnessed no commotion among the assistants. So he kept quiet, but as soon as we came out of the church he could no longer refrain from speaking of the prodigy he had beheld with his own eyes: he spoke of it to all who wished to hear, and with much eagerness.[52]

The life of this holy pastor was graced by many other wonders which are recounted throughout this book. He is numbered among the Incorruptibles and his preserved body, his living quarters and the old church in which he ministered are frequently visited by pilgrims.

To tell us of the wonders witnessed in the life of ST. CATHER-
INE OF SIENA (d. 1380), we have none other than her confessor,
Bl. Raymond of Capua, who was also her first biographer. He, himself, witnessed many of the phenomena, and he interviewed others
who had seen marvels performed by the Saint. He also spoke to St.
Catherine's mother, who told him that the Saint was privileged even
as a child. Bl. Raymond writes:

> I asked her (the mother) for confirmation in secret.
> She replied that more often than not, when she (St.
> Catherine) was going up and down stairs she felt herself
> being lifted up into the air and her feet no longer
> touched the stairs. Her mother assured me that she used
> to go up the stairs so quickly that it made her quite
> frightened . . .[53]

Another time, after receiving Holy Communion, she felt weak
and was helped to her cell, where she immediately fell down on her
plank bed "and remained there for a long time like one dead." Bl.
Raymond reports:

> Later, her body rose into the air and remained there
> without anything supporting it, as three witnesses I shall
> name claim to have seen. Finally she came down again
> onto the bed, and then in a very hushed voice she began
> to utter words of life that were sweeter than honey, and
> so full of wisdom that they made all the people there
> cry.[54]

Bl. Raymond tells us that the three witnesses "were a certain
Catherine, the daughter of Ghetto da Siena, the Saint's sister-in-law
Lisa, who is still alive, and Alessia, as well as a number of the Sis-
ters of Penance of St. Dominic."[55]

Another time, after St. Catherine received Communion, she went
as usual into ecstasy. Bl. Raymond continues:

> We were waiting for her to come back to herself, so
> as to receive some kind of spiritual encouragement from
> her, as we often did on these occasions, when to our sur-
> prise we saw her little body, which had been lying pros-

trate, gradually rise up until it was upright on its knees, her arms and hands stretched themselves out, and light beamed from her face; she remained in this position for a long time, perfectly stiff, with her eyes closed, and then we saw her suddenly fall, as though mortally wounded. A little later, her soul recovered its senses.[56]

It was during this levitation and ecstasy that the Saint received the Holy Stigmata.

ST. IGNATIUS LOYOLA (d. 1556), the founder of the Jesuit Order, also levitated in a kneeling posture. Early in the Saint's quest for holiness he spent months in prayer and penance and experienced such severe spiritual trials that it seriously affected his health and strength. Andres Amigant, head of a noble family, on hearing of the Saint's illness brought him home. Together with his good wife, he nursed the Saint back to health. The annals of the Amigant family relate various wonders they experienced while nursing him, especially the time when the Saint appeared to be at the point of death. It was then that the Saint became enraptured, and to the surprise of everyone was lifted into the air, where he knelt without visible support. He prayed aloud, "O, my God, how can I love You as You deserve. If men but knew You, they would never offend You; for they would love You too much to do so."[57]

The same phenomenon of levitating in a kneeling position was also related in the biography of ST. BENEDICT JOSEPH LABRÉ (d. 1783), the holy, unkempt pilgrim who spent his life travelling through various countries visiting shrines, especially those shrines and churches in Rome. During contemplation, he was often seized by ecstasies. One day, while praying in the church of the Gesu in Rome, other worshipers saw him levitating in a kneeling position. The sacristan who was sweeping the church was notified by the amazed witnesses, but he, accustomed to such levitations by the Saint, continued sweeping and replied calmly, "The Saint is in ecstasy."[58]

ST. ROSE OF VITERBO (d. 1252) was holy from childhood and became a member of the Third Order of St. Francis. She once experienced a vision of Our Lord, who appeared all bloody and wounded. "The sins of men have done this to Me," Our Lord explained. Afterward, by divine inspiration, Rose walked up and down the street and in public squares holding a cross in her hand while entreating people to do penance for their sins.

The town of Viterbo, which belonged to the Papal States, had revolted against the authority of the Pope. Moral decay and a disregard for religion were prominent. The Saint continued to talk to anyone who would listen, and often people came in crowds to hear her. One day, while standing on a stone platform, she and the stone were raised in the air. They remained there for a considerable time, while words of inspiration issued from her lips. This miracle brought about the desired effect, since the people resolved to do penance and to return to legitimate papal allegiance. As a result, Rose and her parents were expelled by the civil authorities.[59]

Levitation seems to be one of the most frequently mentioned phenomena in the lives of the Saints. Many more Saints have experienced this marvel in addition to those mentioned here. An abbreviated list contains the names of St. Angela of Brescia, St. Antoinette of Florence, St. Arey, St. Peter Celestine, St. Colette, St. Margaret of Hungary, St. Stephen of Hungary, St. Mary of Egypt, St. Joseph Oriol, Bl. Bentivolio Buoni and St. John of St. Facond.

All the foregoing levitations were of Saints who were living, but what of the levitation of a dead body? Strange as it may seem, the levitations of ST. RITA OF CASCIA (d. 1457) took place on a number of occasions and were witnessed by the nuns of her convent, many of the clergy and countless members of the laity.

Around the time of St. Rita's Beatification, and the day before her feast, the town of Cascia was crowded with many clergy and crowds of visitors who came from all parts of Italy to be present at the celebration. It is reported that never before or since has Cascia seen so many religious. One situation, however, could have marred the celebration—had not the Saint intervened.

At the time of Vespers of the Office of the Saint, the secular clergy claimed the right to conduct the function, but the Augustinian priests argued that it was their right, since Rita had been an Augustinian nun. Into the dispute came the laity, whose voices blended with the loud voices of the clergy. The nuns of the convent, frightened by what was taking place, prayed to Rita for a solution. To the surprise of the nuns the body of the Saint rose to the top of the glass-sided reliquary. In addition, the eyes, which had been closed since the Saint's death 171 years earlier, were now open. The nuns immediately hurried to ring the convent bell, which alerted the people, so that thousands are said to have witnessed the miracle. Peace among the clergy was quickly restored when the Augustinians permitted the secular clergy to conduct Vespers.[60] The eyes seem to have remained open for some time, as paintings executed during that time indicate.

Another elevation took place in the year 1730 when earthquakes in the outlying towns and villages forced people to hurry for protection to Cascia and the church of St. Rita. When Cascia itself began to tremble, the body of St. Rita rose inside the reliquary, to the great joy and comfort of the frightened people who had earnestly prayed for protection. Although the earthquake outside of Cascia destroyed many houses, Cascia itself survived without experiencing any damage whatsoever.[61]

The body of St. Rita was also seen to move to one side, and after a lapse of some years to have changed position to the other side. The elevation of the entire body to the top of the sarcophagus was also observed on a number of occasions, a circumstance that was carefully recorded by the eyewitnesses to this prodigy. The documents pertaining to these occurrences are preserved in the archives of the Archdiocese of Spoleto.

The nuns of the convent of St. Rita readily affirm that the elevations did indeed occur in past times, as documents affirm. However, the nuns reported to this writer that other works are incorrect which state that the elevations often occurred on the feast days of the Saint or during the various visits of bishops.[62]

In his biography of the Saint, Rev. Corcoran quotes the official witness for the Canonization this way:

> Many persons who have been questioned from the time of the first Process in 1626 and again successively in 1739, in 1751, and even at the time of the writing, 1893, give testimony to have seen the body of St. Rita move . . . some there are who say that they saw with their own eyes her head turned toward the people; according to some, the body raised itself to the top of the urn; and some moreover note the fact that her habit was moved and disordered . . .

PRIVILEGED, EVEN AS A CHILD. St. Catherine of Siena's mother related to her biographer that even as a little girl Catherine was known to levitate, especially when going up stairs.

EVIDENCE OF SANCTITY. When St. Alphonsus Liguori fell into ecstasy and was raised several inches from the floor, witnesses were convinced of his holiness. Countless conversions resulted.

UPLIFTED BY GOD. After giving a mission, St. Peter of Alcantara would erect a cross in a conspicuous place to remind the people of the truths he had preached. He is levitating here before one of these crosses.

LEVITATING DURING HOLY MASS. St. Joseph of Cupertino in rapture while celebrating Mass. His garments were never disturbed when he levitated. The number of his flights cannot be estimated, they were so frequent.

FIRSTHAND ACCOUNT. St. Teresa of Avila, pictured levitating, wrote of the experience of levitation in her autobiography: "It seemed that I was being lifted up by a force beneath my feet so powerful that I know nothing to which I can compare it."

DEEP IN PRAYER. St. John of the Cross is depicted here levitating. The Saint was once found in the chapel with his head touching the ceiling, having been lifted high by divine favor.

THE POPE WITNESSES A LEVITATION. While visiting Pope Urban VIII, St. Joseph of Cupertino became enraptured and rose in the air. The Pope marvelled at the phenomenon.

— 3 —

ODOR OF SANCTITY

"And when he had opened the book, the four living creatures, and the four and twenty ancients fell down before the Lamb, having every one of them harps, and golden vials full of odours, which are the prayers of saints."—Apocalypse 5:8

At the very beginning of the Christian era, perfumes were introduced as elements proper to the worship of God. Myrrh, an aromatic gum resin, and frankincense were offered to the Christ Child by the Three Magi. We also read of the reverential act performed by Mary Magdalen when she "took a pound of ointment of right spikenard, of great price, and anointed the feet of Jesus, and wiped his feet with her hair; and the house was filled with the odour of the ointment." (*John* 12:3).

It is not surprising that the sweet aroma of perfumes should be associated with virtues, goodness and holiness of God's Saints, and it is not surprising that one of the phenomena most frequently mentioned in the lives of the Saints is that of a perfume in which the Saints, by the grace of God, emitted a sweet fragrance from their bodies either during their lifetime or after death. In this chapter we will consider the fragrances emitted from the bodies of the Saints while they were alive, or the perfumes that lingered about the articles they used in life. Another chapter will deal with the fragrances of the dead.

POPE BENEDICT XIV (d. 1758), in his work, *De Beatificatione et Canonizatione*, acknowledges this phenomenon and even indicates the procedure to be followed in verifying its existence when a soul is being considered for beatification. According to the Pontiff, it should be considered whether the odor is both sweet and persistent and whether it could be explained as having come from anything other than the person under consideration.

Long before the recommendations were given by Pope Benedict XIV, perfumes were mentioned in the early days of the Church and were properly recorded by those who perceived them. This was first noted in a famous letter of the Christians of Smyrna, who described the martyrdom of their bishop, ST. POLYCARP (d. 155). The Christians wrote:

> When he had offered up the Amen and finished his prayer, the firemen lighted the fire. And a mighty flame flashing forth, we to whom it was given to see, saw a marvel, yea and we were preserved that we might relate to the rest what happened. The fire, making the appearance of a vault, like the sail of a vessel filled by the wind, made a wall round about the body of the martyr; and it was there in the midst, not like flesh burning but like gold and silver refined in a furnace. For we perceived such a fragrant smell, as if it were the wafted odour of frankincense or some other precious spice.

The letter continues that the executioners, on seeing that the body could not be burned, killed the Saint with a dagger.

Thurston tells that "No critic nowadays contests the authenticity of this letter. It was undoubtedly written by . . . eye-witnesses."[1]

Eusebius tells in his *Ecclesiastical History* of another letter dated about the year 177 A.D., written by the Christians of Vienna and Lyons to their brethren in Asia Minor concerning the martyrdom of some of their fellow believers. Part of the letter reads:

> They went out rejoicing, glory and grace being blended in their faces, so that even their bonds seemed like beautiful ornaments, as those of a bride adorned with variegated golden fringes; and they were fragrant with the sweet odour of Christ, so that some even supposed that they had been anointed with earthly ointment.

A few centuries later we learn that the odor of sanctity was so strong about the body of ST. BENEDICT (d. 543) that it even penetrated and was perceived about his clothing. An early biographer, Cassidorus, who knew the Saint, reports that:

> His tunic—and he had but one—just like his skin, gives forth a sweeter fragrance than all the perfumes of

India, thus proving that the human body can have its own good odor, provided it be not defiled with surfeiting, by reason of which it gives forth a stench. It can easily be seen that divine Omnipotence deigns to visit such a man, when we ourselves are delighted by his presence . . . After treating at length of the soul, we have also put down with regard to the human body what we ourselves have seen.[2]

Another early example reveals that one day St. Colomban was giving a lecture to his monks when the room was suddenly filled with a celestial fragrance. The holy Abbot asked who it was who had just entered, and being told it was ST. VALERY (d. 619), Colomban—detecting the fragrance as a sign of advanced spirituality—cried aloud, "It is you, not I who are the veritable head of this monastery."[3]

BL. MARY OF OIGNIES (d. 1213), who was born at Nivelles in Brabant, was married against her wishes when she was only fourteen, but with the consent of her husband they lived in perfect continence—and with him she cared for lepers in their home.

Attracted by her virtues and spiritual gifts was Jacques de Vitry, who under her guidance became a priest; later he was elected to the College of Cardinals. Having witnessed some of her austerities, he was quick to note in his writings that her example was not recommended for general imitation.

In her biography, which the Cardinal wrote soon after her death, he testified that her body, even in winter,

> when the frost was so severe as to turn all the water into ice, she gave off a warmth so that sometimes she even perspired, and her clothes were scented with a sweet aromatic fragrance. Oftentimes also the smell of her clothes was like the smell of incense, while prayers were ascending from the thurible of her heart.

Butler is quick to note in his chapter about Bl. Mary of Oignies that Cardinal Jacques de Vitry, in telling of her extraordinary experiences, "was undoubtedly a devout and honest man, who told the truth fearlessly."[4]

Every time ST. HERMANN (d. 1230) said grace at table, he exhaled sweet odors like roses, lilies or violets, which were very agreeable. Because of his humility he was never aware that the perfumes proceeded from himself, but thought that it was his brethren who carried about them the sweet odor of sanctity.[5]

BL. IDA OF LOUVAIN (d. 1300), who was a Cistercian nun at Roosendael near Mechlin, was remarkable for her devotion to Our Lady and the Holy Eucharist. Her devotion to the Sacred Passion was eventually rewarded with the stigmata in her hands, feet and side, with the additional wounds of the Crown of Thorns. Her ecstasies were frequent and her miracles numerous. Witnesses stated that she was often radiant with light and that a fragrant perfume was perceived by many who approached her.[6]

ST. LYDWINE OF SCHIEDAM (d. 1433) was a victim soul and a stigmatic whose body was ravaged with numerous afflictions so that she was said to be hideous to all who saw her. Since her bandages needed constant monitoring and changing, it seemed that the good Lord wished to spare her attendants the unpleasant odors that the sores and soiled bandages would normally produce. Perhaps it was for this reason that, by a constant miracle, the wounds were veritable censers of perfume. Huysmans reports that from her body came a delicate aroma, like "an exquisite atmosphere of shells and spices of the East, a fragrance at once keen and sweet, something like the smoke of cinnamon and spices."[7]
According to Gerlac, the perfume was perceptible to the taste so that when one breathed it, one also tasted a celestial dainty which the perfume recalled. He, too, reports that the scent coming from St. Lydwine's body was like ginger or cinnamon.[8] Later the scent of ginger or cinnamon was replaced when the stigmata began to exhale the perfume of certain flowers. Brugman says that even in the depths of winter the Saint gave off the scent of the rose, the violet or the lily, symbols of humility and chastity.[9]

In his desire for advancement in the spiritual life, BL. JOHN BAPTIST DA FABRIANO (d. 1539) practiced extraordinary penances. He observed rigorous fasts and busied himself in his priestly ministry and in charitable endeavors. After reciting the night office, it was his custom to remain in the church instead of retiring to his cell for rest. One night, when the sacristan entered the church to prepare it for the night, he became curious about the sweet perfume that drifted about. Tracing the scent to a corner of the church, he discovered Bl. John in a profound ecstasy while the fragrance emanated from his body. After his death, his body was found to be incorrupt. Because of the many miracles worked at his tomb, Pope St. Pius X confirmed his cultus in 1903.[10]

VEN. DOMINICA OF PARADISO (d. 1553) was born to humble parents in a small country village near Florence called Paradiso. As a child she exhibited an attraction to prayer and early in her life experienced visions and mystical favors. She was a stigmatist with unusual manifestations and experienced the mystical exchange of hearts with Our Lord. Immediately after this experience, although she had been ill before the vision, afterwards she was promptly restored to health. At this time it was noticed that her body emitted a wonderful fragrance which communicated itself to everything she touched.[11]

ST. TERESA OF AVILA (d. 1582) was a Discalced Carmelite nun who became the first woman to be declared a Doctor of the Church. She experienced perhaps every phenomenon peculiar to the mystical state, yet she remained a shrewd businesswoman, administrator, writer, spiritual counselor and foundress. During her lifetime a delightful fragrance frequently enveloped her.

St. Teresa, in turn, tells about one of her contemporaries, the Spanish ascetic CATALINA DE CARDONA (d. 1577), who also emitted an extraordinary perfume. St. Teresa tells about one of Catalina's visits to the Carmelite convent of Toledo in Chapter 28 of *The Book of Foundations*. St. Teresa writes:

> When Catalina left the house where she was staying, she wasn't able to protect herself from the crowd. This happened wherever she went. Some cut pieces from her habit, others from her mantle. She then went to Toledo, where she stayed with our nuns. All of them have affirmed to me that the odor of sanctity emanating from her was so great that it permeated even her cincture and habit, which she exchanged for another given her by the

nuns; it was something to praise God for. And the closer they came to her the greater was this fragrance, even though her manner of dress, because of the intense heat, would rather have caused a bad odor. I know they (the nuns) would not say anything but the complete truth, and thus they were left with great devotion.[12]

ST. CATHERINE DEI RICCI (d. 1589) was well-known for the perfume that issued from her body. One of her biographers wrote that:

she sent forth a most sweet odor which surpassed every known perfume in the world. This did not happen always nor continuously . . . It was chiefly when she was in prayer, or when she came out after Holy Communion, and during her hours of ecstasy . . . Once all the nuns of the monastery of Prato had the joy of breathing these heavenly perfumes for twenty-four hours without a break whilst her ecstasy lasted. This odor clung to her clothing and every object she touched . . . Sometimes the very places in which she communed with heaven remained sanctified through the presence of this heavenly balsam.[13]

During the official investigation prior to her canonization, twenty to thirty nuns who were present at the death of St. Catherine were questioned about the fragrance that was pronounced in the death chamber. Under oath these nuns also testified that a similar perfume clung to her on certain occasions in her lifetime. Some of the nuns described the scent as resembling that of vivuole mammole, while others maintained that it could not be compared to the odor of any flower or to any artificial perfume.[14]

Articles used by ST. JOSEPH OF CUPERTINO (d. 1663) retained a delightful fragrance, as told by Cardinal Brancati:

The best proof of Joseph's purity was given to all those who associated with him or only touched an object belonging to him; for there emanated from him a most pleasant perfume, which clung for a long time to all the things he used. Even the rooms through which he passed long retained this unusual fragrance, and to find the way he had gone, it sufficed to follow this scent.[15]

A most remarkable case is that of VEN. JOAN MARIE OF THE CROSS OF ROVERETO (d. 1675), which was reported by her biographer, B. Weber. Having access to all the official documents and depositions of witnesses, the biographer tells of her mystical espousal with Jesus in which a mystical ring was given to her. He then writes:

> From this time onwards her finger exhaled a delicious fragrance, which she was unable to hide, and which all the community soon became aware of. Consequently they sought every opportunity to touch it and kiss it. The perfume which it gave out was so powerful that it communicated itself to the touch and persisted for a considerable time. Thus it happened that Sr. Mary Ursula, having touched that finger in the holy nun's first illness, her hand for several days afterwards retained an exquisite fragrance. This scent was particularly perceptible when Ven. Joan Marie was ill, because she could not then take any precautions to disguise it. From her finger the perfume extended gradually to the whole hand and then to her body, and communicated itself to all the objects which she touched. It could not be compared to any earthly scent because it was essentially different, and transfused soul and body with an indescribable sweetness. It was more powerful when she came back from Communion. It exuded not only from her body but also from her clothes long after she had ceased to wear them, from her straw mattress and from the objects in her room. It spread through the whole house and betrayed her comings and her goings and her every movement.
>
> The religious who were in choir were aware of her approach from the perfume which was wafted before her before she came into view. This phenomenon, which lasted for many years, was the more remarkable because naturally she could not endure any form of scent. It was

necessary to keep all such things as musk and amber out of the house altogether, because they acted upon her from a considerable distance even though they were hidden in the cellar, and produced a most distressing effect, so much so that she would even faint away on the spot. The only scent which did her no harm was that which breathed from her own person. Often new novices who joined the order came to the convent wearing, according to the fashion of the times, scented necklaces of pearl or coral. She was so painfully affected by these objects that she could not come near the wearers, and it was found necessary to require them to lay them aside at the convent gate in order to save the Mother Abbess from the risk of a swoon or some other indisposition.

Another unusual aspect of this phenomenon is that this mysterious perfume waxed and waned according to the events of the ecclesiastical year. The odour was notably more pronounced upon the feasts of Our Lady and reached its greatest intensity on the feasts of Our Lord. On ordinary days of the year the scent was present, but less powerful.[16]

BL. MARY OF THE ANGELS (d. 1717) was the ninth of eleven children of Count John Donato Fontanella of Turin, the city of her birth and death. After some difficulties with her family, she was admitted in her sixteenth year to the Discalced Carmelite Convent of Santa Christina.

She served her Order as both novice mistress and prioress, and also dispensed advice and prayers for many people who asked her help in times of trial. Bl. Mary of the Angels experienced extraordinary mystical favors during the last twenty years of her life, especially that which is known as the odor of sanctity.

One of the princesses of the royal house of Piedmont, in a deposition made under oath for the process of beatification, testified in this manner concerning the fragrance:

> As a proof of the holiness of this servant of God I would appeal to the incomparable fragrance which made itself manifest in the places where she lived or through which she passed. The sweetness of this perfume

resembled nothing earthly. The more one breathed it the more delicious it became. It was especially perceptible on the feasts of Our Lady, of St. Joseph, of St. Teresa, during solemn novenas and at the holy seasons of Christmas, Easter and Pentecost. The ladies of my suite were conscious of it as well as myself, and what astonished me more than all else was the fact that after the death of the servant of God I noticed and still continue to notice this perfume in the cell she occupied, although every object which it formerly contained has been taken out of it.[17]

One biographer tells that:

The scent emanated from her person, and was communicated to her clothes and even to things that she touched, from which it was sometimes difficult to eradicate. From about 1702 this phenomenon was permanent, and among the witnesses to it was Fr. Costanzo, afterwards Archbishop of Sassari in Sardinia. He characterized it as "neither natural nor artificial, not like flowers or aromatic drugs or any mixture of perfumes, but only to be called an odour of sanctity."[18]

Another witness testified at the process for Bl. Maria: "When we wanted Reverend Mother and could not find her in her cell, we tracked her by the fragrance she had left behind."[19]

ST. VERONICA GIULIANI (d. 1727), a Capuchin nun at Citta di Castello for 34 years, was distinguished for her level-headedness and efficiency. Her personal experiences, which were unusual and extraordinary, were also carefully witnessed, making her case outstanding for mystical phenomena.

In his life of St. Veronica, Fr. F. M. Salvatori relied mainly on the depositions of witnesses who were questioned in the process of canonization. He writes of the stigmatic:

It is worthy of remark that when the above-mentioned wounds were open (the stigmata), they emitted so delicious a fragrance throughout the whole of the

convent that this alone was sufficient to inform the nuns
whenever the stigmata had been renewed, and on several
occasions the religious were convinced by ocular
demonstration that they had not been deceived. When
the bandages which had been applied to these mysterious wounds were put away, they communicated the same
sweet perfume to everything near them. This fact is
attested by her confidant, the Blessed Florida Ceoli.[20]

In addition to the scent proceeding from the wounds of the stigmata, the scent of Veronica Giuliani was also communicated to the
water in which she washed her hands. This water was occasionally
saved and, according to reports, it effected many cures.[21]

When ST. GERARD MAJELLA (d. 1755) was still in the bloom
of health the perfume of Paradise was often detected in his cell, so
much so that, as the Saint's physician, Giuseppe Salvadore, testified, when the people of Oliveto came to speak to him the sweet
odor guided them to his room.[22]

The same took place when St. Gerard was dying. At that time the
entire infirmary was filled with a heavenly odor and was of such
intensity that the infirmarian thought it his duty to notify the Father
Rector. After investigating, the priest declared that God was dis-
playing a great favor. St. Gerard was dying from tuberculosis and
had frequently vomited as a normal function of the disease. To the
astonishment of the infirmarian, it was realized that the heavenly
fragrance was actually coming from the Saint's expectorations.[23]

The holiness of ST. PAUL OF THE CROSS (d. 1775) was overwhelmingly demonstrated during his lifetime by extraordinary
occurrences, and at his death by a most sweet fragrance that radiated from his body. His biographer relates that during the Saint's
lifetime:

> In the retreat of Toscanella, his room preserved this
> heavenly fragrance for about six months. After the mis-
> sion at Aspra, a town of Sabina, the master of the house
> where Paul had lodged during the time, going into the
> room that the Saint had occupied, perceived an odor so
> sweet and delicious that in astonishment he called in all

the family exclaiming, "Come and smell here . . . what a scent!" The same happened at Fianello, another town of Sabina where those who smelled the scent remarked that it excited devotion.[24]

ST. MARY FRANCES OF THE FIVE WOUNDS (d. 1791), a Franciscan nun and a stigmatist, died in the odor of sanctity. Again we are told that a delicious fragrance clung not only to her habit, but to everything she had touched. After a careful examination of the papers introduced during the process of beatification, her biographer wrote:

> There is hardly one of the numerous witnesses whose evidence is reported in the Summarium who does not speak in explicit terms of this perfume, and in order that there might be no doubt that the favor came to her from her Mother Mary and from her divine Spouse, it was regularly observed that this phenomenon manifested itself with special intensity on the great festivals of Our Lady and on Fridays in March on which she participated mysteriously in the sufferings of Christ's Passion.[25]

People believed themselves singularly blessed to be able to draw near ST. ANTHONY MARY CLARET (d. 1870), or to touch the hem of his cassock, or to kiss his hand. His body and his garments seemed to exhale a perfume of purity and a fragrance from Heaven which calmed temptations and pacified spirits.[26]

A Carmelite nun, SR. MARY OF JESUS CRUCIFIED (d. 1878) of Pau, died at Bethlehem after a very saintly life. Her biographer, Père Estrate, wrote:

> Since the death of the holy sister, several Carmelites both at Bethlehem and Pau have been conscious of a delicious perfume in many places which she once frequented. This fact reminds us that the same sweet fragrance was often noticed to proceed from her when she was still living. In addition to this, all those who visited the room in which she died came away with the perfume clinging to their clothes.[27]

Known as the "Wonder Worker of the Nineteenth Century," FR. PAUL OF MOLL (d. 1896) was one day distributing Holy Communion when one of the communicants tells us that he "perceived a perfume so delicious that I was quite distracted by it. I imagined that one of the lay brothers must have brought a bouquet of flowers . . ." Looking up, the communicant saw that Fr. Paul had levitated several inches above the floor while holding the Sacred Host. During the several minutes that he remained in ecstasy, ". . . the atmosphere was scented with the most delicious perfume of roses and other flowers, such as I had never before experienced."[28]

VEN. MARIE CELINE OF THE PRESENTATION (d. 1897) was a member of the Poor Clare Order, having been accepted by them when she was only eighteen years old. Soon after she entered the novitiate she became seriously ill, and when death seemed to approach, she was permitted to make her perpetual vows. During the last ten days of her life the scent of roses was often noticed in her room and in the corridor, although there were no flowers anywhere near the area. The heavenly perfume was also noticed about her dead body and sweetly scented many of her relics.[29] Ven. Marie Celine of the Presentation died at the age of nineteen and was declared Venerable in 1957.

In modern times we have the case of PADRE PIO (d. 1968), the stigmatist who exercised a number of mystical favors. One favor appeared often about his wounds and the blood that issued from them. Of course, this was a heavenly perfume that was noticed by many. His doctor, Giorgio Festa, M. D., once took a piece of cloth from the side of the holy priest that was saturated with blood. Dr. Festa himself was "entirely deprived of the sense of smell," and did not notice the perfume, but on his way to Rome in an open automobile, his companion, a "distinguished official," not knowing what the doctor had with him, asked about the perfume. In spite of the air continually rushing through the car, and the fact that the cloth was enclosed in a box, the perfume was still detected. The doctor reports, "In Rome . . . for a long time after, the same cloth conserved in a cabinet in my study, filled the room with perfume— so much so that many patients who came to consult me spontaneously asked me for an explanation of its origin."[30]

What did the perfume resemble? Carmela Marocchino said it was like the scent of roses and violets. Padre Rosario of Aliminusa described it as "a strong and pleasant odor, whose characteristics I cannot describe." Padre Gerardo Di Flumeri recalled, "I don't know how to describe it: very beautiful and very nice, but you can't describe it." Dr. Giuseppe Gusso was one of five or six people standing at Padre Pio's door one evening when all of them detected a perfume, "but it wasn't the same perfume for everyone present. I was with Padre Pio every day. There was never any perfume on him, so this was supernatural." Dr. Eduordo Bianco recorded that the aroma was likened to roses, violets and carnations—and eluded "all scientific explanation." Countless others had detected the fragrance which they were also unable to describe, except to say that it was somewhat like roses and violets.[31]

It is said that after the good Padre's death, a heavenly fragrance accompanied him as he was placed in his tomb.

Rev. Herbert Thurston, S.J., the historian, liturgical scholar and hagiographer, was skeptical of all claims of the unusual until he had thoroughly investigated and studied all that pertained to them. He likewise investigated, studied and wrote about the perfume of the Saints. He considered the question: Could the detection of a pleasant aroma about the Saints be an hallucination? In answer he wrote,

It would mean the collective hallucination of the innumerable witnesses in whose presence the Saints lived, as well as that of the scholars, physicians, philosophers and theologians who drew up their processes of canonization or who have directed the causes for verification of relics for centuries, and continue to do so in our own day.

He then concludes, "To question the existence of an odor of sanctity is a supposition that should be condemned."

— 4 —

ODOR OF SIN

It would seem only proper that if sanctity has a perceptible fragrance, that sin would have the opposite effect—that is, sanctity emitting a perfume; sin emitting an unpleasant odor. Because of these scents a number of Saints have had the ability to detect the difference between a person in the state of grace and another in need of confession.

Of the women who had this ability there is ST. CATHERINE OF SIENA (d. 1380), who related to her confessor, Bl. Raymond of Capua, that "the stench of sin" was so overpowering in many of her callers that she could not endure it.[1]

Bl. Raymond of Capua tells us more about St. Catherine's ability to detect sin, especially the time they were both visiting the Supreme Pontiff, Gregory XI.

Bl. Raymond was serving as interpreter, since St. Catherine could not speak Latin and the Pope could not speak Italian. During their conversation, St. Catherine complained to the Pontiff that in the Vatican—a place which should have been "a paradise of heavenly virtues"—there was instead a "stench of all the vices of Hell." The Pontiff is reported to have been bewildered about the statement and how the Saint knew of such a condition, when she had been in Rome only a few days. St. Catherine responded,

> To the honour of Almighty God I dare to say that I could smell the sins being committed in the Roman Court better when I was in Siena, where I was born, than the people who committed them and are still committing them today.[2]

Bl. Raymond added, "The Pope was speechless, and I in my bewilderment puzzled over the matter, and above all wondered how such words came to be spoken with such authority in front of such a high Pontiff."

Another example is given us by St. Catherine's confessor. One day they met a woman who was leading an evil life. Bl. Raymond writes:

> While this woman and Catherine were talking together, I was present too, and while the woman seemed decent enough in her dress and behaviour, I noticed that she was never able to look the virgin straight in the face. Wondering at this, I took the trouble to find out who the woman was, and was told that she was as described above (a decent woman). I mentioned this to the virgin, and she told me privately, "If you had smelt the stink that I could smell while I was talking to her you would have been sick."[3]

BL. ANNA MARIA TAIGI (d. 1837) was also repulsed by the odor of sin. Her biographer tells that her sense of smell "was infected by the atrocious stench of the sins of the world, an affliction which increased when sinners came near her. Neither the smell of flowers nor burning aromatic herbs could lessen this stench, as of rotting corpses, that choked her."[4]

ST. GEMMA GALGANI (d. 1903), who is known as "The Passion Flower of Lucca" because of her sufferings, upon being introduced to a person for the first time would know at once the state of his or her soul. If the person were in the state of sin, the horrible stench given off by the person would make her shudder and become physically ill.[5]

It is told elsewhere in this volume about the heavenly fragrance emitted by ST. PAUL OF THE CROSS (d. 1775), the founder of the Passionist Order. Whereas he himself gave forth a perfume, he easily detected the sin in others by a foul odor. It is told that he could

> smell such a stench from the bodies of persons guilty of impurity that he could not endure it and almost fainted. In fact he did so once when someone guilty of many of these sins went to his confessional. Another time a young man asked to be admitted to St. Paul's order. The Saint knew nothing of the young man's character, but

took both the young man's hands in his and remarked, "You know how much you have offended God with these hands, and you would say Mass!"[6]

The biographer of St. Paul of the Cross writes: "He (God) caused him to smell a horrible stench, as a token of the foul sins with which their souls were defiled, and Paul availed himself of this knowledge for their spiritual good."

ST. JOSEPH OF CUPERTINO (d. 1663), like St. Paul of the Cross, emitted a perfume which was noticed by many. However, he also could perceive sinful persons by the stench emanating from their bodies. One time he appeared to be exceedingly restless and perplexed. On being asked the cause, he replied that he had just spoken to a licentious person, "who had filled his nose with such a stench that he could not remove it, not even by using snuff." He often mentioned that "the impure stink before God, before the angels and men."[7]

Another time, while speaking with the Guardian, he suddenly exclaimed, "Oh, what a stench! Oh, what a hellish stench!" The Guardian detected nothing, but St. Joseph knew the cause and obtained permission to journey to the town. Upon reaching a certain house he persistently knocked at the door until he was admitted. Running up the stairs he came upon a number of sorcerers, men and women alike. Seeing a number of vases and pots with salves and oils, he thrashed about with his cane until he had broken all the vessels. The sorcerers became so terrified at the Saint's fury that they all fled in dismay.[8]

The odor of sin, especially that of impurity, was also detected by ST. PHILIP NERI (d. 1595). It is reported that this extraordinary sensitivity was attributed to his perfect chastity, as he himself told a penitent by way of encouragement.[9]

So many miracles took place in the church of Montserrat through the prayers of ST. ANTHONY MARY CLARET (d. 1870) that it became known as the Church of Miracles.

One afternoon when the Saint was preaching in a church filled with people, he suddenly paused, and as though speaking to an invisible person, he reproached someone, saying, ". . . Do you not know, miserable man, that one should not jest with God? Do you not know that death is certain and that it may surprise you at this very moment?" A few seconds passed before a man in the middle of the church rose from his place and then fell to the floor dead. Many attempted to help him, but it was too late. One of the Saint's biographers who was present attested to the fact that the body emitted an unbearable stench. The Saint is said to have stood silently.[10]

"God has given me the gift of discerning hypocrites," declared ST. JOHN BOSCO (d. 1888) to one of his spiritual sons. "When one of them comes near me, I discover his presence by a nauseous odour which I can hardly bear." Don Rua and some superiors of the house he founded for boys once heard him confess: "The good God really displays His goodness with regard to my youngsters. Whenever I happen to be amidst them, if there is one impure soul in the group, I know it immediately by its evil odour."[11]

MYSTICAL HEARTS

"The charity of God is poured forth in our hearts, by the Holy Ghost, who is given to us."— Romans 5:5

Since the heart is regarded as the seat of affections and emotions, it seems appropriate that the heart would figure in the mystical life of the Saints, since it is God Himself who repeatedly tells His Saints that it is there He wishes to reside . . . that He wants to capture our hearts and our love, as He has repeatedly expressed through visions and Holy Scripture.

As a reward for those Saints who have permitted His dominion over their hearts and have proved by their sanctity that He has all their love, the good Lord has seen fit by many miracles to reward them and has blessed them with signs and wonders that are related here.

Transverberation

The spiritual wounding of the heart, known as transverberation, is explained for us by ST. JOHN OF THE CROSS in his *Living Flame of Love.* The work was originally a poem, but the Saint wrote a commentary, his first redaction, between the years 1585 and 1587. Since the commentary was written three to five years after the death of St. Teresa of Avila, St. John might have used her experience in explaining how transverberation takes place. St. John of the Cross writes:

> It will happen that while the soul is inflamed with the love of God it will feel that a seraphim is assailing it by means of an arrow or dart which is all afire with love. And the seraphim pierces and cauterizes this soul which, like a red-hot coal, or better a flame, is already enkindled. And then in this cauterization, when the soul is transpierced with that dart, the flame gushes forth, vehemently and with a sudden ascent, like the fire in a fur-

nace or an oven when someone uses a poker or bellows to stir and excite it. And being wounded by this fiery dart, the soul feels the wound with unsurpassable delight.[1]

This is what transpired in most of the cases mentioned here, especially in that of ST. TERESA OF AVILA (d. 1582). Above the main altar of the Church of S. Maria della Vittoria in Rome is a magnificent sculpture by Bernini depicting a life-sized Angel holding a spear which is aimed at the heart of a slightly reclined and ecstatic figure of St. Teresa of Avila. The figures reflect an event that actually occurred which is undoubtedly the best-known case of a heart mystically wounded by an arrow of love. In her *Autobiography,* the Saint describes how her wounding, or transverberation, took place. St. Teresa writes:

> It pleased the Lord that I should see this angel in the following way. He was not tall, but short, and very beautiful, his face so aflame that he appeared to be one of the highest types of angel who seem to be all afire . . . In his hand I saw a long golden spear and at the end of the iron tip I seemed to see a point of fire. With this he seemed to pierce my heart several times so that it penetrated to my entrails. When he drew it out, I thought he was drawing them out with it and he left me completely afire with a great love for God. The pain was so sharp that it made me utter several moans; and so excessive was the sweetness caused me by this intense pain that one can never wish to lose it, nor will one's soul be content with anything less than God.[2]

During an exhumation of the Saint's body, the heart was removed and placed in a crystal reliquary. The heart has been medically examined on a number of occasions, especially in 1872, when it was meticulously studied by three physicians of the University of Salamanca. They noted the perforation made by the dart of the Angel and agreed that the preservation of the organ could not be credited to any natural or chemical means.[3] The relic is kept at the Incarnation, one of the Saint's convents of the Carmelite reform.

St. Teresa's transverberation is perhaps the best known, but there are several other Saints who had an *almost* similar experience, although few have had an apparition of an Angel in conjunction with the happening. One of these Saints was a spiritual daughter of St. Teresa of Avila. Popularly known as "The Little Flower," ST. THÉRÈSE OF THE CHILD JESUS AND OF THE HOLY FACE (d. 1897) was on her deathbed when she described the event to her sister Pauline, whose name in religion was Mother Agnes of Jesus. During the Little Flower's final illness, Mother Agnes made notes of all the Saint's conversations, counsels and spiritual experiences. These were later published in a little book entitled, *Novissima Verba*, and it is from this little book that we learn about the Saint's experience.

Soon after the Little Flower had composed her *Oblation to Merciful Love,* she experienced the following, which she related to Mother Agnes:

> I had commenced the Stations of the Cross in the choir, then all at once I felt myself wounded by a dart of fire so ardent that I thought I must die. I do not know how to explain it; it was as if an invisible hand had plunged me wholly into fire. Oh, what fire, and what sweetness at the same time! I was burning with love, and I thought one minute, nay, one second more, and I shall not be able to support such ardour without dying. I understood then what the Saints have said of those states which they had experienced so often. For me I have but experienced it that once, only for an instant, and afterwards I fell back again into my habitual dryness. From the age of fourteen I have also experienced the assaults of love. Ah! how much I love God! But it was not at all to be compared to what I experienced after my offering to Love . . .[4]

The Saint also revealed:

> I have had several transports of love, and one in particular during my Novitiate when I remained for a whole week far removed from this world. It seemed as though a veil were thrown over all earthly things. But, I was not then consumed by a real fire. I was able to bear those

transports of love without expecting to see the ties that bound me to earth give way; whilst, on the day of which I mentioned (the dart of fire), one minute, one second more and my soul must have been set free . . . True, the Divine Hand had withdrawn the fiery dart—but the wound was unto death![5]

A great admirer of St. Thérèse of the Child Jesus was PADRE PIO (d. 1968), the stigmatic priest of Pietrelcina, Italy. He too experienced a mystical wounding of love, but unlike the Little Flower, he, like St. Teresa of Avila, received the wound during a vision. The event took place on August 5, 1918 and was explained by Padre Pio in these words:

> I was hearing the confessions of our boys . . . when suddenly I was filled with extreme terror at the sight of a heavenly Being who presented Himself in the eye of my intellect. He held some kind of weapon in His hand, something like a long, sharp-pointed steel blade, which seemed to spew out fire. At the very instant that I saw all this, I saw that Personage hurl the weapon into my soul with all His might. It was only with difficulty that I did not cry out. I thought I was dying. I told the boy to leave because I felt ill and did not feel that I could continue . . . This agony lasted uninterruptedly until the morning of the 7th. I cannot tell you how much I suffered during this period of anguish. Even my internal organs were torn and ruptured by that weapon . . . From that day on I have been mortally wounded. I feel in the depths of my soul a wound that is always open and causes me continual agony.[6]

Padre Pio's biographer recorded in a deposition made in February, 1967 that Padre Pio "stated unambiguously that a visible, physical wound in his side resulted from the experience. For a time, he was able to conceal it so successfully that not even Padre Benedetto or Padre Agostino knew that the wound was physical as well as spiritual."[7]

Both of the religious companions of Padre Pio identified the experience as a "transverberation," or piercing of the heart. Padre

Benedetto once wrote in response to Padre Pio's question about the event: "Everything that is happening to you is the effect of love. It is a trial, a calling to co-redeem, and therefore it is a fountain of glory!" And again Padre Benedetto writes: "Kiss the hand that has given you the transverberation and sweetly cherish this wound, which is the stamp of love."[8]

A fiery dart also figures in the life of SR. MARY MARTHA CHAMBON (d. 1907), whose cause for beatification has been introduced. While Sr. Mary Martha was seriously ill in September of 1867, a great light illuminated her humble cell. In this light was the Holy Trinity. She watched with great joy as God the Father presented a Host to her while saying: "I give you Him Whom you have offered to Me so often." He then placed the Host upon her tongue. Next He revealed to her the mysteries of Bethlehem and the Cross, filling her soul with special insights into these mysteries. Then He bestowed upon her the Holy Spirit as a fiery dart, saying, "Here are light, suffering and love! Love will be for Me; for you light to discover My will. Finally suffering in order to suffer from moment to moment as I wish you should do."[9]

Sometime after this vision Our Lord revealed to Sr. Mary Martha the Devotion of the Holy Wounds with the accompanying chaplet, which bears numerous promises for the good of souls.

In his biography of VEN. MARIA VILLANI OF NAPLES (d. 1670), which was written four years after her death, Fr. Francis Marchese, O.P. revealed that Ven. Maria believed she had been wounded in the side and heart by a fiery spear of love. The wound was definitely apparent and was carefully examined by three of her confessors, who signed affidavits to what they had seen and touched. One of these confessors was Dominican Leonardo di Lettere, a man of great reputation and sanctity whose cause for beatification was introduced soon after his death.

The fire of love sparked by the flaming arrow produced a great deal of heat which brought about a great thirst, so that Maria was compelled to drink an excessive amount of water.

Following her death and autopsy, her biographer declared that a formal affidavit regarding the condition of the heart was made by the surgeons, Domenico Trifone and Francesco Pinto. They recorded that the open wound found in the heart corresponded exactly to the wound on the outside of the body. The biographer wrote that he had seen and touched and examined the wound in the heart and described the wound this way: "The lips of the wound are hard and seared, just as happens when the cautery is used, to remind us, no doubt, that it was made with a spear of fire."[10] (See Chapter 12, "Fire and Heat of Love," for more details about the heat produced by the heart.)

What *might* be the first case of transverberation took place in favor of ST. LUTGARDE (d. 1246), a Cistercian mystic who was a devotee of the Roman martyr, St. Agnes. For some time she had had a burning desire to suffer martyrdom as St. Agnes had done, and often expressed this wish to Our Lord. One night, when she entered her room, she began praying beside her bed when the thought of St. Agnes' martyrdom again stirred her heart. As Thomas Merton writes in his biography of St. Lutgarde:

> Suddenly a vein near her heart burst, and through a wide open wound in her side, blood began to pour forth, soaking her robe and cowl. As she lost her senses and sank to the floor, Jesus appeared to her in glory, His face radiant with joy, and said to her: "Because of the great and fervent desire of martyrdom with which thou hast now shed thy blood, know that thou shalt receive the same reward in Heaven as the most blessed Agnes received, in the severing of her head for My faith: because by thy desire even unto the shedding of blood, thou hast equaled her martyrdom."

Thomas Merton's biography of the Saint continues, "Thus wounded once, with a wound like the spear wound in Christ's Heart, Lutgarde was never wounded again: but she kept the scar until the end of her life."[11]

ST. CHARLES OF SEZZE (d. 1670) was reared by his grandmother, whose influence led him to a great love of God. At the age of seventeen, due to his love of the Virgin Mother of God, he made a vow of chastity and thereafter was seized with a great desire for holiness. After joining the Franciscan Order he was sent to Rome, where he received remarkable enlightenment concerning mysteries of the faith, so that learned theologians were astonished by his knowledge and consulted with him on difficult questions. Even cardinals, and especially Pope Clement IX, sought his advice.

One day, while St. Charles was adoring the Holy Eucharist, "a ray of light like an arrow went out from the Sacred Host and impressed a wound in his left side. This wound was still visible after his death."

Symbols of the Passion

ST. CLARE OF MONTEFALCO (d. 1308), an Italian mystic of the Augustinian Order, was graced with an apparition of Our Lord during which He said to her: "I have sought a place in the world where I might plant My Cross, and have found no better site than your heart." She later told her sisters in religion, "If you seek the Cross of Christ, take my heart; there you will find the suffering Lord."

After her death, the Sisters remembered her words and had the heart extracted. The larger-than-average heart, when it was opened, revealed clearly distinguishable symbols of Our Lord's Passion, all composed of cardiac tissue. These figures included:

• The crucifix, which is about the size of one's thumb. The head of the Crucified is inclined toward the right arm. The clearly formed corpus is pallid white except for the tiny wound of the lance, which is a livid reddish color. White tissue covers the loins of the Crucified.

• The scourge is formed of a hard, whitish nerve which has knobbed ends representing the cruel instrument of the scourging. The column is formed of a round white nerve, hard as stone, that is entwined by a nerve representing the cord which fastened Christ to the pillar.

• The Crown of Thorns is composed of tiny sharp nerves.

• The three nails are formed of dark fibrous tissue, exceedingly sharp. A nerve represents the lance, while the sponge is formed of a single nerve with a tiny cluster of nerve endings resembling the sponge at its tip.[12]

The incorrupt heart is enclosed in a bust of the Saint and can be viewed under a crystal which is located in the chest portion of the figure. The incorrupt body of St. Clare can also be viewed in the Sanctuario S. Chiara da Montefalco. In art the Saint is depicted holding a crucifix, the bottom of which penetrates her heart.

Some four hundred years after the death of St. Clare of Montefalco, ST. VERONICA GIULIANI (d. 1727) was the recipient of a similar manifestation. A stigmatist and visionary, St. Veronica told her companions at the Capuchin Monastery at Citta di Castello that symbols of Christ's Passion were kept in her heart. She even drew a picture indicating their location. A post-mortem examination, performed in the presence of a bishop and many witnesses, revealed the symbols of the Passion which corresponded to those she had drawn. Although the body was incorrupt for many years, it was eventually destroyed by an inundation of the Tiber River. However, the heart is still kept in a special reliquary and is said by physicians to be well preserved, although the figures of the Passion have become less defined in recent years.[13]

An Exchange of Hearts

One day while ST. CATHERINE OF SIENA (d. 1380) was in prayer she continued to recite these words from *Psalm* 51 v. 12: "Create a clean heart in me, O God: and renew a right spirit within my bowels."

Over and over again she asked the Heavenly Father to take her own heart and will from her. Our Lord heard the prayer and appeared to her. It then seemed to the Saint that He opened her left side, took out her heart and then went away with it. The Saint afterward told her confessor that she no longer had a heart. Needless to say, even though she attempted a number of times to convince him, he did not believe it and in a kind and charitable manner dismissed her claim.[14]

Another time, when St. Catherine was in the Dominican church in Siena, she fell into an ecstasy. After retreating from it a light from Heaven encircled her, and in this light appeared the Saviour, who held in His hands a bright red human heart. Approaching Catherine, He opened her left side once again and placed the heart within her chest, saying: "Dearest daughter, as I took your heart away, now, you see, I am giving you Mine, so that you can go on living with it forever." He closed the opening He had made, but as a sign of the miracle, a scar remained.

St. Catherine's biographer, Bl. Raymond of Capua, reassures us that the Saint's companions saw this scar and told him and the others about it. Bl. Raymond writes:

When I determined to get to the truth, she herself was obliged to confess to me that this was so, and she added that never afterwards had she been able to say, "Lord, I give You my heart," since He already had it.[15]

The scar was not the only sign that proved the reality of what had taken place. Bl. Raymond continues:

Seeing or receiving the Sacrament of the Altar always generated fresh and indescribable bliss in her soul, so that her heart would very often throb with joy within her breast, making such a loud noise that it could be heard even by her companions. At last, having noticed this so often, they told her confessor Fra Tommaso about it. He made a close inquiry into the matter and on finding it was true, left the fact in writing as an imperishable record. This noise bore no resemblance to the gurgling that goes on naturally in the human stomach; there was nothing natural about the noise at all. There is nothing surprising in the fact that a heart given in a supernatural way should act in a supernatural way too, for, as the Prophet says, "My heart and my flesh have rejoiced in the Living God."[16]

St. Catherine seemed to reaffirm the prophet's words when she declared: "My mind is so full of joy and happiness that I am amazed my soul stays in my body."[17]

VEN. DOMINICA A PARADISO (d. 1553), a Florentine member of the Dominican Order, received word from Our Lord that He no longer wanted her concealed and retired from the world, but to do great things for His glory. She prayed that she was not fit for great things unless He changed her. To this Our Lord replied,

And I will change you and will give you a noble and magnanimous heart; wherefore prepare for keen and terrible sufferings; for it is by them that your heart and blood are to be purged and renovated, and fitted for My service in the eyes of men.[18]

The Venerable immediately felt the approach of sufferings and began to experience faintings and weakness. After a number of weeks in this state, she received another vision of Our Lord, who extracted her heart from her chest and substituted one of burning fire. She rose immediately from her sick bed and realized a renewal of her body and mind. Her sight became keen, a fragrance emanated from her body which attached itself to everything she touched, her smell, touch and hearing were acute to an extraordinary degree. A strange eloquence was now heard to flow from her lips while infused knowledge enlightened her mind.[19]

Ven. Dominica's spirituality soon attracted a number of young ladies, who placed themselves under her direction. After moving into a small house they began to observe the Dominican Rule. Eventually a regular convent was built in which Dominica served as superior until her death.[20]

ST. MARGARET MARY ALACOQUE (d. 1690) had many apparitions of Our Lord in which He gave instructions for the implementation of the Devotion of the Sacred Heart. In her autobiography she writes that Our Lord "asked me for my heart, which I begged Him to take. He did so and placed it in His own adorable heart, where He showed it to me as a little atom which was being consumed in this great furnace, and withdrawing it thence as a burning flame in the form of a heart."[21]

When only twelve years of age, ST. MICHAEL OF THE SAINTS (d. 1625) left his hometown of Vich in Catalonia to join the Trinitarian Order that had been founded some five hundred years earlier by St. John of Matha. It has been said of St. Michael of the Saints that he lived in a constant state of rapture, although this mystical experience ebbed at times and seemed less vehement. He is said to have performed every obligation of his religious and priestly life. Appearing more as an angel than a man, it was written of him:

> Wherefore Our Lord was pleased to bestow a very great and singular grace upon His faithful servant, and on a day when Miguel was in ecstasy, He deigned to make the mystical exchange of his Most Sacred Heart with the heart of the Saint.

St. Michael of the Saints died at Valladolid in 1625 and was canonized by Pope Pius IX on Whit Sunday, 1862.[22]

Mystical Hearts

BL. MARGARET OF CITTA-DI-CASTELLO (d. 1320), who is also known as Bl. Margaret of Metola, was abandoned by her parents when a cure for her blindness was not granted at a favorite shrine. Margaret was adopted by a poor family, even though she was blind, dwarfed, hunchbacked and lame. In spite of these afflictions she served her neighbors, taught catechism, and recited by heart and memory the Office of the Blessed Virgin, as well as the Psalter. She became a Dominican tertiary and, although she was blind all her life, she was the recipient of many visions. She performed many miracles and was often heard to exclaim: "Oh, if you only knew what I have in my heart!"

After her death at the age of thirty-three, permission was received to open the heart which she had mentioned so often. In it were found three pellets, or pearls, on which were carved religious symbols which some recognized as being the images of Our Lord, the Blessed Mother and St. Joseph. This, of course, is what Margaret referred to when she often sighed, "Oh, if you only knew what I have in my heart!"[23] The body of Bl. Margaret remains incorrupt.

Toward the end of his life, ST. GERARD MAJELLA (d. 1755), the mystic member of the Redemptorist Order, was inundated with the love of God—so much so that he often heaved sighs to relieve the excessive ardor and sweetness that he felt for Our Lord. Sometimes these sighs were so audible that he received looks of curiosity and astonishment. One day Fr. Cajone reproved him for the sounds, which he felt could be restrained. Without a word, the Saint took the priest's hand and laid it on his heart. Thoroughly surprised by the vehemence of the beating, Fr. Cajone asked how he could possibly endure the beating and live?

Concerned about the condition of the Saint's heart, Dr. Santorelli was called to examine him. Taking the doctor's hand, the Saint placed it on his heart, which was beating with unnatural violence as though trying to escape from his chest. To the doctor's amazement, the Saint exclaimed: "Were I alone on a mountain, it seems to me that I would set fire to the world with my flames of love."[24]

A different case is submitted by ST. JOSEPH OF CUPERTINO (d. 1663), who is known for his many ecstatic levitations. When St. Joseph was sixty years old and on his deathbed, he expressed his love for Our Lord and the Blessed Mother in many ways and even encouraged his companions to suggest ejaculations of love for him. Then, turning to the crucifix, he spoke these words: "Take this heart, burn and rive this heart, my Jesus." "Rive" means "to tear, split or cleave." After praying the *Ave Maris Stella,* he surrendered his soul to his Creator.

It was decided by his superiors that his body should be embalmed. During this process the body was opened and the heart examined. The attending embalmers must have been quite surprised to find that the pericardium, the tissue around the heart, was shrivelled. Their amazement must have reached a peak when they discovered that the ventricles of the heart were without blood and the heart itself withered and dry.[25]

The Saint had apparently lived by means of the mystical workings of God. It would seem his deathbed request, that his heart be taken and burned, had actually been realized long ago, since the consensus of opinion was that the condition of the heart was the effect of his burning love of God.

The Heart Enlarged and Enflamed

When ST. PHILIP NERI (d. 1595) was twenty-nine years old he was praying with extreme earnestness for the gifts of the Holy Spirit in preparation for the feast of Pentecost. During his prayer he seemed to see a globe of fire that entered his mouth and fell into his heart. At once he felt an intense physical heat that was so overwhelming that the Saint took off his shirt and threw himself on the ground in an attempt to cool himself. When he stood up he was overwhelmed with joy. Instinctively he placed his hand on his chest and felt a swelling as large as his fist. At once there began the loud palpitation of the heart, similar to that experienced by St. Gerard Majella. St. Philip was to experience this unnatural palpitation of the heart for the rest of his life, particularly when he was praying, hearing confessions, offering Holy Mass or distributing Holy Communion.

Those who heard these palpitations described them as being like the blows of a hammer, and they observed a shaking, or trembling, that shook the chair on which the Saint sat.

The Saint always felt a burning heat in the region of the heart and throat, so that he sought relief, even in the depths of winter, by opening his windows wide.[26]

After the Saint's death physicians and surgeons who had known St. Philip were called to investigate the mysterious swelling on his chest. The Saint's biographer writes:

> Examination proved that the two ribs over the heart were broken and arched outwards; the heart was unusually large, while the great artery leading from it was twice the normal size; there was no sign of any disease.[27]

The situation was so unusual that the physicians, after their lengthy examination and a detailed consultation, attested in the form of a written oath that the cause of the phenomenon was supernatural and miraculous.[28]

Recalling that St. Gerard Majella had a strong and audible beating of the heart through an excess of love, so too did ST. PAUL OF THE CROSS (d. 1755) experience this, and like St. Philip Neri, he also experienced the displacing of ribs due to an enlarged heart. St. Paul's biographer writes:

> His heart, burning with love, and in continual excitement for the Sovereign Good, and put thereby into continual vehement action, produced in his bodily frame a quick, strong palpitation, which, on certain days and occasions—as on Friday, on feasts, and when he was absorbed in prayer—became so impetuous that it caused him excessive pain, and forced him to break forth into groans and deep sighs of love, which it was most touching to hear.

There also took place the elevation of two ribs on the Saint's left side which he did not succeed in keeping concealed because of the physical evidence it produced. The biographer again writes:

> Among others, an experienced professor of medicine observed it, and in the *processes* deposed to the fact as one resulting from a supernatural cause. This interior

furnace of the love of God can alone account for what
the religious remarked from time to time about the under
garments which the Saint had used, and especially the
linen vests which, where they had touched his heart,
were found scorched, as though they had been near a
great fire.[29]

Manna and the Heart

Following the death of ST. FRANCIS DE SALES (d. 1622) the
founder, with St. Jane Frances de Chantal, of the Visitation Order,
his heart was extracted for placement in a silver coffer and is of particular interest since it began to exude a clear oil (or manna) at
intervals throughout the years. Because the crystal in which the
heart was kept was not hermetically sealed, permission was
received in March of 1948 for the wrapping of the heart in a new
piece of linen. Found dry at this time, the heart was covered with a
piece of linen and an outer layer of tissue the same color as the
heart. Spots of white appeared between the relic and the sides of the
crystal container during the spring of 1952. The superior then
ordered another examination of the relic, which took place the same
year on August 27. At this time the heart was not examined scien-
tifically. The witnesses thought the powder resembled salt, which
was considered a natural phenomenon because the seal of the container was not perfect, permitting the penetration of air.

After the white powder and the layer of tissue were removed, the
linen cloth that was wrapped around the heart was found to be
imbued with blood. This cloth was placed in a container for safe-
keeping. The heart was then wrapped in a new linen and was placed
in a hermetically sealed crystal especially made for the enshrinement of the heart. This, in turn, was then placed inside the original
reliquary.[30]

The heart was carefully examined on August 28, 1953 by two distinguished men of medicine and Church officials, who declared that
the preservation of the heart was "Not a common occurrence." One
of the professors surmised that the bleeding of the heart was actually caused by "atmospheric humidity which soaked the external
material." But others declared that the irregular pattern of the stain
and its depth within the fabric could only have been, and was
indeed, human blood.

A theory was suggested as a reason for the appearance of blood.

Following World War II, religious houses in Europe were in a sad condition, with their religious suffering various kinds of privations. To remedy the situation, Church officials decided to organize various orders into federations and confederations. The Visitation Order was the first to be organized by Rome with the appointment of the order's first mother general. Since all the foundations of the Visitation Order were previously independent in following the Rule of St. Francis de Sales, this appointment was thought to be the reason that the heart bled as a sign of the founder's dissatisfaction with the arrangement. The confederation was eventually dismissed, although the federation of the order is still functioning for the purpose of offering mutual assistance.[31]

The incorrupt heart is still kept by the Visitation nuns of Treviso.

The co-founder of the Visitation Order with St. Francis de Sales was ST. JANE FRANCES DE CHANTAL (d. 1641). Just as his heart was attended by a phenomenon which was an exudation of oil and blood, the heart of the foundress also displayed a prodigy, but one of a different kind. During one of her body's exhumations, the heart was extracted and was given to the convent of the order at Nevers. The heart was always somewhat shrunken in size, but at times:

> It would swell like a heart under the pressure of sorrow. On the eve of great crises that have desolated the Church, it has been seen to expand and swell like a heart about to burst into groans.[32]

The heart is kept in a bronze and crystal urn that is found in the sanctuary of the Basilica of the Visitation in Annecy, France.

MYSTICAL HEARTS.
(Left) The reliquary that contains the incorrupt heart of St. Jane Frances de Chantal (d. 1641).
(Below) The reliquary containing the incorrupt heart of St. Francis de Sales (d. 1622) and the cloth that absorbed its blood in 1948, more than 300 years after the Saint's death.

Both hearts are kept by Visitation nuns in Europe.

EXCHANGE OF HEARTS. St. Catherine of Siena asks the Heavenly Father to take her heart and will from her. Our Lord appeared to her holding a human heart and said, "Dearest daughter, as I took your heart away, now, you see, I am giving you Mine."

WRITTEN IN HER HEART. St. Mary Magdalene de' Pazzi's heart is mystically inscribed by St. Augustine with the words, "*Verbum caro factum est*" ("The Word was made flesh").

HEAVENLY WOUND. St. Teresa of Avila is pierced by an arrow of divine love.
(Below) The reliquary containing the heart of St. Teresa of Avila, which bears the wound of divine love.

TRANSVERBERATION, or piercing of the heart, was delivered to Padre Pio by a heavenly Being while he was in the confessional. A physical wound was visible as a result. (Used with permission, *The Voice of Padre Pio* magazine.)

SYMBOLS IN HER HEART. The transverberation of stigmatist and visionary St. Veronica Giuliani resulted in the imprint of symbols of Christ's Passion within her heart.

MIRACULOUS TRANSPORT

"And they went down into the water, both Philip and the eunuch: and he baptized him. And when they were come up out of the water, the Spirit of the Lord took away Philip; and the eunuch saw him no more. And he went on his way rejoicing. But Philip was found in Azotus; and passing through, he preached the gospel to all the cities, till he came to Caesarea."—Acts 8:38-40

Chapter 1 deals with bilocation, the phenomenon in which a Saint is in two places at the same time. Miraculous transport deals with those Saints and holy persons who, at one time or another, moved about in unusual ways, sometimes moving with unusual speed, or by using an unlikely vehicle for travelling, or by arriving at their destination without being aware of having travelled or of what took place while they were between one destination and the other.

A good example of miraculous transport is given in the *Acts of the Apostles*. An Angel instructed the Apostle Philip to travel south, down from Jerusalem into Gaza. Philip did as he was directed and came upon an Ethiopian eunuch, a court official of great authority, who was sitting in his chariot reading Isaias the Prophet. Philip asked if he understood what he was reading, and after receiving a negative response, began to explain it to him. When the eunuch understood, he proclaimed that Jesus was the Son of God and asked Philip to baptize him. For what happened next, please see the above Bible quote.

In the lives of the Saints we have many instances of miraculous transport. One of the first is given in the writings of St. Athanasius. In his *Life of St. Antony*, he tells about ST. AMMON THE GREAT (d. 350), who was travelling with his disciple, Theodore. When they reached a stream they had planned to cross, they saw that the water had risen and overflowed the banks. They realized that they had to swim instead of walk across. The two separated to undress, but St. Ammon, being too shy to swim across naked, was trying to make up his mind what to do when suddenly he was transported to the other side. Theodore, coming up and seeing that he had crossed over without getting wet, pressed the Saint for an explanation and was so insistent that the Saint finally confessed the miracle, making his companion promise not to tell of it until after his death.[1]

Another early case is given by St. Gregory in his *Dialogues*. This miracle is attributed to the sanctity of ST. BENEDICT (d. 543). Because of the Saint's reputation for holiness, noble families brought their children to him for their education. In his care were Maurus, a boy of twelve, and Placidus, who was seven. One day, while Placidus was fetching water at the lake in Subiaco, he stumbled and fell into the water. St. Benedict, even though he was at the monastery, knew of the accident through supernatural means and called for the nearby Maurus to run quickly to the lake, saying, "Make haste! The child has fallen into the water." Maurus ran quickly to the lake and, not realizing what he was doing, began to run on the water. After travelling the distance of a "bow-shot" from land, he saw Placidus, who was struggling, and taking him by the hair he dragged him quickly to land. When Maurus reached the shore, he looked back and realized that he had walked upon the water, which he had not thought about until then. St. Benedict ascribed the miracle to the obedience of Maurus, while others realized that it had taken place because of the mystical gifts of the Saint.[2]

We are told that ST. DOMINIC (d. 1221), founder of the great order that carries his name, was travelling one evening in the company of a Cistercian monk when they approached a neighboring church. According to the Saint's custom, he wanted to spend the night in prayer before the altar, but was disappointed on finding the church tightly locked for the night. Both religious decided to spend the night in prayer on the church steps when suddenly, "without being able to say how, they found themselves before the high altar inside the church, and remained there until break of day."[3]

One time when St. Dominic was in Rome, he was approached by the newly consecrated Bishop Ivo of Cracow, who was travelling with his two recently ordained nephews, ST. HYACINTH (d. 1257) and Bl. Ceslaus. The Archbishop had heard of St. Dominic's ideals and his newly founded order and asked St. Dominic to send friars to

Poland. Since none of the friars were acquainted with the Polish language, St. Dominic looked around until his gaze fell on Hyacinth and Ceslaus. The Saint gave the two young priests the habit, trained them himself and sent them to evangelize Poland. So successful was Hyacinth that he was called "the Polish St. Dominic."

St. Hyacinth was especially devoted to the Blessed Mother, and she appeared to him on a number of occasions. The Holy Virgin once called on him for help when the Tartars were about to invade a convent. The Saint was hurrying to remove the Blessed Sacrament to hide it when he heard Our Lady telling him not to leave her statue behind to be desecrated. Since the statue was very large, the Saint did not know how he could possibly carry it, but he heard Our Lady's voice saying, "I will lighten the load." Trusting in the Blessed Mother, he picked up the statue in one hand with ease, while carrying the Blessed Sacrament in the other. Not only did he carry the statue without difficulty, but he also escaped without harm from the burning convent and walked across the Dnieper River bearing the Blessed Sacrament and the statue of Our Lady.[4]

A similar miracle is reported by Butler, who states that St. Hyacinth was a notable wonder-worker. In the Saint's bull of canonization another miracle of walking on water is noted. It took place at Moravia and is said to have been witnessed by over four hundred people. We are told that St. Hyacinth was on his way to preach at Wisgrade and approached the banks of the Vistula with three companions. The river was unusually turbulent, so much so that boats refused to leave land. Accordingly,

> Hyacinth, having made the Sign of the Cross, walked upon the waters of that deep and rapid river as if it had been firm land, in the sight of a multitude of people waiting for him on the opposite bank. Another incident is related later in his life, when he was preaching to the Russians.[5]

A like incident occurred when ST. SERAPHIN OF MONTE-GRANARO (d. 1604) intended to visit the Blessed Mother's shrine at Loreto, near his home. But the River Potenza stood in the way, and on that particular day the water was so high that boatmen refused to venture across. In his eagerness to get to the shrine, Seraphin stepped out onto the water. Instantly it became like solid ground beneath him so that he was able to cross the river both going, and again on his return. This holy Capuchin was favored with other spiritual gifts that were displayed during his assignment as porter of his monastery.[6]

One of the many wonders worked by the great ST. ANTHONY OF PADUA (d. 1231) was that of helping his father, Don Martino de Bouillon, in a time of great distress. The event began in Lisbon when a young nobleman was murdered as he was leaving a cathedral. He was seized and murdered by assassins, and his body was thrown into the nearby garden of Don Martino de Bouillon. Don Martino was arrested on suspicion of the crime and was imprisoned. After his father's situation was made known to St. Anthony through supernatural means, he asked his superior for permission to leave the monastery in Padua, where he then lived. Since St. Anthony was the Provincial, permission from the superior was not necessary, but we are told St. Anthony did this out of humility.

Since the trial was already in progress, the Saint began the journey, praying that he would reach Lisbon in time to rescue his father from what threatened to be a condemnation. His biographer relates: "Filled with hope and perfect trust, suddenly he found himself miraculously transported to Lisbon." Just as suddenly, the Saint appeared in the courtroom and presented himself before the judges, who were startled and amazed by his miraculous appearance.

The Saint asked to speak in defense of his father and declared that his father's innocence would be made known by the murdered man himself. All things seemed to be possible for the Saint. He led the way to the victim's grave, had it opened and the body uncovered. Then, commanding the dead man to speak in the name of God, the corpse sat up and declared in a loud voice that Martino de Bouillon was guiltless. He then asked absolution from the Saint and then assumed his former position. The judges, who were thoroughly bewildered, yet begged the Saint to reveal the name of the murderer. The Saint humbly replied, "I come to clear the innocent, not to denounce the guilty."

The biographer continues: "When Anthony reappeared at Padua he had been absent two nights and a single day."[7]

BL. BENTIVOGLIA DE BONIS (d. 1232) joined the Franciscan Order during the lifetime of St. Francis of Assisi and was known for his zeal for souls and his love of poverty and simplicity. In quoting an ancient source, Butler tells us that

> . . . while sojourning once alone at Trave Bonanti, in order to take charge of and serve a certain leper, Bl. Bentivoglia received a commandment from his superior to depart thence and go unto another place, which was about fifteen miles distant, and, not willing to abandon the leper, he took him with great fervour of charity, and placed him on his shoulders, and carried him from the dawn till the rising of the sun all the fifteen miles of the way, even to the place where he was sent, which was called Monte San Vicino, which journey, if he had been an eagle, he could not have flown in so short a time, and this divine miracle put the whole country round in amazement and admiration.[8]

Bl. Bentivoglia De Bonis died on Christmas Day in San Severino, the city of his birth. The Franciscan Order observes his feast on January 2.

PÈRE LAMY (d. 1931) was a parish priest who worked countless wonders that amazed those who witnessed them. He was closely affiliated with the Angels, who helped him in countless ways. The holy priest admits:

> I have been upheld by the holy angels many a time, when I have been exhausted with weariness, and have been brought from one place to another without knowing anything about it. I used to say, "My God, how tired I am." I was in my parish, far away, often at night, and I found myself to the Place St. Lucian all at once. How it happened I don't know.[9]

When the holy priest was seventy years of age and suffering from heart disease, we are told by M. Maurice Berthon (from the *Bulletin* of January, 1937) that:

> He used to walk slowly and with the help of a stick. Now we have often had occasion to see him go round without

support at full speed. Fairly well accustomed to calculate speed, I can assert that he went about eight miles an hour. A young man even excessively hurried could not have walked so fast without running. Needless to say, we were dumbfounded at this extraordinary fact.[10]

A similar phenomenon took place in 1926 which so amazed the witnesses that two of them wrote lengthy accounts of what took place. The event occurred while the holy Père and his companions were visiting the little village of Mattaincourt, the parish and shrine of St. Peter Fourier. They visited the church, the reliquary and the tomb of the Saint.

Père Lamy expressed a desire to cross to the other side of a nearby river and climb a hill that was topped by a little oratory which was probably used by St. Peter Fourier. The account, again given by M. Maurice Berthon, tells what took place.

> M. Caillier refused to go beyond the bridge, for the hill is both muddy and slippery. So Mme. Caillier and I took the road on foot, leaving the Abbé to take the short cut . . . He set off in front of us, but we could not believe our eyes. He, who dragged his feet so painfully these last days and seemed out of breath after the least walk, went on with agility up this abominable road. At the little circular oratory which crowns the hill, we saw him kneel and fall to prayer.
>
> He came down as fast as he went up. When we rejoined him near the car I said, laughing, "But you have wings, Father, what about your heart?" "My heart, I did not feel it for an instant. I asked the Saint (St. Peter Fourier) to help me climb. It is a mark of mercy from this holy priest to an old scallywag, who isn't worth the trouble."[11]

Mrs. Caillier gives her impression of seeing the unusual transport of Père Lamy on their visit to the shrine of St. Peter Fourier:

> Guess our surprise, both of us, to see the dear old man literally run up that hill, without a trace of breathlessness. It took us all our time to follow him at a dis-

tance. Coming down, on being told that he was walking like a young man, his answer was, "The Saint helped me to go up and took me by the hand."[12]

During the many travels of ST. COLETTE (d. 1447), she found it necessary to avail herself of the services of muleteers to carry the bundles of provisions and religious articles she was bringing to one or other of her convents. Usually of profane tongue, the men are said to have given the Saint courteous considerations and to have resisted their usual inclination toward vulgarity. Her biographer tells us that when the road was exceptionally rough, they would seat her on one of the animals. Typically engaged in contemplation, she "nevertheless held herself so steadily, without leaning to one side or the other, that it seemed as if the Angels upheld her." Her biographer continues:

> It also seemed to the mule-drivers and to the others in the party that at times when she was on foot and the roads were at their worst, "she did not touch the earth" and no one, no matter how strong or how good a walker, could keep up with her.[13]

ST. GERMAINE COUSIN (d. 1601) was a little shepherdess who endured a number of ailments that repulsed her stepmother. In consequence she was not allowed in the house, could not play with her stepbrothers and sisters, was poorly fed, was forced to sleep outdoors under a staircase and was assigned the duties of shepherdess. Every morning she attended Holy Mass, but in order to reach the church from the pasture she had to cross a stream that was sometimes swollen by rainwater. On one occasion the stream was so high that many were afraid to cross it. People who were accustomed to seeing her walk across the stream when it was shallow predicted that Germaine would not possibly attempt to cross, now that it was fearfully deep. But two villagers strongly asserted that as Germaine approached the stream, the waters parted to provide a safe passageway, just as the Red Sea had parted for the Israelites.[14]

Among the many mystical gifts of ST. MARTIN DE PORRES (d. 1639) was that of miraculous transport. Three examples are given in one of his biographies.

One case involved two young religious of St. Martin's monastery
who decided they would leave the order and left without notifying
Martin or the prior. After journeying for some hours they entered a
place called Zercedo and found a room in which to spend the night.
St. Martin, because of his mystical knowledge, knew where they
were, and with the permission of the novice master and the superior
set out to retrieve them. On arriving at the house, the Saint is said
to have entered the room through a locked door and awakened the
boys, who were greatly surprised to see him. After he had spoken
with them about the grace of their vocation, the boys readily
decided to return.

We are told that their speedy repentance was rewarded with a new
miracle, since the three were suddenly transported back to the Convent of the Holy Rosary. The next morning the novice master and
the prior saw the two boys quietly at prayer without anyone else
having found out about their departure the night before. St. Martin's
prophecy that the two boys would become worthy members of the
order was realized. It is said they cherished to the day of their death
the remembrance of the Saint's sudden appearance before them and
their inexplicable return to the priory.[15]

Another time, the prior sent thirty novices to picnic in a wood
about a half mile away and asked St. Martin to accompany them.
The young men enjoyed their lunch and the relaxation, but
whether they were too taken with the beauty of the place, or their
conversation, they soon realized that it was later than they had realized and that they would certainly not return to the monastery in
time for their usual prayers. St. Martin himself was concerned, but
after a few moments of prayer, he asked the novices to gather
around him and to have confidence in Almighty God. Then he said,
"Follow me." "Instantly, without their having taken a single step,
they found themselves at the door of the monastery."[16] The novices
took their places in choir and began their prayers without being a
moment late.

The third example given of "the Flying Brother," as his companions called him, took place when St. Martin and his faithful assistant were busily planting medicinal herbs and fruit trees in the
highlands of Los Amancaes. Before they had completed their work,
it began to grow dark. Once again the Saint resorted to prayer. To
the great astonishment and terror of the companion, he and the
Saint were suddenly transported to the banks of the river that flowed

close by the Dominican monastery. Their transport had taken place in the brief space of a moment.[17]

The following example is unusual in that it was not only a Saint who experienced a miraculous transport, but also an article belonging to him. When ST. JOHN JOSEPH OF THE CROSS (d. 1734) was advanced in years, he found it necessary to use a walking stick, which he was using on the feast of St. Januarius while walking to the Naples cathedral to venerate the Saint's relic. Due to the great press of people also going to the cathedral, the stick slipped from his hands and was lost in the crowd. Unable to walk without it, the Saint sat on the steps of the cathedral and prayed to St. Januarius to help him in his difficulty. Immediately he was transported, first to the pulpit and then to the door of the cathedral.

Arriving at the cathedral was the Duke of Lauriano, the Saint's spiritual son, who was astonished at seeing the elderly Saint sitting in such an undignified position. On being asked if he could be of help, the Saint cheerfully refused his offer and motioned for him to enter the cathedral, saying, "You will see the walking stick in there." The duke did as he was instructed and walked up the aisle, but before he reached the high altar he heard the cries: "A miracle!" "A miracle!" On turning around, he saw the walking stick moving through the air at a distance of about a foot above the heads of the congregation. Those who were outside saw the stick pass through the door, strike the Saint gently on the chest and then settle in his hand. Because of the excitement it caused, St. John Joseph hobbled home with his stick to avoid the people who were following him and exclaiming at the miracle they had just witnessed.[18]

This incident seems extraordinary, but we are assured by the Saint's biographer that it caused quite a sensation, and that a great many people both inside and outside the cathedral witnessed the miracle.

After ST. PAUL OF THE CROSS (d. 1775) had preached a mission at Piombino, his friends and some of the people who had attended the mission accompanied him to the sea, where he was seen to set sail with a number of passengers. Among those who were seeing him off was Dr. Gherardini, who remained on the pier until he had lost sight of the ship. On returning to Piombino, the doctor was entering the home of a friend when he saw the Saint coming out of a room. Not believing his eyes, since he had witnessed the Saint sailing away, he went to him and asked how he could have returned so quickly. "I have been with you down at the pier, I have watched you to a distance out at sea, and now I find you here?" To this the Saint replied, "Hush. Be still. I came here for an act of charity." The Saint then disappeared.[19]

While ST. ANTHONY MARY CLARET (d. 1870) was a seminarian, he resided at Vich in the rectory of Don Fortunato Bres, his very good friend and advisor. A number of years later, the venerable old priest, while on his way to the cathedral to celebrate Holy Mass, slipped on the ice, fell and broke his leg. Don Fortunato asked a friend to notify St. Anthony Mary of his accident and his wish to see his former protégé. St. Anthony Mary was then in Olost. The distance between Olost and Vich was four leagues. Depending on the country in which a league is measured, this could be from two and a half to four and a half miles.

The young man hurried to Olost to relay the message, but before he reached the city, St. Anthony Mary knocked on the elderly priest's door and walked in. Although it had been snowing, his clothes were not damp. He had had to walk through places that were muddy from melting snow, nevertheless his feet were dry and clean. When asked how it was that he arrived so soon, when the messenger had only left a few minutes earlier, the Saint replied that an irresistible impulse had brought him there.

Don Fortunato asked if the Saint had celebrated Mass that morning, and he received an affirmative reply. Not only had St. Anthony Mary celebrated Holy Mass, but he had heard confessions and had eaten his breakfast.

On being asked what time it was when he left Olost to arrive so soon, since it was then seven-fifteen, the Saint replied that he had heard confessions until seven and then started on his journey to the old priest's bedside.

Everyone was amazed that a journey of four leagues, over mountain paths covered with snow, could have been undertaken in ten minutes.

The people of Vich, astonished at this wonder, asked the Pastor of Olost how this event could have taken place. The pastor's sister replied:

I saw him in the confessional until seven. He came out suddenly, saying that he was going to Vich; I ordered a servant to saddle the horse. He followed Fr. Claret with all possible speed, but could not overtake him, nor could he even catch a glimpse of him. Strange to say, no footprints were left upon the falling snow.[20]

Another case of miraculous transport involves St. Anthony Mary Claret and another of his friends, Fr. Don Juan Coma, a priest known for his virtue. On that day, St. Anthony Mary was preaching at Figueras and left quickly so as to arrive at Gerona that same afternoon. The distance was about six leagues. The Saint invited his friend, Fr. Don Juan, to accompany him part of the way. While engaged in spiritual conversation, they suddenly found themselves at the Orriols Inn, three leagues from Figueras. Fr. Don Juan was amazed that they had travelled so quickly and asked how it could have happened. St. Anthony Mary replied simply, "I do not know."[21]

Other Saints have also been known to have travelled in a miraculous fashion, including ST. PETER REGALADO (d. 1456), who is said to have possessed the agility and ease which our glorified bodies will once have, because, as his biographer relates, "he crossed over rivers as though they were solid ground . . ."[22]

ST. PETER OF ALCANTARA (d. 1562), the Franciscan mystic and one-time director of St. Teresa, is said to have done the same, "walked upon the waves of the sea as though it were dry land."[23] Others who are reported as having done the same are St. Peter Nolasco, St. Maria de Cervellione and St. Peter Gonzalez.[23]

BL. CATHERINE OF RACCONIGI (d. 1547) is said to have travelled with great speed from place to place to bring spiritual help to those in need.[24]

Unusual Vessels

Not a ship, nor a boat, not even a row boat or a canoe—but a mantle was used by the following Saints for their miraculous transport over water.

What might be one of the most extraordinary miracles produced by ST. GERARD MAJELLA (d. 1755) was witnessed by an immense crowd. We are told that he was one day journeying along the seashore at Naples when he heard a crowd of people screaming in horror. A sudden squall on the bay began its fury while a ship with many passengers appeared to be in danger of capsizing. Moved to compassion, St. Gerard made the Sign of the Cross and called out to the vessel: "In the name of the Most Holy Trinity, pause!" He then threw his mantle onto the water, and stepping onto it, he approached the ship, took hold of it, and as though it were a floating cork, he pulled it to shore as he walked among the waves.

Needless to report, the crowd was awestruck by what had taken place and hurried toward the Saint while shouting, "A miracle! A miracle!"

The humble Saint, not wishing to take credit for what Our Lord had worked through him, hurried toward the city, where he took refuge in the house of a friend. Later, Fr. Margotta asked the Saint how he had been able to draw the vessel to safety. The Saint simply replied, "Oh, Father, when God wills, everything is possible."

Another priest, Fr. Cajone, asked him the same question. The Saint humbly replied, "I caught the ship with two fingers, and drew it to shore. In the state in which I then was (in ecstasy), I could have flown in the air."[25]

The news of what had taken place was repeated by the witnesses to all who would listen, so that the wonder was made known throughout the region and eventually made its way into the Saint's biographies.

ST. FRANCIS SOLANO (d. 1610), a Franciscan friar, left his native Spain for the New World to evangelize the countries of Argentina, Bolivia, Paraguay and Peru. Relying on the mercy of God for the poor of those countries, he performed numerous miracles that benefitted the local Indians. According to his biographer, "Francis would lay his mantle on roaring streams and sail across on it to the opposite shore."[26]

One of the most spectacular of miraculous transports took place through the faith and confidence placed in the Heavenly Father by ST. FRANCIS OF PAOLA (d. 1507). He was one day travelling with some companions, hoping to take a ferry from Villa S. Giovanni to Messina, about a four-mile journey. The Saint approached one of the ferry captains, Pietro Coloso, and asked if he, for the love of Jesus Christ, would be kind enough to transport him and his companions to the Sicilian shore. The captain replied that he would be happy to do so if they would pay him for his trouble. When the Saint replied that they had no money, Coloso replied scornfully, "If you do not have money to pay me, I do not have a boat to carry you."

Accepting the remark in a kindly manner, the Saint walked down to the beach and knelt in prayer. He then stood up, blessed the waves, and to the amazement of all the people who were watching—including his religious companions—the Saint spread his mantle on the waves, picked up one corner with his staff, and holding the corner high, used it as a sail to calmly navigate across the strait toward Messina. The witnesses on shore cried out in wonder while the greatly troubled Coloso shouted for the Saint to return to shore—he would gladly ferry him and his companions to the opposite shore. The Saint continued on his journey, while Coloso hurried Fr. Rendacio and Brother Giovanni onto the ferry and went in pursuit of the Saint, who was sailing along without the least difficulty.

On reaching Messina, the Saint saw a large number of people watching him and moving toward the area where they expected him to land, but the Saint shifted his direction so that he would land beyond the lighthouse, near an isolated place with a great many rocks. The place was called the Holy Sepulchre. We are told that in 1503, a monastery of the Saint's order was built there to commemorate the Saint's miraculous landing in Sicily.

Captain Coloso, truly repentant, begged the Saint's forgiveness, which he readily received. Afterward, the Saint and his companions hurried away to avoid the attention of the witnesses.[27]

The mantle used during this miracle is a prized possession of the Order of Minims and is kept in the Sanctuary at Paola. Canonized in 1519, St. Francis of Paola was declared the patron of seafarers by Pope Pius XII in 1943 because of this miracle and many others he worked involving the sea.

A similar mode of transportation was used by ST. RAYMOND OF PENAFORT (d. 1275), who was born in a castle in Catalonia which almost three hundred years later was transformed into a Dominican monastery. He made rapid progress in his studies and at the age of twenty was teaching philosophy at Barcelona. After joining the Dominican Order, and after his ordination, he labored "without intermission" in preaching, instructing, hearing confessions and converting heretics. It is said that he "was a perfect model to the clergy by his innocence, zeal, devotion and boundless liberalities to the poor."

St. Raymond was once taken by King James to Majorca to cultivate the Faith on the island. The king, however, was leading a scandalous life, which the Saint attempted to regulate. Because the king delayed in reforming, the Saint asked to be released of his duties. The king not only refused to let him leave, but threatened to punish with death anyone who would assist him in doing so. Full of confidence in God, the Saint said to his companions, "An earthly king withholds the means of flight, but the King of Heaven will supply them." Butler records:

> He then walked boldly to the sea, spread his cloak upon the water, tied up one corner of it to a staff for a sail, and having made the Sign of the Cross, stepped upon it without fear whilst his timorous companions stood trembling on the shore. On this new kind of vessel the saint was wafted with such rapidity that in six hours he reached the harbor of Barcelona, sixty leagues distant from Majorca. Those who saw him arrive in this manner met him with acclamations. But he, gathering up his cloak dry, put it on, stole through the crowd, and entered his monastery.[28]

This incident was recounted in the bull of his canonization and is chronicled by the earliest historians of his life.

A chapel and a tower were soon built at the place of his landing as a commemoration of the miracle. The king, incidentally, after learning of the miraculous transport of the Saint, became a sincere convert "and governed his conscience, and even his kingdoms, by the advice of St. Raymond from that time till the death of the Saint."

The previously mentioned Saints were not the only ones who miraculously used a mantle to travel over water. The same is reported in the life of BL. ALVAREZ OF CORDOVA (d. 1420 or 1430). This holy Dominican, renowned for preaching, built several chapels on the monastery grounds of Scala Coeli, each chapel representing a scene of Our Lord's Passion. It is told that one night, while he was praying in one of these chapels, the stream he was to cross to return to the monastery became flooded from a violent storm, making a crossing entirely impossible. When the bell rang for Matins, his virtue of obedience impelled him to lift his eyes to God in prayer. He then removed his mantle, spread it on the water, stepped upon the mantle and crossed the stream in this fashion. On reaching the opposite shore he retrieved his mantle and assumed his place in choir.[29] It is also reported that after his burial, when the Dominicans decided to remove the body of Bl. Alvarez to another tomb, a violent storm frustrated each of their efforts.[30]

BL. JANE OF SIGNA (d. 1307), a poor shepherdess born near Florence, was a member of the Franciscan Order, but before her entrance—while she was shepherding her father's flocks—she and her sheep were supernaturally preserved from storms and rain. Other shepherds, learning of this protection, gathered near her when storms threatened. Another miracle involved the River Arno, swollen by rain or melting snow which sometimes made it impossible for Jane to cross on her return home. "Full of confidence in God, Jane would then spread her cloak on the waters, and kneeling on it, she would reach the opposite shore in safety."[31]

ST. HYACINTH WALKS ON WATER. Especially devoted to Our Lady, St. Hyacinth miraculously carried her very heavy statue—and the Blessed Sacrament—as he walked across the Dnieper River, fleeing an attack by the vicious Tartars. The Saint is also reported by hundreds of witnesses to have walked on water at least two other times.

CLOAK FOR A BOAT. St. Francis of Paola was refused transport across a body of water by a ferryman because he lacked the fare. The Saint then spread out his cloak, or mantle, upon the waves and calmly navigated across the strait of water to the other shore. Witnesses cried out in wonder at the sight.

UPHELD BY ANGELS. St. Colette was accompanied by muleteers when she carried provisions and religious articles to the houses of her order. The men found it difficult to keep up with St. Colette when she was walking, since it seemed that her feet did not touch the earth. And when she rode, as depicted above, she was typically engaged in contemplation and miraculously maintained her balance without support.

MONEY MYSTERIOUSLY PROVIDED

". . . go to the sea, and cast in a hook: and that fish which shall first come up, take: and when thou hast opened its mouth, thou shalt find a stater [coin]: take that, and give it to them for me and thee." (Words of Our Lord to St. Peter.)—Matthew 17:26

The miraculous appearance of money, or its multiplication in desperate situations, is noted in the lives of some Saints, but appears to be an uncommon occurrence. The times when money was mysteriously provided were not only phenomenal, but of extreme interest for the manner in which the miracles took place. In the majority of cases, the multiplications occurred during the lifetime of the Saints, but there are a few instances when the miracles took place after death. There is, for instance, the little-known case involving St. Thérèse of the Child Jesus who provided money after her death on a number of occasions—miracles that will be explored later.

For now, we will consider perhaps the earliest non-Biblical instance of money being provided as a result of prayer. This case is given us by Pope St. Gregory the Great (d. about 604), who tells in his biography of ST. BENEDICT (d. 543) about the disciple, Peregrinus, a Catholic layman who was heavily burdened with debt.

The man was being constantly tormented by creditors so that he felt his only hope was to confide his problem to the man of God, St. Benedict. The saintly abbot expressed his sorrow at not having the necessary amount to relieve the debt and advised the man to return in three days. In the meantime, the Saint devoted himself to prayer. When Peregrinus returned, the monks went, at the Saint's urging, to inspect a store of grain.

To their surprise, they discovered thirteen gold pieces lying on top of a chest that was filled with grain. The Saint had the coins brought to him and gave them to Peregrinus, instructing the man to use twelve of the coins to settle the debt and to spend the thirteenth coin in any way he pleased. ("Life and Miracles of St. Benedict," Book Two of the *Dialogues*).[1]

Next we learn about BL. GONSALVO OF AMARANTE (d. 1259), who was already a priest and a hermit when he joined the Dominican Order. People flocked to hear him preach and begged him to heal their sick. One of his most astounding miracles, apart from those of healing, involved the building of a bridge across a swift river that prevented people from reaching a little oratory in wintertime. In trying to raise money for the bridge, he took to begging and once approached a man who was apparently annoyed, but who quickly devised a simple means of dismissing the priest. The man wrote a note to his wife and instructed Bl. Gonsalvo to bring it to his home. The wife, on reading the note, began to laugh. The note read: "Give him as much gold as will balance with the note I send you." On Bl. Gonsalvo's insistence, the woman placed the slip of paper on one balance of a scale and a coin in the other. To her surprise, the slip of paper outweighed the gold and continued to do so until a sizable amount of coins balanced with the paper.[2] One wonders what must have been the attitude of the man when he learned about the miracle and his loss of a considerable amount of money.

ST. LYDWINE OF SCHIEDAM (d. 1433) had a brother, William, who died leaving many debts that proved an insurmountable burden to his two children, Petronille and Baudouin. To settle the debts the Saint sold some little family heirlooms which her brother had kept as souvenirs. She placed the money in a purse and gave it to her cousin, Nicolas. He, in turn, paid the debts and returned the empty purse to St. Lydwine. Although she knew the money was gone, she nevertheless opened the purse and turned it over. Out fell eight coins, the exact amount she had given her cousin to pay the debts of her brother. After seeing the miraculous supply of money, she decided that the purse should be called the purse of Jesus. It is said that the Saint could always draw upon it for the needs of the poor. "It did not become exhausted, since even on the day of her death it was still half full."[3]

ST. RITA OF CASCIA (d. 1457), who is known as the Saint of the Impossible, obtained by her prayers many favors for her community and the people of Cascia. At one time the superior was in urgent need of money to pay a bill and requested the prayers of St. Rita. Later that very day the superior found in the alms box the exact amount needed to discharge the debt—an answer to prayer which she credited to those worthy prayers of the Saint.[4]

ST. GERARD MAJELLA (d. 1755) was known for his generosity in clothing and feeding the poor. At times there was insufficient money to discharge the ministry that obedience had imposed on him. Fr. Cajone related that "Three or four times the good brother came to bring me a considerable sum of money which, he said, he had found in the box at the gate. Whence did this money come? That is the secret of God and the good brother. As for myself, I know nothing about it."[5]

On another occasion, while the convent of Caposele was being built, the Father Rector confided to St. Gerard that a considerable amount of money was needed to finish the project. Fr. Cajone composed a formal petition to Almighty God and gave it to the saintly brother to present to His Divine Majesty. Gerard went immediately to the church, laid the letter on the altar and with a holy audacity of faith knocked at the door of the tabernacle saying, "Here, Lord, is our petition. Please answer it." Since the money was needed the next day to pay the workmen, Gerard passed the night before the Blessed Sacrament begging Our Lord to come to the aid of the community. At daybreak he knocked again at the door of the tabernacle to commend his request to Our Lord. At that same instant, the bell at the gate rang. Gerard ran there and found two bags of money— more than was needed to discharge the community's debt.[6]

Stories of miraculous and prophetic powers are recounted in the life of BL. FRANCIS XAVIER BIANCHI (d. 1815). Two very remarkable cases of the multiplication of money are mentioned. When a debt needed to be paid and an insufficient amount of money lay in a drawer, the amount increased so that the debt was promptly paid. This multiplication took place twice and must have been properly witnessed, since they were mentioned in sworn testimony in the process of beatification.[7]

During the process of beatification for ST. GASPAR DEL BUFALO (d. 1837), the founder of the Congregation of the Precious Blood, evidence of a miracle was given by Fr. Blaise Velentini. During the Saint's absence from the monastery of San Felice at Giano, Fr. Velentini wrote to the holy founder that it was impossible to pay a debt. He declared that there were no resources but the many stones in the area. In reply the Saint wrote: "Bless the stones and they will turn into *piastres*." Fr. Velentini took this as a jest, but later, being pressed to pay a debt, he and the bursar looked in the money box and found fifty *bajocchi*, which amounts to about ten cents. Remembering the message of St. Gaspar, and in a spirit of faith, Fr. Velentini blessed the coins. He and the bursar then began to count the coins and found, to their surprise and delight, five *piastres* and five *paoli*, the exact amount that was needed. Fr. Velentini credited the miracle to the holy founder and, in his sworn testimony he deposed that there was not the slightest chance of trickery, nor was there any possibility of an oversight in counting the coins in the first instance.[8]

Known as the "Italian Vincent de Paul," ST. JOSEPH BENE-DICT COTTOLENGO (d. 1842) was a friend of beggars, cripples and the destitute and was a worker of miracles and wonders. He opened the first of many "little houses" which provided free medical care and other help to the poor and afflicted. Working without a budget or a firm source of income, there was always enough money, medicine, food and other necessities.

The Saint's biographer relates one of the miracles which surprised the Saint, as well as his witness. It seems that Joseph Cottolengo bought food on credit for his destitute patients and neglected to pay the bill for five or six months. Finally the creditor became impatient and approached the Saint, raving and demanding his money. Cottolengo was at a loss to pay the man, since he had no money, and proved it to the creditor by opening his pockets and opening drawers in the house. Nothing was found. Finally, the creditor became so enraged he began to physically abuse the Saint. In desperation, and probably because of an inspiration, the Saint reached once more in his pocket and drew out several pieces of gold. Both were amazed since each of them knew that moments before not a penny could be found, even when the creditor himself had examined the pockets.[9]

We read in the life of ST. JEAN MARIE BAPTISTE VIANNEY, the Curé of Ars (d. 1859), that he was much devoted to Our Lady of La Salette, a vision that took place in 1846. The following is reported in the *Procès apostolique ne pereant:* "I was in need of money to complete the requisite sum for the foundation of a mission. I prayed to Our Lady of La Salette to procure that sum for me, and I found just what was needed. I looked upon the incident as miraculous."[10]

The following are miracles that took place after death, in one instance by a holy priest, the other by a well-known Saint.

The first is given us by an unmarried lady living in Termonde who relates,

> For thirty-seven years I enjoyed a small life annuity. In 1897 (the year following the death of Fr. Paul of Moll), on account of unforeseen expenses, I found myself short of money. Full of confidence in the protection of FR. PAUL OF MOLL [d. 1896] whom I had known in life, I put his portrait in my empty safe and said, "Fr. Paul, I am in need, you must help me!" Two days later I opened the safe and to my astonishment I saw lying next to his portrait more money than I had ever had at my disposal.[11]

The most documented incident in which money was miraculously provided is credited to ST. THÉRÈSE OF THE CHILD JESUS AND OF THE HOLY FACE (d. 1897). The account is given in a book entitled, *Soeur Thérèse of Lisieux, The Little Flower of Jesus,* which was published in 1912. Here we find the Autobiography that was edited by Thérèse's sister, Mother Agnes of Jesus. Also included are many other chapters regarding the life of the future Saint and a chapter recounting the Shower of Roses which are the early favors provided through St. Thérèse's intercession. Foremost among these is the miraculous supply of money which was witnessed and documented by the nuns at the Discalced Carmelite convent in the town of Gallipoli, Italy, as well as declarations given by the bishop of the diocese.

It is told that the convent at Gallipoli had been suffering for three years from an insufficient supply of money with which to pay their debts. An adequate supply of food was also lacking, so much so that at times a visit to the chapel substituted for the nuns' dinner. Several months before the miracle, the life of Soeur Thérèse had been read in the community, and now the prioress decided to make a special appeal for three days to the Trinity through the intercession of the Little Flower of Jesus. The triduum ended on January 16, 1910. On that day Soeur Thérèse kept her promise of "doing good upon earth" and of "coming down." The astounding facts of this miracle are given in letters written by Mother Mary Carmela, prioress of the Carmel of Gallipoli, to Mother Agnes of Jesus (the future Saint's sister), who was then the prioress of the Carmel of Lisieux. The first letter from the convent of Gallipoli was dated February 25, 1910 and reads as follows:

> Dear Reverend Mother, I send you the account of the miracle wrought on our behalf. But a long document signed by the whole community, by a commission of priests and by the bishop himself, has been forwarded to Rome. On the night of the 16th of January, 1910, I was in great suffering, and was also worried about certain grave difficulties. Three o'clock had struck, and, almost worn out, I raised myself somewhat in the bed in order to breathe more easily. Then I fell asleep, and in a dream, it would seem to me, I felt a hand touch me, draw the bed clothes about my face, and cover me up tenderly. I thought one of the sisters had come in to perform this act of charity.

Without opening her eyes, Mother Mary Carmela gently protested that the movement of air might be harmful, since she was then covered in perspiration, but a sweet voice she had never heard before replied,

> "No. It is a good act that I am doing. Listen! The Good God makes use of the inhabitants of Heaven, as well as those of earth, in order to assist His servants. Here are 500 francs with which you will pay the debt of your community." Taking them from her hand, I answered that the debt amounted to only 300 francs. "Well," she replied, "the rest will be over and above. But as you may not keep this money in your cell, come with me."

Since the night was bitterly cold and she was bathed in perspiration, Mother Mary Carmela wondered how she could follow the apparition. She continues,

> The heavenly apparition, however, divined my thoughts, adding with a smile: "Bilocation will help us." Suddenly I found myself outside my cell, in the company of a young Carmelite nun, whose veil and robes shone with a brightness from Paradise that served to light up our way. She led me downstairs to the turn-room or parlour, and made me open a wooden box wherein was enclosed the bill which had to be paid. There she deposited the 500 francs. I looked at her lovingly, and threw myself at her feet crying out: "O my holy Mother!" But she raised me up and, caressing me affectionately, replied: "No, I am not our holy Mother St. Teresa of Jesus. I am the servant of God, Soeur Thérèse of Lisieux. Today in Heaven and on earth, we keep the feast of the Holy Name of Jesus."
>
> Then the angelic sister, putting her hand on my veil as if to adjust it, gave me a sisterly embrace and slowly withdrew. "Wait," I called to her, "you might mistake your way." "No, No" she answered with a heavenly smile, "My way is sure, and I am not mistaken in following it."

The next morning, despite her exhaustion, Mother Mary Carmela went to the choir and received Holy Communion. The two sacristans, however, recognized her weakened condition and insisted on calling for the doctor. To prevent this, Mother Mary Carmela told them that she was deeply moved by the impression of a dream, and in all simplicity told them her story. The letter continues,

> Both of them urged me to examine the box. Finally, as they insisted, I did as they desired. I went to the parlour, opened the box, and . . . there I found in reality the miraculous sum of 500 francs! The rest, dear Mother, I leave to your own imagination. Overwhelmed by such goodness we are one and all praying that our great protectress, little Soeur Thérèse, may be beatified. Signed: Sr. Mary Carmela of the Heart of Jesus.[12]

Seven months later Mother Mary Carmela at Gallipoli was obliged to write once more to the convent at Lisieux with details of other miracles. The letter was dated September, 1910 and reads as follows:

> It costs me very much to confide to you what the dear little Soeur Thérèse has done for us since the month of February. But I can no longer resist your prayers, or my little Saint who obliges me to make manifest the prodigies which God has wrought through her.
>
> At the end of the month of January, in spite of the care with which the sisters who have charge of the income and expenditure kept their books, we found a surplus of 25 lire. This we were unable to explain unless on the supposition that Soeur Thérèse had slipped it into our cash box. The bishop therefore desired me to place apart from the money of the community, the two bank notes that still remained of the ten which Heaven had sent. At the end of February, March and April the same strange thing happened, but the amount varied. In the month of May I saw my little Thérèse again. She spoke to me at first upon spiritual matters, and then she added: "To prove to you that it was indeed I who brought you the surplus of money that has been noticed in the settling of your accounts, you will find in the cash box a bank note of 50 francs . . . With God, to say is to do."

Following this appearance of Thérèse, Mother Mary Carmela hesitated to inspect the cash box, but when two of the sisters came a few days later and asked to see the bank notes out of devotion, the box was opened. Mother Mary Carmela writes,

> Mother, what shall I say? You may understand our emotion. Instead of two notes, there were . . . three. In the month of June we found 50 lire in the usual way. During the night between the 15th and the 16th of July (the Feast of Our Lady of Mount Carmel), I saw my beloved Thérèse once more; she promised to bring me before long 100 lire. Then she wished me a happy feast and offered me a bank note of 5 lire. As I did not dare accept it, she placed it at the foot of the little statue of the

Sacred Heart in our cell, and shortly after, when the bell
had rung, I found the note where I had seen her put it.

During a visit to the convent several days later, the bishop mentioned that he had lost a bank note of 100 lire and expressed the
hope that Soeur Thérèse would bring it to the sisters. Mother Mary
Carmela continues:

> It came on the 6th of August, the eve of the feast of St.
> Cajetan, whose name the bishop bears. Again I saw my
> dearly loved Thérèse. In her hand she held a bank note
> of 100 lire, and she said: "The power of God takes away
> or gives with the same ease in matters temporal as in
> matters spiritual." Having found the note of 100 lire in
> the box, I hastened to send it to the bishop with the good
> wishes of the community. He, however, returned it to us.
> Since then she has brought us no more money, for our
> distress has become known through these marvels, and
> alms have been sent to our Carmel.

On the eve of the exhumation of Thérèse's remains, September 5,
Mother Mary Carmela saw her once more.

> After having spoken to me, as she always did, of the
> spiritual welfare of the community, she announced that
> they would find only her bones in the grave. Next, she
> made me understand something of the prodigies she
> will accomplish in the future. Count it for certain, my
> dear Mother, that her blessed remains will work great
> miracles and will be as mighty weapons against the
> devil. Soeur Thérèse appeared to me generally at dawn
> and when I was engaged in prayer. Her countenance
> was radiant and extremely beautiful; her garments glit-
> tered with a light as of transparent silver; her words
> had the sweetness of a heavenly melody. She revealed
> to me the great, though hidden, crosses she bore so
> heroically upon earth. Little Thérèse has indeed suf-
> fered deeply. What more shall I say? It is enough, my
> dear Mother, that you know we feel near us the spirit
> of your angelic child. All the sisters affirm, with ten-

der affection, that, besides the temporal favours granted to the community, each one has been the recipient of very great and personal graces. Signed: Mother Mary Carmela.[13]

The reader will remember the Saint's words to her novices during her lifetime:

> Have faith in all I have told you about the confidence we should have in God; have faith in the way I have taught you of going to Him through self-abandonment and love. I shall come back and shall tell you whether I am mistaken, or if my way is sure. Until then, follow it faithfully.

One year after the first apparition at Gallipoli, the Little Flower returned with another miracle, this one prompted by Bishop Giannattasio of Nardo, near Gallipoli. The bishop was unaware of that particular lesson given to the novices by Soeur Thérèse, and he regretted that the words to Mother Carmela had not been explained: "My way is a sure one." Troubled by this idea, Bishop Giannattasio decided to celebrate the anniversary of the first apparition by presenting the Carmelite convent with a bank note of 500 lire which someone had given him. He enclosed the bank note in an envelope together with his visiting card, on which he wrote: "IN MEMORIAM! My Way is a sure one; I am not mistaken. Sr. Thérèse of the Child Jesus to Sr. Mary Carmela, Gallipoli, January 16, 1910. Pray for me daily that God may have mercy on me." The bishop inserted this envelope into a larger one, which he carefully sealed. On the envelope he wrote: "To be placed in the cash box, and to be opened by Mother Prioress on January 16, 1911."

We return to the account given in the book, *Soeur Thérèse:*

> It was a simple act of devotion by which he intended to obtain the blessing of the Servant of God on himself and his diocese. No miracle was asked. His Lordship knew that several of the community were anxious to have their poverty-stricken chapel decorated. Three hundred lire were needed for this, and Mother Carmela had opposed the project, but she had finally consented to a

novena to the Little Flower. His Lordship intended to give them a pleasant surprise. He forwarded his envelope about the end of December, and on January 16 he himself arrived at the Carmel for the purpose of giving a retreat. He was informed that his letter was still in the cash box. Mother Carmela now took it out and was told to open it, the bishop watching her narrowly as she did so. She passed her finger under the upper flap, thus leaving the seal intact, then handed him the envelope with the remark: "My Lord, take what belongs to you." His Lordship found, to his amazement, that, in addition to the smaller envelope he had placed inside, there were four bank notes, two of 100 lire and two of 50 lire. His own note of 500 lire lay still untouched in the inner envelope. "The money is yours, my Lord," said the Mother Prioress, "but please count it. If there are 300 lire, might it not be the sum which the community has been so confidently asking from Soeur Thérèse?"

Mother Mary Carmela called for the sisters to assemble so that the bishop could present them with the bank note. But before they arrived, the bishop exchanged one of the notes that emitted a perfume of roses for another of the same value. He then examined the seal of the envelope, which was unbroken.

Mother Mary Carmela confessed to the bishop that she had noticed some days previously that the envelope had increased in bulk and thought their heavenly benefactress had heard the prayers of the sisters. The bishop replied that he

saw a higher purpose in the miracle—the confirmation, namely of the Saint's remark: "My way is a sure one." He then showed the astonished Prioress the contents of the inner envelope, the note of 500 lire and his visiting card with its inscription. Sometime after, Msgr. Muller of Gallipoli held a strict canonical investigation into the whole matter, the result of which was to place beyond question the intervention of the Little Flower of Jesus.

The above account is drawn from the Articles for the Cause of Beatification, second edition, July, 1911.[14]

The preceding was carefully considered by a distinguished Jesuit who presided over the first tribunal considering the Cause of Beatification. After having emphatically attributed the whole affair to diabolical intervention, the priest was converted by the overwhelming evidence and became an ardent apostle of Sister Thérèse of the Child Jesus and of the Holy Face.[15]

One may wonder where St. Thérèse obtained the bank notes, since currency is not used in Heaven. One author quotes a bank employee as saying that,

> There are a good many bank notes issued that never come back. They are lost, and thus become *res nullius*, no man's property. Some are so effectively hidden away by misers that they are never found by their heirs; others are dropped and blown away by the wind; others are burned when houses catch fire; others go down with foundering ships. The lost notes give a supply exceeding all demands that miracles will ever make.[16]

"HERE, LORD, IS OUR PETITION. PLEASE ANSWER IT." St. Gerard Majella's prayers for badly needed funds to build a convent at Caposele were answered when two large bags of money miraculously appeared at the monastery door.

MULTIPLICATION OF FOOD

"And Jesus took the loaves: and when he had given thanks, he distributed to them that were set down. In like manner also of the fishes, as much as they would. And when they were filled, he said to his disciples: Gather up the fragments that remain, lest they be lost. They gathered up therefore, and filled twelve baskets with the fragments of the five barley loaves, which remained over and above to them that had eaten."—John 6:11-13

This miracle of the New Testament is, of course, well known. Perhaps a lesser known miracle of multiplication of food is told in the Old Testament and took place during a devastating drought. Elias, who was suffering greatly because of it, was told by God to "Move on to Sarephta." There Elias met a widow at the entrance of the city and asked her to kindly bring him a cup of water. As she was leaving to get it for him, Elias added, "Bring me also, I beseech thee, a morsel of bread." She then explained, "I have no bread, but only a handful of meal in a pot, and a little oil in a cruse." She also mentioned that she was going to prepare something for herself and her son and that ". . . when we have eaten it, we shall die." Elias told her not to worry and to bake him a little cake and bring it to him, telling her, "For thus saith the Lord the God of Israel: The pot of meal shall not waste, nor the cruse of oil be diminished, until the day wherein the Lord will give rain upon the face of the earth."

The widow did as Elias recommended and was blessed. "She went and did according to the word of Elias: and he ate, and she, and her house: and from that day the pot of meal wasted not, and the cruse of oil was not diminished." (*3 Kgs.* 17:10-16).

Not only the Prophet, but a great many Saints have also multiplied food through their trust in the power of God. In mentioning those Saints who performed this gift, it would seem appropriate to begin by relating a miracle performed by a farmer who is known simply as ST. ISIDORE THE FARMER (d. 1130). Born into a poor family, he was sent out to work at a tender age and entered the service of John de Vergas as a day laborer and farmer. He remained in his employ for the rest of his life.

The miracle took place on a snowy winter's day as St. Isidore was carrying a sack of corn to be ground. Along the way he saw some birds who were suffering miserably from the cold and, according to the Saint's reasoning, appeared to be hungry. In the presence of witnesses who ridiculed him, he poured half the sack's contents on the ground. The men who jeered at the generosity of the poor farmer also witnessed that the sack proved to be still full of corn, and when it was ground, it produced double the usual amount of flour.[1]

One of the earliest miracles of food being miraculously supplied is attributed to the faith of ST. BENEDICT (d. 543). It is a matter beyond dispute that,

> Heaven sent a gift of two hundred sacks of flour. But that was a very munificent boon of divine Providence, intended to supply the needs not only of the monks, but also of the guests and the many poor who daily knocked at the door of the monastery.[2]

The miracle took place one day when the cellarer at St. Martin's went to inform the Saint that his generosity toward the poor had almost exhausted their supply of bread, since only five loaves remained. The Saint exhorted the community to have faith—but the monks, in their hunger, were downcast. The Saint had the five loaves distributed among the most famished and addressed the monks: "Why are you saddened at the lack of a little bread? Why do you not rather put greater trust in God? He treats us according to the measure of our faith. Today your faith is small and bread scarce. But console yourselves; tomorrow you shall have in abundance." The following morning there were found outside the gate two hundred sacks of flour. After giving gratitude to the Lord, they became curious about the origin of the flour and who had sent it. They searched through the countryside and could find no trace or clue as to where it had come from. Finally they remembered the prophetic words of their holy founder and concluded that such a large quantity of flour had been provided through the generosity of God. This miracle made such an impression on the monks that a number of the sacks were kept as relics. These, however, were later destroyed in a fire at the monastery of Teano in 896.[3] Through his prayers the Saint also multiplied oil.

Another early miracle was effected through the prayers of ST. DOMINIC (d. 1221). It seems that one day at the friary of St. Sixtus, St. Dominic sent Br. John of Calabria and Br. Albert to the city to beg alms. They were unsuccessful until they met a woman on the return journey who gave them a loaf of bread. But before they reached the friary, they gave the loaf of bread to a poor man who was in great need.

On meeting St. Dominic they explained all that happened to the satisfaction of the Saint, who explained that it must have been an angel who was testing their generosity. As there was no food in the friary, St. Dominic trusted in Divine Providence and summoned all the brethren to the refectory. The table was prepared, dishes and cups were placed and, as the friars sat down, Br. Henry the Roman began to read, as was the custom during meals. St. Dominic, with his hands on the table, bowed his head and began to pray. As the Saint's biographer writes:

> Suddenly two beautiful young men appeared in the midst of the refectory, carrying loaves in two white cloths which hung from their shoulders before and behind. They began to distribute the bread, beginning at the lower rows, one at the right hand and the other at the left, placing before each brother one whole loaf of admirable beauty. Then, when they were come to the blessed Dominic, and had in like manner placed an entire loaf before him, they bowed their heads and disappeared, without any one knowing, even to this day, whence they came or whither they went.

Another miracle at this time took place when there was only a little wine in the cellar. The Saint, by his prayers, increased the amount so that the friars ate and drank all they wanted, both for that day, the next and the day after that. After the third day, St. Dominic would not allow any of the multiplied bread to remain in the house and gave a beautiful discourse warning the brethren never to distrust the Divine goodness, even in time of greatest need.

Br. Tancred, the prior of the convent, Br. Odo of Rome and Br.

Henry, Br. Lawrence of England, Br. Gandion and Br. John of Rome and many others were present at the miracle, which they related to Sr. Cecilia and the other sisters who were still living at the monastery of Santa Maria. It is also related that some of the bread and wine were preserved for a long time as relics.[4]

More is told to us by Fr. Ludovico Prelormitano of other miracles of St. Dominic. According to his account, after St. Dominic had finished some business with the Holy Pontiff at Rome, he went to Bologna and lodged there with the friars of his order at Santa Maria Mascharella. While there the miracle mentioned above was renewed, with enough bread remaining for three days. The miracle is said to have taken place twice at Bologna and twice at Rome. After one of the miraculous distributions of bread, the two beautiful young men gave each friar a handful of dried figs, of which one brother testified to Pope Gregory IX under oath: "Never had I eaten better figs."[5]

Three centuries later, in 1528, the rector of Santa Maria Mascharella reported that every year, on the same day when the holy Angels brought the heavenly bread, a most delightful perfume was perceived in the place where the refectory had been located— a scent that lasted forty hours. Additionally, the table on which the miraculous loaves had been placed was still to be seen (in 1528), protected behind iron bars in the wall. [6]

We read in *The Little Flowers of St. Francis* about the journey of ST. FRANCIS OF ASSISI (d. 1226) to Rieti and the great crowd of people who came to meet him outside the city. Instead of travelling on to Rieti, he went instead to a little church about two miles away from the town. People continued to go to him, many travelling through the vineyard belonging to the priest who was assigned to the church. The vineyard, as a result, was ruined from the many people who were availing themselves of the grapes. After learning by supernatural means of the priest's regret that he had allowed the Saint to spend so much time at his church, Francis bargained with the priest. He first asked the priest how many measures of wine were produced by the vineyard. The answer was twelve. Francis then asked the priest to be patient with the people who were deriving much spiritual benefit by their visit to the church, and to allow them to eat the grapes. In return, Francis promised that, through the mercy of God, the vineyard that same year would produce twenty measures of wine instead of the usual twelve.

The Little Flowers continues: "It seemed to the Saint better that the material vineyard should be damaged than that the vineyard of the Lord of Hosts should be sterile in heavenly wine."

The priest trusted the promise and the sanctity of the Saint and freely allowed the people to eat the grapes. Toward the end of the Saint's visit only a few grapes remained, but these he put in the wine press. "As St. Francis had promised, the priest miraculously obtained twenty measures of the very best wine."[7]

Another incident of multiplication took place when the Saint sailed to Ancona to spread the Word of God among the infidels. Unfortunately, a great storm arose so that the men who had been rowing the boat, requiring great energy, consumed all the food, so that only the provisions of the Saint and his companions were left.

> These, by divine grace and power, were multiplied to such an extent that, though the voyage was to last through several days, they had enough to take care of their needs generously all the way to the port of Ancona. Therefore, when the sailors saw that they had escaped the dangers of the sea through the servant of God St. Francis, they thanked Almighty God who always shows Himself wonderful and lovable in His servants.[8]

ST. ELIZABETH OF HUNGARY (d. 1231) is often pictured with roses falling from her apron. This miracle is said to have taken place when her husband inquired about the bulging contents of her apron, which moments before had contained loaves of bread for the poor. This generosity of the Saint in supplying the needs of the poor was repeated a number of times, but once another kind of miracle took place which was witnessed by her companions.

The report tells that the Saint was carrying bread in her apron to give to the poor when she realized that there was not enough bread to give to all who were about to ask. According to her biographer:

> She then began to pray interiorly while distributing the food, and found that, according as she gave pieces away, they were replaced by others, so that after giving each beggar his share there was still some left.

The report continues that on the return to her castle, she and her companions "sang praises to God, who had deigned to communicate to her His all-powerful virtue."[9]

During a time of great famine, ST. CATHERINE OF SIENA (d. 1380) was staying in the home of one of her great admirers, a young widow named Alessia. It was at that time impossible to buy good flour, even if one had the money to pay for it. All that was available was old wheat that had become moldy. Alessia was forced to buy this old wheat, but at harvest time good wheat became available. Alessia then told St. Catherine that she would throw away the old, moldy wheat and buy some of the new. The Saint suggested that it not be wasted, but given to the poor, but Alessia replied that it would strike her conscience to give the poor what she hesitated to use herself. Since the Saint would not hear of throwing the old wheat away she said: "Get the water ready because I would like to make some bread for the poor of Jesus Christ myself."

Using the moldy flour the Saint produced so many loaves and at such a high rate of speed that Alessia and her servant were amazed. As Bl. Raymond of Capua, the Saint's friend and biographer writes:

> In point of fact the number of loaves that Catherine with her virginal hands presented to Alessia to put on the trays could not have been made with four or five times as much flour as she had used, nor did they smell sour as the others had done that had been made formerly with the same flour. The loaves were served and the people at dinner found nothing wrong with them. In fact, they remarked that they had never before eaten such sweet bread.[10]

When St. Catherine's confessor, Fra Tommaso, heard of the miracle, he, a few friars and other interested and devout people went to see Catherine and investigate the affair. They too were astounded to see how much bread was made with such a small amount of flour and were enchanted by its delightful sweetness.

Another miracle was added when St. Catherine asked that the bread be distributed among the poor and supplied to the friars. It is reported that the bin remained always full, even though the amount of bread distributed was generous.[11]

Four miracles of St. Catherine are here noted. First, the moldy condition of the flour was corrected. Secondly, the sour smell of the flour was eliminated and made sweet. Thirdly, the dough increased and multiplied in size. And fourthly, the loaves of bread increased in number so that for several weeks the bread bin was never empty, although bread was generously distributed to the poor.

Bl. Raymond of Capua also reports that the miracle was widely known, so that many people kept pieces of the bread as though they were relics.[12]

Another time while St. Catherine was staying in Rome, she offered hospitality to "a number of servants of God." Giovanna, a Sister of Penance of St. Dominic, was in charge of housekeeping and was charged to inform the Saint when supplies were low. Giovanna, however, forgot to notice that the supply of bread was insufficient until it was time for dinner. When she humbly reported her failure to St. Catherine, the Saint instructed that everyone should gather at the table and that the bread, which was only enough for four, be distributed in pieces to the sixteen people who were present.

Giovanna carried out the order, giving each a small piece which they knew would be consumed in one bite and would not be enough to satisfy their hunger following a fast. To their surprise, the small piece of bread increased. Bl. Raymond writes:

> They went on eating, and nevertheless that small amount of bread remained as much as it was at first; each person made a meal of it, and yet there was always bread on the table.

After the meal, St. Catherine ordered that the remaining bread be given to the poor.[13]

The concern of ST. FRANCES OF ROME (d. 1440) for the poor was of great importance to her since she and her friends often distributed food to the needy, the sick and to prisoners. But a time of privation forced them to use extreme measures to find enough corn for their usual distribution. Frances at that time suggested to her sister-in-law, Vannozza, that they should go to the now empty corn loft and search among the straw for whatever they could find. They, with a faithful old servant named Clara, mounted to the loft and on their knees sifted through the straw. All they were able to find was a measure of corn. One of St. Frances' early biographers wrote:

> Lorenzo (her husband) had entered the granary just as they were carrying off their hard-earned treasure, and, looking about him, beheld in place of the straw which was lying there a moment before, 40 measures of bright yellow corn, so shining and so full . . . that it seemed as though it had been raised in Paradise and reaped there by angels . . .

Grain, however was not enough. Many asked the Saint for wine to give them strength. In her generosity St. Frances drew from the single cask that remained in the cellar. Day after day she drew from it for all who asked. Finally not a drop remained, much to the annoyance of Andreazzo, her father-in-law, who raved at her, saying that in order to assist strangers she had introduced privation into her own family. The Saint remained calm under his accusations, but finally suggested that they see if the cask was filled through the mercy of God. Following her to the cellar were her husband, father-in-law and other members of the family. They watched in bewilderment as wine flowed freely when she turned the cock of the barrel. In Andreazzo's estimation, the wine was far superior to any he had ever tasted. He is alleged to have said: "Oh, my dear child, dispose henceforward of everything I possess, and multiply without end those alms that have gained you such favor in God's sight."[14]

Many other miracles are reported in the life of St. Frances of Rome in which the bountiful God provided food for her distribution to the poor.

During the course of ST. COLETTE'S (d. 1447) work in reforming the Poor Clare Order, she met with opposition from Frère Jean Fourcault, guardian of one of the nearby monasteries. It was he, together with some adherents, who retaliated against the Franciscan friars of Dôle who accepted the reform by cutting off their supply of food. Colette was ill at the time at Besançon, but it was unquestionably because of her saintly influence that Agnes de Vaus, the abbess at Auxonne, was able to perform a spectacular miracle.

For a whole year she was able to provide the reformed friars with all their bread, although the amount of wheat in the convent's granary was insufficient for such generosity. The bread was always carried from Auxonne to Dôle on an exceptionally small donkey, which became the object of much interest by people in both towns and the little villages in between. After a year the donkey's work came to an end. According to St. Colette's biographer, "No one knew exactly where the wheat in the nuns' granary had come from, still less how it never ran short, no matter how many loaves were baked."[15]

Bread is said to have multiplied on numerous occasions at the hands of ST. GERARD MAJELLA (d. 1755). There was one occasion when, because of his generosity to the poor, there was no bread in the monastery—but Gerard, after instructing the brother baker to look once more in the bread-press, found it full of loaves.

Another time, a student who assisted at the distribution of bread to the poor affirmed that as soon as the baskets were emptied, they were at once refilled without visible help. Another student testified that, having distributed with his own hands all the bread that was in a large box, he suddenly found it miraculously full.[16]

One of the most remarkable of St. Gerard's gifts of multiplication involved a poor blind woman named Lucretia. She related to Br. Antonio of Cosimo a miracle performed earlier for her by St. Gerard, who was dead at the time of the telling. The poor woman told the brother that during a time of great need the Saint had predicted to her that the only remaining bushel of meal would last her a whole year, that is, until the next harvest. She further stated:

> The prophecy was accomplished to the letter. With that one bushel of meal, I was able for a year to feed not only my whole family, but all my workmen besides, and there even remained some over, which I sold for the other necessities of my family. The year following, on the anniversary of Brother Gerard's prophecy, the miraculous meal suddenly gave out.[17]

The confidence that St. Gerard placed in the generosity of God was always met in accordance with the Saint's great faith and fervent prayer. The instances of multiplication of food for the poor, and for his brethren, are far too numerous to mention here. The witnesses of impeccable integrity and reputation are also numerous, so that the many miracles of multiplication cannot be placed in question.

Such also is the case regarding the miracles of ST. FRANCIS OF PAOLA (d. 1507), who had 300 witnesses for one of his multiplications of food. The miracle took place while the 300 workmen were engaged in building an aqueduct for the city of Corigliano. Present were two noblemen who had brought with them two focacce, which are flat, round loaves of bread. The noblemen began to eat one of the loaves while they were watched by the workmen, who did not have food of any kind. St. Francis approached the noblemen, and after telling them that it was right for them to nourish themselves, nevertheless, he said it was also right that they should share what they had with the others. The Saint then took the second loaf, blessed it, and began to distribute pieces to the workmen. All of them, although receiving only a small portion, were fully satisfied.[18]

The same happened during a great famine that visited Calabria. The people, mostly farmers, saw their desolate fields and keenly felt their inability to properly feed their children. The pride they had always felt in their formerly productive work was crushed, so that now they were reduced to begging for help from the holy Wonder Worker. To some he would give a piece of bread, or a portion of cooked beans or vegetables, and to some other fruit. It is said that although they received only a little helping, their hunger was miraculously satisfied.[19]

It was also during this famine, when the supply of food was very low, that the Saint would enter the church and pray fervently. In time the trees, fields and gardens would produce more for the Saint's distribution. During the canonization process, it was declared that this food was of superior taste and flavor.[20]

Another miracle worked by St. Francis of Paola took place after a sea voyage when he and his companions, Fr. Rendacio and Br. Giovanni di S. Lucido reached the town of Palmi. Tired from their voyage and with appetites sharpened by the fresh air, they discovered they had nothing to eat. A welcoming committee of nine was unable to correct their difficulty, since none had thought to bring anything with them.

The Saint then said to one of them: "Give me your pouch, I am certain there is bread in it." Before the eyes of all, the Saint pulled from the pouch a loaf of hot bread, as fresh as if it had just been baked. The Saint with casual ease blessed the bread and distributed pieces to his companions and the people who had come to greet him. All remarked about the superb flavor and their interest that so much of the bread still remained after all had been fed.

The people who had witnessed this miracle followed the Saint for two days on his journey to Catona. All the while they continued to eat from the same loaf of bread, which continued to be fresh and delicious.[21]

Still another time, while the Saint was travelling with three companions, they entered the town of Castelluccio very tired and thirsty. The Saint approached a man who was standing outside his home and asked if he might spare the travellers a small cup of wine. The man replied that he would gladly give them all they wanted, but his barrel had been empty for days. Sensitive to the man's embarrassment, the Saint told him to once again test the contents. Knowing full well that the barrel was empty, the man nevertheless turned on the spigot and discovered, to his complete amazement, that the barrel was now full of wine. He quickly filled goblets for the four weary travellers while thanking the Saint profusely for the miracle. He then knelt down for Francis' blessing.

The people of the town soon learned of the miracle and rushed to see the Wonder Worker. It is reported that, because of the crowd that flocked around the Saint asking for prayers or blessings, "It was with great difficulty that the four could resume their journey to Naples."[22]

When ST. TERESA OF AVILA (d. 1582) was having repairs made to a house for her Discalced Carmelite nuns, she engaged some twenty-five workmen. One hot day, the Saint looked out the window and noticed that the workmen looked very tired and hot. She asked Pedro Hernandez, a carpenter, to give them something to drink. Since wine at the time was very expensive, the carpenter protested that it would cost too much to satisfy all the men. The Saint, however, insisted. William Thomas Walsh writes:

> Wine was very expensive that year, and cost a *real*
> and a half for an *azumbre* (about two quarts), but Her-

nandez obediently sent a man to a tavern with about fifty *maravedis* (at least he says he got two *maravedis'* worth for each workman) to buy some. There was so little of it that he poured some water in to make it go further, and handed it to one of the toilers. After three or four had drunk, he looked into the jar again, and found (so he testified for the beatification of La Madre) that there was just as much as before.

When St. Teresa asked Pedro Hernandez if he had done what she had asked, he told her about the increase of wine. To this the Saint replied, "God has done this."

Returning to the workmen, Pedro Hernandez cried, "Brothers, you can drink hearty now, for this is wine of benediction!"[23]

Among the many mystical gifts of ST. MARY MAGDALENE DE' PAZZI (d. 1607) was that of providing food for her community. On more than one occasion when the supply in the cupboard was insufficient, the cook would express the need to the Saint, who would always recommend: "Do not doubt, but trust in God!" Sister Jerome Pucci, the cook, recorded: "I saw that things grew in my hands. And when I divided them there were things left over."

One day in Lent there was nothing to eat in the convent except a few herring, which was not enough for the community. Sr. Mary Magdalene then decided that they should pray for their Guardian Angels to inspire Mr. Lapo del Tovaglia "to send us as many herring as will be needed for all the sisters." But a difficulty existed that would prevent the fish seller from venturing out of doors to perform this act of charity—a relentless rain storm. Nevertheless, within an hour a deliveryman appeared at the convent door with a basket full of herring, more than enough for the community. Sr. Mary Archangela, amazed at the precise answer to prayer since only herring was prayed for and only herring was delivered, credited the Saint with the miracle, while the Saint credited the sister's prayers. It is said that this friendly contest went on for some time.[24]

Two miracles of multiplication are mentioned in the biography of ST. ROSE OF LIMA (d. 1617). At one time, the family of St. Rose was having financial difficulty and one evening had only a thin soup and a little bread for their meal. The barrel of honey, a cheap staple food in Peru at the time, was empty. Since they customarily had some with their meals, the mother asked one of the children to go to the cellar and try to scrape a little from the barrel. The child reported that the barrel was completely dry. St. Rose then offered to see if the good Lord would provide and took the honey crock with her. She returned with the crock full of honey, much to the amazement of the family, all of whom knew that the barrel had been completely empty only moments before.[25]

Another time when there was no bread in the house, Rose found the cupboard full, although the others had seen it empty a short time before.[26]

During a time of scarcity at Le Puy, ST. FRANCIS REGIS (d. 1640) was offering Holy Mass one day when he pleaded with the rich and the middle class to be generous in giving donations that would relieve the needs of those suffering from hunger. The response was successful. With the money, as well as funds provided by the city authorities who committed the whole relief problem to the Saint, Francis purchased a large quantity of grain for the poor. This he stored in the granary belonging to a devout widow, Marguerite Baud, whom Regis secured as the keeper and distributor of the grain. Marguerite was quite busy during the fall of 1637, distributing to the long lines of the destitute who came every day to her door.

Finally the grain gave out. One day Marguerite travelled to the college to tell the Saint that there was no grain to give the poor who were begging for it. St. Francis Regis remained silent and cast his eyes down in prayer. In a few moments he smiled at Marguerite and said, "Don't worry. There is still some grain in your bin." To this Marguerite replied insistently that the bin and the granary were both quite empty. The Saint smiled and quietly remarked, "You have poor eyesight, my daughter." Marguerite, mistaking his meaning, felt insulted and began a defense when the Saint interrupted, "Go, I tell you. They are hungry, so give them a large portion."

Marguerite returned home and decided to prove to the poor that the granary was empty. She also decided that after she had enough witnesses, she would send the poor to report to St. Francis that the granary was indeed empty, as she had reported. But when she turned the knob to open the small door of the bin, the grain cascaded out on all sides. She quickly distributed to those present and then hurried to report the marvel to St. Francis Regis. Seeing him near the college, she told what had taken place, to which the Saint replied: "God's granary will always be full."[27]

The Saint's prayers were instrumental in multiplying grain at least three times during the scarcity of 1637. Marguerite Baud tells of another of these remarkable incidents in these words:

> Another time, not having any more grain in the bin, I swept it clean. When I asked the Father if he wanted me to buy some more, he told me that he should have some there. I replied that I had swept the bin and locked it with a key. Nor had I given the key—a peculiar one— to anyone else. The Father persisted and said that there was some grain in the bin. Just to obey him, I went to my dwelling and opened the bin and found it full of grain. It held about forty bushels. I can guarantee you that, during the famine, I took out of this bin a prodigious quantity of grain.

News of the multiplications naturally spread abroad, so that those who were in positions of authority felt obliged to investigate. Afterward, they found it necessary to confirm the truth of the miracles. In a brief statement, the Council General of Le Puy summed up the case in this manner: "When the grain was lacking, Fr. Regis made some in order to give it away; he many times refilled the empty granary, finding a crop and a harvest for which no seed had been sown."[28]

Two hundred years after the death of St. Francis Regis (d. 1640), ST. JEAN MARIE BAPTISTE VIANNEY, the Curé of Ars (d. 1859), received one of his relics which was instrumental in the multiplication of corn. The facts regarding this miracle were given by the eyewitnesses, who testified for the *Proces de l'Ordinaire* for the eventual canonization of the holy Curé. They declared that in the year 1829 the orphanage named the Providence, that was instituted by the Curé, was very low on its supply of corn. Only a few handfuls of grain remained scattered on the floor of the attic of the presbytery. Since the whole countryside was in distress because of a poor harvest, the holy priest could not ask the support of the villagers.

Knowing of the multiplications of food worked by St. Francis Regis, the Curé turned to prayer and implored the intercession of the Saint. Sweeping the scattered grain into one little pile, he hid in it his small relic of the Saint. Together with the orphans, he prayed fervently and then waited. Jeanne Marie Chanay, the baker of the Providence, knew about the shortage, yet the Saint told her, "Go and gather what corn there may be in the attic." Presently she returned in great excitement exclaiming, "Your attic is full." She had experienced the miracle firsthand when she found it difficult to open the door and then saw a stream of corn escaping through the small opening.

According to Abbe Raymond, who also testified for the *Proces,* "The colour of the new corn differed from that of the old." The corn covered the entire floor and was arranged in a pyramid shape.

People who converged on the scene were amazed that the main beam, that was somewhat worm-eaten, had not collapsed under the weight. A little later, when Msgr. Devie asked, "The corn reached up to here, did it not?" pointing to a high mark on the wall, the answer was, "No, my Lord, higher still."

During the same *proces* M. Toccanier quoted the words of the Saint when the holy Curé explained the miracle to him.

> I had many orphans to feed, and there was but a hand-
> ful of corn left in the attic. I thought that St. Francis
> Regis, who during his life had miraculously fed the des-
> titute, would do likewise after his death. I had a relic of
> the Saint. I put it in the handful of grains that remained;
> the little ones prayed, and the attic was then found to be
> full.[29]

The kneading trough of the Providence became a place of special interest because of another miracle that took place sometime later. Because of a drought that had spread affliction over the country-side, flour was scarce and very expensive. Jeanne Marie Chanay, the baker, tells about this second miracle.

> We felt very anxious because of our children. Cather-
> ine Lassagne and I thought that if M. le Curé would pray
> to the good God, he could obtain that the handful of
> flour that was left should yield an ovenful of loaves. We

went to inform him of our predicament. "You must make the dough," he said. So I set to work, not without a certain apprehension. I began by putting a very small quantity of water and flour in the kneading trough, but I saw that the flour remained too thick. I added some water and more flour, without my small stock being exhausted. The trough was full of dough, as on a day when a whole sack of flour was emptied into it. We baked ten big loaves, each weighing from twenty to twenty-two pounds, and the oven was filled as usual, to the great astonishment of all present. We told M. le Curé what had happened; his reply was: "The good God is very good! He takes care of His poor."[30]

ST. ANDREW HUBERT FOURNET (d. 1834) was a secular priest who founded an order of women known as the Daughters of the Cross. With the assistance of Ven. Elizabeth Bichier, the order was established for the purpose of educating the poor in the spiritually neglected part of western France. Because the holy founder's reputation for advanced spirituality was well known, the order was often called the Sisters of St. Andrew. These nuns were witnesses to many of the miracles worked by the Saint, including that of multiplying grain. The details of the miracle became known when two of the sisters gave depositions to the Congregation of Sacred Rites in 1877, when Andrew Hubert Fournet was being considered for beatification. Of these good sisters, one, Sr. Bartholomew, who was under the spiritual direction of the Saint for the first thirteen years of her religious life, related the following under oath, as reported in the writings of Rev. Herbert Thurston, S.J. :

While I was still at La Puye, there was committed to my charge the care of the granary and of the laundry. Just before the feast of St. John the Baptist (in 1824) we were looking forward to the annual retreat, which is made by all the sisters in common, when our good Mother Elizabeth (the foundress) told Father Andrew that it was impossible for that year to assemble all the sisters who were scattered throughout the different parishes of the diocese and in other parts of France, because we had not corn enough in the house and there was no money to buy more. The Father answered: "My child, where is your faith? Do you think God's arm is shortened, and that He cannot do here what He did of old when, as we read in the Gospels, He multiplied the loaves? Go and write to the sisters to come to the retreat." Afterwards, the Servant of God climbed up to the granary, where I was occupied at the moment with one of the other sisters.

As usual he brought his manservant with him, for it was his custom never to come among the sisters without a companion. He walked around the two little heaps of grain, one of which consisted of wheat and the other of barley. I do not remember whether he blessed the heaps, nor can I say exactly, not having measured them, how many bushels they each might have contained, but the heaps were very small. Accordingly the sisters arrived and, when added to those in the motherhouse and to a score of orphans, they brought up the number that had to be fed to about 200. I went every day to the granary to take the corn that was needed and during two months and a half, in other words, from the beginning of July to the middle of September, I drew my supplies from those two little heaps without their showing any sign of diminution. I cannot say for certain how long the sisters from the parishes remained at the motherhouse. As I mentioned before, I had not measured the two heaps. They contained, perhaps, more than twenty bushels . . . and this was the quantity which, for two hundred people, would at the very most have lasted a week. In the middle of September I quitted La Puye to go to Angles, leaving the two heaps of grain in just the same condition in which they were when the Servant of God came to the granary. I heard it said that the same two heaps continued to serve the needs of the community until Christmas . . ."[31]

After Sr. Bartholomew left for another house of the Order, the granary was placed in the care of Sr. Mary Magdalen, who was no longer living when the depositions were taken. Sr. Mamertus reported to the Commission this second miracle which took place a year or two after the first. Sister tells what happened in this manner:

> Sister Mary Magdalen came to me one morning and said: "I don't know what to do. There are not more than eight or ten bushels of corn left in the granary". . . . Sister Mary Magdalen went off to the Father and told him that the community would soon be without bread. He replied: "My dear child, how little faith you have! God's Providence watches over our needs. Send the corn you have to be ground." Shortly afterwards I noticed that the Servant of God was making his way to the granary, and my curiosity having been aroused by what Sister Mary Magdalen had told me, I followed him. He went into the granary and closed the door behind him, but I was able to watch him through the keyhole. He knelt down beside the little heap that was there and began to pray very fervently. I don't know that he did anything else, because in my fear that he himself might catch me spying and might reprimand me for my curiosity, I withdrew almost at once. But in due time, after the Father had left, Sister Mary Magdalen came along with the men from the mill, and I heard from her on that same day that she measured the corn and found that there were sixty bushels.[32]

ST. ZITA (d. 1278), the patroness of domestic workers, was the holy maidservant of Signor Fatinelli, for whom she worked all her life. She generously aided the poor to the extent of giving them her food, while she subsisted on scraps from the master's table. During a time of great scarcity those families with a large supply of provisions shared what they had with the unfortunate. After giving away all she had, she began distributing beans from her master's supply.

One day Signor Fatinelli decided to inspect the household's stock of beans, since he thought to sell it at a considerable profit. Zita was very worried by this new development, since her generosity would be noted, to the master's violent temper. As a result of her prayers and to her great relief, the supply of beans had not been diminished. The miracle of multiplication was given as the only possible explanation.[33]

St. Charles Borromeo not only collected information about the life of BL. GERARD OF MONZA (d. 1207), but also promoted his cause and obtained its confirmation. After the death of his parents, Gerard spent his inheritance in building a hospital for the poor and caring for those who came for healing. Once, during a great famine, the appeals for food were such that the storerooms of grain were exhausted and starvation seemed inevitable. After hearing about the sad situation from the steward, Bl. Gerard placed his trust in God and prayer. When the steward next visited the storerooms he found the granary so full of corn that it was difficult to open the door. The cellar was also found stocked with good wine.[34]

Another miracle is related in the biography of Bl. Gerard. It states that once in midwinter he asked permission to spend the night in prayer in the church of St. John Baptist. The doorkeepers resisted, but then bargained that they would permit the Blessed to do this if, in the morning, they were supplied a quantity of cherries—which, of course, were out of season. The bargain was accepted. The following morning, although he did not leave the church, Bl. Gerard presented each doorkeeper with a cluster of fresh, ripe cherries. Because of this miracle, Bl. Gerard is depicted in artwork holding a quantity of cherries in his hands.[35]

Cherries also figured in an important incident in the life of ST. JOSEPH BENEDICT COTTOLENGO (d. 1842). During the *Proces* Canon Vogliotti and another priest testified to the miracle worked by Joseph Benedict which they had witnessed. Someone had brought to the Saint a little basket of cherries which the Saint began distributing to all of his students, handful by handful. Although the students are described as being a "crowd," each student received the same amount, but the miracle "was that the amount thus distributed was quite out of proportion to anything which the basket could possibly have contained." Canon Vogliotti and his companion went away astonished "to observe how Divine Providence seemed to be taking part in a game with the generous-hearted servant of God."[36]

It was not cherries, but another foodstuff that was multiplied under the hand of ST. JOHN BOSCO (d. 1888) in an almost similar situation. The day this took place was January 1, 1886, when a number of the students from the Saint's school came to offer him good wishes for the new year. Fr. Saluzzo was witness to the exchange of wishes when Don Bosco added, "My dear boys, I wish I had something to give you."

Looking around, he saw on a table a little paper bag with nuts in it. He immediately took out a handful and gave it to one of the boys, who was replaced by another who received a generous handful, and so it went. Those at the end of the line realized that the bag did not contain a sufficient amount for the Saint's generosity, yet he withdrew handful after handful to all thirty-five boys. When the last boy received a share and the bag was empty, someone told Don Bosco that three or four students had left, thinking that there would not be enough for them. The Saint immediately put his hand into the empty bag and drew handfuls out of it. One of the witnesses testified, "Whence he fished them out of the bag I cannot tell; the bag was quite empty."[37]

Another time, when only a few rolls were available for the boys' breakfast and the local baker refused to extend credit, the Saint told Dalmazzo, the boy in charge, to bring what rolls he had in a basket, adding that God would provide. The number of rolls placed in the basket numbered exactly fifteen—and there were three hundred boys waiting to be fed. As the boys assembled in a line and each approached to receive a roll, Don Bosco smiled and continued to steadily draw out the rolls, giving one roll to each boy. When the last boy received his roll young Dalmazzo counted what remained in the basket—exactly fifteen rolls. Dalmazzo, some years later, became a Salesian priest, the order founded by Don Bosco.[38]

Many marvels are reported in the life of BL. ANNA MARIA TAIGI (d. 1837), who was a wife, mother and mystic. Among her miracles was that of the multiplication of food. She is said never to have refused an alms to anyone coming to her door, but one day, during her absence, her mother sent a poor beggar away empty-handed. On returning, Anna Maria gently reproached her, saying, "In the name of Heaven, my good mother, never send anyone away without giving him an alms." Domenico, her husband, was always amazed that the cupboard was never empty especially during a famine, when countless beggars came to their door.[39]

Known as the principal ornament and propagator of the religious order known as the Servites, ST. PHILIP BENIZI (d. 1285) also served as its superior general. During his first year in this office he was on a visitation of the order in Arezzo where his first miracle was reported. The Servites in Arezzo were unable to secure food and were on the verge of starvation when they assembled for supper one evening. There was nothing to eat until St. Philip exhorted them to have faith, and then went to pray in the church before Our Lady's image. Presently a knock was heard at the monastery door. Found on the steps were two large baskets of good bread, whose existence was credited to the faith and prayers of the Saint.[40]

A mysterious benefactor also came to the assistance of BL. ALVAREZ OF CORDOVA (d. 1420), who founded the Dominican monastery of Scala Coeli near Cordova. On one occasion when there was no food for the community except a head of lettuce, Bl. Alvarez called the community together in the refectory for prayer. Afterwards, through his faith in Divine Providence, he sent the porter to the gate. Outside the astonished porter found a stranger leading a mule whose cart was filled with bread, fish, wine and all things needed for the meal of the community. In relief and gratitude for the supply, the porter turned to thank the benefactor and found that he had completely disappeared.[41]

A long-commemorated tradition among the religious at the University of Cracow resulted from an incident involving ST. JOHN CANTIUS (d. 1473), who taught at the University. The story is told that once while he was dining, he

> glanced up and saw a poor man passing by. Surmising that the man was also hungry, the Saint brought him his plate of food. At St. John's place at table was found a plate full of food that had been miraculously provided. The others at table, realizing what had taken place in honor of the generous saint, began the tradition of setting aside a place at table every day for a poor visitor. When the dinner was ready a cry in Latin would sound, "A poor man is coming," to which was replied, "Jesus Christ is coming." The man would then be served. St. John Cantius worked many miracles during his lifetime, many of which were recorded by contemporaries.[42]

The same took place for the founder of the Passionist Order, ST. PAUL OF THE CROSS (d. 1775), when his monastery, named St. Angelo, was found to be without bread and oil. Since all communication was hampered by a heavy snowfall, it was impossible to obtain provisions or to beg for them. After the fervent prayer of the holy founder there came to the door an old man with two mules. One mule was laden with bread, the other with oil. The religious received the provisions with expressions of gratitude and joy. St. Paul then instructed the religious to give some refreshments to the benefactor. They were astonished at finding that both man and mules had disappeared and had not even left their footprints in the snow.[43]

The confidence that St. Paul of the Cross placed in Divine Providence was always rewarded. When the Saint was at the monastery near Toscanella, one of the brothers noted in the early morning that there would not be enough food for dinner. St. Paul merely replied, "This morning we will take a little collation, this evening God will provide." Before the evening meal a basket full of food was delivered to the monastery door. The next day the Saint exhorted all to trust in God and not to doubt and to pray when in need, which they did. Later that day some beasts laden with provisions were sent by a pious benefactor.[44]

Having entered the Dominican Order at an early age, BL. JOHN LICCIO (d. 1511) holds the record for longevity in the order, having worn the habit for ninety-six years. His life was studded with miraculous happenings even from childhood. But most of his wonder-working seems to have taken place during the building of a monastery at Caccamo, when building materials were either multiplied or were supplied under miraculous conditions. Water was miraculously supplied as well, as was bread and wine to feed the workers. Another unusual incident involved a poor widow whose six small children were crying for food. Bl. John happened to visit her that day and blessed them. On leaving he told them to look in the bread box. Knowing that nothing had been in it for days, the poor widow obediently did as she was directed. The bread box was full, "and it stayed full for as long as the need lasted."[45]

In a biography of ST. RITA OF CASCIA (d. 1457) we read that sometime after her death, and before her beatification, the nuns of her convent in Cascia found themselves without wine for their meals. Sr. Costanza, the superior of the convent, knowing that she had no money with which to buy what was needed, decided to visit Rita's tomb and tell the Servant of God of their need. A short time later the superior answered a loud knocking at the convent door and saw a man standing there who said he had a barrel of wine for the convent. As soon as the barrel was placed in the cellar, the man disappeared, together with the donkey and the cart that had brought the answer to her prayer.[46]

A case in which there was a subtraction of wine is reported in the biography of BL. PETER OF TIFERNO (d. 1445) when he was begging supplies for his brethren. He approached a wine merchant, who refused the priest with a lie: "the barrels down cellar are all empty." A short time later, the merchant had cause to remove some wine from the barrels. It was then he discovered that they actually *were* empty, although they had been quite full before Bl. Peter's visit.

Realizing this was a punishment for his lack of generosity and the lie he told to a priest of God, he hurriedly ran after Peter, apologized profusely and begged him to bless and restore the wine. Peter did so without hesitation. Although the biographer does not mention the result of Peter's kindness, we can well imagine that the wine merchant was exceptionally generous to Peter that day and more than likely on the following visits of the Blessed.[47]

Some of the other saints in which the multiplication of food or drink is mentioned in their biographies can be numbered: Bl. Crispin of Viterbo, St. Benedict the Moor, St. Cuthbert, Bl. Jane Scopelli, Bl. Louis Guanella, St. Joseph of Cupertino, St. Lupicinus, St. Clare of Assisi, St. Richard of Chichester, St. Mary Magdalen de Pazzi, St. Aloysius Gonzaga, St. Francis Xavier, St. Cunegund, St. Elizabeth Queen of Portugal, Bl. Mother Pelletier, Bl. Gaspar del Bufalo, Ven. Gertrude Salandri, Bl. Andrew Ibernon, Ven. Joan Marie of the Cross, St. Veronica Giuliani, St. Aidanus, St. Bridget, St. Cronin, St. Hermenland, Bl. Crispin, St. Dorotheus, Venerable Bede, St. Peregrine Laziosi, Bl. Eustochia Calafato, Bl. Luchesio, St. Ives of Brittany and many others.

The multiplication of food items has taken places in all ages, in many different countries by religious people and members of religious orders—people of unquestionable integrity. There are too many instances in which these miracles have taken place for them to be dismissed as an impossibility.

As one reputable author wrote: "This multiplication of food, though the evidence at times may be inadequate, cannot lightly be dismissed as a phenomenon belonging merely to the domain of legend."

GENEROSITY REPAID. A relief depicting St. Dominic and friars being served by angels after their last loaf of bread was selflessly given to the hungry poor.

ST. JOSEPH OF CUPERTINO multiplies bread, wine and honey.

MYSTICAL MARRIAGE
AND HEAVENLY JEWELRY

*"I will greatly rejoice in the Lord, and my soul shall be joyful
in my God: for he hath clothed me with the garments of salvation:
and with the robe of justice he hath covered me, as a bridegroom
decked with a crown, and as a bride adorned with her jewels."*

—Isaias 61:10

The highest spiritual state that can be attained this side of Heaven
is that of Mystical Marriage, wherein the divine love of God is
united to the soul in a state of heavenly embrace so that the spirit
becomes one with the Lord. Souls who are privileged to receive this
divine gift are those who have been purified and who have spent a
lifetime of complete fidelity and submission to God with a pure and
unconditional love.

Many writers of the spiritual life have explained this state, but all
depend on the writings of ST. TERESA OF AVILA (d. 1582) and
ST. JOHN OF THE CROSS (d. 1591), who are Doctors of the
Church in addition to being masters of mystical theology. Both
Saints have written about this subject, and it is from them that the
following brief explanation is given.

Before participating in mystical marriage there is a time of mystical espousal which is comparable in a small way to an earthly
courtship, but the soul must already have reached a high degree of
sanctity. St. Teresa describes the mystical espousal in this way:

> The contract is already drawn up and the soul has
> been clearly given to understand the happiness of her lot
> and is determined to do the will of her Spouse in every
> way in which she sees that she can give Him pleasure
> . . . His Majesty is pleased with the soul and desires
> that she shall get to know Him better and that, as we
> may say, they shall meet together and He shall unite her

with Himself . . . All giving and taking have now
come to an end and in a secret way the soul sees Who
this Spouse is that she is to take . . . For it is all a matter of love united with love.[1]

St. Teresa again describes the betrothal:

When Our Lord is pleased to have pity upon this
soul, which suffers and has suffered so much out of
desire for Him, and which He has now taken spiritually
to be His bride, He brings her into this mansion of His,
which is the seventh, before consummating the spiritual
marriage. For He must needs have an abiding place in
the soul, just as He has one in Heaven, where His
Majesty alone dwells. So let us call this a second
Heaven.[2]

St. John of the Cross explains the difference between the espousal
and the marriage in this way:

In the espousal there is only a mutual agreement and
willingness between the two, and the bridegroom graciously gives jewels and ornaments to his espoused. But
in marriage there is also a communication and union
between the persons. Although the bridegroom sometimes visits the bride in the espousal and brings her presents, as we said, there is no union of persons, nor does
this fall within the scope of the espousal."[3]

St. John of the Cross further explains:

Spiritual marriage is incomparably greater than the
spiritual espousal, for it is a total transformation in the
Beloved in which each surrenders the entire possession
of self to the other with a certain consummation of the
union of love . . . I think that this state never occurs
without the soul's being confirmed in grace . . . It is
accordingly the highest state attainable in this life . . .
Just as in the consummation of carnal marriage there are
two in one flesh, as Sacred Scripture points out (*Gen.*

2:24), so also when the spiritual marriage between God and the soul is consummated, there are two natures in one spirit and love, as St. Paul says in making this same comparison: "He who is joined to the Lord is one spirit with him." (*1 Cor.* 6:17).[4]

ST. BERNARD OF CLAIRVAUX (d. 1153) also considers the quotation of St. Paul when he explains mystical marriage:

> It is a chaste and holy love, sweet and strong, intense and lively, which of two makes but one, according to the testimony of St. Paul . . . The union of man with God consists not in a confusion of natures (the divine with the human), but in a conformity of wills.[5]

And as St. John explained, the marriage is the union of love to love and of God with the soul of the human.

Since mystical marriage is a spiritual union, it should not be surprising, then, that not only female Saints have been so privileged, but a number of male Saints have been graced as well with this exalted state. One of these was the Curé of Ars, whose experiences will be recounted later.

Just as in earthly marriages a ring is given as a visible sign, so the good Lord often gives a heavenly ring to those who are privileged to participate in this mystical union. Sometimes the ring is not visible to others, although the recipient can always see it. At other times the ring is visible to others, or it might be a reddening of the skin as it encircles the finger. The marriage and the ring-giving sometimes take place in a ceremony in which the Blessed Virgin, or one or more of the Saints, takes part, as we shall see.

How many Saints have experienced this mystical state? Dr. Imbert-Gourbeyre once compiled a list of almost 100 persons who either had experienced the mystical espousal or mystical marriage. Fifty-five of these had received the mystical rings.

ST. TERESA OF AVILA experienced this state and frequently in her writings tells us that God dwells in the very center of the soul, a point she repeats: "In the spiritual marriage, the secret union takes place in the very interior center of the soul, which must be where God Himself dwells."

As mentioned previously, the good Lord gives jewels to those He embraces in the spiritual marriage, but to St. Teresa He gave a "jewel" of another nature. The Saint tells of her own mystical marriage that took place after receiving Holy Communion.

> He revealed Himself to me in an imaginary vision (with the eyes of the soul) most interiorly, as on other occasions, and He gave me His right hand, saying to me: "Behold this nail. It is a sign that from today onward thou shalt be My bride. Until now, thou hadst not merited this; but henceforward thou shalt regard My honour not only as that of thy Creator and King and God but as that of My very bride. My honour is thine, and thine, Mine." This favour produced such an effect upon me that I could not restrain myself but became like a person who is foolish and begged the Lord either to exalt my lowliness or to show me fewer favours, for I really did not think my nature could endure them. For the whole of that day I remained completely absorbed. Since then I have been conscious of receiving great benefits and of still greater confusion and distress when I see that in exchange for such great favours I am doing nothing.[6]

Three of St. Teresa's contemporaries were favored with the mystical espousal. One of these was ST. CATHERINE DEI RICCI (d. 1590). Having left a position of honor in the world, St. Catherine entered the Dominican convent of St. Vincent at Prato, Italy when she was only thirteen years old. She advanced rapidly in the mystical life so that by the age of twenty (some report nineteen), during Holy Week of 1542, she experienced the first of her ecstasies in which she saw enacted, in sequence, the scenes of Our Lord's Passion. The ecstasies were repeated every week for twelve years, beginning at midday every Thursday and ending on Friday at 4:00 p.m. She also received the sacred stigmata, which included the wounds of the hands, feet and side in addition to those inflicted by the Crown of Thorns.

On Easter Sunday of that same year, St. Catherine dei Ricci experienced the mystical espousal. Our Saviour appeared to the Saint radiant with light, and drawing from His own finger a gleaming ring, He placed it upon the forefinger of her left hand, saying, "My daughter, receive this ring as a pledge and proof that thou dost now, and ever shalt, belong to Me." Catherine described the ring as being of gold and set with a large pointed diamond. Thankfully, we have a great deal of information about this ring and how it was viewed by others.[7]

The question of the ring was of particular interest to Prosper Lambertini, the future Pope Benedict XIV, when the cause for Catherine's canonization was being considered. Acting as the Promoter of the Faith, which is popularly known as the Devil's Advocate, Rev. Lambertini posed several questions that were answered by the Postulator of the Cause and various witnesses.

Since the event took place in 1542, and St. Catherine lived another 48 years after the event, there were still alive a number of people who had seen the ring when witnesses were questioned in 1614.

One of those questioned was Sr. Dorothea Vecchi, then 83 years old, who deposed that she had seen the ring and described it as having a hoop of gold, but in place of the diamond, she saw a protrusion of the flesh of the finger. Sr. Mary Magdalen Ricasoli, 69 years of age, had seen the ring twice, once during her childhood; the second time after the Saint's death. She testified that while St. Catherine's body was lying before the altar she clearly saw a livid mark around the index finger of the left hand. She added that the circle of red remained until the body was buried.

Also questioned was Donna Isabella de' Bonsignori, aged 50, who saw the ring not long before the Saint's death. The ring was on the index finger of the left hand and appeared to be "flesh raised up like a ridge." When the Saint saw that she was looking at it, the Saint placed her hand under her scapular, where she usually kept it.

Another witness who was not a religious testified that she saw the ring two years before the Saint's death. She described it as a bright gold ring upon the Saint's left hand. She saw nothing unusual in the Saint wearing such a ring, since she felt it was a token which a prioress wore in virtue of her office.

One of the oldest nuns recalled that when she was a child she was allowed to hold the Saint's hand for a long time. It was then that she saw upon the Saint's finger a gold ring with a brilliant white stone, "so that I could see myself reflected in it." One nun said that there was such a bright light coming from the finger that she could not see what kind of ring it was.

The most valuable testimony of all was contained in two written documents dated 1549, seven years after the mystic espousal. One was a letter of Dominican Fr. Neri dated 1549, which reads:

> Within a fortnight of Easter, the true ring, that is to say the ring of gold with its diamond, was seen by three very holy sisters at different times, each of them being over forty-five years of age. One was Sister Potentiana of Florence, the second Sister Mary Magdalen of Prato, the third Sister Aurelia of Florence. A command was laid upon this holy virgin (Catherine) by her superior to ask a favour of Jesus Christ; and by Him the favour was granted that all the sisters saw the ring, or at least a counterfeit presentiment of it, in this sense, that for three days continuously, i.e., the Monday, Tuesday and Wednesday of Easter week, all the sisters beheld on the finger beside the long finger of the left hand, and in the place where she said the ring was, a red lozenge to represent the stone or diamond, and similarly they saw a red circlet around the finger in place of the ring, which lozenge and circlet Catherine averred she had never seen in the same way as the sisters, because she always beheld the ring of gold and enamel with its diamond. Also the ring was seen in this way as a reddening of the flesh throughout the whole of Ascension Day, 1542, and also on the day of Corpus Christi, when it was accompanied by a most wonderful perfume which was perceived by all.[8]

Father relates further that the reddening of the finger could not be ascribed to any paint or dye since on the feast of Corpus Christi, Catherine was brought into the church, where the governor of the city hoped to see the ring. Although the circlet had been red moments before, as Catherine entered the church all sign of redness disappeared. When Catherine returned to the convent the circlet reappeared.

What is certain is that this nun, a contemplative who had devoted her life to the practice of virtue, declared on numerous occasions when questioned about it that she saw the ring as a circlet of gold with a huge white diamond.

What is also certain is that others, if they did not see the ring itself, saw instead a circle of red and protruding flesh which unmistakably indicated the presence of a mystical ring.

A contemporary of both St. Teresa and St. Catherine dei Ricci was BL. CATHERINE OF RACCONIGI (d. 1547). In this case we have two betrothals, one ceremony in which Our Lady took part as well as two Saints; in the second ceremony the appearance of only one Saint.

Catherine was a mere child of five when she began to have mystical experiences, which continued throughout her life. Although it seems inconceivable that a child of that age would be granted extraordinary experiences, we are told that Our Lady appeared to her as she was praying alone in her room and told her that the Child Jesus wanted to take her for His spouse.

> Accompanied by many saints and angels, among whom were St. Catherine of Siena and St. Peter Martyr, Jesus appeared as a child of Catherine's own age. It was Our Lady who placed on her finger the ring of the espousal. The ring remained visible to Catherine for the rest of her life, although it could not be seen by others.[9]

Another biographer tells that while Catherine was praying to St. Stephen on his feast day in the year 1500 (when she was 13 years old), the Saint appeared to her and spoke encouraging words, promising that the Holy Spirit would come upon her in a marvelous way.

The second espousal took place when three rays of light fell upon her and a heavenly voice sounded: "I am come to take up my dwelling in you and to cleanse, enlighten, kindle and animate your soul." After she made a vow of virginity the mystical espousal took place and "the mark of a ring appeared upon her finger . . ."[10]

Catherine became a Dominican tertiary, had many mystical experiences and performed many miracles both during her life and after her death.

Another of the contemporaries was BL. STEPHANIE DE QUINZANIS (d. 1530), whose mystical experiences began at the age of seven when she made vows of poverty, chastity and obedience.

She later became a Dominican tertiary and was favored with visitations of Our Lord and several Dominican Saints. During one of Our Lord's visits she was given a beautiful ring as a token of her espousal. Little else is given us about this experience, but we do know that she led a life of almost constant penance, was especially devoted to the Holy Eucharist and bore the wounds of the sacred stigmata.[11]

ST. GERTRUDE THE GREAT (d. 1302) was a mystic who experienced mystical favors and numerous visions, which are recounted for us in her *Life and Revelations*. Our Lord once gave her extraordinary graces which are given in Chapter XXI of her book. Soon after, she was so full of joy that she rather boldly, but lovingly, mentioned to Our Lord that He "had not assured me of these favours by solemn contract." To this Our Lord replied, "Do not complain of this; approach and receive the confirmation of My promises." Our Lord then opened both His hands to reveal His Heart and commanded Gertrude to extend her hands. Our Lord then promised to preserve the gifts He had given her. St. Gertrude continues:

> After these most sweet words, as I withdrew my hand,
> I perceived thereon seven golden circlets, in the form of
> rings, one on each finger, and three on the signet finger;
> which indicated that the seven privileges were confirmed to me, as I had asked.[12]

This mystical favor is commemorated by the Church in St. Gertrude's Office. This appears during the third antiphon at Lauds which reads: "My Lord Jesus has espoused me to Him with seven rings, and crowned me as a bride." St. Gertrude's feast is observed worldwide on November 16.

We have in the case of ST. CATHERINE OF SIENA (d. 1380) an example of a ceremony witnessed by the Blessed Virgin and four Saints. We are fortunate in having Bl. Raymond of Capua, the Saint's confessor, relate for us what took place.

It was almost the time of Lent, Bl. Raymond writes, "when men celebrate the vain feast of the stomach," before the time "when the faithful must abstain from meat and fats." While others in the household feasted, St. Catherine was alone in her room "seeking through prayer and fasting the face of her eternal Bridegroom." Suddenly Our Lord said to her:

> "Since for love of Me you have forsaken vanities and despised the pleasure of the flesh and fastened all the delights of your heart on Me, now, when the rest of the household are feasting and enjoying themselves, I have determined to celebrate the wedding feast of your soul and to espouse you to Me in faith as I promised."
>
> Before He had finished speaking, His most glorious Virgin Mother appeared with the most blessed St. John the Evangelist, the glorious Apostle Paul, St. Dominic, the founder of the order, and the prophet David with his harp. While David played sweet strains on the harp, the Mother of God took Catherine's hand in her own most holy hand and, presenting her to her Son, courteously asked Him to marry her to Himself in faith. The Son of God, graciously agreeing, held out a gold ring with four pearls set in a circle and a wonderful diamond in the middle, and with His most holy right hand He slipped it onto the virgin's second finger saying, "There! I marry you to Me in faith, to Me, your Creator and Saviour. Keep this faith unspotted until you come to Me in Heaven and celebrate the marriage that has no end."[13]

After the vision disappeared Catherine saw the ring on her finger, although no one else could see it. Bl. Raymond tells that "she frequently confessed to me in all humility that she could always see it on her finger and that there was never a moment when it was out of her sight."

Known as the reformer of the Poor Clare Order and the foundress of a branch of the order which is still known as the Colettines, ST. COLETTE (d. 1447) was especially devoted to St. John the Apostle, and it is this Saint who is featured in her mystical espousal. The Saint's spiritual experiences were told to only a few intimate friends, two being Fr. Pierre de Vaux and a nun of her order, Sister Perrine. Early in her work of restoration, St. John the Evangelist appeared in splendor and placed a miraculous ring on her finger, saying that he did so "by my own right and on behalf of the sovereign King and Prince of virginity and chastity." Fr. Pierre described the ring as: "of gold, very precious and beautiful."

Whereas the other recipients of mystical rings wore them on their fingers, St. Colette is an exception. Fr. Pierre writes that she customarily kept her treasure in a gold or silver case and showed it occasionally to "her friars, confessors, and other persons who were much gladdened and consoled by the sight of it." Not only did she keep it secured in a case, but she also entrusted the ring to friars she sent on difficult missions so "sufferings and dangers might be averted."

In his life of the Saint, *Vie de Sainte Colette,* written in 1594, Benedictine Dom M. Notel wrote that the ring was given to the Benedictines of Saint-Pierre in Ghent after the Saint's death in 1447. Unfortunately, it disappeared during the sixteenth century.[14]

ST. VERONICA GIULIANI (d. 1727), a Capuchin nun, endured accusations, doubts and great humiliations at the hands of her community because of her many spiritual favors, including that of the stigmata. After enduring the sufferings for some time, she experienced the mystical espousal. The event took place on April 11, 1694. She received a mystical ring from the hand of Jesus which many witnesses were privileged to see. One witness related, "This ring encircled her ring finger as ordinary rings do. On it there appeared to be a raised stone as large as a pea and of a red color." The ring was not always visible, but at times was seen clearly.[15]

Among the men who have experienced the mystical marriage is ST. JEAN MARIE BAPTISTE VIANNEY, the Curé of Ars (d. 1859). Many of the Saint's mystical experiences are related in this volume, but we will now consider that which took place after a life of "continual prayer."

During the Process of the Saint's canonization, Baronne de Belvey related that he once had heard him exclaim: "Oh! the beautiful union of the soul with Our Lord! The interior life is a bath of love into which the soul plunges. God holds the soul, when she has reached that stage, as a mother embraces the head of her child in order to cover it with caresses. Our Lord hungers after such a soul!" Another time he was heard to say: "I wish I could lose myself and never find myself except in God."

We are not told how the espousal took place, but the ring given him during the event was clearly seen by a witness and was attested to by the Curé himself. These facts are related in a letter written by a devout woman to one of the Curé's successors which reads:

> Monsieur Le Curé,
>
> I deem it a duty to inform you that I was at Ars on July 2, 1856, and not having succeeded in seeing the Saint in the confessional, owing to the crowd of strangers that thronged round it, I promised myself the satisfaction of at least throwing myself at his feet to ask for his blessing. As soon, therefore, as I came into the presence of that wonderful man, I endeavoured to grasp his sacred hand so as to kiss it reverently. But he withdrew it, saying to me in a grave, yet gracious manner: "Oh! do not rob me of my ring."
>
> At the same moment I saw what I had not noticed until then: on the fourth finger of his left hand there shone a golden ring of extraordinary brilliancy. So he had received, because he deserved it, the wonderful favour which other saints have also had bestowed upon them.

The devout woman, Jeanne Clairet of Villefranche-sur-Saone, wrote the letter, which is kept in the archives of the presbytery of Ars. Although the letter itself is undated, the date within the letter indicates that the marriage must have taken place before 1856, which would be three years before the Saint's holy death.

Knowing of the Saint's loving intimacies with God, M. Toccanier once alluded to the experiences and the happiness he must have derived from them. The Saint is said to have replied: "Oh! my friend, there is much more besides!" Perhaps, by this remark, the Saint referred to his spiritual marriage?[16]

Jeweled Crucifixes

Throughout her lifetime there was one article that ST. COLETTE (d. 1447) yearned for: a relic of the True Cross. As mentioned earlier, St. Colette was given a mystical ring. Records also reveal that her desire for the precious relic was satisfied. She received this small piece of Our Lord's Cross in this way. In the presence of her community, she was one day contemplating Our Lord's sufferings when she was drawn into an ecstasy. When it ended she discovered in her hand a small golden crucifix that had not been there before the ecstasy.

The upright beam of the Crucifix measured 0.035 millimeters and the crossbar 0.008 millimeters. On one side are five precious stones: a blue stone on each extension, and a red stone in the middle. Surrounding this red stone are four pearls with a fifth pearl added at the foot of the cross. On the other side is a figure of the Crucified. The rectangular section, to which the figure is attached, can be turned back or removed, revealing the relic, which is identified with an inscription. The receptacle is backed by the red stone and fronted by the head of Jesus.[17]

When St. Colette's good friend, St. Vincent Ferrer, was told about her experience and the heavenly gift of the Crucifix, he held out his hand to receive it. But when he saw it in the hand of St. Colette, he fell to his knees and for a time was oblivious to everything around him.

Toward the end of her life, St. Colette distributed her few possessions to her spiritual daughters. A breviary was given, as was the tall wooden cross of St. Vincent Ferrer, and lastly the golden Crucifix with its relic of the True Cross. Placing it in the hands of the abbess of Besançon she said simply, "Keep it and treasure it, for it is from Heaven."[18]

The reliquary, known as the Cross from Heaven, is kept with great reverence at the *Monastere de Ste. Claire* in Besançon, France.

ST. TERESA OF AVILA (d. 1582) tells us about the vision she had in which she was given a jeweled crucifix by Our Lord. She explains the experience in this manner:

> Once, when I was holding in my hand the cross of a rosary, He put out His own hand and took it from me, and, when He gave it back to me, it had become four large stones, much more precious than diamonds— incomparably more so, for it is impossible, of course, to make comparisons with what is supernatural, and diamonds seem imperfect counterfeits beside the precious stones which I saw in that vision. On the cross, with

exquisite workmanship, were portrayed the five wounds. He told me that henceforward it would always look to me like that, and so it did. I could never see the wood of which it was made, but only these stones. To nobody, however, did it look like this except to myself.[19]

The crucifix was later given by St. Teresa's sister Juana to Dona Maria Enriquez de Toledo, Duchess of Alba. After the Duchess' death the Carmelites claimed possession of it and, until the end of the eighteenth century, it was preserved in their Valladolid convent. It was lost during the religious persecutions of 1835.

Jewels and Blood

Perhaps the most amazing situation regarding heavenly jewels is that concerning the blood of ST. PHILOMENA (d. 1st century). The discovery of her remains took place on May 24, 1802 while workmen were clearing away sand in a subterranean cemetery, under the road that leads out of the Porta Salaria from Rome to Ancona. When one of the workmen's picks hit a cemented surface, three tiles were found that marked the tomb of St. Philomena. Markings on the tiles identified the name as being Philomena. Also on the tiles were: a lily, which identified her as a virgin; a palm, signifying the victory of martyrdom; and arrows and an anchor, which were later revealed to have been used in an effort to kill her.

Revelations made later to three persons who were unknown to each other indicated that Philomena had been shot with arrows and had been thrown into a river with an anchor tied to her neck. An examination of the bones revealed that Philomena was about 12 or 13 years of age at the time of her death.

Under the gaze of Church and civil authorities who were called to the scene the next day, workmen searched for a vial or ampoule containing the dried remains of blood which would confirm that the subject had been martyred for the faith. After a brief search near the head, a vase was found which was embedded in the concrete of the tomb. Since the vial was cracked, the dried reddish-brown substance was carefully placed in a vase of clear glass. While the distinguished witnesses gazed at the substance, they were surprised by a wonderful chemical reaction. Gems became visible, as well as kernels of silver and gold in a substance that later was chemically proven to be human blood.

This chemical change has been noted on many occasions since its discovery. Cardinal Ruffo Scilla deposed: "And we have seen her blood changed into several brilliant little precious stones of various colors; also into gold and silver."[20]

Cardinal Victor Auguste Dechamps in 1847 witnessed the change. He testified: "Need I tell you what happiness I saw . . . the phial of blood, of that precious blood shed for love of virginity . . . It is a thing marvelous to see . . . I had read of it in descriptions, but now I have seen it with my own eyes."[21]

Fr. Paul O'Sullivan, O.P. in his biography of the Saint which was written about the year 1925, relates the following:

> The blood is not in a liquid state, but quite dry and in appearance resembles ashes. It is preserved in a small crystal vase which allows the visitor to see it . . . I had the happiness of examining this priceless treasure as many as thirty or forty times. Each time, without fail, I saw the blood change most marvelously, and the transformation was so clear and distinct as not to allow room for the smallest doubt or misconception. Precious stones, rubies and emeralds, pieces of gold and particles of silver appeared mingled with the blood. One might shake the reliquary, and again the precious stones appeared, not always in the same way, but still clearly and distinctly.[22]

Sometimes dark particles appear in the blood, which signifies impending evils or sorrows for those who are handling or gazing at the relic.

The vial containing the jeweled blood is kept in the Sanctuary of St. Philomena located in Mugnano, Italy. It is found in a glass-fronted reliquary above the main altar, which also contains a figure representing the Saint. The bones of the Saint are arranged inside the figure.

St. Philomena was a favorite of St. Jean Marie Baptiste Vianney, the Curé of Ars, and it was to her that the Curé attributed all the miracles that were worked in Ars.

MYSTICAL MARRIAGE. The Blessed Virgin assists at the Mystical Marriage of St. Catherine of Siena. Witnessing the ceremony are (from left) King David, St. John the Apostle, St. Dominic and St. Paul the Apostle. (*Painting:* A. Franchi. *Photo:* B. N. Marconi, Genoa.)

MIRACULOUS PROTECTION

"Be thou unto me a God, a protector, and a place of strength: that thou mayest make me safe."—Psalms 70:3

We will never know, until we reach the Heavenly Kingdom, how many times we were preserved during childhood from accidents or death through the intercession of the Blessed Mother, some of the Saints, or our Guardian Angel. Many in later life are aware of their unusual safety from accidents. By the irreligious it might be attributed to "luck," while the religious and devout will attribute their safety to heavenly intervention. For the following Saints, their safety from accident or death can only be regarded as miraculous.

The first presented for our consideration is ST. THOMAS BECKET (d. 1170), who was to become the Archbishop of Canterbury and a martyr. During his adolescence he was employed by Sir Richer de l'Aigle, who introduced him to the joys of hawking, hunting and other field sports.

One day when Thomas was in pursuit of game by a river, his hawk made a dive at a duck and went with it into the water. Thinking he would lose his hawk, the Saint leaped into the water to retrieve it. Unmindful of the swift current, he was swept down the river in the direct path of a mill whose water-wheel was turning. As soon as Thomas neared the wheel, it abruptly stopped—an occurrence that was regarded as miraculous.[1]

Every biographer of ST. PHILIP NERI (d. 1595) seems to relate an incident that took place when Philip was about eight years old. His parents one day took him to Castelfranco, where his father owned some property, and while the adults conducted business he was left alone in the courtyard of the house. Bored with waiting, he saw a donkey that was loaded with fruit standing near a flight of stone steps leading to a cellar. Without realizing the danger, Philip jumped on the donkey, which startled and fell down the steps. When they landed, Philip was under the donkey and the fruit. Everyone thought Philip would be found dead, but when he was pulled free he was not only alive, but was almost entirely unharmed. Philip "always looked on his preservation on this occasion as a miracle, for which he never forgot to thank God."[2]

Two preservations from drowning are recorded in the life of ST. JOHN OF THE CROSS (d. 1591). One event was mentioned by the Saint when he was passing by a lagoon at Andalusia. He recalled that it took place when he was five years old at a similar lagoon at Fontiveros, where children often went to play on the banks. In the company of some children, one being the youngest child of the weaver Catalina Alvarez, he began to throw sticks in the water. "The game consisted in throwing a stick sharply downward into the water, perpendicularly, so that it would quickly rise to the surface, permitting them to grasp it again as it rose." While playing this game, John lost his balance, fell into the water and sank below the surface. In a moment his head rose out of the water, but then sank again. This is how the story was told.

When he was at the bottom of the water, he saw a very beautiful lady who stretched out her hand, but he was afraid to grasp it because his own was so muddy. He was about to drown when suddenly, on the bank, a peasant came forward bearing a pole in his hand, and with this pole John was drawn from the water.[3] Can anyone doubt that it was Our Lady who sent the peasant with the pole at precisely the right time?

The second protection from drowning took place when John was playing with other boys in the courtyard of a hospital near the school. One of his companions pushed him, causing him to fall into a "low-lipped" well. As he fell he called for help, which no doubt caused a great deal of confusion. Everyone thought he was drowning, but instead of sinking, John floated to the surface and calmly called for a rope. He tied it under his arms and was pulled up without suffering the least scratch. Everyone present called it a miracle.

One of those present was a certain Pedro-Fernandez Bustillo, who also called the preservation a miracle and often told the story. Juan Gomez, who was entering his house at the time John was emerging from the well, heard it said that a miracle had been wrought by the Blessed Virgin. John, himself, always asserted that it was Our Lady who had personally kept him afloat.[4]

Another Saint who was spared from drowning was the young ST. ANTHONY MARY CLARET (d. 1870), who went with friends to wade in the water at Carceloneta, which boasted of a beach that attracted huge crowds. Anthony was seated near the water when a huge wave swept over him and drew him into turbulent water. Thinking he had drowned, his friends began to weep while some ran for help. Although Anthony was in the midst of an agitated sea, he is said to have remained serene in spite of his condition. While huge waves tossed him about in the air and submerged him in the water, the future Saint appealed for help to the Blessed Virgin. As soon as his brief prayer was sounded, a wave gently carried him to the beach. Without knowing how it happened, he found himself safe on the shore. There was no doubting that Our Lady had miraculously intervened in saving his life.[5]

MOTHER LOUISE MARGARET CLARET DE LA TOUCHE (d. 1915), whose cause for beatification was introduced in 1973, was saved through the intercession of the Blessed Virgin. When she was still a young child she suffered successive attacks of bronchitis which at one point threatened her life. The distraught mother promised to erect a votive tablet on Our Lady's altar in the Church of Obezine if she were cured. The tablet remains today as testimony to the protection of the Blessed Virgin.

Yet another time her parents were prostrate with grief when the child suffered a different ailment which robbed her of speech, weakened her pulse and gave all signs that she would soon die. Once again the Blessed Mother was called upon, when the mother felt herself prompted to pour a few drops of Lourdes water between the lips of the dying child. A minute later the child opened her eyes, smiled sweetly and fell into a peaceful slumber.

In her autobiography, Mother Louise Margaret tells of this experience, which reads: "I remember very well this painful illness and the evening that I was so sick. I had lost consciousness. Suddenly I experienced a very pleasant sensation, something inexpressibly sweet . . . it was in 1874 when the miraculous water of Lourdes cured me."[6]

LIGHTS AND RAYS OF LOVE

"And it came to pass, as I was going, and drawing nigh to Damascus at midday, that suddenly from heaven there shone round about me a great light . . . And they that were with me, saw indeed the light, but they heard not the voice of him that spoke with me." (St. Paul's conversion.) — Acts 22:6, 9

Ecstasy is sometimes accompanied by a luminous phenomenon wherein the Saint's head is aglow, a light might encompass the entire body, or rays either come toward or proceed from the body. Sometimes called "luminous effluvia," it is recounted numerous times in the lives of the Saints and has been described and attested to by persons of unquestionable integrity, and more often than not, by members of the Saints' own religious orders.

During the eighteenth century, when a candidate's case was being considered in whose lifetime lights and rays were reported, the guidelines of Pope Benedict XIV (1740-1758) were considered, he being the first to present such directives.

In the work, *De Beatificatione et Canonizatione*, the Pontiff lists the five conditions:

1) Did the phenomenon take place in full daylight, or during the night? If the event took place at night, was the light more brilliant than any other light?

2) Was the light a mere spark, or was it prolonged so that the observer had time to gaze upon it and become convinced of its reality? Did the phenomenon take place more than once?

3) Was the light produced during a religious act—an ecstasy, a sermon or a prayer? It would then possess a religious character.

4) Since God does not permit such manifestations to satisfy vain curiosity, but only for the good of souls, was there some beneficial result—an intervention of divine grace or a lasting conversion?

5) Are the lights and rays associated with a person who is (was) holy and virtuous?

The lights and rays mentioned in the lives of the Saints in this chapter have either been scrupulously examined under the Pope's conditions or, if the Saint's life preceded the Pope's guidelines, they were observed by reputable persons whose truthful depositions, together with the holiness of the person in question, were acknowledged by the person's canonization. Pope Benedict XIV admits to the miraculous nature of lights and rays mentioned in the lives of the Saints by declaring, "There are hundreds of such examples to be found in our hagiographical records."

The following are some examples of luminous phenomena which are mentioned in the lives of Saints which confirmed their sanctity, edified those who observed the illumination, produced converts to the Faith, reconciled sinners, but most of all demonstrated the love of God for these souls and the love of these souls for God.

The first example of an illumination which proceeded from one of God's holy ones is mentioned in the Old Testament in the Book of *Genesis.*

> As Moses came down from Mount Sinai with the two tablets of the commandments in his hands, he did not know that the skin of his face had become radiant while he conversed with the Lord. When Aaron, then, and the other Israelites saw Moses and noticed how radiant the skin of his face had become, they were afraid to come near him.[1]

In the New Testament we learn of light surrounding Our Lord when He was on the mountain with Saints Peter, James and John. Scripture tells us: "He was transfigured before their eyes. His face became as dazzling as the sun, his clothes as radiant as light."[2]

Following the death of Jesus, during the first centuries of the Church, there are a number of instances in which lights and rays are mentioned. We will give an example recorded by Ven. Bede (d. 735), who wrote *The Ecclesiastical History of the English Nation.*

Ven. Bede tells about the death of ST. OSWALD, King of Northumbria, who was killed in a battle on August 5, 642, and the discovery and translation of the King's bones. Since his niece, Queen Osthrida of the Mercians, wanted the remains to be buried in the province of Lindsey called Beardeneu, the bones were placed on a wagon and carried to the venerable monastery in Lindsey. The monks knew the King to be very holy, but were hesitant to accept the remains since the King was originally of another province. While they debated the issue, the bones of St. Oswald remained during the night in the open air with a tent spread over them. But during the night a spectacular miracle took place.

> A pillar of light, reaching from the wagon up to the heavens, was seen by almost all the inhabitants of the province of Lindsey. In the morning, the brethren who had refused it the day before began themselves earnestly to pray that those holy relics, so beloved by God, might be deposited among them.[3]

Ven. Bede also writes about an unusual light that appeared at the monastery of Barking about the year 676. Around that time in England there existed what are called "double monasteries," that is, buildings that were divided, with the monks on one side being completely separated from the women religious on the other side. Ven. Bede writes that a disease among the monks was claiming many lives, so that the gravediggers were quite busy. The women religious were spared the sickness, but began to wonder where they would be buried should the disease claim some of their number. The location of their cemetery was a source of confusion until Heaven indicated where Our Lord's beloved should be buried. One day when the morning psalm ended, they proceeded to the cemetery of the monks to chant prayers for the departed when

> a light from the heavens, like a great sheet, came down upon them all and struck them with so much terror that, in consternation, they left off singing.
>
> But that resplendent light, which seemed to exceed the sun at noonday, soon after rising from that place shifted to the south side of the monastery—that is, to the west of the oratory. Having continued there some time, it covered those parts in the sight of them all and withdrew itself up again to heaven, leaving conviction in the minds of all that the same light, which was to lead or to receive the souls of those servants of God into Heaven, was intended to show the place in which their bodies were to rest, awaiting the day of Resurrection.

Two of the monks who were praying in the oratory at the time, one being elderly and the other much younger, stated later that "the rays of light which came in at the crannies of the doors and windows, seemed to exceed the utmost brightness of daylight itself."[4]

Lights are also noted in the life of ST. ELIZABETH OF HUNGARY (d. 1231), the daughter of King Andrew II of Hungary. She was married at the age of 14 to the landgrave of Thuringia, Ludwig IV, who died during the Crusades. Because of problems with his family, Elizabeth was forced out of her castle with her three children and was their sole support under trying circumstances. She joined the Third Order of St. Francis and suffered dreadfully under the strict directions of her spiritual advisor. She nevertheless worked tirelessly among the poor and the sick and advanced rapidly in the spiritual life. Count De Montalembert, in his biography of St. Elizabeth, mentions the time she was irradiated in light. He writes:

> Now it happened one day that during the Canon of the Mass, while she prayed fervently, with her hands folded and modestly hidden under her mantle, and her veil raised in order that she might contemplate the Sacred Host, a celestial light beamed around her. The celebrating priest, a man renowned for a holy life, saw at the moment of the consecration the face of the duchess refulgent with so great a splendor that he was dazzled by it, and until the Communion he found himself surrounded by a light radiating from her as from the sun. Filled with surprise, he returned thanks to God for having thus manifested, by a visible and wonderful light, the interior brilliancy of that holy soul, and he related afterwards what he had seen.[5]

ST. CLARE OF ASSISI (d. 1253) also experienced this illumination. After being appointed by St. Francis of Assisi as the abbess of his congregation for women, she governed her convent with humility and dependence upon the providence of God. The sisters of her community noticed at times that: "She came from prayer with her face so shining that it dazzled the eyes of those that beheld her."[6]

BL. HENRY SUSO (d. 1365) was a hard-working Dominican, a poet, an outstanding preacher and a great devotee of the Blessed Virgin. He had a great veneration for the Holy Name of Jesus and went so far as to cut the Name into the flesh above his heart with a pointed styletto so that at every beat of his heart, the Name moved with it. Although this would seem to be an extreme demonstration of love, the good Lord seems to have been pleased with it. One day when Bl. Henry was in ecstasy, it seemed that a light streamed from his heart. Although he had never before revealed that the Name was imprinted on his chest and had held his mantle tightly around him while the light was pulsing from him, the radiance was so brilliant that all his efforts at concealment proved useless.[7]

In his biography of ST. CATHERINE OF SIENA (d. 1380), Bl. Raymond of Capua writes that he was one morning offering the Holy Mass and turned to give the blessing when he "saw that her face had become like an angel's and was sending out bright rays of light." Following this marvel, a strange occurrence took place when the Host seemed to rise several inches from the altar onto the paten he held in his hand. Bl. Raymond writes: "I cannot remember whether It came to rest on the paten Itself or whether I put It there, for what with the brilliance of the Virgin's face and then this second miracle, I was absolutely dumbfounded . . . "[8]

BL. JOHN RUYSBROECK (d. 1381) was fond of leaving his monastery to spend hours in the forest, where he was free from human distractions while he engaged in prayer. Once when he was missing at supper a canon went to look for him. He was discovered sitting under a lime tree in apparent ecstasy, while surrounded by a brilliant light. It is claimed that the writings of Bl. John assure him a place among the greatest contemplatives of the Middle Ages.[9]

Miracles of all sorts abounded during the lifetime of ST. FRANCES OF ROME (d. 1440), so that it was not surprising, as she continued her advancement in spirituality, that her very body would display the indwelling of the Holy Spirit. It was noticed by her companions that she ate very little and that usually she "turned her face to the window, and her eyes fixed on the sky, while rays of light seemed to play around her and her countenance grew dazzling from the celestial brightness which overspread it."[10] Her ecstasies were frequent and her visions of heavenly wonders were numerous, including the ever-abiding vision of her Guardian Angel.

ST. COLETTE (d. 1445) once had a vision of St. Francis of Assisi in which he charged her to reform the Poor Clares, since the Order had relaxed some of its rules. Authorized by the Pope to undertake the reform, she corrected existing convents and founded seventeen more. Many mystical favors were granted this holy nun, who was a friend of the illustrious St. Vincent Ferrer. More than once St. Vincent saw her with her face streaming with light during ecstasies. Not only this holy priest, but also the nuns of the Order, the peasants outside Besançon and the friars at Dole had marveled at the spectacle.[11] Especially after receiving Holy Communion, "She was all enraptured and transfigured, and remained in this state as if she were in a trance. And when she returned to herself, sometimes her face was like an angel's, so beautiful and bright."[12]

When ST. FRANCIS OF PAOLA (d. 1507) and three of his friars were visiting the castle of King Ferrante of Naples, they shared a room in which four luxurious beds were provided. The King, who could not believe the four led lives of strict self-denial and prayer, had arranged with his servants to cut peep-holes in the door. When the King thought they would be asleep, he looked through the holes and saw the three friars sleeping on the floor next to the beds. In their midst was the Saint, floating in mid-air, his whole body glowing with light, as he prayed fervently to God! It is said that from then on King Ferrante treated the Saint with "unaccustomed respect."[13]

A similar condition was known to exist with ST. THOMAS OF VILLANOVA (d. 1555), the Archbishop of Valencia, Spain. The Saint fell frequently into raptures at his prayers and especially during Holy Mass when his face, according to Butler, "shone like that of Moses and as it were dazzled the eyes of those that beheld him." Although he endeavored to hide such graces, he was unable to do so.[14]

Butler tells us that ST. PHILIP NERI (d. 1595) lived in such constant touch with the supernatural that sometimes it was with the greatest difficulty that he could pursue his worldly avocation. "He would fall into an ecstasy when saying his office, when offering Holy Mass, or even while he was dressing. Men looking upon his face declared that it glowed with celestial radiance."[15]

ST. IGNATIUS OF LOYOLA (d. 1556) once suffered from a severe sickness brought about by various troubles and fatigue. After he entered a hospital two of his near relatives, Dona Maria d'Oriola and Dona Simona d'Alzaga, attended him; it is from their testimony that we learn of a wonderful event. One night before retiring, they wanted to leave a light burning in the Saint's sick room, but he opposed it, saying that God would provide a light if he needed it. He then arose, according to his custom, to pray. The fervor of his devotion prompted frequent sighs and murmurs. The two ladies, on hearing these sounds, assumed the Saint was moaning in pain and rushed to his room. On opening the door they found him in prayer, surrounded by a brilliant light. The Saint, greatly confused on being discovered in this state, begged them not to mention what they had seen.[16] Another time, while St. Ignatius was sitting on the steps of an altar with a group of children listening to a sermon, a lady of position, Elizabeth Roser, saw the Saint's head encircled with a bright light.[17]

The depositions of witnesses and other documents presented before the Roman authorities when the beatification of ST. STANISLAUS KOSTKA (d. 1568) was being considered reveal that this Saint's face "appeared all on fire as soon as he entered the church." Many times he was seen in ecstasy at Holy Mass and after having received Holy Communion. Devoted to Our Lady's Assumption during his brief life, he died on that feast day at the age of 18, having reached perfection in a short time.[18]

We read in the process for the canonization of ST. TERESA OF AVILA (d. 1585) that her extraordinary encounters with Our Lord often produced results visible to the eye. Maria de San Jose tells about the time the Saint's face began to glow when a priest spoke to her about the love of God. Maria Bautista deposed regarding these ecstasies that "on those occasions her face became so radiant, beautiful and devout that one who saw it could never forget it."[19]

Bl. Anne of St. Bartholomew spoke of Teresa's face "shining

resplendently" on two occasions, while Isabel of St. Dominic also saw the Saint's "resplendent face" on several occasions.[20]

Ana of the Incarnation lived with St. Teresa at the convent in Segovia during the year 1574 and gave a juridical deposition for the Cause of Teresa's canonization. She testified that one night she went to the door of Teresa's cell to ask if she needed anything. The Saint did not hear her and continued to write while her face was lit by a brilliant light. In addition, the Saint was surrounded all about by rays of gold. When the Saint stopped writing, the light immediately vanished, leaving her in darkness.[21]

The face of ST. BENEDICT THE MOOR (d. 1589) likewise shone with a celestial light, especially when he was in chapel. As the son of African slaves, he was granted his freedom and joined the Franciscan Order at Palermo, where he was employed as a cook. It was quietly whispered about that Angels were seen assisting him in the kitchen and that, moreover, food seemed to multiply miraculously under his hands. He has been chosen as patron by the blacks of North America and is regarded as the protector of the town of Palermo.[22]

In the process for the beatification of ST. LOUIS BERTRAND (d. 1581), testimony was given that his cell often appeared illuminated by a bright light, although no such lights were in his cell. Other witnesses testified that when they were keeping watch at his bed as he lay dying, "a brilliant light flashed from his mouth, illuminating the whole cell with its splendor—and this lasted for about the length of time that is needed to recite a 'Hail Mary.'"[23] Other phenomena attended his death, when perfume rose from his dead body and heavenly music was heard in the church.

ST. CATHERINE DEI RICCI (d. 1590), a member of the Dominican Order and a stigmatist, often fell into ecstasy while surrounded by a radiant light. In addition, a sweet fragrance often filled the room.[24]

Those who gave testimony to the virtues of ST. BERNARDINO REALINO (d. 1616) for the process before his beatification tell that an extraordinary radiance transformed his countenance. Some declared that they had seen sparks coming from all over his body like sparks from a fire, while others declared that the glow coming from his countenance dazzled them on more than one occasion, so that they could no longer distinguish his features and had to turn their gaze away for fear of straining their eyes. A priest in Naples tells how one day, when he had gone to call Fr. Bernardino in the early morning, he found the Saint on his knees with his face so radiant that it dispersed the darkness of the room.[25]

ST. ROBERT BELLARMINE (d. 1621), who served the Church as Archbishop of Capua, became a Cardinal and is now numbered among the Doctors of the Church. He was regarded as an authority on ecclesiology and Church-State relations, and is known as one of the greatest theologians the Church has ever produced. Butler tells us that the Saint "was small of stature and had to stand on a stool in the pulpit to make himself seen and heard . . . Men declared that his face shone with a strange light as he spoke and that his words seemed like those of one inspired."[26]

JOHN OF ST. SAMSON (d. 1636) was a humble lay brother of the Carmelite Order. Blind from the age of three, he nevertheless learned to skillfully play the organ and several other musical instruments. Because he advanced so quickly in the spiritual life, he was appointed spiritual master and director of the monastery of Rennes, France. He possessed many mystical gifts and would often fall into ecstasy when a religious work was read to him. It is said that the spiritual light that flooded the lay brother's soul, and the flames that consumed his interior, were revealed externally by a certain radiance that was clearly visible. Fr. Donatien of St. Nicholas, O. Carm., who was a member of the same community and a close friend of John of St. Samson as well as his first biographer, tells us:

> In these extraordinary states we often saw his face glowing and radiant with, I know not what kind of luminous ray, which used to be reflected from it. I myself witnessed it with a number of other trustworthy religious. No one can doubt the truth of this since John himself wrote in his Mystical Cabinet that he often experienced this light, which spread from the center of his soul to all his faculties, even to the exterior senses.[27]

We learn of a number of luminous manifestations in the life of ST. MARTIN DE PORRES (d. 1639), a humble Dominican lay brother who served his order in Lima, Peru. One night while the whole community of the Saint was engaged in the recitation of Matins, they saw a bright light near the main altar. Investigation disclosed that the heavenly splendor was focused on the countenance of St. Martin, who was obviously experiencing a profound ecstasy.[28]

Another time, when the Saint was at the Convent of the Most Holy Rosary, he nursed back to health a young man named Juan Vasquez. In gratitude for his restoration to health at the hand of the Saint, Juan became a willing assistant in the work of distributing alms to the poor. One night a violent earthquake shook the city. When the terrifying jolts awakened the young man, he rushed to the Saint's cell for refuge. When loud knockings on the door were not acknowledged, the young man walked into the cell. To his amazement he saw the Saint prostrate on the floor, his arms extended in the shape of a cross and a rosary in his hand. Although no candles or lamps were lit, the room was flooded with a supernatural light. At this, Juan Vasquez was terrified and ran from the room. Meeting Br. Miguel of St. Dominic in the hallway, he revealed the situation, but the brother, who was familiar with the supernatural gifts enjoyed by the Saint, simply told the young man that the condition would soon pass.

Juan Vasquez, thoroughly shaken by the experience, was unable to sleep for the rest of the night. The next morning, when Martin saw Juan, he charged the young man not to tell anyone what he had seen.[29]

At various times a certain religious saw Martin reflecting many brilliant rays of light. This usually occurred after the Saint had been engaged in prayer. According to J.C. Kearns, O.P., the Saint's biographer: "These celestial rays converged on the saintly Negro, extending, we are assured, from the high choir to the door of the chapter hall, a distance of one hundred and fifty yards, and were raised some sixteen to eighteen yards, gradually dying out in the darkness."[30]

While ST. JOSEPH OF CUPERTINO (d. 1663), who is known for his extraordinary levitations, was on his deathbed, he was awaiting the reception of the Holy Eucharist when he heard the sound of the bell that announced the approach of the Sacred Host. According to the Saint's biographer, Pastrovicchi, "The Saint suddenly rose from his bed and flew in rapture from the door of his room to the stairs above the chapel. There on his knees, with a supernatural light diffused about his face, he received his Lord for the last time."[31] Many were the supernatural gifts experienced by this Saint, whose body is preserved in the basilica at Osimo.

A heavenly light is also reported to have encompassed ST. FRANCIS OF POSADAS (d. 1713), especially while celebrating Holy Mass and while reading the Gospel of the day. Rays of light are said to have issued from his mouth so as to lighten the missal he held in his hands. Twice during Pentecost, observers saw a brilliant light issue from his body so that the whole altar was illuminated.

In the life of this Saint there are many instances of levitation which he tried to resist, but without success.[32] On two occasions during the Feast of Pentecost, "A similar splendor emanated from his whole body and illuminated the altar."[33]

ST. GERARD MAJELLA (d. 1755), who is known as the "Wonder-Worker of Our Days," once fell into an ecstasy and became so inflamed with the love of God that rays of light spread from all parts of his body. Observers reported that the brilliance from this phenomenon was such that the room in which he was praying appeared to be on fire.[34]

ST. PAUL OF THE CROSS (d. 1775), Founder of the Passionist Order, was one day praying alone in the house of a benefactor when his companion came to call him. On entering the room where the Saint was on his knees, the companion saw rays of light flashing from the Saint's face as from the sun.

On another occasion, St. Paul of the Cross visited the home of Maria Giovanna Grazi and spoke to her of heavenly matters. The lady had apparently glanced away because, as the Saint's biographer relates, ". . . upon hearing him speak with extraordinary fervor, she lifted her eyes and saw his face so lighted up and shining that her eyes could not bear it." After speaking a while longer, the Saint suddenly returned to himself and left quickly with his companion.[35]

When the young ST. ALPHONSUS LIGUORI (d. 1787) was unsure of his vocation to the religious life, he walked to the Hospital for the Incurables and began helping his beloved sick. As he went from one ward to another on August 28, 1723, he suddenly saw a dazzling light around him while a voice sounded in his ears: "Leave the world and give yourself to Me." Somewhat frightened, he started to leave the hospital when, for the second time, the light appeared about him and the voice repeated: "Leave the world and give yourself to Me." With a generous heart the Saint replied: "Lord Jesus, too long have I resisted Your grace; do with me what You will."

From the hospital he walked to the church of Our Lady of Ransom. While kneeling before the altar of Our Lady, he saw the bright light around him for the third time. He then promised to become a priest and later founded the order known as the Redemptorists. While taking recreation with his students at Ciorani some years later, he told them that the next day was the anniversary of his "conversion." He then revealed everything that had taken place at the Hospital for the Incurables and in the church of Our Lady of Ransom.[36]

Still another time St. Alphonsus was favored with an extraordinary light. This took place while the Saint was preaching a mission in Foggia. It was in this city and in the same collegiate church some fourteen years earlier that he was favored with a vision of the Blessed Virgin. The miracle was repeated while he was preaching the mission in preparation for Christmas of 1745. While Alphonsus was preaching about the patronage of the Blessed Mother, the people saw the portrait of the Virgin Mary become animated and moving, as though she were alive. While the congregation gazed in wonder, a ray of light darted from the face of the Virgin Mary to that of St. Alphonsus, illuminating him in a heavenly light. After asking the vision, "My Lady, is it your pleasure to play with me?" he not only entered into a profound ecstasy, but also levitated several inches into the air. His biographer tells us that "The cries of 'miracle' rent the air, and from that moment the conversions and public demonstrations of sorrow for sin were innumerable and extraordinary."[37]

ST. FRANCIS DE SALES (d. 1622) was also preaching when he was illuminated. The event took place on a feast day of the Blessed Mother, while the Saint was delivering a homily to a crowded congregation. Suddenly his face glowed with an unearthly light so that all present marveled at it.

Because the event was immediately recorded and attested, it was said that there can be no question that it was miraculous.

People from throughout France flocked to the confessional of ST. JEAN MARIE BAPTISTE VIANNEY, the Curé of Ars (d. 1859), who had the mystical gift of reading hearts. It is estimated that in one year he was visited by over a hundred thousand pilgrims and that for thirty years he spent from sixteen to twenty hours a day in the confessional. It is not surprising then, that in March of 1852, the Curé was hearing confessions at half past one in the morning. When he saw a nun named Sr. Clotilde of the Congregation of the Child Jesus waiting in line, the Saint summoned the sister to confess ahead of the others. In the chapel of St. John the Baptist, where the Saint's confessional was located, there was only one candle lit, but when the Saint opened the little shutter of the confessional, the nun saw the Saint wholly enveloped in a transparent and unearthly radiance. The Saint remained in this supernatural light throughout the confession, but when the nun left, the holy priest recovered his normal aspect.

On another occasion Marie Roch was waiting in line to confess and to consult the Saint about severe interior trials she was experiencing. From where she stood in line, she was able to see into the dark corner where the Saint was seated in the confessional. To her amazement she saw two fiery rays projecting from the priest's face, his features being completely hidden by the brightness of their light. Fascinated by the dazzling countenance, she gazed at it for at least eight to ten minutes. Finally, she felt unworthy to approach the Saint and left the chapel. The Saint, however, had already read her heart and perceived her difficulties. The next day, as he passed near her, he whispered, "Fear nothing, my child, all will be well."[38]

ST. ANTHONY MARY CLARET (d. 1870), whose life is resplendent with numerous mystical experiences, was the founder of the Claretian Fathers and served for a time as Archbishop of Santiago, Cuba. He was renowned for his parochial missions and the retreats he gave in his native Spain, where he also served as spiritual director to Queen Isabella II. Of the many wonders that surrounded the Saint was a heavenly light that occasionally enveloped him. One of the many witnesses of this marvel was Fr. Paul Coma of the Oratory of St. Philip Neri. His declaration reads:

> When I was fifteen years of age I entered the parish church of St. Eugenia of Berga, diocese of Vich. At the Rosary altar I noticed an unusual splendor surrounding the then unknown celebrant. I drew near and then recognized Father Claret, whose face was transformed. This strange brightness spread its rays as far as the sacristy. . . . This happened while the servant of God was giving missions in Catalonia.[39]

Another time, when the Saint and a companion were preaching a mission, they were praying together in the morning as was their custom when the Saint's face became lighted as he whispered ejaculatory prayers. His companion gazed in amazement as the Saint began to rise from the floor in ecstasy. His companion tells that:

> I feared that he would rise higher and that he would run the risk of injuring himself and fall to the floor when coming out of his ecstasy. I declare frankly, that I tried to make all the noise possible to awaken him from his rapture. It lasted a long time . . . After descending to the floor the Saint, crowned with rays of light, continued his prayers as before.[40]

We also have the testimony of Queen Isabella II of Spain, who was under the Saint's spiritual direction. In the sworn declaration the Queen sent to the *Proceso Informativo*, one of the six parts reads: "In regard to his sanctity, I can assure you that one day I saw him saying Holy Mass in my oratory, surrounded by splendor, and that I have seen his predictions fulfilled. Thus, my conscience obliges me to consign it to writing, adding that while I had the good fortune of having Father Claret as confessor, I saw nothing but prudence, humility, abnegation and all the other virtues found in a real Saint."[41]

FIRE AND HEAT OF LOVE

In another chapter we learn that the mystical state often produces a light or sparks of light proceeding from or directed toward a holy person which indicates a high degree of sanctity and a great intimacy with God. There is also a mystical fire, known as *Incendium Amoris,* that produces an unearthly glow or transformation which also gives visible evidence of sanctity. St. Gerard Majella, who experienced this mystical phenomenon, tells us that "God is a consuming fire. When He enters a soul, He inflames it, and its affections become sometimes so intense that they appear even on the body."[1]

The mystical state is also visited by a heat which actually raises the bodily temperature so that the ardor of love experienced by the mystic becomes almost unbearable. It is often mentioned in the lives of the Saints that such transports of love produce glows of heat that force the recipient to reach for cold water to tame the temperature, or the Saint is forced to find relief by throwing open doors and windows, even in the middle of winter.

From where does this fire and heat originate? Nowhere else but the Heart of Jesus. This proof is given us by ST. MARGARET MARY ALACOQUE (d. 1690) during her visions that resulted in the devotion to the Sacred Heart of Jesus. In her *Autobiography* the Saint tells of one vision of Our Lord in which

> The Sacred Heart was represented to me as a resplendent sun, the burning rays of which fell vertically upon my heart, which was inflamed with a fire so fervid that it seemed as if it would reduce me to ashes . . . His Five Wounds shining like so many suns. Flames issued from every part of His Sacred Humanity, especially from His Adorable Bosom, which resembled an open furnace and disclosed to me His most loving and most amiable Heart, which was the living source of these flames.[2]

During another apparition the Saint tells that "His Divine Heart being opened, there issued from it a flame so ardent that I thought I should be consumed, for I was wholly penetrated with it . . ."[3] Another time St. Margaret writes: "One day, as I went up to receive Him in Holy Communion, Our Lord showed me His Sacred Heart as a burning furnace . . ."[4]

It is quite understandable, then, that the beloved Saints of Our Lord, those who were overtaken with love for Him, should experience from this Sacred Heart a fire and heat which sometimes even betrayed itself by a glow and radiance that was readily observed by others.

One of the Saints who experienced this heat of love was ST. GER-ARD MAJELLA (d. 1755). He also had many other supernatural gifts and is known as a wonder-worker. We are told that while in ecstasy his face glowed, and sometimes his body as well. Once while speaking to the Dominican nuns of Corato, his face became radiant as he looked toward Heaven. With his hands grasping the bars of the grate, he heaved deep sighs under the flood of celestial emotions. His biographer, an unknown religious brother, writes:

> He remained a long time in this state. At last, return-ing to himself, he called for cold water, of which he swallowed a few mouthfuls; then withdrawing, he bathed his breast to temper the heat of divine love.[5]

On another occasion, while visiting the Carmelites of Ripacan-dida, he fell into an ecstasy and became, according to the reli-gious: "as luminous as the sun and incandescent to such a degree that the iron grate with its ornamental points bent under his hands like soft wax."[6]

In his biography of ST. CATHERINE OF SIENA (d. 1380), Bl. Raymond of Capua tells of the time her first confessor, Fra Tom-maso, celebrated Holy Mass under divine inspiration. He did not know that St. Catherine was in attendance, but when he turned to offer her Holy Communion he saw her face "bathed in tears and sweat, but shining and as though on fire, and received the Sacra-ment with such devotion that he marvelled at it and was greatly edi-fied." The next day Fra Tommaso approached the Saint "whom he had seen with such a burning face" and asked her what had happened to her. The Saint then described an extraordinary contact with Our Lord and ended by saying: "I wonder how ever I managed to go on living in such an excess of ardour and love."[7]

Similar sentiments were often expressed by ST. MARY MAGDALENE DE'PAZZI (d. 1607). She often found it necessary to visit the well. There "she immersed her arms in the icy-cold water, drank of it and poured it on her breast. She was on fire."

When others touched the Saint, "She was like a burning coal . . . her face was inflamed and her eyes shone so that she seemed a seraph."[8]

The Rev. Cepari, a Jesuit of advanced spirituality who was a confesssor of the Saint and later her biographer, tells us that St. Mary Magdalene was transformed by sudden overwhelmings of love,

> for her face, losing in a moment the extreme pallor which had been produced by her severe penances and her austere cloistral life, became glowing, beaming with delight, and full; her eyes shone like twin stars, and she exclaimed aloud, crying out "O love! O Divine Love!"

Moreover, such was the excess and abundance of this celestial flame which consumed her that "in the midst of winter she could not bear woolen garments, because of that fire of love which burned in her bosom, but perforce she cut through and loosened her habit."

As a priest of the Society of Jesus, ST. BERNARDINO REALINO (d. 1616) dedicated his life to the education of youth and to the care of prisoners, slaves and all who needed assistance. His life of self-sacrifice was rewarded with mystical favors. According to his process of beatification, he was seen surrounded by light while sparks of fire emanated from his body. It was deposed that the radiance was so intense that the features of the Saint could not be clearly identified—and in fact, the radiance was so brilliant that the viewer was required to look in another direction.

Testimony also indicated that he was seen one morning before dawn kneeling in prayer while the light surrounding him brightened the whole room.[9]

Cardinal James de Vitry, who was led to take Holy Orders under the inspiration of BL. MARY OF OIGNIES (d. 1213), wrote a biography of the Beata in which he tells about the mystical heat of love that she experienced:

> In the depth of winter she needed no material fire to keep off the cold, but even when the frost was so severe as to turn all the water into ice, she, wonderful to say, burned so in spirit that her body partook of the warmth of her soul, especially in time of prayer; so that sometimes she even perspired, and her clothes were scented with a sweet aromatic fragrance. Oftentimes also the smell of her clothes was like the smell of incense, while prayers were ascending from the thurible of her heart.[10]

Butler assures us that "Cardinal de Vitry was a devout and honest man, who told the truth fearlessly." Lest we think that what he wrote was an exaggeration, Butler again tells us that "Jacques de Vitry was a man of scrupulous integrity and of sober judgement."

The saintly housewife and Trinitarian tertiary, BL. ANNA MARIA TAIGI (d. 1837), often received Holy Communion at the Roman church of Santa Maria della Pieta from the hands of Cardinal Pedicini. It was he who noticed that streams of perspiration poured down her face as she wept abundantly and uttered deep sighs. Her cheeks at this time became rose-red as she was gripped by a spasm of divine ecstasy which caused her to faint. The Cardinal noted: "I have seen her fall after receiving Communion as if struck by lightning, and thus remain a long time burned in the sweet flames of divine love."[11]

When Anna Maria became too ill to attend Holy Mass in the churches of Rome, Pope Gregory XVI granted her the extraordinary privilege of a private oratory in her home. Anna Maria was delighted with the arrangement, since she would be able to hide herself from the eyes of men while she "surrendered to the transports of her faith."

Cardinal Pedicini, a frequent visitor to her home, described the exterior manifestations that followed her reception of the Holy Eucharist.

The Cardinal again tells: ". . . her face was suffused as with fire, and a noise such as a sparking flame makes was heard, and her bosom heaved as if it would burst."[12]

ST. STANISLAUS KOSTKA (d. 1568) was a Polish youth who entered the Jesuit order at Rome. According to his novice master, "Stanislaus was a model and mirror of religious perfection, who did not spare himself any penance in spite of his very delicate constitution." After only 10 months of religious life, Stanislaus died at the age of 18.

St. Francis de Sales, in writing about him, tells us that "Stanislaus was so violently assailed by the love of our Saviour as often to faint and to suffer spasms in consequence, and he was obliged to apply cloths dipped in cold water to his breast in order to temper the violence of the love he felt."[13]

One night, during a bitterly cold winter, Stanislaus was found by his superior walking alone in the Novitiate garden. When he was asked what he was doing there, the Saint replied with all simplicity, "I am burning, I am burning." The novice master, Fr. Lelius Sanguigni, was well aware that Stanislaus had to frequently bathe his chest with cold water to temper the heat of the love he felt. A fountain in the garden where the young Saint availed himself of the cool water for this purpose bears a plaque which identifies the fountain as the one whose waters were used by St. Stanislaus to cool the ardor of his love for God.[14]

ST. PHILIP NERI (d. 1595), known as "The Apostle of Rome," was only 29 years old when he received an extraordinary experience which he confided to Cardinal Federigo Borromeo. The event took place in a chapel in the catacombs of S. Sebastiano in the year 1544 while he was praying with special devotion to the Holy Spirit. Suddenly a globe of fire entered his mouth and sank down into his heart. At the same time he was seized by a fire of love so intense that he threw himself on the ground in an effort to cool it. When he stood up and felt his chest, he discovered a swelling as big as a man's fist, which caused pain neither then nor later. It did, however, cause violent palpitations during times of spiritual emotion, and caused heat to such an extent that he often had to bare his chest to relieve it.[15]

Even in winter the Saint found it necessary to open his clothes from the waist upwards to cool the heat. One day at Rome, after a great snowfall, he was found walking in the streets with his cassock unbuttoned, and at nighttime, the windows were left open to allow the cold to relieve him. Cardinal Crescenzi, one of St. Philip Neri's spiritual children, said that whenever he touched the Saint's hand it felt as though the Saint was suffering from a raging fever.[16] We are also told that "Sometimes in saying the Office, or after Mass, or in any other spiritual action, sparks, as it were of fire, were seen to dart from his eyes and from his face."[17]

The palpitations of his heart, which the Saint experienced at the time of his mystical experience, continued for the remainder of his fifty years of life. The heartbeat was also heard by those near him. Described as "being like the blows of a hammer, it was particularly noticed while he was praying, hearing confessions, saying Mass or giving Communion, or when he was speaking on some subject which stirred his emotions."[18]

After the Saint's death physicians and surgeons who had known the Saint "proceeded to open the body to investigate the mysterious swelling on his breast. Examination proved that the two ribs over the heart were broken and arched outwards; the heart was unusually large, while the great artery leading from it was twice the normal size; there was no sign of any disease."[19] The unusual arch of the ribs provided extra room for the mystical beatings of the heart. Herbert Thurston, S. J. relates that,

> In view of the positive testimony of the surgeons, there can be no dispute that the injury was there and had been there for many years. His biographers seem therefore fully justified in tracing it to that strange incident of the coming to him of the Holy Ghost in 1544 under the guise of a globe of fire.[20]

ST. PAUL OF THE CROSS (d. 1507), the founder of the Passionist Order, was afire with the love of God so much so that there took place the same effect which we read about in the life of St. Philip Neri; that is, a marvelous elevation of two ribs on his left side. According to his biographer, the unusual aspect of the ribs could not always be concealed. "An experienced professor of medicine observed it, and in the process deposed to the fact as one resulting from a supernatural cause."

The biographer continues:

This interior furnace of the love of God can alone account for what the religious remarked from time to time about the undergarments which he had used, and especially the linen vests, which, where they had touched his heart, were found scorched, as though they had been near a great fire.[21]

VEN. ROSA MARIA SERIO (d. 1725), the prioress of the Carmelite convent of Fasano, had an almost similar experience to that mentioned in the life of St. Philip Neri. The event also involved the Holy Spirit, since it occurred on the feast of Pentecost. Her biographer tells us that while the whole community was engaged in communal prayer, a ball of fire descended on the holy prioress. Perhaps her clothing began smoking as a result, or some other condition presented itself, since the nuns felt the need to undress her. What they found on the underlinen above the breast was a burn in the form of a heart.

The same burning took place six more times in as many years, but without the appearance of the ball of fire.[22]

Thomas Merton tells us in his biography of ST. LUTGARDE OF AYWIERES (d. 1246) that the Saint became so fervent in choir that a flame was seen to shoot out of her mouth and rise into the air. "A young nun, who happened to look up just in time to catch sight of this strange phenomenon, was so panic-stricken that she fell over in a dead faint."[23]

The Dominican nun, VEN. MARIA VILLANI OF NAPLES (d. 1670), is believed to have had a similar experience. Ven. Maria died at the age of 86 having within her body, according to her own declaration, a furnace of love. Her life, written four years after her death by Fr. Francis Marchese, O.P., reveals that Ven. Maria believed she was wounded in the side and heart by a fiery spear of love. The wound was definitely apparent and was carefully examined by three of her confessors, who signed affadavits to what they had seen and touched. One of these confessors, the Dominican Leonardo di Lettere, was a man of great reputation and sanctity whose cause for beatification was introduced soon after his death. The fire of love sparked by the flaming arrow produced such heat that Ven. Maria was forced to drink an excessive amount of water each day. Witnesses claimed that the drinking of the water was accompanied by a hissing sound like that of water falling on a sheet of hot iron.

In her letters and other writings it was often expressed by the Venerable that she was continuously consumed by an almost insupportable flame of love. The heat from this flame was quickly brought to the attention of a surgeon after her death when he conducted an autopsy. When an incision was made in the area of the heart, the witnesses were amazed to see "smoke and heat which exhaled from the heart, that veritable furnace of divine love." The heat was so intense the surgeons found it necessary to stop and wait until the body cooled somewhat. After a time the surgeon returned. "He put in his hand to extract the heart, but he found it so hot that, burning himself, he was compelled to take his hand out again several times before he succeeded in effecting his purpose."

The biographer declares that a formal affidavit regarding these facts was made by the surgeons Domenico Trifone and Francesco Pinto, who also described the open wound found in the heart. It corresponded exactly to the wound on the outside of the body. Her biographer, writing just four years after the autopsy, writes:

> This wound (in the heart) I have seen and touched and examined. The lips of the wound are hard and seared, just as happens when the cautery is used, to remind us, no doubt, that it was made with a spear of fire.[24]

Like Ven. Maria Villani, VEN. FRANCESCA DAL SERRONE (d. 1601) also had a wound in the side placed there during a transport of love. We read in the life of this Franciscan nun of San Severino that the wound occasionally bled, while at other times blood was vomited from the mouth. The unusual aspect of this bleeding is that the liquid was so hot that it cracked an earthenware vessel used to receive it. In consequence, the blood had to be collected in a metal bowl.[25]

ST. IGNATIUS LOYOLA (d. 1556), the founder of the Jesuit Order, had the gift of tears and experienced many ecstasies during his Holy Masses. An unusual manifestation was noted during one of his Masses which was attended by Fr. Nicholas Lannoy. During the Memento of the Mass, a flame of fire hovered above St. Ignatius' head, much to the horror of Fr. Lannoy. Rushing forward to extinguish it before the Saint was harmed, the priest suddenly stopped when he realized that the Saint's face clearly indicated he was lost in contemplation. The flame, moreover, was causing no harm. This amazed the priest, and he stared at the spectacle for some time in complete amazement.[26]

It is recorded of the VEN. SERAFINA DI DIO (d. 1699) that while she was rapt in prayer following Holy Communion, the community saw her face glowing like a red flame as her eyes sparkled fire. "It burned them if they but touched her," and she herself declared that she was consumed and shrivelled with heat, that her blood was as molten lead in her veins.[27]

ST. FRANCIS DE POSADAS (d. 1713) was remarkably pious as a child, and after becoming a Dominican he preached successfully in southern Spain and was noted as a confessor who could read hearts and discover sins that had been willfully concealed. He experienced many levitations and other mystical favors. One of these favors took place while he was celebrating Holy Mass and was pronouncing the words of Consecration. His body rose in the air and remained suspended, to the utter amazement of the congregation. When he descended, they saw that he was encompassed with a great light, the wrinkles of his face had disappeared, his skin looked transparent as crystal, and his cheeks were red and hot as fire. This indicated to many the burning love of God within his soul.[28]

A more recent example of this "fire and heat of love" is demonstrated in the life of PADRE PIO and begins in the year 1917 when he became ill. When his temperature was taken, the mercury in the thermometer was found to have reached the highest point at 108.5 degrees, as recorded by Padre Paolino, the superior at that time of the San Giovanni Rotondo friary. The Padre writes,

> Curious to know how high Padre Pio's fever had reached, I took my large thermometer from its wooden case and went to the patient to take his temperature again. To my surprise I saw the mercury reached 52 degrees, or 125.6 degrees fahrenheit . . . I immediately

called the doctor, who verified his high temperature
. . . but finding the patient free from any specific illness, prescribed him the common remedies for a strong
bout of flu . . .

Dr. Giorgio Festa, who visited Padre Pio several times, noted
these extraordinarily high fevers and wrote that they broke all natural and scientific rules.

Another doctor, Giuseppe Avenia, surgeon at Agropoli (Salerno),
wrote a letter on July 14, 1967 to Padre Mariano of San Giovanni
Rotondo and enclosed it in a package which also contained a thermometer. The doctor wrote:

. . . I include also the thermometer that broke when I
visited Padre Pio as a patient when he suddenly fell ill.
The Father Guardian Damaso and Padre Ezechia of
Pietrelcina were present. Many years have since gone by
and I have always jealously preserved this as a relic. I
am sorry to have to part with it, but realise the necessity
of its being collected together and kept in the friary.

In this instance Padre Pio's temperature was so high that it actually broke the thermometer at its end. The thermometer is now preserved in the Padre Pio archives of the friary, as are other
thermometers which show the mercury at its extreme.

Gennaro Preziuso, who wrote about the high temperatures in an
article from which this information is gleaned, equates the Padre's
temperatures with that phenomenon known in the mystical life as
the fire of love. He also notes that Padre Pio's phenomenon passed
through different states, from a simple burning heat of the heart to
the physical burning of very high fevers. Padre Paolino notes that
the temperatures were also of an apostolic nature. He writes in his
memoirs:

In considering the illness that struck Padre Pio during
my stay with him in San Giovanni Rotondo, I must
accept what a number of serious-minded people, who
knew Padre Pio well, told me, that these crises of health
that took place in him were more often caused for moral
reasons, e.g., the conversion of a sinner, the cure of

someone seriously ill, etc., which would then be taken out on him so that he would be physically tormented, sometimes in unimaginable ways.

Padre Pio himself confirmed that the fevers were those of the fire and heat of love when he wrote in a letter to Padre Benedetto on November 20, 1921:

> I confess in the first place that for me it is a great misfortune to be unable to express and pour out this ever active volcano which burns me up and which Jesus has placed in this very small heart. It can all be summed up as follows: I am consumed by love for God and love for my neighbour.[29]

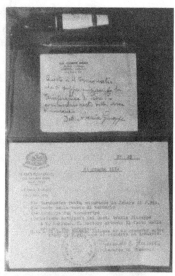

**BROKEN BY PADRE PIO'S
FEVERS.** Thermometers and their
documentation telling of Padre
Pio's extraordinarily high fevers.

(Voice of Padre Pio, Vol. XXIV, No. 6, 1994.)
Used with permission.

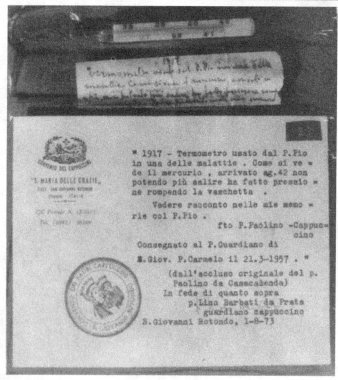

FLAME OF LOVE. St. Ignatius Loyola, lost in contemplation, is depicted at Holy Mass with a flame hovering above his head. Onlookers stared at the flame for some time in total amazement.

— 13 —

PROPHECY

"No prophecy of scripture is made by private interpretation. For prophecy came not by the will of man at any time: but the holy men of God spoke, inspired by the Holy Ghost." —2 Peter 1:20-21

Prophecy in this chapter has nothing to do with matters of faith or the prediction of future world events, but simply tells how the Saints, inspired by the Holy Spirit, have been able to reveal things concerning people with whom they came in contact or those persons who were suggested to them. These prophecies might take the form of a Saint predicting the time and place of a person's death, the future loss of someone's vocation, revealing the safety of persons at sea who were thought lost, the recovery of persons who were at the point of death and similar revelations. Some prophecies were given as a form of consolation, others as a warning. Some might involve happenings that we will call short-term events; other prophecies might concern events that would take place in years to come, as the prophecy given by St. Benedict concerning Monte Cassino.

Converted to the Faith by ST. BENEDICT (d. 543) was a certain nobleman named Theoprobus. One day, on entering the Saint's cell, Theoprobus found St. Benedict weeping bitterly. Although the Saint occasionally wept during prayer, this time he was making, according to the writings of St. Gregory the Great, "doleful lamentations." After a time, Theoprobus asked the cause of his grief. The Saint replied, "All this monastery which I have built, with whatsoever I have prepared for my brethren, are, by the judgment of Almighty God, delivered over to the heathen; and I could scarce obtain from God to save the lives of those in this place."[1] This prophecy hung over the heads of the monks for forty years. Finally around the year 590, the Lombards invaded the monastery in the middle of the night, jolting the terrified monks from their sleep. Remembering the prophecy that they would all be spared, the monks quickly collected their valuables: the autographed copy of the Rule, the daily bread ration, a number of manuscripts from the library and several of the 200 sacks that contained the miraculous supply of flour. (Cf. Chapter on multiplication of food.) The monks quickly left the abbey, made for the woods and safety and eventually found their way to Rome and the Lateran monastery.

Just as the Saint had predicted, Monte Cassino, which had been built on a mountain, was destroyed in the year 590 at the hands of the Lombards, who wanted it for a strategic location from which to observe the surrounding countryside. After its rebuilding, Saracen hordes overtook and damaged the monastery in 883, and in 1349 a violent earthquake razed it.

The most devastating destruction after it was rebuilt took place on February 15, 1944, during the Second World War, when Monte Cassino was bombarded by the Allies in an effort to annihilate the Germans who occupied the many caves on the mountain. The Germans had not only fired artillery on the troops below, but also noted the movement of the Allies, thus preventing every attempt of the Allies to open a way toward Rome. Because of repeated attacks, it was thought best to destroy the abbey, where it was believed the German forces had established headquarters. The abbey was left a tragic ruin, but after the war it was lavishly and splendidly rebuilt by the Allies. On one of the abbey's coats of arms is the motto, *Succisa Virescit* ("Struck down, it comes to new life"), a reality which gives luster to the memory of St. Benedict.[2]

At a time when King Louis VI of France was in disagreement with the Pope and the local bishops and remained obstinate in settling the matter under dispute, ST. BERNARD OF CLAIRVAUX (d. 1153), knowing that the King's position was contrary to the will of God and seeing into the future, offered this prophecy in a quiet and mournful voice: "Well, then, expect the chastisement which your crime deserves. Your eldest son will be taken away—he will die an early death."

The accident that claimed the life of Philip, the presumptive heir to the throne, was recorded in the Life of Louis de Gros, which quotes the Abbot of St. Denis as follows:

> Two years afterwards the young prince, who was about sixteen, was riding one day in a faubourg of the city of

Paris (Rue de Martroy St. Jean, near the Greve); suddenly a detestable little pig threw himself into the way of
the horse; he suddenly fell, threw his noble rider against
the curbstone, and stifled him by the weight of his body.
All hurried to raise the half-dead and tender youth, and
to carry him into a neighboring house.

Towards night he expired. On that very day the army
had assembled for an expedition, so that all the warriors,
as well as the inhabitants of the city, were struck with
grief and poured forth sighs and groans. As to the
despair of the father and mother and their friends, no
words can describe it.[3]

The preaching of ST. DOMINIC (d. 1221) was often accompanied by miraculous powers. His gift of prophecy was displayed
while preaching in the country of Segovia, where a long drought
had afflicted the people. The Saint had been speaking only a few
moments to a large crowd that had gathered outside the walls when
he stopped abruptly, as though receiving heavenly inspiration. He
then announced: "Fear nothing, my brethren, but trust in the Divine
mercy. I announce to you good news, for today God will send you
a plentiful rain and the drought shall be turned into plenty." The
atmosphere gave no hint that rain was expected, still the people
trusted in the Saint's words. Towards the end of his discourse rain
began falling in torrents so that the people had difficulty traveling
to their homes. The miracle seemed so spectacular to the people that
a little chapel was erected at the place where the Saint preached, in
commemoration of the event.[4]

On another occasion St. Dominic began preaching before the senate of the city by saying: "You listen to the words of an earthly king,
hear now those of Him who is eternal and divine." One of the sen-
ators took offense at the words and mounted his horse, but before
he rode off, he contemptuously remarked: "A fine thing for this fellow to keep you here with his fooleries." The Saint looked sorrow-
fully at the senator as he rode away and then predicted: "He goes,
as you see, but within a year he will be dead." The Saint's biographer writes: "And, indeed, not many months after the occurrence,
he was slain on that very spot by his own nephew."[5]

ST. ANTHONY OF PADUA (d. 1231) was the most famous

preacher of his day and was called "The Hammer of the Heretics" because of his eloquence and boldness in preaching against error. He was also mindful of the sufferings of those he met, including a lady of position who once approached the Saint and recommended herself to his prayers. The Saint told her: "Be of good heart, my daughter, and rejoice; for the Lord will give you a son who, as a Friar Minor and a martyr, will shed luster upon the Church." His prophecy was fulfilled.[6]

Another prediction of St. Anthony involved a notary at Puy-en-Velay who was leading a sinful life and had a violent temper. There were several occasions when the two met on the street. Each time the Saint saw the notary, he would bow in respect.

Finally the notary, believing the Saint was mocking him, cried out in rage, "What does this mean? But for fear of the anger of God I would run you through with my sword!" The Saint then explained, "O my brother! you do not know the honor in store for you. I envy your happiness. I longed for the martyr's palm, but the Lord denied it to me. But He has revealed to me that this grace is reserved for you. When that blessed hour arrives, be mindful, I beseech you, of him who foretold it to you." St. Anthony eventually converted the notary, who died a martyr's death, just as the Saint had predicted.[7]

BL. CONRAD OF ASCOLI (d. 1289) was pious from childhood and even then had the gift of prophecy. There were times when he would go on his knees before his friend and companion, Jerome, and always showed him the greatest respect. When he was asked why he did this, he replied, "I have seen the keys of Heaven in his hands." The two would vie with one another in the practice of virtue and eventually entered the Franciscan Order. They studied together in Assisi and Perugia, and after receiving their degrees in theology, were ordained and began teaching, always remaining fast friends. When Jerome went on to higher offices in the Order, Conrad went as a missionary to Africa. Jerome rose through the ranks in the Vatican and was elected Pope in 1288, just as Conrad had predicted in their childhood. Known as Pope Nicholas IV, he intended to raise his lifelong friend, Conrad, to the Cardinalate, but Conrad died before this could be performed. The Pope bewailed the death of his friend, saying that the Church had suffered a great loss.[8]

BL. MARGARET OF CASTELLO (d. 1320) is also known as Bl. Margaret of Metola, the hunchbacked and blind Dominican tertiary who was rejected by her parents. She lived for a time in the home of a wealthy family named Offrenduccio. Sharing this house was a family named Macreti, who also belonged to the higher class of society. The daughter of the Macreti family was sixteen-year-old Francesca, who grew close to Margaret and was instructed by her in the practices of the Faith. One day when the two families were entertaining guests, Margaret suddenly announced that Lady Macreti and her daughter, Francesca, would someday become Mantellate (Dominican tertiaries). The statement met with laughter, since all knew that Lady Macreti was indifferent to religion and that Francesca was likely to be married. Still, Bl. Margaret repeated the prophecy, declaring that mother and daughter would wear the Dominican habit for as long as they lived. Once again, everyone laughed at the implausibility.

Several months later Mr. Macreti took sick and died. Lady Macreti was inconsolable and sought comfort in the practice of religion. Finally she and her daughter begged to be admitted to the Dominican Order. They became faithful members until death, as prophesied by the humble Margaret.[9]

ST. FRANCES OF ROME (d. 1440), who had the privilege of constantly viewing her Guardian Angel, knew a woman named Palozza Altieri, who was much taken with the world and its vanities. When her husband, Lorenzo, was dying, Palozza, who had several young children, was in great despair at the thought of losing her husband. After all medical treatments had been utilized, the physician declared the case hopeless. Palozza, heartbroken at the announcement, bewailed what seemed imminent and immediately sent for St. Frances. The Saint comforted Palozza and told her compassionately, "Dear sister, give up the love and the vanities of the world and God will take pity upon you. Lorenzo will yet recover; he will be present at my burial." Palozza was transformed at that moment and led thereafter the life of a Christian wife and mother. Just as the Saint had predicted, Lorenzo recovered completely and later assisted at the funeral of the Saint.[10]

Another time, St. Frances of Rome was consulted by the superioress of the Sisters of the Third Order of St. Francis regarding the admission of a young girl into the Order. St. Frances had never seen the girl and knew nothing about her when she recommended that the girl be refused admittance. The Saint added, "She will enter another monastery and after remaining in it a short time, will return to the world, and soon after she will die." All happened as predicted. The girl, Francesca da Fabrica, entered the convent of Casa di Cento Finestre, on the shores of the Tiber. She left before the end of the year and soon contracted a fever which claimed her life.[11]

Another woman who had the gift of prophecy was ST. COLETTE (d. 1447), who became a Franciscan and was made superior general of the Poor Clare Order. Reformer of those convents already in existence, she became the administrator of the convents she had established. Toward the end of her life she began to divulge events that were to take place in the future, including the Protestant Reform. At the convent in Besançon she foretold an event that would take place in the next century. A great fire, she said, would burn the building to the ground. The nuns were horrified and pressed the Saint to tell them if the fire could be stopped. Colette shook her head sadly and told the nuns, "When the big cross out there in the cemetery falls down across the graves, they will know the fire is about to come. Let them be warned and run out of the house. But they will not be able to prevent the disaster." The nuns who heard this prophecy from the Saint's lips wrote the warning in the convent's archives for their sisters of the next century.

Approximately 60 years later, in 1510, the great cross fell over the graves. The nuns were terrified and began at once to take every precaution to prevent the fire that had been predicted. However, their precautionary endeavors were to no avail. The fire began and destroyed the convent the next day. It is said that perhaps God wanted to show the indestructibility of the spiritual edifice Colette had built, since the convent was rebuilt soon afterwards and remains in full operation even today.[12]

Another prophecy of St. Colette concerned her good friend, St. Vincent Ferrer. After coming out of an ecstasy, which he had witnessed, she asked St. Vincent if he wanted to know what she had been told about him. She asked as though it were a thing of joy. When he replied that he wanted to know, she told him death would come for him in less than two years. As a native of Valencia, Spain, he asked, "Well, tell me at least that it will be in Spain." This appeal she answered with a "No. In France." And so it happened. Two years later St. Vincent Ferrer died when 69 years of age in Vannes, France, a country in which he had labored so long and diligently in the service of God.[13]

ST. FRANCIS OF PAOLA (d. 1507), who is called "God's Miracle Worker Supreme," was sixty-seven years old when he approached Pope Sixtus IV about giving papal approval for the strict vegetarian fast practiced by his Order, the Minims. He presented himself as an example of one who had always practiced this diet and, in spite of his age, was enjoying robust health.

The Pope refused to give his sanction, but the Saint pleaded, saying that this fast would give a good example of self-denial to those in the world who were engulfed in corruption and sensuality. Pope Sixtus IV still would not give his sanction. The Saint was disappointed, but he accepted the decision as the will of God.

Looking about at the many ecclesiastics who were gathered in the room, Francis, using his prophetic abilities, pointed his finger at the young Cardinal Giuliano della Rovere, nephew of the Pope. Addressing Pope Sixtus, the Saint exclaimed, "Holy Father, there is the one who will concede what your Holiness is now denying me!"

The Cardinal was elevated to the Papacy as Julius II in 1503, twenty years after the Saint's prophecy. Two years later he approved the perpetual fast as a requirement of the Saint's order.[14]

One of the Saint's visitors when he was in Rome was the famous Duke of Florence, Lorenzo de Medici, who presented his son, Giovanni, to the Saint, asking that he bless the boy. Looking upon the seven-year-old child while peering prophetically into the future, St. Francis embraced him and told him: "I shall be made a Saint when you are Pope." All took place just as the Saint had predicted. Giovanni de Medici was elected Pope as Leo X on March 2, 1513. He beatified Francis during the first year of his reign and canonized him on May 1, 1519.[15]

During the time that ST. MARY MAGDALENE DE PAZZI (d. 1607) served her community as Mistress of Externs (those who lived in the convent to test their vocation), there was one young lady who had stayed only four days. After that time she had doubts about her vocation to the Carmelite Order and told the Saint of her troubles.

The Saint began to pray and then experienced an ecstasy. Finally she turned to the young lady and sweetly announced that God wanted her consecrated to Himself in that convent. For three hours the two conversed on the difficulties that were apparently produced by the devil and other matters that troubled the extern. Finally, with great dignity, the Saint declared: "I tell you, on the part of God, that it is His will that you consecrate yourself to Him as a virgin in this place!" According to the extern: "And suddenly, I felt such a great change in my heart that I resolved so firmly to consecrate myself to God in this place that I would have undergone any kind of death, howsoever terrible, rather than forsake my resolution." The young lady became Sr. Catherine Angelica and lived in virtue, to the edification of the community.

Another young lady who wanted to enter the Saint's convent had difficulties with her mother, who "resolutely opposed her entry." The Saint warned the mother that if she did not relent and permit her daughter to enter religious life, God would punish her with death. The mother continued her opposition. The prophecy was realized, with the result that the mother died within a few months and the young lady received the veil.[16]

During one of ST. MARTIN DE PORRES' (d. 1639) visits to a prison to relieve the spiritual and temporal needs of the prisoners, one of the men, who was condemned to die the next day by hanging, implored the Saint to pray that he would have the strength and courage to die a truly Christian death. The Saint did so and retired to the monastery, where he was given the light to foretell what would take place. He promptly sent word to the prisoner that he should not fear, since he would not be hanged. It seemed that the Saint would be wrong in this prediction, since the man was led through the streets and actually stood at the foot of the gallows. He was about to ascend the steps leading to the place of execution when suddenly a woman's voice was heard. From the balcony of the viceroy's palace, the wife of the viceroy, the Countess of Chinchon, exercised her prerogative as the wife of the chief executive of Peru to stop the execution and surprisingly ordered a reprieve. One can only imagine the shock and relief of the prisoner who was set free. We are told that St. Martin, a practical person, sent the man a new shirt and a pair of linen breeches, together with some coins for his immediate needs.[17]

Don Juan de Figueroa, who held one of the highest offices in Lima, was a good friend of St. Martin and often consulted the Saint in times of distress or when his advice was needed. St. Martin had often told Don Juan that he would be overwhelmed by a number of serious matters, and so it happened. A large amount of money was lost after he invested it in property. Physical sufferings of all sorts plagued him, but the most trying of all was that his enemies took advantage of his sick confinements to spread malicious rumors about him. Finally, he felt that he was about to die and called for the Saint to assist him in his last moments. When St. Martin arrived he smiled at the sick man and announced that he, Martin, would be the first to die. Don Juan recovered completely, and sometime later, while visiting the Saint in his humble cell, he revealed that he was planning on erecting a tomb for himself in the Church of Our Lady of Mercy.

St. Martin told him that instead he should donate the money for decorations in the church, and to "Prepare this chapel, but do not reserve a tomb there, for it is here that they are going to bury the both of us." The place indicated by St. Martin was his own cell.

Two years later the Saint died. Sixteen years later the Dominicans began to transform Martin's cell into a shrine and remembered the prophecy made by the Saint that Don Juan would participate in the transformation. When Fr. Gaspar Saldana approached Don Juan about the matter and proposed that he too could be buried there, Don Juan immediately produced funds. Some years later, when the chapel was transformed and embellished, the remains of the Saint were transferred into the shrine called Christ's Chapel. When Don Juan died at a venerable old age, he was buried beside his good friend and adviser, St. Martin de Porres. Thus the prophecy was fulfilled exactly as it had been uttered by the holy Dominican.[18]

ST. JOSEPH OF CUPERTINO (d. 1663), who is known for his ecstatic flights and numerous mystical favors (mentioned elsewhere in this book), was also favored with the gift of prophecy. His visions of the future revealed those persons who, though looking healthy, nevertheless were to die unexpectedly. He had knowledge of those priests who would achieve ecclesiastical office, of plans that would go awry, of events that would take place soon and those that were in the distant future. It is said that all his predictions came true to the smallest detail.[19]

The prophecies of ST. GERARD MAJELLA (d. 1755) were numerous, and many were recorded. One of them concerned a young professed student of the Redemptorist Order named Pietro Blasucci. The Saint told him one day that he would become Superior General of the Institute. Forty years later, in 1793, Pietro was made Superior General, just as the Saint had predicted.[20]

One prediction was particularly sad and took place at Oliveto. Gerard was gazing fixedly at a certain child and in a mournful voice predicted that the child would lead a sinful and disordered life. As the child grew, he began to engage in crimes of all kinds. One day he made an attempt on the life of his father, who killed him in self-defense.[21]

Very often St. Gerard predicted the death of certain persons, even giving the exact date when it would take place. There was, for instance, the time the Saint was visiting the house of Carmin Petrone of Muro, who had a child three years of age. The Saint warned the father that the child would soon be taken from him, saying: "He will die with a musical instrument in his hand." He died exactly as the Saint had predicted.

St. Gerard once told a religious of Foggia, "Keep very close to God, for in eight days you will no longer be alive." She died eight days later.[22]

Whenever the Saint was in Muro, he accepted the hospitality of a certain clockmaker. During one visit he took the man's wife aside and revealed to her certain sins she had hidden in the confessional. He added: "Prepare for death by a good confession, for soon you will appear before God." Although the woman appeared to be in perfect health, she died shortly afterward. To another woman who was leading a wicked life, this one at Vietri, the Saint gave a picture of the Blessed Virgin and told her to commend herself to Mary, since she had only a few days to live. The woman died three days later, after being reconciled to God.

To a man who was leading a sinful life and was completely taken with worldly matters, the Saint warned that he should make a retreat in the monastery of Caposele. The man excused himself, saying he would see to it in October—but the Saint replied that he would never see October. The man died in August of an overwhelming fever.

And finally, there is the case of a Carmelite nun of Ripacandida who was already in her agony when the Saint said she would get well. He explained that she still had to make progress in perfection. To the amazement of those who had witnessed her dying, the nun recovered and became one of the most devout members of the community.[23]

Shortly after Pope Pius VI was elected in February, 1775, he went to adore the Holy Sacrament exposed for the Forty Hours' Devotion in the church of Saints John and Paul. The church was attached to the monastery in which ST. PAUL OF THE CROSS (d. 1775), founder of the Passionist Order, was then living. The Pope sent word that he wanted to visit the holy man, who was then too ill to rise from his bed. Because of his illness, the Saint was granted the rare privilege of having the holy Pontiff journey to his bedside.

After a very edifying visit in the Saint's poor cell, each recommended himself to the prayers of the other. After the Pope left, the Saint prophesied to Antonio Frattini, who later recorded all that took place, that the Pope would have a glorious and long pontificate but would suffer many calamities and at length would be forced to leave Rome—a thing that seemed improbable. St. Paul died the same year, but all his predictions concerning Pope Pius VI took place.[24]

The Pope reigned for twenty-five years and had great difficulties with Emperor Joseph II, who limited papal power in his jurisdiction, suppressed monasteries and changed Church regulations, all of which caused great distress to the Holy Father. Then some outrageous decrees were passed in the Synod of 1786, which the Pope was forced to condemn. In addition, the Febronian Manifesto was a doctrine which held that the pope was not superior to the bishops, thus reducing the papal power. The French Revolution also caused the Pontiff great stress. Other difficulties, too numerous to mention here, also plagued the Pope. The most bitter of all was his being taken captive by Napoleon, who dragged him to France, just as St. Paul had prophesied. After leading the life of a prisoner in exile for two years, Pius VI died on August 22, 1799 in Valence, France. It is his kneeling statue which is situated at the entrance of the crypt in St. Peter's Basilica in Rome.

We learn the following incident from a deposition made by Archbishop Saporiti for the process of St. Paul's canonization. The Archbishop's mother, while visiting a church in Genoa, saw St. Paul and noted his devotion and penitential appearance. She remarked to her son, the Archbishop, that she would like to meet Paul, but the Archbishop, thinking her request to be a "piece of womanish curiosity," did nothing to advance the meeting.

But the mother, acting on a strong impulse, approached the Saint and spoke to him. The impulse proved to have been an inspiration from God, since Paul gave her a startling reply. He told her that she must prepare to die and even mentioned the very day of her death, which happened on the feast of St. Joseph. The prophecy and its exact fulfillment astonished her son, the Archbishop, who gave testimony about it, as mentioned previously.[25]

St. Paul not only predicted the imminent deaths of people who appeared to be in robust health, but also predicted that many persons would recover from what appeared to be life-threatening situations. Such was the case with Signor Fabio, who was dying when the Saint passed the shop where the coffin was being constructed. After learning for whom the coffin was meant, the Saint replied, "This time this coffin will be kicked aside." Signor Fabio got well and lived several more years.

The same took place when an eighty-year-old benefactor of St. Paul's order was dying from a severe heart attack. Because of the patient's advanced years and frail health, no hope was given for his recovery. The elderly gentleman's nephew hurried to ask for the Saint's prayers, but was unexpectedly told that the patient would recover and that in three days he would resume his normal activities, which, in fact, he did.[26]

The Passionist Order, founded by St. Paul of the Cross, had a student of the congregation named Valentine of St. Mary Magdalene, whom physicians pronounced to be a victim of tuberculosis. He was continually spitting up blood according to the progress of the disease and would normally have been released by the Order, but the Saint would not allow it. Instead the Saint told him that the sickness was of no consequence and that it was a trial given him by God. The Saint also predicted that the young man would completely recover and serve the Church as a missionary. It all happened as the Saint had predicted. Valentine of St. Mary Magdalene lived many years and worked in the missionary field without experiencing any further difficulty or weakness in his chest.[27]

BL. ANNA MARIA TAIGI (d. 1837) was a Roman housewife and mother who saw past, present and future events in a mysterious "sun" that was always before her. Of special concern to her were the tribulations endured by Pope Pius VII, the second pope taken prisoner by Napoleon.

Because of the mysterious sun, a small orb that was framed with thorns and which always remained slightly above and in front of her, she was able to tell the sufferings endured by the Pope to the cardinals and the prelates who often visited her home. In the presence of many witnesses and of the Marquis Bandini, she told, two years before the event, the exact date when he would return to the Vatican. All took place exactly as she had predicted. In the palace of Fontainebleu, where the Pope was imprisoned, Napoleon signed his Act of Abdication. While the Pope left the palace in freedom, Napoleon began his journey to the island of Elba. The Pope's triumphal return to St. Peter's took place on Whitsunday, May 24, 1814, exactly as Anna Maria had predicted.[28]

Another prediction of Bl. Anna Maria concerned the same Pontiff, Pius VII, who fell and broke his thigh on July 6, 1823. Although he seemed to be making a rapid recovery, Anna Maria warned Cardinal Pedicini to give him the Last Sacraments without delay. Her recommendation was taken. The holy Pontiff died a month later, at the age of 81. At almost the same time the 1,400-year-old Basilica of St. Paul's-Outside-the-Walls, where the Pontiff had been rector, experienced a devastating fire, exactly as Bl. Anna Maria had predicted.[29]

Pope Pius VII was followed by Pope Leo XII, who reigned six years. He, in turn, was followed by Pope Pius VIII. We are told by Cardinal Pedicini that the new Pope became ill, although the illness was not thought to be serious. The Pope was ready to resume his normal activities when Anna Maria warned Msgr. Natale, a priest of the Vatican, that the Pope would soon die. Cardinal Pedicini writes: "Mgr. Natale came to tell me that the servant of God had seen in her sun the catafalque crowned with the Tiara set up in St. Peter's. I warned the secretary, who was thunderstruck, but he had no doubts upon the matter, and three days later the Pope died." He had reigned only 20 months.

Bl. Anna Maria had predicted that the pontificate of Pope Pius VIII would be a short one, and it was.[30]

The miracles of ST. ANTHONY MARY CLARET (d. 1870) were so numerous that a whole book is dedicated to telling them. Among these are, of course, various prophecies. One recounts that Fr. Claret organized a mission which, because of his heavy schedule, was unfortunately planned during harvest time when the wheat was ripe and the people were obliged to work in the fields. In order for his words to reach most of the people who were in need of spiritual inspiration, he visited the homes of the principal workmen and told them that they should attend the mission and that God would bless them for doing so. Many respectfully countered that it was impossible, since the entire harvest could be lost in a single day. To this the Saint uttered this prophetic warning: "In God's name I say to you, that if you come to the Mission your wheat fields will be more productive, and all danger of rain and hailstorms will be averted. If, however, you do not come, your harvest will be destroyed."

The Saint began the mission. Some farmers attended; others did not. Two days later the farmers who had not attended the mission saw their crops completely ruined by a fierce hailstorm that unexpectedly appeared. Those who had attended the mission saw that not only had the hail spared their crops, but their wheat stalks were also more heavily laden with grain than had been anticipated, just as the Saint had predicted.[31]

Another miracle took place in the diocese of Vich, in the province of Barcelona, where a couple named Jose Rovira and Rosa Malats had two daughters. One died in childhood; the other daughter, Candida, secretly yearned to enter the religious life and eventually told her parents of her vocation. They asked her to think well about it. The father and daughter consulted Fr. Canals, Prior of the Carmelites of Vich. After speaking with Candida and seeing the poverty and age of the parents, the priest was reluctant to make a decision since the parents were no doubt expecting Candida to be the joy and help of their old age.

Fr. Canals sent them to Fr. Claret, who interviewed the daughter, reflected for a few moments, prayed and then made this prophetic pronouncement to the father: "It is the will of God that Candida become a religious. Do not fear to give your consent, because within a year God will grant you the blessing of becoming the father of a son, who will be your consolation in your old age." The father smiled, realizing that his wife was well past the age of childbearing, but he replied to the Saint: "If within a year we have a son, we shall give our daughter permission to enter the convent."

Needless to report, a son was born exactly one year later. The whole town had heard of the prophecy, and all declared that it was a miraculous birth. Candida, now relieved of responsibility, was accepted into the Third Order of the Carmelites of Charity. Her brother grew in health and virtue and became, as the Saint had predicted, the consolation and joy of his aged parents.[32]

On many occasions ST. JOHN BOSCO (d. 1888) foretold events that would take place to people he knew and to many whom he met for the first time. Such was the case in 1853, when a young girl spoke to the Saint of her vocation to the religious state. The Saint hesitated only a moment before replying, "You will have to wait long before you can realize your design, but at last you will join a congregation which was founded in the year of your birth."

Twelve years later the young girl joined the Little Sisters of the Assumption, which had been founded, as the Saint had predicted, in the year of her birth. It is said that the Saint had never met the girl, but perhaps knew of the many difficulties that had detained her so long in the world.[33]

One of the lay brothers, named Nasai, a member of John Bosco's Order, the Salesians, was entrusted with a prophecy in February of 1882 regarding Fr. Bologne, one of the founders of a Salesian Mission at Marseilles, France. The Saint told the lay brother to continue helping Fr. Bologne and to follow him to France, where the good priest would govern several houses of the Order. The Saint added, "Yet he will not end his life in France, but at Turin (Italy). When you hear of his death, get ready; your own will be close at hand."

Fr. Bologne died on January 4, 1907, of apoplexy, at Turin. Br. Nasai entered eternity eight months later, on September 25.[34]

St. John Bosco predicted the untimely death of a number of his students. The Saint, in addressing the boys in his school, once warned: "Let us be ready for death, for before a month is over one of us has to appear before God." One of the young Latin scholars named Berardi, who was experiencing robust health, heard the prophecy and felt it was meant for him. Several days later a sore developed on his lip and kept enlarging, until a fever kept him in bed. A doctor examined the boy and had him immediately brought to the hospital, where the boy died the next day of blood poisoning caused by the bite of an insect. The prophecy had been realized in only sixteen days.[35]

Two priests, one named Cagliero, went in February, 1862 to tell Don Bosco that one of the pupils of the Oratory had died. The Saint replied sadly: "He will not be the only one. Within two months from now two others will appear before God." The two priests begged to be given the names. Fr. Cagliero wrote them down on a piece of paper and slipped it into an envelope, which he sealed. Before the end of two months both youths mentioned in the prophecy took sick and died.[36] There are too many such prophecies to mention here, but almost all were documented, with many slipping into the pages of the Saint's biographies.

Having lived the humble life of a Discalced Carmelite nun for nine years, ST. THÉRÈSE OF THE CHILD JESUS and of the Holy Face (d. 1897) began to prophesy on her deathbed and seemed to know that she would be the instrument of much good to souls after her death. Mother Agnes of Jesus (her sister Pauline), realizing there was extraordinary holiness in her sick sister, kept notes of all that the Saint uttered on her deathbed, and it is from these notes that we learn more about Thérèse's spirituality and her prophecies.

We learn from Mother Agnes of Jesus' notations that just a few months before Thérèse died of tuberculosis, Sr. Marie of the Sacred Heart (the Saint's sister, Marie) told the Saint, "What sorrow we'll experience when you leave us!" To this the Saint replied, "Oh, no, you will see; it will be like a shower of roses." She then added: "After my death you will go to the mailbox, and you will find many consolations."[37] This prophecy was indeed fulfilled, since the convent at Lisieux was deluged with mail telling of a worldwide devotion to the Saint, of favors received and graces showered from Heaven.

Another reference to roses was made one day when she was given a flower which she unpetalled over her Crucifix with great piety and love. When the petals began slipping off her bed she said "quite seriously," "Gather up these petals, little sisters, they will help you to perform favors later on . . . Don't lose one of them."[38] Some of these petals were later given as precious relics.

Mother Agnes of Jesus asked Thérèse one day, "You will look down upon us from Heaven, won't you?" The Saint replied, "No, I will come down,"[39] as she did for countless souls who have received consolations in times of distress and answers to their prayers.

Under obedience, St. Thérèse had written her autobiography,

which is entitled, *The Story of a Soul.* While on her deathbed the Saint made many references to the book's future appeal and bene- fit to souls. The Saint gave this warning concerning the book: "After my death, you mustn't speak to anyone about my manuscript before it is published; you must speak about it only to Mother Pri- oress. If you act otherwise, the devil will make use of more than one trap to hinder the work of God, a very important work!"

Mother Agnes' notes continue:

> A few days later, having asked her to read again a pas- sage of her manuscript which seemed incomplete to me, I found her crying. When I asked her why, she answered with angelic simplicity, "What I am reading in this copy- book reflects my soul so well! Mother, these pages will do much good to souls. They will understand God's gen- tleness much better." And she added, prophesying her future popularity, "Ah, I know it; everybody will love me!"[40]

One day the Saint prophesied: "Little Mother [Agnes] will be the last to die . . . when she will have finished working for me." Another time she re-stated the prophecy after her sister Marie had said to her, "Ah! if I were alone in suffering from your death, it would not be so hard; but how will I be able to console Mother Agnes of Jesus, who loves you so much?" The Saint predicted: "Don't worry, she will not have time to think of her pain, for until the end of her life she will be busied about me, she won't even have time to do everything."[41]

Mother Agnes of Jesus was indeed busy working for the little Saint, since she engaged in correspondence with the Saint's devo- tees from around the world.[42] In addition, she helped prepare the Saint's manuscript for publication and all the matters that attended its release, as well as testifying at various times for Thérèse's beat- ification and canonization. Although she was a cloistered nun, she was obliged at times to meet priestly and episcopal dignitaries who wished to express their love for and devotion to the Saint of the Lit- tle Way.

It was with good reason that Pope St. Pius X once told a mis- sionary bishop privately that Thérèse was "the greatest Saint of modern times."[43]

A contemporary of St. Thérèse was ST. GEMMA GALGANI (d. 1903), who is known as "The Passion Flower of Lucca" because of her intense sufferings and her great love of Jesus Crucified. She was favored with the Holy Stigmata and received many extraordinary graces and heavenly revelations. During her brief life of 25 years she had an abiding desire to enter the Passionist Order, but each request was denied. Realizing that she would never enter the Order she once predicted: "The Passionists did not wish to receive me, and notwithstanding, because I wish to stay with them, I shall when I am dead." The prophecy was realized. Today St. Gemma's mortal remains are treasured by the Passionist Nuns in the convent in Lucca, Italy.[44]

A contemporary of both St. Thérèse and St. Gemma was BR. ANDRE (d. 1937), the great Canadian devotee of St. Joseph who entered his eternal reward at the venerable age of ninety-one. Born Alfred Bessette, he joined the Congregation of the Holy Cross as a lay brother and worked as a porter for many years. He was fond of saying: "On my entrance into the community they showed me the door, and I remained there for forty years." During his lifetime he cured many by touching the afflicted with a medal of St. Joseph. He had other mystical gifts, including the knowledge of when certain persons would die (examples are found in the chapter, "Mystical Knowledge") and prophecy. One prophecy seemed highly unlikely to those who witnessed the action and words of the holy brother. It took place in this manner:

The steamship Cymbeline, docked at Vicker's Dry Dock in Montreal, caught fire. Since other ships and boats were at risk, Fire Chief Gauthier boarded the burning ship and was standing on the deck directing his firemen, who were spraying water down the open hatches. Suddenly the ship was destroyed when a tremendous explosion ripped her apart, hurling the fire chief and three of his men skyward together with blazing timbers, hot chunks of steel and angry gushes of fire.

Immediately after the fire was contained, the river was dragged for the bodies. Three corpses were recovered, but that of Chief Gauthier could not be found. Br. Andre was notified of the disaster and was called to the edge of the dock. With a great crowd, he watched mournfully as the bodies were brought ashore. Finally, one of the district firemen told him all that had taken place and remarked that they would never find the body of the chief, since it was believed the body had been carried downstream by the swift current.

Br. Andre thought for a moment and then said quietly, "I don't think so." Then taking a medal of St. Joseph, he threw it as hard as he could into the busy waters of the river; pointing to the spot, he predicted: "He will come up there."

Leopold Lussier, who had served the district as fire chief before Chief Gauthier, assumed the responsibility of the recovery. He related: "I was there, all of us were, out in boats. We had dragged that spot twenty times. Yet the following morning the body of our chief appeared floating on the water." The place of discovery was, of course, the exact place where the medal of St. Joseph had been cast into the river by Br. Andre.

Today the great Canadian church of St. Joseph of Mount Royal in Montreal stands as testimony to its founder, the holy lay brother, and his great devotion to the foster-father of Our Lord.[45]

The gift of prophecy was also given to PADRE PIO (d. 1968), who on one occasion obliged three priests who wanted to know the order in which they would die. Time proved the Padre correct in all cases. One of the priests was Padre Romolo, who asked on another occasion who would die first, he or Padre Pio, since they were about the same age. The holy Padre replied, "We will both live a long time, but I will die first." He then added, "It has been determined that you will die very old." Padre Romolo survived Padre Pio by thirteen years and died at the age of ninety-five.

Maria Pyle, a great friend of the stigmatic, also asked a question of Padre Pio: "What am I going to do when God calls you?" To this the holy priest replied, "You are going to greet me." Maria Pyle was in good health when she asked the question, but she did, in fact, predecease Padre Pio. And because the holy man had predicted it, we can be assured that she joyously greeted him in Heaven when he entered his reward.[46]

To Archbishop Barbieri, who asked Padre Pio to assist him on his deathbed, the holy Padre responded, "No, I will die before you, but I will assist you from Heaven." The Archbishop lived to the age of eighty-seven and survived Padre Pio by eleven years.

The next case might be consigned to the chapter on "Mystical Knowledge," but it is also a prediction and concerns one of Padre Pio's spiritual sons, an eminent plastic surgeon named Piero Meililo, who had suffered a brain hemorrhage. His attending physicians were of the opinion that the bleeding resulted from a severe aneurysm in one of the major blood vessels in his brain and wanted to operate immediately. The patient was forbidden to move for fear of a massive stroke that would undoubtedly kill him. But Dr. Meililo hesitated and decided to ask the opinion of Padre Pio. We are told that Padre Pio was passing the phone when Meililo called and that the Padre promptly told Meililo not to have the operation. In fact, he insisted that the operation be canceled, and it was. The doctors were confused by Meililo's decision and predicted that if he got out of bed he would drop dead on the floor. In fact as he walked to the hospital door, doctors and nurses followed him, waiting for him to collapse. But Meililo had faith in Padre Pio's prophecy that he would be well and continued his normal routine. The stroke did not take place. Dr. Meililo resumed his practice and was perfectly well twenty years later.[4]

— 14 —

INVISIBILITY

"And it came to pass, whilst he was at table with them, he took bread, and blessed, and brake, and gave to them. And their eyes were opened, and they knew him: and he vanished out of their sight." (The Resurrected Lord at Emmaus.) —Luke 24:30-31

One of the most mysterious and astounding wonders exercised by the power of God was that of Saints who became invisible before the eyes of witnesses. Present for a time, they were promptly lost from view to perform works of mercy, or in some cases, to be able to pray without interruptions.

One of the Saints who possessed this extraordinary ability was ST. FRANCIS OF PAOLA (d. 1507), who was known during his lifetime as "The Miracle Worker." We are told that the Saint was visiting the city of Bormes as the guest of the governor, and while there he confirmed his great reputation by performing a number of miracles. When he was about to leave, people swarmed around the governor's palace to see and be near him. Their great enthusiasm for the Saint was expressed by tearing off bits of his clothing— which the Saint, surprisingly, permitted. According to his biographer, "God would renew his clothing as fast as it was being torn away. Spectators were amazed to see that after scores of people had torn away pieces from his hood and tunic, they both were still miraculously whole."[1]

The great miracle of invisibility took place while the people were still crowding around him. Finding it impossible to make his way through the crowd which was closely packed in the square, and being somewhat embarrassed by the adulation, the Saint suddenly disappeared before the people's eyes, much to their confusion. One moment he was there, the next moment he was gone. His companions, much to their amazement, found him waiting for them outside the walls, ready to begin their journey.[2]

When St. Francis of Paola was away from his monastery, people who recognized the Miracle Worker would approach him, asking for his prayers or petitioning him for a cure. While visiting Grenoble, the Saint found a remarkable way to obtain peace and seclusion while he committed himself to prayer and meditation. Seeing a church a short distance away, he went in to pray. After a time, a merchant and a man named de Bussieres, who had seen the Saint enter the church, went in to remind him of the time. The Saint was nowhere to be found, even after a thorough search of the building. Others are said to have also helped in the search. Finally, while they were standing outside the church in bewilderment, the Saint appeared at the church door. He offered no explanation for his disappearance, but as his biographer noted: "Evidently he had willed to become invisible to human eyes during his period of deep prayer, as he had done on occasions before."[3]

ST. CLEMENT MARY HOFBAUER (d. 1820) was a member of the Redemptorist Order who was noted for his preaching. On numerous occasions, the devil attempted to interfere in the work St. Clement did for the good of souls. While the Saint was preaching to a great crowd in his Warsaw church during the year 1801, cries were heard in the church, especially those of a voice shouting "Fire! Fire!" There were flames and smoke, yet nothing was damaged. Understandably the people were in the grip of panic. Firemen arrived, but they found the building perfectly intact.

That same afternoon, while St. Clement was praying before the altar of St. Joseph, hundreds of people in the church saw a cloud forming above the altar. The cloud slowly enveloped the figure of the Saint, until he completely disappeared from their sight. Gradually, in his place, appeared a beautiful woman who smiled at the worshippers, who had been frightened only a few hours earlier by devilish activity. St. Clement was regarded as a great Saint during his lifetime and is said to have appeared many times to various friends after his death.[4]

Another member of the Redemptorist Order who is known to have had the gift of becoming invisible was the holy lay-brother, ST. GERARD MAJELLA (d. 1755). One day at the monastery at Caposele the Saint received permission to make a day's retreat of prayer and recollection in his room. A little later the Father Rector needed him and sent someone to fetch him. The Saint could not be found, although everyone in the house searched for him. Dr. Santorelli, the monastery's physician, at one time exclaimed, "We have lost Brother Gerard!"

Dr. Santorelli took one of the brothers with him for another search and went to the Saint's room, which measured ten feet square. The room contained only a poor bed and a little table, without any other furniture which would prevent his being seen. He was nowhere to be found. Finally, one of the religious realized that the Saint would surely come forward at the time of Holy Communion, and so they waited. Exactly as predicted, the Saint was seen at that particular moment. On being asked where he had been, the Saint answered, "In my room." When the religious told the Saint about the various times and places they had searched for him, he made no reply. Then, under obedience to tell what happened, the Saint explained, "Fearing to be distracted in my retreat, I asked Jesus Christ for the grace to become invisible."

Dr. Santorelli's curiosity was not satisfied, so he asked again, "How could you say that you were in your cell, when I searched every nook and corner of it with Brother Nicolo, and yet could not find you?" Taking the doctor by the arm, the Saint guided him to his cell and pointed out the little stool where he had been sitting the whole time they were searching for him. Then the Saint whispered to the doctor, ". . . sometimes I make myself very little."

The miracle became so well known outside the monastery that children, in playing hide-and-seek, were accustomed to say, "Let us play Brother Gerard!"[5]

ST. MARTIN DE PORRES (d. 1639), also a humble lay-brother, is another who experienced the phenomenon of invisibility. Once it was exercised in favor of two escaped criminals who fled to the Convent of the Holy Rosary and the cell of St. Martin, begging him for the love of God to hide them. Martin asked them to kneel down in all humility and confidence to petition Almighty God for His protection. Together they knelt and prayed for a solution to their difficulty. Whether the authorities saw the criminals enter the monastery, or whether they suspected that St. Martin would help them, as he tried to do for all God's children in difficulty, the authorities entered the monastery and searched the cell assigned to St. Martin. They thoroughly inspected the humble room—even turning over the bare planks which served as a bed—but could not find the two escapees. After the authorities left, the two men were overjoyed that they had not been detected. They thanked Martin, but were told by him that they must amend their lives as a true sign of repentance and in gratitude for such an extraordinary favor from Divine Providence.[6] We are not told if the two men were innocent of the crime of which they had been accused, or if they were returned to justice.

FR. PAUL OF MOLL (d. 1896) was a Flemish Benedictine who is known as "The Wonder-Worker of the Nineteenth Century," and with good reason since he exercised many of the phenomena mentioned in this volume and was the worker of countless miracles. He, too, experienced the wonder of invisibility. A working woman of Thielt reported that since Fr. Paul took up residence in Termonde, she saw him on two occasions praying in the church in Thielt. A few moments later he disappeared from view. The woman knew him well enough to write to him and ask if she had really seen him in the church and if he had disappeared from sight. His answer was a simple, "Yes." The holy man had become invisible for reasons not given.[7]

SAINTS WHO KNEW THE DATE
OF THEIR DEATH

"Watch ye therefore, because you know not what hour your Lord will come."—Matt. 24:42 (This quotation is true for all men except for those faithful servants of God who were divinely inspired.)

Most of us would prefer not to know when we will die, but there were countless Saints who were pleased to be spiritually informed of the date and time of their entrance into eternity. Heavily laden with graces and merits after years of love, devotion and service to God and man, they were eager for the embrace of their Redeemer and grateful to know the time when this would be realized.

The number of Saints who were supernaturally informed about the date of the end of their exile on earth is very great, but here are a few examples.

Perhaps one of the earliest Saints to be so informed was ST. BENEDICT (d. 543). For details of his death we have the biography written by St. Gregory the Great. The Saint wrote:

> The same year in which Benedict departed out of this life, he foretold the day of his most holy death to some of his disciples who conversed with him . . . giving strict charge . . . to keep in silence what they had heard . . . Six days before his departure he caused his grave to be opened, and immediately after, he fell into a fever, by the violence whereof his strength began to wax faint, and the infirmity daily increasing. The sixth day he caused his disciples to carry him into the oratory, where he armed himself for his going forth by receiving the Body and Blood of the Lord; then supporting his weak limbs by the hands of his disciples, he stood up, his hands lifted towards heaven, and with words of prayer at last breathed forth his soul.

St. Benedict died on March 21, 543 on the Saturday preceding Passion Sunday, the day he had predicted.[1]

ST. DOMINIC (d. 1221), the founder of the Order of Preachers, an order otherwise known as the Dominicans, left Bologna on his last missionary journey in June, during the year of his death. Before he left Bologna he had received from God an intimation of his approaching death. One day, while in familiar conversation with some of the students and clergy of the university,

> . . . he spoke with his usual cheerfulness and sweetness for some time, then, rising to bid them farewell, he said, "You see me now in health, but before the next feast of the Assumption, I shall be with God." These words surprised those who heard them, for indeed there were no signs of approaching sickness, or of the failure of that vigorous and manly spirit for which he had been ever distinguished.

On his return to Bologna, after speaking with the procurator and the prior of the monastery of St. Nicholas, St. Dominic spent hours in prayer before the Blessed Sacrament. When he had finished his prayer, "he was obliged to give way to the violence of the fever, the advances of which he had hitherto disregarded . . ." Although suffering grievously, he counseled his brethren and during his last hours exhorted them to practice the ways of virtue.

Just as the Saint had predicted, he died before the feast of the Assumption, which is observed on August 15. He died on August 6, being 51 years of age.[2]

BL. GANDULPHUS OF BINASCO (d. 1260) entered the Franciscan Order while the holy founder, St. Francis of Assisi, was still alive. His life was one of continual penance and abstinence. In addition, he had a great zeal for the salvation of souls and was known for his long hours of prayer, which were rewarded by ecstasies.

When he heard himself commended for his inspiring sermons, he and a companion decided to embrace the solitary life to escape the temptation to vainglory. While setting out for the wild district of Petralia, they passed through the town of Polizzi. While there Bl.

Gandulphus arranged for lodging in the hospital of St. Nicholas. On Wednesday of Holy Week in the year 1260, while preaching in the church and while in perfect health, Bl. Gandulphus announced that would be his last sermon, since he would soon die. On his return to the hospital of St. Nicholas he prepared for death and soon experienced a violent fever. On Holy Saturday he announced that he would not see the dawn of the next day. He died as he had predicted.

His sanctity was soon recognized by a sweet perfume that fragranced the whole house for a fortnight. Sixty years later, because of the many miracles taking place through his intercession, it was decided to remove his body to a more honorable place. At that time his body was found perfectly incorrupt.[3]

ST. ALOYSIUS GONZAGA (d. 1591) was the son of the duke of Mantua. Ignoring the worldly spirit of his family, he had some difficulty in realizing his desire to become a priest, but finally entered the Society of Jesus and journeyed to Rome to begin his novitiate. Unfortunately, the Plague was then vigorously attacking the people, and many succumbed to its onslaughts. In Rome he became one of the many victims of the Plague—"with the difference that he knew the date of his death in advance."[4]

When ST. ROSE OF LIMA (d. 1617) was 31 years of age and in relatively good health, she announced that she would die in four months, a prophecy which she received during a vision of the Sacred Heart. Not only did she know the date of her death, but also the pains she would suffer. She mentioned the details to Fr. Lorenzana and added that she would die at the end of August, on the eve of the feast of St. Bartholomew.

Because of the severe pains she would suffer at the end, she begged for prayers. And suffer she did. In addition to a paralysis on one side of her body and a fierce headache, "She felt as though a hot iron were being passed over her whole body." She suffered agonizing pains in her joints and hemorrhaged a great deal. In addition, a great thirst was present which reminded the dying Saint of the thirst suffered by Our Lord on the Cross. She died as she had foretold, surrounded by loved ones and after having received sacramental blessings.[5]

One day an archbishop from Mexico, in search of a miraculous cure from pleurisy, visited ST. MARTIN DE PORRES (d. 1639) in Peru. After the Saint touched the side that was causing the most pain to the archbishop, an immediate cure was detected. The archbishop then made a request of the Saint's provincial. He wanted to bring the Saint to Mexico, where he would draw down blessings upon the Mexican people. Reluctantly the provincial agreed, but the Saint, informed by spiritual means, knew he would never leave Peru and that he was soon to die in his native city.

Before he could leave for Mexico, the Saint was one day walking past the procurator, Fr. Juan de Barbaran, who quickly realized that St. Martin was dressed in a fresh new habit instead of the tattered, worn garments he always wore. Fr. Juan could not help but ask the Saint why he was dressed that way and received the answer, "This is the habit in which they will bury me."

Soon after, Martin was in the grip of an acute fever which would prove fatal. He confided in various religious that his death was not far off and even foretold the precise day and hour in which he would die. While waiting for Heaven to claim him, he experienced visions of various Saints, including the Mother of God. St. Martin was fully awake when the friar who kept watch asked if it was time for the bell to be rung which would summon all the friars to bid him farewell. His answer was, "No." But some hours later, when asked another time, Martin agreed. Surrounded by various dignitaries of the order, a goodly number of his confreres, as well as Don Feliciano, the Archbishop of Mexico, Martin quietly died. The day was November 3, 1639, between the hours of eight and nine in the evening, the day and time he had predicted. He had lived 60 years, 45 of which he had spent in the Dominican Order working miracles and experiencing many mystical favors.[6]

When ST. JOSEPH OF CUPERTINO (d. 1663) arrived at the monastery at Osimo, after having served God in other houses of the order, he declared, "This is my rest," meaning that Osimo would be the place of his death. He went so far as to predict to his brethren that he would die on the day on which he would not receive the Holy Eucharist.

A fever invaded his body on August 10, 1663, and for five days ebbed and waned so that he was able to rise each morning to say Holy Mass in his private oratory. During these Masses he experienced miraculous ecstasies and levitations, as was his custom, especially during his last Mass, which was offered on the feast of the Assumption.

Thereafter, because of the violent fever, he was unable to offer the Holy Sacrifice and instead received the Holy Eucharist daily. His last Holy Communion was received on September 17, the day before his death, thus fulfilling his prophecy. While reciting ejaculations to the Blessed Virgin Mary he joyfully departed this life, after days of unrestrained expressions of his love of God.[7]

One of the biographers of the holy Redemptorist lay brother, ST. GERARD MAJELLA (d. 1755), wrote that several large volumes would be necessary to record all the many miracles worked by the Saint. One of his mystical favors was to predict the death of a number of people. He also predicted his own death, six months in advance, telling Dr. Santorelli that he would die of consumption, although he was then in perfect health. When questioned by the doctor, the Saint explained that he had prayed to die in that manner, since few nurses would care to tend him and he would thereby die practically abandoned.[8]

The Saint contracted the disease, which progressed swiftly. While he was dying, a heavenly fragrance, which filled the whole monastery, was found to originate from his expectorants. Always regretting the expensive medications that were prescribed for him, he bore his pains with admirable patience, declaring that he joined his sufferings to those of the Saviour.

The Saint received Holy Communion every day and received his Lord with exceptional devoutness on the feast of St. Teresa of Avila, the 15th of October. On that day he reminded his confreres that the feast of St. Teresa was a recreation day and one for the relaxation of the Rule. "Tomorrow, it will again be recreation. Why? Because I shall die tonight." A little later he asked for the time and was told it was six o'clock. To this he remarked, "I have still six hours to live." St. Gerard Majella died on the night of October 15-16, 1755 around midnight. He was only 29 years of age.[9]

Among the other Saints and Blesseds who prophesied the time of their death were these holy Dominicans: BL. STEPHANIE DE QUINZANIS (d. 1530), who predicted the day of her death and the place of her burial. BL. NICHOLAS PALAEA (d. 1255) was given the date during a vision of a brother who had died years earlier. BL. JAMES OF BEVAGNA (d. 1301) received his notice from the Blessed Mother, who assured him that she would accompany him to his heavenly reward. ST. LOUIS BERTRAND (d. 1581) also prophesied the day on which he would die, as did BL. BERNARD SCAMMACCA (d. 1486).

Among the many Franciscans who knew the date of their death was ST. JOSEPH OF LEONISSA (d. 1612), who prophesied that he would die on February 4, which he did.

BL. GERARD OF VILLAMAGNA (d. 1242) knew that he would die in the month of May. His confessor verified that the Blessed had died on the very day he had predicted well in advance.

The Servite BL. FRANCIS PATRIZZI (d. 1328) knew that he would die on the feast of the Ascension. While walking to the church in Siena where he was to preach, he collapsed on the roadside and died on the day he had predicted.

ST. MADELINE SOPHIE BARAT (d. 1865) died on the day she had foretold, Ascension Thursday, May 25, 1865.

And ST. CATHERINE LABOURÉ (d. 1876) of the Miraculous Medal visions always predicted that she would never see the year 1877. She died during the evening of December 31, 1876.

THE STIGMATA

"And I will pour out upon the house of David, and upon the inhabitants of Jerusalem, the spirit of grace, and of prayers: and they shall look upon me, whom they have pierced: and they shall mourn for him as one mourneth for an only son, and they shall grieve over him, as the manner is to grieve for the death of the first-born."—Zacharias 12:10

Stigmatists are those Saints and holy persons whose bodies bore wounds corresponding to those suffered by Our Lord during His Passion and Crucifixion. There are many differences among the Saints regarding the number of their wounds. Most of the stigmatists had five wounds, while others had only the wound on the shoulder representing the one suffered by Our Lord while carrying the Cross. Another might have marks representing the Crown of Thorns. Still another might have the marks of the Scourging, and so forth. It has been noted that few of the stigmatists have had all the wounds representing those of Our Lord. Some of the wounds never bled; others bled on Fridays or at other times.

Some of the stigmatists experienced an ecstasy in which, by gestures and remarks, they re-lived the sequences of Our Lord's Passion as though they were present during His ordeal. The ecstasy and sufferings usually began for these Saints on Thursday and ended on Friday afternoon around 3 or 4 o'clock. All the recipients of this mystical wounding suffered dreadfully, as did Our Lord during His Passion and death. Dr. Imbert-Gourbeyre notes that "The life of stigmatics is but a long series of sorrows which arise from the Divine malady of the stigmata and end only in death." It has also been observed that, historically, only ecstatics have experienced the stigmata.

Many of the stigmatists experienced cruel rejection and suspicion before their wounds were authenticated. Among the many methods employed during the investigative process has been the covering of the wounds with gloves or bandages, the Saint being carefully watched day and night so that tampering with the wounds could not be performed. When these methods were used, a number of false stigmatists were exposed. It was suggested that their false wounds were either developed through their own intervention or, as some thought, were produced by hypnotism, auto-suggestion or another function of the mind. The authentic wounds were, in all cases, a matter of careful study and examination by medical personnel and representatives of the Church.

ST. JOHN OF THE CROSS mentions the stigmata in the *Living Flame of Love* and explains:

> When the soul is wounded with love by the five wounds, the effect extends to the body and these wounds are impressed on the body and it is wounded, just as the soul is wounded with love. God usually does not bestow a favor upon the body without bestowing it first and principally upon the soul.[1]

When the body of a Saint has been wounded, and the Saint asks out of humility for the wounds to disappear, according to St. John of the Cross the wounds are still impressed upon the soul. The Saint continues:

> The greater the delight and strength of love the wound produces in the soul, so much the greater is that produced by the wound outside the body, and when there is an increase in one there is an increase in the other. This so happens because these souls are purified and established in God and that which is a cause of pain and torment to their corruptible flesh is sweet and delectable to their strong and healthy spirit. It is, then, a wonderful experience to feel the pain augment with the delight.[2]

The first stigmatist to experience this pain and delight was ST. FRANCIS OF ASSISI (d. 1226), whose condition was so marvelous that the Church observed the feast of the Impression of the Stigmata of St. Francis every September 17 until the Roman Calendar was revised in recent times. His stigmata were of a character never seen in any other stigmatist and were bestowed in the early morning hours on the Feast of the Holy Cross in the year 1224, two years before his death.

The Little Flowers of St. Francis tells that during the apparition:

> All of Mount Alverna seemed to be on fire with very bright flames which shone in the night and illumined the various surrounding mountains and valleys more clearly than if the sun were shining over the earth. Shepherds who were guarding their flocks in that area witnessed this. And they were gripped by intense fear when they saw the mountain aflame and so much light around it, as they later told the friars, declaring that the fiery light remained above Mount Alverna for an hour or more.[3]
>
> The light also shone through the windows of houses and inns in the area, and muleteers who were resting in the area got up, thinking the sun had risen. They were busy loading their animals when the mysterious light faded and the sun rose.[4]

Thomas of Celano, the first biographer of the Saint and one of his first companions, tells what took place during the apparition:

> Two years before Francis gave his soul back to Heaven, while he was living in the hermitage which was called Alverna, after the place on which it stood, he saw in the vision of God a man standing above him, like a seraph with six wings, his hands extended and his feet joined together and fixed to a cross. Two of the wings were extended above his head, two were extended as if for flight, and two were wrapped around the whole body. When the blessed servant of the Most High saw these things, he was filled with the greatest wonder, but he could not understand what this vision should mean. Still, he was filled with happiness and he rejoiced very greatly because of the kind and gracious look with which he saw himself regarded by the seraph, whose beauty was beyond estimation; but the fact that the seraph was fixed to a cross and the sharpness of his suffering filled Francis with fear. And so he arose, if I may so speak, sorrowful and joyful, and joy and grief were in

him alternately. Solicitously he thought what this vision could mean, and his soul was in great anxiety to find its meaning. And while he was thus unable to come to any understanding of it and the strangeness of the vision perplexed his heart, the marks of the nails began to appear in his hands and feet, just as he had seen them a little before in the crucified man above him.

His hands and feet seemed to be pierced through the middle by nails, with the heads of the nails appearing in the inner side of the hands and on the upper sides of the feet and their pointed ends on the opposite sides. The marks in the hands were round on the inner side, but on the outer side they were elongated; and some small pieces of flesh took on the appearance of the ends of the nails, bent and driven back and rising above the rest of the flesh. In the same way the marks of the nails were impressed upon the feet and raised in a similar way above the rest of the flesh. Furthermore, his right side was as though it had been pierced by a lance and had a wound in it that frequently bled so that his tunic and trousers were very often covered with his sacred blood . . .[5]

Following the apparition, St. Francis attempted to hide his holy wounds from his brethren, but they soon noticed that he did not uncover his hands or feet and that he had difficulty placing the soles of his feet on the ground. In time, his companions were made aware of his condition, not only because of the blood on his clothing, but also because of the unbearable pain he suffered from the wounds. Eventually,

He let Brother Leo see and touch those holy wounds, and St. Francis entrusted his wounds only to him to be touched and rebound with new bandages between those marvelous nails and the remaining flesh, to relieve the pain and absorb the blood which issued and flowed from the wounds. When he was ill, he let the bandages be changed often, even every day in the week except from Thursday evening all through Friday until Saturday morning, because he did not want the pain of the Passion of Christ which he bore in his body to be eased at all by any man-made remedy or medicine during the time when our Saviour Jesus Christ had for us been arrested and crucified, had died and been buried.[6]

Although St. Francis attempted to conceal the stigmata to avoid worldly curiosity and glory, it nevertheless became well-known, as did his gift of healing, which was demonstrated many times during the remainder of his life. The Saint lived only two years after the imprinting of the stigmata and died at the age of forty-five. Two years later, in 1228, Pope Gregory IX went in person to Assisi for Francis' canonization.

An unusual bloody sweat and the wound in the side were given to ST. LUTGARDE OF AYWIERES (d. 1246). Thomas Merton, in his biography of the Saint, reports that she had a particular devotion to St. Agnes, the Roman virgin martyr. She was one day praying to St. Agnes when "suddenly a vein near her heart burst, and through a wide open wound in her side, blood began to pour forth, soaking her robe and cowl." She then sank to the floor and "lost her senses." She was never wounded again, but she kept the scar until the end of her life. This took place when she was twenty-nine years old.[7] Witnesses to this event were two nuns, one named Margaret, the other Lutgarde of Limmos, who washed the Saint's clothes.

Thomas Merton also tells that on many occasions, this saintly Cistercian, in meditating on Christ's Passion, would fall into ecstasy and sweat blood. A priest who had heard of this sweat of blood watched for an opportunity to witness it himself. One day he found her in ecstasy, leaning against a wall, her face and hands dripping with blood. Finding a pair of scissors, he managed to snip off a lock of the Saint's hair which was wet with blood. As he stood marvelling at the blood on the lock of hair, the Saint suddenly came to herself. Instantly the blood vanished, not only from her face and hands, but also from the lock of hair in the hand of the priest. Thomas Merton writes, "At this, the investigator was so taken aback that he nearly collapsed."[8]

St. Lutgarde's thirteenth-century biographer, Thomas of Cantimpré, writes that "the influence of her ecstatic soul was the proximate cause of the bloody sweat on her body."

The biography of BL. ELIZABETH THE GOOD (d. 1420) was written soon after her death by her confessor, Rev. Conrad Kügelin, who tells us of the sufferings she endured at the hands of her companions in the Third Order Regular at Reute. Since she had many mystical favors and visions, she was misunderstood and suffered many spiritual trials as a result. But she was given the grace of perseverance and endured her trials and her physical maladies with patience and humility. She was also given the wounds of the stigmata which appeared "from time to time." To the five wounds were added those marks resembling the Crown of Thorns and the stripes and marks of the scourging. These, her biographer relates, bled copiously on Fridays and in Lent and the pain continued with few respites until the end of her life.[9]

Immediately after her death at the age of thirty-four, people began to honor her as a saint. Her cultus was approved by Pope Clement XIII in 1766.

ST. LYDWINE OF SCHIEDAM (d. 1433), a victim soul who endured excruciating pains from physical ailments, was also favored with the stigmata, which she received during a vision of the Holy Child Jesus. Our Lord, first appearing as a child, was transformed during the vision into a man whose face was disfigured and scarred. The wounds He suffered during His Crucifixion appeared, while drops of blood ran down from the Crown of Thorns. Lydwine was ravished by the vision, but was also saddened by Our Lord's sufferings. Then luminous rays darted from the wounds of Jesus and pierced her feet, her hands, and her heart.[10]

When the Saint realized that she had the wounds of Our Lord, she prayed that the marks be hidden so that the stigmata would be a secret between them. As Michel d'Esne, Bishop of Tournai, relates: "Marvellous to relate, a little skin immediately covered these wounds, but the pain and the bruise remained." According to her prayer, the pain of the wounds endured until the end of her life.[11]

A phenomenon associated with the stigmata of St. Lydwine was that of an extraordinary perfume. Don Jan Angeli, a new curate of Schiedam, visited the Saint after learning of her holiness and tried to catch sight of the Saint's hands, which were carefully concealed under her blanket. Under obedience she withdrew her left hand for his inspection. On the palm of the hand was the bruise of the stigmata, which exhaled and filled the room with the perfume of spices.[12] The perfume wafted from her wounds, as mentioned elsewhere in this book.

In the Bull of Canonization for ST. CATHERINE DEI RICCI (d. 1589), mention is made that her sufferings began when she was twenty, and that for twelve years they recurred regularly. Her biographers report that her ecstasies lasted exactly twenty-eight hours, from Thursday noon until Friday afternoon at four o'clock.

The Saint conversed aloud while witnessing the drama of Our Lord's Passion in seventeen scenes while moving in conformity with the movements of Our Lord. Afterward, at the end of the ecstasy, in addition to her bleeding wounds, she was covered with the injuries produced by the whips and cords of the scourging. In addition, she suffered from the wound on her shoulder which was that of the carrying of the Cross.[13]

The wounds of her stigmata, located in her hands, feet and side, and those wounds inflicted by the Crown of Thorns, were variously described by people who saw them. Many declared that the hands were bleeding and pierced through. Others saw a brilliant light that dazzled their eyes, while others saw the wounds as being healed, but red and swollen.

One of the Saints who experienced only one wound of the stigmata was ST. RITA OF CASCIA (d. 1457). One day, she went with the sisters of her convent to the Church of St. Mary to listen to a sermon preached by Bl. James of Mount Brandone. The Franciscan friar had a great reputation for learning and eloquence and spoke about the Passion and death of Jesus, with particular emphasis on the sufferings endured by our Saviour's Crown of Thorns. Moved to tears by his graphic account of these sufferings, she returned to the convent and retreated to a small private oratory, where she prostrated at the foot of a crucifix. Absorbed in prayer and grief she declined, out of humility, to ask for the visible wounds of the stigmata as had been given to St. Francis and other Saints, but asked instead for one of the thorns so that she could experience this suffering for love of our Saviour.

Concluding her prayer, she felt one of the thorns, like an arrow of love flung by Jesus, penetrate the flesh and bone in the middle of her forehead. The wound, in time, became ugly and revolting to some of the nuns, so that St. Rita remained in her cell for the next fifteen years of her life, suffering excruciating pain while engaged in divine contemplation. Added to the pain was the formation of little worms in the wound. At the time of her death a great light emanated from the wound on her forehead while the little worms were transformed into sparks of light. The wound can still be seen on the forehead, since her body remains marvelously incorrupt.

BL. LUCY OF NARNI (d. 1544) received her stigmata during a meditation on the Passion while she was in the choir with the rest of her community. Suddenly she became pale and gave all appearances of suffering acute pain. The nuns rushed to help her, but in a few moments the agony was such that Lucy swooned. On recovering in her cell, where her companions had taken her, she could not hide her hands; they were livid, and the skin was raised and inflamed. By the end of the week the wounds became large and shed an abundance of blood. The religious authorities were notified, resulting in a minute investigation by the bishop of Viterbo. Afterward three successive commissions of inquiry were appointed by the Pope. After these inquiries, declarations were issued which maintained that the stigmata were beyond all dispute.[14]

The Saint participated in all the sufferings of the Passion, which were accompanied by a great loss of blood every Wednesday and Friday for the three years she remained at Viterbo.

Before she entered the Capuchin order at Siena, VEN. PASSITEA CROGI (d. 1615) experienced an ecstasy on Palm Sunday that was so intense it lasted for days. On Good Friday, between two and three o'clock, she suddenly rose and knelt down with outstretched arms. Suddenly a dazzling ray like lightning flashed through the room, accompanied by a loud noise like thunder. Passitea immediately cried in pain and collapsed. When her two sisters ran to lift her up, they were astonished to see blood pouring from her hands, feet and head. Blood also splattered the bedrail and the bed's coverlet. The Rev. Domenico Marchi, a priest familiar in the ways of mysticism, was urgently summoned. Upon arrival he at once recognized that Passitea had received the sacred stigmata and began to gently ask questions concerning it. Passitea obediently replied that she had had a vision of Christ crucified, livid and bruised and covered with wounds streaming with red blood. She heard the words, "Daughter, drink of My Chalice," after which rays of transparent glory struck her hands, feet, side and encircled her head.

At the instigation of Church authorities, physicians tried every method then known to science to close the wounds, all to no avail.

The wounds in her hands and feet did not pierce through, but four years later, in 1593, while Passitea was in deep contemplation, a Seraph encircled in light, crucified and covered with wounds, appeared to her. As the vision approached, another loud noise like that of thunder shook the house, alerting Passitea's two sisters. They rushed to her room and found that once again Passitea had fainted, her body covered with blood.

Whereas the first stigmatic wounds did not pierce through, this second incident produced wounds that bore completely through the hands and feet. On certain days, especially during Holy Week, the wounds bled profusely and caused excruciating pain. At other times the flow was staunched, while less pain was experienced as the wounds throbbed.

It was only after receiving the stigmata that Passitea founded in Siena, in 1599, a convent of Capuchin nuns who followed the strict, primitive rule. She served the Siena community as its abbess and founded other convents of the order. Described as a sublime contemplative and a mystic of a very high order, Passitea Crogi exercised many other mystical phenomena, which are recounted elsewhere in this book.

After her death, her community of nuns, as well as many witnesses, saw the wounds of the stigmata that Passitea had always kept closely guarded, and "gave their official testimony to the fact and set their hands to all necessary formal documents."[15] (Some of the blood from these wounds was collected and has displayed a phenomenon that is described in the chapter of this book entitled "Blood Miracles.")

The stigmata of ST. VERONICA GIULIANI (d. 1727), a Capuchin nun at Citta' di Castello, were quite unusual since her confessor and her bishop seem to have exercised some control over one of the wounds. The Saint first received the wounds of the Crown of Thorns, then a year later, during a vision of the Crucified on April 5, 1697, the wounds in her hands, feet and side. The Saint describes the reception of the five wounds in this manner:

I saw five brilliant rays of light dart forth from the Five Sacred Wounds, and all seemed to concentrate their force upon me. And I saw that these rays became small flames of burning fire. Four of them appeared in the form of great pointed nails, whilst the fifth was a spearhead of gleaming gold, all aquiver as thrice heated hot. And this, a levin flash, lancing upon me, pierced my heart through and through, and the four sharp nails of fire stabbed through my hands and my feet . . . When I had thus been wounded the rays of light gleaming with a new radiance shot back to the Crucified and illumined the gashed side, the hands and feet of Him Who was hanging there . . .

When I came to myself I found that I was kneeling with my arms wide outspread, benumbed and sore cramped, and my heart, my hands and my feet burned and throbbed with great pain. I felt that my side was gashed open and welled and bubbled with blood. I tried to open my habit and see the wound, but I could not because of the wounds in both my hands. After much suffering, I succeeded in loosing my habit and I then saw that the wound in my side purled forth with water and blood. I wished to trace a few lines but I could not hold the quill in my hand for very agony. Whereupon I prayed to my Spouse, begging Him that my fingers might at least have power to guide the pen. Being under obedience I wished to write a screed for my confessor and with the ink of my blood I wrote upon a paper the name Jesus . . .[16]

Great mental anguish was experienced when the Holy Office and Bishop Eustachi began rigorous examinations to determine if the wounds were authentic. To guard against fraud, Veronica was forbidden to receive Holy Communion and was kept under constant supervision. She was also isolated from the rest of the community and had her hands placed in special gloves that were fastened with the bishop's signet. All medical treatments to heal the wounds were unsuccessful. The Saint prayed for the wounds to disappear, but she was told during a vision that they were to remain visible for three years. They, in fact, disappeared on April 5, 1700, exactly three years later. After that date they appeared intermittently. The wound in the side, however, remained and bled profusely.

When asked by her confessor how long the wound in the side would remain, the Saint replied as quoted in her *Relations:*

> Our Lord seems to wish it should remain open for so many hours or days, according as I had been given to understand and exactly at that time it would close again. But sometimes he, the confessor, said to me, "I do not wish it to close before such a day or such an hour." And in fact it would happen so . . . If I am not mistaken the bishop on one occasion did the same thing. He came here with certain of God's servants and they wished to see this wound in the side open, to my great sorrow. Then the bishop told me that he would come again the next day but wished the wound to be closed. And so precisely it came about. These things have been a very great suffering for me. May it be all for the glory of God.[17]

Just as in the case of St. Veronica, in which she received the wounds of the stigmata on different occasions, so it was with BL. OSANNA OF MANTUA (d. 1505), who was twenty-eight years old when she received the first wound, the Crown of Thorns, on February 24, 1476. The wound in her side next appeared on June 5 of the following year. On Friday in Passion Week of the year 1478, while she was weeping over the sufferings of Calvary, Our Lord appeared to her. From the four red wounds of the Crucified there "darted four forked flambent rays which pierced through, like the thrust of white hot daggers, her feet and hands."

On Wednesdays and Fridays the wounds felt as though "huge two-penny nails were being remorselessly hammered through the tender flesh, whilst during Holy Week so fierce was the agony that she herself declared, 'Had I not been miraculously holpen of [helped by] Heaven, I had surely died.' "[18]

Bl. Osanna died at the age of fifty-six and was beatified in 1694. After her death the stigmata became quite pronounced. The visible change in appearance of these mysterious markings, after all apparent signs of life had left the body, completely challenges the opinion of those who would attribute the stigmata to auto-suggestion.[19]

A twentieth century mystic, ST. GEMMA GALGANI, who is known as the "Passion Flower of Lucca" (d. 1903), also had wounds that appeared at intervals. She tells what took place when she received the holy stigmata on June 8 in the year 1899, a Thursday, the eve of the Sacred Heart's feast. The Saint discloses:

> I felt an inward sorrow for my sins, but so intense that I have never felt the like again . . . My will made me detest them all, and promise willingly to suffer everything as expiation for them. Then thoughts crowded thickly within me, and they were thoughts of sorrow, love, fear, hope and comfort . . .

Gemma then experienced a rapture in which she saw her Guardian Angel in the company of the Blessed Virgin. Gemma tells what took place after the Blessed Mother told Gemma that her Son loved her very much and was giving her a special grace:

> The Blessed Mother opened her mantle and covered me with it. At that very moment Jesus appeared with His wounds all open; blood was not flowing from them, but flames of fire which in one moment came and touched my hands, feet and heart. I felt I was dying, and should have fallen down but for my Mother, who supported me and kept me under her mantle. Thus I remained for several hours. Then my Mother kissed my forehead, the vision disappeared and I found myself on my knees; but I had still a keen pain in my hands, feet and heart. I got up to get into bed and I saw that blood was coming from the places where I had the pain. I covered them as well as I could and then, helped by my Guardian Angel, got into bed.[20]

The wounds were not always present, but appeared in her body every Thursday evening towards eight o'clock and stayed until three p.m. on Friday, the hour of Christ's death on the Cross. Fr. P. Germano, who was an eyewitness more than once to the appearance and disappearance of the wounds, tells that no warning was given, no particular feeling, but the Saint did experience a recollection and then an ecstasy. Fr. Germano explains:

. . . red patches would suddenly appear on the back of her hands, and in the center of the patches a jagged wound gradually formed under the skin, rising to the surface. This wound was oblong on the back of the hands and measured three quarters of an inch in length by an eighth in width; the wound in the palm of the hand was roundish but irregular and measured just under half an inch in diameter. On the feet the wounds were longer and wider and there was considerable discoloration round the edges and the measurements were somehow reversed, being larger in diameter on the back and smaller under the foot. The open wounds formed themselves gradually and took about five minutes before commencing to bleed, growing from the inside of the outer skin and ending with the perforation of the latter . . .

On other occasions the phenomena would come upon her much more suddenly, like a sudden and violent tear of the flesh, breaking through from the inside, and the shock this gave her caused her to tremble from head to foot and the muscles of her arms and legs would jerk from the dreadful pain in them. It was a terrible thing to witness. The blood that spurted out from the wounds was fresh and bright in color and this vivid shade was retained until all trace of a wound had disappeared. It also remained the same bright red when it splashed onto the floor or on her clothes. The wound from the heart always bled copiously and her undergarments were invariably saturated with it.

As to the disappearance of the stigmata, Fr. Germano reveals:

Nor was the manner of the disappearance of these wounds any less marvellous than their coming. When her ecstasy came to an end on the Fridays, the flow of blood ceased abruptly from all the five wounds and her skin would regain its look of healthy flesh and close up, leaving no trace of any laceration. This complete obliteration generally took from Friday evening to Saturday, but it sometimes was slower and took until Sunday. The flesh was natural in color and in texture, and the same as that of the rest of her body. It was almost unbelievable that those dreadful gaping wounds, which had been bleeding and sore only the day before, would heal, and again, in a few days' time, when Thursday evening came round would bleed again.[21]

Another twentieth century case is that of PADRE PIO (d. 1968), a Capuchin friar of whom many books have been written. Padre Pio received permission from his spiritual director to ask Our Lord to accept him as a victim soul to alleviate the sufferings of the souls in Purgatory and to win souls for Heaven. God apparently accepted the offer, since Padre Pio received signs in his body which suggested the Wounds of Christ's Passion. On the afternoon of September 7, 1910 Padre Pio appeared at the office of his former professor and pastor of the parish in Pietrelcina, Archpriest Salvatore Maria Pannullo, and showed his friend what appeared to be puncture wounds in the middle of his hands. These were about a half-inch in diameter on both the backs and palms of Padre Pio's hands. The wounds did not bleed, but seemed to extend through the hands. A few days later he asked Pannullo to pray with him that the visible marks would disappear, although he wanted to continue the pains he was experiencing. The two prayed and the wounds went away "for a season."[22]

This was only the forerunner of a more extensive and phenomenal condition.

Eight years later, on August 5, 1918, Padre Pio had this extraordinary experience, which was told to Padre Benedetto, his confessor. Padre Pio's account reveals,

> I was hearing the confessions of our boys . . . when suddenly I was filled with extreme terror at the sight of a heavenly Being who presented Himself to the eye of my intellect. He held some kind of weapon in His hand, something like a long, sharp-pointed steel blade, which seemed to spew out fire. At the very instant that I saw all this, I saw that Personage hurl the weapon into my soul with all His might. It was only with difficulty that I did not cry out. I thought I was dying. I told the boy to leave because I felt ill and did not feel that I could continue . . . This agony lasted uninterruptedly until the morning

of the 7th. I cannot tell you how much I suffered during
this period of anguish. Even my internal organs were
torn and ruptured by that weapon . . . From that day on
I have been mortally wounded. I feel in the depths of my
soul a wound that is always open and causes me continual agony.[23]

A month later, Padre Pio received the other wounds of the Passion. The whole event was described by the Padre in 1918, as well
as in depositions made years later, and took place in the following
manner.

On the morning of September 20, while the students were in the
garden, Padre Pio went to the choir between nine and ten and sat on
the "vicar's bench" to make his thanksgiving after offering the Holy
Sacrifice. Padre Pio relates:

I was overtaken by a repose similar to a deep sleep.
All my internal and external senses and even the very
faculties of my soul were steeped in indescribable quiet
. . . I was filled with great peace and abandonment that
blotted out every worry or preoccupation.

It was then that he was surrounded by a great light, and in the
midst of the light the crucifix before him was transformed into the
same *misterioso personaggio* who had wounded him on August 5.
The Padre tells that blood was dripping from the vision's hands,
feet and side. "This great Exalted Being, all blood, from whom
there came forth beams of light with shafts of flame that wounded
me in the hands and feet. My side had already been wounded on the
fifth of August of the same year." He continues that the countenance of the celestial visitor frightened him. "I thought I should die
and really should have died if the Lord hadn't intervened to
strengthen my heart, which was ready to burst out of my chest."
Padre Pio affirmed that the Exalted Being was indeed Jesus Christ,
who said not a word to him before He disappeared.[24]

Following the vision, Padre Pio found himself lying on the floor,
and from his side, hands and feet there issued large amounts of
blood. After dragging himself to his cell, he cleaned the wounds,
and while doing so, "I looked at the wounds and wept, singing
hymns of thanksgiving."[24]

A number of physicians were called to examine the wounds. Dr. Cardone declared that the wounds "pierced the palms of the hands completely through, so much so that one could see light through them." Padre Alessi Parente concurred, saying, "The wounds went all the way through the hands. If he held his hand in front of a window, you could see light." The wounds in the feet were said to be similar. There were times when both the hands and feet were covered with reddish-brown scabs or thick crusts of dried blood.

As to the wound in the side, most witnesses attested that it was shaped like a cross, a slash about three inches long that cut parallel to the ribs.

As a test to judge the genuineness of the stigmata, the authorities of the Order at first ordered that the wounds be bandaged and sealed in the presence of two eyewitnesses, Padre Paolino and Padre Placido. After eight days, when the bandages were removed, there was no sign of healing—in fact, the hands bled more than before. During the offering of Holy Mass the wounds in the hands bled so profusely that the holy Padre constantly had to wipe them to keep blood from falling on the altar cloths.[25]

Padre Pio would have preferred that the wounds be invisible and that he continue to suffer the pains, but it was not God's will. To hide the wounds he was permitted to wear fingerless gloves. Padre Pio bore the wounds of Christ for fifty years. By the spring of 1968 God seemingly answered his long-time prayer. The stigmata became less evident on the feet, although the pain continued. On the hands there were only scabs and a bit of redness. Seeing this as a sign of approaching death, Padre Onorato said, "The ministry was finished, so the signs were finished."[26] Padre Pio died on September 23, 1968.

Most of the Saints and holy persons mentioned above were members of religious orders. BL. GERTRUDE VAN OOSTEN (d. 1358) was a laywoman, a Beguine, of Delft, Holland. Beguines were women who lived in a settlement of connecting houses. Although they lived alone, sometimes with a companion or two, they performed religious exercises in common and occupied their time in works of charity. In the strict sense they were not members of religious orders, but they did take vows of chastity and obedience—however, not of poverty.

After years of austerity and contemplation, Gertrude received the sacred wounds of Jesus on Good Friday, in the year 1340. The wounds had the unusual capability of bleeding seven times every day. When news of these bleedings became known, crowds converged on her house to witness the marvel. As a consequence, and out of humility, Bl. Gertrude prayed for Our Lord's help. In answer to her prayer the wounds no longer bled, but the marks continued to be visible. During the remaining eighteen years of her life she continued to suffer and to display many mystical favors.[27]

The Invisible Stigmata

All the cases previously mentioned were of stigmatics whose wounds were visible. There are many cases in which the wounds of the stigmata were invisible, yet most of the recipients suffered as much as those who had the visible wounds, without the usual bleeding, of course. In some cases the wounds were visible at first, but were rendered invisible by Our Lord when the Saint asked this grace out of humility.

An unusual case is that of ST. CATHERINE OF SIENA (d. 1380), whose reception of the stigmata is told us by her confessor, Bl. Raymond of Capua. The event took place at Pisa after the reception of Holy Communion. Entering into an ecstasy, as was her custom, St. Catherine lay prone for a time. Then to the surprise of everyone present, "We saw her little body, which had been lying prostrate, gradually rise up until it was upright on its knees, her arms and hands stretched themselves out, and light beamed from her face. She remained in this position for a long time, perfectly stiff, with her eyes closed, and then we saw her suddenly fall, as though mortally wounded."[28]

After the ecstasy, Catherine called for Bl. Raymond, who suspected that she had received a remarkable grace. The Saint quietly began to relate what had taken place.

> You must know, Father, that by the mercy of the Lord Jesus I now bear in my body His stigmata. I saw the Lord fixed to the Cross coming towards me in a great light, and such was the impulse of my soul to go and meet its Creator that it forced the body to rise up. Then from the scars of His most sacred Wounds, I saw five rays of blood coming down towards me, to my hands, my feet and my heart. Realizing what was to happen, I

exclaimed, "O Lord God, I beg You—do not let these
scars show on the outside of my body!" As I said this,
before the rays reached me their colour changed from
blood red to the colour of light, and in the form of pure
light they arrived at the five points of my body: hands,
feet and heart.

Bl. Raymond then asked if a shaft of light had reached the right
side. She replied, "No, it came straight to my left side, over my
heart; because that line of light from Jesus' right side struck me
directly, not aslant."

When Bl. Raymond asked if she felt any pain, St. Catherine
replied, "I feel such pain at those five points, especially in my heart,
that if the Lord does not perform another miracle I do not see how
I can possibly go on, and within a few days I shall be dead." Strange
to relate, Bl. Raymond, together with her companion, prayed that
the good God would relieve her of the pain—a prayer that was
promptly answered. On being asked by Bl. Raymond if she still suffered, the Saint answered, "The Lord, to my great displeasure, has
granted your prayers, and those wounds no longer give my body any
pain, instead they have made it stronger and healthier and I can feel
quite clearly that the strength comes from the places where the agonies came from before."[29] This is one of the few cases in which the
stigmata did not cause considerable discomfort.

The invisible stigmata were given to ST. MARY MAGDALENE
DE PAZZI (d. 1607) in the year 1585, one year after Our Lord had
placed His Crown of Thorns upon her heart and her head. It was
Holy Monday when the Saint began to contemplate the Wounds of
Our Lord. After a few moments Sr. Mary Pacifica saw the Saint
begin to lose consciousness and guided her to her curtained cell in
the corner of the novitiate dormitory.

A sister by the same name, but known to us as Sr. Mary Magdalene Mori, wrote in her *Book of Colloquies* about what then took
place.

She took her place kneeling by the bed in order not to
be seen. And so she remained with her hands extended
and her eyes fixed on an image of Jesus that she had
over her bed.

Five luminous rays left the wounds of her Crucified Spouse to find their places in her hands, her feet and her side. Immediately she prayed that the wounds would not be visible. The rays then disappeared, but not before they left the Sacred Wounds impressed upon her soul.

During many ecstasies she was also privileged to accompany Our Lord during His Passion and Crucifixion and experienced many of the sufferings He endured. Her movements and facial expressions were such that the nuns could identify exactly what part of the Passion was being re-enacted. But it did not appear that she was always watching Our Lord, but actually, at times, taking His place. When she was asked by one of the nuns if, during the various scenes and mysteries, she actually saw Jesus, Sr. Mary Magadalene Mori recorded, "She told us yes, that she saw Him and suffered with Him in such a way that sometimes she seemed herself to be Jesus."

It appears that these participations in Our Lord's Passion were not repeated on a regular basis, such as some have endured every Friday, or during Holy Week, but were suffered by the Saint at various intervals.[30]

Another Saint who bore the invisible stigmata was ST. MARY FRANCES OF THE FIVE WOUNDS OF JESUS (d. 1791), who joined the Franciscan Third Order at the age of 16. Pious from childhood, she received the stigmata which took no outward, visible appearance, but, as with the other stigmatics who bore the invisible wounds, she suffered the pains of the Passion. While making the Stations of the Cross on Fridays, especially the Fridays during Lent, she would experience pains corresponding to the Agony in the Garden, the Scourging, the Crowning with Thorns and those other pains experienced by Our Lord during the rest of His Passion. In the end she appeared as though dead.[31]

She experienced many other mystical favors that are reported elsewhere in this book.

ST. COLETTE (d. 1447), the foundress of the Colettine division of the Poor Clare Order, did not have the visible or invisible stigmata as in the cases previously mentioned, but was favored in another way. We are told that she had a special devotion to the Passion and that during Holy Week she was wholly absorbed in bemoaning the sufferings of Our Lord. Sometimes during her contemplation and ecstasies, she participated in the sufferings, so much so, that she was left with visible marks on her body. Her biographer writes:

> One time, on a Friday, at the hour of Matins, she set herself to meditate on the grievous pains that Our Lord had suffered. During this meditation she endured such great torments that the sisters, who were coming out from chapter, meeting her, looked at her in great amazement. For it seemed as if her beloved face had been beaten with sticks, and there remained only the skin and the bone, which appeared all bruised.[32]
>
> In this manner, she at least, for a time, bore some of the sufferings of Our Lord. These visions, we are told, took place on Fridays and lasted from six in the morning until six in the evening.[33]

There are many more stigmatists not mentioned here, but others who were identified as stigmatists are: Ven. Benoite Rencurel, Bl. Eustochia Calafato, Bl. Anne de Paredes, Bl. Margaret Colonna, Bl. Angela of Foligno, St. Margaret of Cortona, St. Gertrude, St. Frances of Rome, St. Catherine of Genoa, Bl. Baptista Varani, Bl. Catherine of Racconigi, St. John of God, Bl. Marie de l'Incarnation, Bl. Mary Anne of Jesus, Bl. Carlo of Sezze, St. Margaret Mary Alacoque, Bl. Beatrix d'Ornacieu, St. Miguel de los Santos, Bl. Stefana Quinzani, St. Joan Marie of the Cross, St. Christina of Stommeln, St. Catherine of Veszprim, Bl. Emilia Bicchieri of Vercelli, Bl. Christina d'Aquila and Bl. Vanna of Orvieto.

The question arises: how many stigmatists have there been? Dr. Imbert-Gourbeyre, a French physician, numbered 321 genuine stigmatists in his two-volume work, *La Stigmatization*, which was written in 1894. A few more stigmatists have been added since then. One source reports that all of these were Roman Catholic, the majority being female and Italian. Of the several hundred stigmatists whose lives have been studied since the thirteenth century, only sixty-two have been either canonized or beatified.[34]

Dr. Imbert-Gourbeyre gives other statistics. Of those stigmatists he regarded as being genuine, he calculated that 229 were from Italy; Sicily claimed 10; France, 70; Spain, 47; Germany, 33; Belgium, 15; Portugal, 13; five each from Switzerland and Holland; three from Hungary and one from Peru.

With regard to religious affiliations, Dr. Imbert-Gourbeyre tells us there were 109 stigmatists from the Dominican Order, the Franciscans numbered 102, of which a quarter were Poor Clares; Carmelites, 14; Ursulines, 14; Visitation nuns, 12; Augustinians, 8; Jesuits, 3; and the others were laymen or members of smaller religious orders. Because the doctor's book was published in 1894, there are, of course, no twentieth-century cases mentioned.

The subject of the stigmata is a vast subject, too broad to cover thoroughly in a single chapter, but it is a matter which has been explored in a number of books which are readily available.

ST. CATHERINE OF SIENA receives the stigmata. She later told her confessor, "I saw the Lord fixed to the Cross coming towards me in a great light . . . I saw five rays of blood coming down towards me, to my hands, my feet and my heart . . . before the rays reached me their color changed from blood red to the color of light, and in the form of pure light they arrived at the five points of my body: hands, feet and heart."

ST. RITA OF CASCIA is among the hundreds of Saints who were stigmatics. She received only one wound—a wound in the forehead—produced by a thorn from Our Lord's Crown of Thorns.

MARKED BY GOD'S FAVOR. St. Francis of Assisi is honored as the first to carry the holy wounds, which were imprinted upon his body in 1224, two years before his death. Wounding by the holy stigmata imparts a mixture of pain and spiritual joy.

THE GIFT OF TONGUES

"And they were all filled with the Holy Ghost, and they began to speak with divers tongues, according as the Holy Ghost gave them to speak . . ." —Acts 2:4

What might come immediately to mind when considering the gift of tongues are the charismatic prayer meetings in which one person speaks a message or offers a prayer in a foreign language. Most in the group cannot understand the message or prayer until it is translated or interpreted by another. This chapter does not deal with tongues as they pertain to the charismatic movement. Instead, the gift of tongues in this instance involves Saints' speaking in their own language, but being understood by many others who speak a different language. It is not one speaking and one interpreting, but one speaking in his own language and everyone else, of a different tongue, knowing what was said, with no interpreter needed.

This gift of tongues as exercised by the Saints recalls that which took place after the Apostles received the gifts of the Holy Spirit and spoke "in divers tongues. And when this was noised abroad, the multitude came together, and were confounded in mind, because that every man heard them speak in his own tongue." (*Acts* 2:6).

This gift of speaking in one language, but being understood by people who speak another language, was not reserved to Apostolic times. Many Saints were given this ability, including ST. ANTHONY OF PADUA (d. 1231), whose gift of tongues is described in *The Little Flowers of St. Francis*. This little book, written by Br. Ugolino, who lived a century after the death of St. Francis of Assisi, was based on early documents of the order. In this book we are charmingly told that:

> St. Anthony was preaching one day . . . before the
> Pope and Cardinals in a consistory where there were

men from different countries—Greeks and Latins, French and Germans, Slavs and English—and men of many other different languages and idioms.

And being inflamed by the Holy Spirit and inspired with apostolic eloquence, he preached and explained the word of God so effectively, devoutly, subtly, clearly and understandably that all who were assembled at that consistory, although they spoke different languages, clearly and distinctly heard and understood every one of his words as if he had spoken in each of their languages. Therefore they were all astounded and filled with devotion, for it seemed to them that the former miracle of the Apostles at the time of Pentecost had been renewed, when by the power of the Holy Spirit they spoke in different languages.

And in amazement they said to one another: "Is he not a Spaniard?[1] How then are we all hearing him in the language of the country where we were born—we Greeks and Latins, French and Germans, Slavs and English, Lombards and foreigners?"[2]

It was not only at this consistory that St. Anthony's gift of tongues was utilized. It is said that while preaching in Italy he spoke in perfect Italian, and while in France he preached in French, although he had never studied these languages. Also remarkable is the fact that "the simple-minded and the most ignorant listeners were capable of fully comprehending all he said; and his voice, though gentle and sweet, was distinctly heard at a very extraordinary distance from the speaker."[3]

The grace of being heard at a great distance was also related in the life of ST. PAUL OF THE CROSS (d. 1775). This took place in La Tolfa, at Civitacastellana, and on the Isle of Elba, where he was heard a full five miles away. Not only that, but his Italian language was understood by members of different nationalities who listened to him.[4]

ST. DOMINIC (d. 1221), the founder of the Dominican Order and the great champion of the Holy Rosary, exercised the gift of tongues when he was one day on a journey to Paris with his companion, Bertrand of Garrega, and a number of other disciples. On the road they visited the sanctuary of Rocamadour, where they spent the night praying before a miraculous image of Our Lady. The next day, as they journeyed along, they sang litanies and recited psalms and the divine office, which attracted the attention of two German pilgrims, who began to follow them. When they came to the next village the two German pilgrims, being greatly attracted by the devotion of the little band, made motions to them indicating that they should sit down and dine with them. It was somewhat of an awkward situation since the Germans could not understand the Dominicans, nor could the Dominicans understand the Germans. This continued for four days, with the Germans sharing their food with the Dominicans.

On the fifth day St. Dominic addressed Bertrand in this manner: "Brother Bertrand, it grieves me to reap the temporal things of these pilgrims without sowing for them spiritual things: let us kneel down and ask God to grant us the understanding of their language, that we may speak to them of Christ." Accordingly, they knelt down and prayed. When they rose up, they were able to converse with the Germans in their own language and did so without difficulty for the rest of the journey.

As they drew near Paris, the Germans, now filled with spiritual consolations, departed from them. The earthly food which the Germans had provided had been exchanged by Dominic for spiritual food which nourished their spirits and was beneficial to their eternal salvation.

St. Dominic, for his part, charged Bertrand to keep silent about the matter and to keep it secret until his death, "lest the people should take us for Saints who are but sinners."[5]

ST. VINCENT FERRER (d. 1419), the celebrated Dominican and friend of St. Colette who spent the last twenty years of his life on missionary journeys, delivered his sermons in Latin or Limousin, the language of his native Valencia. It is reported that he was followed by an army of penitents and that while speaking only Latin or Limousin, he was understood by persons of many nationalities. His contemporary biographers maintain that he was endowed with the gift of tongues, an opinion that was supported by Nicholas Clemangis, a doctor of the University of Paris who was a witness to the marvel.[6]

Often the audience of strangers who came to hear him preach was enormous, sometimes amounting to ten thousand souls. Peter Ranzano, the bishop of Lucera, who wrote a biography of the Saint, affirms that the people of all nationalities understood the Saint in their own languages, and that the people furthest away from the Saint heard him as distinctly as those near him.

Another Dominican, ST. LOUIS BERTRAND (d. 1581), who was also a native of Valencia, exercised the gift of tongues when he and two brothers were sent as missionaries to the territory of New Granada. Arriving there he was thoroughly disappointed, since the territory was inhabited by devil worshippers. The situation was doubly complicated since they spoke a number of dialects. Finding it impossible to learn the languages, Louis had recourse to prayer and begged for the gift of tongues, which he received. Records have it that the people understood him and were converted.[7]

ST. MARTIN DE PORRES (d. 1639), the humble black lay brother who was also a Dominican, often used the grace of bilocation to further his apostolate in far off countries. Fr. Francisco d'Arce declared that an elderly religious, "whose proven virtue made him a reliable authority," assured him that St. Martin often visited Japan, where persecutions threatened to destroy the Faith, and that he there assisted the martyrs. His early biographer reports, "It has been positively declared that Martin spoke with fluency in strange tongues."[8]

ST. PHILIP BENIZI (d. 1285) was a member of the Order of the Servants of Mary, which is also known as the Servite Order. Summoned by Pope Gregory X to be present at the Second General Council of Lyons, he made a profound impression "and the gift of tongues was attributed to him."[9]

During the Proces de l'Ordinaire previous to the canonization of ST. JEAN-MARIE BAPTISTE VIANNEY, the Curé of Ars (d. 1859), Sr. Marie-Francois of the Third Order of St. Francis related that she went to Confession to the Saint during Holy Week of 1849 or 1850. She declared that she asked the Saint, "Father, what is it God wants of me?" The Saint responded, "Ah! my child . . ." and then a soft voice began mumbling on the other side of the grate. Sr. Marie-Francois continued:

After that M. Vianney spoke as if to himself for the space of five minutes and in a tongue unknown to me; at any rate, I could not understand him. In my astonishment I looked into his face. He seemed to be out of himself, and I thought that he beheld the good God. Deeming myself unworthy to remain in the presence of so great a Saint, I withdrew, feeling quite overcome with fear.[10]

What language could the Saint have spoken that was not understood, since he is known never to have left his native France?

Barnaby of Siena, a contemporary of ST. BERNARDINE OF SIENA (d. 1444), relates that the Saint on one occasion had to preach to Greeks, but not knowing the Greek language, he spoke in his native Italian. Barnaby of Siena writes that the Greeks understood St. Bernardine as well as if he had spoken to them in their own language.[11]

The biography of ST. PACOMIUS (d. 348) was written by one of his disciples, a monk of Tabenna, who tells us of the Saint's instantaneous knowledge of the Greek and Latin languages. It seems that St. Pacomius knew only one language, his native Egyptian, but one day a religious from Italy came to consult him on a case of conscience. Pacomius, kneeling in prayer, said,

O God, if the knowledge of languages is essential in order that I may make known Thy will to strangers, why hast Thou not given me this gift? If it seemeth good in Thy sight, give me now the gift of tongues, that I may be useful to this stranger.

The biographer relates that when the Saint rose from his knees he found himself a perfect master of the Greek and Latin languages.[12]

ST. FRANCIS SOLANO (d. 1610) was a Franciscan friar who was sent to South America from his native Spain to convert the Indians in Argentina, Bolivia and Paraguay. Later he was to labor in Peru. St. Francis Solano was known as a Saint during his lifetime, and the Indians at once welcomed him and always rejoiced in his presence. God assisted him in extraordinary ways, and it was through the grace of God that the Saint learned the difficult Indian languages in a very short time and was understood wherever he went.

Once when he was in the city of La Rioja, a horde of armed Indians, counted in the thousands, went out in a frenzy to slay all Europeans and Christianized Indians. The Saint went out bravely to meet them and spoke words that disarmed them. All understood what he said, although they spoke different dialects. They begged for instructions and were baptized. The converts to the Faith numbered nine thousand.[13] Because of his many miracles, he became known as the "Wonder-Worker of the New World."

An unusual situation existed with regard to PADRE PIO (d. 1968) in that sometimes, when a penitent spoke in his own language in the confessional, a language unfamiliar to the Padre, he replied in Italian, with the result that they both understood each other. In these cases Padre Pio attributed the interpreting to his Guardian Angel.[14]

NOTE: When the gift of tongues is mentioned, St. Francis Xavier is almost always presented as having been a recipient of this gift. But there is a problem with this claim. According to the Rev. James Broderick, S.J., the Saint "learned to speak and write, serviceably, if not elegantly, Portuguese, Spanish, French, Latin and Italian." His mother tongue was Basque. While laboring in Italy we learn that "he never had any inhibitions about speaking a new and unfamiliar tongue. His accent might be execrable and his grammar deplorable, but he made no apologies and went brazenly ahead."

When he began his missionary endeavors and was laboring among the pearl-fishers in the region of Cape Comorin, St. Francis "wrote despondently to his Jesuit brethren in Rome that he could not hold converse with his humble neophytes and had to employ such interpreters as knew a little Portuguese, 'because their mother tongue is Tamil and mine is Basque.'"

Eventually we find that he learned a little Tamil: "He did not speak their Tamil tongue at all fluently or well, but he had enough of it, at least by heart, to convey to them the most extraordinary story of a supreme God . . ."

We also learn that ". . . one man and one man alone was responsible for creating the hoary and still persistent legend that St. Francis Xavier possessed the gift of tongues, and that man was Antonio Pereira." He testified on oath before an ecclesiastical court at Malacca in November, 1556 about his unfounded claims.

Because of this controversy, the Saint is not mentioned in the body of this chapter. The claim of his having had the gift of tongues has been placed in doubt.

ST. DOMINIC exercised the gift of tongues.

MYSTICAL FASTS

"And the angel of the Lord came again the second time, and touched him, and said to him: Arise, eat: for thou hast yet a great way to go. And Elias arose, and ate, and drank, and walked in the strength of that food forty days and forty nights, unto the mount of God, Horeb." — 3 Kgs. 19:7-8

It is an indisputable fact of nature that if a person fails to eat and is malnourished for a lengthy time, he will die. How long he can survive without food or nutritious liquids, or can consume such a meager amount of food as would not encourage proper health, depends on his physical and psychological makeup. But what about those persons who have lived for years without eating, yet who lived in health? How did they do it? They had one meal each morning at the sacrificial Altar: the Holy Eucharist, the Bread of Life that nourished the soul and, through mystical means, the body.

What about those holy persons who ate meager amounts of food: a little flour and water, a small piece of bread soaked in milk, a piece of potato? They, too, credited the Holy Eucharist for their health and vigor. These were not periodic fasts, but ongoing abstinences from food. These were the mystics who contradicted the laws of nature and, through the inspiration of God, either consumed small amounts of food such as would not maintain proper health, or refrained from eating altogether. Yet they continued their ordinary activities, sometimes in the rigors of the monastic life, and in many cases continued schedules that the ordinary person would find difficult or impossible to imitate, even with a proper diet.

Because the prolonged fasts of these Saints were the cause of much attention and curiosity, they were carefully watched; the Saints' activities were scrutinized and studied.

The cases mentioned in this chapter are true accounts of Saints whose fasts were affirmed by holy companions, in many cases by physicians, and in the cases of those in religion, by physicians and religious authorities. Here then are a few of those privileged souls.

One of the earliest accounts of a mystic who lived for years upon the Blessed Eucharist alone is BL. ALPAIS (d. 1211), a peasant girl who was born at Cudot, which is now in the diocese of Orléans, France. Her biography was written while she was still alive by a Cistercian monk of Escharlis who knew her personally. Other contemporary reports still exist in the public records.

During her early youth she was stricken by a disease that was cured during a vision of Our Lady. Although she lost the use of her limbs and was confined to her bed because of that condition, she was otherwise perfectly well. The Cistercian monk, after closely observing her way of life, wrote that nothing in the way of food or drink, except the Blessed Sacrament, passed her lips for a very long time. Her abstinence from food was brought to the notice of the Archbishop of Sens, who was also the legate of the Holy See. To test the truth of the report, he appointed a commission, which conducted an examination and confirmed the truth of her fast. Her perpetual fast, as well as her miracles and ecstatic experiences, made her home a place of pilgrimage, with even prelates and nobles arriving from all parts to visit her.[1]

A contemporary of Bl. Alpais, BL. MARY OF OIGNIES (d. 1213), also observed an unusual fast, but a strange aspect of it was her physical repulsion for food. Her biographer, Cardinal Jacques de Vitry, carefully observed her fast and wrote:

> On one occasion she went for as long as thirty-five days without any sort of food, passing all the time in a tranquil and happy silence. . . . She would say nothing for many days but "Give me the Body of our Lord Jesus Christ," and as soon as her request was granted she returned to her former silent converse with her Saviour . . . At length, after five weeks, returning to herself, to the wonder of those who were present, she began to speak and to take food. But for a long time afterwards she could not in any way endure even the smell of meat, or of anything cooked, nor of wine, unless it was an ablution after the Blessed Sacrament, which was sometimes given her, in which case she minded neither the smell nor the taste.[2]

Following a vision in which the Blessed Mother complained about the sins of heretics and bad Christians, ST. LUTGARDE OF AYWIERES (d. 1246) began the first of her three seven-year fasts of reparation. During these years she lived on nothing but bread and the ordinary drink of the convent, which was weak beer. She was ordered, under obedience, to take other food, but it was physically impossible for her to do so. It is noted that the fasts, "instead of weakening her health, only increased her strength and her power of resistance."[3]

The second seven-year fast was the result of another vision. This time her fast of reparation was for sinners at large. In addition to the bread and weak beer, Lutgarde added a few vegetables.

The third seven-year fast followed still another vision, when Jesus appeared and warned that His Church was exposed to attack by a powerful enemy which would bring terrible harm to souls unless someone undertook to suffer and win grace from God. The fast was observed, and though she was to die during its seventh year, "her death would be serene with the confidence of victory." In the year before her death she told Thomas of Cantimpré, her biographer, "Do not worry: this man who secretly desires the overthrow of the Church is either going to be humbled by the prayers of the faithful, or else he will soon depart this life and leave the Church in peace."[4]

The enemy who was causing difficulties for the Church was Emperor Frederick II, who was "devoured with pride and ambition, was given to a life of indulgence and scarcely concealed his contempt for the Church and for the Christian religion—indeed, for all religions and for the very notion of God."

Soon after Lutgarde's death both her prophecies were realized when Frederick II was first deposed, and then died suddenly at the age of fifty-six.[5]

Another example of a Saint who observed a mystical fast is ST. CATHERINE OF SIENA (d. 1380), who travelled a great deal in the interests of the Church. Her fast began after a vision of the Sacred Heart. Our Lord promised that He would work wonders through her, although she would suffer much from the suspicion of those who knew her. And so it happened. As her confessor, Bl. Raymond of Capua, writes in his biography of the Saint:

After the vision there began to descend into her soul, especially when she received Holy Communion, such an abundance of graces and heavenly consolations that, overflowing and pouring out into her body . . . changing the nature of her stomach in such a way that not only did she have no need of food but she could not in fact take any without it causing her pain. If she forced herself to eat, her body suffered extremely, her digestion would not function and the food had to come out with an effort by the way it had gone in. It is difficult to estimate the amount of suffering that this holy virgin experienced through swallowing food.[6]

Just as the vision had promised, the people in her own home considered the fast incredible, ". . . and what in fact was an extraordinary gift from God, they called a temptation and a trick of the devil."

The confessor who was guiding her spiritual progress before Bl. Raymond of Capua did so decided that Catherine had indeed been led astray by the enemy and forced her to eat every day. St. Catherine finally convinced him that she felt stronger and healthier when she refrained from eating, and was tired and ill when she did eat. The confessor relented and said, "Do as the Holy Spirit prompts you to do, for I can see that God is doing great things in you."[7]

Not only was her family unhappy with her abstinence from food, but also others found fault, while some were even scandalized by it. Out of humility and charity, the Saint at one time decided to attempt eating, but this produced such pains in her body that those who saw her were entirely sympathetic with her condition. Bl. Raymond writes:

. . . her stomach could not digest anything, with the result that what she had taken in had to come out by the same way as it had gone in, otherwise it caused her acute pains and swellings over most of her body. The holy virgin did not swallow any of the vegetables or other things that she chewed, for she spat out all the large bits; but because it was impossible for some little bits of food or juice not to go down into her stomach, and because she liked to drink fresh water to refresh her throat and jaws,

she was obliged to throw up everything she had swallowed every day. To do this she often had to introduce a
small branch of fennel or some other shrub into her
stomach, despite the great pain it caused her, as this was
generally the only way in which she could get rid of
what she had swallowed. She did this throughout the rest
of her life because of the grumblers, particularly those
who were scandalized by her fasting.[8]

Bl. Raymond, out of compassion, tried to persuade her to stop this
practice, but the Saint insisted on continuing, adding that she
wished to perform this penance for the salvation of souls.

The stigmatist BL. ELIZABETH THE GOOD (d. 1420) was frequently tormented by the devil, who once appeared as her confessor and ordered her to break her fast of three years, which she did.
During those three years she had eaten nothing at all. It is also
recorded that "For years and years, Bl. Elizabeth lived on an amount
of food far short of the minimum normally required to keep a
human being alive." When she died, she was attended by Fr. Conrad Kügelin, who had been the witness of her extraordinary life and
who has given us information regarding her mystical favors.[9]

The Saint who perhaps suffered the most excruciating pains as a
victim soul is ST. LYDWINE OF SCHIEDAM (d. 1433), whose
diseased body was literally falling apart. It was a wonder she
remained alive. Her biographer relates:

> The sum of her maladies continued to overwhelm her
> and she was attacked by a furious recrudescence of dis-
> ease. Her stomach burst like a ripe fruit, and they had to
> apply a woolen cushion to press back her entrails and
> prevent them from leaving the body. Soon, when they
> wished to move her to change the sheets of her bed, they
> had to bind her members firmly with napkins and cloths,
> for otherwise her body would have fallen to pieces and
> come away in the hands of those who tended her.[10]

In addition, her detractors who came to investigate the marvels
that accompanied her

saw only a head riven from forehead to nose; a face fur-
rowed like a melon, a body whose flesh had to be com-
pressed like that of a mummy by the interlacing of
bandages, and disgust overcame them at the sight of so
many infirmities.

In spite of these horrible physical conditions, St. Lydwine's life
was preserved by an unusual fast. As her biographer wrote:

By a miracle evidently intended to certify the super-
human origin of these ills, Lydwine no longer ate food,
or scarcely ate any. In thirty years she only ate as much
as a healthy person is accustomed to consume in three
days.

Her biographer continues:

During the first years of her life as a recluse her only
food from morning to night was one round of apple of
the thickness of the Sacred Host . . . if she occasionally
attempted to swallow a mouthful of bread steeped in
beer or milk, she was only able to do so with great difficulty. After a time the slice of apple became too much
for her and she had to content herself with a drop of
wine and water flavoured by a dash of spice of muscade,
or by a morsel of date . . . Finally she ceased to take any
food at all.

In answer to her detractors who accused her of eating greedily
when she was alone, the Saint replied: "You believe it is impossible to subsist without the help of food; but God is Master and can
act as He wishes. You affirm that my maladies should kill me; but
they will not kill me till the Saviour wishes it."[11]
St. Lydwine died at the age of 53, after a lifetime in which numerous mystical phenomena were manifested.

ST. NICHOLAS VON FLÜE (d. 1487) was a father of ten children who set his affairs in order and, with the permission of his
wife, left the world to live in solitude, a vocation to which Our Lord
was calling him.

One night, while he was in the forest near Liechstall, the sky was ablaze with lightning during a severe thunderstorm. Afterward, the Saint was seized with such violent gastric spasms that he felt he was about to die. When the pains passed, he discovered that he had lost all desire for ordinary food or drink and even felt himself incapable of taking either one or the other.

After he began to reside in a little hermitage, strangers sought him out for spiritual and temporal advice. Not talkative by nature, he said little to those who came to him out of curiosity. And to those who had heard reports of his abstinence from food and inquired about it, he merely answered: "God knows."

To satisfy themselves that Nicholas did not eat or drink, the cantonal magistrates blocked all approaches to his cell for a month. Archduke Sigismund sent his physician, and envoys from Emperor Frederick III also investigated. All satisfied themselves that the abstinence was correct and true and were, moreover, impressed with the Saint's sincerity and sanctity.[12]

It is said that St. Nicholas' fast endured for twenty years—from 1467 until his death in 1487.

BL. COLUMBA OF RIETI (d. 1501), a Dominican tertiary, was known during her lifetime for her intense devotion to the Blessed Sacrament and for the miraculous events that began when she was still a girl. She began to practice austere penances during her youth and subsisted for the greater part of her life on the Holy Eucharist alone. One of her biographers relates that Columba kept five Lents a year, fasted on bread and water, and went to Mass and received Communion as often as she was allowed in those days of infrequent Communion.[13]

She endured many trials and was consoled by a visit of Pope Alexander VI, who went himself to see her. He was fully convinced of her great sanctity and set the seal of his approval on her mode of life. She was beatified in 1697.

During the thirty-six years of her widowhood, ST. CATHERINE OF GENOA (d. 1510) practiced penance and enjoyed the most sublime graces while caring for the poor and sick. She also maintained an unusual fast which was recorded for us by her biographer, Baron Friedrich von Hügel, who wrote:

As to food, it is clear that, however much we may be able or be bound to deduct from the accounts, there remains a solid nucleus of remarkable fact. During some twenty years, she evidently went, for a fairly equal number of days—some thirty in Advent and some forty in Lent, seventy in all annually—with all but no food; and was, during these fasts, at least as vigorous and active as when her nutrition was normal . . . Practically the whole of her devoted service (in her hospital at Genoa) fell within these years, of which well nigh one-fifth was covered by these all but total abstinences from food.[14]

The Baron also mentions that she received Holy Communion daily, and also, as was customary at Genoa, she took a draught of wine by way of ablution, and occasionally at other times a little water rendered unpalatable by the addition of salt or vinegar. The fast, he mentions, was continuous for forty days without any interruption on Sundays.

The Saint's confessor, Marabotto, informs us that it was impossible for her to take any solid food or other form of drink during these times. Once she was ordered under obedience to eat something, but her stomach instantly rejected it.[15]

ST. PETER OF ALCANTARA (d. 1562) was a Franciscan friar and a friend and adviser of St. Teresa of Avila, and it was to her that he confided many of his mystical experiences. St. Teresa relates the following in Chapter XXVII of her *Autobiography*:

It was a very common thing for him to take food only once in three days. He asked me why I was so surprised at this and said that, when one got used to it, it was quite possible. A companion of his told me that sometimes he would go for a week without food. This must have been when he was engaged in prayer, for he used to have great raptures and violent impulses of love for God, of which I was myself once a witness . . .

St. Peter of Alcantara died at the age of 63, after a life of great activity, in which he founded and maintained a number of religious houses whose members adopted his name and are known as the

Alcantarine Franciscans. He observed extreme poverty, slept but an hour and a half every night for forty years and wrote books of prayer and meditation. Apparently his energy was sustained by his reception of the Holy Eucharist, which he received during his holy Masses.

BL. MARY ANNE DE PAREDES (d. 1645) attained sanctity by living in solitude in her own home, apart from all worldly cares, but closely united to God. She practiced austerities and observed an unusual fast in which she "took scarcely an ounce of dry bread every eight or ten days. The food which miraculously sustained her life, according to the sworn testimony of many witnesses, was the Holy Eucharist which she received every morning in Holy Communion."[16]

ST. ROSE OF LIMA (d. 1617), a Dominican tertiary, also attained sanctity while living outside the cloister. Her diet was also austere. One biographer reports that as a child Rose was very fond of fruit, "but from the age of four, she would not touch it." Later she never ate meat. Her ordinary fare consisted of hard crusts, water and bitter herbs; "during Lent she omitted the bread."[17]

One particular Lent, when the archbishop was trying to call a council to deal with an Indian scandal, the penance which she offered to God for the success of this endeavor was to stop eating completely. It is reported that "nothing but Holy Communion passed her lips, except for five pomegranate pips a day, which she chewed slowly in order to keep their bitter taste in her mouth as long as she could."[18]

During a good part of her life "she lived on her gazpacho, or bread soup. Her very life was a quasi-miracle." In spite of this meager amount of food, the Saint lived a busy life in support of her family and worked ten hours a day. She maintained a flower garden whose blossoms she sold. She also sold fine embroideries and nursed many of the poor to health. She was known as a Saint during her lifetime of 31 years and was the first canonized Saint of the Americas.

ST. JEAN MARIE BAPTISTE VIANNEY, the Curé of Ars (d. 1859), was always a frugal eater, sometimes partaking of a potato or a few vegetables, but he admitted that at times he required no nourishment other than the Eucharistic Host. One morning he revealed to Catherine Lassagne: "Oh! how hungry I felt during Mass. When the moment of the Communion came, I said to Our Lord: 'My God, feed my body as well as my soul!' and the pangs of hunger vanished at once."[19]

Concerning the holy Curé, a priest was heard to remark: "I think a time will come when the Curé d'Ars will derive his sustenance from the Holy Eucharist alone."[20]

Others who have maintained their vitality and received their sustenance from the Eucharist alone include the following:

BL. ANGELA OF FOLIGNO (d. 1309), who remained twelve years without taking any other nourishment. BL. CATHERINE OF RACCONIGI (d. 1547), a stigmatist, was sustained on the Eucharist alone for ten years.

ST. GEMMA GALGANI (d. 1903), also a stigmatist, is known as the "Passion Flower of Lucca." She "partook of no food of any kind, except the Blessed Sacrament, from Whitsunday in June, 1902 until her death on April 11, 1903."[21]

Even closer to our own day, there is BL. ANDRE (d. 1937), who is known for his great devotion to St. Joseph and who was the driving force behind the erection of St. Joseph's Oratory on Mount Royal in Montreal, Canada. It is known that Bl. Andre suffered from childhood with chronic stomach problems which prevented him from eating solid foods. He was much weaker than his brothers and sisters and always appeared frail. His stomach affliction also rendered him unable to persevere at various trades that required strength and stamina.

Despite this condition, Andre, at the age of 25, entered the Congregation of the Holy Cross, a teaching order, and served as the barber and doorkeeper. He liked to repeat humorously, "When I left the novitiate, my superiors gave me the door . . . I remained there forty years without ever leaving."

Surprisingly, while serving the community as doorkeeper, he had the necessary strength to counsel countless people, and because of his gift of miracles, many others came for a physical cure. When he was being thanked for their restoration of health or the correction of a physical handicap, the little Brother would always attribute what had taken place to the intercession of St. Joseph.

During Bl. Andre's life as a religious, his usual fare was "a mixture of flour and water, preferably without seasoning." He once confided to a friend, "Often, I did not bother to take breakfast. I'd slip a few biscuits into my pocket and go to the Oratory. Sometimes at night, on returning from the Mount, I noticed that I had forgotten to eat them."[22]

Another witness reported that Bl. Andre "had to stay at the door. So he took his meals on his desk in the porter's cell. Because his stomach still troubled him, his meals almost always consisted of a bowl of milk, watered down, in which he soaked a few pieces of bread."[23]

Later, when he was able to live at St. Joseph's Oratory, "he would take with him, on Monday mornings, his weekly ration: a kettle of potatoes."[24]

During his advanced years Bl. Andre was forced to his bed with various ailments. His biographer reports that the only thing which troubled the Brother's nurses was his refusal to eat proper food. According to Fr. Cousineau,

> Sr. Le Royer reported to me that during all three of Br. Andre's illnesses she had great difficulty making him eat. He would accept nothing but wheat flour softened in hot water and seasoned with salt. One day Sr. Le Royer said to him, "But is it glue that you wish?" "Yes," replied Br. Andre, "it is glue."[25]

When in his final illness, in the hospital of Saint Laurent, Br. Andre was asked by one of the nuns what he would like to eat. He answered, "Boil some water. Mix a little flour and salt in the water, and then dump it in the boiling water, stirring it so as to make a little gruel." In trying to provide a little more nourishment, the nun substituted cornstarch for the flour. Br. Andre immediately recognized the difference, so that the nun "made the flour gruel six or seven times following Brother Andre's instructions." The nun added almost in disbelief: "And strangely, this stuff that I called paste, this unappetizing mélange, Br. Andre appeared to enjoy and his stomach retained it."[26]

This unappetizing gruel that the Brother ingested throughout most of his life, this gruel that was moreover devoid of vitamins and nutrients that are regarded as necessary to maintain health and vigor, was apparently supplemented by Divine intervention so that Br. Andre could maintain a hectic schedule. Long lines of people were always waiting to speak with him. For example, once when he was visiting a friend in Ottawa, a local newspaper reported the name and address of Br. Andre's host: "consequently he received more than 1,400 visitors."[27]

In addition to speaking with countless people who came to him for cures or advice, he travelled to many sickbeds and journeyed tirelessly in an effort to collect funds for the Oratory. He oversaw the building of the Oratory, but, unfortunately, did not live to see its completion. Br. Andre died at the age of 92 and was beatified in 1982 by Pope John Paul II.

How is it that the Saints mentioned here, and many others, who abstained completely from food or who subsisted on flour gruel or meager servings of other foods, could live active lives filled with penances and works of mercy? The question is answered by the Jesuit, Herbert Thurston, who studied and wrote extensively about mystical phenomena. He reports:

> If it can be proved that this absence of nourishment is maintained concomitantly with the continual discharge of ordinary duties, then natural causes supply no explanation of the phenomenon, and we are justified in inferring the intervention of miracle.[28]

MYSTICAL KNOWLEDGE

"Shall not God search out these things: for he knoweth the secrets of the heart."—Psalms 43:22

It has been said of ST. JOHN BOSCO (d. 1888) that he had the ability to know "the mystery of hearts, the secrets of consciences, men's innermost thoughts; also the future and the end of anyone's life." We are told that he could read all of this with "marvelous lucidity and unrivaled clairvoyance."

Many other Saints were similarly blessed, but mystical knowledge also embraces a number of other exceptional abilities, such as that which enabled the unschooled ST. GERARD MAJELLA (d. 1755) to answer difficult questions concerning the Holy Trinity. Of him it was said, "In his mouth the most obscure mysteries became luminous."

Mystical knowledge would also explain how ST. ANTHONY OF PADUA (d. 1231) "knew the Holy Bible by heart," or how BL. JORDAN OF PISA (d. 1311) memorized "the Breviary, the Missal, the greater part of the Bible with its marginal notes, the second part of the *Summa* of St. Thomas and various other things."

Mystical knowledge would also account for the fact that some Saints knew of events that were taking place at a distance, or of past events that had taken place even in foreign countries, involving, in many instances, people the Saint had never met.

It must be noted that this gift of mystical knowledge was not given to the Saints for their own benefit, but was given solely for the spiritual benefit of those persons for whom it was exercised.

Many Saints possessed the above-mentioned forms of mystical knowledge and another form by which they knew the secret thoughts, sins and the condition of another's soul.

If Heaven permitted, this ability also allowed the gifted soul to tell the sinner the date, time and circumstances surrounding a forgotten sin that had not been confessed, or one that had been deliberately withheld from a past confession. The sinner, needless to relate, would be astounded that his hidden sin should be known to another, and in most cases would seek the confessional.

It would seem that confessors would have been given exclusive possession of mystical knowledge that would involve the revelation of sins and the condition of souls, yet a number of women Saints have been given this gift, which has helped many sinners to set their spiritual lives in order.

One of these women was ST. CATHERINE OF SIENA (d. 1380), who had a great reputation for miraculous conversions. One of these conversions involved a soldier of aristocratic family known as Niccolo dei Saracini, who had neglected the Sacrament of Penance for many years. Despite the efforts of his good wife to have him receive the Sacrament, he was totally engaged in the things of this world and laughed when she suggested that he speak with the Saint.

One night St. Catherine appeared to the soldier in a dream and warned him of eternal damnation and his need to confess his sins. Intrigued by the dream, he decided to visit the Saint to see if she had been the one who had appeared to him. He immediately recognized St. Catherine and promptly confessed his sins to the Saint's confessor, Fra Tommaso.

The soldier then wanted to speak with the Saint about other matters and told her of his confession. She seemed pleased, but then asked him if he had confessed everything he could remember. When he replied that he had, she again asked him to examine his conscience. After due consideration, he replied that he had mentioned all his sins. Taking the soldier aside, she reminded him of a certain sin which he had committed very secretly when he was in Apulia. When the soldier was reminded of the sin, he immediately returned to the confessional.

From that time on, he told everyone of the Saint's ability to read souls, saying, "Come and see the virgin who has told me of the sins I committed in distant parts. She reminded me of a sin that no one in the world knew of apart from myself."

Soon afterwards, the soldier became desperately ill and died before the end of the year, being well prepared.[1]

Bl. Raymond of Capua, St. Catherine's biographer, relates another case of mystical knowledge which involved Friar Giorgio Naddi and her confessor at the time, Fra Tommaso. Both men of

God decided to visit St. Catherine and borrowed two horses for the journey. They were well aware that their trek would take them into territories that were infested with thieves who often murdered their victims. Nothing happened along the way until they reached a narrowing in the road. There the friars were stopped by ten or twelve ruffians carrying swords and lances, who knocked both religious to the ground. After being robbed of what little they had, the religious were dragged into a thicket where, from all appearances, the thieves intended to kill them.

Fra Tommaso quickly appealed to St. Catherine: "Come to our aid in this tremendous danger." Suddenly, just as one of the thieves was about to murder him, the scoundrel said, "Why should we kill these good friars, who have never done us any harm? . . . Let us let them go in the name of the Lord . . ."

Surprisingly, all agreed. They returned to the friars their clothes, horses and all that had been stolen, except for a little money. When the two friars reached the convent of the Saint they told Bl. Raymond all that had taken place. Bl. Raymond writes:

> When Fra Tommaso got back to Siena, he discovered—as he relates in his writings and told me by word of mouth—that at the very hour, in fact at the very moment that he had prayed for help, the virgin, St. Catherine, had actually said to the companion who was with her at the time, "My Father (Fra Tommaso) is calling me, and I know that he is in great distress," and had got up and gone off to the place where she was accustomed to pray. In this way Fra Tommaso was saved by the prayers of the saint.[2]

Many of the visitors to the sickroom of ST. LYDWINE OF SCHIEDAM (d. 1433) were skeptical of the reports they had heard regarding her mystical gifts and decided to test her. Many of her gifts are recounted in this book, but the one that caused the most consternation among her visitors was that of reading their souls and disclosing to them transgressions known only to God and themselves.

One such visitor was a woman who actually "had relations with a demon" but who pretended virtue and claimed to be a virgin. St. Lydwine scoffed at the claim and exposed the hypocrite, who did not contradict the Saint, but left, furious at having been exposed.

A young girl who was a witness to this event questioned the Saint about her severity with the woman and was told by the Saint to make this experiment to prove the woman's worth. The young girl was to go to the woman's house and speak with her. If the woman listened patiently, it would prove that St. Lydwine was wrong. If the woman responded with rage, it would prove that the Saint was correct in her appraisal of the woman's sinful condition. The young girl did as the Saint suggested and was met with furious insults. The woman died soon afterward. When the Saint began praying for the woman, Lydwine's Guardian Angel revealed that "she is in the abyss from which there is no escape."

One visitor to St. Lydwine's sickroom was overwhelmed with her holiness and his own wretched sinfulness and felt compelled to mention his sins to her, perhaps in the hope that she would pray for him to overcome his failings. The visitor, Dom Angeli, recounted his sins through his tears, but out of shame withheld the sin of adultery. The Saint mentioned the sin to him, but he denied ever having committed it. During another visit the Saint confronted him with the sin, telling him the day, hour and place where it had been committed since their last conversation. To this Dom Angeli exclaimed, "Who has been able to reveal my misdeeds to you?" After crying for a time for having offended God, he promised to amend his ways, and did so.[3]

Another woman who had the gift of mystical knowledge was a widow, ST. HEDWIG (d. 1243), a native of Bavaria who was the mother of six children. One of her sons, Duke Henry II, led his army in 1340 against the Mongol Tartars who were plundering their way through Ruthenia and Poland. In what might be the first instance of chemical gas being used in wartime, such is reported to have happened in a great battle near Wahlstatt when "a thick and nauseating smoke, issuing from long copper tubes shaped like serpents, stupefied the Polish forces."

During this battle Henry was killed. St. Hedwig, a goodly distance away, knew that her son had been killed and announced it to her companion, Dermudis, saying: "I have lost my son. He has gone from me like a bird in flight and I shall never see him again in this life." A messenger arrived three days later with news of Henry's death—a fact already known by the grieving family.[4]

BL. MARY FORTUNATA VITI (d. 1922) was a Benedictine nun who spent more than seventy years as a religious in the cloister and died at the age of 95, having exhibited rare supernatural gifts. One was that of knowing the minds and hearts of others. This gift was once exercised in favor of a fellow sister, Maria Teresa Cianchetti. Before entering the convent and while working alone in her father's shop, Maria Teresa was threatened by a man with sinful intentions. Unable to escape, she picked up the first heavy object she could find and struck the man in the head. He did not die, but from that time on she was extremely distressed over her actions. She sought advice from many confessors, particularly those at two famous shrines, who reassured her that she had done nothing wrong—yet she maintained her distress, even to the cloister.

One day Bl. Mary Fortunata saw her deep in thought and approached her, saying, "Won't you try to get hold of yourself and remember what the confessors told you at Loretto and Casamari." Startled, the young nun asked how Bl. Mary Fortunata knew her problem and what to say. The old nun replied, "God told me." Maria Teresa adds, "She helped me to place all my trust in Him."[5]

A number of other women Saints have had the ability to know the condition of souls and distant events, but men, especially priests, have had the greater share of the gift.

One of these confessors was ST. FRANCIS OF PAOLA (d. 1507). This Saint is known as "God's Miracle Worker Supreme." When his reputation for miracles and supernatural gifts reached the ear of Pope Paul II in 1469, the Pope sent a chamberlain to inquire of the local archbishop if the rumors were correct. When the chamberlain, who was in disguise, and his companion approached St. Francis, who was busy with the stonemasons during the construction of a church, the Saint immediately left his work and, falling to his knees before the chamberlain, asked to kiss the hands which for thirty years had been sanctified by offering the Holy Sacrifice. The chamberlain was astounded that he, a stranger, had been identified as a priest by the Saint. After experiencing this display of supernatural knowledge and many others of a different nature, the chamberlain returned, full of veneration for the Saint. He reported to the Pope that St. Francis was even greater than his reputation.[6]

The Saint was also gifted with knowledge of events taking place at a distance. This gift was displayed when a young man named Ludicissa visited St. Francis of Paola in Naples in the hope that he would be permitted to accompany St. Francis on his trip to France. While the young man was making his request, the Saint tilted his head as if listening to something in the distance. When the young man attempted to hear what the Saint was listening to, he could not. St. Francis took him to a window overlooking the Gulf of Naples. It was then that Ludicissa heard bells in the distance. St. Francis explained, "These bells are tolling the death of your dear father. Accept the will of God, and return to your home without delay so that you can arrange your family's affairs." The young man left immediately for Spezzano, where the Saint's words were sadly confirmed.[7]

After the death of St. Francis of Paola an important testimonial of his holiness was given when his canonization was being considered. At that time the bishop of Grenoble wrote to Pope Leo X, "Most holy Father, he revealed to me many things which were known only to God and to myself."[8]

ST. PHILIP NERI (d. 1595), who is known as the Apostle of the city of Rome and who was the founder of the Congregation of the Oratory, also had the gift of reading souls and hearts. This gift was exercised frequently in the confessional when a sin had been forgotten or a penitent withheld the telling of a grievous sin out of shame. One time, when a young man found it difficult to describe a certain sin, the Saint had pity on him and revealed for him exactly how it had taken place.[9]

Another time when a penitent began his confession, the Saint started relating his sins for him and revealed the young man's secret thoughts. As a result, the young man placed himself under the spiritual direction of St. Philip. He became a priest and was later designated an archbishop and a cardinal.[10]

St. Philip was visited one day by a young man who brought along a friend named Rafaelle Lupo. The young man, hoping to effect Rafaelle's conversion, told the Saint that Rafaelle wanted to make a good confession. Since Rafaelle had not expressed this intention he was extremely indignant, but rather than cause a disturbance, he made a false confession. At the end, the Saint pressed Rafaelle's head to his heart and declared that the Holy Spirit had informed him that there was not a word of truth in all that he had confessed. Surprised by this revelation, Rafaelle made a general confession and later, on the Saint's advice, became a Franciscan friar.[11]

The humble lay brother ST. MARTIN DE PORRES (d. 1639) had many exceptional gifts, including that of knowing the needs of others. This was demonstrated many times when he appeared at homes with baskets of food desperately needed by the poor occupants, although no one had notified him of their need.

One case involved a poor woman who was in dire need of exactly six dollars. Knowing of St. Martin's supernatural powers, she prayed over and over again, "Br. Martin, I require your help in the great affliction in which I find myself." She continued her appeal in prayer when, to her amazement, the Saint appeared at her door and pressed into her hand the six dollars she so desperately needed.[12]

The Saint financially assisted so many of the poor that he became known as "the treasurer of the poor."

St. Martin was also alert to the difficulties experienced by the novices of his order. One day, two of the novices decided to leave the order and did so without notifying anyone. After the master of novices had searched everywhere for them, he notified St. Martin of the loss and was reassured by the Saint that they would soon return. After fervent prayer, the Saint secured permission of the superior to leave during the night to search for them.

Arriving at a place called Zervedo, a few miles distant, the Saint entered the locked room where the two young men had found refuge and found them quietly asleep. Startled by the Saint's mysterious appearance, they listened as he gently spoke of the beautiful life they were abandoning. They quickly repented and agreed to return.

It is reported that God rewarded their new resolve by speedily transporting them and the Saint to the Monastery of the Holy Rosary, where they entered without the doors being unlocked by the porter, and without any scandal being given. The next morning the novice master was surprised to see the two delinquents quietly assisting at the religious services of the community as though nothing unusual had taken place. The superior was also pleased that the matter had been resolved in such a speedy and quiet manner.[13] The two runaways confirmed St. Martin's prophecy that they would become worthy members of the order.

One example of the Saint's ability to know the secret activities of another involved the wife of a certain Agustin Galari, whom the Saint met as she was going into church one morning to hear Holy Mass. The Saint detained her for a moment and then asked her: "Do you think it is right for you to rob your husband by having a false key for his desk? Make haste and give me this key at once; and I will take care of all your wants." The woman was about to make a denial when she realized that only God could have revealed her secret to St. Martin. She gave the key to the Saint and promised not to steal from her husband again.[14]

Another example of his spiritual knowledge took place one night and involved a foreigner who was hospitalized in Lima. The man professed to be a Catholic, but it was later suspected that he did so in order that he might receive better treatment—yet the man had never been baptized.

St. Martin, supernaturally enlightened about the matter, rushed to the hospital one night and insisted on speaking with him. In his customarily gentle manner, the Saint spoke about the condition of his soul and urged the man to repent. The foreigner soon begged for Baptism and, if one may interpret the urgency of the Saint in this matter, the foreigner died soon afterward with the blessings of the Church.[15]

ST. JOSEPH OF CUPERTINO (d. 1663) is known for his many levitations and other mystical gifts, including that of knowing the consciences and sins of those with whom he came in contact. He would often approach people to remind them to confess hidden sins. When they replied that they were not conscious of any hidden sins, the Saint would reveal the time, place and circumstances of the offenses against God.

Such was the case when he advised a novice to write his general confession. While reading it the Saint remarked, "My son, here you have not expressed yourself well; for it was not as you have written here . . ." The Saint then proceeded to describe the sins and the circumstances surrounding them.[16]

The Saint always received a heavenly light by which he knew if certain persons had withheld sins in the confessional. To these he would say, "Go wash your face, which you have sullied with ink," or other expressions which were understood by the guilty.

The Saint was also aware when these sinners had confessed to another priest, even though no words concerning the matter had been expressed.[17]

St. Joseph of Cupertino not only read consciences and hidden sins, but he also knew the faults and failings of the novices of his order.

On numerous occasions they were amazed when he revealed their hidden faults and exactly described certain distractions they had entertained when they should have been praying. Such was the case when a novice was dreaming of climbing a fig tree and eating his fill. The Saint exactly described the distraction and gently reproved him for it.

He was likewise aware of good deeds performed in secret and often knew of penances performed by certain persons. We are told that he once thanked a lady named Elizabeth for having recited a *Salve Regina* for him.

He also mentioned to another person that he was aware of certain mortifications which she had practiced. Other times, he was aware of troubling anxieties. Such was the case when Cardinal Rapaccioli, Bishop of Terni, was about to write the Saint for spiritual direction. The Cardinal was surprised to receive a letter from the Saint giving his opinions on the as yet unasked questions.[18]

St. Joseph was also aware of events that were taking place at a distance. One case involved the Father General of his order, who was traveling near the village of Monte Falco when the mule he was riding became frightened and threw the holy cleric from a bridge into the water below. During his fall, Father General commended himself to St. Joseph of Cupertino, who was then still living. The next time St. Joseph saw the cleric, who had escaped harm, the Saint said: "Certainly, my dear Father General, you were in great peril; for you had a dangerous fall at ten o'clock, just as I was saying Mass, and I prayed to God for you."[19]

One of the biographers of St. Joseph of Cupertino relates that the Saint knew of sick persons at a great distance who had regained their health and that he knew when both Pope Urban VIII and Innocent X had died. The biographer further relates that:

> Many other instances of his knowledge of things that had happened long before or at a great distance, could be adduced on sworn testimony of trustworthy witnesses.[20]

Similar abilities were known of ST. FRANCIS OF ASSISI (d. 1226). Thomas of Celano, one of his early biographers, writes:

> How often, without any man telling him, but by means of a revelation of the Holy Spirit, Francis knew the

actions of his absent brothers, laid open the secrets of their hearts, and explored their consciences! Of how many he admonished in their sleep, commanded them things to be done, forbade things not to be done! Of how many did he not predict future evils, though their present conduct seemed good! Thus, knowing in many cases that certain brothers would end their evil ways, he foretold the future grace of salvation for them.[21]

Thomas of Celano includes in his biography of St. Francis many instances of the Saint knowing the thoughts of his brethren so that, by the grace of God, he was able to give advice to the confused before the matter was told, or had a solution to a problem before it was presented.

BL. ANTHONY GRASSI (d. 1671) had the gift of reading consciences, not just in generalities, but in specific terms, according to the declarations made for the process of his beatification. Convincing testimony proved that he could not possibly have known, by natural means, of the details he revealed to penitents in the confessional and to those who came to him for spiritual direction. As he grew older, his knowledge of future events and of those taking place at a distance increased, so that it was a consolation to many—and to others a warning.[22]

ST. GERARD MAJELLA (d. 1755), the holy Redemptorist, also could detect the sins of certain persons. He was once in the gallery of a church during Holy Mass when he quickly left his place and hurried to the altar rail to remove a man who was about to make a sacrilegious Communion. Taking the man aside, the Saint explained the nature of the grievous sin he was about to commit and revealed to him the sins he had deliberately withheld from confession. The man, filled with repentance, left the church, declaring that such was the case and crying aloud, "I was ashamed to confess my sins to the priest, but Br. Gerard revealed them to me. Now I wish, to my own confusion, to confess them to the whole world." He would have related his sins to those outside the church, had not a priest restrained him.[23]

On another occasion St. Gerard approached the notary, De Robertis of Muro, and without the usual pleasantries promptly declared that the man's conscience was in a bad state since he had refused to confess the sin of murder. The Saint even revealed that the sin had been committed under a cherry tree in the man's vineyard. The unexpected and precise revelation had its effect, in that the man promptly confessed the sin in the confessional. Afterwards the notary would declare, "Yes, Gerard is a great saint. He revealed to me what was known only to God and myself."[24]

In addition to revealing sins, St. Gerard Majella also had the ability to read souls and hearts. We are told about a young man, a consumptive named Nicholas Benincasa, who was often in the Saint's company. Having witnessed the many miracles of healing performed by the Saint, he was one day wondering why the Saint did not pray for the restoration of his health, since the Saint knew quite well the dangerous state of his condition. He had scarcely finished the thought when the Saint turned and remarked that he did indeed pray for him, but that God did not wish to cure him, adding, "You are not for this world." The young man died soon after his thoughts had been read by the holy Redemptorist.[25]

Another time, after a two-month effort, several priests grew weary of attempting to exorcise a woman who seemed to be terribly tormented by demons. When Gerard Majella saw the woman, he declared that she was not possessed. Taking her aside, he told her to stop her antics or he would make everything known. The woman, thoroughly frightened, never again feigned diabolical possession.[26]

We are told that St. Gerard detested the practice of some men who pretended to be crippled in order to live on the charity of others. On one occasion the Saint saw a man dragging himself along on his crutches, one leg bandaged in old rags, pleading for alms from the pious who were on the road leading to a convent. Outraged by such deception, Gerard approached the man, tore off his bandages and ordered the man to stop the pretense for the good of his soul. "Beholding his fraud discovered, the pretended cripple ran off on both legs, forgetful even of his crutches."[27]

St. Gerard Majella read hearts and thoughts so frequently, and sent so many sinners back to the confessional to confess sins they had deliberately withheld, that a whole chapter could be written about his experiences. Suffice it to say that he was regarded as a Saint during his lifetime and that many souls were saved because of his spiritual gifts.

Fraud was also detected by ST. PAUL OF THE CROSS (d. 1775). However, the person in question was not a beggar, as in the life of St. Gerard Majella, but a certain married woman who was constantly in prayer and who professed to receiving visions and favors from God and the Blessed Virgin. "Everyone believed this, and even her own director looked upon her as a saint." In time she was sent to St. Paul, who was not yet ordained, for him to consult with her. After listening patiently to all she said and after pondering her words carefully, he reported that the woman's experiences were completely unreliable. Everyone defended the woman, claiming that St. Paul was incorrect. They continued believing in the woman until clear signs were given that the woman was indeed experiencing illusions.[28]

The Saint also had knowledge of situations taking place at a distance, such as the time that wives of some poor sailors at Gaeta were deeply distressed because it had been months since they had heard from their husbands. In desperation they went to the Saint, who was living in Gaeta at the time, and implored him to pray for the safe return of their husbands. St. Paul immediately prayed and then saw the condition of the men. He told the afflicted women that the ship had fallen into the hands of the Turks, who would have made their husbands slaves, except for the grace of God. It is said that this escape from captivity was effected by the prayers of the Saint. St. Paul gave the women the welcome news that the vessel with their husbands and all on board would return safely in four days. All took place exactly as the Saint had revealed.

St. Paul not only knew the condition of souls and their forgotten or unconfessed sins, but also correctly advised many on the correct course they should take in spiritual and temporal matters. In addition, he also knew those who had a religious vocation. Such was the case during his occasional lodgings in the home of Signor Ercolani, his benefactor, who had a daughter named Elizabeth, who was about eight years of age when the Saint first started visiting. St. Paul would call the child his little nun, a name that the child disliked to the point of tears. Yet the Saint continued using the name until the child insisted during the years that she would never enter religious life. Even the mother thought Elizabeth would never be a nun because of her daughter's frequent illnesses. To this the Saint replied: "Never mind, the Blessed Virgin will see to that." To the child he once said, "Do not be afraid; they won't make you prioress."

Elizabeth continued her aversion to the religious life until she was nineteen years old, when she suddenly realized a calling to serve God in the cloister. She entered a convent at Vetralla, never became prioress and died after many happy years in the service of God.[29]

Another time, while visiting in Rome, St. Paul of the Cross called upon Signora Margherita Sabatini, who presented her three sons to the Saint for his blessing. As the Saint blessed the first boy he remarked, "What a fine friar this one will make." To the second boy he revealed: "This one will remain at home." He caressed the third boy, the youngest, and said, "This one is a little angel." It happened that the first boy became a Franciscan friar; the second married; the third child died soon after the blessing.[30]

Even bishops consulted St. Paul. One in particular asked the Saint's opinion about his intention to ordain his nephew and to renounce in his favor his own rich bishopric. St. Paul expressed his disapproval of the plan, citing the reason that the plan was in consideration of affection and blood, and not by the spirit of God. The bishop was dissatisfied with the Saint's opinion, and in spite of it, the bishop ordained his nephew. When St. Paul heard of the ordination, he is said to have shrugged his shoulders and to have prophesied, "He will never get what his uncle intends for him." And so it happened that the bishop died before making his renunciation, leaving the nephew to remain a poor priest for the rest of his life.[31]

ST. JOHN MARIE BAPTISTE VIANNEY, who is more affectionately known as the Curé of Ars (d. 1859), spent from sixteen to eighteen hours in the confessional each day. We are assured that many were the penitents which the holy Saint assisted in the revelation of their sins, which were known to the Saint through Divine inspiration.

One such incident, recorded by a nun who was a witness, took place in 1853. During that year a happy group of men set out on a pilgrimage to Ars to attend the Holy Mass of the Saint. They were all devout Catholics, except for an older man who had joined them. After reaching their destination they entered the church, while the older man remained in the back. At about that time the Saint came out of the sacristy and entered the chancel. He knelt down, stood up and turned toward the back of the church, looking in the direction of the holy water font. Then he signalled for the older man to come forward. According to the nun, the older man, greatly embarrassed, proceeded toward the Saint, who asked him how long it had been since he confessed. The man replied that it had been thirty years. The Saint corrected him, saying that it had been exactly thirty-three years, and then revealed the town where his last confession had taken place.[32]

Because of the holy Curé's gift of knowledge, the number of penitents was such that there was always a long line waiting to confess. These lines were so long that many had to wait thirty, fifty, even seventy hours before reaching the confessional. When the church was about to be locked for the night, the people numbered themselves and assumed their position the next day.[33]

There was one young lady named Louise Dortan, who had never met the Curé, who arrived at the church to confess and consult the Saint on the subject of her vocation. After waiting three days in line, she was about to leave in despair of ever seeing the Saint when he approached her and said, "You are not very patient, my child, you have been here only three days and you want to go home? Remain fifteen days and go pray to St. Philomena, who will tell you about your vocation." The young lady did so, and later became Sr. Marie of Jesus.[34]

From the *Proces de l'Ordinaire* we are told about the mother of sixteen children who was in line, but quite a distance from the holy tribunal, when the Saint left the confessional and pointed to her to come forward, saying, "You, madame, you are in a hurry. Come at once!" To another woman who was about to leave the church after being in line a long time, the Saint sent a messenger to fetch the lady and told how she could be identified. When the messenger, M. Oriol, could not find her, he returned. This time the Saint replied, "Run quickly. She is in front of . . ." and he described the house where she could be found. According to M. Oriol, "I ran and overtook the lady, who was going away, grievously disappointed, for she could wait no longer."[35]

On another occasion, there was a poor woman who was too timid to assert herself when, on two or three occasions, others slipped before her in line. She had been in Ars eight days when she was about to leave the church. The Saint himself made his way through the crowd to the back of the church and told her to follow him. "Quite happy now, she held onto his cassock and slipped through the passage he opened for her."[36]

According to M. Claude Rougemon, who was the vicar of Ars in

1871, the Saint often drew from the line certain persons who were invited to confess before the others. "These he had seen by means of an interior light that it was necessary that they should speak to him without further delay." To the complaints that arose because of this, the Saint replied, "I am accused of being somewhat easy with certain pilgrims. Surely I must take into account the trouble it cost them to come from so far and the expense to which they are put. There are some who come secretly and who do not wish to be recognized; these are in a great hurry to leave."[37]

The Curé of Ars' biographer, Abbe Francis Trochu, writes: "How blessed was the holy Curé to know such unspoken matters about his penitents, and how charitable and considerate he was in all situations."

Other spiritual gifts were also given to the holy Curé, such as that exercised by ST. ANTHONY MARY CLARET (d. 1870), who knew the sins of those with whom he came in contact. Such was the case one day while he was walking near Manresa and met a woman on the road whose sinful life was revealed to him by God. After a polite conversation, the Saint mentioned certain immoral sins she had committed and her need for confession. Surprised that this priest, who was unknown to her, could mention her hidden sins, she hastened to confess these offenses against God, and from that time onward led an exemplary and fervent life.[38]

It was not only the consciences of sinners that were revealed to him, but the dispositions of consecrated souls. So it was in Vich that St. Claret was giving the Spiritual Exercises to the Discalced Carmelite nuns. As Mother Prioress, Sr. Maria Esperanza of the Conception relates:

> Fr. Claret had heard our confessions. He told us in one of his conferences not to be uneasy about these confessions because at that very moment he was reading our consciences. All of us have experienced that he was telling the truth; he knew the faults of each one better than the interested person.[39]

This ability to read consciences in an extraordinary way was also a gift of ST. JOHN BOSCO (d. 1888), who relates:

I see consciences in the confessional as if they were open books. That happens especially on the eves of great feasts and at the close of retreats . . . This facility in reading the depths of the heart is granted me by God at intervals of greater or lesser length . . . Give me a young man I have never seen; I have merely to look him in the face to reveal to him the faults he has committed since his earliest childhood.[40]

This ability to read the thoughts of others was demonstrated in a significant way in 1858 and took place in this fashion. Mr. deCamburzano, ex-deputy of Nice, was speaking one day with a group of distinguished people about the Saint's mystical powers when a lady in the gathering decided to try an experiment, saying: "If this worthy man will be so good as to reveal to me the state of my conscience, I shall then be ready to believe anything you like." Her proposal was met with a round of applause.

The experiment took the form of a letter written to the Saint in which the woman mentioned nothing about the test nor gave any hint of what was expected of him. The Saint's reply to the letter was this: "One, go back to your husband; two, renew your confession since . . . (a period of almost twenty years). When you have done these two things, you can be easy in your mind."

The woman, a person whom the Saint had never met, declared that the Saint's God-given ability to read her thoughts was proven by these two revelations.[41]

St. John Bosco also knew when an act of charity was performed or a secret mortification was offered to God. Such was the case when the Saint met one of the students. As the boy relates,

One day I had done an act of charity which had cost me a good deal. God alone had witnessed it. How astonished I was to hear Don Bosco, as soon as we met, say to me: "Oh, what a pearl for paradise you have won by your sacrifice!" I asked, "What sacrifice?" And the act which I believed was known to God only, he described in full detail.[42]

Not only did the Saint know the good deeds of the boys in his school, but also their misdeeds, an ability he demonstrated time and time again. One such example took place while the Saint was hearing confessions. After one boy confessed, the Saint asked him to go to the loft of a building, where he would find a certain lad smoking. "Call him and tell him to come to Confession." The boy climbed to the third floor and found the other smoking, just as the Saint had said he would be. A few minutes later the guilty boy was seen making his way to where the Saint was waiting for him.[43]

Many other times Don Bosco saw at a distance his students at mischief or deserting prayertime for activities they found more satisfying, or leaving services prematurely. The Saint once sighed, "Poor children! How little do they think of their souls!"

The order founded by St. John Bosco was named for St. Francis de Sales, to whom he had great devotion and whom he admired greatly. Popularly known as the Salesians, the order developed as a result of John Bosco's work in educating and spiritually directing boys and young men. Among the other marvels worked by the Saint, which were frequently witnessed by the students, was the Saint's ability to discover hidden sins and to relate all the sins of his penitents so that it was practically impossible to leave his confessional with any grave sin on one's conscience.

The gift of knowing about events taking place at a distance, as related above in the lives of some of the Saints, was also a gift of ST. GODRIC (d. 1170). According to the monk Reginald, who often visited the Saint and who wrote his biography, which is still extant, St. Godric often turned from his activities to pray for those whom he knew were in imminent danger of death—especially sailors who were about to be shipwrecked.[44]

ST. ALPHONSUS LIGUORI (d. 1787), bishop, confessor, founder of the Redemptorist Order and Doctor of the Church, was also the author of numerous spiritual books and the possessor of many spiritual gifts. Like a number of the Saints mentioned above,

> He was permitted a knowledge of secret and hidden
> things, and frequently told those around him of some
> event taking place at a distance that could not have been
> known without a supernatural inspiration from God.[45]

Two proofs of the Saint's ability to know of events at a distance were duly verified. One took place in March, 1786, when St. Alphonsus foretold the death of Rev. Alexander de Meo, who was suddenly stricken with apoplexy while in the pulpit, and in October of the same year, the Saint had knowledge that his friend, Fr. Caputo, was dying at Naples.

BL. MARY OF OIGNIES (d. 1213) also knew of events taking place at a distance. Cardinal James de Vitry, who was a spiritual son of Bl. Mary and who was her biographer, tells that Mary, while remaining in Brabant, knew of the ordination of a dear friend, which took place at Paris. She related to the cardinal all she had seen, the vestments he had worn, where he had stood, how he had been anointed and even his thoughts and disposition. She immediately sent a letter to him by messenger in which she wrote: "A new tree is now in bloom, the first fruits of which God has destined for me."

The newly ordained did not understand its meaning until he journeyed to see her. "And, indeed, it so happened by the direction of Heaven, that though he had purposed to celebrate his first Mass in France, yet he actually did so in Oignies, and this holy woman was present at it." Because of this rearrangement of plans, Bl. Mary received the first fruits from the "new tree."[46]

ST. VINCENT PALLOTTI (d. 1850) is the founder of the Society of the Catholic Apostolate, which is also known as the Pallottine Fathers. His deep spirituality and his many mystical favors were well known, including that of knowing future events. Such was the case when he called a young boy from play and asked him if he would like to make his confession. The boy humorously protested, saying that there was plenty of time the next day. The boy, in fact, made his confession before he left the priest, and although seemingly in robust health, he died suddenly during the night.

Another time, while a Conclave was being conducted to elect a new pope, St. Vincent announced that Cardinal Cappellari, Pope Gregory XVI, had been nominated. An hour later this fact was confirmed when it was publicly announced.[47]

In Canada, the great promoter of devotion to St. Joseph and the driving force behind the building of the great basilica on Mount

Royal was also a miracle worker and one who possessed many mystical favors. Beatified in 1982, he is known as BL. ANDRÉ (Alfred Bessette) (d. 1937). Many were the gifts of healing that he performed with oil that he took from a lamp burning before the image of St. Joseph. And in the cases when he knew death would take place according to the will of God, pain and fever were diminished through his prayers. In these cases he would know the exact time of death.

Arthur Ganz was witness to a visit made by Bl. André to a little girl eleven years old. Dr. Letendre was in attendance and had diagnosed the child's condition as meningitis. After a moment, Bl. André mentioned to the doctor that the child's temperature was now normal. The doctor gently protested that her temperature was higher than a child would normally survive. When the doctor again took the child's temperature, it was indeed normal. Thinking that the Brother had saved her child's life, the mother expressed her gratitude, but Bl. André told her quietly, "Madame, your child will die tomorrow morning between eight o'clock and half past eight, but she will not suffer." The next morning the child died at exactly 8:22. When told of the child's death, Bl. André replied quietly, "I know it."[48]

On another occasion Bl. André visited a young man in the hospital who was very ill with tuberculosis. After praying with him, Bl. André rubbed his chest with St. Joseph's oil. Almost immediately the young man's temperature dropped to normal and his sufferings came to an end. Bl. André warned, however, that he would die "a week from today, but do not be afraid. St. Joseph is watching over you, and you will not suffer." The young man died exactly as Blessed André knew he would.[49]

Monsieur Michel Albert Trudel, who often accompanied him on his trips, once explained: "For myself, I believe that it was not that Bl. André had a knowledge of the future, but that he was in constant contact with St. Joseph, who put the words on his lips."[50]

Another beatus who knew the date and time of another's death was BL. PETER OF TIFERNO (d. 1445), but because of a fire that destroyed the archives of the friary of Cortona, little is known of him. What is known is that at the age of fifteen he received the Dominican habit and was instructed by many famous friars, including Fra Angelico and St. Antoninus. Several of his miracles are remembered, and his ability to read consciences was also evident. One such event took place when he met a young man on the street. Bl. Peter stopped him and said, "What wickedness are you up to now? How much longer are you going on adding sin to sin? You have twenty-four hours to live, and at this time tomorrow you will have to give God an account of your sins." The young man was no doubt startled by this declaration, but after a moment of concern, took no more notice of it. That night he had a bad accident. Bl. Peter was hurriedly sent for and heard the young man's confession moments before the penitent died.[51]

The humble lay brother, BL. FRANCIS OF CAMPOROSSO (d. 1866), of the Friars Minor Conventual, who had the assignment of begging in the city of Genoa for the needs of his fellow religious, was a familiar figure in the dockyards and in the city, where he was well known for his sanctity. He was frequently stopped so that people could ask him for news of their friends and relatives who were overseas. The information he gave of people he had never met, in places far distant, always proved to be correct.[52]

A similar gift was possessed by PADRE PIO (d. 1968), who exercised it frequently during the Second World War when worried parents asked about the welfare of their sons who were on the battlefield.

This knowledge even extended to the other world, as when one worried mother asked about her missing son. Padre Pio replied, "Poor son, he suffered so much! He suffers no longer. We must resign ourselves to the will of God." Later the Red Cross notified Signora Gagliardi that her son Italo had been killed in action.

Padre Pio's knowledge of souls in the other world was again exercised when another worried mother asked about her son, who was also missing in action. Padre Pio paused for a moment and then said, "He must be alive, for I cannot find him in the other world." Eventually the son returned home.[53]

Many such accounts are given in which Padre Pio relieved the minds of the worried, or consoled those who grieved.[54] Many peacetime cases are given in which he knew of distant occurrences. For example, there was one Silvio Scocca, who often visited Padre Pio and was about to leave on another visit. While on the way he stopped at the home of his Aunt Mary, who knew Padre Pio, to see if she had any messages for the holy Padre. She prepared coffee for Silvio and then penned a note, which Silvio put in his pocket. When he arrived at the friary he went to confession and was asked by Padre Pio how things were in Pietrelcina. After a little discussion, Silvio was silent. The Padre asked, "Is there anything else?" Silvio answered, "No." Padre Pio then continued, "You had coffee with Aunt Mary and she gave you a letter for me, and you say you have nothing more to say!" Silvio had forgotten the letter, which he promptly handed to the holy priest.[55]

One more case involved Alberto Cardone, who visited the Padre in May of 1944 and asked about certain relatives. One was his father, but he purposely did not tell Padre Pio that he was in the United States. Alberto was astonished when Padre Pio replied, "Your father is in America and is better than you or I." Alberto then asked about his uncle Francesco, who was with the Italian army in Libya and had not been heard from in a long time. Padre Pio replied, "It could be he is a prisoner. When you get home, maybe you will hear some good news." When Alberto returned home from the visit he found a letter from his uncle Francesco in which he revealed he was a prisoner in England and was working as a cook. "He eventually returned home in excellent health and spirits."[56]

These are but a few instances of Padre Pio's gift of distant knowledge. Many, many more are given in his biographies.

The list of those who possessed these gifts of knowledge is lengthy, but to mention a few more, we have BL. FRANCIS OF POSADAS (d. 1713), whose preaching was rivaled only by his gifts as a confessor. Known for reading the hearts of his penitents and visitors, he also revealed in the confessional sins that had been deliberately concealed. He was also led interiorly to the bedside of the dying who were in need of the Last Sacraments.[57]

BL. FULCO OF NEUILLY (d. 1201) also had exceptional gifts, as did ST. JOHN OF SAHAGUN (d. 1479), who "was endowed with a judicious discernment and with an extraordinary gift for reading the secret thoughts of his penitents."[58]

It is said that ST. JOHN JOSEPH OF THE CROSS (d. 1734) "could read the thoughts of those who came to consult him as clearly as though they had been written words."[59]

Some might think that the Saints mentioned above violated the seal of confession by divulging these facts regarding their penitents' confessions or the state of their souls. This was not the case. The privacy of the penitents was respected in all the cases. The penitents themselves, surprised at being told their sins by priests they did not know, eventually divulged the facts in order to indicate the power of God in giving this gift for the salvation of their souls. Moreover, the gift of spiritual knowledge was given to these holy persons solely for the benefit of those for whom it was exercised.

We will conclude this chapter with the case of POPE ST. PIUS V (d. 1572), who was one day discussing important business with Cardinals when he rose from his chair, left the table and went to the window, which he opened. For a moment his eyes were fixed on the sky. Then, returning to the table, he announced: "It is not now a time to talk about affairs, however pressing; it is the time to give thanks to Almighty God for the signal victory at the Battle of Lepanto which He has vouchsafed to the Christians over the Turks." It was established that the Pope had made his announcement at the exact time the battle was being won decisively. The Cardinals in attendance carefully recorded the time and words of the Pope, which attested to the authenticity of his experience of mystical knowledge.

St. Veronica Giuliani

Bl. Angela of Foligno

St. Ignatius Loyola

St. John Bosco

—Part II—

THE MIRACULOUS BODIES
OF THE SAINTS AFTER DEATH

St. Nicholas of Tolentino

St. Patricia

Ven. Mary of Agreda

St. Catherine of Siena

THE INCORRUPTIBLES

What is perhaps the most unusual phenomenon regarding the bodies of Saints is that of the preservation of a great number of them after being interred for years in conditions that should have provoked their destruction according to the laws of nature. All of the bodies mentioned in this chapter were *not* embalmed, with the exception of one unusual preservation. In spite of not being embalmed or treated in any fashion, the bodies remained lifelike, flexible and often sweetly scented many years after death. Many are now displayed under altars in glass-fronted reliquaries, to the admiration and wonder of many.

According to natural laws, moisture in the body or in the atmosphere of the tomb is the chief reason for the decomposition of the body. Yet the bodies of many Saints have survived this condition, as well as other unfavorable conditions. We will here examine those remains that were subjected not only to moisture, but to the application of quicklime, and one whose mutilated condition should have hastened the body's destruction.

Since this subject is more thoroughly explained in the author's Introduction to her book, *The Incorruptibles,* we will pass over further examination of it and proceed to relating the wonders associated with the blessed bodies of God's special friends.

There is, for instance, the case of ST. CATHERINE OF SIENA (d. 1380), who died at the age of thirty-three. She experienced many mystical favors and labored tirelessly for the interests of the Church and the Apostolic See.

Bl. Raymond of Capua, the Saint's confessor and first biographer, relates that after her death, large crowds visited her remains, "and those who succeeded in touching them, considered themselves highly favored." Three days following her death she was buried in the cemetery adjoining the Church of Santa Maria Sopra Minerva. Sometime later Bl. Raymond had the casket removed and placed at the foot of a column facing the Rosary Chapel.

Bl. Raymond at this time had the casket opened and wrote that the opening of it was:

> . . . a thing easily done, as in point of fact it was not actually buried beneath the ground and [he] found that the clothes had suffered somewhat from the dampness of the place where the body was deposited, and where it was much exposed to the rain.[1]

In spite of the damp garments against the skin of the Saint, the body was not affected. Since churches were requesting relics of the body, parts were removed and distributed, especially to those churches that had been dedicated to her memory.

ST. CATHERINE OF GENOA (d. 1510) was entombed in the hospital chapel where she had labored for many years in the service of the poor. Eighteen months later it was discovered that a conduit of water ran behind the wall near the tomb. To determine if the casket of the Saint had been affected by the moisture, an exhumation was conducted. These fears were realized when the casket was found in a deplorable condition due to the moisture, but to the surprise of all present, the body of the Saint was found perfectly incorrupt, even though the shroud was thoroughly moist. Following an examination and re-clothing of the body, it was left exposed for eight days in the chapel to satisfy the devotion and curiosity of the faithful.

The body is now enshrined in a glass-sided reliquary high atop the main altar of the church built in her honor in Genoa, Italy. The shrine of the Saint recorded for the author: "The conservation is truly exceptional and surprising and deserves an analysis of the cause. The surprise of the faithful is justified when they attribute this to a supernatural cause."[2]

Nine months after the death of ST. TERESA OF AVILA (d. 1582) the nuns of her community wondered about the condition of her body and the heavenly perfume surrounding her tomb. The provincial of the order, Father Jerome Gracian, gave permission for the exhumation of the body and described the proceedings in this manner:

> The coffin lid was smashed, half rotten and full of mildew, the smell of damp was very pungent . . . The clothes had also fallen to pieces . . . The holy body was covered with the earth which had penetrated into the coffin and so was all damp too, but as fresh and whole as if it had only been buried the day before.[3]

After the washing and re-clothing of the body, ". . . there spread through the whole house a wonderful penetrating fragrance which lasted some days . . ."[4]

Three years later the body was thoroughly examined by two doctors in the presence of the community and the bishop. The doctors declared the condition of the body to be

> truly miraculous . . . for after three years, without having been embalmed, it was in such a perfect state of preservation that nothing was wanting to it in any way, and a wonderful odour issued from it.

This in spite of the mildew and moisture that had visited the remains for the original nine months of its entombment.[5] The body remains incorrupt.

When the Cause for the Beatification of ST. CHARLES BOR-ROMEO (d. 1584) was underway, delegates from Rome were sent to Milan for the identification of his body. The Saint had been buried under the pavement in the middle of the cathedral of which he had served as archbishop. The authorities found that the "natural humidity of the place . . . had corroded the cover of both coffins (of lead and another of wood) . . . and allowed the moisture to penetrate even to the corpse."

Even so, they found that "the body was still preserved in spite of the condition to which the coffins had been reduced . . . After being re-vested, the body was placed in a new coffin and entombed." This exhumation of the body took place twenty years and four months after the death of St. Charles Borromeo.

The body is still preserved and can be found in a jewel-like reliquary of rock crystal which is found in a magnificent oratory in the Cathedral of Milan. During an examination of the body in 1880, it was discovered that the body had been embalmed, but this was not held directly responsible for the preservation of the body almost three hundred years after the Saint's death.[6]

One year following the death of ST. MARY MAGDALEN DE PAZZI (d. 1607) the sweet odors that emanated from her tomb beneath the high altar of the church of the monastery prompted the community to exhume the body. A biographer reports:

> When the casket was opened, the corpse was found to be still entire, fresh-looking and fleshlike in its softness. Blond hairs still adhered to the head; the whole body was flexible. The Saint appeared as one recently deceased. Yet the clothing was wet, for the place of burial was a damp one with running water nearby.[7]

The body of the Saint remains incorrupt, surrounded by crystal in her artistically crafted shrine which is located in the Carmelite Church of Florence, Italy.

The body of ST. MADELEINE SOPHIE BARAT (d. 1865), the foundress of the Society of the Sacred Heart, was exhumed 28 years after her death for the recognition required for the advancement of her Cause for beatification. In the presence of distinguished witnesses they discovered that:

> The coffin, which was falling to pieces owing to the damp of the vault, was with great difficulty lifted out, chiefly through the help of a faithful old servant who had seen it placed there twenty-eight years earlier. It was feared that scarcely anything would be found intact when Msgr. Caprara cried, "See, the veil is hanging from her head," and when the debris of wood and the mildewed garments were removed, the body was found entire, the features quite recognizable . . . the slender fingers still clasping a small crucifix.[8]

Still incorrupt, the body is now found in Jette, Belgium.

One of the most amazing preservations is one that took place at the turn of the century. It is the case of ST. CHARBEL

MAKHLOUF, who died in 1898. Having entered the Monastery of St. Maroun at Annaya, Lebanon, he began his studies for the priesthood and after ordination spent sixteen years as a member of the community. He lived the next twenty-three years in the Hermitage of Saints Peter and Paul, a little distance from the monastery. He was especially devoted to the Holy Eucharist and was stricken with a fatal illness while saying Holy Mass. Burial of the body took place in the monastic cemetery, where many saintly monks before him had been buried. According to the Rule of the monastery, the body was not embalmed and was consigned to the grave without a coffin. Because of a mysteriously bright light that surrounded the tomb for forty-five nights, and due to the curiosity of the people, ecclesiastical authorities who witnessed the phenomenon gave permission to exhume the body, a ceremony which took place four months following the Saint's death.

When the grave was opened in the presence of the superiors of the order, the monks of the monastery and many villagers, the body was found to be in perfect condition, in spite of frequent rains that had deluged the cemetery several times since the burial. In fact, the body was actually found floating in mud in a flooded grave.[9] Since the unembalmed body had been assaulted by this abundant moisture for four months, who can explain its preservation?

Another mystifying event took place sometime later, after the body was cleaned and re-clothed in fresh garments. From the pores of the body a liquid exuded which is described in another chapter of this book entitled "Manna."

The body of this holy hermit produced this manna and remained whole, entire, and had every appearance of an elderly man who was sleeping, for almost sixty-six years, until the time of his beatification on December 5, 1965. Only the bones now remain, and these are of a distinctive reddish color.

The incorrupt bodies mentioned above were all exposed to moisture, which would hasten destruction. However, the body of ST. JOSAPHAT (d. 1623) was actually "buried" in water, and it later experienced moisture in the tomb, yet the conservation of his body was maintained.

Born in Vladimir, Poland, the Saint entered the Order of St. Basil the Great, was ordained and quickly advanced in the order, culminating in his consecration as the Archbishop of Polotsk in 1617.

Josaphat labored gallantly on behalf of the Roman Primacy, but in the process secured many enemies among the Orthodox factions who refused allegiance to the papacy.

During one of his sermons he announced that he was willing to sacrifice his life for the cause of Church unity if it pleased God. Perhaps inspired by the Saint's remark, the unfaithful Orthodox factions antagonized the supporters of the bishop. During the confusion that followed, the dissenters stormed the bishop's residence, hacked and beat the bishop to death, and threw his remains in a nearby river.

The martyrdom took place on a Sunday, with the water "burial" taking place the next day. The body remained in the river until the following Friday. It was retrieved by St. Josaphat's followers, who found it normal in all respects, in spite of the ordeal it had experienced during its five-day submersion. The mutilated body was interred at Biala in Podlesie.

Because of the many miracles taking place through Josaphat's intercession, King Sigmund, together with Ukrainian and Polish ecclesiastics and civil authorities, petitioned Pope Urban VIII for Josaphat's canonization. During the ecclesiastical process the identification of the remains took place. It had been five years since the death of the martyred archbishop, yet his body—in spite of the water "burial"—was found perfectly incorrupt and pliable, although the vestments and interior clothes had rotted away because of the dampness of the tomb.

To satisfy the great crowd of people who flocked to the church to view the miracle, the body was dressed in new vestments and was actually propped in a sitting position upon the episcopal throne for all to see.

An emotional event took place when the Bishop of Milton, George Tishkevick, raised the right hand of the dead archbishop and blessed the throng. At that moment, on the face of the Saint, miraculous droplets of moisture developed, which were collected on handkerchiefs as precious relics.

The body was again examined in 1637. When a magnificent reliquary was crafted and presented in 1650, the body was exhumed once more. In addition to the body's preservation, another wonder was presented when the mortal wound on the forehead of the Saint opened and discharged fresh red blood.[10] This was truly an amazing occurrence, since the Saint had been dead twenty-seven years.

Josaphat Kuncevyc, "The Apostle of Union," was canonized in 1867 by Pope Leo XIII.

Next we will consider the amazing results after the deliberate and speedy destruction of the bodies of three Saints was attempted. With regard to the remains of St. Francis Xavier and St. John of the Cross, the hasty destruction was anticipated so that their pending translations could be more conveniently and hygienically undertaken by the transference of their bones, rather than the removal of partially decayed remains. Concerning the remains of St. Pascal Baylon, the hasty dissolution of the body was hoped for so that no offensive odors would be detected by the many visitors to his shrine, a condition which might detract from the devotion lavished on his memory. In all three cases the incorrupt condition of the bodies was maintained, as explained in the following accounts.

ST. FRANCIS XAVIER (d. 1552), after meeting St. Ignatius Loyola, became one of this Saint's original seven followers. His missionary career took him to Ceylon, India, Malaya and Japan, but his dream of evangelizing China was never realized. After traveling toward China by ship, he died within sight of Canton on December 3, 1552 at the age of forty-six.

The Saint's young Chinese companion, Antonio, in writing to the Jesuit Manuel Teixeira at Goa, India, described the lonely burial and what was done to the body. After securing vestments, he and his companions made a wooden coffin, in which they reverently placed the body. In the company of some people from the ship,

> We took the body in a boat to another part of the island opposite to where the ship and its people lay . . . It was very cold, so most of them stayed aboard and there were only four of us at the burial, a Portuguese, two slaves and a Chinaman . . . Having dug a deep grave we lowered the coffin into it and were about to cover it with earth when one of the company suggested to me that it might be a good idea to pack the coffin with lime above and below the body, as it would consume the flesh and leave only the bare bones, in case anyone in time to come should wish to take them to India. This seemed to us an excellent suggestion, so we withdrew the coffin,

obtained four sacks of lime from the ship and poured
two underneath the body and two above it. Then we
nailed on the lid again and filled in the grave . . . I put
some stones around it as markers, so that if I or any
member of the Society happened to come to the lonely
spot in the future and desired to see where the body of
the blessed Father rested, we would be able to find it.
Thus did we bury him, full of bitter sorrow, on the afternoon of Sunday, December 4, the day following his
death.[11]

Ten weeks later, on February 17, 1553, the casket was raised and
the body found to be perfectly preserved under the layer of lime.
The body, still encased in lime, was then placed on board a ship
bound for Malacca. Upon its arrival at the Church of Our Lady, it
was placed in a grave near the high altar where "it lay under and in
full contact with the earth for nearly five months."[12] At that time the
body was removed and taken to Goa, India, where the Saint had so
successfully evangelized. The body was in such a remarkable state
of preservation that it was left exposed in the Basilica of Bom Jesus
for four days. Although the preservation of the body was widely
acclaimed as miraculous, there were some skeptics who suggested
that the body had been carefully embalmed. To settle the issue the
Viceroy had the body examined by the chief medical authority in
Goa. After his thorough examination he testified:

I, Dr. Cosmas Saraiva, physician to the Senhor
Viceroy, have been to examine the body of Fr. Master
Francis, brought to this city of Goa. I felt and pressed all
the members of the body with my fingers, but paid special attention to the abdominal region and made certain
that the intestines were in their natural position. There
had been no embalming of any kind nor had any artificial preservative agents been used. I observed a wound
in the left near the heart and asked one of the Society
who was with me to put his fingers into it. When he
withdrew them they were covered with blood which I
smelt and found to be absolutely untainted. The limbs
and other parts of the body were entire and clothed in
their flesh in such a way that, according to the laws of

medicine, they could not possibly have been preserved by any natural or artificial means seeing that Fr. Francis had been dead and buried for about a year and a half. I affirm on oath that what I have written above is the truth. Signed: Dr. Cosmas de Saraiva.[13]

One hundred forty-two years after the death of St. Francis Xavier, his body was given another examination. Following this procedure, which was conducted in the presence of the bishop and other dignitaries, the medical report states the following:

The Saint's hair is black and slightly curling. The forehead is broad and high, with two rather large veins, soft and of a purple tint, running down the middle, as is often seen in talented persons who concentrate a great deal. The eyes are black, lively and sweet, with so penetrating a glance that he would seem to be alive and breathing. The lips are of a bright reddish colour and the beard is thick. In the cheeks there is a very delicate vermillion tint. The tongue is quite flexible, red and moist, and the chin is beautifully proportioned. In a word, the body has all the appearance of being that of a living man. The blood is fluid, the lips flexible, the flesh solid, the colour lively, the feet straight and the nails well formed. The loss of two toes left a darkish trace on the right leg. But for this, there can be found no other body so clean and sound as the body of the Apostle of the Indies. It is so great a marvel that on seeing it, while I was present, the Commissary of the Dutch East India Company, Mynheer Vandryers, became at once a convert to the Catholic Faith.[14]

Newsweek Magazine, in its December 30, 1974 issue, described the body as being "surprisingly well preserved." The body of the Saint is enshrined in the Basilica of Bom Jesus in Goa. The right arm of the Saint that had been raised so often in blessing, and which had been amputated in 1614, sixty-two years after his death, was taken on a pilgrimage in 1949 through Japan in observance of the 400th anniversary of the Saint's arrival in that country. It was then taken to the United States, where it was venerated by crowds in every city it visited during its three-month tour. The arm is now reverently kept in the Church of Il Gesu in Rome.

Pope St. Pius X proclaimed St. Francis Xavier the "Patron of Missions," a title he shares with St. Thérèse of Lisieux. He is considered the greatest individual missionary to the heathens since St. Paul.

St. Teresa of Avila once said of ST. JOHN OF THE CROSS (d. 1591) that "He was one of the purest souls in the Church of God." It was with St. Teresa that St. John of the Cross often conferred on their experiences in the spiritual life. And it was at Avila that the Sisters witnessed some of his levitations during ecstatic prayer. Because of his many writings, which include *The Ascent of Mount Carmel, The Dark Night of the Soul* and *The Spiritual Canticle,* his works have been regarded as possessing the same authority in mystical theology as the writings of St. Thomas Aquinas possess in dogmatic theology.

St. John died at the age of forty-nine and was buried in a vault beneath the flooring of the church at Ubeda, where a few nights later the friars observed a great light, which burned for several minutes.[15]

Nine months later the tomb was opened for the first time since the Saint's death. Doña Ana de Penasola wanted the body of the Saint removed to the house she had established for him in Segovia and obtained a legal order for the removal of the bones. One of the king's sergeants, Francis de Medina Zavallos, was sent to Ubeda to negotiate the translation. In obedience to the order, the prior admitted him to the church at night and found the body perfectly preserved, wreathed with a heavenly fragrance. Since the legal document specified the removal of the bones and not the body, the relic was again entombed, but not before a layer of lime was placed over it to hasten the reduction of the body so that, in time, the bones could be removed according to the legal order. Before doing this, however, the sergeant removed a finger to present to Doña Ana as proof of the body's preservation. When the finger was removed, "blood flowed profusely, as would be normal in a living person."[16]

After another nine months Sergeant Zavallos was again sent to Ubeda to arrange for the transfer. When the tomb was opened and the lime removed, they found, once again, the perfectly preserved body of the Saint, completely unaffected by the lime. The body was then taken on a journey to Segovia, where it was placed in the chapel of the house which Doña Ana had prepared for it. The preservation of the body, as well as the reputation of the Saint, prompted the devotion of huge crowds of people who visited and viewed the relic for the next eight days.

Examinations of the incorrupt body were conducted in 1859, 1909, 1926 and 1955. The body is still in Segovia, enshrined in a reliquary composed of beautifully colored marble and bronze. St. John of the Cross was canonized in 1726 and was numbered among the Doctors of the Church in 1926.

As a lay brother in the Alcantarine Franciscan Order, ST. PASCHAL BAYLON (d. 1592) served his community in various capacities and lovingly cared for the sick and poor. His great love for the Blessed Sacrament earned him the title, "The Saint of the Eucharist." After his death at the age of fifty-two, many wonders took place, including the "miraculous sweat" and the movement of his eyes toward the Blessed Sacrament, both of which are mentioned in other chapters of this work. For three days the body was left exposed to the veneration of the people, who marveled at the heavenly radiance of his countenance.

Before the body was placed in a vault under the altar of the Immaculate Conception, the guardian of the house covered it with a thick layer of quicklime so the flesh would be quickly consumed, producing clean white bones, which he felt would look impressive in a shrine. He also believed that by quickly destroying the flesh of the body, he would prevent unpleasant odors from escaping which might shock people and detract from the reputation the Saint had acquired by many miracles.[17]

The body of St. Paschal rested under this caustic element for eight months, until the time it was exhumed in the presence of various friars and the provincial of the order, Fr. John Ximenes. The Provincial related the following about this event:

> The lid was raised and we all approached the shrine and attested the presence of the crust of lime which concealed the Saint from sight. I would not allow anyone else to have the honor of removing this crust, but detached it bit by bit, beginning with the portion which covered the face. In proportion as I lifted the veil, the features of our blessed brother were disclosed, full of

life and animation. It was indeed himself, miraculously preserved in the flesh; intact from head to foot, even down to the tip of the nose, ordinarily the first part to show signs of decomposition. When we raised the eyelids, the eyes seemed to gaze at us and smile. The limbs were so supple and flexible that they lent themselves to every movement we imparted to them. Nothing recalled death . . . A crystalline liquid like balm distilled from the face and hands. When each of the Religious had satisfied his devotion, a fresh layer of quicklime was spread over the body.[18]

Nineteen years after the Saint's death an official exhumation was made for the Process of beatification. Witnessing this exhumation were the Bishop of Segorbe, the provincial of the order, doctors, surgeons and a notary. Part of the report made at this time reads:

As soon as the lid was raised, an agreeable fragrance resembling the perfume of flowers, or scent, arose from the sepulchre. Armed with a pair of scissors, the bishop proceeded to cut open the habit of the Saint down to the girdle in order to give the medical faculty every opportunity of making an examination of the body, which had now been nineteen years lying in the tomb. The doctors and surgeons acquitted themselves of the delicate task with carefulness and reverence . . . On the following day the Commission reassembled to hear the reading of the medical report. The conclusion arrived at, which was based upon the principles of medical science, was in the affirmative as to the miraculous state of the body.

The report concluded:

We, the undersigned doctors and surgeons, affirm on oath before God and according to our conscience, that the body of the said Brother Paschal Baylon is incorrupt and that the manner of its preservation is supernatural and miraculous.[19]

This, in spite of being twice covered with quicklime.

St. Paschal was canonized in 1690, and his extraordinary devotion to the Blessed Sacrament was rewarded by Pope Leo XIII in 1897 when he was made the patron of Eucharistic Congresses and all organizations dedicated to increasing love and devotion to the Holy Eucharist.

The preservation of the mutilated body of ST. ANDREW BOBOLA (d. 1657), a Polish priest in the Society of Jesus, is one of the most extraordinary among the Incorruptibles. During religious and political unrest between Poland and Russia, the Saint was captured by the Cossacks who were traveling the countryside beating the Poles into submission. After severely beating the Saint, two Cossacks tied him to their saddles and dragged him to Janow, where he endured horrific sufferings. It was recorded that:

> No horror in the passions of the early martyrs, nor in the sufferings of the victims of the Indian savages, surpassed what was inflicted on his living body; he was burned, half-strangled, partly flayed alive, and finally dispatched by a saber cut.[20]

The body was found incorrupt forty years later when his tomb was discovered under the ruins of a Jesuit church in Pinsk, Poland. The discovery prompted an immediate devotion to the Saint throughout Lithuania and Poland. This resulted in the introduction of his cause for beatification, and he was eventually beatified in 1853 and canonized in 1938.

Since the body of the Saint was never embalmed, treated or conditioned in any manner, many declared the preservation to be miraculous in spite of the mutilated condition which had resulted from the Saint's cruel martyrdom. Eighty-eight years after the Saint's death, the body was examined by Drs. Alexander Pascoli and Raymond Tarozzi of the College of Physicians in Rome and professors of medicine at the University of Rome. They stated in their medico-physical dissertation that the condition of the body would normally hasten dissolution, since it was a large specimen covered with livid wounds. In addition, it should have corrupted after the Cossacks mutilated the body since it was buried during the summer months in a spot where the ground was moist and where, for sixty years, it was near the contagious elements of

decaying bodies. All these conditions would normally act upon a
body in a destructive manner.[21]

The two doctors also declared that the survival of the body, considering the many harmful conditions already noted, was beyond
their ability to explain. They unanimously declared the preservation
to be of a miraculous nature.[22]

Another doctor, Marco Cingelo Marcangeli, a physician who was
a professor of theoretical medicine in the University of Rome and
a Medical Director of the Holy Ghost Apostolic Hospital, examined
the body for the Cause of Beatification and Canonization. Part of
his lengthy deposition dated 1827 reads:

> Having been asked to present my opinion on the
> question of the preservation of the body of the Servant
> of God, the Venerable Andrew Bobola, Priest of the
> Society of Jesus, I do not hesitate to repeat and confirm
> the opinion of the many witnesses who have seen and
> touched the body and who are unanimous in acknowl-
> edging its integrity, which experienced persons have
> described as eyewitnesses and which well-known med-
> ical professors have asserted to be nothing less than
> miraculous.[23]

Dr. Marcangeli concluded in favor of a miraculous preservation.

The body was sent to Polotsk in White Russia, where it was
examined by the Imperial Commission in 1866. It was examined
another time in 1896. During the solemn exhibition of the relic on
September 17, 1917, the body was found pliable and in a good state
of preservation.

A cordon of troops of the Red Army surrounded the church on
June 23, 1922 and approached the altar to see for themselves if the
rumors concerning the incorruption of the body were true. A terrible sacrilege was committed when they withdrew the body from the
casket, disrobed it, threw the body on the floor and mutilated it. The
relic was then sent under guard to Moscow, where it was concealed
by the Bolshevik government in a museum.

Several petitions were made by the Pope for the relic's return. In
1938 it was taken to Rome; then, shortly after the Saint's canonization it was returned to Poland, where it was eventually enshrined
in the Warsaw church bearing his name.

Over four hundred authenticated miracles are attributed to this holy martyr whose body remains incorrupt—the face still bearing the deadly wound it suffered more than three hundred years ago.

There are so many preserved bodies of Saints and holy persons enshrined around the world that it would be virtually impossible to determine the exact number. One hundred two cases are given in the author's book, *The Incorruptibles*, and there are many more. The examples given in this chapter are samples of a few Saints among many whose remains endured the most unfavorable conditions, yet their preservations were secured.

— 21 —

SAINTS' BODIES TRANSFORMED, MOVED OR WEIGHTED AFTER DEATH

The ravages of illness, the wounds of victim souls, the results of mystical fasts, the marks of martyrdom, all were transformed after the death of the Saints mentioned here. The admiration of those who witnessed these transformations immediately developed into confirmation of their saintliness.

Who can explain how someone, after suffering months from tuberculosis without benefit of pain killers, could become beautiful soon after death without the least trace of her suffering? How is it that someone, after dying of gangrene in a discolored and bloated condition, would soon return to her natural color, comely features and slim body?

Who can explain how bodies could become temporarily weighted to an abnormal degree or how dead bodies actually moved under the gaze of many witnesses? Lights and perfumes at the time of death also added to the mystery.

Who can doubt that these changes were God's way of signifying His love for the holy person and of testifying to their sanctity. Here then are a few of God's chosen ones whose holiness was confirmed by these miraculous happenings.

Known as "The Holy Abbot," ST. GERVINUS (d. 1075) was the friend of St. Edward the Confessor and King Henry I of France and once met St. Stephen, the King of Hungary. Noted as a preacher of extraordinary virtue, he was often thronged by pilgrims who came to him for Confession. He practiced great austerities and for the last four years of his life suffered from a form of leprosy. Although in pain and very weak, he was able to say his last Mass and was then placed before the altar of St. John the Baptist, where he died. When his body was being prepared for burial it was washed, according to the usual monastic custom. It was then noticed that all traces of leprosy had disappeared.[1]

At the death of ST. FRANCIS OF ASSISI (d. 1226) his brethren gazed at his body and wept in jubilation,

> For in truth there appeared in him a true image of the cross and of the passion of the Lamb without blemish who washed away the sins of the world, for he seemed as though he had been recently taken down from the cross, his hands and feet were pierced as though by nails and his side wounded as though by a lance.[2]

The first biographer of St. Francis, Thomas of Celano (d. 1260), was a member of the Franciscan Order and a contemporary of the great Saint. He tells that the stigmata remained on the hands and feet of the Saint, but that a transformation took place. Thomas of Celano writes:

> They saw his flesh, which before had been dark, now gleaming with a dazzling whiteness and giving promise of the rewards of the blessed resurrection by reason of its beauty. They saw, finally, that his face was like the face of an angel, as though he were living and not dead; and the rest of his members had taken on the softness and pliability of an innocent child's members . . . his skin had not become hard, his members were not rigid. And because he glowed with such wondrous beauty before all who looked upon him, and his flesh had become even more white, it was wonderful to see. In the middle of his hands and feet, not indeed the holes made by the nails, but the nails themselves formed out of his flesh and retaining the blackness of iron, and his right side was red with blood. These signs of martyrdom did not arouse horror in the minds of those who looked upon them, but they gave his body much beauty and grace.[3]

ST. ANTHONY OF PADUA (d. 1231) died at the age of 36, having been perfected in a short time. His life as a Franciscan friar was tireless in preaching and in defense of the Church, so that he was called in his lifetime "The Hammer of Heretics." At the time of his death he was described as being wasted, his face haggard from continuous fasting and unceasing labors, and he was "enfeebled to the verge of decrepitude." However, those who looked upon him after his death saw a body restored

> to the incomparable beauty of youth. A smile played upon those fair features; a delicate flush suffused them; the limbs were once more softly rounded and more pliable to the very last, as if he were but dreaming a sweet dream of rest. There he lay, wrapped in the innocent slumber of a child, fragrant as a dew-drenched rose—a very lily of purity plucked in its perfect prime.[4]

Also dying in the year 1231 was ST. ELIZABETH OF HUNGARY. She went to her eternal reward at an earlier age than St. Anthony, being only 24 years old. Although persecuted by her in-laws during her marriage and for a time despised by others, she labored tirelessly in the interests of the poor and the sick. It was they and the faithful women she had attracted to a life of service and prayer who flocked to the church when they heard of her death. Love and devotion were everywhere expressed when her remains were brought into the church.

Although she was but 24 years old, historians report that before her death her countenance was like that of one who had passed her life in bitter sufferings. But when viewed in the church after her death,

> her face became so smooth, so majestic, and so beautiful, that this sudden change could only excite admiration; and one might say that death, the ruthless destroyer of all things fair, visited her but to obliterate the traces of sorrow and austerity, as if that grace which hitherto replenished her soul, would now in turn animate her body.

One of the Saint's biographers reported that an unknown artist who sculptured the principal events of her life upon the altars at Marburg followed the report which says that physical beauty was renewed and increased in the remains of the Saint. The artist is said to have represented her exposed on the bier "as far more lovely in her death-sleep, than in all the other representations of her."[5]

At the age of eighteen, BL. VILLANA DE BOTTI (d. 1360)

experienced an immediate conversion from a life of gaiety and worldly interests into one of penance and prayer. As a married woman, she put aside her rich clothing and jewels, devoted herself to works of charity and became a Dominican tertiary. She is said to have been able to read the secrets in the hearts of those who visited her. Villana died at the age of 28 after a long bout with fever. Her biographer reports that: "Miraculously, the ravages of the long fever did not show, and, in death, her face possessed a beauty it had never had in life."[6]

ST. LYDWINE OF SCHIEDAM (d. 1433) was a Dutch mystic and a victim soul who endured such serious ailments that her visitors wondered not only about her ability to withstand the pain, but also how life was sustained in such an afflicted body. Lydwine died at the age of 53 amid the sorrow of many who had loved and tended her. The day after her death, as she lay on her poor bed, the veil which had covered her face since the time of her death was removed. Huysmans, her biographer, tells:

> Lydwine had become again as she had been before her illnesses, fresh and fair, young and dimpled; one would have thought it was a girl of seventeen, who smiled there in her sleep. Of the cleft in the forehead, which had so disfigured her, there was not the least trace; the ulcers and wounds had disappeared, except the three scars of the wounds made by the Picardians, which ran like three threads of purple across the snow of her flesh. All were astounded at this spectacle and eagerly inhaled a scent which they could not analyze, so sustaining, so fortifying, that for two days and three nights they felt no need of sleep or nourishment.[7]

One of St. Lydwine's early biographers was Thomas à Kempis, the author of *The Imitation of Christ*. He, as well as two other biographers, place the number of visitors to her bier as being close to several million, although we can safely assume that this number was a complete exaggeration.[8]

We do know that a great concourse of visitors from throughout the country passed in procession through the poor room where St. Lydwine's body lay in the repose of death.

When ST. FRANCES OF ROME (d. 1440) died at fifty-six years of age, the sweet scent of sanctity filled the room. Sr. Margaret of the Oblate sisters, who had a withered arm, was engaged in washing the body when her arm was immediately cured. This caused all the Oblates to fall on their knees at the sight of the miracle. It was soon noticed that:

> Frances' face, which had recently borne the traces of age and of suffering, became as beautiful again as in the days of youth and prosperity; and the astonished bystanders gazed with wonder and awe at that unearthly loveliness . . .[9]

Because of the many miracles of healing that were taking place for those who visited the body, the burial was delayed a few days.

> . . . and in the meantime, day and night, there is no limit to the concourse of people that assemble in the chapel. Still the Saintly body exhales its perfume; still the sweet features retain their beauty . . .[10]

The relics of St. Frances of Rome are now arranged in a crystal-fronted reliquary and can be viewed in a chapel of the Roman church named in her honor.

One day in February, in the year of her death, when ST. COLETTE (d. 1447) was 66 years old, she told her community that she would soon die and added, "Do not wait for me to say anything to you at my death, for I shall say nothing." Exactly one month later she placed on her head a veil of special significance. It was the veil which Pope Benedict XIII had placed on her head in 1406 when he named her the abbess-general of all Poor Clares who would embrace her restoration of the primitive Rule. She had worn this veil on special occasions and she was now wearing it on the most important day of all, that being the day of her entrance into eternal life. After lying down on her bed of straw she announced: "This is the last time I shall lie down." She died two days later. As she had predicted, she said not a word at her passing.

Attending St. Colette at her death was her secretary, Sr. Perrine, who reported that the appearance of the Saint remained unchanged for twelve hours. Age and suffering marked her features. Then "suddenly," she writes, "her body was transformed into a great and marvelous beauty; it was white as snow, and her veins showed through the white like fine azure; her whole body was so lovely, so supple, so fragrant, that it seemed entirely spiritualized with an angelic purity."[11]

For three days the Saint was visited by the "admiring and the curious," as recorded by Sr. Perrine. Her biographer notes: "they buried her with none of her unearthly loveliness diminished . . ."[12]

ST. RITA OF CASCIA died in the year 1457 at the age of seventy-six, forty-one years of which were spent in the cloister in Cascia.

In his biography of the Saint, Rev. M. J. Corcoran reports that the bells of the convent and of the castle of Cascia, as well as other church bells throughout the city, rang out in jubilee although untouched by mortal hands.

> Her poor cell was cloaked with vivid splendor, and an odor, sweet with the sweetness of Paradise, spread through all the convent. The wound which was produced by the thorn and which at other times inspired disgust, all at once was changed into a sign of election; and her body, worn and poor through fast and penance, took on a beauty that was not of this earth.[13]

Another author tells us that "Her body had not the sign of a corpse . . . she did not appear to be a prey of death, but only sleeping peacefully. She appeared years younger than she was, and her face was more beautiful in death than in life."[14]

After she pronounced the name of Jesus three times, a heavenly perfume signaled the death of ST. CATHERINE OF BOLOGNA (d. 1463). She had received many mystical favors as a member of the Poor Clare Order. The Saint's biography was first written by her fellow religious, Sr. Illuminata, whose manuscript is still preserved in the convent at Bologna. We are told that immediately after her death, the face of St. Catherine "became so fresh and beautiful that she looked like a young girl of fifteen who was sleeping."[15] The

Saint was 50 years old at the time of her death. Her body remains incorrupt and is situated in her shrine in a sitting position.

BL. JEANNE DE LESTONNAC (d. 1640), a mother and a widow, founded the Order of Notre Dame and served for a time as its superior. The usual signs of aging progressed in the normal fashion during her lifetime, but at her death at the age of 84, all testified to the beauty of her countenance.

A sweet fragrance surrounded the body for days after her death, while a brilliant light is said to have played about the bier.[16] In addition, miracles worked at her tomb testified to her virtue and closeness to God.

At twenty-three years of age, ST. TERESA MARGARET OF THE SACRED HEART (Anna Maria Redi) (d. 1770), a Discalced Carmelite nun at Florence, developed a gangrenous condition of the intestines and died after severe sufferings. She had advanced rapidly in perfection in a short time, and Our Lord seemed to signal His favor by the remarkable events that took place. The Saint's biographer reports:

> The gangrenous condition of the intestines, the direct cause of her death, naturally presaged early dissolution. In fact, the Saint's form became rigid almost immediately after death, her face and neck livid, and the abdomen fearfully swollen. The religious charged with preparing the corpse for the grave had good reason to fear that its condition would prevent its being exposed to view at the public funeral the next day, so they got ready a box to receive it.[17]

During the night a group of the nuns accompanied the body of the Saint from the cell in which she had died to the grille that opened into the chapel. When they reached the grille they noticed that "the swelling of the body had increased so much that it was necessary to place pillows underneath the head and shoulders, so that the face might be seen by those outside the grate."

A great crowd was in attendance at the funeral rites, while throughout Florence word was spread about the saintly young nun who had just died.

After the funeral services, when the church was cleared and the doors locked, the body was carried below ground to be buried underneath the monastery. It was then discovered that:

> the lividly purplish hue of her face, hands, and feet had changed to a faint rose-like color, which gave her a more angelic beauty than she had when alive. The nuns decided to put off the burial for awhile. The ninth of March, that is, two days after her death, the religious went to her uncovered tomb again, and were astounded to see that the lifeless and pallid color of her hands and feet had now changed to the glow of living flesh; her cheeks, now rosy, gave a heavenly look to her face . . . she seemed truly to be alive, just quietly sleeping. The Father Provincial and Doctor Antonio Romiti, the monastery surgeon, marveled at the beauty of her countenance . . . even the eyelids were dewy and in color, even her lips seemed fresh and naturally red.[18]

Two days later they returned to see the corpse.

> Their astonishment reached its peak on discovering that the face was even more beautiful and that the body had regained its former size and shape without exuding a drop of moisture. Her limbs had become so pliable and so easily moved as to give the impression of being animated. It was at this time that a new and most delightful odor, not to be compared with any earthly fragrance, clearly revealed what had been brought about in these precious remains . . . God had glorified them by the gift of incorruption.[19]

The body was entombed in the wall of the monastery, but it is now presented to the view of the public in the chapel of the Monastery of St. Teresa in Florence, Italy.

ST. THÉRÈSE OF THE CHILD JESUS AND OF THE HOLY FACE (d. 1897) was called by Pope Pius XI "the star of my pontificate." She endured tremendous sufferings from tuberculosis, which were described in the writings of her sisters and members of her community. The onset of tuberculosis presented itself on April 3, 1896, when she experienced her first hemoptysis, or vomiting of blood. Thérèse continued her duties until May of 1897. She was then relieved from all her responsibilities, including the charge of the novices.

The Saint's sister, Pauline, Rev. Mother Agnes of Jesus, recorded in June, "The illness makes rapid progress." In July, "Thérèse is at the end of her strength." She also experiences "strong fever; she vomits blood continually. Suffocation; she is dying."

The July 20 reports states: "Her right lung is damaged; several cavities in it . . . Continual hemoptyses; suffocations." In August there are "heavy perspirings; violent pains in her side." August has her suffering

> intense pain in her left side . . . the right lung is totally lost; the left is diseased in its lower region . . . intestinal pains . . . It is feared she has gangrene . . . Intestinal pains bad enough to make her cry out. The patient suffers violently at each breath.

In September, "Her suffering is extreme. Her breathing is very short." Sr. Thérèse of the Child Jesus and of the Holy Face died on September 30 at 7:20 at night, surrounded by the nuns of her community.[20]

After such prolonged sufferings, one can only imagine the gaunt and sickly look that must have languished upon her features, remembering that the Saint was never given morphine or any drug to relieve pain. After her death, however, all signs of her agony disappeared. Her sister, Celine Martin, a member of the community under the name Sr. Genevieve of the Holy Face, wrote:

> In her sleep of death, on Thérèse's countenance there was a reflection of eternal happiness and a celestial smile. That which struck me most, however, was a certain vitality and joy with which her closed eyelids seemed to vibrate. Death was forgotten while this consolation lasted. I might add that in all my contact with our Sisters who have died since then, I have never noticed anything like it . . . Thérèse was beautiful in death . . .[21]

Another report states that: "a mysterious smile was on her lips. She appeared very beautiful; and this is evident in the photograph taken by Celine after her sister's death."[22]

Sr. Marie of the Trinity and of the Holy Face, the Novice of the Shell (this novice will again be mentioned later in this chapter), agreed that the transformation was unusual. In her deposition she stated, "Immediately after her death, the countenance of the Servant of God became remarkably beautiful, animated by a heavenly smile; it radiated peace and happiness!"[23]

Bodies That Were Temporarily Weighted
And Those That Moved

We read in the biography of the Dominican, BL. BERNARD SCAMMACCA (d. 1486), that his body was found incorrupt fifteen years after his death. During this exhumation the church bells are said to have rung of their own accord. Sometime later a nobleman organized a raid with the object of carrying off the incorrupt body to his own castle. Bernard is said to have thwarted the nobleman's armed raiders who came at night. He knocked on the doors of every cell to alert the sleeping friars. When this did not arouse most of them, the great bell rang, which proved an effective stimulus. The Dominican community rushed to the church to investigate the disturbance and found the body lying at the door, surrounded by the armed raiders who were trying with all their strength to lift it from the floor. The body had become miraculously heavy, but reverted to its normal weight when the friars, without any difficulty, restored the body to its shrine.[24]

ST. DROGO (d. 1189) was of Flemish noble parentage, but at the age of eighteen he felt called to a penitential life and left home, country and his inheritance to work as a shepherd. After a few years he embarked on the life of a pilgrim and visited many of the major shrines.

He also visited Rome nine times. After developing a repulsive hernia he was forced to abandon his travels and retired to a room adjoining a church at Sebourg. He lived as a recluse in this room for forty years, dying with the reputation of sanctity at the age of eighty-four.

Drogo's kinsmen at Epinoy, his birthplace, demanded his body and sent a cart to fetch it. A great difficulty arose when his body became too heavy to be lifted from the ground. Several strong men exerted all their power, but were unsuccessful. The relatives were therefore obliged to leave the body at Sebourg, where it was buried. The place where the cart stopped to take the body is called "Mount Joie St. Drogo." Although the Saint resisted the move to Epinoy, his relics were transferred in the thirteenth century to Binche, where for many years an annual procession was made in his honor on Trinity Sunday.[25]

As the founder of the order which has given so many celebrated Saints to the Church, it is not surprising that ST. DOMINIC (d. 1221) was attended by many marvels both during his lifetime and after his death. Because the ideals of his order attracted a large number of new members, the monastery at Bologna had to be enlarged. At the same time the religious seized the opportunity to repair and alter the church in which the Saint's body had been buried under the flagstone. These alterations required the removal of the Saint's remains, which was undertaken on May 24, 1233 in the company of distinguished prelates, civil authorities and a representative of Pope Gregory IX. As soon as the flagstone was removed and a little of the earth disturbed, a wonderful perfume filled the church. (See the chapter, "Perfume from the Sainted Bodies of the Dead," for more details.) When the lid of the casket was opened, "there were once more exposed to their eyes, unchanged, and with the same look of sweetness and majesty they had ever worn in life, the features of their glorious Father."[26]

Attending the ceremony was Bl. John of Vercelli (d. 1283), whose zeal and sanctity had been especially dear to St. Dominic. He worked extensively in the interests of the Church and later became the master general of the Dominican Order. Bl. John stood for several minutes beside the body during the ceremony, but then moved aside to make way for William, the Bishop of Modena. Immediately, without help of any sort, St. Dominic's head turned in the direction in which he stood. On seeing this marvel, Bl. John decided, out of humility, to change his place again. But the head once more turned in his direction. One biographer reports:

> On this the first day when the public honours of the
> church were about to be paid to the holy patriarch, he
> was willing by this token to show that he counted his

chiefest glory to be less in such honour than in the sanctity of his children.[27]

The intelligence and holiness of ST. AGNES OF MONTEPUL-
CIANO (d. 1317) so impressed the nuns of her order that she was
elected prioress, but before she could assume the position, a special
dispensation was obtained from Pope Martin IV. This was necessary
because Agnes, at the time, was only fifteen years old. After her
order was placed under the rule of St. Dominic it flourished under
her guidance. She served as prioress until her death at the age of
forty-nine.

Bl. Raymond of Capua, St. Catherine of Siena's biographer, was
also the biographer of St. Agnes. Having served for many years as
confessor of the convent in which the body of Agnes was conserved,
he was able to study the documents in the archives relating to her.
He tells of the manna that issued from her body after her death, and
of the miracle of movement that was witnessed by many of the sisters. Bl. Raymond tells of a visit of St. Catherine to the shrine of St.
Agnes and relates this incident, which is frequently depicted in St.
Agnes' iconography:

> She (St. Catherine) had entered the cloister and
> approached the body of St. Agnes, with almost all the
> nuns of the Convent and the Sisters of Penance of St.
> Dominic who had accompanied her. She knelt at her feet
> and prostrated to embrace them piously; but the holy
> body that she intended honoring, unwilling that she
> should stoop to kiss it, raised its foot, in the presence of
> the whole assembly. At this sight Catherine, much trou-
> bled, prostrated profoundly and gradually restored the
> foot of Agnes to its usual position.[28]

When Bl. Raymond became the confessor of St. Agnes'
monastery there were still many sisters living who had witnessed
the miracle. Having received authority over the convent from the
prior provincial, Bl. Raymond tells that: "I assembled all the sisters
in conference according to the Rule of the Order, and made a
minute examination of this miracle under a precept of holy obedience. All present declared positively they had seen it perfectly."[29]

St. Catherine of Siena visited the body of St. Agnes once again, but this time, "She did not place herself at the feet, but joyfully approached the head; she designed, by humility we presume, to avoid what had happened when she attempted to kiss the feet at her first visit."[30]

One hundred fifty-two years after the death of ST. RITA OF CASCIA (d. 1457), her body was found incorrupt. Twenty-two years after the beautifully preserved body was found, the eyes of the Saint opened and remained so for many years, as paintings executed during the time indicate.[31] Not only was this prodigy noted, but also observed by many were the movements of the body. From time to time the body would turn and remain for some years on one side, and then turn to the other side. The nuns of the convent gave testimony under oath of the fact that these movements of the body did indeed take place. Another phenomenon, the elevation of the body, was such that the Saint's face touched the screen of wire that formerly enclosed the top of the old coffin. This is said to have happened each year on St. Rita's feastday, the twenty-second of May. Details regarding the elevation of the body to the top of the sarcophagus were carefully recorded by eyewitnesses whose testimonies are still reserved in the archives of the Archdiocese of Spolet. One of the longest elevations of the body took place on January 14, 1730. At that time the city of Cascia was in great anxiety because of an earthquake that destroyed many houses in outlying towns and villages. As the people fled the area, they sought refuge in the church of St. Rita and saw the elevation of the Saint's body. They interpreted it as an indication of the Saint's concern and protection. Cascia also experienced the earthquake with some damage, but St. Rita's convent and church remained unharmed.

The movements of the body are described by the official witness for the canonization of St. Rita. Rev. Corcoran gives this account from the official document:

> Many persons who have been questioned from the time of the first Process in 1626 and again successively in 1739, 1751 and 1893, gave testimony to have seen the body of Saint Rita move. Other persons tell the same story on the testimony of trustworthy witnesses.
> Amongst the first class, some there are who say that they saw with their own eyes her head turned toward the

people; according to some, the body raised itself to the
top of the urn; and some moreover note the fact that her
habit was moved and disordered; and some add to the
facts of sight the facts of hearing.[32]

Many others also gave witness to the heavenly perfume that
came from the body, which is described in more detail elsewhere
in this volume.

After her death, did the fingers of ST. THÉRÈSE move? It
appears that they did, according to Sr. Marie of the Trinity and of
the Holy Face. Sister was a novice under the Little Flower, the one
who is known as the Novice of the Shell. The former novice tells
how she acquired this name.

> I often cried, and for nothing, and this caused my dear
> Mistress a lot of sorrow. One day she had a brilliant
> idea: taking from her painting table a moulding shell and
> holding my hands so I could not wipe my eyes, she
> started to gather my tears in the shell. Instead of con-
> tinuing my crying, I could no longer keep from laugh-
> ing. "All right," she said, "from now on you can cry as
> much as you want, providing you cry into this shell."
> Then eight days before her death, I cried all night, think-
> ing about the fact that Sister would soon leave us. She
> noticed it and said, "You have been crying; did you cry
> into the shell?"
> I could not lie, and my denial made her sad. She
> answered, "I am going to die, and I will not rest easy
> because of you, if you do not promise me to obey faith-
> fully my recommendation, since I attach primary impor-
> tance to it for the benefit of your soul." I promised her,
> asking only as a favor, the permission to cry freely when
> she died. She replied, "I pity your weakness and I per-
> mit you to cry for the first few days, but after that you
> have to go back to the shell."[33]

After the death of the Little Flower, Sr. Marie of the Trinity wrote
about the phenomenon of movement:

When Sister Thérèse of the Child Jesus was laid in state at the choir grille, as is the custom, many persons came to see her, and to touch her out of devotion with objects of piety, and even with toys. At this moment a rather curious thing happened. Contrary to the directions of the Servant of God, I did not stop crying and could not console myself about her death. Then approaching her in order to touch her with a rosary that a person had handed to me, she held it in her fingers. Very delicately I lifted her fingers to move the rosary, but just as soon as I detached it from one finger, it was caught again by another. I repeated this five or six times without any result, and my Little Thérèse said to me interiorly: "If you don't smile for me, I will not give it back." And I answered her, "No, I am too unhappy and want to cry." In the meantime the people behind the grille were wondering what I could be doing for so long a time. I was very embarrassed and begged my Little Thérèse to let me return the rosary.

I pulled on the rosary; it was useless! Then, completely defeated, I began to smile. That was just what she wanted, for immediately, she let go of the rosary of her own accord, and I was able to return the rosary![34]

Sr. Marie of the Trinity received many heavenly favors after the death of her Novice Mistress, especially that of patience in enduring her final illness, which was lupus, a tubercular skin disease. We are told that the disease had completely consumed her left ear, the side of her face up to the eye, and the whole top of her head to the right ear. Her sufferings were described as a martyrdom which she endured with such patience that the sisters and even her doctors were amazed. In the end the Reverend Mother wrote that by her heroic abandonment, Sr. Marie of the Trinity proved herself "a faithful pupil of her holy Mistress, Saint Thérèse."

When ST. MARY MAGDALEN DE PAZZI (d. 1607) died, the city of Florence mourned the loss with many of the citizens retiring to the convent church to gaze for the last time on the features of the Saint who had counseled many in the ways of virtue. Men and women from all walks of life, nobles as well as the poor, went to recommend themselves to the prayers of the holy Carmelite. People were constantly approaching the body, but all were astounded when a certain young man approached the Saint. It was then that the Saint actually turned her face from him. The Saint's biographer reports that the young man had been living an unchaste life. The turning of the Saint's face away from him "was for the young man's good, because he changed his manner of life."[35]

Unusual marvels have taken place regarding the relics of ST. PHILOMENA (d. Roman era) in that her relics, placed in a papier-mâché figure, exhibited the three wonders mentioned previously. That is, the figure not only moved and became temporarily weighted, but also was transformed into a thing of beauty.

Many witnesses have testified to the marvels that attended the remains of the young maiden who had been entombed in the catacombs from Roman times until the year 1802. Although she had been unknown before that year, devotion to her spread with amazing speed during the relics' journey from Rome, through Naples and then to their final destination at Mugnano, Italy. Within 35 years Pope Gregory XVI had named her "The Wonder-Worker of the 19th Century." The Curé of Ars was especially devoted to the little Saint, and it was to her that he attributed the miracles worked at Ars.

Sometime after the discovery of the relics, they were awarded to Mugnano and were taken to Naples. There the bones were joined with wires and wrapped in cloth for placement in a papier-mâché figure that was clothed in sumptuous robes. The figure that had been prepared for the reception of the bones proved to be a disappointment. "It was far from being a work of art. The face was a morbid white color; the lips were thick and a grimace was noticeable about the mouth."[36]

In addition, the glass-sided ebony shrine that had been made to fit a five-foot corpus was too short. It was then necessary to arrange the figure in a most unbecoming manner with the knees of the figure bent and elevated, while the rest of the figure was somewhat reclined.

During its journey to Mugnano, and while the entourage was in the vicinity of Cimitile, the shrine suddenly seemed to be weighted with lead. The bearers, unable to support the weight, placed the shrine on the ground and heard a strange metallic sound. Everyone was mystified by the strange weight and the sound until it was real-

ized that thousands of martyrs had suffered there under Roman con-
querors. The unusual heaviness of the shrine and the sound were
taken as a sign of respect from the young virgin to her fellow victims who also had been granted the grace of martyrdom.[37]

Don Francesco di Lucia, pastor of the church in Mugnano, tells
in his *Memoirs* that the shrine was lifted and carried with great difficulty so that men from Mugnano were called to help in carrying
it. These extra men later joined the procession when their help was
no longer needed, since the shrine once more became light after
they passed the village of Schiawa. The change in weight was so
instantaneous and unexplainable that it was regarded as miraculous.

The arrival of the relics in Mugnano was met with grand ceremonies and many astounding miracles of healing. Because of the
popularity of the Saint, Don Francesco di Lucia dedicated a special
altar to the Saint in September 1805, with the shrine arranged above
the altar. After its placement Don Francesco and the people witnessed the first miraculous re-arrangement of the figure. Much to
their surprise they saw that the right arm was elevated and stretched
out, holding arrows (a symbol of her martyrdom) that were now
aimed toward the feet instead of the heart where they had formerly
pointed. The mouth, now smiling, was slightly opened to reveal the
teeth, and the color and shape of the face changed into one of
appealing beauty.[38]

The change was so extraordinary that a legal deposition was made
by Donna Angela Terres of Naples. While the relic was in her city,
the only key to the shrine was given to her as a consolation for losing the relics to Mugnano. She testified that the key to the shrine
that had been entrusted to her care had never left her, thus quelling
any possibility that the shrine had been opened so that the changes
could be effected through human assistance. The artist was also
called to testify under oath that he had not repainted the image—
that it was of a white color when last he saw it. In addition, the
triple seals impressed in Naples by the episcopal ring were still
intact, further indicating that the shrine had not been disturbed, at
least not by human intervention.[39]

Another miraculous change took place in 1824, when the shrine
was replaced with one that was more beautiful and elegant. This
shrine was a foot longer than the former one, but for some reason
the figure seemed to lengthen so that, while she assumed the same
position, her figure lengthened so that her feet touched the end of

the case. The hair at this time also seemed to be more abundant. While tourists prayed before the image in 1841, the Saint turned so that three-fourths of her face was visible. The witnesses testified that she had given them a pleasant smile—an extraordinary privilege which both pleased and amazed them.[40]

The image assumed yet another position on May 27, 1892, which was witnessed by a large group of pilgrims. Their statements were accepted by ecclesiastical authorities.[41]

A good description of his experiences before the shrine of St. Philomena was given by Fr. Paul O'Sullivan, a Dominican priest of Lisbon who spent nine days in Mugnano during the year 1909. Fr. Paul wrote a book about the Saint and gave a description of yet another marvel, a blood miracle which is described in another part of this work. In describing the statue containing the relics he writes:

> During my own stay in Mugnano, I saw the statue changing color very frequently, passing from pale to a light blush and again to a darker red. The lips were sometimes compressed and sometimes opened. No interference with the statue is possible, since it is placed in the wall and closed in by a thick plate of crystal glass and locked with three keys, which are held by three different authorities. One of these is the bishop of Nola.[42]

The opening of the eyes has also been reported. Don Francesco, in his *Memoirs,* mentions such a miracle which involved a cynic, Marianna Masuccia, wife of Andrew Tedeschi. Marianna had heard of the miraculous opening of the statue's eyes and brazenly approached the shrine one day, demanding a miracle. Sarcastically she asked the Saint how she could open her eyes when there were none beneath the closed eyelids.

She questioned how such a thing could happen to a face made of papier-mâché and wondered, if others could see the miracle, why she could not.

According to Don Francesco, the statue of the Saint opened its eyes and looked contemptuously and severely at Marianna, and then sweetly closed its eyes, leaving the woman completely confused and contrite.[43]

The popularity of St. Philomena has spread worldwide, and astounding miracles have been reported.

Another Saint who opened his eyes after death is ST. PASCHAL BAYLON (d. 1592). He is known for his great devotion to the Holy Eucharist, and for how, as a Franciscan lay-brother, he tended the sick and the poor. We also read elsewhere in this book about the miraculous manna that distilled from his body after his death and of the "Golpes" with which many were favored.

In addition to these wonders, miracles of healing were occurring on all sides while his body was displayed to the devotion of the people. But one miracle in particular caused great astonishment. This was the opening of the eyes of the corpse—a miracle that was viewed by many of the people who filled the church to capacity.

An eyewitness to this event was a person who was previously repulsed by dead bodies, Eleanora Jorda y Miedes. She related in her deposition:

> I went up to Br. Paschal as though he had been alive, kissed his hands and feet and saw the miraculous dew upon his forehead. In short, I felt so much at my ease at the side of the holy man, that in order to remain the longer under his blessed influence, I resolved not to quit the chapel before the end of High Mass. I must confess, to my own shame, that I was more attentive in watching what was going on round the holy man, than in following the Holy Sacrifice. When I saw him open his eyes at the Elevation, I was so astounded that I gave a loud scream. "Mamma, Mamma!" I exclaimed to my mother, who had come with me, "Look, Look! Br. Paschal has opened his eyes."

She looked, and she too saw the eyes of the Saint open and then shut at the second Elevation.

> All who were witnesses of this miracle, like ourselves, had one and the same idea about it, namely that Our Lord wished in this way to reward Paschal's extraordinary devotion to the Sacrament of the Altar, and that He gave him a new life so that even on the other side of the tomb, he might still have the consolation of adoring Him in the Holy Eucharist.[44]

Paschal was canonized in 1690, and his devotion to the Holy Eucharist was rewarded when, in 1897, Pope Leo XIII named him the patron of Eucharistic Congresses and all organizations dedicated to increasing love and devotion to the Holy Eucharist.

ST. AGNES OF MONTEPULCIANO's incorrupt body was conserved in the convent of her order and effected a miracle when St. Catherine of Siena attempted to embrace the Saint's feet out of devotion. One foot raised up to keep St. Catherine from stooping to kiss it.

— 22 —

LIGHTS ABOUT THE
BODIES OF SAINTS

In a previous chapter we learned that lights and rays were noted in the lives of many Saints, but mysterious lights were also seen about the bodies of some of the deceased children of God. Sometimes lights were noticed about their graves, which sparked special interest in the sanctity of the deceased, and in some cases signalled the incorruption of their bodies.

It seems that the earliest Saints favored with these mysterious lights were British princesses, ST. MAURA and ST. BRIGID (d. 5th century), who made a pilgrimage to Rome. On their return journey they were set upon by heathen outlaws who put them to death at Balagny-sur-Therain and quietly buried them. St. Gregory of Tours relates that his predecessor, St. Euphronius, was told of a mysterious light that was seen over a bramble-covered hill and of a vision of two maidens asking for a chapel to be built for the two holy souls who had died there. The relics of the two were discovered, a chapel was built, and a cultus that immediately began is said still to exist at Tours. Their feastday, January 28, is observed with special ceremonies.

St. Louis IX had a great devotion to these Saints and was a benefactor of their shrine and church. The cessation of the Plague at Beauvais is attributed to their intercession.[1]

Lights also indicated the place where BL. DOMINIC and BL. GREGORY died in the year 1300. Both were dedicated priests who accepted as their mission in life the preaching of the Gospel in out-of-the-way districts. Once while preaching to the people who lived in the hilly hamlets of the Pyrenees, they took refuge under a cliff during a severe thunderstorm and were buried there when rocks, loosened by the torrential rains, fell upon them. The whereabouts of their bodies would have been lost had not the villagers been alerted by the mysterious ringing of bells and a strange light that revealed the scene of the catastrophe. The bodies of the two missionaries

318

were recovered and buried at Besiano, where they were honorably entombed and greatly venerated.[2]

This prodigy was also noted when the body of ST. RITA OF CASCIA (d. 1457) was placed on a catafalque before the altar of the church where her funeral was held. All present were amazed at a brightness that radiated from her, but especially from the stigmatic wound on her forehead that shone and glistened like a jewel.[3]

Known as the Doctor of Mystical Theology, ST. JOHN OF THE CROSS (d. 1591) assisted St. Teresa of Avila in the reform of the Carmelite Order and authored such masterful works as *The Ascent of Mount Carmel* and *The Dark Night of the Soul*.

When the Saint was 49 years old and was on his deathbed, he occasionally asked about the time, saying, "At midnight I shall be before God, saying Matins." When the bell finally chimed to call the friars to the chapel for the recitation of Matins, the Saint reached for his crucifix and said, "Into Thy hands, Lord, I commend my spirit." One biographer writes:

> And with these words John quietly died—the death of love. It was then that the friars saw above the bed a great sphere of light, like that of sun and moon and stars together, sparkling, soft and intense: a sweet perfume filled the room. Those around perceived that he whom they watched no longer breathed: a triple crown seemed to circle his head: his face shone with a brilliant pallor: his expression was one of peace and joy.[4]

After the death of the Saint huge crowds hurried to the church to touch religious objects to his body. He was buried beneath the flooring of the church, where a great light burned brightly for several minutes on the Monday night following the funeral.[5]

The body was first exhumed nine months after his death and was found perfectly preserved. Since then there have been a number of exhumations of the body, with many witnesses marvelling at its wonderful preservation, the same condition in which it is found today. St. John of the Cross was declared a Doctor of the Church by Pope Pius XI in 1926. St. Teresa of Avila once said of him that "He was one of the purest souls in the Church of God."

The huge crowd that gathered on October 16, 1895 at Caposele to honor ST. GERARD MAJELLA (d. 1755) on his feastday were destined to witness a phenomenon that would leave them animated with great confidence in the Saint's wonder-working power.

It took place two years after his beatification and the 140th anniversary of his death. Fr. Bozzoatra delivered the panegyric of the holy brother and ended with an eloquent prayer. It was then that a brilliant light, like a flash of lightning, came from the chapel where the tomb of the Saint was located. After some moments the prodigy was repeated, and then, after a few more moments, the light flashed for a third time. At this, a great cry sounded in the church, "A miracle! A miracle!" The lights were accepted by many as confirmation of all that Fr. Bozzoatra had mentioned moments earlier about the virtues and graces St. Gerard had experienced in life.[6]

ST. CHARBEL MAKHLOUF (d. 1898), a monk of the Monastery of St. Maroun at Annaya in Lebanon, spent 16 years in community and then lived 23 years in a hermitage near the monastery. In this secluded place he practiced corporal discipline, slept on the hard ground and ate only one small meal a day. After suffering a seizure while saying Mass, he died eight days later and was buried in the monastery cemetery.

In all probability, he would have been forgotten had not a certain phenomenon occurred at his grave in the form of an extraordinarily bright light which surrounded his tomb for 45 nights following the interment. Because of this and the enthusiasm of the many witnesses of this prodigy, the officials of the monastery requested permission from the ecclesiastical authorities to exhume the body—a ceremony that took place four months after the Saint's death.

To the amazement of all present, the body was found completely and marvelously incorrupt, even though, as the result of frequent rains which had inundated the cemetery several times after the burial, the body was found floating on mud in a flooded grave.

Because of the lights and miraculous events that surrounded the incorrupt body, the humble monk's sanctity was examined by ecclesiastical authorities and confirmed by his canonization in 1977.[7]

Other prodigies were noted after his exhumation—namely, the exudation of a clear oil, which is mentioned elsewhere in this book.

BLOOD MIRACLES

The miracles we will consider in this chapter take a number of forms. One is that of liquefaction, which Webster defines as "The act or process of making or becoming liquid; esp., the conversion of a solid into a liquid by heat." While dried or solid blood might be liquefied in the laboratory by the application of heat, heat was not required and was not used for the liquefactions mentioned here.

A number of miracles have taken place, and in some cases are still taking place with blood that was collected soon after the death of certain martyrs—but most of the miracles have taken the form of liquid blood flowing from the body of a Saint long after death. There is a well-documented history of these samples of blood liquefying at various times of the year, especially on the Saints' feast-days. These samples have been known to liquefy under various circumstances, at different seasons of the year, in various countries and in varied ways. Many samples still display wonderful reactions in our day, as we will soon consider.

It is a matter of common knowledge that once removed from the body, blood soon coagulates and eventually spoils. This natural condition was well-known among the medical faculty of the Middle Ages, so that a claim made by them of prodigious liquefactions can hardly be ignored. Some of their records still exist telling of blood miracles that were clearly above and beyond the scope of normal experience.

In three articles written on this subject in 1927 for the English magazine, *The Month*, Rev. Herbert Thurston, S.J. mentions a number of holy persons whose samples of blood liquefied in the past. Many of these samples were lost or misplaced, but many still remain and are marvels of activity.

The practice of collecting blood for relics began in the days of persecution, when the early Christians soaked cloths in the blood shed by martyrs, or if possible, actually collected the liquid in flasks to keep as devotional items. In the catacombs these flasks were buried with the dead, their discovery indicating that the person so interred had died a martyr's death. Such was the case when a tomb in the catacomb of St. Priscilla was opened on May 24, 1802. Three tiles with an inscription in red paint read: LUMENA—PAX TE—CUM FI. It was generally accepted that the mason either had closed the vault in a hurry or perhaps could not read, since the tiles were in the wrong order. When rearranged the inscription reads: *"Pax tecum Filumena,"* or "Peace be with thee, Filumena," a name which is also spelled, PHILOMENA (d. Roman era).

Inside the vault were the bones of a female about thirteen to fifteen years of age. Embedded in the cement near the head was a slightly broken glass vial with a dark red or brown substance which scientific testing proved to be congealed blood. The finding of this "blood-ampulla," plus the symbols on the three tiles of an anchor, two arrows, a javelin, a palm and a flower, were accepted as proof that the young girl had died the death of a martyr in defense of her virginity. The Congregation of Sacred Rites likewise accepted this conclusion, especially when the blood in the vial began sometime later to display an extraordinary phenomenon.

When experts were transferring the congealed parts of the blood into a clear vial they were startled on seeing shining gems, as well as pieces of gold and silver. The Court of Inquiry was amazed, as were all those who gazed on the marvel, which they accepted as a guarantee of sainthood. Cardinal Ruffo Scilla, who placed the seals on the new reliquary, testified to its authenticity in this way: "And we have seen her blood changed into several brilliant little precious stones of various colors; also into gold and silver."[1]

After the bones were removed from the catacomb, they were carefully deposited in the *Custodia Generale* of sacred relics.

When the Reverend Don Francis di Lucia heard of the discovery of the virgin-martyr who had died in the early days of the Church, he asked permission to enshrine the remains in the church at Mugnano in the diocese of Nola, and was given the relics in 1805 by Pope Pius VII. When the relics were carefully enshrined in Mugnano, devotion to St. Philomena began in earnest; miracles both temporal and spiritual were reported.

When Cardinal Victor Auguste Dechamps visited the shrine in 1847, he witnessed the miracle of the blood and in a written statement testified:

I saw above all, that precious blood shed for the love

of virginity. It was at first dull and hardened, and behold! Jesus Christ, by communicating to it a ray of the glory of the soul which offered it to Him, renders it dazzling as the rainbow. It is truly marvelous. I had read accounts of it, but now I can say that I have seen it with my own eyes.[2]

Sixty-two years later, in 1909, the Rev. Paul O'Sullivan, O.P. visited the Sanctuary of St. Philomena for nine days and often accompanied the pilgrims who were allowed to kiss the reliquary containing the blood of the martyr. "Sometimes, when the chaplain was not present, it was my privilege to offer the relic for the veneration of the visitors, and frequently, when the church was closed, I was allowed to extract it from its repository for my private devotion."

In his biography of St. Philomena he describes the phenomenon of the blood.

The blood is not in a liquid state, but quite dry and in appearance resembles ashes. It is preserved in a small crystal vase which allows the visitor to see it as perfectly as though it lay on the palm of one's hand. I had the happiness of examining this priceless treasure as many as thirty or forty times. Each time, without fail, I saw the blood change most marvelously, and the transformation was so clear and distinct as not to allow room for the smallest doubt or misconception.

Precious stones, rubies and emeralds, pieces of gold and particles of silver appeared mingled with the blood. One might shake the reliquary, and again the precious stones appeared, not always in the same way, but still clearly and distinctly. At times, too, small black particles appear, which are supposed to presage some cross or affliction or foretell impending evils. These black particles were very noticeable when the great Pontiff, Pius IX, venerated the blood of the Saint. The black particles were supposed to be prophetic of the sorrows in store for the Holy Father.

At times the blood takes the form of black earth, and this appears to denote unworthiness of those who are venerating the relic. One very notable case was that of a priest whose life was far from what the sacred ministry demanded. When he knelt to kiss the reliquary, the blood became very dark. On his departure it regained its natural appearance. Some days after, he fell dead in the midst of a feast.

These extraordinary transformations are witnessed daily by the crowds who flock to the Sanctuary and have been verified and declared authentic by the highest ecclesiastical authorities.[3]

St. Philomena was a favorite of St. Jean Marie Baptiste Vianney, the Curé of Ars, who attributed all the miracles worked at Ars to his "dear little Saint." St. Philomena was likewise a favorite of St. Madeleine-Sophie Barat, Bl. Peter Eymard, Bl. Peter Chanel and the Venerable Countess de Bonnault d'Houet, among many others.

The remains of the Saint have prompted other phenomena which are mentioned elsewhere in this book.

Better known is the liquefaction of the blood of ST. JANUARIUS (d. 305), the bishop of Benevento, who died during the persecution of the Roman Emperor Diocletian. After his decapitation, his followers removed the remains and collected two vials of blood, as was the custom regarding martyrs. The relics were finally brought to Naples, where a great cathedral rose over his tomb. Veneration to the Saint was profound.

The miracle of liquefaction first took place in 1389 while a priest was holding the flasks during a procession. The coagulated blood began to liquefy and bubble, an occurrence that took place afterward 18 times a year.

In more recent years the liquefactions and viewings have taken place three times a year: on September 19, the feastday of the Saint; on December 16, which is the anniversary of the eruption of Vesuvius in 1631; and on the first Sunday in May, which commemorates the translation of the relics to Naples.

The two flasks of blood are not equal in volume, one having more coagulated blood than the other. The vials are hermetically sealed and are solidly fixed side by side in a silver ring which touches the bottom of the vials and the top. On both sides of the ring are circular coverings of crystal which protect the vials and permit easy viewing of the miracle. At the bottom of the ring is a stick-like handle. The cathedral is always filled to capacity when the resident cardinal or a priest holds the reliquary for all to see, being careful not to touch the crystal sides. When the bust reliquary containing the head of the Saint is brought near, the blood in the vials begins to liquefy. The cardinal then announces, "The miracle has happened," words that cause great excitement and the chanting of the *Te Deum*.

The blood of St. Januarius has failed to liquefy several times, each time coinciding with the outbreak of disease, famine, war or political oppression.

When the liquefactions occur, these dreaded occurrences are not expected to take place, and this gives vent to great rejoicing and notices in many secular presses throughout the world.

After the blood liquifies, and at the completion of the ceremony, the reliquary is placed in a silver case and enshrined inside the altar. The blood might be found the next day in a coagulated state, or it might still be liquid and might remain in that condition for days or months.

The liquefaction presents a puzzle to those who have studied it since it takes place under diverse circumstances and physical conditions. The miracle takes place at different temperatures, as indicated by the records kept by the cathedral for a century and as reported by Professors Pergola, Punzo and Sperindeo, who have pronounced that there is no direct relation between the temperature and the time and manner of liquefaction. The blood has been known to liquefy at temperatures of 77 degrees or higher, which might take as much as 20 to 40 minutes. A smaller amount of time might be required when the temperature is 20 degrees or less. Sometimes when the temperature has stood as high as 86 degrees, more than two hours passed before the liquefaction began. Again, when the temperature has been 15 to 20 degrees lower than this, the complete liquefaction has occurred in from 10 to 15 minutes.

Many skeptics have argued that the candles, the lights, the press of the people or the temperature of the priest's hand increases the temperature, which influences the rate of liquefaction. But, since the vials are protected by crystal and do not come in contact with the hand of the priest, and because it has taken place in the sanctuary away from the crowd of people—as well as in the bitter cold of December, the heat of Summer and in the Spring—there is no constant temperature at which the liquefactions take place. The miracle is contrary to physical laws. Also, there have been occasions when the blood has failed to liquefy under what appear to be ideal circumstances.

Several anomalies exist after the liquefaction takes place. There is a variation in volume, since it sometimes decreases, while other times it almost doubles. Sometimes the coagulated blood occupies almost half the vials; at other times the vials are almost full. There is also a difference in its weight. The reliquary was weighed in 1902 and 1904, with findings that the weight increased as much as 25 to 27 grams.

Another strange element is that an increase in weight takes place when there is a decrease in the volume, and a decrease in weight when the vials are almost full. The color of the blood also changes from dark red to almost black to a bright vermillion. The viscosity changes as well, with the blood being sometimes gummy, at other times very fluid—and this being independent of any movement. Sometimes only some of the coagulated blood liquefies, leaving a small lump that floats in the liquid—a situation that cannot be explained.

Skeptics have also wondered if the substance in the vials is real blood. Constant tradition has maintained that it is real blood, a fact that is confirmed by documents that are impossible to refute. Scientific examination has also confirmed this, especially when Professor Sperindeo was permitted to pass spectroscopic beams of light through the liquefied material. This test yielded the distinctive lines of the spectrum of blood with the characteristics of hemoglobin.

Everything concerning this blood is phenomenal, especially the times when the blood liquefies and forms tiny bubbles that rise to the surface and collect into a foam. Another mystery is presented when these bubbles form, since the color of the blood changes from dark to light red.

The liquefaction of the blood of St. Januarius has occurred for over 600 years. Concerning these occurrences, Thurston notes that "so far no natural explanation has been found." It clearly remains a challenge to the skeptic, a mystery to the scientific community and a true phenomenon.[4]

Dying the same year as St. Januarius was ST. PANTALEON (d. 305), who was born in Nicomedia, Turkey, the son of a pagan senator and a Christian mother. His reputation as a talented physician brought him to the court of Emperor Galerius Maximian. Although raised a Christian, he fell into apostasy until a Christian named Hermolaos awakened Pantaleon's conscience and brought him again to the fervent practice of virtue. When Diocletian's persecution began, Pantaleon remained steadfast and refused to apostatize to escape certain martyrdom. He was finally beheaded after being cruelly tortured. The greater part of the Saint's relics are found in the church of Lucca, but the blood that was collected according to custom found its way to Ravella, some 22 miles from Naples, and is now kept in the cathedral consecrated to St. Pantaleon.

The blood remains in its ancient flask and is held fast in its reliquary by two iron clasps. The reliquary is kept amid the stonework of the altar where the flask cannot be touched or turned or shaken.

The blood is clearly divided into four strata. When the blood is inactive, it occupies only half the container. The empty portion contains traces of fat and blood adhering to the glass. The substance at the bottom level appears to be very dark blood mixed with sand. The next layer appears to be dirt mixed with a greater amount of blood. The third strata is pure blood of a ruby color when liquefied. The highest level consists of a whitish foam.

When liquefaction takes place, the layer of blood turns transparent and ruby-colored like fresh blood, while little bubbles reach almost to the top of the container. The traces of dark blood that adhere to the top of the vial when the blood is inactive turn reddish and wet during the miraculous liquefaction. The blood is never in a coagulated condition, but in a perfect state of viscousness, in an almost fluid state.

On the feastday of the Saint, July 27, the blood may liquefy, but then might not. Sometimes it gradually begins to change and may continue for a month or longer. Sometimes the liquefaction takes a week, while at other times a few days. At other times it can liquefy very quickly when a relic of the True Cross is brought into the church. This has been found to happen on a number of occasions.

According to tradition, the blood of the martyr has liquefied from the earliest times. Apparently the blood displayed some unusual activity since merchants of Amalfi, Italy heard of it and journeyed to Nicomedia to obtain it for enshrinement at Ravella. Records of 1112 reveal that the blood was carefully guarded in the cathedral at Ravella which was consecrated to the Saint. The blood's activities have been been carefully documented since 1577. The untouched

vial with its unusual activities has been of interest and spiritual benefit to all who have witnessed the liquefaction of this ancient blood
which dates to the year 305.[5]

Another early Christian Saint who is the cause of great interest is
ST. PATRICIA (d. circa 665), who was born in Constantinople and
is regarded as a relative of Emperor Constantine. She vowed her virginity to God at an early age, and while on a journey to Rome her
ship found it necessary to weigh anchor at Naples due to a violent
storm. After a few years of penitential life in Naples she died a
saintly death at the age of 21.

Her history records that her body was placed on a cart for transport to the cemetery, but the animals pulling the cart wandered
through the streets, finally arriving at the church of Saints Nican-
dro and Marciano. They stopped there and refused to move. It
seems that she had visited this church before her death and had
prophesied, "Here my body will rest." Her prediction was fulfilled
with her burial inside the church. The nuns who cared for the
church and her shrine soon adopted the name Patrician Sisters.

Apparently St. Patricia's shrine became known as a place of miracles, since we are told that a Roman knight, suffering for a long
time with unbearable pains, was cured after fervent prayers at the
shrine. He obtained permission to express his gratitude to the Saint
by spending the night in prayer before her relics. When all alone in
the empty church he opened the glass case in which St. Patricia's
bones were kept, and out of an excess of devotion, drew from the
skull a tooth that he wanted to keep as a precious relic. At once
fresh, red blood began flowing from the cavity made by the
extracted tooth. We are told that the knight was found the next
morning on the floor in a faint.

Church authorities hastened to the church on learning from the
nuns what was taking place. The warm blood that continued to flow
was quickly collected into two ampules. Since that time the miracle has been renewed for over 12 centuries. The liquefaction takes
place every year on the feast of St. Patricia, August 25, and frequently in the presence of pious pilgrims who visit the shrine. Witnesses to the miracle watch as the dry mass of dark blood in the
ampules begins to liquefy slowly. It increases in volume, fades to a
ruby red, and then reacts as fresh, living blood.

The liquefactions have been thoroughly investigated a number of times by both ecclesiastical and scientific authorities, and they have all concluded that the blood's activity cannot be explained by science and is, therefore, a genuine miracle.

In Naples, every Tuesday is dedicated to St. Patricia. Large crowds which assemble on that day to honor St. Patricia receive a blessing with the ampules containing the miraculous blood. The miracle occurs so frequently that tourists are almost constantly visiting the shrine to view the liquefaction, since the miracle is often mentioned on travel itineraries.

When a suppression of the convent took place in 1864, the shrine was transferred to the Monastery of St. Gregorio Armeno, where the relics are now kept in a crystal case decorated with gold, silver and precious gems. The cloistered Sisters, Adorers of the Blessed Sacrament, have been the guardians of the relics for many years, and it is to them that we are indebted for this information.[6]

Among the other early Saints whose blood experienced some unusual activity can be numbered ST. STEPHEN (d. circa 35), the first martyr, whose blood liquefied as late as 1674 when the hymn *Deus tuorum militum* was sung. Sabbatini, a learned and reliable witness, observed the relic in the Church of San Gaudioso in Naples when the hard substance in its vial was seen to liquefy "many times."

ST. NAZARIUS (Roman era) was a martyr whose remains at Milan were exhumed by St. Ambrose about the year 395. In the tomb was a vial of the Saint's blood that was found "as fresh and red as if it had been spilt that day." St. Ambrose also gave an account of the exhumation of the early martyrs ST. GERVASE and ST. PROTASE when "very much blood" was found. When the martyrs STS. MARCELLINUS and PETER were exhumed, the relics exuded blood for several days, although the Saints had been dead for 500 years. This exhumation was witnessed by Abbot Einhard, "whose credit as a veracious chronicler stands high." Liquefaction also took place regarding the blood of ST. LAWRENCE. For many years his blood would liquefy for eight days in August.[7]

Centuries later we have the case of ST. NICHOLAS OF TOLENTINO (d. 1305), an Augustinian who was known for his preaching, the administering of the Sacraments in the homes of the poor, in prisons and in hospitals, for the long hours he spent in the confessional and for countless miracles for which he would caution, "Say nothing of this. Give thanks to God, not to me."

Following a painful illness, the Saint died on September 10. Forty years after his death, his incorrupt body was disinterred and exposed to the faithful in the wooden casket in which it was first consigned. One night, during this exhibition, when the doors of the church were locked, the arms were secretly detached from the body. It is not certain, but the suspect is believed to have been a German monk, Teodora, who probably intended to take the arms to his native country. This amputation began the strange, almost 400-year history of the bleeding arms—discharges that were verified and recorded, according to the present representatives of the shrine.

As soon as the arms were detached a great flow of blood signaled the sacrilegious act. Later, the incorrupt body and the two arms were again consigned to the tomb, but 100 years later, during another exhumation, the body of the Saint was found to have conformed to the natural laws of dissolution, while the arms remained perfectly incorrupt and imbued with blood. Once more the remains were placed beneath the pavement of the *Cappellone*, a small chapel adjoining the church where the body had previously been interred. This time the arms were not buried, but were placed in beautifully crafted silver cases.

Fresh blood spilled in profusion toward the end of the fifteenth century, an occurrence that was repeated twenty times at various intervals. The most astounding seepage took place in 1699. The flow of blood began on May 29 and continued until September 1.

The discharges of 1671 and 1676 were also noteworthy. According to the custodians of the shrine, their Augustinian monastery and the archives of the Bishop of Camarino possess many authoritative documents concerning these effusions.

The Basilica of St. Nicholas in Tolentino was built in the fourteenth century and contains the Chapel of the Holy Arms, where relics of the blood are kept in ornate vessels. Here, behind a crystal panel in a gem-encrusted seventeenth-century urn, can be seen the cloth that was used to staunch the blood at the amputation. The crypt, built between 1926 and 1932, contains the remains of St. Nicholas. His bones are arranged in a simulated figure that is clothed in the Augustinian habit. The mummified arms, still in their silver casings, are arranged in their normal positions beside the figure. Pope Pius XI personally blessed the reliquary in which the remains are enshrined.[8]

The Church of the Holy Cross in Montefalco, Italy, possesses some remarkable relics of ST. CLARE OF MONTEFALCO (d. 1308), including her miraculous heart with its symbols of the Passion, three pellets which in a unique manner represent the Holy Trinity, and the incorrupt body of the Saint. The church also has a reliquary of the Saint's blood that liquefied at various times during the centuries.

The Saint had once mentioned to her Sisters in the Augustinian community, "If you seek the Cross of Christ, take my heart; there you will find the suffering Lord."

Again on her deathbed she repeatedly murmured, "Know that in my very heart I have and hold Christ crucified." Soon after her death, the community, as though inspired to do this, decided to extract the heart. While they did so, the blood which rushed out was collected in a large vial which had been previously washed and purified. On opening the heart and seeing the symbols of the Passion clearly defined, the Sisters realized that this extraordinary phenomenon should be witnessed and verified by others. They then locked the heart and the vial of blood in a box and carefully secured it. The next morning the box was opened in the presence of the Chief Magistrate, Gentile di Gilberti, together with the leading physician of the town, Messer Simone da Spello, and a public notary named Angelo di Montefalco. Also attending was Fr. Guardian of the Franciscan house at Foligno. After viewing the phenomenon, they prepared a report for the Bishop of Spoleto. The heart and the blood of St. Clare were later examined carefully by other church and political dignitaries. (For more details of the heart, see the chapter, "Mystical Hearts.")

Three hundred years later, in the year 1608, when it became necessary temporarily to remove the incorrupt body of St. Clare from its shrine, the nuns noticed that the vessel containing the Saint's blood had become very dusty during the course of the years. One of the nuns picked up the vessel and began carefully to wipe it when, despite all her efforts at handling the vial with utmost caution, it nevertheless slipped from her fingers and crashed on the floor. Sobbing bitterly, the distraught nuns picked up every particle of the blood and every shard of glass. All of this was placed in a larger crystal vessel. At some point during the years a crack in this vessel was noticed, and it was placed in a third vessel. The blood and the shards of glass, together with the second cracked vessel and the third crystal covering, are all perfectly transparent. The coagulated blood can be clearly viewed.

It has been noticed through the years that this blood of St. Clare of Montefalco, which is normally dry and coagulated, has been known not only to liquefy, but also to boil and bubble. Many of these ebullitions have been historically recorded and attested. These phenomena seem to have preceded "untoward and serious events," as, for instance, the liquefaction of October, 1495, when the combined forces of the Baglioni and of the Orsini swooped down and for two months pillaged and harassed the countryside. When the dreaded Duke Valentino (Cesare Borgia) established himself and his eleven thousand soldiers in Montefalco in 1500, the blood of the Saint remained in a liquid state, bubbling and frothing in its vial until he left. Other liquefactions connected to unfortunate political disturbances took place in 1508, 1560 and 1570. And still other notable liquefactions took place in 1601, 1608 and 1618.

During the seventeenth century a commission was established to study the mystery surrounding the blood of St. Clare. Again in 1880 the phenomenon was scrutinized by experts. Their conclusions coincided exactly. Their reports stated that there was something unexplainable which was outside and beyond the ordinary causes of natural law.[9]

Almost one hundred and fifty years after the death of St. Clare of Montefalco there lived the Spanish Franciscan, ST. PETER REGALADO (d. 1456), who served his order in many positions of authority while observing a strict penitential life. God rewarded his faithful service with many extraordinary graces and mystical phenomena. St. Peter of Regalado died in the sixty-sixth year of his life and was acknowledged a Saint by the great crowds that visited his body before its interment, and afterward his grave, where many miracles were worked.

Because of these miracles it was decided to remove his relics to a more honorable resting place. This was accomplished in 1492, 36 years after his death. During this exhumation several fingers were removed at the request of Queen Isabella, who wanted them as precious relics. The amputation of the fingers introduced a flow of fresh, red blood that continued "for some time." This wonder was duly noted in the records of the order, since it took place 36 years after Peter's death.[10]

We read in a biography of ST. CATHERINE OF BOLOGNA (d. 1463) that this holy abbess of a community of Franciscan nuns died at the age of forty-nine in early March and was buried, according to the custom of the order, only a few hours after death. She remained interred for eighteen days, until a heavenly perfume caused the confessor of the community to permit the body's exhumation. Phenomena soon became apparent which were described by the abbess who succeeded St. Catherine. She wrote:

> On Good Friday . . . we opened the sepulchre and on lifting the silk veil which covered the virginal body, we found it quite bathed in sweat; while we were wiping it with linen cloths it exhaled a most agreeable odour. One of the Sisters seeing a little bit of skin which hung from one of the feet, pulled it off, and instantly red blood flowed out from the place as if the body were alive . . . When morning came the Saint appeared more beautiful than ever; her forehead seemed to shine, her face was red as a rose and a mild light filled her eyes, which were quite open . . .

What is more surprising is that, ". . . three months after death, she twice bled at the nose so copiously as to fill a cup with the blood."[11]

ST. FRANCIS XAVIER (d. 1552) is regarded as one of the Church's most illustrious missionaries. While laboring in the East Indies he performed miracles of all kinds. After a brief illness, the Saint died at the age of 46. His body remained incorrupt and was eventually taken to Goa, India, where it was exposed and interred in the Basilica of the Bom Jesus.

A year and a half after the Saint's death, the body was thoroughly examined by the chief medical authority in Goa. Part of his statement reads: "I, Doctor Cosmas Saraiva, have been to examine the body of Fr. Master Francis . . . I observed a wound in the left part of the chest, near the heart and asked one of the Society who was with me to put his fingers into it. When he withdrew them they were covered with blood which I smelt and found to be absolutely untainted . . ."[12]

Eighteen months after the death of ST. JOHN OF THE CROSS (d. 1591) a legal order was issued for the removal of his bones to a monastery that had been established for him in Segovia by Doña Ana de Penasola. One of the king's sergeants, Francis de Medina Zavallos, was sent to Ubeda to negotiate the translation. In obedience to the order, the prior admitted him to the church during the night and opened the sepulchre. Immediately they both detected a heavenly fragrance and discovered the body to be perfectly intact. Because the order asked for the removal of the bones, the prior refused to obey it, since the body was fully incorrupt.

To prove to those concerned that the body was indeed incorrupt, it was decided to amputate the three fingers of the right hand which had held the pen used by the Saint in his writings. As soon as these were detached the hand filled with blood, which continued flowing freely, "as from a living person."[13]

The incorrupt body, which had been covered with lime to progress its corruption, was miraculously preserved in spite of this, and was finally taken to Segovia nine months after the amputation of the finger. The last examination of the body was made in 1955, when it was again found incorrupt. St. John of the Cross was canonized in 1726 and assumed a position among the Doctors of the Church two hundred years later, in 1926.

The poor little shepherdess ST. GERMAINE COUSIN (d. 1601) was neglected by her father, despised by her step-mother and denied the companionship of the step-children. Several miracles are recorded of her: Once, while she was on her way to church, the waters of a swollen stream separated for her passage, as did the Red Sea for Moses. While she attended Mass, her sheep were known never to stray from the staff which she stuck in the ground, and once, when she was bringing her own food scraps to the poor, only roses fell from her apron when she was accused by her step-mother.

The little Saint died alone one night on her straw pallet under the outdoor staircase where she always slept. Because of her saintly life, she was buried in the village church of Pibrac.

Once again she was neglected and forgotten until the year 1644, when workmen were preparing a grave beside that of Germaine. Upon lifting the flagstone the workmen were astonished to find the perfectly incorrupt body of a beautiful young girl who was readily identified as Germaine. A tool used by one of the men had slipped and injured the nose of the corpse, causing it to bleed. This was quite a marvel, since Germaine had died 43 years earlier.[14]

ST. ANDREW AVELLINO (d. 1608) became a doctor of law and was ordained at Naples, where he pleaded cases in the ecclesiastical courts. He eventually renounced the profession for that of saving souls and entered the Theatine Order, which he served as novice master and founder of houses in Piacenza and Milan. He refused a bishopric offered him by Gregory XIV and returned to Naples. There he became known for his preaching and miracles.

During his eighty-eighth year, on November 10, he approached the altar to begin Mass when he was suddenly struck with an attack of apoplexy. Later that afternoon he died.

While his body lay in state in the Church of St. Paul, crowds of people visited the remains, with many of them snipping off locks of his hair as relics. Because of this, some cuts were accidentally made in the skin of his face. The next morning, thirty-six hours after death, these cuts began to exude fresh, red blood. It was naturally assumed that the Saint was not really dead. When death was confirmed by physicians, a few more incisions were made and for another thirty-six hours the blood that continued to trickle from them was carefully collected.[15]

Four days later it was seen to bubble in its vial while being held by a professor of medicine. Three years later, on the anniversary of his death, the blood, by that time hard, is said to have liquefied when exposed for veneration. Again it frothed and boiled in the presence of eight religious of the Theatine Order, who signed a formal deposition to what they had witnessed.[16] Since then, records tell us that the solidified blood liquefied every year on the anniversary of St. Andrew's death.[17]

Known as a Saint during his lifetime, ST. BERNARDINO REALINO (d. 1616) was ordained a Jesuit in 1564 and earned this recognition by his devotion to the sick, the poor and the inmates of prisons, by his inspired preaching, his self-sacrificing zeal and his apostolic fervor. Because of the cultus that promptly sprang up after his death, there were many persons who were able to testify on oath to what they had witnessed for the Process of beatification. The activity of his blood samples was duly recorded and sworn to by reputable witnesses.

During his last illness two open wounds discharged a great deal of blood which, by virtue of his saintly reputation, was carefully collected in various vials. Some of these samples are said to have remained liquid for over a century; in other vials the blood foamed and appeared to increase and decrease in volume.

The Saint died at the age of 86 and was buried at Lecce in Apulia. His tomb was opened by ecclesiastical authorities in 1634. Both Butler and Thurston give some gory details regarding the remains which are nevertheless necessary in order to complete this report on the phenomenon.

The witnesses, on examining the remains, found a good deal of fleshy tissue which was removed from the bones and put into two glass containers. These were reburied with the skeleton, but 78 years later, in 1711—that is 95 years after his death—the tomb was again inspected by the bishop of Lecce for the official recognition of the relics. One of the glass vessels had broken, but the other contained a mystery since the tissue remained in the same state, but was now floating in an inch and a half of dark red liquid. Physicians promptly examined the contents and found the liquid to be human blood which exhaled a heavenly fragrance.

Two years later, the phenomenon was investigated by three bishops appointed by the Congregation of Sacred Rites. They heard the testimony of the witnesses to the 1711 experience and watched as the blood, still bright crimson, began foaming into little bubbles. Much later, in 1804, Don Gaetano Solazzo, the custodian of the vial of blood, left a statement in which he declared that the liquid had twice foamed and bubbled in his presence. Some visiting nuns also witnessed the foaming, as did a Jesuit priest who gave a sworn declaration that he had personally witnessed the bubbling in 1852.

Inserted into the official Process were depositions made by certain witnesses that one vial of the Saint's liquid blood began to boil and froth on the anniversary of Bernardino's death and also whenever it was brought into the presence of the silver reliquary containing his tongue.

According to Butler, in 1895 the blood was no longer in a liquid state.[18]

VEN. PASSITEA CROGI (d. 1615), a stigmatic, the foundress of several houses of Capuchin nuns and the abbess of the house in Siena, bled freely during her ecstatic re-enactments of Christ's Passion. On certain feastdays, as, for instance, Good Friday and the Feast of the Stigmata of St. Francis, the blood was carefully gathered in vials of various shapes. These were hermetically fastened and sealed. Because of her intense ecstasies at this time, she was totally oblivious of what was taking place around her and was unaware that her blood was being collected.

One particular vial of blood is described for us as being about two and a quarter inches in height. It is thick clear crystal which has been authenticated as having originated from the time of the stigmatic bleedings of Ven. Passitea. The stopper is covered with parchment, which has been tied down and sealed. Normally the dried blood, dark in color and resembling particles of grit, covers an eighth of an inch at the bottom. This blood, as well as the blood in other vials, has been known to change into a rosy-hued fluid that increases in size until it fills almost the entire vial.[19]

The mutilated body of ST. JOSAPHAT (d. 1623) remains marvelously incorrupt in the Church of St. Sophia in his native Poland. When a costly reliquary was crafted of precious metals and engraved with mother-of-pearl pictures depicting scenes of his martyrdom, the body was exhumed for the third time. While the incorrupt body of the martyr was being prepared for its enshrinement, the mortal wound on the forehead of the Saint opened and discharged fresh red blood. This amazed the witnesses, since St. Josaphat had been dead 27 years.[20]

The Franciscan ST. PACIFICUS DI SAN SEVERINO (d. 1721) died while wreathed with the fragrance of sanctity. More than four years later, when his body was disinterred, it was found incorrupt, flexible and emitting the same sweet perfume. Much to the horror of those who were moving the body, the head of the corpse struck a stairway and detached from the trunk. As if that were not enough to cause great confusion, blood flowed freely from the neck and splattered the shirt of one Francesco Tarquinio, who was helping to move the body. A century later, Fr. Melchiorri, who wrote a biography of the Saint, claimed that the shirt was still kept as a relic.[21]

Other Miracles of Blood

Another kind of blood miracle is that of blood exuding from a crucifix. Such a miracle took place during the lifetime of BL. JAMES OF BEVAGNA (d. 1301), a holy Dominican about whom much is mentioned in this book. It seems that the mother of Bl. James was shocked at seeing the poor condition of his habit and gave him money to buy a new one. Instead, he bought a crucifix for his cell, reminding his mother of the Bible text, "Put ye on the Lord Jesus Christ." The crucifix, he told his mother, was the "garment" with which he wanted to be clothed.

Once while praying before this same crucifix, he was overwhelmed with his own unworthiness and begged Our Lord for some sign that his soul would be saved. Immediately, blood gushed from the hands and side of the figure on the cross while a heavenly voice reassured him of his salvation. Some of the miraculous blood was collected and kept for two centuries, but it was eventually stolen by heretics.[22]

The Saint who is known as "God's Miracle Worker Supreme," ST. FRANCIS OF PAOLA (d. 1507), was in disagreement with the Neapolitan King Ferrante, who was regarded as being corrupt and cynical. During one of their meetings, St. Francis expressed a desire to construct a monastery of his order in Naples. Hoping to win the Saint's gratitude and make him less critical of the way he treated his subjects, the king sent Francis a large vessel with gold coins as his contribution toward the construction of the monastery.

Realizing the intentions of the king, the Saint went himself to the royal court to return the coins. In doing so he delivered a long, loud and stern rebuke to the king, saying among other things, "This gold that you offered me to build a monastery in your capital city, this gold is not your gold; this is the blood of your people that has been squeezed out of them through your ruinous taxes and vicious tax collectors . . ."

He warned the king of God's vengeance and the strict account he would have to give to God for all the injustices, acts of extortion, and the cruelty of his ministers upon poor and helpless people. The king answered the Saint quietly, in a strong reversal of his usual bad temper, and promised to correct the matters expressed to him.

As a final testament to the king, the Saint reached for one of the gold coins and with ease broke it in two. The king and the court moved away in shock when blood dripped from the two halves. This is a scene that is often depicted in the Saint's iconography. The king, badly shaken by this sign from God, promised to reform his government and begged for the Saint's prayers.[23]

A very unusual blood miracle, and one drastically different from those mentioned above, involved POPE ST. PIUS V (d. 1572), who is regarded as one of the greatest Popes of all times. The miracle of blood took place when the Polish ambassador, while speaking with the Pope, asked for a relic to take back with him to his country. Pope Pius V stooped down and gathered a little dust from the ground. He put the dust in a piece of clean linen and gave it to the ambassador saying, "These are very precious relics." No doubt the ambassador was somewhat surprised and shocked by the Pope's actions, and was also disappointed at not receiving a precious relic for his country. But on arriving home he found the cloth stained with blood, which was recognized as that of the holy martyrs— blood that had sanctified the Roman terrain.[24]

The Blood of St. John the Baptist?

The examples of blood liquefactions mentioned in the beginning of this chapter concerned early martyrs whose blood relics are still performing this unique activity. There is still another vial of blood of an early martyr. This sample of blood is not very well known. Additionally, it is not known if the blood still liquefies, nor is it absolutely certain that the blood came from the person mentioned, but because of the reputable persons who wrote about it, the author feels compelled to mention it here. The blood is said to belong to none other than St. John the Baptist.

Attention shifts to a convent named Sant' Arcangelo a Baiano, which belonged to nuns of the Order of St. Benedict. Recalling that the blood of martyrs was customarily collected in little vials, Pietro di Stefano, "the pious and well-informed antiquary" who wrote about the miracle in the mid-16th century, tells that the nuns had a little cruet with "blood which was harder than a stone." It had been given to the convent about the year 1265.

The abbess was anxious to learn to which martyr it belonged and sought advice from an aged priest. The priest replied: "My dear Sister, the only thing to do is to have recourse to prayer and to ask God to reveal to you what martyr it belongs to. And so I suggest that on every martyr's feast you set the relic with all honour upon the altar, and have the Vespers of the martyr solemnly sung in the hope that our God may grant you some miracle . . ."

The abbess did as she was directed on every feastday of a martyr. Finally, on the feast of The Beheading of St. John the Baptist, a day which is still observed worldwide, she placed the cruet on the altar and began the first Vespers. "And lo! on that same day the blood liquefied miraculously . . . and the same thing has happened each year on the feast of St. John the Baptist's Beheading."

Pietro di Stefano continues by telling of his personal observation:

> I myself, being anxious to witness so great a miracle was present there on the same feast, which is the 29th of August, in the year 1558, in order to see what happened. There was brought in a little cruet full of blood which was as hard as a rock, and they set it with great veneration upon the High Altar, and the priests of San Giovan' a Mare sang the Vespers, and when the Vespers were over, all the bystanders could see that the blood had liquefied, whereupon all gave praises to God Almighty. And surely this is a most glorious miracle and a great testimony to our holy faith that the said most holy martyr, than whom there hath not arisen a greater born of woman, should vouchsafe to give such a sign on the day he died for the love of Christ our Redeemer.[25]

The book by Pietro di Stefano which detailed the above was printed in 1560. Sometime later the membership of the convent of Sant' Arcangelo a Baiano dwindled and the convent was closed. The relic was then divided into two parts which were given to the convent chapels of Santa Maria Donna Romita and San Gregorio Armeno. St. Alphonsus in his theological work entitled *Evidenza della Fede* mentions the blood of St. John the Baptist as being kept in these two convent chapels. Cardinal Newman also mentions the blood of the Saint.

Before he was consecrated bishop, Sabbatini, a scholar of vast learning who was mentioned previously, saw the liquefaction and wrote: "One morning I had the consolation while celebrating Mass in the church of Donna Romita to see that the said blood began gradually to dissolve, and eventually it all liquefied."

Sabbatini wrote about the year 1750 that the blood of the Saint at Donna Romita was often exhibited to gratify the devotion of casual visitors, and that it liquefied every time, especially when Holy Mass was offered in its presence. However, the relic kept at San Gregorio Armeno usually remained hard until the first Vespers of the Saint's feastday, August 29.

A Jesuit priest who accompanied Count Palatine on a visit to Naples in 1676 went to the church of San Gregorio Armeno, where a votive Mass of St. John the Baptist was celebrated. He wrote:

> I said the first Mass and before I had ended drops were already trickling from the solid substance in the glass phial before me. Another Mass followed during which it became fluid, and by the time a third was begun it all sparkled and bubbled like blood freshly spurting from the veins of a living man.[26]

The blood is known to have liquefied in 1846 and might still be liquefying on the Saint's feastday, August 29. The relics are still kept in two convent chapels, Santa Maria Donna Romita and San Gregorio Armeno, both in Naples.

The account of this miracle was included in the *Acta Sanctorum*, a scholarly hagiographical collection which began in the first years of the seventeenth century and continues to be published in our day by the Bollandists.

"THIS IS THE BLOOD of your people that has been squeezed out of them . . . ," said St. Francis of Paola as he returned coins that had been given to him by Neapolitan King Ferrante for construction of a monastery. The Saint demonstrated his disapproval of the King's corrupt ways by breaking one of the gold coins in two. The King and his court moved away in shock when the two halves of the coin dripped blood.

THE LIQUEFACTION of the blood of St. Januarius was captured in the photograph above, taken during ceremonies in the Naples cathedral. (From *The Book of Miracles*, by Zsolt Aradi; Farrar, Straus & Cudahy.)

BLOOD RELICS of St. Nicholas of Tolentino, kept in ornate vessels in the Basilica of St. Nicholas, Tolentino. The vessel at right contains a blood-stained cloth that was used at the amputation of the relic's arms in 1345. (From *Un Asceta E Un Apostalo S. Nicola da Tolentino*, P. Domenico Gentile.)

VOICES OF THE DEAD

Few facts are given about the life of BL. PETER OF GUBBIO (d. circa 1250), although we know that he joined the Brictinian Hermits of St. Augustine and later became its provincial. But interest in him was suddenly generated when an unusual occurrence was reported at his tomb. Often, when the hermits had gathered for the night office, a voice was heard chanting the alternate verses of the *Te Deum*. An investigation proved that the voice was proceeding from the tomb of Bl. Peter.

Because such a wonder called for investigation, the vault in which he was buried was opened. To the amazement of all present, his body was found in a kneeling posture with the hands joined in prayer and the mouth wide open. The incorrupt body was moved to a more honorable resting place, where it is said to have remained incorrupt. The wonder also attracted pilgrims, and many flocked to Gubbio to pray at the tomb.[1]

The Monastery of St. Augustine in Gubbio, Italy, can prove by a great collection of documents contained in its archives that the voice of the Blessed was heard emanating from his tomb many years after his death, as testified and sworn to by many distinguished authorities of the Augustinian Order and the reports of many reliable witnesses.

BL. EUSTOCHIA CALAFATO (d. 1485) had spent eleven years in the convent of the Poor Clares at S. Maria de Basico when she was inspired to found a new convent where the original rule of St. Clare was to be observed in greater strictness and in absolute poverty. Since the first convent was in poor condition, she and her sisters were forced to move to Montevergine (Maiden's Hill) in northeast Sicily. Montevergine observed the fifth centenary of its founding in 1964.

In the biography written by Sr. Pollicino, one of the Beata's original companions in the new community, there are many testimonials to the heroic nature of the virtues practiced by Eustochia, and to numerous miracles—especially regarding the multiplication of food. Bl. Eustochia died a saintly death on January 20, 1485 after spending fifty-one years in the performance of God's Will and after having borne in her flesh for many years the stigmatic wounds of Our Lord's Passion.

The most dramatic miracle performed by the Beata, who had so often protected the city from damaging earthquakes, occurred in 1615 when the city was shaken day and night by almost constant vibrations. Unable to quiet the earthquake by their own prayers, the senate and people of the city petitioned the Sisters to pray to Bl. Eustochia for protection. The Sisters promised their prayers and then decided on a strange scenario.

They removed the perfectly preserved body of Bl. Eustochia from the oratory where it had been conserved for almost a hundred fifty years, and placed it in an upright position in the Saint's old choir stall. After they had charged Eustochia to pray for the protection of the city, the lips of the obedient Beata opened and her voice was heard chanting the first verse of the psalm of the night office.

The Sisters, completely terrified, nevertheless joined in the recitation and bowed their heads during the *Gloria* in unison with their holy foundress. Needless to add, the earthquake is said to have ceased at that moment.[2]

The miracle is related in papers composed by the sisters of Monastero Montevergine in 1964 at the time of the observance of the fifth centenary of the founding of the monastery.

VEN. MARIA VELA (d. 1617) entered the Cistercian Convent of Santa Ana in Avila, where she lived in great sanctity for the rest of her forty-two years on earth. In addition to being an accomplished musician, she was useful to the community as sacristan and seamstress. She also suffered both physical and spiritual afflictions and was often rapt in ecstasies. She was also known to have levitated frequently during prayer.

Reports of her sanctity spread beyond the walls of her enclosure so that, at the time of her death, the convent was besieged by crowds seeking relics. She was declared a venerable by popular acclamation, which could legally be done in those days with the permission of the Church.

Because of her great sanctity she was not buried on the cloister grounds, but at the foot of the altar dedicated to Our Lady of the

Sun, to whom she had shown particular devotion. Attending the service were the bishop, Don Francisco de Gamarra, the canons of the cathedral and the nobles and gentry of Avila.

After the Venerable's death many mysterious occurrences were recorded, and there were instances when her voice was heard speaking to her dear friend and fellow religious, Maria de Avila, during the community recitation of Matins. During Benediction services her singing voice was recognized accompanying the sisters in the hymns.[3]

Two years after her death, with the permission of the bishop, the casket was transferred to a new position in the chapel. It was during that function that her body was found to be in a perfect state of preservation, in which it remains today.

VEN. MARY OF AGREDA (d. 1665) wrote the well-known book, *The Mystical City of God*, which is regarded as the autobiography of Our Lady. It is said that the information in the book was revealed by the Blessed Virgin and was in part dictated by her.

At the age of only twenty-five, Mary of Agreda was elected abbess of her community because of her talents and extraordinary virtues. She fulfilled her obligations in this position for the remainder of her life. Her ecstasies, levitations, bilocations and other mystical phenomena were such that she was investigated at the instigation of her bishop, who was satisfied with the findings.

After rigorous examinations of her life and graces, Abbe J. A. Boullan, Doctor in Theology, declared:

> In the highest rank among the mystics of past ages, who have been endowed with signal graces and singular privileges by the august Queen of Heaven, must be placed, without hesitation, the Venerable Mary of Jesus called of Agreda, from the name of the city in Spain where she passed her life . . . No more perfect model can be found of the most elevated ways of mystical perfection . . . She is unique, and most valuable as a study in the progress of the soul . . .[4]

Being divinely informed of her impending death, she notified her community. With the townspeople weeping outside, and with the members of her community praying beside her sickbed, she died peacefully at the age of 62, having been a nun for 46 years and abbess for 35 years.

The community attested to the fact that at the moment of her death they heard a heavenly voice repeat, "Come, come, come," the Venerable expiring at the last summons.[5]

In another chapter of this book we read about the wonders performed by ST. THÉRÈSE OF THE CHILD JESUS AND OF THE HOLY FACE (d. 1897). Some of these marvels took place when the Saint multiplied money that was desperately needed by the community of Gallipoli, Italy. Following the miracles, a Carmelite nun in another convent wrote to the Carmel at Lisieux to report what she had experienced while writing a letter which included information about the Saint's multiplication of money. Unfortunately, we do not know the name of the correspondent or her location, but she begins her letter in this way:

Dear Reverend Mother,

On July 20, 1910, writing to a friend, an exiled nun in Belgium, I had mentioned, as I invariably do in my letters, the marvels wrought throughout the whole world by our dear little Sister of Lisieux. I gave an account of the wonderful miracle of the 500 francs of Gallipoli, but, forgetting the name of the town in Italy where it had happened, I left a blank space for it.

That evening after Compline, wishing to finish the letter, I noticed that, contrary to my intention, I had forgotten to ask some one or other of the Sisters at recreation for the name of Gallipoli, which during the day I could not remember. Then, having recourse to my little Thérèse, I begged her to recall it to my memory: "Little Thérèse, do remind me of that name which escapes me!" Immediately I heard a voice sweet as that of an angel sound in my ear, and I caught perfectly this word, "Gallipoli." "Oh, I whispered to myself, Thérèse is here!" At the same moment I felt her near me at the window where I was writing. "Yes," she made answer. Then there were several seconds of a pause and she went on: "That is just what you must do. You must make me known everywhere. I desire to do so much good." With my wonted familiarity I replied: "O my little Thérèse, how much you have changed since you have gone to heaven! In this world you wished only for forgetfulness and contempt." Then she gave an interior light which made me understand that the more we humble ourselves, the more God exalts us. Presently I knew that my celestial visitor, whom I did not see, but whose presence I could feel, was about to leave me. I said a few words more to her, and she withdrew—leaving my soul inundated with a heavenly joy. I went to Matins, my heart overflowing with gratitude for the grace just given me. All my life long it will be an indelible memory.[6]

The letter was signed simply, "A Carmelite."

In the 1912 edition of the Saints' autobiography published as *Soeur Thérèse of Lisieux*, the letter is found in the section called "The Shower of Roses," which contains letters received by the convent at Lisieux telling of prayers answered and cures obtained.

The Voice of St. Clelia Barbieri

The previous examples of voices heard after death all happened years and centuries ago, but we have a present-day example that was heard and is still being heard in the convents and hospitals that are under the direction of the order known as Suore Minime dell'Addolorata in LeBudrie, Italy.

The voice belongs to ST. CLELIA BARBIERI (d. 1870). Her brief life edified everyone who came into contact with her. Clelia was born into a poor family of hemp farmers. When she was eight years of age her father died during a cholera epidemic. Without Giuseppe Barbieri, Clelia's mother, her two sisters and her seventy-five-year-old grandfather were faced with a difficult future. But Clelia was a great consolation for her mother and assisted her by learning to use the loom and weave hemp. Even at this age Clelia was devout and learned all she could about the Faith from her mother and the parish priest. After she had learned to read and write, Clelia's favorite book was her catechism, because it taught her about God and encouraged her in the way of virtue.

Her biographer reports that she was regarded as a little angel, and people outside of church, on seeing her leave, would respectfully exclaim, "Let the little Saint by." After receiving the Sacrament of Confirmation, she determined to become a saint and at the age of eleven, she was already wholly dedicated to Christ.

When she was fifteen, the parish priest, Fr. Guidi, formed a group known as "The Christian Doctrine Workers," a group of young teachers of which Clelia was a member. She taught children their catechism and ran a small primary country school in which the students were only a few years younger than herself. Eventually, both men and women attended her classes along with their children.

Having pledged herself to Our Lord, she refused a number of proposals of marriage and is believed to have taken the vows of chastity, obedience and poverty under the guidance of Fr. Guidi.[7]

When she was almost twenty-one years old, Clelia inspired a small group of young ladies of similar religious ideals to join her in the performance of good works. After acquiring a small house near a church in LeBudrie they began living a community life, but they retained their secular status throughout Clelia's lifetime. They devoted their energies to the teaching of Christian doctrine, to sewing, to aiding the sick, and to providing every manner of charitable assistance to those in need.

Many unusual things began to take place. When there was no food in the house, the community prayed; the doorbell rang, and food was provided. Praying to St. Francis of Paola, the patron of the group, was also effective in obtaining bread, flour, wine and other staples. Clelia seems to have been blessed with other mystical favors, as was demonstrated when she was given a quantity of apples from the mother of Anna Forni, a member of the community. Clelia placed them on a table and divided them into three parts, saying, "I will keep these you picked in your orchard, and those you found on the ground, but I cannot accept this third group because you did not come by them honestly." In fact, the woman had gathered some of the apples from the trees on someone else's property.

In addition, Mother Clelia, as she was then known, cured many people by using the oil from the lamp that burned before the portrait of St. Francis of Paola.[8]

One day, while standing at the window of the community's house, she pointed to a nearby field and prophesied, "Do you see that field next to the church? There the new house will rise. I will no longer be here . . . You will increase in number and will spread out on the plains and in the mountains to work in God's vineyard. Many will come with carriages and horses . . ."[9]

All of this was eventually realized. Clelia died of tuberculosis on July 13, 1870 when she was only 23 years old. Her last words were prophetic: "Be brave because I am going to Paradise; but I shall always remain with you, too; I shall never abandon you!" This prophecy was also realized, since she proved her presence by the sounding of her voice. The miraculous phenomenon of her voice first took place during the evening of July 13, 1871, exactly one year after Clelia's death, while the sisters were at prayer in the chapel. The Sisters declared that:

> Suddenly there was the sound of a high-pitched, harmonious and heavenly voice that accompanied the singing in the choir; at times it sang solo, at other times it harmonized with the choir, moving across from right to left; sometimes it passed close by the ears of one or other of the sisters.[10]
>
> The joy which it brought filled our hearts with a happiness impossible to put into words. This wasn't of this world. We lived that day in paradise. From time to time, one had to leave the room . . . The emotion that we experienced was so strong that it left you breathless until one had to call out: "Enough, dear Lord, enough!"[11]

The miraculous event dismissed all thought of their night's rest. Instead, since the Blessed Sacrament was not then reserved in their chapel, they decided to pass the night adoring the Blessed Sacrament in a nearby church. They again declared, "But how great was our surprise when we realized that the voice had followed us and accompanied us as we began our prayers."[12]

Clelia's voice prayed with them until dawn. Since that day she has never left them, joining them in the most diverse surroundings and conditions.

At the time of Clelia's death there were only ten girls who lived in the community. After the Rule of the Order was approved by the Vatican, more members joined the community, many being inspired by the voice of the holy foundress. After the Second World War there were 236 members. During the 1950's the sisters numbered almost three hundred. In recent years the flourishing order maintained over thirty-five institutions throughout Italy. Then mission fields beckoned. Houses of the order were opened in Keralia, India and in Tanzania, Africa with a number of the local young women joining in practicing the ideals of the holy foundress.

In the communities of Usokami and Wadakanchery, the Sisters hear Clelia's voice which sings and prays with them in Swahili and Malayalam. When they pray in Latin, Clelia prays in Latin as well.

During the past one hundred and twenty-five years since her death, Clelia's heavenly voice has been periodically heard in the houses of the order. Especially at LeBudrie the voice is heard accompanying the sisters in their hymns, in religious readings and in their conversations. It is also heard accompanying the priest during the celebration of Holy Mass and during the sermons. Even in the parish churches it is heard lingering among the faithful.

The Mother Superior of the order in LeBudrie stated to the author in 1970, ". . . this prodigious gift stimulates us to do well, increases our faith, is a relief to the trials of life, and gives us a great desire for heaven."[13]

In a more recent letter received before publication of this book, the Mother Provincial of the order, Sr. Silvana Magnani, confirms that the prodigy is still taking place. She writes that "The voice accompanies us in our prayers which are in Italian and with prayers that are in diverse languages: in Tanzania where we have a mission, the voice speaks in the language of Swahili; in India, the language [is] Malayalam."

The voice has been described as one unlike any of this earth. Always sweet and gentle, it is sometimes sad, and not only is it frequently accompanied by angelic strains but is itself often transformed into the purest celestial music. Many witnesses of unquestionable integrity, including her original companions, various superiors and sisters of the order, priests and lay workers in the order's hospitals have adequately testified that they have heard the voice. Moreover, many witnesses have given sworn testimony before ecclesiastical tribunals who investigated the prodigy prior to Clelia's solemn beatification on October 27, 1968, and before her canonization on April 9, 1989.

The vocal manifestations confirm the protective promise made by Clelia to her companions before her death, "Be brave, because I am going to Paradise; but I shall always remain with you, too; I shall never abandon you!"

St. Clelia's biographer reports in a recent book:

> And St. Clelia continues to let us hear her voice like
> that first anniversary of her death.
> Her nuns, together with many others, continue to hear
> her voice which prays, sings and intercedes. It is a voice
> full of happiness when announcing good news for her
> "family," the Church and the world. It is full of sadness
> when suffering is nearby. It is always calm and encour-
> aging, a true sign that God never leaves us.[14]

At Le Budrie, in the sanctuary of the Saint, people are always
kneeling before the beautifully crafted urn that contains her relics.
It is from there that blessings have proceeded throughout Italy and
the world.

ST. CLELIA BARBIERI died in 1870, but her voice is still heard
by the sisters of her order.

DEATH WARNINGS AND OTHER SIGNALS FROM THE DEAD

Rappings and knockings, also known as "Golpes," have proceeded from relics of certain Saints. The knockings have been instinctively interpreted according to their intensity and have been frequently accepted as a friendly signal or as a warning of an approaching death. Needless to relate, the friendly signals instilled in the hearts of the beneficiaries an intense religious joy and an overwhelming consciousness of the Saint's presence. When the rappings were interpreted as a signal of an approaching death, they were accepted with holy resignation and timely preparation.

Knocks of a friendly nature were given by ST. PHILOMENA (d. Roman times) in favor of Giovanni Maria Ferretti, who was to become Pope Pius IX (d. 1878). He was devoted to St. Philomena the child martyr from the time he was cured of epilepsy in his childhood through her intercession. During the days when he served the Church as Archbishop of Spoleto, he frequently visited St. Philomena's sanctuary in Mugnano, Italy and encouraged devotion to her.

Some years later, when he was Archbishop of Imola, he became seriously ill and close to death. With a statue of the Saint beside his bed, he and others prayed fervently for his recovery. Those around his bed heard distinct tappings, then known as "St. Philomena's knocks of assurance," which usually signalled the granting of a miracle. A great improvement was then seen in the condition of the Archbishop, and a speedy recovery followed.[1]

This devotee of St. Philomena, Pope Pius IX, holds the honor of being the Pontiff who reigned the longest, from 1846 to 1878. He also holds the distinction of having proclaimed the dogma of the Immaculate Conception.

The Pontiff's devotion to St. Philomena was confirmed when he bequeathed his pectoral cross to her. It is now worn around the neck of the image that contains her bones. Additionally, the Pontiff honored St. Philomena with a visit to her shrine and also honored her on November 7, 1849, when he offered Mass on the altar dedicated to her. A plaque in the sanctuary bears testimony of this visit. The same Pope immortalized St. Philomena in 1849 when he named her Patroness of the Children of Mary and declared her to be Secondary Patroness of the Kingdom of Naples.[2]

From time to time, friendly knockings are also given to the Saint's clients who visit the shrine. One such occurrence took place when the Rev. Paul O'Sullivan, the Saint's biographer, visited the shrine for a number of days. One day while he was praying in a side chapel of the church where the relics are kept, one of the Sisters approached him and asked, "Father, have you received the sign?" When the good priest indicated that he did not know about the sign, the nun insisted, "Father, you have come from a long distance and have remained here so many days; the Little Saint must give you the sign." Saying this, she directed the priest to the altar where the miraculous image is enshrined. As Fr. O'Sullivan writes:

> We knelt in front of the urn and began a short prayer. Suddenly, a sharp report rang out, as if the crystal glass had been struck sharply by something hard. The little Sister jumped up, radiant with smiles, and said to me: "Now you have got it." The report was so distinct and sharp that the Reverend Mother, further up in the church, ignorant altogether of what we were about, jumped round and asked, "Whom is it for?"[3]

Fr. O'Sullivan reports that the knock of St. Philomena is looked upon as a special mark of her good pleasure, "and surely it was a harbinger of good for me." The knockings of St. Philomena, a Saint beloved by St. Jean Marie Vianney, were experienced by many priests in the nineteenth century who verified these occurrences. Their depositions are recorded in the annals of 1850-1855.[4]

Among other relics that demonstrated a friendly signal were those of ST. PASCHAL BAYLON (d. 1592), especially known for his devotion to the Holy Eucharist. When the Saint's body was found to be incorrupt, fragments of bone were carefully removed from the feet of the corpse. Tiny pieces of these bones were enclosed in little cases and were distributed to the faithful, with one being given to a child named Antonio Pascal. Antonio was one of the first to hear the holy rappings.

While Antonio was wearing the relic around his neck, it began to emit light taps on the child's chest, as though the relic were alive. To those who discounted the miracle, the child had merely to take off the reliquary and recite devoutly, "Blessed be the most Holy Sacrament of the Altar," after which the knockings would immediately resound.

Hearing of this phenomenon, Archbishop Don Luis Alphonsus de Cameros expressed his skepticism until the child was brought to him. After the customary prayer, the knockings were immediately heard coming from the reliquary. So great was the emotion of the Archbishop that he kissed the relic and exclaimed, "Verily, God is wonderful in His Saints."

The Ven. Fr. Diego Danon, who was renowned in the Province of St. John the Baptist for his great holiness, also wore a relic of the Saint about his neck. The sounds coming from the relic were like those of a ticking clock which were distinctly heard by everyone around him. The holy priest maintained that the Saint bestowed many favors upon him by means of the relic and that the holy effects it produced would be known only on the day of judgment.

The celebrated preacher, Fr. Alphonsus of St. Thomas, a Discalced Trinitarian, testified in a deposition that the relic he wore was a source of copious graces and blessings. During one of his meditations he counted sixty raps. The sounds were frequently heard during his offering of Holy Mass, when the sounds filled him with devotion or aided in his recollection.[5]

Golpes as warnings of approaching death were also used by BL. ANTHONY VICI OF STRONCONE (d. 1461). Anthony died after having spent sixty-eight years as a Franciscan friar. As in the case of St. Philomena, his rappings were heard coming from the glass-sided reliquary which holds his incorrupt body. The rappings were first heard soon after the second exhumation that took place in 1599 at the church of San Damiano in Assisi.

Following the examination, the body was placed above a side altar. One of the marvels that took place before this altar consisted of distinct knockings heard by many priestly witnesses immediately prior to the death of a member of the community. For example: the Rev. Pietro of Cibottola heard the sounds before the death of Friar

Giuseppe of Gandino. Rev. Bartolomeo of Costacciaro and Rev. Girolamo of Amelia heard the rappings immediately before the death of Sebastiano of Monte Tezio. The Rev. Isidoro of Carniola heard the knockings before the death of the Rev. Antonio di Castelnuovo, as did Friar Bonaventura before the death of the Rev. Egidio of Bonveglio.

Accounts of these and other phenomena were recorded and can be found in the archives of the monastery of St. Francis at Stroncone, the place where the incorrupt body is still enshrined.[6]

Another unusual incident related to the prophetic warnings of a death revolved around the incorrupt body of BL. MATTHIA NAZZAREI OF MATELICA (d. 1319). Throughout the years a miraculous flow of "blood-fluid" was seen proceeding from her corpse, to the amazement of many witnesses, physicians and ecclesiastical authorities. Known as "manna" (see the chapter on Manna in this volume), the liquid began flowing in December of 1758 and commenced and stopped at various times, until it was realized that it flowed as a warning before the outbreak of wars, plagues, events of epic proportions or just prior to the death of members of the community. The mysterious formation of the "blood-fluid," which flowed intermittently for over 200 years, stopped when the condition of the incorrupt body deteriorated.[7] In recent years the relics have been enclosed in a plastic form representing the Saint's body.

We also have the case of BL. BEATRICE D'ESTE (d. 1226), the aunt of the Beata of the same name who is mentioned elsewhere in this book. Bl. Beatrice was born in the castle of Este and became a nun in the convent of Santa Margherita at Solarolo. Not finding herself sufficiently secluded from the world, she founded a religious house in a deserted area of Gemmola. After her holy death she was buried in the church of Santa Sophia at Padua. According to traditional accounts, a great noise which reverberates throughout the church proceeds from her tomb whenever important events are to befall the family of Este.[8]

A signal of another sort, which was experienced at the tomb of BL. CLARITUS (d. 1348), warned of approaching deaths and might be mentioned here.

Bl. Claritus, a married man of considerable means, founded in

1342 a convent for Augustinian nuns at Florence which was dedicated by him to Our Lady, the Queen of Heaven. When his wife, Nicolasia, entered the order, Claritus disposed of his wealth and joined the order, living at the convent as a servant. In this humble capacity he remained until he died of the plague that tormented Florence in 1348. Buried in the convent church, his body was credited with the property of emitting a heavenly fragrance whenever one of the nuns was about to die.[9]

BL. ALVAREZ OF CORDOVA (d. 1420) was a member of the Dominican Order and is best remembered as a builder of churches and convents and the worker of miracles. A short distance from Cordova, where he was born, he built the famous convent of Scala Coeli, and there he died and was buried. Sometime after his death the people of Cordova wanted to remove his relics to his birthplace, but each time an attempt was made a violent storm began which stopped only when the relics were returned to their original resting place. Deprived of the body of their Saint, the nuns at the convent at Cordova nevertheless dedicated a chapel to Bl. Alvarez.

Located in this chapel is a bell which rings of its own accord when anyone in the convent is about to die. It has also been noted and documented that it also rings when a member of special note in the order is going to die.[10]

Signals of the Blessed Virgin Mary

We now turn to the Queen of Saints, the BLESSED MOTHER, who used a statue, that of Our Lady of Santa Anita, to announce the approaching death of certain people. Located in Santa Anita, Jalisco, Mexico, the statue is a small wooden sculpture a foot and a half high that was brought to Mexico by a European hermit sometime before the year 1700. Before his death it was given to a pious native named Agustina, who began the custom of carrying the statue to the bedside of the sick. It was also the custom for Agustina, upon arriving home, to light a candle before the image and pray for the health of the patient. Agustina soon began to notice that the face of the statue became bright and glowing if the patient was going to recover, and would turn dark if the patient was destined to die. In the case of a forewarned death, Agustina would exhort the patient to receive the Sacraments and die in the grace of God.

When the Franciscans at Tlajomulco learned of the prophetic

image, they questioned Agustina about the phenomenon. As a test, they carried the statue to their monastery. One of the religious was gravely ill, and as the image was brought to the bedside, the sick friar exclaimed: "You are very beautiful, O Lady, but very dark." Shortly thereafter he died a holy death. The Franciscans eventually became custodians of the statue.

According to tradition, Our Lady of Santa Anita notified the friars by means of knockings, or "golpes," when a death was to occur in their community. One incident is particularly remarkable.

Many years ago, when an elderly friar was ill, his brethren were participating in their daily period of recreation when the sound of shattering glass was heard coming from the sanctuary. They rushed into the church, but found everything in order. They had just returned to the common room to continue their recreation when the sound was repeated. For a second time they ran to the sanctuary, thinking that perhaps the glass case protecting the holy statue was broken, but they again found everything in order. The sound of breaking glass was distinctly heard a third time—with the same result. It was the Father Superior who declared that perhaps Our Lady wanted to warn the community that one of their members was about to die. They, of course, thought of their elderly confrere who was ill. Entering the friar's cell the Father Superior whispered in his ear, "My brother, I have a message for you from Our Lady." Holding his rosary in his hands, the old religious replied, "I know already. I am going to die. Just a few moments ago Our Lady knocked on the door three times to tell me."

It was usually by three knocks that the Blessed Virgin warned the friars that one of their brethren was soon to die.

The miraculous statue, usually vested in fine fabrics and crowned with gold, is serenaded each year on the feast of the Purification during a grand fiesta held in honor of Our Lady.[11]

— 26 —

MANNA

During the 40 years that Moses and the chosen people were wandering in the wilderness, they were sustained with manna which

> . . . was like coriander seed, of the colour of bdellium.
> And the people went about, and gathering it, ground it
> in a mill, or beat it in a mortar, and boiled it in a pot, and
> made cakes thereof of the taste of bread tempered with
> oil. And when the dew fell in the night upon the camp,
> the manna also fell with it. (*Numbers* 11:7-9).

In contrast to its use above, the word "manna" has been used for a variety of fluids: oil from the lamps that burned before the shrines of some Saints, oil or water that was spilled over their relics, or water from wells near their burial places, all of which were used for the cure of bodily and spiritual ailments. The favorable results from their application were not obtained from any intrinsic power of the oil or water, but through the intercession of the Saints with whom the water or oil had some connection.

What we are considering here is not the manna of the Old Testament, nor the substances described in the preceeding paragraph. For the purposes of this chapter, manna takes the form of a granular powder, or a powdery substance like flour, or, what is the most common form: a colorless, tasteless, often odorless oil or liquid which has mysteriously appeared on, and often flowed from the bones of many Saints and from some incorrupt bodies of Saints. The word "manna" has been borrowed, since the formation of this liquid is as mysterious and miraculous as was the creation of the Old Testament food.

The formation of this oil is truly mystifying, since it has been known to collect on the bones and bodies of Saints that are located in many different countries with various atmospheric conditions and under circumstances that are considered unfavorable and unusual.

Manna from the Bones of the Saints

The oldest relics known to have exuded manna are those of ST. ANDREW THE APOSTLE. It is believed that St. Andrew labored in Turkey and Greece, where his life ended in the city of Patras on November 30 in the year 60. According to the Greek document that was translated by St. Gregory, Bishop of Tours (d. 594), the manna first presented itself on the anniversary of the Apostle's death as a perfumed oil that flowed from the sepulchre. Sometimes the manna took the form of a powder that collected on the tomb. For years the oil was so abundant that at times it dripped from the tomb and flowed down the aisle of the church.

The relics were moved about the year 357 to Constantinople, and there also the manna continued to flow. Cardinal Baronio commented at the time that the entire Christian world knew about the substances that collected on the Apostle's tomb. The manna was gathered as a relic and as such was distributed.

At the time of the fourth Crusade in 1204, Cardinal Peter of Capua collected the bones of the Apostle in a silver urn and brought them to safety in Italy, where he placed them in the Cathedral of Amalfi. A century later an elderly gentleman worshiping in the church was somehow alerted to the miracle and notified the priest. A white granular substance was discovered inside the tomb, and when this substance was applied to a man his vision was restored after several years of blindness.

Sometime later the location of the tomb was "lost to oblivion" until January 2, 1603. A stonemason, while working in the church, discovered a slab of marble with the inscriptions *Corpus s. And. ap.* After being recognized by the bishop, the relics were interred with a notarized document signed by the mayor and many witnesses. Unfortunately, the tomb was again lost to memory.

The relics were delivered from obscurity on January 28, 1846, when restorations were being conducted in the church. Work on the flooring had progressed very slowly, since the masons had heard that a treasure had been buried centuries before. After they removed some stones from a wall, the marble slab and the urn were discovered. The next day, in the presence of the archbishop, the document of 1603 was found in the urn with the relics of the Apostle. To prevent their being misplaced again, the urn was removed to the main altar, and there the relics are still found. A silver basin rests beneath the urn to collect the manna.

Since that time manna has been collected punctually on the 28th of January, the anniversary of the relics' discovery, when the substance never fails to appear. Some years there is a great quantity; other years less. In addition to the anniversary when the relics were found in the Basilica of Amalfi, the manna is also collected during the main holidays of the basilica: the 26th of June and during the month of November, which is dedicated to the Apostle—and especially November 30, the anniversary of his martyrdom.

A chronicle started by Bishop Bonito in 1908, which has been maintained to the present day, contains a record of the phenomenon and the amount of manna collected. Under the date of November 29, 1909 it is recorded that two silver bowls and a glass vial were needed to collect the flow of manna.

Of particular interest is what took place on November 30, 1915. The canonical secretary, Antonelli, tried to collect the manna, but found none. Responding to an inspiration, he and those with him began to recite the *Miserere*. After the third recitation of this prayer the manna began to collect. In later years it was found that the recitation of the Creed also produced a quantity of manna. Even today, if the manna fails to appear (with the exception of January 28, when it always appears), the Creed is recited—with miraculous results.

An exceptional amount of manna was found on January 28, 1933. The flow continued until 15 vials were filled with it.

Some may argue that the manifestation is due to natural causes, but the skeptic should consider that the chronicle, which is still kept, presents a phenomenon that has been constant, not related to season, not fixed to a liturgical rite, and which takes place at all times of the year. Moreover, it has occurred in three countries: Greece, Turkey and Italy, all of which have different climatic conditions. Just as Jesus multiplied in Andrew's presence the five barley loaves and two fish, so it is that the good Lord has multiplied in a wondrous way the manna of St. Andrew—a phenomenon that has spanned more than fourteen centuries.[1]

As we have seen, the manna of St. Andrew the Apostle appeared both in liquid and powdery form, but the secretions exuding from the bones of ST. NICHOLAS (d. 324) are presented only as a liquid and have been a curiosity for more than 1600 years. Known as St. Nicholas of Myra, after a city he served as archbishop, and as

St. Nicholas of Bari, after the city where his relics are enshrined, St. Nicholas is perhaps better known as the progenitor of Santa Claus. His reputation for gift-giving originated when he secretly provided dowries for three girls by throwing small bags of money through the open window of their father's room.

Traditions are unanimous in telling us that St. Nicholas was born at Patara in Lycia, a province of Asia Minor (Turkey), and that he died in the year 324 at Myra. A basilica was later built there over his tomb. When the shrine at Myra fell into the hands of the Saracens in 1034, several Italian cities vied for possession of the relics because of the Saint's popularity and the phenomenon that attended his remains. Bari won the treasure and greeted the arrival of the relics on May 9, 1087. As a suitable shrine for the relics, a new basilica was built. It was consecrated by Pope Urban II.

The oil that exuded from the Saint's bones was first observed while the relics were still enshrined in Myra. From that time until today the fluid has been called unction, myrrh, medicinal liquor, balm, oil or manna. In addition to these names yet another name was given in 1304 when Carlo II d'Angio presented the church with a sizable donation. He is recorded as having said, "I wish to endow the church of Bari which has the bones of St. Nicholas that exude distilled bone oil."

Scientists from the Institute of Hygiene of the University of Bari have concluded that the manna is a combination of hydrogen and oxygen which is biologically pure.[2] Other scientific studies have determined that the manna was not sea water, water from rain, water from infiltration or water from a spring. A priest named Lequile noticed that the manna distilled from the pores of the bones little by little until the tiny collections touched one another and then dripped into a container.[3] The manna has always been seen to collect along the bones, and never on the walls of the tomb nor around the hole through which the interior of the tomb can be viewed. This hole, cut into the altar table, is securely closed when not in use. Since the tomb of the Saint is about 90 centimeters deep, with the walls of marble measuring 15 centimeters thick, it is little influenced by outside temperatures, nor can it be penetrated by humidity.

When the relics were temporarily removed from the altar in the crypt during the restoration of the basilica in 1953, the receptacle was closely examined in the presence of a pontifical commission,

the archbishop of Bari and distinguished members of the Dominican Order. No breach was found through which outside waters
could penetrate. The tomb was then subjected to procedures that
further guaranteed its security. It must be mentioned that at this
examination, in the presence of the distinguished persons previously mentioned, the bones were found immersed in a clear liquid
measuring two centimeters in depth.[4]

The flow of manna from the bones was interrupted on four occasions, the first being in the year 887, when a legitimate successor
of the Saint was expelled from office—the cessation appearing to
be a protest until the bishop was reinstated. The second instance
occurred in the year 1086, the year before the relics were transferred to Italy. The third interruption took place from 1916 to 1917.
This was taken as another protest, this time because of the First
World War. The fourth cessation occurred during the restoration of
the basilica that lasted from 1953 to 1957.

When the relics were returned to the altar in the crypt, the flow
of manna appeared for a few months and then stopped. It appeared
again on April 10, 1961 and continues to this day.

For those who believe the manna to be the result of humidity, saturation or condensation, we should consider that the manna ceased
to collect between the years previously mentioned, but especially
the latter period, which lasted a full four years. During that time
such conditions as humidity, saturation or condensation had every
opportunity to exert their influence, but did not.

Before the relics were transferred from Myra, Turkey, records
indicate that a knight took from the reliquary a tooth, which he
placed in a small golden case. From this tooth a clear liquid formed.
Additionally a group of people actually stole some fragments of
bone and placed them in a bag, which was soon saturated with
manna. We have here instances in which manna was collected in
two different locations: Myra, Turkey and Bari in southern Italy,
both inside and outside places of enshrinement.

In Eichstätt, located in southern Germany, a similar event takes
place involving the remains of ST. WALBURGA (d. 779), an Eng-
lishwoman who belonged to a family of Saints. St. Walburga governed a Benedictine convent at Heidenheim, in the diocese of
Eichstätt, for almost 25 years until her death on February 25, 779.
The remains were transferred to Eichstätt between 870 and 879 and

were placed beside those of her brother, St. Wunibald, in the Holy Cross Church, where the Church of St. Walburga stands today. At this time the bones of St. Walburga began secreting "pearls," according to the record kept by Wolfhard of Herrieden dated 983. When Holy Cross Church fell into decay and a new structure was built around 1035, the remains were exhumed and placed in a shrine situated in a chapel directly behind the main altar. At this time another historian from Herrieden wrote that,

> a clear liquid like fresh water flows today from the tomb containing her revered remains, much in the same manner as the flow of oil from St. Nicholas' tomb in Bari. It is a continuous flow wonderfully effective and a cure for many ills.

The relics of the Saint are kept in a reliquary resembling a tabernacle, but one with two compartments that are separated by a shelf. The bones are kept in a bowl of precious metal placed on top of the shelf. A shell of silver is kept on the bottom. Attached to the bottom of the top bowl are silver pipes which pass through the shelf to the silver shell. In this way the oil that collects on the bones drips through the silver pipes into the silver shell, and there it is collected by the Benedictine nuns. The manna is then placed in tiny ampules that are distributed to the faithful who believe in its effectiveness, as so many have believed for over 10 centuries.

Because the manna of St. Walburga develops slowly it has been identified as an oil. It is also called an oil because so many of the faithful use it as a medicinal ointment. Since the fluid has no color, taste or odor it more accurately resembles water, although it is much more precious.

There is still a more phenomenal element to the flow of manna from the bones of the Saint who died 1,200 years ago. According to records carefully kept, the oil flows each year from October 12, the day St. Walburga's remains were transferred to the present location, until February 25, the anniversary of the Saint's death, when the flow abruptly stops. This four-month activity has been carefully observed for several centuries.[5]

The bones of ST. GERARD MAJELLA (d. 1755) also produced manna. Born in Muro, a small town south of Naples, Gerard was a tailor who joined the newly founded Congregation of the Most Holy Redeemer (The Redemptorists) as a brother. While Gerard was serving the order as a tailor and infirmarian, St. Alphonsus Liguori, the founder of the order, immediately recognized Gerard's holiness. St. Gerard possessed a number of supernatural gifts: ecstatic flight, bilocation, the gifts of prophecy and healing, multiplication of food and infused knowledge. Suffering from tuberculosis, he died in a house of the order in the small village of Caposele at the exact time and date he had predicted, midnight of October 15-16, 1755.

Atop the hill against which Caposele is nestled stands the Basilica of Materdomini, which contains the sanctuary of the Saint. His bones are enclosed in a reclining figure which is seen beneath the altar. One hundred years following his death, the ecclesiastical authorities ordered the recognition and examination of the relics as required for the Process preceding beatification. At this time it was noted that,

> After the head and other bones were placed in a vessel prepared to receive them, there was seen to ooze from them a mysterious, perfumed oil in such abundance that the basin was filled with it, and it even ran over. This marvelous manna, as the Italians call it, was gathered up with great care on handkerchiefs and linens, of which the sick soon proved the virtue.[6]

The remains were again examined by ecclesiastical authorities and two physicians on October 11, 1892.

> The bones were found more or less humid; but as this phenomenon might be attributed to the dampness of the ground, no attention was paid to it. They were carefully dried and inclosed in a casket ornamented with white silk. Four hours later the casket was opened. A kind of white oil of a sweet odor was oozing from the holy relics and lying like drops of dew on the silk lining.

After a rigorous examination, the physicians drafted an official report stating that the formation of the liquid was "beyond the natural order."[7]

The oil did not appear again.

One of the miracles offered to the Congregation of Rites during the process preceding Gerard Majella's canonization was the cure of Dominico Beneducce on May 13, 1893. After enduring a condition known then as the *miserere*, Dominico was at the point of death when he swallowed a thread from a cloth that had been steeped in the mysterious oil that had oozed from the bones of the Saint. It is recorded that he was instantaneously restored to health.[8]

Some reports claim that the oil still exudes from the relics, a claim denied by the priests of the shrine. The "Oil of St. Gerardo," which is distributed in the basilica souvenir shop, is only oil blessed with a relic of the Saint.

A perfumed oil is noted in the history of ST. ELIZABETH OF HUNGARY (d. 1231). The Saint's biographer, Count de Montalembert, reported that after her death the bishop affixed his seals to the coffin of the Saint after it had been exposed throughout the day to receive the last respects of the faithful. The next year, after the seals on the coffin were broken,

> they found it full of a pure and delicate oil which gave forth a perfume like to that of the most precious spikenard. This oil flowed drop by drop from the relics of the Saint, like the bounteous dew of heaven; and when they collected or wiped these drops away, there came others, almost imperceptibly, and forming a kind of vapoury exhalation . . . this oil flows principally from her feet, because they so frequently bore her to the cabins of the poor, and to every spot where misery required consolation.[9]

The biographer continues, "This precious oil was gathered with great care and zeal by the people and many cures were effected by its use in serious maladies and dangerous wounds."

Manna from the Bodies of the Saints

The preceding cases involved manna secreted from the bones of Saints. A similar oil, frequently perfumed, is also known to have proceeded from some of the incorrupt bodies of Saints. In only a few cases, however, has the liquid or "manna" continued to exude into modern times.

One of the first incorrupt bodies of Saints to exhibit this phenomenon was that of ST. HUGH OF LINCOLN (d. 1200), a Carthusian whose abilities were recognized by King Henry II of England. The King appointed Hugh to the post of Bishop of Lincoln. At that time Lincoln was the largest diocese in England. As administrator of this diocese he engaged in almost continual confrontation with three temperamental kings over royal control of Church affairs and their demands on Church monies. In spite of this, the kings held him in highest regard.

In addition to his ecclesiastical duties, Hugh frequently conducted funerals for the abandoned dead, defended the Jews who were being persecuted and regularly visited and cared for the lepers in their hospitals. Having spent himself in laboring for the Church, and having reached a high degree of sanctity, he died in England after making a sentimental visit through his native France.

Eighty years after his death, when the tomb of St. Hugh was opened prior to the body's transfer to a worthier shrine, the Saint's body was found to be incorrupt. An eyewitness account relates that, to the surprise of everyone:

> As soon as the Archbishop laid his hand on the glorious head of the Saint, it separated from the shoulders, leaving the neck fresh and red, just as if death had been recent. Many of those present considered this separation to be miraculous, because the magnificent reliquary which had been prepared to receive the sacred remains was not long enough to have contained both head and body together . . .[10]

After the body was placed in an elaborately prepared receptacle, it was noticed that a great quantity of a pure clear oil had collected at the bottom. The body was then taken into the vestry, where it and the head were washed and carefully dried. The following morning, during the conclusion of the solemn ceremony, witnesses related that,

> the Bishop of Lincoln took up the head of St. Hugh and held it for a while reverently before him. As he did this, an abundance of the same pure oil flowed from the jaw over the Bishop's hands, and this notwithstanding that

the venerable head had been carefully washed a few hours before, and had been found quite dry in the morning. The oil only ceased to flow when the Bishop had placed his precious burden upon the silver dish upon which the relic was to be carried through the crowd.[11]

The relic was then enclosed in a coffer of gold, silver and precious stones. Although the body of St. Hugh had been embalmed at the time of his death, no explanation was ever given for the flow of oil eighty years later.

For the facts concerning the unusual miracles that took place after the death of the Dominican nun ST. AGNES OF MONTEPULCIANO (d. 1317) we turn to Bl. Raymond of Capua (d. 1399), her biographer, who was also the confessor of St. Catherine of Siena. As the confessor of the monastery in which the incorrupt body of St. Agnes was conserved, Bl. Raymond was able to study at length the documents in the archives relating to the phenomena surrounding her. Based on these documents and the testimony of eyewitnesses, Bl. Raymond wrote of the Saint's miracles and prodigies.

He tells us that the body of the Saint was meant to be embalmed, but a wonderful miracle took place that prevented it because,

> from the extremities of her feet and hands a precious liquor issued drop by drop. The convent sisterhood collected it in a vase of crystal and still preserve it. This liquor is similar to balm in color, but it is without doubt more precious. God deigned thereby to show that the Saint's pure flesh that distilled the balm of grace had no need of earthly embalmment.[12]

And the good Lord proved this in another extraordinary way, since her body remained incorrupt for over two hundred years. But another more wondrous miracle took place a few years after the death of St. Agnes—a miracle that recalls the manna of Moses' time. St. Catherine of Siena on this occasion visited the incorrupt body of St. Agnes in the company of her two nieces and their mother, Lysa. Catherine remained at the head of St. Agnes for a long time in prayer and then said smiling, "What, do you not observe the present that heaven sends us? Do not be ungrateful!" At these words Lysa and the others lifted their eyes and saw very fine and very white particles falling like heavenly dew which covered not only Agnes and Catherine, but also all the persons present, and with such abundance that Lysa filled her hands with it.[13]

But this was not the first time such a substance fell. The archives contain documents which disclose that mysterious cross-shaped particles frequently fell upon Agnes during her ecstasies. To confirm this Bl. Raymond questioned the witnesses, all of whom affirmed that the occurrences took place as reported. Bl. Raymond reports:

> . . . several nuns belonging to the convent have equally affirmed before me and before the friars who were with me, that thus the occurrences took place. Many are now dead; but myself and my brethren recall perfectly their depositions: further, Lysa collected the manna which fell, showed it frequently, and gave it to several persons.[14]

During the sixteenth century the body was reduced in the normal manner, but the parts that remained are enclosed in a figure representing the Saint which is kept by the Dominican Fathers in Montepulciano, Italy.

BL. MATTHIA NAZZAREI OF MATELICA (d. 1319) fled to the Poor Clare convent when her father insisted that she marry. She became a valued member of the order and served her community as abbess for forty years. Having predicted the date of her death, she died on December 28, the day she had specified, surrounded by a heavenly fragrance and a mysteriously bright light. Interment was in an elegant urn deposited near the major altar. Two hundred seventeen years later the incorrupt body that was never embalmed was exhumed and carefully examined. The community was astonished at that time to see the body sweat profusely; in fact, the moisture was so abundant that it became necessary to dry the body with linen towels—an incident that was carefully recorded in the documents pertaining to the history of the Beata.[15]

The tomb was once again disturbed, this time in 1756 when

repairs were being made in the chapel. The bishop seized the opportunity to examine the relic. Again it was found perfectly incorrupt, flexible and emitting a sweet fragrance. Two years later, in December 1758, an extraordinary condition was noticed when a "blood-fluid" was seen proceeding from the corpse, to the amazement of the witnesses and the physicians called to the scene. Other men of science and renowned ecclesiastical authorities have witnessed and affirmed the miraculous formation and nature of the liquid throughout the years.[16]

Another mysterious aspect of this "blood-fluid" is the fact that it commences at various times, especially prior to the death of members of the community or before the outbreak of wars, plagues, or events of epic proportions.

The linens kept under the Beata's hands and feet were changed in 1920. In 1969 the shrine of the Beata affirmed that the linens were still saturated with this miraculous fluid.

The incorrupt body of Matthia Nazzarei with its mystifying issue of "blood-fluid" has miraculously existed for over 650 years.

There seems to be no phenomenon peculiar to the mystical state that was not experienced by the great reformer of the Carmelite Order, ST. TERESA OF AVILA (d. 1582). She attained the heights of mysticism, enjoyed countless visions and experienced the phenomenon of levitation. She was also a shrewd business woman, administrator, writer, spiritual counselor and foundress of several convents. When she died at the age of sixty-seven, her body was not embalmed; nevertheless, it was found to be incorrupt nine months later and remains so. At this exhumation, unpleasant as it may sound, the provincial of the Order, Fr. Jerome Gracian, requested that the left hand of the Saint be removed for a relic. The holy priest gives us an interesting report concerning what took place: "I took the hand away wrapped in a coif and in an outer wrapping of paper." Then as though exclaiming at the wonder, he states, "Oil came from it." He left this precious relic ". . . at Avila in a sealed casket . . ."

Not only the left hand, but also the left arm was amputated. This was given to the convent at Alba de Tormes when the body was removed to the Saint's native Avila.

We are told that during the exhumation of the body in 1588, "the shoulder from which the arm had been detached exudes a moisture which clings to the touch and exhales the same fragrant scent as the body."[17]

Canonized in 1622, St. Teresa of Avila, of the Discalced Carmelite Order, was officially proclaimed a Doctor of the Church by Pope Paul VI in 1970. She is the first woman so designated.

ST. PASCHAL BAYLON (d. 1592) was a member of the Franciscan Order who had an extraordinary devotion to the Holy Eucharist. His first biographer, Fr. John Ximenes, the provincial of the order and a personal friend of the Saint, reports that Paschal spent all his free time before the tabernacle, kneeling without support, with his hands clasped and held up above his face. He delighted in serving several Masses in succession and often spent nights in prayer before the tabernacle. He was also solicitous for the poor and often performed miracles of healing. He was only fifty-two when he died in 1592. When all was in order, the body of the Saint was carried from his humble cell to one of the chapels in the church of Our Lady of the Rosary, where it was displayed to the veneration of the people. The mourners who filed past the bier were astonished to see the heavenly radiance on his countenance and the perfumed moisture that had collected on his forehead since the time of his death. But there was another wonder when, during the three days of exhibition, the "miraculous sweat which distilled from the members of the Saint flowed copiously and continuously."[18]

We are told that armed guards were required to control the people, many of whom were permitted to collect the scented moisture on small cloths, which were later to occasion many cures by their application in previously hopeless maladies.

Before the burial of the Saint, the guardian of the house covered the body with a thick layer of quicklime so that the flesh would be quickly consumed, producing glossy white bones which he felt would look impressive in a shrine. The body rested eight months in this caustic element. After that time the body was exhumed for the provincial of the order, Fr. John Ximenes. All were amazed that, in spite of the caustic quicklime that had been applied to the body at the time of its burial, it remained perfect in every respect. Then, after Fr. Ximenes took the hand of the Saint in his, "A crystalline liquid like balm distilled from the face and hands."[19]

Nineteen years after the Saint's death an official exhumation was made for the process of beatification. After a thorough examination of the body, the conclusion reached by the physicians and surgeons was that "the preservation is supernatural and miraculous."

The devotion to the Blessed Sacrament which Paschal Baylon exhibited so devoutly during his life was reflected in the phenomena and miracles performed by the Saint after his death. It would then seem more than appropriate that Paschal, having been canonized in 1690, was declared by Pope Leo XIII in 1897 the patron of Eucharistic Congresses and all organizations dedicated to increasing love and devotion to the Holy Eucharist.

BL. BEATRICE D'ESTE OF FERRARA (d. 1262) is the niece of her namesake, Bl. Beatrice d'Este of Gemmola. Little is known of the life of Bl. Beatrice of Ferrara, although one source reveals that she belonged to the family of the Norman Dukes of Apulia and was herself the daughter of the Marquess of Ferrara. She was betrothed to Galeazzo Manfredi of Ferrara, who on the very day of the nuptials died of the wounds he suffered in battle. Seeing the will of God in this tragedy, Beatrice and some of her maidens turned themselves to the service of God and followed the rule of St. Benedict. Bl. Beatrice died with a reputation of great holiness in her convent at Ferrara, which had been founded by her powerful family. Five hundred years after her death, an oily liquid flowed from her marble tomb. This mysterious liquid was highly regarded by her devotees; they applied it to the sick and witnessed many miracles as a result.[20]

ST. MARY MAGDALEN DE'PAZZI (d. 1607) was a nun in the Carmelite convent of Santa Maria degli Angeli in Florence who withstood almost unbelievable physical and spiritual distress. These sufferings, however, were rewarded with mystical experiences and remarkable visions of Our Lord, the Blessed Virgin and a number of Saints. She experienced the phenomenon of levitations, performed many miracles, suffered the Passion of Our Lord and was granted the privilege of viewing in Purgatory the souls of persons she had known.

The holy Carmelite died during her forty-second year and was buried beneath the high altar of the monastery church. From the tomb there issued the sweet odor of sanctity which has been recognized about the body on numerous occasions, even to the present day. During the year following her death, the body was exhumed and found to be in a perfect state of preservation, despite conditions that should have had a reverse effect.[21]

The body of the Saint soon exhibited the phenomenon of tran-spiration, the secretion being described as ". . . a liquor as oil, more odoriferous than balm." The Saint's biographer relates,

> When the nuns took their precious charge back with them into the cloister, they discovered a new circum-stance. From the knees of the sacred body trickled a liq-uid of exquisite scent. It looked like oil, but it was not. It was examined, but its nature could not be ascertained. At any rate, this liquid absorbed into pieces of cloth was distributed to the faithful and carried afar.

The biographer adds, "For twelve years the phenomenon per-sisted, until the year 1620; then it stopped."[22]

The feastday of the Saint is celebrated by crowds of pilgrims who visit the church to view the body of St. Mary Magdalene de' Pazzi, preserved for almost four hundred years.

The symbol of the Red Cross, representing mercy and help to per-sons in need, is thought to have originated in recent times, but it was first used when ST. CAMILLUS DE LELLIS (d. 1614) founded the Order of Ministers of the Sick in 1586. Also known as the Camil-lians, members of the order wore such a symbol on the front of their black habits. The members are still distinguished by the wearing of this symbol of charity.

In his early life Camillus fought the Turks at Lepanto. He then turned to gambling and then to begging. He experienced a complete reform and a rekindling of faith when a Capuchin monk took him aside one day for counseling. It was during one of his hospitaliza-tions for a recurring ulceration of his leg that he decided to found the religious order which is devoted to the care of the sick and dying.

After intense suffering, the Saint died in 1614. Eleven years later Pope Urban VIII gave permission for the exhumation of the body, which was found to be in excellent condition.[23] During the nine days in which the body was exposed for viewing, enormous crowds wit-nessed "the flow of a pure, fragrant liquid which proceeded from an incision which had been made by the doctors during the examina-tion of the body. The faithful soaked cloths in it, and it effected many cures."[24]

Camillus was canonized by Pope Benedict XIV in 1746. With St. John of God, his Spanish counterpart, St. Camillus has been given a triple designation by Pope Leo XIII as the patron of the sick, of nurses and of hospitals.

After experience as a tradesman, ST. JOSAPHAT (Josaphat Kuncevyc) (d. 1623) entered the Monastery of the Trinity at Vilan which was conducted by the Order of St. Basil the Great. He was ordained four years later, his quick advancement in the Order culminating in his consecration as the archbishop of Polotsk in 1617. Six years later, in October of 1623, his residence was stormed by enemies of the Church. The holy archbishop was beaten and hacked to death, and his remains were thrown into a nearby river. Retrieved by the faithful, the mutilated body was interred at Biala in Podlesie. Because of the numerous miracles that were occurring through Josaphat's intercession, appeals were made to the Vatican for his canonization. During the required opening of the grave which took place five years after his death, Josaphat's body was found perfectly preserved. The body proved to be so pliable that it was dressed in new garments and was propped up on the episcopal throne for all to see. In an emotional gesture, George Tishkevick, Bishop of Milton, raised the right hand of the dead bishop and blessed the throng. The Saint would seem to have been touched by the unusual benediction since his face broke out in droplets of manna, which were collected in handkerchiefs.[25]
Josaphat was canonized in 1867 by Pope Leo XIII.

When VEN. MOTHER MARIA OF JESUS (d. 1640) was seventeen years old, her sanctity was recognized by none other than St. Teresa of Avila, who intervened when the girl's acceptance into the Discalced Carmelite Order was being debated by the sisters of the convent to which she had applied.

After spending sixty-three years in the religious life, during which Mother Maria of Jesus served her order as novice mistress and prioress, she died in the odor of sanctity at Toledo, where she had spent many fruitful years. The body of the Saint was found to be incorrupt during one of its exhumations and has been examined several times throughout the years.

The last exhumation took place in 1929 in the presence of distinguished personages and Church authorities. After the body was placed on a table, its perfect flexibility was noted. The garments were then discovered to be saturated with a perfumed oil which exuded from the skin and not only coated the flesh of the entire body, but also kept it constantly moist. A sample of the saturated clothing was taken for laboratory examination. The mysterious oil and the heavenly scent surrounding the body were declared to be unexplainable by the attending physicians and distinguished men of science who were present at the exhumation and those who studied the laboratory sample.[26]

The body of the Venerable is now enclosed in a marble sarcophagus at the Carmelite Convent of San Jose in Toledo, Spain, where it might repeat similar manifestations at its next exhumation.

ST. JULIE BILLIART (d. 1816), foundress and first superior general of the Congregation of the Sisters of Notre Dame of Namur, was still young when her piety and virtue became known. When twenty-two years of age she suffered a nervous shock that left her with paralysis. A miraculous cure restored her to health on June 1, 1804, during a novena to the Sacred Heart of Jesus. From the time of her miraculous recovery in 1804 until her death in 1816, the Saint established fifteen flourishing foundations in the larger cities of Belgium. Having died at the motherhouse of the Order at Namur, Belgium, the Saint was buried two days later in the city cemetery. Sixteen months later the body of the blessed Foundress was transferred from the public cemetery to a tomb on the grounds of the Motherhouse. During this removal, the coffin was opened to reveal the incorrupt body. Wrapped in linen clothes, it was conveyed to the cloister.

The Saint's biographer wrote, "From it exuded a quantity of clear oil which stained the cloths in which it was wrapped, and even the wooden floor of the room whereon it was laid for a moment."[27] Sometime later, owing to an inundation of the Sambre and Meuse Rivers, the flesh was reduced in the normal manner and only the skeleton remained. Julie Billiart was canonized by Pope Paul VI in 1969.

Perhaps the most amazing phenomenon in the modern world was the existence of the perfectly incorrupt and lifelike body of the holy Maronite monk, ST. CHARBEL MAKHLOUF (d. 1898). Born in 1828 to poor, religious parents, he was given the name of Joseph at his Baptism. He received the name Charbel, the name of an early martyr, when he entered the Monastery of St. Maroun at Annaya, Lebanon. He was ordained in 1859 and spent sixteen years in the practice of the monastic life until he received permission to retire to the Hermitage of Sts. Peter and Paul, a short distance from the monastery. In this secluded place he spent the remaining twenty-three years in the practice of severe mortification.

Death was due to a seizure suffered during the offering of Holy Mass. Interment was in the monastery cemetery, where so many saintly monks before him had been buried. The body was never embalmed and was consigned to the grave without a coffin. As a result of strange lights appearing near the tomb for forty-five nights following the burial, the body was exhumed and was found perfectly incorrupt, in spite of lying on mud in a flooded grave. After being cleansed and reclothed in fresh garments the body was laid in a wooden coffin and placed in a corner of the private chapel.

A strange phenomenon was soon noticed. A liquid described as perspiration and blood, which had the characteristic odor of blood, began to exude from the pores of the body. As a result of this transpiration, the blood-stained clothing on the body was changed twice a week. Small pieces of cloth soaked in this mysterious fluid were distributed as relics, and these frequently relieved pain and effected cures.

The body of the Saint was thoroughly examined on July 24, 1927 by two physicians of the French Medical Institute of Beirut. Documents were drawn up by various officials and placed in a zinc tube which was entombed with the body in a new vault especially prepared in the wall of an oratory.

The tomb was undisturbed for twenty-three years until February 25, 1950, when pilgrims to the shrine noticed a liquid streaming from a corner of the tomb and coursing its way along the floor. Fearing water damage to the tomb, the casket was removed. At this time it was noticed that a liquid was dripping through a crack at the foot of the casket. This liquid flowed in the direction of the west wall, eventually finding its way into the oratory.

Permission to examine the contents of the casket was obtained from ecclesiastical authorities, who witnessed the opening with various men of science. The body was found completely free of any trace of corruption and was perfectly flexible and lifelike. The liquid and blood had continued to exude from the body, and the garments were found stained with blood. Some of the white content of the fluid had collected on the body in an almost solidified condition. Part of the chasuble had rotted, and the zinc tube containing the official documents was covered with corrosion.[28]

The body was eventually placed in a casket under glass for various visitors to visually examine and venerate. Many remarked that the body appeared to be an elderly man fast asleep.

After the exhumation in 1950 the monastery began keeping records of well-authenticated miracles of healing. Within a two-year period they had collected reports numbering over 1,200.

The fluid constantly exuded from the body so that at times it was discovered to have collected in the casket to a depth of three inches.

By the time that Charbel was beatified on December 5, 1965 the body had reduced according to the natural process. The bones are carefully kept and these are inexplicably reddish in color. It should be noted that the bloody sweat had exuded from the body for sixty-seven years.

Manna from a Statue of a Saint

Manna has also been known to distill from certain statues of the Blessed Mother, such as the event at Akita, Japan, and from crucifixes and some statues of Our Lord. It also formed on a statue of ST. PHILOMENA (d. Roman era).

The relics of this child martyr are now found in Mugnano, Italy, but they were discovered in the Catacomb of St. Priscilla in Rome during the year 1802. Brought to Mugnano three years later, the bones were positioned in a papier-mache figure which is located in a shrine high atop the altar. The church in which the relics are kept has been a place of miracles, as well as the scene of various phenomena.

One of these mystical events involves a wooden statue of the Saint which was given by the archbishop of Naples for use during processions. In observance of the anniversary of the translation of St. Philomena's remains to Mugnano, the customary procession took place in 1823. Presently the bearers began to complain of the heaviness of the statue, a condition not noted in the eighteen previous years. While this difficulty was noted by the people, they also observed that a rosy tint seemed to color the face.

The next morning, August 11, visitors exchanged remarks about a moisture that seemed to glisten on the face and neck of the statue.

Upon close examination the liquid was described as a kind of "crystalline manna." A broad red ribbon which held a relic around the statue's neck was soaked with the fluid. The formation of this liquid was regarded as an extraordinary miracle which prompted the composition of two documents, one signed by the pastor and priests of the district who witnessed the phenomenon, the other signed by public officials. The first document reads as follows:

> We the undersigned pastor and priests in the locality of Mugnano del Cardinale, in the diocese of Nola, hereby testify as eyewitnesses, that on the eleventh of August, the day following the celebration commemorating the translation of the body of Saint Philomena, Virgin and Martyr, which took place on the tenth of the said month, in the course of the Jubilee octave, and previously on Monday (twenty-one o'clock), to the Church of Santa Maria delle Grazie, where rests the body of the said Saint Philomena . . . we noticed that till midnight the statue of the said martyr was copiously exuding a fluid of clear manna in the manner of natural perspiration coming in abundance from her face and neck. While this prodigy was noticed on the statue of Saint Philomena, the other statues in the Church of Santa Maria delle Grazie were examined, those of Our Lady of Grace, Saint Joseph and also the marbles and the stuccos of the church, which were found to be dry, moistless and dusty as were the other parts of the statue of Saint Philomena, namely her feet, hands, forehead and mantle, which were covered with the dust accumulated during the procession of the preceding day, which had taken place amid the scorching heat of the season and of a long dry spell.
>
> This exudation continued until late at night on Tuesday the 12th of the month, when the exudation ceased, but the liquid manna remained on the face and neck of the statue without drying up, until the octave of the feast, which was on the 17th, observed and venerated by out-of-town people. In like manner, the wide, red silk ribbon on which is fastened the relic and which hangs around the neck of the statue, remained soaked and on

the date given below, August 22, 1823, the exudation on it is still fresh, for it has not dried at all.

Of all these happenings, we have been eyewitnesses, together with a great number of the inhabitants of our district and out-of-town people who had hastened here to observe the manifest prodigy.

For the glory of God so marvelous in His Saints, for the triumph of the Catholic Church, to the honor of the Holy Virgin and Martyr Philomena, for the edification of the faithful, and for the everlasting remembrance of posterity, we have drawn up the present document under our hand and seal and confirmed by the parochial seal, on this day, the 22nd of August, 1823.

The document was signed by eighteen priests and continues:

We, too, the undersigned, Mayor, Councilmen, and officials of the locality of Mugnano and Cardinale, together with other citizens, attest the public miracle of the emanation of manna from the statue of Saint Philomena, Virgin and Martyr, which took place on the eleventh of last August in the year 1823, in the village church of Santa Maria delle Grazie, where rests the very body and the phial of blood.

This was signed by the Mayor, the Police Deputy, the Council Notary and twenty-four distinguished citizens.[29]

Rev. Herbert Thurston, S.J., who wrote a great deal about physical phenomena in the lives of the Saints, and who was very skeptical about such reports until he had thoroughly studied them, once noted, ". . . however we may explain the phenomenon or fail to explain it, the exudation of some sort of viscous oil fluid from many incorrupt bodies seems to be a fact beyond dispute . . ."

The men of science who have analyzed the manna and who have watched its formation on the bones and bodies of God's elect have been unanimous in declaring the miraculous nature of its formation. But why this phenomenon took place with regard to some Saints and not others is known to God alone. It would seem to those of us who read about these miraculous events that the good Lord wants to draw special attention to these, His faithful sons and daughters, by anointing their remains with an oil of special origin.

As early as the eighth century, St. John Damascene recognized the miraculous nature of manna and wrote for the skeptics,

> Christ gives us the relics of Saints as health-giving springs through which flow blessings and healing. This should not be doubted. For if at God's word water gushed from the hard rock in the wilderness . . . yes, and from the ass' jawbone when Samson was thirsty, why should it seem incredible that healing medicine should distill from the relics of the Saints?

ST. NICHOLAS, Archbishop of Myra, died in 324, his relics eventually being enshrined in Bari, Italy. In both Myra and Bari, the Saint's bones exuded manna, a liquid that collects on the relics of St. Nicholas, and never on the walls of his tomb. The flow of manna from the Saint's bones continues to this day.

AN ANCIENT BOTTLE of manna (left) from the bones of St. Nicholas bears testimony to the occurrence of this phenomenon in past centuries.

AMPULES containing manna (below) from the bones of St. Walburga. For more than 10 centuries, the clear, odorless fluid has been distributed to the faithful. The miraculous liquid flows each year from October 12, the day on which the Saint's remains were transferred to their present location in Eichstätt, Germany, until February 25, the anniversary of the Saint's death. (Picture from *Heilige Walburga*, by Maria Anna Bergitta zu Munster, O.S.B., St. Walburg, Eichstätt, 1979.)

MANNA ISSUED from
the miraculous statue of
St. Philomena (above) on
August 10, 1823.

ST. WALBURGA (right)
is shown holding a vial
of her "oil."

PERFUME FROM THE
SAINTLY BODIES OF THE DEAD

Perfumed oils were not needed, and indeed were not used, to scent the bodies of God's beloved Saints since their bodies, by the grace of God, gave forth perfumes of their own as confirmation of their sanctity.

Because of the great number of these cases, and in consideration of the great number of clergy and religious, as well as reputable members of the laity who perceived the scents and gave testimony to the fact under oath, the subject of these fragrances around the sainted bodies can hardly be questioned and is a matter far beyond dispute.

The fragrances that have been noted about the bodies of holy persons have been chronicled since the early days of the Church. It is evident that the presence of perfume, as early as the second century, was familiar to the Christian world and was accepted as evidence of high virtue.

This fact was registered when the Christians of Smyrna, eye witnesses to the martyrdom of ST. POLYCARP (d. 155), left this account:

> When he had offered up the amen and finished his prayer, the firemen lighted the fire. And a mighty flame flashing forth, we to whom it was given to see, saw a marvel, yea, and we were preserved that we might relate to the rest what happened.
>
> The fire, making the appearance of a vault, like the sail of a vessel filled by the wind, made a wall round about the body of the martyr; and it was there in the midst, not like flesh burning but like gold and silver refined in a furnace. For we perceived such a fragrant smell, as if it were the wafted odour of frankincense or some other precious spice.[1]

We are told that no critic nowadays contests the authenticity of this letter.

Eusebius in his *Ecclesiastical History* tells us what happened to the Christians who were martyred at Vienne and Lyon about the year 177.

> They went out rejoicing, glory and grace being blended in their faces, so that even their bonds seemed like beautiful ornaments, as those of a bride adorned with variegated golden fringes; and they were fragrant with the sweet odour of Christ, so that some even supposed that they had been anointed with earthly ointment.[2]

The body of ST. GREGORY NAZIANZEN (d. 389) is said to have been identified by its sweet fragrance from those of other members of his family who had been buried in the same vault.

From more than one source we learn about the death of ST. SIMEON STYLITES (d. 459) and how his disciple, Anthony, unable to obtain a response from the Saint, climbed up to the platform on which he lived. There he found the dead body of St. Simeon, "exhaling the perfume as it were of many spices."

St. Gregory the Great in his *Dialogues* recounts what was witnessed at the death of ST. SERVULUS (d. 590), whom he knew personally.

> While he lay giving ear within himself to that divine harmony, his holy soul departed this mortal life; at which time all that were there present felt a most pleasant and fragrant smell . . . A monk of mine, who yet liveth, was then present, and with many tears useth to tell us that the sweetness of that smell never went away, but that they felt it continually until the time of his burial.[3]

ST. CLARUS (d. circa 660) was a monk and an abbot of St. Marcellus Monastery at Vienne. He also served as the spiritual director of the convent of St. Blandina, where his own mother and other widows took the veil. Many miracles are said to have confirmed his holiness, especially that of a perfume that was emitted from his body after his death.[4]

While on his deathbed, ST. GUTHLAC (d. 714) "turned himself and recovered his breath when there came forth fragrance from his mouth like the odour of the sweetest flowers." After his death those around the body "heard angelic songs thro' the regions of the air, and all the island of Crowland was profusely filled with the exceeding sweetness of a wondrous odour."

The next day St. Pega visited the remains of her brother, St. Guthlac, and she found the death chamber and the buildings filled with an odour like the herb ambrosia.[5] These quotes are taken from the life of St. Guthlac which was written by his contemporary, Felix. It is said that because of the trustworthiness of the biography, the facts are disputed by no one.

ST. ANNE OF CONSTANTINOPLE (d. circa 918) lived a monastic life in the world and eventually retreated to one of the Ionian Islands. There she passed the rest of her life, dying at about the age of 80. Her tomb was a place of pilgrimage where many cures were effected. When her tomb was opened many years later, her body was found not only incorrupt, but also exhaling a delightful fragrance.[6]

Many extraordinary events took place in the life of the great ST. DOMINIC (d. 1221). One of these concerns the angels who once supplied bread to St. Dominic's brethren when many visiting monks were present and not enough bread was available to satisfy their hunger. The angels' supply multiplied so that there remained enough for three days. This miracle was commemorated every year in a special way at Santa Maria Mascharella in Bologna, the place of the miraculous supply.

Three hundred years after the Saint's death, the rector of the monastery recorded (in 1528) that every year, on the anniversary date when the heavenly bread was brought to the monks, a sweet odor was detected in the space that had formerly been occupied by the refectory. The heavenly scent is said to have lasted forty hours.[7]

During the year 1233, twelve years after the Saint's death, an enlargement of the friary and the church required the removal of the Saint's remains. Gathered in the church on May 24 of that year were officials of the order, bishops, prelates and magistrates. Standing around the grave, they witnessed the removal of the flagstone and immediately detected a sweet fragrance which grew stronger as the earth was removed. Then, when the casket was raised to the surface, "the whole church was filled with the perfume, as though from the burning of some precious and costly gums."[8] When the casket was opened, the body of St. Dominic was discovered to be completely incorrupt. Eight days later the casket was again opened.

The religious of the order approached one after the other, "and kissed the features that still smiled on them like a father; all were conscious of the same extraordinary odour; it remained on the hands and clothes of all who touched or came near the body."[9]

The fragrance apparently lingered about the Saint's relics, since Flaminius wrote almost three hundred years later: "This divine odour of which we have spoken, adheres to the relics even to this present day."[10]

Bl. John of Alverno, the companion of ST. FRANCIS OF ASSISI (d. 1226), reported that sweet odors came from cloths that had been stained with blood from the Saint's stigmata. We are told that the linens are still preserved at Assisi, and that on certain feasts the sweet perfume is renewed.[11]

Count de Montalembert, in writing about ST. ELIZABETH OF HUNGARY (d. 1231), reports that soon after her death the Saint's body exhaled a delicious perfume which "served to console the poor and all the people who deeply felt her loss."[12]

ST. FRANCES OF ROME (d. 1440), a daughter of the Roman aristocracy, was married at the age of thirteen to Lorenzo de' Ponziani and became the mother of several children. After the death of her husband to whom she had been married for forty years, St. Frances joined the religious community she had founded. St. Frances is known to have had mystical experiences and revelations, and to have had the constant apparition of her guardian angel. Miracles of healing attended her death and the odor of sanctity was intensely noted in the room in which she died. During the time that the funeral was delayed due to the press of people who wanted to pay their respects, the fragrance continued to linger—to the delight of the visitors.

When a monumental tomb was prepared a few months after her death, the first tomb was opened to effect the transfer of the Saint's remains. At this time the body was found perfectly preserved and still exhaling the same sweet fragrance as before.[13] The Saint's body is no longer incorrupt.

At the age of twenty-one, ST. COLETTE (d. 1447) joined the Franciscan Third Order. Later she had a vision of St. Francis of Assisi, in which he charged her to bring the Poor Clare nuns back to their original strict rule of life. She met with great success in this endeavor and founded seventeen convents of the strict observance. The Poor Clares of the Colettine reform are found in many parts of the world. At the death of the Saint, "the body that had been dominated so completely by the soul issued an odor of sweetness which pervaded the place of death and the adjoining rooms."[14]

An interesting story is told of one mourner named Germain, who it is said lived a "rather easy life." Refusing to demonstrate any grief as did those who approached the bier of St. Colette to kiss the body and to press medals and rosaries to the remains, he stood aloof. But without realizing what was happening, he found himself among the mourners, kissing and pressing his rosary to the body of the Saint. He soon became aware that a delightful perfume lingered on the rosary. This perfume had the effect of making him mend his ways so that he thereafter lived a holy and devout life.[15]

The scent associated with ST. RITA OF CASCIA (d. 1457) is truly astounding. After the Saint's death it was noticed in her cell, but then it spread throughout the entire monastery. Then too, after the nuns had prepared the body of St. Rita for burial and had taken it to the church for the throngs of people who wished to view it, everyone was amazed at the celestial odor that surrounded the remains. The official witness for her canonization wrote that:

> Not only do witnesses, with perfect accord, but likewise well-founded reports speak of an odor of sweetness issuing from the body of Bl. Rita, and moreover from objects which have touched the holy body. No one seems to be able to classify this fragrance; they simply

say it is not of this world. It has been perceived beyond the limits of church and convent; it grows at times as one draws near the church and spreads even to the farthest quarters of the convent. It does not depend on sweet spices placed in the body of the Saint—there are none; nor can it be accounted for by flowers within the church. In this church flowers that carry perfume are not used, so that no one might declare that in the flowers the fragrance found an explanation. The intensity of this fragrance, its spread, its prevalence in every century make this quite a different matter from the fragrance which at some times and in various places has marked the presence of the relics of the Saints. For these reasons and from a hundred others which have their basis in the character of the witnesses that have testified, I do not hesitate to declare that the fragrance emanating from the body of Bl. Rita is supernatural—in other words, a miracle.[16]

Confirmation of this prodigy was given by no less than Pope Leo XIII. He approved the three miracles that were required for St. Rita's canonization, which took place in 1900. The Decree reads:

The first miracle approved consists of that pleasing scent emanating from the remains of the Saint's body, the existence of which is confirmed by many reliable witnesses and trustworthy tradition, so that to doubt concerning this fact would be absurd; moreover, no natural cause can be given for the existence of this odor, as we see from the physical research which has been made by men most skilled in such things. Furthermore, this odor diffuses itself in a manner above the usual laws of nature. Hence we should be persuaded that this fragrance has its origin through divine intervention.[17]

The scent that proceeded from the body of St. Rita continues to make itself known, although it is not continuous. The Sisters who are the guardians of the incorrupt body revealed to the author that the perfume is still noticed, especially on the occasion of an extraordinary miracle.

Because of his keen intelligence and many talents, Antonio Vici, known as BL. ANTHONY OF STRONCONE (d. 1461), seemed destined for the priesthood, but he declined the privilege and remained a humble lay brother for the rest of his life. He died at the age of eighty, after having spent sixty-eight years in the religious life.

The body of the holy friar was buried in the common sepulchre beneath the flooring in the sanctuary of the church of San Damiano. A year minus one day after his death, a flame was seen burning brightly on the slab, which was accepted by St. James of the Marches as "a sign from Heaven" and resulted in an almost immediate exhumation. St. James assisted at the undertaking, which brought to light the perfectly intact and sweetly perfumed body of Bl. Anthony, which remains incorrupt in the Church of St. Francesco in Stroncone, Italy.[18]

ST. CATHERINE OF BOLOGNA (d. 1463) rejected the proposals of a number of suitors and joined a group of Franciscan tertiaries who later adopted the rule of St. Clare. She was both a writer and an artist who enjoyed many visions and mystical experiences. Johann Joseph von Görres, the great German Catholic philosopher and writer, describes what took place after the death of the Saint:

> When she died and the grave was dug, the Sisters carried her body to be buried without a casket. As the body of the Saint was lowered into the grave an incredibly sweet fragrance emanated from it, filling the entire cemetery and regions beyond. After several days, when the sisters visited the tomb, the fragrance was still there. There were no trees, flowers or herbs on the grave or in the vicinity, and it was safely established that the scent came from the grave. Eighteen days after the interment, miracles began to happen at the grave. Persons incurably sick were cured. The Sisters then felt guilty because they had buried the body without a casket and that, as a result, masses of earth might have fallen on her face. They thought the body should be exhumed and placed in a casket. The Sisters went for advice to the confessor of the convent, who was quite surprised to learn that after eighteen days the body had not yet started to decay. And when the nuns told him of the fragrance still emanating

from the grave he gave his consent for the exhumation.
When the body was brought into the church, the fragrance became even sweeter, pervading the church and
the immediate neighborhood.[19]

After the death of her parents, BL. JANE (JOAN) SCOPELLI
(d. 1491) fulfilled her desire of founding a convent of Carmelites
in Reggio, which she virtuously served as prioress. Two years after
her death her body was found to be incorrupt and giving forth a
delightful fragrance. On learning about this perfume, which was
noted by many witnesses, the bishop of Reggio ordered that her
body be entombed near the high altar of the church. This was done
with all solemnity in 1771.[20]

One supernatural token after another declared the holiness of BL.
LUCY OF NARNI (d. 1544), a stigmatist whose wounds exhaled a
delightful perfume during her lifetime. After her death all the sisters declared that they had heard angelic singing in her cell while
an extraordinary fragrance filled the chamber and the whole house.

Four years after the burial, the body was exhumed and exposed to
the veneration of the faithful. They were impressed by the scent of
violets which issued from it. As a token of the Blessed's favor with
God, the fragrance attached itself to all the articles pressed to her
body.[21]

ST. JOHN OF GOD (d. 1550), a native of Portugal, lived a carefree life, but repented of his transgressions. Through the counseling of St. John of Avila, he pursued virtue and dedicated himself to
the care of the sick.

The men who were drawn to imitate St. John of God's charity
eventually became known as the Brothers Hospitallers and are
sometimes called the Brothers of St. John of God.

Upon the Saint's death, the Archbishop hastened to pay his
respects and was astonished to find a heavenly fragrance which
invaded the sickroom and the whole house. This fragrance was
attested to in depositions made by order of the Holy See and was
also recognized on many occasions in the room in which St. John
of God had died.[22]

During the nine days before his burial, the perfume in the death
chamber was "looked upon as a sure mark of sanctity by the judges

of the city, who came with the archbishop's deputies to make an inventory of the things that belonged to him . . ." Because of the perfume, the owner of the house in which the Saint had died, Dona Anna Ossorio, converted the death chamber into a chapel with the cooperation and assistance of the archbishop. In this chapel the same fragrance was renewed every Friday at midnight until Saturday evening—Saturday being the day on which the Saint had died.

Fifty years after the Saint's death, a certain Dona Ursula Romas visited the house, not knowing of its past history, and questioned Mary, the daughter of the owner, about the sweet fragrance that she detected. Mary asked her,

> Do you not know that this oratory was the room in which St. John of God died? Though it is now more than fifty years since his death, the odour you speak of is still renewed by him, but it is on Saturdays chiefly that we perceive it . . . This which seems to you so surprising a favor is a common thing with us; we enjoy it every Saturday.[23]

We read in the life of ST. STANISLAUS KOSTKA (d. 1568) that he once received Holy Communion from St. Barbara (d. fourth century) when he was seriously sick, and that the Blessed Mother herself advised him to enter the Society of Jesus. He joined the order at Rome, and there he met St. Francis Borgia. St. Stanislaus died ten months later, at the age of seventeen.

Two years after his death, when a house of the order pleaded for a relic of the young Saint, permission was given for the exhumation of the remains. A biographer wrote,

> At the opening of the grave, which had been closed for more than two years, the novices went, vested in surplices, and each bearing a lighted torch, to receive with fitting respect the promised treasure. But no sooner was the coffin uncovered than a fragrance, more delicious than that of the sweetest flower, issued from it. So delicate, so pure, so exquisite was this scent, which, moreover, instead of only delighting the senses, seemed to penetrate to the souls of those present, that one and all felt that it was perfume not of earth but of Paradise.[24]

ST. TERESA OF AVILA (d. 1582) was a Discalced Carmelite nun and the first woman to be declared a Doctor of the Church. She experienced perhaps every phenomenon peculiar to the mystical state, yet she remained a shrewd businesswoman, administrator, writer, spiritual counselor and foundress. The delightful fragrance which frequently enveloped the Saint during her lifetime was so strongly noted at the time of her death that the door and windows of her cell had to be opened. We are told that the fragrance continued to emanate from the grave.

At her exhumation nine months after her burial, "a wonderful penetrating fragrance which lasted some days" was noted by the provincial of the order, Fr. Jerome Gracian, who was the Saint's confessor and first biographer.[25]

Once again the scent was noted when the body of the Saint was removed in 1585 to the monastery of St. Joseph's at Avila. This exhumation was witnessed by the bishop, Don Pedro Fernandez de Temino, and two doctors, P. Diego de Yepes and Julian de Avila. After examining the incorrupt body the doctors decided that its perfect condition was supernatural,

> . . . for after three years, without having been opened or embalmed, it was in such a perfect state of preservation that nothing was wanting to it in any way, and a wonderful odour issued from it.[26]

ST. JOHN OF THE CROSS (d. 1591), St. Teresa of Avila's counterpart in the reform of the Carmelite Order, was, according to Teresa, "one of the purest souls in the Church of God." The Saint died at the age of forty-nine at Ubeda and was buried beneath the flooring of the church. Nine months later the body was exhumed and found to be perfectly incorrupt.

Approximately one and a half years after his death, one of the king's sergeants, Francis de Medina Zavallos, was sent to Ubeda to transfer the body to Madrid.

At this exhumation the body was again found perfectly preserved. Zavallos then wrapped the body carefully and took it on its first journey. The perfume which surrounded the body was so intense and pleasing that it aroused the curiosity of the people whom he passed along the way, so that Zavallos was frequently asked about the contents of his cargo.[27]

The Saint's body was eventually taken to Segovia, where it is reverently enshrined.

After the death of ST. MARTIN DE PORRES (d. 1639), one of the religious, Fr. Cipriano de Medina, was somewhat surprised that nothing unusual had taken place—especially since the Saint had experienced and performed so many extraordinary wonders when alive. Following an irresistible impulse he reproached the deceased wonder-worker: "How is it, Brother Martin, that your body is stiff and rigid? All these good people are waiting to behold wonders wrought by you in order to glorify the Lord. Ask your Master to show His supreme power by making your body supple and lifelike!" Immediately the fragrance of roses and lilies emanated from the body, and it was found to have regained its flexibility.[28]

During the transfer of the Saint's remains in March of 1664, the casket was opened in the presence of political and ecclesiastical representatives. As soon as the lid was removed everyone present instantly perceived a sweet perfume like the odor of roses.

As soon as the casket of Martin de Porres was properly situated in its new location, throngs of people went to pray before it. Although the friars announced that Martin had not as yet been declared worthy of veneration, the people nevertheless felt that the sweet fragrance that lingered around the casket gave ample proof of Martin's sanctity.[29]

When VEN. MOTHER MARIA OF JESUS (d. 1640) applied for acceptance in the Discalced Carmelite Order, her entrance was debated by the nuns; they questioned the wisdom of accepting the 17-year-old girl because of her poor health. St. Teresa of Avila intervened and welcomed her, "even though it should prove necessary for her to remain in bed all her life." Apparently the health of the young girl improved, since she served the community as prioress and novice mistress and died after having spent 63 years in religious life.

Buried at Toledo, her incorrupt body was examined several times during the years. The last exhumation took place in 1929 in the presence of many distinguished persons. When the vault was opened there immediately rose from the incorrupt body the sweet perfume of roses and jasmines. The garments on the body were found saturated with a perfumed oil which coated the flesh of the entire body. It was also observed that everything that the Venerable had used in life retained the same flowery fragrance. These articles included an instrument of penance, books, manuscripts and the clothing she had used. The delightful phenomenon was considered particularly mystifying since the Venerable had last touched these objects 289 years earlier.[30]

A very painful death was experienced by 23-year-old ST. THERESA MARGARET REDI (d. 1770), who died of intestinal gangrene after an agony of eighteen hours. Immediately after her death her body began to swell and became discolored, but when the body miraculously returned to its natural color and assumed a glow of health, the burial of the Saint was delayed for a number of days. It was then noticed that "a most delightful odor, not to be compared with any earthly fragrance, clearly revealed what had been brought about in these precious remains . . . God had glorified them by the gift of incorruption."[31]

Fifteen days following her death, the archbishop and other dignitaries went to the monastery to view the remains and to learn all the details concerning the mysterious transformation. It was then noticed that a little moisture lingered about the nose of the Saint. The archbishop asked that it be removed with a handkerchief. At once the handkerchief produced such a sweet scent that the archbishop could not keep from weeping. Smell the little piece of cloth he exclaimed, *"Virgineo fragrat odore"*—"fragrance of virginity." The handkerchief is still kept as a precious relic.

Not only the handkerchief, but other objects the Saint had used in life also emitted a mysterious and fragrant odor. One woman detected this sweet perfume on at least three occasions when she was washing clothes formerly worn by the Saint.[32]

This phenomenon occurred not only in Florence, but also, and quite frequently, in the Saint's native city, Arezzo. St. Theresa Margaret's mother was the first to experience it. She remembered that she had cut off a lock of her daughter's hair before she entered Carmel and had put it away as a keepsake. After a brief search she found the hair in a small box which, when opened, "set free a delicate, fragrant, extraordinary odor that filled the room, to the wonder of all who smelled it."

Much more thrilled were both parents when, on opening a package—which the nuns had sent to Arezzo for memory's sake—containing a piece of her tunic and the bronze crucifix that the Saint had so closely pressed to her lips when she was dying, they smelled the very same extraordinary odor, with which God was glorifying their beloved daughter.[33]

ST. MICAELA DESMAISIERES (d. 1860), a Viscountess, founded a religious order in Madrid known as the Adoratrices. Known in religion as Mother Sacramento, she also experienced mystical favors during life and again after her death when a heavenly perfume spread throughout the chapel of the Adoratrices.
One biographer wrote:

> The celestial fragrance which was perceived in that chapel by many religious and pupils is a historic fact which is corroborated by a declaration made under oath. It figures in the Process of the beatification of the Saintly Viscountess.[34]

Micaela was canonized in 1934, the same year that her friend, St. Anthony Mary Claret, was beatified.

VEN. MARIE CELINE OF THE PRESENTATION (d. 1897) was born into a poor family, the fifth of twelve children. At the age of eighteen she entered the Poor Clare Order at Bordeaux, but soon afterward she became seriously ill. When death seemed to approach, she was permitted to make her perpetual vows. During the last ten days of her life the scent of roses was often noticed in her room and in the corridor, although there were no flowers anywhere near the area. The heavenly perfume was also noticed about her dead body and sweetly scented many of her relics.[35] Marie Celine of the Presentation died at the age of nineteen and was declared venerable in 1957.

ST. THÉRÈSE OF LISIEUX died in 1897, and her remains were exhumed on September 6, 1910. As soon as the coffin was opened a strong scent of violets was noticed, a scent which none of the observers could explain. It was soon noticed that a fragrance of incense was emitted from some boards that had been removed from the coffin, as well as bits of clothing and the palm which had remained fresh in the hands of the Saint. Another board from the top of the coffin had been removed, but was brought to the convent a week after the exhumation. The extern sister, discovering the board, but not knowing for certain if it was from the coffin, asked the Little Flower for some token of its origin. Her prayer was granted when several of the nuns, who knew nothing of the matter, noticed a wonderful perfume of incense coming from the board. One of them could even perceive it from a considerable distance.[36]

The holy remains of the following Saints were also blessed with perfumes:

The body of BL. ANGELO OF BORGO SEPOLCRO (d. 1306), an Augustinian, was found incorrupt in 1583, exhaling a delightful perfume. An intense fragrance was also noted about the body of ST. DIDACUS OF ALCALA (d. 1463) at the time of his death and again five days later. During the Process of beatification, witnesses testified that shortly after the death of ST. LOUIS BERTRAND (d. 1581), a heavenly perfume arose from his body which was accompanied by an illumination and seraphic music. The perfume that emanated from the body of VEN. CATALINA DE CRISTO (d. 1589) perfumed not only the cell in which she had died, but the entire convent as well.

When the incorrupt body of ST. PASCHAL BAYLON (d. 1592) was exhumed nineteen years after his death, "an agreeable fragrance, resembling the perfume of flowers, or scent, arose from the sepulchre." The body of ST. MARY MAGDALEN DE'PAZZI (d. 1607) also exhaled the odor of sanctity, which was detected about her tomb soon after her interment and again on numerous occasions throughout the years. Eighteen months after the death of ST. ROSE OF LIMA (d. 1630) her incorrupt body was found exhaling a delightful perfume.

When Onulf was sent to fetch the dead body of ST. SEVERIN (d. 508), who had been dead for six years, it was found not only incorrupt, but also giving off a most exceedingly sweet fragrance "though no embalmer's hand had ever touched it." When the body of ST. FRANCIS XAVIER (d. 1552) was brought to Goa, India, where it is still enshrined, the Viceroy took part in the ceremony, which was attended by crowds of people who were aware of the missionary's holiness. It was noted at this time that although no ointment, spices or balm had been used, the body "had a ravishing fragrance."

The body of ST. BENEDICT THE MOOR (d. 1589), a humble Franciscan lay brother, was also discovered incorrupt many years after his death, and it also emitted a pleasant scent. BL. HENRY SUSO (d. 1365), a Dominican mystic, was also favored with a sweet odor about his incorrupt body 250 years after his death.

—Part III—

THE SAINTS AND THEIR
INFLUENCE OVER NATURE

St. Clelia Barbieri

St. Elizabeth of Hungary

St. Joseph of Cupertino

EARTH, SEA AND SKY

It is wonderful to consider that the good Lord gave to many of His chosen souls the power to control the elements and to perform prodigies that would suppress evil and aid their neighbors during difficulties. In many instances it would appear that God gave the power solely to signal the sanctity of those who performed such wonders.

What miracle would present this God-given power better than a humble Saint confronting a roaring volcano? Such a miracle took place while ST. ALPHONSUS LIGUORI (d. 1787) was visiting the area south of Naples during the year 1779. Mount Vesuvius at that time was giving all indications of a fearful eruption. Flames leaped high in the crater while the mountain grumbled its warning. St. Alphonsus was shown the spectacle, which promised a terrible destruction.

According to eyewitnesses of the event who testified before the tribunal considering the holy man's beatification, St. Alphonsus, while looking at the mountain, uttered the holy name of "Jesus" three times and then made a Sign of the Cross toward the eruption. The eyewitnesses testified that after the blessing, the flames instantly disappeared.[1]

It was because of the counsel given by St. Alphonsus Liguori that BL. FRANCIS XAVIER BIANCHI (d. 1815) was able to overcome his father's objections and enter the Congregation of Clerks Regular of St. Paul, commonly called the Barnabites. By special permission of Pope Clement XIII he received the three major orders on consecutive days. After his ordination he was appointed superior to two different colleges simultaneously, positions which he held with distinction for fifteen years. Afterward, although his health suffered, he began to lead an extremely mortified and austere life, spending long hours in the confessional, where thousands sought his counsel.

Because of his service to all who needed his help and the miracles he performed, as well as his prophetic powers, Bl. Francis Xavier was universally regarded as a Saint. Just like his friend, St. Alphonsus Liguori, he too was called upon by the people when Mount Vesuvius once again became active. The year was 1805. Although unable to walk at the time because his legs were terribly swollen and covered with open sores, he was carried to the edge of the lava stream, which he blessed, with the result that the flow promptly stopped.[2]

It was another deadly mountain, this one named Mount Etna, that challenged the prayers of BL. PETER GEREMIA (d. 1452) while he was preaching at Catania. The Mount not only thundered a warning, but also sent forth flames while lava flowed down the mountain toward the city.

Bl. Peter's reputation as a worker of miracles attracted the people of the city, and they fled to him for protection. After preaching a warning about repentance, he went to the nearby shrine of St. Agatha, removed the veil of the Saint which was kept there as a relic and held it up toward the Mount. The activity ceased due to the prayer of Bl. Peter and the intercession of St. Agatha. One biographer notes: "This and the countless other miracles he performed caused him to be revered as a saint."[3]

If the Saints were able to tame volcanoes through their prayers, surely they could stop earthquakes—and that is exactly what took place while ST. ANTHONY MARY CLARET (d. 1870) was the Archbishop of Cuba.

The island at that time was subject to earthquakes, and as a result the people were reluctant to gather in churches, for fear of the buildings' collapse.

One day, while the archbishop was preaching in a public square, a distant thunder gave warning of another quake. The people screamed and began to flee, but the archbishop calmed them, telling them not to fear. The crowd again assembled, but once more the earth trembled. This time the Saint decided to calm the earth in a way that must have seemed dramatic to all the witnesses. The Saint knelt down on the ground, and placing his two hands on the soil, he offered a silent prayer. Rising, he predicted: "The quakes will not molest you again today!" He then continued with his sermon.

His biographer reports: "In the future, the people never believed themselves so well preserved from the dangers of earthquakes, as when they were listening to the sermons of their holy archbishop."[4]

What took place *after* an earthquake is recorded by St. Jerome. He tells of the event in his biography of ST. HILARION (d. 371). The Saint had gone to Epidaurus in Dalmatia for the purpose of obtaining seclusion, thinking that he would be unknown—but his reputation for miracles followed him.

It happened that a violent earthquake shook Epidaurus. The people were fearful that a tidal wave would overwhelm the city, and they went in search of the Saint. Finding him, they brought him to the shore, asking him to offer a prayer against the devastating force of nature.

The Saint looked out to sea, then kneeling in the sand he made three crosses. The sea had adjusted itself into a great wave when the Saint arose and stretched his arms, as though ordering it not to advance. The wave is said to have weakened and to have returned to the sea.[5]

Not a tidal wave, but a tide, was obedient to ST. FRANCIS OF PAOLA (d. 1507). The miracle took place at Ostia when the Saint and his companions were about to sail for France. Upon reaching their ship they were told that the voyage would be delayed, since the tide was unpredictable and not enough water was available to float the ship. Overhearing the captain explain to the disappointed passengers that it was impossible to float the ship, the Saint approached the sailors and requested that they measure the water again, ". . . because, with the help of God, it should prove sufficient." To the amazement of the crew, the water had risen in a short time to six palms, enough to sail, which they did.

But the passengers and crew would witness yet another miracle when they reached the Gulf of Lyons. It was then that a violent storm forced them to drop anchor. While they were waiting for the storm to quiet, a Turkish pirate ship came into view and began bombarding the Saint's ship with their cannons. In great distress the captain and members of his crew told the Saint of their fears, to which St. Francis calmly replied, "Brothers, raise the anchor and have no fear. With the help of God, none of you will be hurt."

It is reported that the pirate ship became immobile at that moment as the Saint's ship sailed away with a favorable wind.[6]

As early as the seventh century the power of the Saints over nature was demonstrated in the life of ST. ETHELWALD (d. 699), who inhabited a hermitage on Farne Island, which had formerly been used by St. Cuthbert. The island was situated in such a way that fierce gales and ocean swells made it impossible for weeks at a time to journey to neighboring islands.

Three monks from Lindisfarne, a neighboring island, had paid a visit to the hermit on a fine day. What then took place is recorded for us by St. Bede the Venerable in his *Ecclesiastical History of the English Nation.*

He relates that as soon as the three monks boarded a boat for their homeward journey and were a distance from the island of St. Ethelwald, a frightening storm arose so that they were in danger of capsizing and losing their lives in the heavy waves. Looking back they saw St. Ethelwald, at the entrance of his hermitage, fall on his knees in prayer. At that moment the wind died down, the waves settled and a soft breeze blew them homeward.

However, as soon as they disembarked and secured their boat, the wind again blew furiously, and the storm that had been interrupted by the prayer of the Saint renewed its anger and raged for the rest of the day.[7]

ST. JOSEPH OF CUPERTINO (d. 1663) needed only one command to stop a storm that threatened the area. Going out of doors, he dismissed the storm with the command, "Go away in God's name." And it left the area immediately.

On another occasion a storm, described as something of a hurricane with a heavy downpour of rain, threatened the area around the convent at Grottella, which badly frightened the townfolk. It, too, ceased at his command. It is reported that the clouds fled before him and the sky cleared, to the wonderment of all.[8]

The great ST. DOMINIC (d. 1221) also tamed a storm. It seems that the Saint often passed through the city of Bolsena. He was accustomed to stay with a certain citizen there who had a great vineyard. One day, during a visit of the Saint, a violent storm arose which threatened all the vineyards in the area. In seeming gratitude for his host's gracious and repeated hospitality, the Saint is credited with saving his vineyard from the storm, even though it devastated all the surrounding vineyards.

The host, in return for this favor and to prove his friendship for the Saint, imposed on his heirs the obligation that they should receive and lodge all the Friars of the Dominican Order when they passed through Bolsena. Theodoric of Apoldia wrote toward the end of the thirteenth century that this condition was still being graciously observed.[9]

ST. ANTHONY MARY CLARET (d. 1870) was another stormtamer. History records that his saintly reputation and his gift as a preacher of extraordinary ability brought huge crowds to hear him speak wherever he went. On this occasion so many gathered that the event could not be held in the church, but was instead held out of doors. The weather was bright and calm as the Saint began speaking, but in a moment dark clouds thundered, lightning flashed and the wind grew in intensity so that the people were immediately alarmed and began to flee in terror.

The Saint shouted over the noise, "Let no one move. It is the evil spirit which comes in the midst of this storm. He will soon flee conquered." The Saint then raised his arm and blessed the clouds. At that moment the clouds parted, thunder quieted and peace was restored, permitting the holy man to give forth words that were the spiritual encouragement of all.[10]

Although many of the preceding miracles were about the quieting of storms, one storm *arose* as a result of the prayers of the Polish people and of BL. LADISLAUS OF GIELNIOV (d. 1505). His native Poland was in danger of being overrun in 1498 by the Tartars, who were in league with the Turks. The combined enemy numbered some 70,000 men, who encamped between the Pruth and the Dniester Rivers prior to their planned attack.

Bl. Ladislaus appealed to the frightened population to pray and put their trust in God. Before the enemy could begin their assault, the waters of both rivers rose to flood stage, thoroughly inundating the area. The flood was followed by an intense frost and then a severe snowstorm. Thousands of the enemy either drowned or perished in the cold. The rest were easily defeated by the Polish Prince Stephen.

Bl. Ladislaus' biographer writes: "The victory was generally ascribed to the prayers of Bl. Ladislaus, whose prestige was enormously enhanced."[11]

If Saints could tame volcanoes, stop earthquakes and calm storms, the diverting of a river might seem a minor miracle in comparison, but the following event in fact involved the reforming of another violent force of nature. The miracle would seem unbelievable, had it not been reported by St. Gregory the Great, who obtained his information from the Ven. Venanzio, Bishop of Luni. This miracle is reported in the *Dialogues* of St. Gregory the Great and concerns ST. FREDIANO, Bishop of Lucca (d. 588). St. Gregory tells of the miracle in this way:

> I learned from the Venerable Venanzio that at Lucca there had lived a bishop of marvellous power of whom the inhabitants relate this great miracle. That the river Auxer (Serchio), running close under the walls of the city and often bursting from its bed with great force, caused grievous damage to its inhabitants, so that they . . . strove to divert its course . . . but failed in the attempt. Then the man of God, Frediano, made them give him a little rake, and advancing to where the stream flowed, he knelt in prayer. He afterwards raised himself to his feet and ordered the river to follow him. As he dragged the rake behind him, the waters left their usual course and ran after it, making a new bed wherever the Saint marked the way. Whence thus ever following on, it ceased to do injury to the fields and to the crops raised by the husbandmen.[12]

The feast of St. Frediano is kept on November 18 in Lucca. His remains are enshrined there under the high altar of the Church of the Three Deacons, which was re-dedicated in his honor.

RAIN, SNOW AND ICE

One of the earliest reports of a Saint demonstrating power over nature took place in favor of ST. HILARION (d. 371), a native of Gaza who was one of the Desert Fathers. He was considered by the people of Egypt, Syria, Palestine and surrounding areas as the successor of St. Antony of the Desert. St. Jerome, Hilarion's biographer, tells that miracles followed St. Hilarion everywhere so that it seemed natural for the people to implore his prayers when they were suffering any kind of distress.

When the Saint went to Aphroditopolis and journeyed into the desert with two of his disciples to fast and pray, he was informed by the people that it had not rained in the country for three years, ever since the death of St. Antony. The Saint, having pity on the people, "lifted his arms and eyes to Heaven, and immediately obtained a plentiful downpour." St. Hilarion's biography was also written by the historian Sozomen, and he, too, gives testimony of the Saint's many miracles.[1]

One of the best-known instances involving rain is reported in the life of ST. SCHOLASTICA (d. 543), the twin sister of St. Benedict. The event is often described in her biographies and that of her holy brother, but we will rely on the biography of St. Benedict written by St. Gregory the Great.

It seems that St. Scholastica customarily visited her brother once a year and stayed in a house separate from the monastery, but on its grounds. One day during the year 543 St. Scholastica joined her brother in the little house and spent the day discussing pious matters. Towards evening, when it was beginning to grow dark, St. Benedict began to prepare for his return to the monastery. It was then that St. Scholastica pleaded with him to stay through the night, but St. Benedict replied: "By no means can I stay out of my monastery."

At these words St. Scholastica bowed her head, clasped her hands and prayed. During the time of her prayer the sky was clear and the atmosphere serene, but when she lifted her head thunder roared and lightning flashed. St. Benedict and the monks he had brought with him were astounded by the ensuing heavy rainfall, which prevented them from leaving the house.

St. Benedict did not seem pleased by what was taking place and complained by saying: "God Almighty forgive you, sister. What is this you have done?" To this his sister answered, "I prayed you to stay and you would not hear me. I prayed to Almighty God and He heard me. Now, therefore, if you can, go forth to the monastery and leave me." Unable to leave, he was forced to stay and spent the night ". . . content in spiritual discourse of heavenly matters."

The next morning, St. Scholastica returned to her convent—and there she died three days later.[2] The two Saints died during the same year and lie buried beside each other in tombs located in the church of St. John the Baptist at Monte Cassino.

ST. HERIBERT (d. 1021) is regarded as one of the most distinguished of the prelates who have ruled over the diocese of Cologne. His generosity to the poor and his service to the sick, as well as reports of his ardent prayer life, have enhanced his biographies. It is in these books that we learn of a miracle involving rain.

During the time of a great drought, the archbishop instituted a penitential procession from the church of St. Severin to that of St. Pantaleon. Butler's biography of the Saint relates the following:

> In fervent words he exhorted the multitude to do penance and to trust in God. Some of those present declared that they saw a white dove flying close to the Saint's head as he walked with the procession. Entering the church of St. Severin, Heribert went up to the high altar and, bowing his head in his hands, gave himself to earnest prayer for his people. Scarcely had he risen from his knees when a torrential rain poured down upon the city and the countryside, and the harvest was saved.[3]

Heribert's biographer continues, "From that time onward the Saint was invoked for rain."

A miraculous rainfall is also noted in the life of ST. DOMINIC (d. 1221), the founder of the Order of Preachers. This took place while the Saint was preaching in Segovia. The area was afflicted by a severe drought; even so, one day while the Saint was preaching out of doors, he felt inspired to announce that a plentiful rain would fall that very day. The sky was clear when he began preaching, but as soon as his words were uttered, dark clouds quickly gathered and rain fell in such torrents that the crowd made their way home with some difficulty. In honor of the Saint, and in commemoration of this miracle, a little chapel was built at the site where the Saint made the prophecy.[4]

The biographies of ST. JOHN BOSCO (d. 1888) mention a great drought that afflicted Montemagno in 1864 when he had been invited there to preach a triduum in preparation for the feast of the Assumption. The peasant farmers were in danger of losing their entire crop of grapes, maize, potatoes and vegetables.

In his first sermon, the Saint felt inspired to promise a plentiful rainfall if the farmers invoked the intercession of the Blessed Mother when in a state of grace. The people were to make a good Confession, attend the three nights of prayer and receive Holy Communion on the feast with heartfelt devotion.

The people flocked to the confessional and the evening services, but no rain was in sight. So it was also on the day of the feast. The sky was clear, and the sun scorched the fields.

That evening, as Don Bosco prepared for the evening service, the sky was still clear. It is reported that when he ascended the pulpit for his final sermon he pleaded with the Blessed Virgin for the rain he had promised.

The church was crowded that evening as the Saint recited a fervent *Ave Maria* with the multitude. Then, as he began his sermon, the sky darkened and a dreadful clap of thunder sounded. Lightning flashed repeatedly as rain began to course down the windowpanes.

The Saint is said to have finished his brief discourse by eloquently exhorting confidence in the goodness of the Blessed Virgin. It is recorded that the rain was so intense that the people had to wait a lengthy time before they were able to leave the church.[5]

Rain also was obedient to ST. GERARD MAJELLA (d. 1755) on a number of occasions. One report tells that he was sent one day on an errand and was only a short distance from the monastery when the rain fell in torrents. The Father Rector, fearful that the

Saint might get sick from being unprotected against the elements, sent a messenger to tell the Saint to return. The holy religious did as he was told and returned, but to the amazement of the Father Rector and the messenger, Gerard and his garments were perfectly dry.

We are also told that the same miracle was repeated in favor of seven postulants he was bringing to the monastery.[6]

Rain obeyed the command of ST. PAUL OF THE CROSS (d. 1775) when he was at Santafiora. Because the church in which the Saint was to preach was too small for the huge crowd that gathered to hear him, they assembled in the square. The weather at first was beautiful, but suddenly clouds gathered and rain began to fall in torrents. The people immediately started to seek shelter, but the Saint ordered them not to leave. Taking his crucifix, he blessed the air. In a moment, the rain stopped falling. This miracle amazed the people, but they were even more bewildered when they realized that the Saint, as well as those who had obeyed him, had remained perfectly dry.[7]

Another time, while again preaching outdoors, he blessed the dark clouds with his crucifix. While the rain fell on the farmlands that needed it, not a drop fell where he was preaching. Twice more his biographer relates stories of similar powers over rain while he was preaching. The Saint interpreted these heavy rainfalls as the work of the devil to prevent, or at least diminish, the good he was accomplishing by his preaching.

A miracle very similar to that worked by St. Paul of the Cross in dispersing the rain while preaching outdoors took place when ST. ANTHONY OF PADUA (d. 1231) was preaching to a large crowd of people in the square known as *des creux des Arenes* in the city of Limoges, France. A violent storm threatened to disrupt the gathering. The downpour was such that the people began at once to disperse when the Saint announced, "Fear not; the storm will pass you by."

Mindful of the many miracles worked by the Saint, the crowd remained. To their great confusion they soon realized that although the storm deluged the city, not a drop of rain fell on the square while the Saint preached to them.[8]

The same miracle was performed again, this time while St.

Anthony was at Brive, where he had established a little hermitage. On one occasion, while the community was suffering hardships, the Saint reluctantly asked alms from a generous and wealthy woman of the city. In response to the appeal, the lady sent a maid servant with the needed relief, although the area was experiencing a severe storm.

St. Anthony's biographer reports that not a drop of rain fell on the servant during her going and coming and that she returned to her mistress dry-shod.[9] It is also affirmed that these two miracles involving rain "are historically certain of the sojourn of St. Anthony in Limousin."

A similar event took place during the lifetime of ST. GASPAR DEL BUFALO (d. 1837), the founder of the Congregation of the Precious Blood. His biographer tells that once while he was preaching to a large crowd outside the church, a heavy rainfall approached.

Immediately reaching for a portrait of the Blessed Mother, he held it high in the air and made the Sign of the Cross with it. The rain is said to have stopped its advance toward the church so that not a drop fell on the crowd, although the rain fell all around the area and in the entire city.[10]

We read in the life of ST. BERNARD OF CLAIRVAUX (d. 1153) about a letter he was dictating to the monk Godfrey. The letter is said to be "a masterpiece of tenderness and eloquence" and was being written for Robert, St. Bernard's cousin. The Saint had gone into the fields with Godfrey and was dictating the letter when a heavy rain fell.

St. Bernard is said to have continued dictating without interruption, without "the paper being wetted." His biographer reports: "This circumstance, joined to the sublime character of the letter itself, was looked upon as miraculous; and an oratory was afterwards built on the very spot where the Saint had seated himself while he dictated this epistle."[11]

The great miracle worked by Moses when the Red Sea parted was worked in a much smaller fashion in favor of one of God's chosen souls, the humble shepherdess, ST. GERMAINE COUSIN (d. 1601). Rejected by her father and stepmother because of her withered right hand and scrofulous neck, she was treated shamefully by her family. But she was also the object of many miracles witnessed by the villagers of Pibrac, France.

We are told that in order for her to reach the village church for Holy Mass, it was necessary for her to cross a stream which was often swollen by rain. On one occasion when the stream was overflowing and the current was particularly strong, the villagers watched in amazement as the rushing water separated to provide a dry passageway for her.[12]

Not rain, but destructive hail was averted by ST. FRANCIS OF ASSISI (d. 1226) while he was visiting the monastery at Greccio. The people had complained to him about the frequent hail storms that were destroying their fields and vineyards. The Saint advised that they should all confess their sins and "bring forth fruits befitting repentance." The Saint also promised that if they did as he recommended, the Lord would look kindly upon them and increase their temporal goods. He also warned that if they returned to their former ways, the punishment of God would be doubled.

The people did as St. Francis recommended, and from that hour the destruction ceased. To this miracle was added another, since if any hail fell on their neighbors' fields, it either stopped short when it got near the borders of their lands, or turned aside to some other region.

Unfortunately, the people eventually reverted to their former ways, which brought about a severe punishment from God in that a pestilence brought many to the grave and a fire destroyed the whole town.[13]

Snow

For a miracle concerning a miraculous snowfall, we turn to Our Lady and a certain Roman aristocrat named John Patrizio who had wealth and position and was completely happy in his marriage, with one exception: he had not been blessed with children. Accepting the disappointment with Christian resignation, he and his wife prayed that the Blessed Mother would designate an heir so that they might bequeath their immense fortune and property to one of Our Lady's own choosing. Since John Patrizio and his wife placed their fortune in Our Lady's hands, Heaven's decision was indicated in a miraculous fashion on the morning of August 5 about the year 352-358.

Tradition reveals that after a warm summer night, a carpet of snow fell upon Mount Esquiline. The next morning, the unexpected brightness alerted the people. Many journeyed to the spot, where the snow remained intact despite the heat. Pope Liberius already knew the meaning of the mysterious snowfall. During the night, by means of a dream, both John Patrizio and Pope Liberius were told of Our Lady's intentions for the property. Upon awakening, John Patrizio hurried to the site, while the Pontiff, wanting to emphasize Our Lady's wishes, went to the area in solemn procession. When the people were told that Our Lady had indicated by the snowfall the exact location of a church she wanted to have built, the area was staked off by the people. When the staking was completed the snow immediately disappeared. John Patrizio lost no time in providing all the money necessary to defray the cost of the building. The church was completed two years later.

For a time the church was known as the Basilica Liberiana, after the name of its consecrator. In the early part of the following century Pope Sixtus III rebuilt portions of the basilica with greater magnificence and enriched it with silver articles and adornments, for which it was then known as the Basilica Sixti. It received other names as well, including the Church of St. Mary of the Crib to commemorate the venerable relic which was later deposited there. Because of its size and splendor it finally became known as St. Mary the Greater or St. Mary Major, a name by which it is now known, although it is also known as St. Mary of the Snows.

While some may speculate as to whether the ancient story of the foundation of this basilica is truth or legend, Pope Benedict XIV settled the matter once and for all by proclaiming, "It must be acknowledged that nothing is wanting to enable us to affirm with moral certainty that the prodigy of the snow is true."[14]

An unusual snowfall is also recorded in the life of BL. LADISLAUS (d. 1505), a native of Poland who entered the Franciscan Order of the Strict Observance. He was several times elected provincial and aided the Church as a missionary and preacher, as well as by his example of personal holiness. He wrote both in Latin and in Polish and composed hymns that were sung by the people at evening services.

Poland at one time was in great danger from the Tartars, who joined the Turks in marching against Poland. Ladislaus called upon the frightened people to pray and put their trust in the protective power of God. While they prayed, the invading army encamped between the Pruth and the Dniester Rivers. Suddenly the waters rose in a flood, inundating a large area. This was followed by a severe frost and then by a blinding snowstorm. The invading armies originally numbered approximately 70,000 men, but thousands died by means of the flood, the frost or the cold. Those that survived were easily routed by the army of the Wallachian Prince Stephen. Although the people had joined their prayers to those of Bl. Ladislaus, the victory was ascribed to the prayers of the saintly Ladislaus, "whose prestige was enormously enhanced."[15]

We now turn to ST. THÉRÈSE OF THE CHILD JESUS AND OF THE HOLY FACE (d. 1897), affectionately known as "The Little Flower." When the time of her Postulancy was completed, plans were made for her to receive the habit in a ceremony conducted by the bishop. She would be dressed like a bride and would venture outside the cloister. There she would take part in a ceremony in the presence of her father and the family. The ceremony was set for January 10, 1889. In her autobiography, *The Story of a Soul,* the Saint writes,

> Nothing was missing, not even the snow! I don't know if I've already told you how much I love snow? When I was small, its whiteness filled me with delight and one of the greatest pleasures I had was taking a walk under the light snowflakes. Where did this love of snow come from? Perhaps it was because I was a little winter flower, and the first adornment with which my eyes beheld nature clothed was its white mantle. I had always wished that on the day I received the habit, nature would be adorned in white just like me. The evening before, I was gazing at the grey skies from which a faint rain was falling every now and again and the temperature was so mild I could no longer hope for any snow. The following morning the skies hadn't changed . . .

After the ceremony was completed she embraced her father for the last time and entered the cloister where she was to be clothed in the habit of the Discalced Carmelite Order. Upon entering the cloister,

> . . . the first thing that struck my eye was the statue of "the little Jesus" smiling at me from the midst of flowers and lights. Immediately afterwards my glance was drawn to the snow: the monastery garden was white like me! What thoughtfulness on the part of Jesus! Anticipating the desires of His fiancée, He gave her snow. Snow! What mortal bridegroom, no matter how powerful he may be, could make snow fall from heaven to charm his beloved?

The snowfall was unseasonal and unexpected, since the Saint continues,

> What is certain, though, is that many considered the snow on my Clothing Day as a little miracle and the whole town was astonished. Some found I had a strange taste, loving snow![16]

Ice

Once again we turn to Our Lady, but this time the miracle concerns the French Jesuits who began to evangelize the eastern parts of Canada. Their great devotion to Our Lady was manifest by the many shrines and chapels they erected in her honor. One of the settlements that benefited from this devotion was the trading post named Three Rivers. Here, in 1634, they dedicated a shrine to the Immaculate Conception. In the mid-seventeenth century a district adjacent to Three Rivers became a separate village which was promptly dedicated to the Blessed Mother. A fort and some houses were built, likewise a church that was placed under the patronage of St. Mary Magdalene. Eventually the settlement became known as Cap-de-la-Madeleine, a name it has retained.

During the eighteenth century, devotion in the settlement waned, with only visiting priests administering the Sacraments on a somewhat regular basis. It was not until 1845 that the bishop appointed Fr. Leandre Tourigny to be the settlement's resident priest. It was during his pastorate that a generous donor presented the little church with a statue of Our Lady in honor of the definition of the

Dogma of the Immaculate Conception. It is this figure of Our Lady that is the focus of Canada's most popular shrine of Our Lady, now known as Our Lady of the Holy Rosary.

Unfortunately, Fr. Tourigny was unable by himself to rouse the people from their indifference. So it was that Bishop Cooke appointed Fr. Luke Desilets to help in revitalizing religious fervor. The method devised for this transformation was the building of a National Shrine of Our Lady. When the bishop granted permission for this undertaking, the stones needed for the new church were cut and dressed at a quarry at S. Angele on the other side of the river. It was the intention of the builders to drag the stones across the frozen water of the St. Lawrence River during the winter, when thick ice customarily formed. But the winter of 1879 proved an exceptionally mild one. During the month of March the parishioners grew increasingly doubtful that they would be able to secure the needed stones from the opposite side of the river.

Realizing that the plans for the new church would likely be abandoned, Fr. Desilets had recourse to urgent prayer and bargained with Our Lady. If the Heavenly Queen would construct a bridge of ice sufficient to transport the stones, he would not supplement the supply of stones by taking the stones from the primitive church. He would instead preserve the old church and cause it to be dedicated for all time as a perpetual shrine of the Most Holy Rosary.

The holy prelate's prayers were answered almost immediately. On March 15, 1879, a violent gale began to pile up ice floes until a bridge of thick ice formed from one shore to the other. The next day, a Sunday, it was found that this bridge of ice could bear the weight of thirty or forty men. The next day saw a steady stream of more than 150 horse-drawn sledges crossing and recrossing this bridge carrying loads of stone. By the end of the week every needed stone was located on the church site. Then, when the ice bridge was no longer needed, a thaw set in. The following day, just as quickly as it had formed, the ice bridge was gone.

We are assured that the formation of the ice bridge is no imagined legend since newspapers of the time told of its mysterious and timely formation, as well as its sudden disappearance. The story of the miraculous ice bridge is also recounted in a detailed letter written by Fr. Frederic, O.F.M. (d. 1916), whose Cause for beatification was introduced in 1940.

Moreover, the events relative to the ice bridge were regarded by everyone as so extraordinary that a permanent marker was erected in the garden.

The church that was built with the stones transported across the ice bridge was opened on October 3, 1880. The miraculous statue that is revered in this church was given to Fr. Tourigny during his pastorate, which began in 1845. This statue is noted for the miracle that took place on June 22, 1888 in the presence of Fr. Desilets and Fr. Frederic and an infirm pilgrim, Pierre Lacroix, who was cured at the time. While they were praying, all three, independently, observed that the eyes of the statue, which had moments before been downcast, were then wide open and looking straight ahead. Details of this miracle were recorded by the three witnesses. These documents are still found in the sanctuary archives.

News of this miracle, as well as that regarding the ice bridge, prompted pilgrimages that have continued ever since and have increased in number until the shrine is regarded as the most frequented shrine of the Blessed Mother in Canada.

A whole complex of buildings developed at Cap-de-la-Madeleine. Today, in addition to the many buildings, there are found serene ponds, a lake, gardens and devotional areas including a Stations of the Cross which is located on the other side of the little Faverel River. Linking the shrine grounds to the Stations is the Rosary Bridge, named in memory of the historic episode of the ice bridge. The Rosary Bridge is uniquely decorated throughout with large chains representing rosaries.

The statue of Our Lady of the Cape (Notre Dame du Cap) was crowned by Pope Pius XII and is the only Madonna to be pontifically crowned in Canada. The shrine was also honored by the visit of Pope John Paul II on September 10, 1984, when 75,000 pilgrims joined in welcoming him.[17]

Our Lady in the Sand

Ice is also mentioned in the history of a statue known as Our Lady in the Sand in Roermond, the Netherlands. An unbroken local tradition relates that Wendelinus, the son of a Polish knight, while looking for work, came upon the farm of Gerard Muggengebroeck. Unable to find more elegant work, and because of his extreme need, he agreed to work for the farmer as a shepherd. The year was 1435. One day while the sheep grazed on the flatlands, Wendelinus became enormously thirsty and went in search of water. Coming upon a well that was known to have run dry, he nevertheless tried to obtain some water and found not only a quantity of fresh water, but also a small statue of Our Lady. It was soon learned that the statue had been enshrined near the well in a tiny, primitive chapel. When a blind girl was cured after a novena in honor of Our Lady in the Sand, a chapel was built at the well where the statue had been discovered. The popularity of the shrine spread rapidly as indicated by Fr. Luncenius, who gave the city council a list of the offerings made by the pilgrims from 1467 to 1495.

Spanish governors and Protestant iconoclasts presented grave problems for the shrine. Finally one of the governors ordered the destruction of the chapel in 1578. The statue was rescued and found refuge in St. Christopher's Church. Another chapel built in 1610 was soon enlarged because of Our Lady's popularity. As the shrine increased in celebrity, so did the number of miracles, which have continued through the years, as detailed in documents of the shrine.

In addition to wonderful cures, a miracle of another kind took place in 1624 when a conflict developed between Spain and the Protestant north. When it seemed that the Protestants would prevail, the Marian Brotherhood made a pilgrimage to the chapel, where devout appeals were made to the Blessed Mother. Almost immediately the water of the Ysel River miraculously froze to permit the crossing of a Catholic army that soon defeated the Dutch Calvinists.

The miraculous statue of Madonna and Child continues to attract pilgrims. Measuring a mere thirteen and a half inches tall, the statue of Our Lady in the Sand was awarded two distinctions in the year 1877. It was recognized as an historic figure by the Dutch government and it was given a papal coronation on the command of Pope Pius IX. Many are the cures that are still reported at the shrine and by use of the water from the well.[18]

THE BRIDGE OF THE ROSARIES. Large chains representing rosaries decorate the bridge which links the grounds of the Cap-de-la-Madeleine Shrine to the Stations of the Cross located across the Faverel River in Canada. The bridge commemorates the miraculous formation in 1879 of an ice bridge that allowed stone to be transported across the river for construction of a chapel (seen in the background).

ST. MARY OF THE SNOWS Basilica was built on a site indicated by Our Lady through a miraculous snowfall. Here Pope Liberius watches the measuring of the plot of land. This picture is from a famous painting by Tintoretto.

LAST MEAL TOGETHER. St. Benedict and his twin sister, St. Scholastica, customarily met once a year for a visit. In this painting they are pictured at supper in the year 543. St. Scholastica was loath to be parted from her dear brother and implored him to visit further with her. When he refused and insisted that he must leave, St. Scholastica asked for and was granted by God a great thunderstorm that prevented St. Benedict from departing. This was to be their last visit, since she died only days later. Her brother followed within a year's time. (Subiaco, Sacro Speco.)

PLANTS, FRUIT AND FLOWERS

Although an Englishman by birth, ST. BONIFACE (d. 755) is known as "The Apostle of Germany." Since parts of Germany had accepted the Christian faith before his arrival, the Saint is credited with evangelizing the other parts of the country. He also organized the Church and created a hierarchy under the direct commission of the Holy See. During a visit to Rome, he was consecrated bishop and returned to the country to eliminate the remaining kernels of pagan superstitions that were a hindrance to the progress of the Gospel and a temptation to the newly converted.

To secure the destruction of pagan worship, a public spectacle was planned which would, in effect, confront the false god, Thor, with the God of the Gospel. The central place of worship for the pagans was a sacred oak dedicated to Thor which stood on the summit of Mount Gudenberg. Boniface and two companions, armed with axes, approached the tree and began striking at it. As Butler relates:

> Almost as the first blows fell upon it, the huge tree crashed, splitting into four parts, and the people who had expected a judgement to descend upon the perpetrators of such an outrage acknowledged that their gods were powerless to protect their own sanctuaries.[1]

From then on, evangelization of the entire country progressed steadily.

ST. PETER OF RAVENNA (d. thirteenth century) was one day preaching at Como on the quotation, "Honor the Lord . . . Then will your barns be filled with grain." *(Proverbs* 3:9-10). This aroused the attention of two farmers. One scoffed at the notion and declared that whether he honored the Lord or the devil, his harvest would depend on his skill at farming. The other farmer commended his labors to God and vowed to dedicate to Him a tenth of his harvest if He would bless his crops.

The days of harvest arrived. The fields of the impious farmer did not produce "one single ear of corn," while the other farmer's fields produced a hundredfold. The farmer whose harvest failed was thereafter diligent in his prayers and "was blessed in his basket and his store."[2]

In a biography of ST. THÉRÈSE OF THE CHILD JESUS AND OF THE HOLY FACE (d. 1897) published in 1912, before her beatification, we find a chapter which gives the details of the exhumation of the Saint's remains that took place on September 6, 1910. Attending the exhumation were members of the clergy, the Vice-Postulator of the Cause for beatification and the Bishop of Bayeux and Lisieux, and His Lordship, Msgr. Lemonnier.

The work of taking up the remains presented great difficulties for the workmen, but while the priests chanted the *Laudate Pueri Dominum,* the coffin finally came into view. To the surprise of many, they saw through the loose boards, as fresh and green as ever, the palm which had been placed in the hands of the Saint on the day of her death. This was considered to be a symbol of the immortal palm she had won by her martyrdom of self—that martyrdom of which she had written: "I desire at all costs to win the palm of Agnes; if not by the shedding of blood, it must be by Love."

The account continues:

> Other palms of exactly the same kind and sterilized in a similar way were placed in the sacristy of the Carmel in 1897, the year of the Saint's death. Though, however, they were kept as dry as possible and wiped over in damp weather to prevent mildew, they had ultimately to be burned.[3]

The palm that was found fresh and green in the Saint's casket is kept at the Carmel of Lisieux.

Fruit

A case of obedience is related in the biography of ST. JOHN THE DWARF (d. fifth century), who placed himself under the direction of an elderly hermit named St. Poemen. For his first lesson in holy obedience, St. Poemen gave St. John a dry walking stick and instructed him to plant it in the ground and to continue watering it every day until it bore fruit. The Saint did as he was told and watered it every day for three years, even though the water source was some distance from the hermitage. Finally, the stick took root, pushed forth leaves, then buds and finally fruit. St. Sulpicius Severus was assured that the tree grew in the garden of the monastery and continued for many years to send out shoots and green leaves.[4]

Also in the fifth century we have a similar incident, but this involved not one, but many dry sticks. ST. TYCHON (d. fifth century) wanted to establish a vineyard soon after he became a bishop. Known as "the Wonder Worker," St. Tychon unfortunately lacked the means to stock the vineyard. He then decided to collect the dead and dried cuttings that the vine growers had thrown away. The Saint planted the sticks and prayed that they would be rejuvenated, that the future vines should produce an abundance of fruit and that the fruit should be sweet and ripen early. The prayer was answered on all counts. In fact, the early harvest of grapes prompted the celebration of the feast of St. Tychon on June 16, while elsewhere in Cyprus the vine-gathering festival was celebrated many weeks later. Because of his miraculous vineyard, St. Tychon is regarded as the patron of vine growers.[5]

Like St. John the Dwarf and St. Tychon, a dried stick also has a prominent place in the history of ST. RITA OF CASCIA (d. 1457). To test the Saint's obedience, the Mother Abbess one day gave the Saint a dry stick and ordered her to plant it in the ground between the cistern and the wall of the convent, and to water it each day until it blossomed. Morning and evening, in good weather and in bad weather, in winter and in summer, St. Rita went to the well and watered the stick. The sisters teased her about the watering, but the Saint merely smiled in reply. For an entire year the Saint continued to water the stick until one day, to the amazement of all in the convent, the stick gave forth leaves and then branches. Blossoms came next and then clusters of grapes. Today, after six centuries, this vine is still thriving and producing fruit.[6] Each year the harvest is distributed among high-ranking ecclesiastics, while the leaves are dried, made into a powder, and sent to the sick around the world.[7]

A miracle concerning grapes is also mentioned in the life of ST. PAUL OF THE CROSS (d. 1775). When Bishop Cristoforo

Palmieri petitioned St. Paul to minister in his diocese, the Saint experienced every kind of physical discomfort while travelling about to preach, give instructions and hear confessions. It was said by outsiders that they had never seen a more devout people as those to whom the Saint witnessed, and it was for these good people that Our Lord was pleased to reward "and at the same time to give increased authority to the word of" His servant. The miracle took place when a tempest threatened extreme damage to their vines, which that year were heavy with fruit. In fear, but with faith in the Saint's intercessory prayers, they begged St. Paul to bless the air with his crucifix. He did so, but the hail continued to fall with apparent violence. After the storm it was joyously noticed that although the leaves had been stripped off the vines, the grapes remained untouched and completely undamaged.[8]

BL. JAMES OF BITETTO (d. 1485) is little known, but deserves to be greatly regarded since he was one of the greatest mystics of the Franciscan Observance. His levitations, prophecies, miracles and mystical gifts were attested to by his fellow religious during the Process for his beatification. Employed as a cook for his community, the humble lay brother was often in ecstasy while preparing meals, but "the Divine Spirit who filled his soul at such times did not permit his work to suffer on that account." In the monastery garden was a grotto with an image of the Mother of God where Bl. James retired often to pray. It was near this grotto that he planted a juniper tree, whose berries were said to possess wonderful healing properties.[9]

As a Carmelite nun, BL. ARCHANGELA GIRLANI (d. 1494) "was the model of every religious virtue, most austere in her practice of penance, charitable to all, and possessed of a marvelous spirit of prayer." Many times she was found in ecstasy, levitated several feet above the floor. After serving as abbess for many years she died a holy death and her body was found incorrupt many years later. Long before her death there was a tradition regarding a certain pear tree. It was believed that the tree produced as many pears as there were nuns in the convent. If a pear fell off the tree, it was accepted by the community as an indication that one of the members would die within the year. As soon as a pear dropped from the tree Bl. Archangela would exhort her sisters to prepare for death, since no one knew for whom the warning was intended. Evidently the tradition was validated by the death of some of the nuns, since the dropping of the pears was accepted as a death warning for many years after Archangela's death.[10]

A pear tree is also mentioned in the life of BL. JAMES THE ALMSGIVER (d. 1304), although Butler expresses some reservations about the authenticity of the report. At any rate, Bl. James was murdered for defending the rights of the Church and the poor. After his death his murderers hid the body, and no trace of him was found until shepherds, passing through a forest, came upon a pear tree and shrubs in full blossom. Greatly surprised at the unseasonable blooming, since it was in the dead of winter, they stood gazing at the wonder when a voice was heard which was that of "James, the priest, who has been murdered for defending the rights of the Church and the poor." The blossoms and the voice prompted a search in the area for the body, which was found incorrupt. First buried in the chapel of a hospice, it was again found incorrupt 174 years later during a translation of the body. The date given for the murder is January 15, 1304.[11]

At the age of twelve, the future ST. MARTIN DE PORRES (d. 1639) was apprenticed to a barber. In those days barbers also served as surgeons, physicians and druggists. It was his training at this time that aided him in successfully performing his lengthy apostolate of generosity to mankind. While he was still in training, he planted a lemon tree in the garden of the rented house belonging to Ventura de Luna, in which he was then living with his mother and sister. Much to the amazement of the neighbors, the tree continued to bear fruit all year round. According to reliable witnesses, the tree was still bearing fruit fifty years after St. Martin's death.[12]

The Saint planted other trees as well. After he entered the Dominican Order, his longing to help the poor prompted him to plant fig and other fruit trees in public areas outside the city. This was to enable the poor to satisfy their hunger with fruit from these trees, rather than be tempted to steal fruit from private orchards nearby. It is said that some of these trees that St. Martin planted may still be seen.[13]

St. Martin also planted olive trees, a great number of them, on the property of the Monastery of the Holy Rosary. These olives were to provide the friars and the poor with the purest of oil. The Saint's biographer relates:

> . . . these trees grew in ways that were certainly not natural. Leaves and sprouts and fruit came forth in miraculous fashion, and we are assured that Martin's olive trees withstood the ravages of pests and blights, of unfavorable weather conditions, and of other obstacles to splendid growth in ways that seemed to be beyond the laws of nature.[14]

At the time the biography was written (1937), the few surviving trees of "the Olive Garden of Brother Martin" were still producing olives at Limatambo.

Like St. Martin de Porres, ST. ANTHONY OF PADUA (d. 1231) also planted a lemon tree. When he landed at Messina, he stayed two months at a monastery of the Friars Minor, where he planted the tree in the monastery garden. It is said that it flourishes "to this hour . . . which time cannot wither and which every year buds, blooms and gives abundant fruit."[15]

A lime tree is mentioned in the life of BL. AUGUSTINE GAZOTICH (Augustine of Lucera) (d. 1323), who became a Dominican and then was elevated to the bishopric of Lucera. It seems that he had the gift of healing, and for this reason huge crowds flocked to him. For reasons of humility, he planted a lime tree and humbly suggested to the people that its leaves would be more efficacious than his hands. And so they were. It is said that even the invading Turks respected the wonder-working tree.[16]

Another Dominican, BL. BARTHOLOMEW OF CERVERIO (d. 1466), distinguished himself by obtaining his licentiate, the doctorate and the master's degree from the University of Turin. It is the only time in the history of the university that anyone had acquired three degrees in one day. In a short apostolate of only twelve years he converted many heretics and worked hard to eradicate heresy. He prophesied that he would die a martyr's death and that he would be known as Bartholomew of Cerverio, even though he had never visited the place. His prophecy was fulfilled when he was on the road which led to Cerverio and was attacked by heretics who desecrated his body with numerous dagger wounds. A chapel was soon erected at the place of martyrdom which was often visited by pilgrimages from Savigliano and Cerverio. At the same place a fig tree sprang up which is always mentioned in the Saint's biographies.[17]

ST. JOSEPH OF CUPERTINO (d. 1663), who is known for his ecstatic flights and levitations, was on his way to the monastery of the Conventuals at Osimo when he and his companions decided to pause outside the city. Since the Saint was well known and would normally attract a crowd of people, the Saint's companions thought it best to wait until nightfall before going further. When a priest companion pointed out the cupola of the Holy House of Loreto a short distance away, Joseph, on looking at it, exclaimed: "Do you not see the angels who ascend and descend from Heaven to yonder sanctuary?" Immediately after saying this he flew without support to an almond tree about fifteen yards away. Thereafter, the tree became known as "the almond tree of St. Joseph," as it is still known today.[18]

The story is told that BL. GERARD OF MONZA (d. 1207) wanted to spend the night in prayer in the church of St. John the Baptist and asked the doorkeepers for permission to do so. The doorkeepers hesitated, since they felt they should receive some recompense for the favor. They apparently were amused at what they decided upon, since it would be impossible for the Saint to give them what they wanted. Because it was mid-winter they told the Saint they would permit him to be locked in the church if, in the morning, he would supply them with fresh ripe cherries. The Saint promised to give them exactly what they wanted and spent the night in prayer. The following morning when the doorkeepers unlocked the doors and approached the Saint, they were amazed when he presented each of them with handfuls of ripe cherries. Pictures of the Saint represent him as carrying cherries in his hands.[19]

BL. THOMAS CORSINI (d. 1345) was a humble lay brother in the Servite community who experienced at least two visions of the Blessed Mother. His main occupation as a lay brother was to beg alms for his brethren. While on his rounds he worked many miracles, but one that is called "famous," and which was duly witnessed, was his visit to a poor woman who was near the time of her confinement. As an expectant mother, she had a craving for fresh figs, which she expressed to Bl. Thomas. Although it was the month of January, he went into the garden and found on a tree three ripe figs in perfect condition, which he took to her.[20] We are also told that, in addition to miracles, Bl. Thomas Corsini had many spiritual graces and gifts.

Flowers

When ST. BENEDICT (d. circa 547) was living in a grotto at Subiaco he was maliciously attacked by a black bird which he dismissed with a Sign of the Cross. Realizing who it was that had sent the bird, he was almost immediately attacked with a temptation against holy purity. The temptation was such that it seemed to him as though his very vocation was at risk. To conquer the evil insinuation, the Saint undressed and threw himself into thorn bushes that grew nearby. Rolling back and forth numerous times, he overcame the temptation so well that he claimed in later life that he never again experienced a similar threat to his purity. The Saint's contact with the thorn bushes apparently became well known, with the bushes, and those that replaced them throughout the years, being regarded as something of a relic.

At any rate, seven centuries later, about the year 1223, the bushes were apparently pointed out to St. Francis of Assisi when he visited the Benedictine abbey. According to Cardinal Schuster, St. Francis "engrafted some rose branches on the thorny bush in which St. Benedict had rolled himself."[21] Other authors claim that the thorns were changed to roses following a blessing by the Saint. This is the opinion of yet another biographer who relates that centuries after St. Benedict dismissed the temptation by rolling in the brambles, "St. Francis went to visit the rocks of Subiaco where Benedict had his cavern. He made the Sign of the Cross over these thorns and brambles, covered with the blood of the young solitary, and they were converted into roses, which have given health to many a pilgrim."[22]

With regard to these rose bushes we turn to FR. PAUL OF MOLL (d. 1896), a Flemish Benedictine who is known as the "Wonder-Worker of the Nineteenth Century."

Among his many mystical favors, Fr. Paul was especially known for healing countless afflictions and diseases. On one occasion a girl of twelve was so severely afflicted with a nervous disease that her mother was advised by the Little Sisters of the Poor to ask the good Father to cure her. A servant girl was sent to the monastery at Steenbrugge to present the mother's appeal to Fr. Paul. His reply was, "That child is in a deplorable condition and cannot live more than two days. However, we shall see what can be done through the aid of St. Benedict." He gave the servant girl two medals of St. Benedict. "Place one around her neck, though you will experience great difficulty in so doing. The other you will dip into whatever she may drink, and also into the water wherewith you bathe her suffering limbs. Give her no medicine, only a small powder of the miraculous roses of St. Benedict." The priest also recommended that they make fervent novenas in honor of the Saint. After the second novena the child was greatly improved, and after a visit to Fr. Paul, the child completely recovered.[23]

The dipping of a medal of St. Benedict into drinking water as a cure was often recommended by Fr. Paul. The use of powder made from the roses of St. Benedict was advised on certain occasions. (See Birds, Bees and Bugs for more about these bushes.)

Just as St. Benedict threw himself into a thorny bush to overcome a temptation, so, too, did ST. FRANCIS OF ASSISI (d. 1226). According to the shrine of the Saint:

> In order to triumph over a temptation, St. Francis threw himself down among thorns which forthwith were changed into thornless rose trees. They bloom in May and can be seen in the garden at the Portiuncula, the Cradle of the Franciscan Order, which is quite close to the railway station of Assisi in the village of Santa Maria degli Angeli, Italy.

Leaves from these thornless rose bushes are distributed by the shrine in small packets.

We read that ST. ELIZABETH OF HUNGARY (d. 1231) was one day accompanied by a favorite maidservant on an errand of mercy. Within her mantle St. Elizabeth was carrying bread, meat, eggs and other food to distribute to the poor. As they were travelling along they encountered the Saint's husband, who was returning from hunting. Count de Montalembert writes in the Saint's biography:

> Astonished to see her thus toiling on under the weight of her burden, he said to her, "Let us see what you carry" and at the same time drew open the mantle which she held closely clasped to her bosom; but beneath it were only red and white roses, the most beautiful he had ever seen—and this astonished him, as it was no longer the season of flowers. Seeing that Elizabeth was troubled, he sought to console her by his caresses . . .

After seeing a shining cross above St. Elizabeth's head, he left, ". . . carrying with him one of those wonderful roses, which he preserved all his life."[24]

An almost similar situation occurred in the life of ST. GERMAINE COUSIN (d. 1601). One wintry day the maiden's stepmother pursued her with a stick, loudly accusing her of stealing bread for the poor. The Saint was sternly ordered to open her apron. Tumbling out from the apron were fragrant roses of a variety unknown to the region. The bread that had been in the apron was only the meager portion given to Germaine for her meal. The Saint had indeed intended it for the poor. The witnesses of this event, Pierre Pailles and Jeanne Salaires, gave sworn testimony concerning this miracle.[25]

When ST. RITA OF CASCIA (d. 1457) was on her deathbed she was visited by one of her relatives from Roccaporena. As this cousin was about to leave she asked St. Rita if there was anything she wished from her native village. The Saint thanked her and said, "Since you are so kind, I ask you for the love of God to go down into the garden of our house and pick a rose there and bring it to me." Thinking the Saint was delirious, the cousin smiled at the sisters present. It was then winter, a time when roses would not be expected to bloom. But on reaching the garden of the house at Roccaporena she found a rose in full bloom, with bright green leaves, surrounded by freezing snow. The cousin plucked the rose and hurried to Cascia to bring the wonder flower to the Saint.[26]
A short time later the same cousin visited St. Rita and asked

once again if there was something she might do for the Saint. Rita answered, "Yes, in your goodness I beg you to go once again to our garden and bring me some figs." This time the cousin did not consider, as before, that the request was a product of delirium. If a beautiful rose could bloom in wintertime for a Saint, then figs would also be made available for her. And so it happened. While the garden was glistening with snow and ice, there, hanging from a single branch which was heavy with leaves, was a collection of fresh figs. Once again the cousin hastened to the bedside of the Saint. After thanking her cousin, the Saint shared the figs with her sisters.

The appearance of the rose and the figs in the midst of winter became known throughout the area and was considered proof of St. Rita's sanctity.[27]

One of the most beautiful and touching incidents regarding roses involves the Blessed Mother and her appearance to BL. JUAN DIEGO (d. 1548) in Mexico. The Blessed Virgin appeared to the poor Indian four times requesting that a chapel be built in her honor. The last apparition took place on Tuesday, December 12, 1531. To provide the bishop with the sign he requested that would identify the apparition and confirm the supernatural aspect of what Juan had alleged, the Lady asked Juan to walk higher up the hill and to collect the roses found there—this in spite of the rocky nature of the place and its unsuitability for the growth of any type of vegetation. Nevertheless, Juan found roses there and these he collected. He took them to the Lady, who arranged the flowers inside the scoop of the tilma, a cloak worn by the Indians. The vision cautioned Juan against disturbing or revealing his burden except to the bishop. When Juan opened the cloak for the prelate, he found not the rejection and skepticism he had received on a previous visit, but the bishop kneeling among the flowers looking in reverential awe at a picture miraculously applied to the cloak—an exact likeness that Juan Diego identified as the Lady he had seen four times on Tepeyac Hill. The miraculous image convinced the bishop of the supernatural quality of all that Juan Diego had related. A church was soon built, where the image was displayed to the admiration and devotion of the Mexican people.

Although the fabric of the tilma would be expected to have disintegrated within 20 years, it is still in perfect condition after 450 years. Art experts state that four media were used in the painting of the portrait, yet no brush strokes can be detected despite scientific inspections. Scientists have remained baffled concerning the other properties of the portrait. It also intrigues its viewers and inflames the hearts of the devout with a deeper love for the Mother of God.[28]

As a means of imitating Our Lord's sufferings, particularly that of the Crown of Thorns, ST. ROSE OF LIMA (d. 1617) planned to wear a headband made of silver and studded with nails that were pointed inward. Her confessor gave wise advice about the wearing of the penitential instrument and restricted its use to a number of times each week. After obtaining his permission, she realized she could not afford the silver and the nails and made plans to raise the money at her gardening. With the money she collected from the sale of flowers she hoped to contribute toward the family income, as well as to save an amount for the headband. While she worked in her garden she prayed. Her labors were rewarded with flowers that kept blooming beyond their time and in such abundance that the situation was regarded as phenomenal. As the weeks passed, her prolific harvest of blooms drew comments, and orders were placed by people who had never come to her before. In time the necessary money was collected. The band was made, and worn.[29]

Because one of his patron saints was St. John the Baptist, ST. JEAN-MARIE BAPTISTE VIANNEY (d. 1859), the Curé of Ars, was presented each year with a bouquet of lilies by Mlle. des Garets. One year she made the presentation of the lilies in the sacristy. The Saint accepted the flowers and politely commented on their beauty and the arrangement of the bouquet. In a moment or two he placed the flowers on the sill of a window facing due south, not realizing as he did so that the June sun, entering the window, would wilt the bouquet in an hour or two. While the hot June sun should have wilted the flowers, it did not. "After eight days the flowers still retained all their beauty and fragrance."[30]

Finally, we have the case of BL. VILLANA DE BOTTI (d. 1360), who led a carefree and frivolous life. She was instantaneously and completely converted after looking in her mirror and seeing a hideous monster with hair of coiled serpents. As a married woman, she joined the Dominican Third Order and quickly advanced in virtue so that she was favored with visions of the Blessed Mother and various Saints. She died at the age of 28 after a long illness, but soon her physical appearance was transformed and she "possessed a beauty she had never had in life." Before her death she had prophesied that she would send her friends flowers from Heaven, and this was accomplished when a friend, a Franciscan tertiary, bent over the dead woman to view the beautiful face. It was then that "great armloads of flowers fell from the sky, fulfilling Villana's prophecy."[31] Villana de Botti was beatified in 1829.

Cappella Della Santa, Cascia

WATERING A DRY TWIG. Out of obedience, St. Rita of Cascia planted a dry stick in the ground and watered it every day for a year. To the amazement of all, the stick sprouted leaves and branches, followed by blossoms and finally clusters of grapes. Six centuries later, the vine continues to thrive and produce fruit. The leaves are made into a powder which is distributed to sick people throughout the world.

BIRDS, BEES AND BUGS

One of the most unusual incidents in which birds came to the assistance of God's people took place during the time of MOSES after the people of Israel were delivered from their Egyptian captors. Two months and two days after leaving Egypt they began murmuring against Moses and Aaron, complaining that they were hungry and that they had been able to eat their fill during the time of slavery.

The Lord then spoke to Moses: "I have heard the murmuring of the children of Israel: say to them: In the evening you shall eat flesh, and in the morning you shall have your fill of bread: and you shall know that I am the Lord your God. So it came to pass in the evening, that quails coming up, covered the camp: and in the morning a dew [manna] lay round about the camp." *(Exodus* 16:12-13).

Sometime later, while the people were encamped, they once again murmured their complaints about the lack of flesh meat and once again the good God came to satisfy them. "And a wind going out from the Lord, taking quails up beyond the sea brought them, and cast them into the camp for the space of one day's journey, on every side of the camp round about, and they flew in the air two cubits high above the ground. The people therefore rising up all that day and night, and the next day, gathered together of quails, he that did least, ten cores: and they dried them round about the camp." *(Numbers* 11:31-32).

The supply of quail was enough to last a month, but before the end of the month the Lord grew angry with the people because of their greed and punished them with a great plague so that the place became known as *Kibroth-hattaavah*, that is, "Graves of Greed." *(Numbers* 11:33-34).

A great number of the Israelites were provided with quail and manna from the hand of God, but in another case one man, the prophet ELIAS, was miraculously fed through the concern of God for his well-being. Instead of quail, ravens were called upon to fulfill a holy mission.

One day the Lord said to Elias, ". . . I have commanded the ravens to feed thee there. So he went, and did according to the word of the Lord: and going, he dwelt by the torrent Carith, which is over against the Jordan. And the ravens brought him bread and flesh in the morning, and bread and flesh in the evening, and he drank of the torrent." (*3 Kings* 17:4-6; in some translations *1 Kings* 17:4-6).

Just as quail were provided for the children of Israel and ravens assisted Elias in the Old Testament, birds and animals have inserted themselves into the lives of numerous saints. Their actions have been holy deviations from the laws of nature that have inspired devotion, warned of danger, protected in marvelous ways and edified those who were fortunate to have witnessed their activities.

One of the earliest New Testament cases of a bird inserting itself into the life of a saint took place in the year 236 when the clergy gathered to elect a new pope after the death of St. Anterus. A number of laymen were also present to observe the proceedings. This, of course, was in the early days of the Church, before the election of a pontiff became a fixed ritual. According to Eusebius in his *Ecclesiastical History* (VI, xxix):

> For when the brethren were all assembled for the purpose of appointing him who should succeed to the episcopate, and very many notable and distinguished persons were in the thoughts of many, Fabian, who was there, came into nobody's mind. But all of a sudden, they relate, a dove flew down from above and settled on his head as clear imitation of the descent of the Holy Ghost in the form of a dove upon the Saviour; whereupon the whole people, as if moved by one divine inspiration, with all eagerness and with one soul cried out "worthy," and without more ado took him and placed him on the episcopal throne.[1]

St. Fabian reigned for fourteen years, dying a martyr in the year 250. St. Jerome bears witness to his glorious martyrdom, as does St. Cyprian, who called St. Fabian an incomparable man, and further declared that the glory of his death corresponded with the purity and holiness of his life.

We learn of the terrible tortures endured by ST. VINCENT (d. 304), who died a martyr in prison as a result of the tortures. He steadfastly defended the Faith and refused to acknowledge the gods of his persecutors. After suffering atrociously in prison, St. Vincent died while thanking God that he was being privileged to surrender his life for Christ. After his death, Dacian, his persecutor, ordered that the martyr's body be thrown among rushes in a marshy field, this to demonstrate how little regard he had for Christians. In this inhospitable place a raven defended the body from wild beasts and birds of prey.

According to the Acts in Ruinart and the Bollandists, as well as a sermon attributed to St. Leo, the body was then retrieved by his enemies. They placed it in a sack, tied it to a great stone and cast it into the sea. Contrary to what was expected, the body miraculously drifted to shore, where it was revealed to two Christians who claimed the body and buried it honorably.[2]

Two saints of the sixth century were troubled by noisy birds, one being ST. SAMSON (d. 565), whose monastery in Brittany was greatly disturbed by the noise of wild geese in the adjoining meadows of Dol. Their cries interfered so much with the serenity of the place that St. Samson felt compelled to reproach them. We are not told exactly what method was used, but we may speculate that the Saint blessed the flock, "and they never afterwards returned."[3]

Another was ST. THECLA OF MORIANA (d. sixth century), who was troubled by smaller birds—but a great many of them. It happened that the oaks around the hermitage of the Saint were so thickly crowded with sparrows that their incessant clack disturbed her meditations.

Besides, they would fly round her in flocks, lighting upon her as she knelt in prayer, peeping, wrangling and hopping about, distracting her contemplation. St. Thecla prayed God to deliver her from their annoyance, and forthwith they all left the neighborhood.[4]

In his biography of ST. BENEDICT (d. 543), St. Gregory the Great tells us of an heretical Arian priest of a church located near the Saint's humble dwelling. The priest greatly envied the Saint because of Benedict's well-known reputation of sanctity. When the priest realized that he could not, after all his efforts, stop the many

pilgrims seeking the Saint's counsels, the Arian priest, "blinded by
envy, sent to the servant of God a poisoned loaf for an offering,
which the man of God received thankfully, although he was not
ignorant of the poison in it." St. Gregory the Great writes:

> There used to come to Benedict at the time of dinner
> a crow from the adjacent forest, which took bread from
> his hand. Coming therefore, as she was wont, the man of
> God cast before her the bread that the priest had sent
> him, saying, "In the name of the Lord Jesus Christ take
> this bread and cast it in some place where no man may
> find it." The crow, gaping and spreading her wings, ran
> croaking about it, as if she would have said, "I would
> willingly fulfill thy command, but I am not able." The
> man of God commanded again, saying, "Take it up, take
> it up and cast it where no man can find it." So at length
> the crow took it up in her beak and flew away with it,
> and three hours after returned again to receive from his
> hand her ordinary allowance.

St. Gregory ended this narrative by reporting, "The venerable
Father Benedict, seeing the priest so perversely bent on seeking his
life, was more sorry for him than grieved for himself."[5]

Another event in the life of St. Benedict took place earlier, when
he was living alone in a cave at Subiaco. The Saint was one day at
prayer when a black bird flew into the cave. It flew around the Saint
so closely that it brushed against his cheeks and struck his head in
a menacing fashion. The bird flew so closely that if he had wanted
to, the Saint could have seized it with his hand.

St. Benedict, however, knew who had sent the bird to his cave. He
made the Sign of the Cross, and immediately the bird left him.[6]

Venerable Bede, who was a priest and is numbered among the
Doctors of the Church, spent his life as a monk in teaching and
writing. One of his works, *The Ecclesiastical History of the English
Nation*, tells about the life and miracles of ST. CUTHBERT (d.
687), a monk, hermit and then Bishop of Lindisfarne. He is numbered among the Incorruptibles and is known to have performed
miracles of all kinds, some of which are mentioned in this volume.
He is known to have sowed a field with barley late in the season and

to have obtained abundant growth. But, no sooner had the grain ripened than birds came and feasted on it. Venerable Bede writes:

> Christ's holy servant, as he himself afterwards told it, drew near to the birds, and said to them, "Why do you touch that which you have not sown? If you have received license from God, do what He allows you; but if not, get you gone and do no further injury to that which belongs to another." He had no sooner spoken, than all the birds departed and never returned to the field.[7]

Venerable Bede also tells of the time that crows were accustomed to build nests on St. Cuthbert's island retreat. One day, the Saint saw a crow pull out the thatch of the hut which he had made for his brethren. The Saint stretched out his hand and warned the birds to do no more harm. Since they neglected the command, St. Cuthbert commanded, "In the name of Jesus Christ, depart as speedily as possible, and do not presume to remain any longer in the place to which you are doing harm." After hearing these words the birds departed, but three days later one of them returned and found St. Cuthbert digging in the field. As though asking pardon for the damage it had done, it drew near the Saint, spread out its wings, and bending its head down as a sign of humility, seemed to ask for pardon and permission to return. Venerable Bede continues:

> It then departed and fetched its companion and when they had both arrived, they brought in their beaks a large piece of hog's lard, which the man of God used to show to the brethren who visited him, and kept to grease their shoes with; testifying to them how earnestly they should strive after humility, when a dumb bird that had acted so insolently, hastened by prayers, lamentation, and presents, to obliterate the injury which it had done to man.

Venerable Bede adds that "the birds remained for many years. They built their nests on the island, and did not dare to give annoyance to anyone."[8]

ST. AGRICOLUS (d. 700) was still a child when his mother died.

His father, a Gallo-Roman senator named Magnus, became a monk at Lerins and was later consecrated Bishop of Avignon. At the age of fourteen, St. Agricolus followed the example of his father and joined the same monastery and quickly progressed in virtue. After spending sixteen years as a monk, he was appointed archdeacon by his father and quickly distinguished himself by his preaching and his administrative abilities, as well as by his care of the poor and the troubled. In the year 660, Magnus was summoned to a synod, but before leaving, he consecrated his son Bishop of Avignon and charged him with the affairs of the diocese during his absence. Ten years later Magnus died and his son, St. Agricolus, succeeded him and assumed all the duties of the office.

One of the figures on the heraldic arms of the see of Avignon is a stork holding a snake in its beak. This is a reference to an incident that took place during the episcopate of St. Agricolus. Storks at that time were numerous in the city of Avignon. Their favorite food was snakes, but they were not very delicate in consuming them since they dropped the half-eaten corpses on the roofs of the houses. When these discarded pieces decomposed in the sun, they produced a very disagreeable stench, as well as producing epidemics of sickness among many of the citizens. It is reported that St. Agricolus put an end to this nuisance by prayer and by blessing the storks with the Sign of the Cross. The storks then withdrew to the fields and did not return.[9]

When ST. MEINRAD (d. 861) established a little chapel in the woods near Lake Lucerne in Switzerland, he enshrined a statue which had been given him by Abbess Hildegarde of Zurich. This statue is now revered as the miraculous image of Our Lady of Einsiedeln. People flocked to the chapel to pray before this image, and soon extraordinary graces were received. Because of these favors, pilgrims soon found their way to the Saint's hermitage.

Two thieves named Richard and Peter eventually heard that crowds of people were visiting the isolated chapel. Thinking that jewels and valuables had been donated in return for benefits derived there, the thieves visited the hermitage one wintry day in the year 861. We are told that the Saint was informed by supernatural means of their coming and their intent; nevertheless, St. Meinrad welcomed them kindly and offered them the hospitality of his humble dwelling. It is uncertain whether the thieves attacked the Saint before they searched for treasure, or whether they killed him from disappointment at finding nothing of value. It is told, however, that after the body was placed on the hermit's bed of leaves, two candles standing nearby were mysteriously lighted. Frightened at this marvel, the thieves hastily left, but two crows that had nested near the hermitage of the Saint followed them to Zurich. The crows' sharp cries and flapping wings attracted the attention of many, including a woodcutter who identified the birds as those which lived near the Saint. Suspecting that danger had befallen his friend, the woodcutter hurried to the chapel and discovered the body.

History reports that the two crows hovered over the scaffold the day the two thieves were brought to justice. A number of historians claim that there exists no reason to doubt the truth of this account.

In addition to many reproductions of the crows in sculpture and illuminations found in Swiss churches, the abbey of Einsiedeln bears the likeness of two crows on its armorial shield, and for many years an inn in Zurich was known as the Inn of the Two Faithful Crows.[10]

ST. VEREMUNDUS (d. 1092) entered the Benedictine monastery of Navarre as a mere boy and in time became its abbot. Known for his love of the poor and his generosity to them, he is especially known for outstanding miracles performed for their benefit. During a time of great famine, when hunger and disease ravaged Navarre, the poor flocked to the good abbot for assistance, since it was known that the monks had granaries and storehouses of goods that previously had been given to them as stipends. The good abbot had distributed all the foodstuffs among the citizens of Navarre when pilgrims began arriving from distant places. Men who had been sent abroad by the Saint to buy provisions had not yet returned, so that the estimated three thousand persons who were assembled could do nothing but suffer and lament their condition. The holy abbot prayed for an alleviation of the situation and prepared to offer the Holy Sacrifice. During that part of the Mass when the priest prays for the people, the Saint made intercession to Heaven with tears. Suddenly a white dove appeared and flew low over the heads of the people, almost touching them as it passed. After it circled over the congregation the bird disappeared as mysteriously as it had arrived. The real wonder was that the people experienced a feeling of contentment. Their hunger was appeased and their mouths experienced a delicious taste, as though they had participated in a heavenly banquet. In their joy and relief they shouted words of praise and thanksgiving to God. St. Veremundus' influence spread far beyond his own abbey. At the time of his death no fewer than twenty-five monasteries were under the jurisdiction of the Saint.[11]

ST. BOTWID (d. 1100) met his death as the result of a most despicable act. A Swedish layman, Botwid converted to the Faith and performed good works and even preached about the glories of the Faith and the benefits of Baptism. He bought a Finnish slave, whom he instructed, baptized and then set free, asking him to spread the Gospel in his own land. Botwid, together with a companion named Asbjorn, acquired a boat to take the former slave across the Baltic. During the night, while Botwid and Asbjorn slept on shore, the former slave murdered them both and left with the boat. When the two men did not return on time, a search party set out to find them, and according to their account, a bird perched on the prow of their boat, singing until the bodies of the martyrs were found. St. Botwid was buried in his native land, where he is venerated as one of the apostles of Sweden.[12]

When the mother of ST. HUGH OF LINCOLN (d. 1200) died, his father, a knight named William, joined the Canons Regular of St. Augustine and took with him the eight-year-old Hugh, who said, "I needed no persuasion to renounce pleasures of which I knew nothing, and to follow my father as a fellow soldier in the spiritual army." He later transferred to the Carthusians, was ordained priest and was eventually consecrated Bishop of Lincoln which at that time was the largest diocese in England. Besides his ecclesiastical duties, he regularly visited and ministered to the lepers in their hospitals, frequently conducted funerals for the abandoned dead and defended the human rights of Jews who were being persecuted. When he died, his funeral was impressive, since his coffin was carried by three kings and three archbishops.

During the exhumation of his incorrupt body eighty years after his death, when the Archbishop laid his hand on the Saint's head, it separated from the body, "leaving the neck fresh and red." At this time manna collected and dripped from the head. This phenomenon is mentioned elsewhere in this book. Because of this miracle, the head was encased in a coffer of gold, silver and precious stones and was placed near the shrine of the Saint.

When England was overrun in 1364 by bands of ruffians who went about violating tombs, profaning the relics of the Saints and pillaging churches, the precious reliquary containing the head of St. Hugh was stolen. After dividing the treasure among themselves the mob discarded the head of the Saint in a field. According to chroniclers at the time, a raven perched beside the relic and left it only after it was recognized and returned to the cathedral. The thieves were themselves robbed, and struck with remorse they surrendered themselves to justice. Being found guilty on their own confessions, they were judiciously hanged at Lincoln. The relics of the Saint were later destroyed by order of King Henry VIII about the year 1540.[13]

The early legends have left us many idyllic stories of how beasts and birds were susceptible to the gentle ways of ST. FRANCIS OF ASSISI (d. 1226) and entered into loving companionship with him. There was the fierce wolf at Gubbio which the Saint tamed; the young hare that sought the Saint's protection against hunters; the half-frozen bees that crawled toward him in the winter to be fed; the wild falcon that fluttered around him, and the nightingale that sang with him in sweet harmony in the ilex grove at the Carceri.

St. Francis preaching to the birds has been the subject of countless works of art, as the result of the incident in which St. Francis paused on the road near Bevagna to speak with his "little brethren the birds." Leaving his companions on the road, he walked to the trees where a great number of birds had gathered, namely, doves, crows, and others popularly known as "daws." As the Saint approached them they seemed to wait expectantly for him. The Saint then preached to them, telling them that they should praise their Creator often for giving them such beautiful feathers, wings so they could fly and pure air through which they could soar. At his words the birds stretched their necks, extended their wings and opened their mouths. The Saint then walked among them, touching their heads and bodies with his tunic. Finally, he blessed them and gave them permission to fly away. The birds are said to have listened so intently that St. Francis chided himself for not having thought of preaching to them before.[14]

Another source tells of an incident when swallows began chirping loudly while circling overhead as St. Francis was preaching at

Alviano. The Saint gently reproached: "My sisters the swallows, it is now my turn to speak. You have been talking enough all this time." The birds are said to have perched around him while he exhorted them to praise their Creator.[15]

In *The Little Flowers of Saint Francis* we read that the Saint, while travelling to the peak of Mount Alverna, stopped to rest for a while under a certain oak tree.

While resting under the tree St. Francis began to study the location and the scenery. While he was absorbed in this contemplation, a great number of all kinds of birds came flying down to him with joyful songs, twittering and fluttering their wings. They surrounded St. Francis in such a way that some of them settled on his head and others on his shoulders—with others on his knees, and still others on his arms and lap and on his hands and around his feet. They all showed great joy by their tuneful singing and happy movements, as if they were rejoicing at his coming and inviting and persuading him to stay there.

The Saint's companions were understandably surprised at seeing the birds tamely perched about their founder and accepted the unusual display, as did St. Francis, as an indication from God that they should live on the mountain. Count Orlando gave St. Francis the property, which soon supported a house of the order.[16]

The evening before the burial of ST. ELIZABETH OF HUNGARY (d. 1231), we are told by her biographer, Count de Montalembert, of a strange event that was witnessed by many people. He wrote:

> On the night preceding the solemnization of the last rites, the Abbess of Wechere, who had come to assist at the funeral ceremony, heard a harmony which astonished her extremely. She went outside accompanied by several persons to learn whence it proceeded, and they saw on the roof of the church an immense number of birds, of a species unknown to men before that time, and these sang in tones so sweet and varied, that all who listened were filled with admiration. These little creatures seemed to celebrate this glorious burial-service. They were, according to the opinions of some, the angels who had borne Elizabeth's happy soul to heaven, and who

had now returned to honour her body by their hymns of celestial gladness.[17]

St. Bonaventure wrote, "These little birds rendered testimony to her purity by speaking of her in their language at her burial, and singing with such wondrous sweetness over her tomb."[18]

BL. NICHOLAS PALAEA (d. 1255) was named for the great St. Nicholas of Bari, and at the age of eight he was already practicing austerities. Later he joined the Order of Preachers founded by St. Dominic and was privileged not only to have met the Saint, but also to have accompanied him on many of his travels.

Just as St. Nicholas of Bari performed miracles of every sort, his namesake did likewise, so that he became known not only as a renowned preacher, but also as a miracle worker. His biographer tells that on one occasion when he was preaching in the Cathedral of Brescia, two irreverent young men began to harass him and disturb the congregation. They soon made such a noise that Bl. Nicholas left the cathedral and walked to a nearby hill. There he called for the birds to listen to him as he preached about the glories of God. Just as the birds had congregated before St. Francis of Assisi, flocks of birds also gathered at the feet of Bl. Nicholas and listened attentively while he preached. At the end of the sermon they chirped happily as they flew away.[19]

BL. GANDULPHUS OF BINASCO (d. 1260) joined the Franciscan Order while its founder, St. Francis of Assisi, was still alive. His life was one of great self-abnegation and virtue. Afraid that he might be tempted to vainglory, he decided to embrace a solitary life after hearing himself commended. With one companion, the holy brother set out for the wild district of Petralia, but while passing through Polizzi they accepted the hospitality of a charitable woman. Since he was known to be an eloquent preacher, he was induced to deliver a course of Lenten sermons. On Wednesday of Holy Week, while he was preaching, the sparrows chattered so loudly that the congregation could not hear the sermon. Bl. Gandulphus appealed to the birds to be quiet, and we are told that they kept silence until the conclusion of the service.

Bl. Gandulphus died soon after the event, but "when his body was elevated, the watchers declared that during the night there had flown into the church a number of swallows who had parted into two groups and had sung, in alternating choirs, a *Te Deum* of their own."[20]

ST. AGNES OF MONTEPULCIANO (d. 1317), who is mentioned often in this book, was born in a village near Montepulciano, Italy. While still a child she felt drawn to the religious life and was attracted to the Dominican Order. On one of her journeys to visit the convent with her mother and women of the household, the group passed a hill on which stood a house of evil reputation. Much to their surprise, a flock of crows swooped down on the little girl and attacked her with beak and claw. Screeching and plunging, they attempted to continue their assault as the women struggled to scare them away.

When the birds were finally dismissed, the women comforted little Agnes and agreed among themselves that the crows must have been devils who resented the purity and goodness of the child. Without realizing they were being prophetic, they speculated that one day the devils would be driven from the hilltop by Agnes, which in fact took place when she, as a member of the Dominican Order, built a convent atop the hill.[21]

BL. BERNARD SCAMMACCA (d. 1486) was born in Sicily to wealthy and pious parents, but despite their good example and his fine education, he led a careless life. It was only after being seriously injured in a brawl that he reformed and entered the Dominican monastery at Catania. Little is recorded of his religious life, although we know he practiced severe penances to expiate for the sins of his youth, that he was given to prayer and solitude and "was particularly kind to sinners in the confessional." Not recognized as a great preacher, he is known to have been content with spending his time in the confessional and in the guidance of souls. He also experienced a number of mystical phenomena and is said to have had great power over animals and birds. Singing birds would flutter down around him while he walked in the garden, but as soon as the Blessed went into ecstasy they quieted of their own accord and remained so until the ecstasy ended. Then they would resume their singing.[22]

Bernard Scammacca's cultus was confirmed by Pope Leo XII in 1825. He is numbered among the Incorruptibles, his body being displayed in the Church of S. Biagio in S. Dominico, Catania.

While ST. ROSE OF LIMA (d. 1617) lived with a pious family in the Maza mansion, many miracles and unusual happenings were recorded by them in a diary. Among the events was one involving a bird that arrived each day at sunset. The children were the first to notice that the bird sang a song with Rose and then would fly off at her bidding. Unnoticed by Rose, members of the family began to witness the event and would position themselves where Rose could not see them, and there listen to the strange duet.

As soon as the bird arrived, Rose would lay aside whatever she was doing and speak gently to the little creature, greeting its arrival. She would then invite the little bird to join her in a song, one that the observers suspected she had written herself. The bird would chirp as she sang these words:

> Tiny singer, flit your wings;
> Bow before the King of kings.
> Let your lovely concert rise
> To Him who gave you songs and skies.
> Let your throat, full of carols sweet,
> Pour them before the Eternal's feet
> That we His praise may magnify
> Whom birds and angels glorify.
> I shall sing to Him who saved me;
> You will sing to Him who made ye.
> Both together, we shall bless
> The God of love and happiness.
> Sing, sing with bursting throat and heart!
> In turn our voices will take part
> To sing together, you and I,
> A canticle of holy joy.

The hidden witnesses estimated that the duet lasted almost an hour before Rose would signal for her feathered visitor to leave. As it flew into the dusk, Rose would sing:

> The little bird abandons me;
> My playmate's wings ascend.
> Blessed be my God, who faithfully
> Stays with me to the end.[23]

ST. MARTIN DE PORRES (d. 1630), the humble Dominican lay brother who was a friend of St. Rose of Lima, labored and worked miracles in Peru. One day he was in the garden of the monastery reciting his prayers in solitude when a wounded hawk fell at his feet. Despite its threatening attitude, Martin picked up the hawk and commanded it not to struggle while he bandaged its broken leg. It is said that the hawk immediately became tame and remained until its leg was healed. When the Saint unwrapped the leg, the hawk flew off to the nearby woods, but whenever it saw its benefactor in the garden, it would fly to him, entirely fearless—much to the community's surprise and delight.[24]

ST. JOSEPH OF CUPERTINO (d. 1663) is known for his ecstatic levitations, as well as other physical phenomena and the working of miracles. He also had experiences with the unusual behavior of animals and birds. The Saint once gave the nuns of St. Clare at Cupertino a lamb which was very tame and demonstrated an unusual intelligence. When the lamb died, the Saint promised to send them a bird which would assist them in their praise of God. And so it happened that one day, when the nuns were reciting the Divine Office, a forest songbird perched on the window of the choir and sang beautifully, as though joining them in praise of the heavenly Creator.

The bird faithfully accompanied and encouraged the nuns in their chanting for five years, until an unfortunate situation occurred. One day two of the novices began to quarrel. Suddenly the bird flew between them as though to restore peace, when one of the novices, in her anger, struck the bird. The feathered creature flew away and did not return until the nuns pleaded with St. Joseph of Cupertino to send it back.[25]

The next time the nuns were in choir the bird not only appeared and chanted with them but, for the first time, entered the building and permitted the nuns to touch it. For whatever reason, one of the nuns tied a small bell to its foot. This prompted the bird once again to fly away. When the nuns told the Saint what had been done, the Saint gently reproved them: "I sent you the bird that it should sing, not that it should ring a bell." At the request of the nuns, the Saint once again promised to have the bird return, which it did. It remained for many more years, to the edification and pleasure of the community.[26]

A finch which often visited the Saint would chirp its praise of God each time the Saint told it to "Praise God," and would stop its song at the Saint's command. The Saint's biographies mention a goldfinch which the Saint set free from an entanglement. Before the bird flew off the Saint said to it: "Go, enjoy what God has given thee; as for me I require nothing more of thee than that thou return when I call thee to praise with me thy God and mine." Others noticed that the bird flew about in the garden, and when the Saint called it, it came immediately to join in praise of the Creator.[27]

One of the brethren of ST. GERARD MAJELLA (d. 1755) tells of an interesting situation involving a flock of birds. He writes:

> One day at table in our convent of Caposele, Gerard called, by a wave of the hand, the birds that were warbling in the neighborhood. The charming little creatures, docile to the orders of him who so faithfully obeyed his God, came at once fluttering around the holy religious and hopping over the table in front of him. Their eyes were fixed on his, and they seemed to listen attentively to the words full of sweetness and simplicity that he addressed them, as if they were endowed with intelligence.[28]

After ST. ANTHONY MARY CLARET (d. 1870) died, the following was written by his biographer:

> Dead: The counsellor of saints; the protector of religious orders; the propagator of the Holy Rosary and of devotions to the Heart of Mary; the ecstatic adorer of the Holy Eucharist and the living ciborium of our Sacramental Lord; the transfigured priest who celebrated Holy Mass amid splendors and who received the Child Jesus in his arms on Christmas Eve.

To this could be added: the founder of the Missionary Sons of the Immaculate Heart of Mary, the founder of three cultural institutions, the propagandist of the Catholic press, the preacher of 25,000 sermons, the author of 144 different works, the wonder-worker, the prophet and the former Archbishop of Cuba.

His biographer also tells of a wonder that took place in the church where the body of the Saint was exposed for veneration. He writes:

> During the funeral Mass, a mysterious little bird appeared in the church. It fluttered over the remains of the archbishop and sang sweetly, joining its *arpeggios* to the psalmody of the monks. The little bird was silent while the celebrant officiated, but when the choir intoned the responses it gave full power to its voice. At the end of the obsequies it disappeared from the church in the same mysterious way in which it had made its appearance at the beginning of the funeral services.[29]

FR. PAUL OF MOLL (d. 1896), who is called "The Flemish Benedictine Wonder-Worker of the Nineteenth Century," also had a mysterious experience with birds. We are told in his biography that whenever he visited Antwerp he would call upon a certain invalid lady and her servant, Theresa.

Fr. Paul, in the year 1887, told the servant Theresa that she would know beforehand of his approaching visits. At his next visit he asked, "Well, have the little birds announced my coming?" The biographer continues:

> As a matter of fact, on the eve of Father Paul's visits to the lady, beautiful little birds, varying in number from two to twelve at a time, began to make their appearance in the garden, singing a joyful air which was always the same. They would also perch on the window-sill of the drawing room which looked out upon the garden, and tap upon the window panes. Although the tune of the mysterious songsters never varied, they had at each successive visit a different plumage.

Not only did the servant, Theresa, see the birds, but also the invalid lady and her nurse. Neither of them could tell where the birds came from any more than Theresa could.

The biographer continues:

> Were the birds from the tropics? But in that case these

delicate little creatures would hardly have ventured into our climate in all seasons, for they came in winter, when it was snowing and very cold, as well as in summer. The nurse tried repeatedly to catch one of the birds, but in vain. She spoke of it to Fr. Paul and he replied, "Oh! they won't let themselves be caught!"

When asked about the beautiful little birds, Fr. Paul replied with a smile, "They are messengers." Fr. Paul then warned Theresa not to speak of the birds to anyone except to an intimate friend of hers. He then warned, "If during my lifetime you spread the news abroad, the birds will never come again."

On the eve of Fr. Paul's death, the birds appeared once more, but they were somewhat dejected and with drooping wings sang a melancholy song which the members of the household understood to be a presentiment of a tragic happening. Six months passed before the birds returned again, and this took place when a photograph of Fr. Paul was hung in the invalid's drawing room. At this time they sang beautiful melodies, but it is reported that afterwards their visits were infrequent.

As reported earlier, the birds appeared each time in a different plumage. Theresa, however, was able to give us a description as the birds appeared on Wednesday, September 30, 1897, a year and seven months after Fr. Paul's death. (See the following page for a similar remarkable occurrence on this same date.)

> Today, at ten minutes to eleven, two little birds of incomparable beauty arrived; their plumage was blue, green and purple, their breasts and heads white, the latter with stripes of deep purple in the form of a garland.

Another lady of Antwerp was favored with a visit of Fr. Paul. She had two small sons who were covered with horrible eruptions which the doctors could not cure. When Fr. Paul saw the condition of the children he advised the mother to make a novena and wash both children with water containing the medal of St. Benedict. Fr. Paul was a promotor of the medal of St. Benedict and often advised this remedy to those who were ill. The mother was surprised by this advice and replied, "But the physician forbade me to wash them in water." Fr. Paul repeated his advice, "I tell you, wash them twelve

times a day for nine days." Before the end of the novena both children were perfectly cured.

The same woman tells us, "I have visited the grave of Fr. Paul
three times, and on each occasion a beautiful little bird came and
sang over the tomb as long as I prayed there. The bird did not fly
away until the moment I left."

During the final illness of ST. THÉRÈSE OF THE CHILD
JESUS AND OF THE HOLY FACE (THE LITTLE FLOWER) (d.
1897), her sister Pauline, in religion Rev. Mother Agnes of Jesus,
began writing day by day the words spoken by the holy patient.
These were published in a little book entitled *Novissima Verba*. At
the end of the book, in telling what took place after St. Therese's
death on September 30, Reverend Mother Agnes of Jesus writes:

> During the long agony of Sr. Thérèse of the Child
> Jesus, a multitude of little birds took their station on a
> tree beside the wide-open window of the infirmary,
> where they continued to sing with all their might until
> her death. I experienced a sorrowful impression caused
> by the contrast between so much suffering within and
> the joyous notes without.
>
> A venerable sister who had not always very well
> understood our Thérèse remarked to me afterwards, very
> much moved: "Have you noticed, my mother, the
> singing of those birds? I assure you that it was really
> extraordinary."[30]

Repeated visits of little birds are also noted in the biography of
BL. MARY FORTUNATA VITI (d. 1922), a humble Benedictine
lay sister who achieved great heights of spirituality and lived to the
age of ninety-five. Birds are said to have flocked about and to have
charmed their visitor by singing, at her request, their songs of praise
to God.

On one occasion a goldfinch with a string entangled on its leg
flew through the window and patiently waited for the nun to
remove it. Once freed, it bowed politely before flying away.
Another time a sparrow flew in the window. After it had hopped
about the nun with unusual friendliness, she placed a little piece of
wool in its beak and said playfully: "Go, now, and build your nest."

The sparrow took a firmer hold on the wool and then flew away to obey the command.

One day a Sister who worked in the kitchen found Sr. Mary Fortunata spinning as usual, but in her lap was a bird, contentedly picking up some bread crumbs that she had placed there. The visitor asked for the bird, but Sr. Mary Fortunata, thinking she would kill and cook it, told the bird to fly away quickly, which it did.

These visitations of the birds were noted by the nuns of the convent, and one of the Sisters left a record for us when she wrote:

> I once saw a pretty chicken sitting close to Sister Mary Fortunata while she was busy with her spinning. After a time she drew back the hem of her habit and said: "Come, sit over here!" At once the chick approached and sat in the place designated, remaining there until it was given other orders.

And finally, another of the Sisters writes that she saw Sr. Mary Fortunata sitting at a window surrounded by a flock of birds who were eating from her hands.

> Wishing to enjoy the charming spectacle at closer range, I approached very cautiously without making any disturbance. But no sooner had I gotten near enough to see the birds than they all flew hastily away. Surprised, Sister Fortunata looked up, turned to me and said: "Ah, you are there! That's why they left me so suddenly."[31]

Following her death, and for many years after, and perhaps even to the present day, numerous miracles have taken place through the intercession of Sr. Mary Fortunata Viti. She was beatified by Pope Paul VI in 1967.

The Doves of Our Lady of Fatima

The miracle of the doves that remained at the feet of a statue of Our Lady of Fatima as quiet sentinals was reported worldwide in the secular and religious press, to the wonderment of many. It all began in the year 1946 when Portugal was celebrating three events: the third centenary of the revolution which gave Portugal its independence from Spain, the crowning of John IV as the king of the country, and the king's declaration naming Our Lady as patroness of Portugal under the title of the Immaculate Conception. By a coincidence, the United States that same year was celebrating the first centennial of the nation being dedicated to the same patroness, Our Lady as the Immaculate Conception.

Every year in Portugal a celebration was held on December 1, the anniversary of the three events, but for the third centennial special plans were made. Pope Pius XII recognized the forthcoming event by sending, as his special legate to Portugal, Cardinal Messela, who on May 13 would bless for the statue a golden crown encrusted with gems donated by the women of Portugal as tokens of love for the Mother of God.

Although Portugal has a number of revered statues, the one selected to take part in the third centennial celebration was the statue of Our Lady of Fatima which is kept at the Cova da Iria, where the Blessed Mother had appeared to the three shepherd children. Plans were formulated for the statue to be placed on a platform and to be carried on the shoulders of priests and laymen through Portugal, and special services were to be conducted in the churches along the way. Its final destination was the cathedral of Lisbon, where special observances were to be conducted on December 8 by Cardinal Cerejeira, the city's Patriarch, who would renew the consecration made three centuries earlier.

The statue left Fatima on November 23, 1946, on a gilt platform, with white flowers surrounding the feet of the image, and was carried in procession from parish to parish. It was jubilantly greeted by thousands of people. At each church where it stopped for the night, great crowds spent the entire night in adoration of the Blessed Sacrament, which ended with the offering of Holy Mass.

The statue finally arrived in Lisbon on the 5th of December, but something extraordinary had already taken place in the city of Bombarral, located about forty miles north of Lisbon.

As a special tribute to the Blessed Mother, a woman named Enra D. Maria Emilia Martins Coimbra bought some white doves from a market in Lisbon and had them sent to Bombarral to be set free as the statue of Our Lady passed in procession. The date was December 1—a day on which the most spectacular public phenomenon since the miracle of the sun at Fatima was to take place.

One of the doves had died, but two little girls released the remaining doves at the proper time. Two doves flew high and then left, but three doves flew to the statue and settled among the flowers at the feet of the Madonna. Many people thought the doves would crush the flowers or soil the statue and tried to make them leave by clapping their hands loudly or waving their arms in front of them, but the doves refused to move.

During the journey from Bombarral to Lisbon the doves contentedly nestled amid the flowers. As one witness wrote:

> The noise and acclamations of the crowds, the hymn singing, the bursting of festive rockets, the lights at night, the heat of the sun or the heavy rain during some days, or the entrance of the image on its flowered stand into the various churches where, during the night, prayer vigils and night ceremonies took place—nothing made the doves abandon the touching and humble image of Our Lady.[32]

The unusual devotion of the doves and their determination to remain at the feet of Our Lady caused some of the people to think they were tied down. At one point the doves flew up and around the statue as though to prove they were being docile of their own accord. One man could not bring himself to believe they were really wild birds behaving in such a tame manner. No sooner had he expressed this thought than one of the birds left the statue and actually perched on his shoulder.

The secular press was quick to take notice and prompt to narrate the facts in the daily papers. The most widely circulated Lisbon daily paper, *Diario de Noticias*, carried the following:

> During the pilgrimage of the Image of Our Lady of Fatima there was a moving and extraordinary episode which created the greatest interest among believers and doubters, which turned to amazement among skeptics, after these had assured themselves that it was a fact— the episode of the three white doves which at Bombarral "freely" of their own accord alighted on the stand of Our Lady, and "of their own accord" accompanied it as sentinels in their post of honor. In many pages of Holy Scripture (as was told in an article published in this same paper under the title of "The Doves of Holy

Mary"), the white dove appears as a symbol of purity, messenger of peace, in all the Old Testament, since Noah had let it from the ark and it had returned with the olive branch.[33]

The Lisbon papers were not the only ones reporting the miracle of the doves, since the secular presses throughout Europe and the United States detailed the occurrences as they were taking place.

The statue arrived at Lisbon on December 5, carried triumphantly through the crowd by Carmelite tertiaries to the new Church of Our Lady of Fatima. It was to remain there for two days. Much to the surprise of everyone, the doves remained with the statue as it was taken into the brightly lit church. Although their site of election was still at the feet of Our Lady, they left now and then during their two-day visit to perch on the dossal, the high roof covering the archbishop's chair at the side of the High Altar.

An all-night vigil was conducted December 5-6, but from midnight on, the Holy Sacrifice was offered, one Mass after the other, until the Solemn High Mass later that morning. The next night, another all-night vigil was observed, conducted by several priests. All that day, as on the preceding day, Our Lady received the prayers and petitions of the faithful.

At about nine-thirty the evening of December 7, the statue was conveyed with all pomp and reverence in a candle-lit procession to the cathedral. But the going was not quiet, since fireworks exploded in celebration, bands played loudly, flowers were tossed to the statue, flags flew and banners flapped, the platform swayed and jerked with the steps of the bearers—all without disturbing the birds, who merely flapped their wings to maintain their balance. The transfer took three and a half hours because of the huge crowd that participated in the procession.

When the image arrived at the cathedral about one o'clock in the morning of December 8, one of the doves flew to the top of the tower and remained there for almost an hour. Throughout the night, with the church filled to capacity and prayers sounding throughout the church, the doves remained quiet and still. The morning of the day of the feast, a Pontifical High Mass was offered by Cardinal Cerejeira; he also repeated the three-hundred-year-old consecration of Portugal to the Immaculate Conception. But during the Holy Mass something extraordinary took place.

The Very Reverend Canon J. G. de Oliveira, a representative of the Bishop of Fatima who was an eyewitness, wrote that at the ringing of the bell that alerted everyone to the imminent elevation of the Sacred Host:

> To the utter amazement of all, two of the doves suddenly flew . . . after days of refusing food or drink and of remaining at the feet of the statue . . . one sped straight to the gospel side of the altar, and the other to the epistle side! There, as the bishop straightened to raise the Consecrated Host, they folded their wings . . . one on each side . . . as though in adoration! As the Mass progressed, the two doves remained there to the bewilderment of the celebrants and servers and the stupefied congregation. But this was still not the end. The third dove had not left the statue. Suddenly, at the moment of Communion, the third dove flew up and perched on top the statue's golden crown . . . placed there by the Cardinal Legate who personally represented the Holy Father the previous May 13 at Fatima . . . and as the celebrant turned and held up Our Lord saying, *"Ecce Agnus Dei"* (Behold the Lamb of God), the dove spread its white wings and held them open![34]

During the Holy Mass the doves remained in silent adoration, as they did throughout the day when crowds of Our Lady's devotees crowded around her platform to express their tender affections.

During the evening of December 8, the image was taken to a decorated frigate for its transport across the River Tagus. During its ride over the water, flaming rockets broke overhead while large searchlights moved back and forth over the sky. Hymns to the Blessed Mother were sung, and handkerchiefs were waved while the noise of engines and whistle blasts from hundreds of boats seemed to echo the cries of the people.[35]

On the opposite shore hundreds of people were waiting to welcome the statue as it began its second journey, back to Fatima.

When the statue, again carried on the shoulders of priests and laymen, arrived at Almada the next day, it was positioned in the courtyard of the seminary and was venerated by the people. Fr. Joseph Cacella, a witness at this time, noted:

The doves did not mind in the least the crushing crowd around the stand and the image, or the children whom the seminarians picked up and raised in their arms so that they might kiss the feet of the image close to the doves, which stood calm and indifferent to all this movement, as if their duty was to guard the Image of Our Lady.[36]

After this, the doves were replaced one after another along the way by three other doves who were just as devoted to the image of Our Lady. It has been noted that after the statue's visit in Bombarral, where the doves were first introduced, Our Lady was never without her faithful sentinels throughout her journey back to Fatima, where the statue arrived on Christmas Eve.

Several days later, on January 9, 1947, the Lisbon paper *Novidades* published an article with a large photograph detailing an interesting event that had taken place in Rio de Janeiro on the same day, December 8, on which the ceremonies were held in the Lisbon Cathedral. The article read:

At High Mass, in the Church of the Immaculate Conception in Rio de Janeiro, celebrated in honor of their Patroness, when the priest in the pulpit began speaking about devotion to Our Lady, a white dove suddenly found its way into the church and flew straight to the altar, where it came to rest on an arm of the cross, and where it remained throughout the ceremony. There was time to send for photographers and journalists, and after Mass the people in the church crowded up near, to see, to comment upon, and to photograph the strange bird, yet without succeeding in frightening it away—just as it had happened in Lisbon when the doves showed an extraordinary calm and dignity and strange tameness.[37]

The Fatima doves, always numbering three, have been taken to symbolize the third centennial of the consecration, the Three Persons of the Holy Trinity, the three children who saw Our Lady at Fatima and the three theological virtues of Faith, Hope and Charity. They could also represent Our Lady as daughter of the Father, Mother of the Son, and spouse of the Holy Spirit. Above all, the doves, being white, represent purity, especially that of our Holy Mother.

* * * * *

Extraordinary as the preceding events were, there was still more to come the following year, when the miracle of the doves was repeated! For three months, from October 13, 1947, until January 12, 1948, the statue of Our Lady of Fatima at the Cova da Iria was taken on another pilgrimage through cities and towns of both Portugal and Spain. We will here mention some of the unusual events that took place, as recorded by Rev. Joseph Cacella, who witnessed most of the events.

At the little town of Borba, the image was carried over a thick carpet of rosemary, lavender and other perfumed plants amid an enthusiastic crowd shouting hosannas and prayers while waving white flags. Rockets flared overhead and candles flickered all around the statue as it passed. Once more, as in the previous year, three faithful guards of honor were nestled at the feet of the Madonna.

At the village of Cabeçao one of the doves was removed from its reserved place at the feet of Our Lady and was placed upon the altar, where it quietly remained until the blessing of the Holy Sacrament. Again, it flew to the feet of the statue.

At Vila Viçosa a number of doves were let loose, with some of them seeking the feet of Our Lady. While the statue was visiting the small village of Bencatel, thirteen doves nestled close by Our Lady, as counted by Rev. Joseph Cacella. During an overnight stay at the property of the House of Braganza, a trusted and respected employee notified several distinguished local men of an unusual situation. Instead of the doves tucking their heads under their wings as birds usually do when sleeping, the doves were all sleeping with their heads resting against the mantle and feet of Our Lady.

After the image crossed into Spain, other wonders took place. In Alemtejo a number of people put doves into the hands of one of the statue's bearers for placement amid the flowers of Our Lady. These wild birds, after settling down, remained as though tame.

To the pleasure and amazement of the crowds inside the various churches, the birds would sometimes fly about, but would always return to their accustomed place.

Sometimes, after the statue left the churches of Mourao and

Evora, the doves remained in the churches, but then, after a few moments, returned quickly to Our Lady's platform. There were times when the birds were removed so that the flowers on the platform could be renewed. In such cases the birds remained obedient until they were again restored to Our Lady. This took place especially at "a certain Alemtejo town."

A skeptic at the village of Gafanheira announced that he did not believe the doves were remaining on the flowered stand by their own choice and would believe it only if he provided a few doves of his own. He soon returned with a number of doves and gave them to a lady. She released them, and without hesitation the doves flew directly to the stand to join the others already there.

At Alcacer another skeptic declared that he would believe only if he would see one of the doves in flight. Then the extraordinary took place. When the procession passed this man's house, one of the white doves flew to his balcony, where the skeptic was standing, and perched near him on the banister. The dove even permitted the man to pick it up and hold it. It is said that the man was promptly converted.

During an all-night adoration of the Blessed Sacrament at the town of Ferreira do Alemtejo, one of the doves flew to the monstrance on the High Altar and gently alighted on it. The dove remained on its perch throughout the night until it was time to restore the Sacred Host to the tabernacle. It then flew back to the Madonna.

These are but a few of the unusual incidents that took place during this second pilgrimage. Other activities of the birds took place in almost every town the statue visited. Since the recording of them might seem tedious to the reader, we will conclude by mentioning that throughout the villages and towns of this second pilgrimage, the statue of Our Lady was greeted by joyous and noisy crowds, as Our Lady was met during her first triumphant pilgrimage. Conversions and miracles of healing also took place, which were duly recognized and the facts recorded.

Two differences are noted, however, in this second journey: One is that the doves in the second instance permitted themselves at times to be held, handled and stroked. Secondly, the number of faithful sentinels varied, as already mentioned, with some flying off at intervals to be replaced by others. When the statue returned to Fatima on January 12, 1948, four doves remained at the feet of Our Lady.[38]

Bees

The eulogy of ST. MODOMNOC (or Dominic) (d. 550) as it was spoken and then recorded, revealed: "In a little boat, from east, over the pure-coloured sea, my Modomnoc brought—vigorous cry—the gifted race of Ireland's bees." Modomnoc is said to have belonged to the Irish royal line of the O'Neils, but to have left his native Wales in the pursuit of holiness. After coming under the direction of St. David, he was given the duty of tending the monastery bees. When the Saint was sent to Ireland, legend states that the bees insisted on following him and swarmed the ship, and in this way were introduced to Ireland. It is said that an Oxford manuscript preserves a short account in Irish of the bringing of the bees and notes that the quantity St. Modomnoc brought was "the full of his bell."[39]

We read in the life of BL. BERTRAND OF GARRIGA (d. 1230) that the southern part of France was ravaged by the Albigensian heresy and civil war during the end of the twelfth and the beginning of the thirteenth centuries. In the year 1200 the Albigensian Raymund VI marched with his troops toward orthodox Catholic monasteries, especially those of the Cistercians, the official missionaries against the heretics. They also marched toward the convent of the Bosquet nuns, who fled for safety. Although what next transpired is in no way phenomenal, nevertheless, God's little creatures aided the interests of the Church since it is reported that the empty convent was saved from destruction by the prompt action of a bee-master. He overturned his rows of hives, forcing the bees to swarm in the face of the heretics, who promptly directed their interests elsewhere.[40]

Because of a fire in the cathedral that destroyed a number of documents, few facts are known concerning BL. BONIZELLA PICCOLOMINI (d. 1300). It is known, however, that she was married to Naddo Piccolomini of Siena and was apparently childless. After the death of her husband, Bonizella retired into the district of Belsederio. There she devoted herself and her possessions to the relief of the needy. After her death, when her body was lying in its casket, a large number of bees alighted on the hands that had distributed so much consolation to the afflicted. Some years later, when bees swarmed numerous times over her tomb at Trequanda, the interest of the people and church authorities was alerted. The result was the discovery of her incorrupt body. Because of this discovery, and the many spectacular miracles that occurred at her tomb, Bonizella is held in great veneration in the dioceses of Siena and Pienza.[41]

Many unusual events graced the life of ST. RITA OF CASCIA (d. 1457), but that of the bees is of special interest. Five days after her birth, in the presence of her mother and at least two other persons, snow-white bees were seen to hover and buzz around Rita's tiny mouth. They also alighted on her lips and were seen to enter and exit from her partially opened mouth—all this without disturbing the sleeping infant. The unusual event remained a mystery to those who witnessed the phenomenon,[42] but later, the bees would again figure in the life of the Saint.

After the death of her husband and two sons, St. Rita felt called to the religious life and presented herself numerous times to the nuns at the Maddalena convent. Each time she was refused entrance because of her previous marital state. Heaven, however, intervened. One night her patrons, St. John the Baptist, St. Nicholas of Tolentino and St. Augustine appeared to her and led her to the convent, where they miraculously opened the doors for her. Leading her inside the cloister they addressed her with the words:

> Rita, remain a rational bee in the garden of the Spouse whom you have so long and ardently loved; so that, collecting the flowers of virtues, you may build a sweet honeycomb. Praise His infinite mercy and publish that there is nothing impossible to God. Rita, the impossible is overcome in your behalf.

After saying these words, the three heavenly helpers disappeared. The next morning, when the nuns found Rita inside the cloister, they realized her entrance could only have been accomplished through supernatural means and permitted her to stay.

Bees once again entered the history of the Saint. One biographer reports that an unusual swarm of bees took residence in the convent wall during the lifetime of the Saint. Another, that they appeared two hundred years after her death. Whichever the case, the bees are still in the wall and are of interest because of their unusual behavior. They remain in hibernation for ten months of the year and emerge during Holy Week of each year. They are never seen to leave the convent enclosure, and after a few weeks of activity about the gardens and rooms of the convent they return to the ancient wall after the feast of St. Rita, May 22, and seal themselves into holes they make themselves. The bees are thought by some to be flies that mimic bees since the little winged creatures never sting and do not gather pollen, yet they definitely resemble bees.[43]

The present-day nuns of the convent do not consider the presence of the insects or their behavior to be miraculous, but only a natural phenomenon that just happens to take place in the walls of their convent.

This view, however, was not held by the nuns who lived there at the time of Rita's beatification. Before the ceremony took place in Rome during the year 1627, the nuns of St. Rita's convent brought one of the bees in a crystal vase to Pope Urban VIII, who conducted the ceremony. They told the pontiff about the unusual event when bees had swarmed around the mouth of the infant Rita. They also told him about the bees that confined themselves in their convent wall and their unusual activity when they emerged from it. The Holy Father was pleased with the visit and blessed both the nuns and the bee, which was brought back to the convent in Cascia.

By a strange coincidence, three bees are depicted on the Coat of Arms of the Barbarini family, of which Pope Urban VIII was a descendant. They likewise appeared on his papal Coat of Arms.[44]

Known simply as PÈRE LAMY (d. 1931), John Edward Lamy was a parish priest who enjoyed many apparitions of the Blessed Virgin and the Saints. He was the founder of the Congregation of the Servants of Jesus and Mary and is known as a wonder-worker. Bees are also mentioned in his life, and he, himself, tells of his confrontation with them.

> Coming back from a little turn in the woods, I was facing the chapel where there are two swarms of bees. I had gathered some flowers and parsnip tops. Lost in my thoughts, I had forgotten the bees, and was startled by their buzzing. I waved the flowers about and that gathered them altogether. I made for the lawn to get into the chapel but I was followed by countless bees, when I distinctly heard these words, "Don't sting, don't sting, Our

Queen would not be pleased!" My idea is that it was the voice of the holy archangel. When we got to the vestibule, all the bees held back.

Before this took place the Blessed Mother had placed the holy priest under the protection of the holy archangel Gabriel—and it was he, apparently, who had saved Père Lamy.[45]

VEN. SOLANUS CASEY (d. 1957), the holy Capuchin priest who died in Detroit, worked many miracles of healing. While performing his duties as the doorkeeper of his friary, he comforted the poor, the sick and troubled souls. He was profoundly affected by God's creation, which he used for contemplative reflection. He admired the beauties of nature and the song of birds, but he was especially fond of bees and liked to observe their movements. Often when strolling through the orchards and vineyards of St. Felix, he would stop near the beehives and reflect on the beauty of the bees who alighted on his hands. He was known to exclaim, "My dear God, how could You have created such a marvelous thing!"

Because he was so relaxed with bees he was made the assistant beekeeper. We learn that sometimes when a bee was found in his room or corridor, he would ask one of the novices to take it outdoors. This request was made of various novices in each class throughout the years. The unhappy novice knew, when asked, what invariably had taken place in previous years when the same request was made by the holy friar. In obedience the novices would take the bee outside, but were usually stung for their trouble.

Sometimes Fr. Solanus would be stung himself, but it had little effect on him. The novice master, Fr. Elmer Stoffel, however, who also helped with the bees, remembers an incident that took place around 1950, when he was stung by three bees and fell to the ground in pain. Fr. Solanus, seeing his co-worker in such a condition, gave him a blessing. Fr. Stoffel recalls that immediately after the blessing the pain completely left him, and with no ill effects.[46] Fr. Solanus Casey was declared Venerable in July of 1995.

Bugs

Strange as it may seem, insects have been mentioned in the lives of many Saints. Their appearance at times was a considerable nuisance, but at other times they were useful to the Saints in helping to defeat enemies of the Faith, or were used by God to indicate the sanctity of holy persons and the power of prayer.

One of the earliest mentions of insects in the biographies of the Saints appears in the life of ST. JAMES (d. 338), the great Doctor of the Syrian Church, who was a native of Nisibis in Mesopotamia. After living the austere life of a hermit, his personal merit, his gifts of prophecy and miracles and his great reputation caused him to be made bishop of Nisibis. He continued his former austerities and fasts, combining these with the difficulties of his episcopal office.

During his bishopric, a siege of Nisibis was instigated in the year 338 when the Persians under Sapor II attacked with a large army of foot soldiers, horsemen, elephants and other armaments of war. After sixty-three days the siege was lifted, due to the miraculous intervention of the holy bishop.

After returning to Persia, Sapor II raised an even greater army and once more besieged the city. St. Ephrem, who had been deacon to the bishop, is said to have looked with fear at the great multitude of men and beasts which covered the whole countryside. Raising his mind and heart to God, St. James or St. Ephrem is said to have prayed: "Lord, Thou art able by the weakest means to humble the pride of Thy enemies; defeat these multitudes by a plague of insects." Butler tells us that:

> God heard the humble prayer of His servant, as He had done on behalf of Moses against the Egyptians, and as He had by the like means vanquished the enemies of His people when He led them out of Egypt. For clouds of mosquitoes, gnats and flies came pouring down upon the Persians, got into the elephants' trunks, and the horses' ears and nostrils, which made them throw their riders, and put the whole army into confusion and disorder. Sapor abandoned the siege and returned home with the loss of twenty thousand men.[47]

ST. SEVERINUS (d. 482) is known as the Apostle of Austria, but two facts concerning him remain a mystery. It is unknown if he was ever ordained, and his history prior to his arrival at Astura on the Danube in 454 is not recorded. Nevertheless, during the next thirty years he evangelized Bavaria and Austria, built churches, founded

monasteries, attracted followers, aided the poor and converted sinners. He led a life of extreme austerity and performed numerous
miracles. One of these took place when locusts descended on farm
lands and threatened to devour the crops that had been expected to
provide food for the year. After the Saint recited a prayer, the
locusts rose in the air and flew away—an event that was regarded
as miraculous.[48]

Another saint who dismissed locusts in the name of God was ST.
FRANCIS SOLANO (d. 1610), a Franciscan missionary who
labored in Argentina, Bolivia and Paraguay. He performed numerous miracles, one of which took place when a swarm of locusts hovered like a black cloud over the fields of the poor Indians,
threatening their entire crop. St. Francis Solano stood by the field
and commanded that none of them alight, but that they depart to the
mountains at once. The locusts immediately flew away.[49]

While ST. BENEDICT (d. 543) was living alone in a cave at
Subiaco, he experienced a fierce temptation against purity. To
defend himself, he undressed and threw himself into thorn bushes
that were growing nearby. As he rolled among the thorns, becoming scratched and bloodied, the temptation left him. Later in life St.
Benedict related that he never again experienced a similar temptation. A monastery was eventually founded at Subiaco.

Centuries later, Subiaco was visited by ST. FRANCIS OF ASSISI
(d. 1226). According to the popular legend, St. Francis either
grafted, or used supernatural means, to grow roses on the thorn
bushes. Aside from the legend, the thorn bushes might have been
rose bushes to begin with. In commemoration of St. Francis' visit
a portrait was painted and hung in the chapel of St. Gregory.

An interesting feature of these rose bushes at Subiaco is that each
leaf contains the outline of a small serpent. This is caused by a par-
asite. In the United States we have what are called leaf miners
which feed within the structure of the leaf. As the larvae eat their
way along, their path can be seen on the leaf by a serpentine trail
which appears light green or pale yellow. At Subiaco, the trailings
are rust-colored and have appeared on the leaves for centuries. This
difference in color could well be a natural feature in that part of
Italy. The serpentine trailings, however, are said to remind the visitor of the hellish serpent that tempted the purity of St. Benedict.

The rose bushes are named for St. Benedict and St. Francis, and are still flourishing in the monastery garden.[50]

A more delightful incident in which St. Francis exercised his influence on little creatures is told by Thomas of Celano, who reports that near the cell of the Saint at the Portiuncula was a tree cricket that perched on a fig tree and made delightful sounds. At times the Saint would extend his hand toward it, and as though it were the most natural thing to do, the cricket would hop on it and listen as the Saint asked it to sing praises to its Creator.

The cricket did as it was asked and made its charming sounds, to which the Saint mingled his own songs of praise. After their little concert, the cricket was told to return to its tree. The Saint enjoyed its company and its own kind of music, and often stroked it. But after eight days the Saint said to his companions: "Let us give our sister cricket leave to go now, for it has made us sufficiently happy. We do not want to glory vainly over things of this kind." With the permission of the Saint, the cricket left and never returned. Thomas of Celano concludes: "Seeing all these things, the brothers were greatly astonished."[51]

ST. CONRAD (d. 975), a member of the great Guelf family, was unanimously chosen to fill the episcopal chair in the year 934. He built and endowed three stately churches at Constance and renovated many old ones. He is also known to have traveled to Jerusalem three times, making his journeys truly pilgrimages of penance and devotion. In pictures and statues he is usually represented with a chalice and a spider.

The reason for this depiction relates to an incident that took place while he was saying Mass one Easter morning. During the Holy Mass, it happened that a large spider dropped into the chalice. It was the common belief of his time that all or most spiders were poisonous, but the Saint, out of devotion and respect for the Precious Blood, deliberately swallowed the spider, without being harmed in any fashion. St. Conrad died in 975, after having served the Church in the episcopal office for over forty years.[52]

St. Gregory of Tours, in his *Lives of the Fathers*, writes about ST. FRIARD (Leufredus), who died in 557. We are told that St. Friard was a farm laborer who was gathering corn in the fields one day with other farm hands when a swarm of wasps descended in the area and delayed their work. One of the Saint's companions began to mock him by saying, "Friar, you are always making the cross on your eyes, ears and mouth; why don't you drive away these devils with the Sign of the Cross?"

The Saint, thinking that this would be an excellent way to show the power of God, knelt on the ground and silently prayed. Then rising, he told his companions to continue their work, since the insects would no longer trouble them. The Saint followed the swarm as it flew away, praying all the while: "Our help is in the name of God." The wasps finally entered a hole in the ground and were never seen again. The miracle made such an impression on the farm workers that they never again laughed at his religious practices, and thereafter regarded him with the utmost reverence.[53]

One day, after returning from the law court where he had gone to obtain papers regarding lands inherited by his monastery, ST. LEUFREDUS (d. 738) stopped at an inn to pass the night. Msgr. Guerin, in his *Lives of the Saints*, writes that the Saint could not sleep because of the many flies that flitted about him in the warm air. Finally the Saint sat up in bed and bent his head in prayer. All the flies flew away, and they never again entered the building.[54]

Flies are also mentioned in the life of ST. BERNARD OF CLAIRVAUX (d. 1153), since they visited the Saint while he was in Foigny for the dedication of a monastery church. During the service the church was filled with a multitude of flies that disturbed the devotion of the faithful with their buzzing. Since no one knew how to disperse them, St. Bernard cried aloud, *"Excommunicabo eas!"* (I shall excommunicate them!) The next day the flies were all found dead. Their number was so great that they blackened the pavement and were removed from the church with shovels. A chronicler of the time adds: "This miracle was so well known, and so celebrated, that the curse of the flies of Foigny passed into a proverb among the people around, who had come from all parts to assist at the dedication of the church."[55]

Not flies, but insects described as lice are mentioned in the biographies of ST. TERESA OF AVILA (d. 1582). The infestation took place when her community of nuns at the monastery of San Jose decided to wear, as a means of penance, certain tunics made of a very rough sackcloth known as horsecloth. All went well until the weather grew warm. It was then that a great difficulty was experienced. It seems that horsecloth was a favorite habitat of lice. William Thomas Walsh writes: "And a lice-infected household devoted to mental prayer and contemplation is a contradiction in terms." Finally, the situation could be tolerated no longer. While the Saint was at prayer one night between ten and eleven o'clock, the nuns carrying lighted candles formed a procession with the first nun in line carrying a crucifix. They went from room to room singing hymns and psalms in petition for the extermination of the bugs. Finally St. Teresa joined the procession. The community then began a chant in this fashion:

Nuns: Since You give us new array, O heavenly King,
    Free this serge from denizens so threatening.
St. Teresa: Daughters, since you take the cross, be stout of heart,
    And ask of Jesus, Light of yours, to take your part.
    He will defend you surely in such a thing.
Nuns: Free this serge from denizens so threatening.
St. Teresa: Ill boots it to be not at ease in mental prayer;
    Devotion when the spirit flees is very rare.
    But let your unaffrighted hearts to God fast cling.
Nuns: Free this serge from denizens so threatening.
St. Teresa: Since you have come that you may die,
    be not dismayed.
    And do not let such scurvy knaves make you afraid.
    In all this trouble God will aid your suffering.
Nuns: Since You have given us new array, O heavenly King,
    Free this serge from denizens so threatening.

Walsh continues: "Not only did the lice disappear from the tunics, but from that time to this the Discalced Carmelite convents have been free from all manner of pedicular intrusion."

A contemporary biographer, Fr. Ribera, S.J., is said to have gone to great pains to verify this.[56] The present author does not know of any surveys that have been made since that time.

Known for his frequent levitations and miracles, ST. JOSEPH OF CUPERTINO (d. 1663) was always anxious to relieve sufferings and aid the poor. This compassion instigated a miracle when he and his companions were on their way to the monastery of the Conventuals at Osimo. During their journey they paused at a farm-house, and while resting, the poor woman of the house complained to the Saint that she usually derived a livelihood for herself and her family from the sale of melons. She explained that the melons then growing in the field were being destroyed by worms. The Saint was moved to pity and blessed the crop. It is recorded that the farm, that same year, produced more and larger melons than ever before.[57]

We read in the life of ST. FRANCIS OF PAOLA (d. 1507) that he was laying the cornerstone of the fourth monastery for his order, the Minims, when he suddenly paused, placed his fingers on the stone and turned to the people saying: "Brothers, have the locusts ruined your harvests, your vineyards, your olive crops? Have the Turks invaded your land?" The answer of all was "No." The Saint then predicted, "Well, then, remember that the day this stone shall be dis-honored, your city will be the victim of these misfortunes." Some 138 years later, in 1596, the monastery was taken away from the Minims and was given over to another order. On the same day clouds of grasshoppers descended and destroyed the crops. One old resident, Andrea Magrino, recalled having heard of the prophecy and advised that the monastery should be returned to the Minims, which it was. When the Minims regained possession, the grasshop-pers rose up and disappeared.[58]

Closer to our own day we learn about the holy monk, ST. CHAR-BEL MAKHLOUF (d. 1898) and the wonders surrounding his one-time incorrupt body which are reported elsewhere in this book. This retiring monk, who was greatly devoted to the Holy Eucharist, spent sixteen years of his religious life at the Monastery of St. Maroun in Lebanon before he retired to the order's hermitage of Sts. Peter and Paul, where he spent the remaining 23 years of his life practicing severe mortifications. Many miracles are recorded in his biogra-phies, but one involves a swarm of grasshoppers that was devour-ing the monastery's farmlands. Under the imposition of obedience, St. Charbel sprinkled the fields with holy water, with the result that the insects immediately rose up and flew away.[59]

St. Charbel is one of the Incorruptibles, but at the time of his beatification in 1965 the body had been reduced according to the natural process.

DOVES OF OUR LADY OF FATIMA. Worldwide attention focused on the statue of Our Lady of Fatima in Portugal when, in 1946 and early 1947, doves "stood guard" by the statue and refused to leave. During Holy Mass they kept completely silent.

RAVENS FED THE PROPHET ELIAS, as commanded by God.
Scripture reports that the ravens brought him bread and flesh in the
morning and again in the evening.

Cappella Della Santa, Cascia

SWARMING BEES were found about the mouth of the infant St. Rita. A strange variety of bees, exhibiting unusual behavior, still inhabit the walls of the monastery in which she lived and died.

— 32 —

ANIMALS, REPTILES
AND CREATURES OF THE SEA

St. John Bosco once wrote: "It is characteristic of the lives of some of the great Saints to find the extraordinary power they exercised over the animal world, making it obediently subserve their desires or needs." The Saint was too humble to credit himself with this gift, which leads us to believe this statement was made rather early in his ministry, since an unusual animal, and its behavior, are prominent later in the Saint's life, as we will soon learn. The quotation, however, is accurate and its truth has been demonstrated in the lives of many Saints.

One of the earliest Saints to have an unusual power over animals was ST. BLAISE (d. circa 316), who was the Bishop of Sebaste in Armenia. When the persecution of Licinius became fierce he withdrew, by divine direction, to a cave in the mountains, where wild beasts came to him peacefully and congregated near the opening of the cave. One day when hunters were scouring the countryside looking for animals to sacrifice in the ampitheatre, they found the Saint, seized him and took him to Agricolaus. On the way they met a poor woman whose pig had been carried off by a wolf, but at the command of the Saint, the wolf released the pig unharmed.

While St. Blaise was in prison and was being tortured, the woman whose pig had been restored to her brought him provisions and also wax tapers to dispel the darkness of his gloomy cell. The Saint was beheaded after suffering atrocious pains.

In the life of St. Blaise we read that the Saint restored to perfect health a little boy who was at the point of death due to a fishbone in his throat. In commemoration of this miracle, throats are blessed on the feastday of the Saint using two tapers held like a St. Andrew's cross. The two tapers, we are told, are used in memory of the tapers brought to the Saint in his dungeon by the woman whose pig had been restored to her.[1]

ST. MARY OF EGYPT (fifth century) had been a harlot at

472

Alexandria before she converted in Jerusalem. Determined to expiate for her sins, she crossed the river Jordan and, for the rest of her days, lived a solitary, penitential life in the wilderness. One day during Lent, a holy monk and priest named Zozimus, after living in the monastery for fifty-three years, was walking near the place where Mary lived and made her acquaintance. He departed after speaking with her about holy matters and learning from her the facts concerning her early life and the events leading to her conversion. Before leaving, he promised to return the following year during Lent, which he did. He brought the Holy Eucharist and a basket of food and again promised to return during the next Lenten season.

When Zozimus returned that year to the place where he had previously conversed with Mary, he found her lying on the ground dead. The holy monk recited fervent prayers for Mary's soul and then began to dig a grave with his bare hands. According to a legendary account, a lion from the desert came to the monk's assistance and with its claws helped him to dig her grave. St. John Damascene, who died in the middle of the eighth century, often quoted from the Life of St. Mary of Egypt.[2]

When the city of Bourges was occupied by the Visigoths, ST. MARIANUS (d. 473) fled to Auxerre and the abbey where St. Mamertinus was then serving as abbot. He received the habit at the hands of St. Mamertinus, and while still a novice he was given the lowly task of caring for the cows and shepherding the flocks. It was then noticed that he had a strange power over all animals: birds flocked to eat out of his hands, while bears and wolves departed at his command. When a hunted wild boar fled to him for protection, he defended it from hunters and then set it free. These and other extraordinary events were remembered after his death so that the abbey was renamed for this humble brother.[3]

ST. BASOLUS (d. circa 600), or Basle, was born at Limoges in the middle of the sixth century and served for a time as a soldier before becoming a monk. Under the direction of the archbishop at Reims, he went to the monastery of Vierzy. He lived there for a time, until the abbot, at the Saint's request, permitted him to live as a hermit in a cave near the top of a neighboring hill. He remained there for the rest of his life. Among his many miracles is one concerning a boar which ran into the Saint's cave while being hunted by the Count of Champagne. The dogs that were chasing the boar approached the entrance of the cell but refused to enter, while the boar took refuge under the skirt of the Saint's habit. The Count, we are told, was so impressed by this spectacle that he gave the holy hermit a large tract of land. St. Basolus is mentioned in the Roman Martyrology.[4]

While ST. CUTHBERT (d. 687) was visiting the monastery at Coludi he piqued the curiosity of some of his companions by leaving the place in the evening and returning at the hour of morning prayer.

Venerable Bede writes in his *Ecclesiastical History of the English Nation* about St. Cuthbert's little excursion and the unusual behavior of two creatures of the sea. The History records:

> One night, a brother of the monastery, seeing the Saint go out alone, followed him privately to see what he should do. But he, when he left the monastery, went down to the sea, which flows beneath, and going into it, until the water reached his neck and arms, spent the night in praising God. When the dawn of day approached, he came out of the water, and, falling on his knees, began to pray again. Whilst he was doing this, two quadrupeds, called otters, came up from the sea and, lying down before him on the sand, breathed upon his feet and wiped them with their bodies after which, having received his blessing, they returned to their native element.

St. Cuthbert returned to the monastery in time to join the accustomed prayers, while the brother who had spied on him came and fell at his feet, asking his pardon. St. Cuthbert reportedly said, "Did you follow me to see what I was about to do? I forgive you for it on one condition, that you tell it to nobody before my death."

The brother is said to have concealed this miracle during St. Cuthbert's life, but "after his death, took care to tell it to as many persons as he was able."[5]

ST. WILLIAM FIRMATUS (d. circa 1090) was a layman when he had a dream or vision in which he saw the devil, in the form of a great ape, sitting on his money chest. He then withdrew into retirement with his widowed mother and at her death embraced an austere lifestyle. He made two pilgrimages to the Holy Land and then settled in Mantille, where he earned a reputation for sanctity and miracles.

The Saint's power over animals came to the attention of local peasants who appealed to him to protect their fields from animals who were ruining the crops. With a gentle tap he admonished the hares and goats, and they immediately regulated their behavior. But there was a particularly destructive wild boar that resisted reform. With this animal he used sterner measures and shut it up one night in a cell. The next morning, and thereafter, the animal proved its complete transformation.[6]

ST. BENNO (d. 1106) was the illustrious bishop of Meissen who, we are told, "was a true shepherd who watched diligently over his flock, enforced discipline on his clergy, preached frequently, made regular visitations, gave liberally to the poor, set the example of a holy ascetic life, restored the public recitation of the office and introduced into his church the chants to which he had been accustomed at Hildesheim." The holy bishop, we are told, was a lover of music and nature.

One day, while he was walking in the fields meditating on the glory of God, he came upon a group of frogs who were croaking loudly. The frogs were so annoying in their persistent bellows that the bishop commanded them to be silent. In a moment there flashed in his mind the words of the Canticle, "O ye whales and all that move in the waters, bless the Lord!" Humbled by the thought, the bishop withdrew his order, permitting the frogs once again to croak their praise of the Creator.[7]

The little book known as *The Little Flowers of St. Francis* tells that: "At a time when ST. FRANCIS OF ASSISI (d. 1226) was staying in the town of Gubbio, something wonderful and worthy of lasting fame took place." This wonderful event involved the Saint and an unusually large and fierce wolf that was attacking and eating not only animals, but human beings as well. The situation became so dangerous that people took to carrying weapons when they were forced to go outside the city gate. But "God wished to bring the holiness of St. Francis to the attention of the people."

Despite warnings, St. Francis decided to go and meet the wolf. Together with some of his companions and many of the bravest citizens, St. Francis went out to see what could be done. To the horror of his followers, the wolf charged toward the Saint with fierce teeth showing in its open mouth. Without the slightest trace of fear, St. Francis made the Sign of the Cross toward the animal, which produced an immediate effect. The wolf closed its mouth and slowed its pace so that it eventually crept to the Saint in humble submission. But that was not all. St. Francis gently rebuked the wolf, ordering it never again to hurt anyone. The Saint also made a pact with the animal, that if it did no more harm, the townsfolk would give it food every day and the dogs would no longer bark at it. The wolf agreed by twists of the body and the wagging of its tail. The Saint then ordered the wolf to walk beside him to the town. "When the people saw this they were greatly amazed and the news spread quickly, so that all of them assembled in the marketplace because St. Francis was there with the wolf."

The Saint then addressed the people: "Brother Wolf, who is standing here before you, has promised and has given me a pledge that he will make peace with you and will never hurt you if you promise also to feed him every day." The people promised to do as the Saint recommended, and the wolf, to show his cooperation and readiness to keep the pact, raised his right paw and placed it in the hand of the Saint. From that day on the wolf and the people kept the peace which St. Francis had made.

> The wolf lived two years more, and it went from door to door for food. It hurt no one, and no one hurt it. The people fed it courteously and it is a striking fact that not a single dog ever barked at it.
>
> Then the wolf grew old and died. And the people were sorry, because whenever it went through the town, its peaceful kindness and patience reminded them of the virtues and the holiness of St. Francis.[8]

This was not the only wolf St. Francis tamed. He once journeyed to Greccio and the little monastery of his order there which he liked to visit. As soon as he arrived, the people told him about a pack of ravening wolves attacking both men and animals. In addition, hailstorms were destroying their fields and vineyards. The Saint's answer to their problems came in the form of a sermon in which he advised that all should confess their sins and bring forth "fruits befitting repentance." He further promised, "I give you my word that every pestilence will depart and the Lord, looking kindly upon you, will grant you an increase of temporal goods." He also warned that if they returned to their former ways, the troubles would return and be doubled in intensity. Needless to report, the people did as he recommended and were not only delivered from the wolves and the hail, but they also prospered and were "filled beyond measure with temporal goods." But in time they relapsed, to the anger of God, who added to their troubles a heaven-sent sickness and a fire that destroyed the whole town.[9]

Another incident in the life of St. Francis of Assisi involved a little rabbit that had been caught in a trap and was brought to him by one of the brothers. When the Saint saw the rabbit he said to it: "Brother rabbit, come to me. Why did you allow yourself to be caught like this?" As soon as the brother placed the rabbit on the ground, it jumped onto the Saint's lap and reclined quietly on his chest. After caressing it and stroking its fur, the Saint placed it on the ground, thinking that it would hop towards the woods, but it jumped again onto his lap—an action that was repeated a number of times, until the Saint directed the brother to carry the rabbit into the woods.[10]

Still another example of St. Francis' influence over animals took place when he was on his way from Siena to the Spoleto Valley. Along the way he was passing a field on which a large number of sheep were grazing. When he greeted them, as was his custom, they all bounded and leaped toward the Saint, raising their heads and returning the greeting with loud bleatings. The Saint's companions were witnesses to this unusual event.[11]

Just as St. Francis of Assisi once quieted some birds in a lagoon from carolling while the friars were praying, ST. ANTHONY OF PADUA (d. 1231) did likewise when he was at the Convent of Montpellier, but the creatures this time were frogs. It seems that the frogs croaked noisily in the monastery's pond at all times of the day, causing great distractions among the brethren until St. Anthony rebuked them. Thereafter, the frogs observed a respectful silence at the hours of prayer.[12]

The monastery of ST. MARTIN DE PORRES (d. 1639) at one time had a terrible problem with mice rummaging in the kitchen and storerooms and even invading the wardrobe room, ruining the clothing and bed linens.

The Saint was ordered to purchase a quantity of poison and spread it around, but the Saint humbly protested, saying that the aim was to get rid of the little animals—not necessarily to kill them—and that he knew a solution. A bargain was reached. The Saint would put scraps of food in the barn and stable to attract the animals outside the building, but if this failed, poison would be purchased.

The Saint then left the infirmary and went to the hole where most of the mice came in on the ground floor. There in the opening was a small gray mouse, who listened as St. Martin spoke to him. It was told to notify the others that they were not to do any more mischief in the monastery, but were to leave the building and retire to the shed and stable, where he would feed them.

In a few moments there was a continuous scuttling sound, then the other friars noticed a large number of rats and mice going out of the building. To the amazement of the prior, Fr. Lorenzana, the rodents were all running out as the Saint had planned. As the last of the intruders was leaving, St. Martin made a small Sign of the Cross in its direction. From then on the rodents were fed by the Saint outside, and the friars and the monastery were left in peace.[13]

Another incident involving mice was experienced by ST. GERARD MAJELLA (d. 1755). Always ready to give aid to the distressed, the Saint was one day walking along the road from Andria to Corato when he met a poor peasant farmer who was greatly distressed. His only means of support was a field he had sown, which was then being ravaged by mice. After listening to the farmer's complaint, the Saint asked if he would rather have the mice die or move elsewhere. The farmer, perhaps fearing that if the mice moved elsewhere they might return once again, replied, "I would rather they would die." The Saint then raised his hand, made the Sign of the Cross toward the field and in a few moments the ground was littered with dead and dying mice. At the sight of this wonder the farmer ran to Corato, crying, "The Saint is here! The Saint is here!"[14]

The history of ST. MARGARET OF CORTONA (d. 1297)

reveals that her attractive appearance came to the attention of a young cavalier from Montepulciano, who persuaded her to live with him in luxury and ease in his castle among the hills. He never married her as he had promised, and for nine years she lived openly with him as his mistress, bearing a son and causing great scandal. One day the young man failed to return from visiting one of his estates. Margaret watched anxiously the whole night and the next day. Finally, the dog that almost always accompanied the cavalier came home alone. The dog tugged at her dress and vigorously indicated that it wanted her to follow him. Margaret went with the animal into the woods and there, at the foot of an oak tree, the dog began to scratch at a shallow grave. With horror she saw the mangled body of her lover, and with great emotion saw in the tragedy the judgment of God. Margaret left Montepulciano with her child and settled in Cortona. She began her penitential life and joined the Franciscan Third Order. Numerous conversions were brought about by her prayers and counsel, and many supernatural communications from Heaven are recorded by her confessor, Friar Giunta.[15]

During his childhood BL. SEBASTIAN APPARICIO (d. 1600) was obliged to work to help support his poor Spanish family. At the age of fifteen he worked as a servant to a poor widow, then was employed as a valet to a wealthy gentleman. He also worked in the fields before he left his native land for America. He settled in Mexico and became a merchant, earning huge amounts of money which he gave to charity. He also provided dowries, freed prisoners, fed the poor and helped poor farmers. He lived a frugal life, and he married twice—although it is said both marriages were never consummated. When the second wife died he received the habit of the Third Order of St. Francis and eventually entered the monastery of the Friars Minor. He was by then in his seventies.

The last twenty-six years of his life were spent in the humble role of a begging brother, taking a cart through the countryside to obtain food for his brethren. The oxen which drew the cart never gave him the least trouble and would promptly obey his whispered commands. Bl. Sebastian is said to have had wonderful power over all animals, and could instantly tame mules and even wild animals. The holy man died at the age of ninety-eight and was beatified in 1787 by Pope Pius VI.[16]

Oxen are also mentioned in the life of ST. PAUL OF THE CROSS (d. 1775). He was one day traveling in the country when he met a farmer whose two oxen were pulling a plow. The animals were giving the farmer a great deal of trouble, so that he took to uttering blasphemies while in a feverish rage. The Saint, full of charity, gave the farmer a gentle admonition, but this only made the farmer more furious. Finally, the farmer reached for the gun he had nearby and leveled it at the Saint. More horrified at the blasphemies than he was at his present danger, the Saint held up the crucifix he always wore around his neck and announced fearlessly, "Since you will not respect this crucifix, these oxen will." As though they understood, the oxen immediately fell to their knees.

This changed the attitude of the farmer. He put down the weapon, threw himself at the Saint's feet and begged forgiveness. He followed the Saint to a church, made his confession and was reconciled to God.[17]

Once a flock of geese was outside a church door making a terrible noise during a service conducted by ST. JOSEPH BENEDICT COTTOLENGO (d. 1842). He is said to have gone outside and gently admonished the geese, asking them if they would kindly go and bathe during Mass and Benediction. The geese promptly obeyed, wobbling away two by two in silence. Thereafter, they did as the Saint had ordered, and peace was restored for all church services.[18]

ST. GODRIC (d. 1170) was a peddler before he took to the sea and became a prosperous trader. Reginald of Durham, who knew him well and learned the particulars of his early life from Godric himself, wrote that Godric's life had been disorderly and his business methods dishonest. Later Godric made several pilgrimages to St. Andrew's in Scotland, to Jerusalem, Compostela and Rome, and became a hermit. He sought with great vigor to make amends for his earlier indiscretions. While observing a very penitential life he progressed quickly in virtue, and, as often happens with solitaries, he acquired a special power over wild creatures which extended even to vipers, which he treated as domestic pets. Shy creatures such as stags, rabbits and birds were not afraid of him, nor did he fear wolves and other animals who fled to him from danger. He is described as being ignorant of music, yet he composed hymns which he said were taught him during visions of the Virgin Mary.[19]

About five years after ST. FRANCIS OF PAOLA (d. 1507) began his life as a hermit, he was one day in his cave praying when suddenly a young goat rushed in, seeking protection from hunters and their dogs. The hunters entered the cave and were startled to see the hermit holding the frightened goat in his arms. Deeply shaken, they called off their dogs and went home to tell everyone of their unexpected experience. As a result, many devout people visited the cave to seek the hermit's blessing and counsel. The Saint accepted the visit of the goat and the hunters as a sign from God that he was to leave his hermitage and work for the good of the Church. This he did with admirable success, performing miracles and exercising many of his mystical favors.[20]

A goat that appears in the history of ST. MARY MAGDALENE DE' PAZZI (d. 1607) was a donation to her convent, but it became rather wild and caused the nuns to worry about being injured by it, especially when it entered the workroom and gave every indication that it was contemplating damage. Mother Evangelist watched as Sr. Mary Magdalene approached the goat without fear. The animal immediately became quiet and permitted the Saint to take hold of it and lead it outside. We can only assume that the animal remained tame from then on, to the satisfaction of all concerned.

The behavior of a little hare must have been extraordinarily disturbing since it is mentioned in the Process of beatification. The hare, apparently a pet of the convent, "one day began to run and jump in a way that was very annoying." A novice whispered to Sr. Mary Magdalene, "Mother, surely you could make the animal keep still." The Saint, looking at the hare, simply said, "Stand still!" The little creature immediately obeyed the command.[21]

It is said of ST. JOSEPH OF CUPERTINO (d. 1663) that "his life was one long succession of ecstasies, miracles of healing, and supernatural happenings on a scale not paralleled in the reasonably authenticated life of any other saint." Among the phenomena mentioned was his influence over animals. On one occasion, when he saw a lamb in the garden of the Capuchins at Fossombrone, he became lost in the contemplation of the spotless Lamb of God and levitated in the air with the animal in his arms. In the opinion of some biographers, the power St. Joseph exercised over animals surpassed even that of St. Francis of Assisi.

We learn that one of St. Joseph's devotions was the Litany of Loreto. Each Saturday, it seems, he was in the practice of reciting the litany with shepherds in a chapel near the monastery at Grottella. One Saturday, however, the shepherds could not attend. If the shepherds could not come, the sheep would. With a loud voice the Saint called to the sheep to gather round him to revere the Mother of God. We are informed that the sheep were at a great distance so that the Saint's voice could not normally have reached them, but they nonetheless ran toward the chapel, disregarding the calls of the shepherds.

The Saint then began the recitation of the litany. After each mention of Our Lady's attributes, the sheep bleated and in this way completed the Litany. After receiving a blessing from the Saint, they happily returned to their pastures.[22]

Another example of his power over animals is given us. Mad dogs, it seems, had bitten a ram, which contracted the madness. Because of the ram's condition it was confined in a fenced garden to prevent contact with animals or people. St. Joseph was warned about the animal, but with a smile he replied that he trusted in God and approached the enclosure. While stroking the animal he spoke gently to it and then told it to return to its flock. On being freed, the ram showed by a change in behavior that it was well and tame, and it contentedly joined its companions.[23]

Yet another example tells that the Saint once gave the nuns of St. Clare at Cupertino a gift in the form of a white lamb which demonstrated an unusual behavior. "The animal was always first in all exercises, abstemious, quiet in the chapel and ever alert to wake the sleepy by butting and jostling, or to remove with hoofs and teeth any vain finery which it observed."[24]

After the lamb's death the Saint replaced the pet with a bird whose unusual behavior is mentioned in the chapter of this book regarding birds.

One of the most mysterious reports of animal behavior mentioned in the lives of the Saints involves the appearance of a mysterious dog that is related in the biographies of ST. JOHN BOSCO (d. 1888). Attempts have been made to account for the animal's appearance when Don Bosco needed protection, while at other times it was nowhere to be found. Those who saw the dog described it as being like an Alsatian, a large ferocious-looking animal, standing about three feet high. We are told that the first time Margaret Bosco, the Saint's mother, saw the dog she cried out in alarm. But the boys at the Oratory were not afraid of it since the Saint wrote in his memoirs, "The boys at the Oratory frequently touched him." The dog first appeared during the mid-nineteenth century when the life of the Saint was in danger because of the attacks made upon him by members of certain religious factions. Once while away from the Oratory teaching catechism to boys, the Saint was fired upon by a hired assassin who stood by a window. Miraculously, the bullet passed under the Saint's arm, producing a hole in his cassock. At certain times ambushes were laid for him and more than once he had to physically protect himself. In the course of his priestly ministry, there were times when he had to walk through deserted areas of land, wastelands they were called, where enemies could hide from detection behind bushes and trees.

One evening when he was returning to the Oratory he found it necessary to walk through the wasteland, "not without fear," when suddenly a large dog, which he later named Grigio (meaning gray), bounded to his side. The Saint wrote in his memoirs:

> Its attitude was not threatening. It was rather like a dog that had just recognized its master. We soon made friends and it went with me to the Oratory. On different occasions it kept me company, sometimes providentially. Towards the end of November 1854, one sleety night I was returning from the town. In order not to be alone I took the road leading from the Consolate down to the Cottolengo Institute. At one point I noticed that two men were walking a short distrance in front of me, matching their pace with mine . . . I crossed over to the other pavement to avoid them, but they did the same. I then tried to turn back but it was too late, for they suddenly faced about and in two steps were on me. Without a word they threw some kind of coat over me. In vain I struggled to set myself free. One of them then tried to gag me with a scarf. I wanted to shout out but I had not the strength.
>
> At that moment Grigio appeared, growling like a bear, and hurled himself at the first man with his paws at his throat, snarling meanwhile towards the other. They

were obliged to let me go in order to deal with the dog
. . . Grigio went on barking. The ruffians made off as
fast as they could and Grigio accompanied me to the
Cottolengo, where I stopped to recover myself a little . . .
Then I returned to the Oratory, this time under safe
escort.[25]

The Saint also wrote: "Every evening when I ventured out into
this deserted quarter alone I always noticed Grigio on one side of
the road or the other."

On one occasion, the dog arrived at the Oratory while Don Bosco
was at table with some priests and his mother. The Saint offered the
animal food, but it would not eat it. "I remember that that evening
I had returned rather late and that a friend had given me a lift in his
carriage; it seemed that Grigio wanted to make sure that nothing
had happened to me."[26]

One evening when Don Bosco was about to leave the house, Grigio placed himself at the door and growled each time the Saint
approached it. A quarter of an hour later a neighbor rushed in to
warn the Saint not to leave, because he had heard of a sinister plot
to attack him. The dog had once again saved the Saint from physical harm.[27]

It is said that Grigio left the Saint's side and went to unknown
regions when conditions settled down and the Saint's enemies
stopped their plots against him. Grigio was not seen again until one
night in 1883, when Don Bosco and a companion arrived late at the
train station at Bordighera. Since no one was around to show them
the way to the Salesian house, they went about aimlessly in the
dark until finally Grigio appeared and escorted them to their destination.[28]

Sometime later, while visiting a friend's house in Marseilles, the
Saint mentioned the dog's appearance after its absence for a number of years. It was then pointed out to him that the dog must have
lived two or three times the normal life expectancy of a dog. The
Saint merely agreed.

The Saint also wrote in his memoirs: "All sorts of stories have
been told about this dog, but I never discovered who his master was.
All I know is that amid the many dangers that threatened me this
animal furnished me providential protection . . ." It was suggested
that perhaps an angel had assumed the appearance of the dog. Oth-

ers wondered about the dog's owner. In answer to all the speculations about the dog the Saint simply responded, "The principal thing is that it was my friend."[29]

A dog is also mentioned in the histories of ST. DOMINIC (d. 1221), and pertains to a vision experienced by the Saint's mother before his birth. The vision consisted of a dog bearing in its mouth a lighted torch, which was understood to indicate the future greatness of her son, who would set fire to the world and kindle and illuminate men's hearts through the ministry of his words.[30]

ST. GERMAINE COUSIN (d. 1606) was born into poor circumstances in Pibrac, near Toulouse, France. Because of her weak constitution, her withered right hand and her scrofulous neck with its discharging sores, her stepmother was repulsed, and she fiercely persecuted her. Germaine was forced to live and sleep in the stable and was fed scraps from the table in addition to being forced at a tender age to shepherd the family's sheep.

Many miracles are recorded with regard to her attendance at daily Mass. It was observed by many of the church-goers that the sheep, which she often took with her to church, never strayed from her staff which she stuck in the ground, and it is known that not once were the sheep threatened by the wolves that inhabited the neighboring forest.[31]

St. Germaine died unattended on her straw mat in the stable at the age of 27. After her body had remained perfectly incorrupt for almost 200 years, it was maliciously destroyed in 1795 during the French Revolution. She was canonized in 1867.

BL. MARGARET OF SAVOY (d. 1464) was of royal birth and was very young when she married the Marquis of Montserrat, who was a widower with two children. After his death some years later, she founded a convent which followed the ancient rule of St. Dominic. Accordingly, she joined the order and lived in the convent for many years. One day the son of one of her stepchildren, having killed a doe in a nearby forest, brought her a motherless fawn to tend. It became a pet and, we are told, was able to find any nun Bl. Margaret would name. For several years the animal had free rein of the halls and cells of the Sisters until the confessor of the convent told her the deer must be returned to the forest. Margaret took the animal to the gate and told it to return to the wild, which it did. The nuns never saw it again until Bl. Margaret was about to die.[32]

Reptiles

The Old Testament mentions serpents a number of times, beginning with the serpent in the Garden of Eden, but more often with regard to Moses. We are told first of all about the rod he threw down before Pharaoh that became a snake. Then we are told that after their escape from Egypt the people complained against God and Moses saying: "Why didst thou bring us out of Egypt, to die in the wilderness? There is no bread, nor have we any waters: our soul now loatheth this very light food." *(Numbers* 21:5). In response the Lord sent a punishment in the form of fiery serpents "which bit them and killed many of them." *(Numbers* 21:6).

The people then repented and asked Moses to pray for them, which he did. "And the Lord said to him: Make a brazen serpent, and set it up for a sign: whosoever being struck shall look on it, shall live." *(Numbers* 21:8).

Moses, accordingly, made a bronze serpent and mounted it on a pole, and whenever anyone who had been bitten by a serpent looked at the bronze serpent, he recovered. *(Numbers* 21:8-9).

This bronze serpent of Moses' existed until the time of King Ezechias (Hezekiah). Scripture tells us that he "broke the brazen serpent, which Moses had made: for till that time the children of Israel burnt incense to it . . ." (*4 Kings* 18:4; *2 Kings* 18:4 in some translations). It was King Ezechias' desire to abolish idolatry, but in attempting to do so he destroyed what could have come down to us as a precious relic.

Snakes, of course, are also mentioned in the life of ST. PATRICK (d. circa 461), who was born on his father's farm beside the sea. Unfortunately, the farm was pillaged by pirates who carried off the sixteen-year-old Patrick. He was sold to an islander and tended his flocks for six years before he escaped and returned to his parents.

After a time Patrick stayed with the monks of Lerins, then went to Auxerre, where he was ordained deacon by St. Amator and was later consecrated bishop by St. Germain. He set about the evangelization of Ireland, which had been ruled with absolute power by a number of minor kings. St. Patrick is remembered as having rid Ireland of venomous reptiles, but some have regarded this as an allegorical way of expressing his triumph over paganism.[33]

St. Gregory the Great in his *Dialogues* tells about the neighborhood of Castoria, which was greatly infested with serpents, and how ST. EUTYCHUS (d. 540) prayed that God would destroy them. This was accomplished in a most extraordinary manner when bolts of lightning flashed and killed them all. Since the bodies of the snakes seemed to be everywhere, his companion wondered, "But who shall remove them out of our sight?" The snakes were soon devoured when a cloud of birds swooped down upon them—this according to St. Gregory.[34]

A number of early Saints are said to have rid certain places of snakes, but we now turn to a twentieth century example which was duly witnessed, and a humble Benedictine nun named BL. MARY FORTUNATA VITI (d. 1922), who served her Benedictine convent as a lay sister.

In the garden of her convent, a large poisonous snake was seen coiled under vegetation. Repeated attempts were made to snare the reptile, all without success. Greatly frightened, the sisters were forced to remain indoors and were denied their outdoor recreations. Bl. Fortunata prayed for a solution of the difficulty and then decided on a forthright approach. Arising early one morning, she went into the garden and raised her voice in prayer: "Most Holy Trinity, show me the snake, and destroy it in my presence." After a moment there was rustling among the bushes and then the snake appeared. It slithered up the stone stairway toward her and waited. Then Sr. Fortunata prayed: "Power and love of God, destroy this serpent." Instantly the reptile tumbled down the steps. With great caution Sr. Fortunata approached the snake and prodded it with a stick to make certain it was dead. She then placed it on the terrace for the nuns to examine. There was no longer a threat, and they could now enjoy the garden without fear.[35]

Creatures of the Sea

We can readily recall the many times Our Lord's attention was drawn to fish. The citations in the Bible concerning these times are numerous. We will remember, of course, the time after the Resurrection when Simon Peter and some of the others went fishing.

And that night they caught nothing. But when the morning was come, Jesus stood on the shore: yet the disciples knew not that it was Jesus. Jesus therefore said to them: Children, have you any meat? They answered him: No. He saith to them: Cast the net on the right side of the ship, and you shall find. They cast therefore; and now they were not able to draw it, for the multitude of fishes. That disciple therefore whom Jesus loved, said to Peter: "It is the Lord." *(John* 21:3-7).

We know that they caught exactly one hundred fifty-three sizable fish and that, "In spite of the number, the net was not broken."

As soon then as they came to land, they saw hot coals lying, and a fish laid thereon, and bread. Jesus saith to them, "Come and dine." *(John* 21:9, 12).

Here we have an instance in which the Redeemer, soon after His Resurrection, not only provided fish for Peter and the others to catch, but also cooked the fish for their breakfast—a most considerate and kindly act performed for His friends who were undoubtedly hungry after having worked all night without success.

Another time, when the temple tax was due, Jesus told Peter to "Go to the sea, and cast in a hook: and that fish which shall first come up, take: and when thou hast opened its mouth, thou shalt find a stater: take that, and give it to them for me and thee." *(Matt.* 17:27). This was enough to pay the tax.

Not a coin, but another object was found in a fish as reported in the life of ST. PAUL, THE BISHOP OF LEON (d. 573). It seems that St. Paul, while visiting King Mark, saw a certain small bell and asked if he might have it. The king refused. Not long afterwards, while visiting the mansion of Count de Witur, someone gave Paul a present of a "very fine fish." As it was being prepared for dinner, the very bell that the king had refused to give him was found in the fish. The report continues that the bell is, or was, preserved in the Cathedral of Leon and is described as having a quadrangular shape. That is, the sides were not all the same, two being large and two smaller. It was a few inches in height and seemed to have been beaten into shape by a hammer. The description continues that it was made of a mixture of copper and silver and had "miraculous virtues attributed to it."[36]

We read in *The Little Flowers of Saint Francis* about an unusual sermon of ST. ANTHONY OF PADUA (d. 1231), a spiritual son of St. Francis of Assisi.

One day St. Anthony was at Rimini where a great many infidels had gathered. Hoping to win them for the Church, the Saint preached to them, setting forth the Faith of Jesus and the Holy Scriptures. Unfortunately, despite his efforts, the infidels would not listen. According to the account of the miracle, the Saint was inspired to:

> go forth to the banks of the river close beside the sea; and, standing thus upon the shore betwixt sea and stream, he began to speak in the guise of a sermon in the name of God unto the fishes. "Hear the word of God, ye fishes of the sea and of the stream, since heretics and infidels are loath to listen to it." And, having uttered these words, suddenly there came toward him so great a multitude of fishes—great, small and middle-sized—as had never been seen in that sea or in that stream, or of the people round about; and all held their heads up out of the water, and all turned attentively toward the face of Anthony. And the greatest peace and meekness and order prevailed; insomuch that next the shore stood the lesser fish, and after them the middle-sized fish, and still after them, where the water was deepest, stood the larger fish. The fish being thus ranged in order, St. Anthony began solemnly to preach . . .

The Saint spoke about God's goodness to them in giving them good water and food so that they could grow and multiply; of how they were preserved during the great flood of Noah; that they were free to roam wherever they pleased and all the other benefits given them by God. *The Little Flowers* continues:

> Upon these and other familiar words and the teachings of St. Anthony, the fishes began to open their

mouths and to bow their heads: and by these and other signs of reverence, according as it was possible to them, they praised God. As St. Anthony continued to preach, more and more fish joined the congregation and none departed.

News of the miracle spread so that

Upon this miracle the people of the town began to hasten forth, and among them were also the aforesaid heretics; the which, seeing so manifest and marvellous a miracle, felt their hearts sorely pricked, and they fell with one accord at St. Anthony's feet to hear his words.

The Saint began to preach to both the people and the fish. We are told that the people were strengthened in their faith, and the heretics converted. This done, St. Anthony dismissed the fish with the blessing of God; and they all departed with marvellous signs of rejoicing, and likewise the people. The account of this miracle ends: "And St. Anthony stayed in Rimini for many days, preaching and reaping a spiritual harvest of souls."[37]

We learn that BL. PETER GEREMIA (d. 1452) of Palermo, Sicily was about to begin a distinguished career as a lawyer when he abandoned his plans and asked to be admitted to the Order of Friars Preachers, the Dominicans. His family was overwhelmingly disappointed that such a promising career would be disregarded for a life of penance and poverty. The father even journeyed to the monastery and demanded his son's return, but when he saw Peter's happiness, he gladly gave his blessing on his son's chosen life. Peter became known as one of the finest preachers in Sicily and even conversed happily on spiritual matters with the renowned St. Vincent Ferrer.

One day, while he was prior of his monastery, he was told that the monastery lacked food for the next meal. Believing in the generosity of the fishermen on the docks, he went to the shore and asked one of the fishermen for some of his catch. To his surprise the fisherman rudely declined, and apparently left to do more fishing. Getting into a rowboat, Peter rowed out on the water and prayed. Before long, a number of fish tore a hole in the fisherman's net and followed Peter's boat. The fisherman, seeing the fish escape through his sturdy net, recognized the miracle and apologized for his rude behavior and lack of generosity. Bl. Peter then made a sign for the fish to return to the net, which they did. The record states, "The monastery was ever afterwards supplied with fish."[38]

The following would seem unbelievable and would be easily dismissed had it not been included in a speech given by Cardinal de Monte before Pope Gregory XV on January 19, 1622.

The incident concerns ST. FRANCIS XAVIER (d. 1552), the great missionary of Japan and India who baptized thousands, founded churches, foretold the future, healed countless persons, calmed tempests, raised several people from the dead and achieved other benefits for the Church which have become legendary.

When Cardinal de Monte addressed the pontiff, he spoke of the time Francis Xavier was sailing from Ambionum, a city of the Molucca Islands, to Baranula when he was overtaken by a storm that threatened to wreck the vessel in which he sailed. All on board pleaded with him to pray for their safety. The Saint took his crucifix, which he wore on a chain around his neck, and held it high against the raging winds. The storm calmed, but a sudden lurch of the vessel snatched the crucifix from his hand and tossed it into the sea.

The ship arrived safely the next day at Baranula. As the Saint disembarked and was walking along the seashore, a great crab leaped out of the sea carrying the crucifix "devoutly and in an upright direction between its claws." The crab made its way directly to the Saint, delivered the crucifix to him and then returned to the sea. The Cardinal tells that St. Francis was unspeakably thankful, and crossing his arms, fell prostrate on the ground and remained for half an hour in devout prayer. All on shore who had greeted the arrival of the vessel were witnesses to the marvel.

This seems to be an almost unbelievable event, but it must have been witnessed by reputable persons who gave sworn statements, since the happening was accepted by the Vatican as one of the three miracles required for the Cause of Canonization. (Mon. Xav. II, 713, Bull of Canonization).[39]

Additionally, we find that when the Jesuits were expelled from Portugal in 1760:

A member of the Company made affidavit that taken from the chapel of their college in Coimbra was a crucifix of wood and silver. On the back of the silver cross was inscribed that this was the crucifix which by "an extraordinary prodigy" the crab brought back to St. Francis Xavier. In Rome, six of his comrades in exile, members of the Company, signed another affidavit that this was the crucifix thus miraculously restored.[40]

ST. GERMAINE PIBRAC'S sheep are known to have remained quietly by the staff she stuck in the ground while she attended Holy Mass. Wolves in the area never troubled them.

ST. ANTHONY OF PADUA holds up the Blessed Sacrament for a hungry donkey to adore, in answer to a heretic who denied the Real Presence. The animal genuflected in adoration, ignoring the proffered food. The heretic was converted.

ST. ANTHONY'S SERMON TO THE FISH AT RIMINI. This painting is found in the vestibule of the sacristy in the Basilica of St. Anthony of Padua.

ST. MARTIN DE PORRES (right), the Dominican mystic and wonder worker of Lima, Peru. The Saint rid his monastery of mice through kindly techniques, rather than poison.

WELLS, SPRINGS AND HOLY WATER

Perhaps the best-known incident in which water was miraculously supplied in the Old Testament was when God alleviated the thirst of His chosen people by making water flow from a rock.

We read in the book of Exodus how the children of Israel, while being led by Moses, encamped at Rephidim. No water could be found in the area, and the people began to grumble and speak against Moses. Finally the holy man cried out to God and was instructed by the Almighty:

> Go before the people, and take with thee of the ancients of Israel: and take in thy hand the rod wherewith thou didst strike the river, and go. Behold I will stand there before thee, upon the rock Horeb: and thou shalt strike the rock, and water shall come out of it that the people may drink. *(Exodus* 17:5-6).

The place was then named "Massah" and "Meribah," which means, "the place of the quarreling."

Once again the Heavenly Father produced water from an unusual source—this time after Samson had killed 1,000 Philistines with the jawbone of an ass. Finding himself thirsty and weak from the ordeal, Samson cried to the Lord:

> "Thou hast given this very great deliverance and victory into the hand of thy servant: and behold I die for thirst, and shall fall into the hands of the uncircumcised." Then the Lord opened a great tooth in the jaw of the ass, and waters issued out of it. And when he had drank them he refreshed his spirit and recovered his strength. *(Judges* 15:18-19).

The first miraculous spring produced in the New Testament is credited to St. Peter. A spring appeared when he was imprisoned in the jail now known as the Mamertine, or the Chapel of San Pietro in Carcere. However, this account is contradicted by a claim that the water was already there at the time of the imprisonment of Jugurtha.[1] Whichever is the case, St. Peter converted his jailers, STS. PROCESSUS AND MARTINIANUS (1st century), and forty others, and baptized them with water from the spring. It is still seen today.

An underground oratory of four rooms located beneath the church of Santa Maria in Via Lata contains paintings of the imprisonment of ST. PAUL (d. circa 65), as well as remnants of an ancient building. Here is found a fountain which is said to have appeared miraculously in answer to the prayers of St. Paul when he baptized his converts. During the Middle Ages this well was frequently used when there were water shortages in Rome.[2]

The Roman Church of San Paolo Alle Tre Fontane (St. Paul of the Three Fountains) was built in the 16th century over the spot where St. Paul was beheaded. In the sanctuary is the low marble column to which the Saint is said to have been bound at the time of his execution. Also found there is a marble block on which he was beheaded. St. Gregory the Great mentions the execution of St. Paul and the place of execution, but sometime later, legend tells that the decapitated head bounded on the grassy slope. At the three places where the head of the Saint touched, fountains sprang up which are now protected by three small marble buildings.[3]

There follows a number of early saints who miraculously produced springs. Perhaps the first was ST. CLEMENT I OF ROME (d. circa 100). Believed to have been ordained by St. Peter, St. Clement was serving the Church as the fourth Pope when he was exiled by the Emperor Trajan to the Chersonese (now Crimea). There he found about 2,000 Christians who were condemned to work in the quarries. Since the only supply of water was two miles away, the prisoners suffered greatly from thirst. In compassion, the Pope prayed for their relief—then, lifting up his eyes, he saw on a nearby hillock a lamb which held up its right foot as though pointing to a certain location. Upon reaching the place, St. Clement made a little hole and praised God—and a spring of clear water appeared. The Pope suffered martyrdom about the year 100.

ST. JULIAN (d. 250), a native of Rome, was named the first

bishop of Mans. In the history of the church of Mans, we are told
that when he arrived to assume his responsibilities, Julian found the
city besieged. The inhabitants soon triumphed over the enemy, but
were greatly exhausted and in need of water. In this emergency and
before the eyes of all, St. Julian made an abundant spring gush forth
by planting his pastoral staff in the ground. This was regarded as a
miracle since the spot selected was wholly destitute of natural
springs. This marvel soon became known throughout the city, with
its citizens receiving him in triumph. He was given the greater part
of a palace to convert into a church, which eventually became the
first cathedral of Mans. St. Julian's spring still flows.

In ecclesiastical art the holy bishop is represented in pontifical
robes, planting his staff in the ground, with a woman at his feet filling her pitcher with water.[4]

ST. JULITTA (d. circa 303) was a very wealthy landowner of
Caesarea in Cappadocia who suffered martyrdom under Emperor
Diocletian. When she refused to offer sacrifice to Zeus she is said
to have exclaimed, "May my estates be ruined or given to
strangers; may I lose my life and may my body be cut in pieces,
rather than that by the least impious word I should offend God that
made me . . ." Butler reports that,

> the pagans were amazed to see a woman of her rank,
> age, and fortune, possessed of all the advantages neces-
> sary to please the world and in a condition to enjoy all
> that is most pleasurable in it, thus to repudiate her good
> fortune and life itself, with such heroic constancy.

After her death by smoke inhalation, St. Julitta was buried by the
Christian community. All we know of her is given by St. Basil in a
homily written about the year 375. In this work St. Basil reports that
her relics ". . . enrich with blessings both the place and those who
come to it." He also assures us that,

> the earth which received the body of this blessed woman
> sent forth a spring of most pleasant water, whereas all
> the neighbouring waters are brackish and salt. This
> water preserves health and relieves the sick.[5]

One of the first martyrs of Britain was ST. ALBANS (d. 304), who was a pagan living at Verulamium (now the town of St. Albans in Hertfordshire) when a cleric, fleeing for his life against persecutors of the Faith, took refuge in St. Albans' house. After a few days St. Albans was converted by his guest and received Baptism. When the persecutors came to examine the house, St. Albans dressed in the habit of his guest and took the cleric's place. After being dragged before the judge, he was scourged and ordered to pay homage to false gods. Bede the Venerable, writing in his *Ecclesiastical History of the English Nation*, reports that,

> When the judge perceived that he was not to be overcome by tortures or withdrawn from the exercise of the Christian religion, he ordered him to be put to death. Being led to execution, he came to a river which, with a most rapid course, ran between the wall of the town and the arena where he was to be executed. He there saw a multitude of persons of both sexes, and of several ages and conditions, who were doubtlessly assembled by Divine instinct, to attend the blessed martyr. Unable to cross the river by way of the bridge which was crowded, and desiring martyrdom, St. Albans stood before the river and prayed. Much to the surprise of all . . . the channel was immediately dried up, and he perceived that the water had departed and made way for him to pass.[6]

Astonished by the miracle, the executioner refused to perform his duty and fell at the Saint's feet, praying that he might suffer with the martyr—or, if possible, instead of him. When no one seemed inclined to execute him, St. Albans and some of the people ascended a nearby mount which tradition claims is Holmhurst Hill. Perhaps the climb encouraged a healthy thirst, since the Saint prayed for water while atop the mount and received a miraculous spring as a consequence.

It is reported that in spite of the two miracles, the Saint received the crown of martyrdom on the mount—his executioner being blinded as a result.[7] During Bede's time (d. 735) the place of the Saint's martyrdom was commemorated by a church and a shrine. The great abbey of St. Albans later rose on the same site.[8]

St. Athanasius, in his life of ST. ANTONY THE GREAT (d. 356), tells that while the Saint was living near the Red Sea he was invited by some monks to visit their monastery. Since there was no drinking water along the route, a camel was used to carry bread and water. After a time the supply of water gave out. Concerned for the welfare of his traveling companions, St. Antony walked a short distance from the caravan and knelt down to pray. Almost immediately a spring of water began to bubble from the ground through the goodness of God. All drank freely from the clear water and filled their vessels. The report states that the travelers continued their journey fully refreshed.[9]

ST. MARCELLINUS (d. circa 374) was an African priest who accomplished the Lord's work in the company of St. Vincent and St. Domninus. Feeling called to evangelize the people of Gaul, he was consecrated bishop by St. Eusebius of Vercelli, who established him as bishop of Embrun.

Arianism, a heresy that denied the divinity of Jesus, was encouraged by Emperor Constantius and was then becoming popular. Sending word to the Christians of Arles, Vienne and Beziers that they should repudiate this heresy, Marcellinus thereby brought persecution upon himself so that he was forced to hide for a lengthy time in the mountains. When Julian the Apostate succeeded Constantius, all orthodox prelates were permitted to continue their work, which Marcellinus did. He successfully Christianized the greater part of the Maritime Alps.

In the baptistry of the church in Embrun which St. Marcellinus built, miracles of healing were often reported. We are assured by St. Gregory of Tours (d. 594) and St. Ado of Vienne (d. 875) that even in their days the font in the baptistry would spontaneously fill to overflowing on Holy Saturday and Christmas Day with water that had healing properties.[10]

ST. SABAS (d. 532) was an outstanding figure among the early monks and was a great influence in the development of Eastern monasticism. Born in Caesarea in Cappadocia, he was left in the care of an uncle when his father, who was an army officer, was obliged to go to Alexandria with the rest of the family. Sabas was so harshly treated by the uncle's wife that he ran away to join the household of another uncle. Here, too, troubles became so intense that Sabas sought refuge in a monastery. Realizing that he was called to a life of seclusion, he placed himself under the spiritual direction of St. Euthymius.

Once when St. Sabas journeyed with St. Euthymius and a recluse named Domitian for their yearly retreat in the desert of Jebel Quarantal, where Jesus is said to have made His forty days' fast, St. Sabas collapsed from thirst. Butler tells us that,

> St. Euthymius moved with compassion, prayed to Christ that He would take pity of His fervent soldier, and it is said that, striking his staff into the earth, a spring gushed forth; of which Sabas drinking a little, recovered his strength.

We read again in the life of St. Sabas that after he founded a community of monks one of their first difficulties was the shortage of water. Butler again relates that, ". . . having noticed a wild ass pawing and nosing at the ground, Sabas caused a pit to be dug at the spot, where a spring was discovered which has subsisted to succeeding ages."

The chief monastery founded by St. Sabas is called after him Mar Saba. It still exists in a gorge of the Cedron, in the desert wilderness between Jerusalem and the Dead Sea. Among the many Saints who lived there was St. John Damascene. Mar Saba is one of the oldest occupied monasteries in the world and is peopled by monks of the Eastern Orthodox church. During his early manhood, Cyril of Scythopolis met St. Sabas and was so deeply impressed with him that he wrote a biography of the Saint. It is regarded as the most trustworthy of early hagiographical documents.[11] Butler reported that St. Sabas' spring was still flowing.

None other than Pope St. Gregory the Great (d. about 604), in writing about the miracles of ST. BENEDICT (d. 543), tells us in Book Two, Chapter 5 of the *Dialogues* how St. Benedict provided water for his disciples. St. Gregory writes:

> Three of the monasteries the Saint had built close by stood on the bare rocky heights (at Subiaco). It was a real hardship for these monks always to go down to the lake to get water for their daily needs. Besides, the slope

was steep and they found the descent very dangerous. The members of the three communities therefore came in a body to see the servant of God. After explaining how difficult it was for them to climb down the mountainside every day for their water supply, they assured him that the only solution was to have the monasteries moved somewhere else.

Benedict answered them with fatherly words of encouragement and sent them back. That same night, in company with the little boy Placid, he climbed to the rocky heights and prayed there for a long time. On finishing his prayer he placed three stones together to indicate the spot where he had knelt and then went back to the monastery unnoticed by anyone.

The following day, when the monks came again with their request, he told them to go to the summit of the mountain. "You will find three stones there," he said, "one on top of the other. If you dig down a little, you will see that Almighty God has the power to bring forth water even from the rocky summit and in His goodness relieve you of the hardship of such a long climb."

Going back to the place he had described, they noticed that the surface was already moist. As soon as they had dug the ground away, water filled the hollow and welled up in such abundance that today a full stream is still flowing down from the top of the mountain into the ravine below.[12]

A native of Ireland, ST. URSUS (d. sixth century) was made archdeacon of Aosta in northern Italy, where he labored against the Arian heresy. One hot summer day, he heard the rural men of Busseia complaining of thirst and emphasizing the need of a fountain in the neighborhood. The Saint was reminded of the words that all things are possible to him who believes. With faith in the power of God he struck the rock on which he was standing with his staff. Immediately water bubbled forth, which flowed in a stream called "St. Bear's Fountain."

Apparently the fountain was still producing water in the year 1290, since a notation in the chapter archives reads that: "One Jacquemet gave to St. Bear's church a parcel of land situated in the locality of St. Ursus' Fountain." In the cloister of the Collegiate, the Saint is represented on a marble column of the twelfth century which bears the inscription, *Fons S. Ursi.* In art St. Ursus is sometimes represented striking a rock with a staff.[13]

A miracle which is said by the Bollandists to be beyond dispute took place in Ireland after ST. FURSEY (d. 648) built a monastery at Lagny-en-Brie and became its abbot. In order to obtain a convenient supply of water, the abbot prayed first to God and then drove his staff into the earth. Instantly a fountain of water bubbled up which was sufficient not only for the needs of the monastery, but also that of the whole town. Healing powers were attributed to the water so that hundreds went to the fountain to be healed of various diseases and physical complaints. These pilgrims were especially numerous on Ascension Day. They formed a great procession during which the relics of St. Fursey were carried to the fountain. It is said that few of the early Irish Saints are better known to us than St. Fursey.[14]

From early childhood, ST. CUTHBERT (d. 687) is known to have performed many miracles, both before and after he entered the English abbey of Melrose. He is known to have obtained food miraculously, and it is to his credit that creatures of the land, sea and air paid him homage. He was tormented by devils, and he sowed a field with barley and received a plentiful harvest out of season; also, he had the gifts of prophecy and healing.

Bede the Venerable tells us that the man of God once felt drawn to live in retirement and built a small dwelling on a tiny island, with the help of a few brethren. Bede reports,

> The place was quite destitute of water, corn and trees; and very ill-suited for human habitation . . . After the man of God built himself a small dwelling, with a trench about it, and the necessary cells and an oratory, he ordered the brothers to dig a pit in the floor of the dwelling, although the ground was hard and stony, and no hope appeared of any spring. Having done this upon the faith and at the request of the servant of God, the next day it appeared full of water, and to this day affords plenty of its heavenly bounty to all that resort thither.[15]

Bede continues that,

> . . . there can be no doubt that it was elicited by the
> prayers of this man of God from the ground which was
> before dry and stony. Now this water, by a most remark-
> able quality, never overflowed its first limits so as to
> flood the pavement, nor yet ever failed however much of
> it might be taken out; so that it never surpassed or fell
> short of the daily necessities of him who used it for his
> sustenance.[16]

Sometime after this, St. Cuthbert was elevated to the episcopacy
of Lindisfarne. He is now counted among the Incorruptibles.

ST. PHARAILDIS (d. 740), a Belgian laywoman, is said to have
used her distaff to strike the side of a hill near Bruay, near Valenciennes, causing a fountain of fresh water to spring out of the
ground to relieve the thirst of the harvesters who were reaping for
her. The fountain is believed to have contained healing virtues,
especially for children's complaints, and so the Saint is invoked by
mothers who are anxious about the health of their little ones.[17]

One hot summer's day, Vargas the farmer, going into his fields,
was overcome with heat and thirst. Turning to ST. ISIDORE (d.
1172), a laborer, he asked if there was a spring in the vicinity.
St. Isidore directed him to a corner of the field, but the farmer
returned in anger, thinking the Saint had misguided him. According
to the Spanish biography of St. Isidore, what next took place is
attested by the very highest authorities. According to the biography,
St. Isidore told his master, "Come with me and I will show you the
spring." They walked to the place St. Isidore had formerly indicated, but when they reached the spot no water was seen. It was then
that St. Isidore pricked the dry earth with his ox-goad. Immediately
a clear spring bubbled up which was not only refreshing, but contained medicinal properties.
The spring still flows near Madrid in a full stream which has
attracted countless numbers of sick persons who visit it daily for the
relief of their infirmities. From the time of the miracle, St. Isidore's
fountain has been held in reverence, and its waters are kept in bot-
tles in case of sudden sickness.[18]

While on a journey to Mount Alverna, ST. FRANCIS OF ASSISI (d. 1226) became so tired that it was necessary for him to travel the rest of the way on a donkey provided by a peasant. Joining the Saint and his companions on the climb up the mountain, the peasant, after a time, began to suffer from the summer heat. Calling to St. Francis, he complained: "I am dying of thirst. If I don't have something to drink, I will suffocate." According to *The Little Flowers of St. Francis*:

> The Saint immediately got off the donkey and began to pray. And he remained kneeling on the ground, raising his hands toward Heaven until he knew by revelation that God had granted his prayer. Then he said to the peasant: "Run quickly to that rock, and there you will find running water which Christ in His mercy has just caused to flow from the rock." The man ran to the place which St. Francis had shown him, and found a very fine spring that had been made to flow through the hard rock by the power of St. Francis' prayer. And he drank all he wanted, and felt better. And it truly seems that that spring was produced by a divine miracle through the prayers of St. Francis, because neither before nor afterward was any spring ever seen there or anywhere nearby. After he had done this, St. Francis, with his companions and the peasant, gave thanks to God for having shown them this miracle. And then they traveled on . . .[19]

BL. CUNEGUNDA (Bl. Kinga) (d. 1279) had several relatives who are counted as Saints, including St. Elizabeth of Hungary and St. Elizabeth of Portugal. At the age of 15 she married Boleslaus, Duke of Cracow, who later became King of Poland. After his death she joined the Order of St. Clare and was in time elected abbess, governing her convent with prudence and maternal charity. Once when there was a scarcity of water and her community was suffering as a result, she pleaded with God to help them. Then she went to a neighboring brook and with her staff traced on the ground the path she would like it to take. The water flowed obediently to her convent.[20] A similar miracle was performed by St. Francis of Paola, as we will soon learn.

ST. COLETTE (d. 1447) became a spiritual daughter of St. Francis when she joined the Franciscan Third Order. At this time she took a vow of seclusion and lived for three years in a cell adjoining the church of Notre Dame in Corbie. After receiving a vision of St. Francis and St. Clare, she joined the Poor Clares and consulted the Pope about her heavenly directive to restore the Poor Clare order to its original severity. Many of the great religious orders, it would seem, experienced periods of heightened activity following their original founding. At one time or another, though, a degeneration of their original fervor was noted following the death of the founders or their immediate successors. With the Pope's permission St. Colette set about the reform with great courage and advanced rapidly in virtue. Besides restoring the order, she founded 20 new houses. The Poor Clares of the Colettine reform are now found in many parts of the world.

While visiting the nuns of the order at Poligny, St. Colette recognized their lack of a water source near the convent and set to praying. While listening to the Gospel reading of the Wednesday in the fourth week of Lent in which the Samaritan woman at the well said to Our Lord, "Give me this water," St. Colette is said to have cried out, "Lord, give me this water!" After a fervent prayer she walked outside and stopped at three places near the building. When each spot was marked with a Sign of the Cross she ordered the workmen to dig. Although the men were doubtful that water would be found, the three places produced clear springs of water which to this day are still providing water for the daughters of St. Francis.[21]

An unusual appearance of water is reported in the biography of BL. EUSTOCHIA OF PADUA (d. 1469). Almost immediately after her incorrupt body was removed from its grave, although the grave had been perfectly dry during the Saint's three-year interment, a fresh spring of water appeared.

"Many afflictions were cured or relieved for those who drank of it and great numbers of people journeyed there on pilgrimages." The water possessed the strange property of never overflowing the tub which had been built around it. Dr. Padre Giamamatteo Giberti kept a record of the miracles which occurred at the spring. His writing was later published as a book in Venice in 1672.[22]

The Saint who produced the most springs through the power of

God is undoubtedly ST. FRANCIS OF PAOLA (d. 1507), who is known as "God's Miracle Worker Supreme." His first well was produced when he was still a boy, after his father complained of thirst while working on the family's property.

Some years later, when the Saint was in the process of building his first monastery, the workers complained about having to travel too far for drinking water. On hearing this, the Saint prayed, struck a tufa rock with a stick, and immediately obtained water, which still flows. Called the *cucchiarella,* or ladle, the spring is now called the Fountain of Seven Canals and can be found near the Church of the Holy Rosary in Paola, Italy. The water is often given to the sick in a spirit of faith, with the prayerful conviction that it can restore them to health.

Another time, while St. Francis was building his fourth monastery, the workmen complained that water had to be carried from a spring that was some distance away. The Saint went to the spring with the workmen and after a few moments of prayer and a blessing, he addressed the spring in these words:

> "In the name of Charity, sister, follow me." The water then began to follow him in a shallow trench made by the Saint's walking stick. The water followed him for four miles until it reached the monastery, providing all the water that was needed. Later the stream was extended to the city, providing enough water for four fountains. The miracle was commemorated by giving the stream the name, "New Water of St. Francis of Paola."[23]

Again, while a monastery was being built in Sicily, a well was dug to provide drinking water for the workers, but the water proved to be salty. With a Sign of the Cross the water became sweet, but the Saint predicted that when the planned cistern would be completed to collect rainwater, the well water would again become salty, and so it did. All was not lost, however, since the salty water was discovered to contain curative elements.[24]

Still another extraordinary miracle is given which was also carefully witnessed. While the Saint was traveling to Lyons, he stopped at a village to ask for a drink of water. On learning that the area was then experiencing a severe drought and had no water, St. Francis of

Paola prayed and then struck the ground with his walking stick. Immediately fresh water gushed out which, in addition to providing drinking water for the village, also proved to have healing proper- ties—especially against fevers.[25]

When the first house of the Discalced Carmelite friars was being established, ST. TERESA OF AVILA (d. 1582) tells us in Chapter 14 of *The Foundations* that there was no well, but she adds: "I don't want to fail to mention the way, considered to be miraculous, in which the Lord gave them water." The Saint writes:

> One day after supper, while the prior, Fr. Fray Anto- nio, was talking in the cloister with his friars about the need for water, he rose and took a staff he was holding in his hands and made a Sign of the Cross on one part of it . . . (after walking outside) he pointed the stick and said: "Now, dig here." After they had dug only a little, so much water came out that it is now even difficult to drain the well so as to clean it. The water is very good for drinking and all that was needed for the remaining construction work was taken from there, and never, as I say, does the well empty out.[26]

An unusual situation has been noted in which springs have appeared where some saints were first buried, or in areas near their tombs. Such was the case regarding ST. OLAV (or St. Olaf) (d. 1030), who as a youngster joined a band of Vikings. Before the age of 20 he had fought for Richard of Normandy and for Ethelred II in England. About the year 1015, when he was 20 years of age, he succeeded his father, Harold Grenske, as King of Norway. Having already been baptized a Christian, he began the complete subjuga- tion of his realm to Christ.

Unfortunately, he was not content with exhortation, and used force without compunction to defeat heathenism and impose the Catholic Faith on his people. Because of this many rose up against him, until he was defeated with the help of Canute the Great, who was the King of England and Denmark.

With the help of the Russians, Olav tried to recover his kingdom but was slain by infidel subjects in a battle fought at Stiklestad, hav- ing reigned only fifteen years. He was buried in a steep sandbank by the river Nid, in the exact place where he had fallen, and there a spring rose of its own accord.

Because of this appearance, and the fact that Olav died for the Faith—although his efforts were regarded as extreme—he was nevertheless regarded as a martyr. Veneration of Olav became widespread when miracles were reported at the shrine that was built over the tomb. In time a large church was built, which was dedicated to Our Lord and St. Olav. This became the great cathedral of Nidaros.

* * * * *

The previous examples took place centuries ago, but here we have an example of a more recent miracle. The wonder-worker in this instance is ST. CLELIA BARBIERI (d. 1870), the foundress of the Order known as Suore Minime Dell'Addolorata, which took St. Francis of Paola as patron.

The miracle took place when preparations were being made for the construction of a convent for her order. But, unlike other Saints—who miraculously provided water while they were living— St. Clelia produced water after her death. Her biographer, Cardinal Gusmini, tells us about the miracle:

> Before setting about constructing the building they thought of sinking a well which was indispensable for supplying them with water, first for the actual construction and secondly for the community, since water was short in that part of the world. They got down to work with high hopes of finding water quickly, but despite the great depth, there was no water to be found. All their efforts were in vain. And then the sisters, concerned about this obstacle, interceded with their Foundress; and with great faith they dropped some hairs of Clelia's head, carefully bound together, into the well. A few hours later, to everyone's great surprise and consolation, the water came forth and so abundantly that they were able to draw it off by hand in buckets without needing chains or ropes. And this water still flows to this very day.[27]

Clelia Barbieri was canonized by Pope John Paul II in 1989.

Holy Water

The use of water for the purpose of spiritual purification is seen in the Old Testament. The Israelites were accustomed to purify cities, houses, persons and implements of war by sprinkling them with water. When a person died, he and the house were sprinkled. Newly married people were sprinkled and sacrifices were never made without it. Scarcely any undertaking was begun without lustration or ceremonial sprinkling, and a sprinkling was even made when the Romans took their census every five years. Thus a period of five years became known as a lustrum.

We read in the book of *Numbers* that God asked Moses and Aaron to make a sacrifice of a red heifer. The ashes of the heifer "may be reserved for the multitude of the children of Israel, and for a water of aspersion." *(Numbers* 19:9). The water was then used to purify unclean persons and objects.

Again Scripture recorded the words of God: "If any man be not expiated after this rite, his soul shall perish out of the midst of the church: because he hath profaned the sanctuary of the Lord, and was not sprinkled with the water of purification. This precept shall be an ordinance for ever." (*Numbers* 19:20-21).

Brewer tell us that the ancients:

> placed lustral water in a vessel at the door of their temples and all persons who entered the temple dipped their fingers in this sacred water and sprinkled themselves, that they might present themselves ceremonially clean. Lustral water was also placed at the entrance door of a house where a person lay dead.[28]

The Israelites' traditions have undoubtedly come down to Christian times with the use of holy water fonts at the doors of Catholic churches and our other ceremonial uses of blessed water, such as the Asperges before High Mass. Catholic holy water is a sacramental which, when used with faith, imparts God's blessing and provides protection from the powers of darkness.

One source relates that sometime during the early Christian centuries it became the custom for holy water to be kept at the back of churches, where an "introducer by water" sprinkled everyone who entered. Gradually those who entered were permitted to bless themselves from the holy water font found at the rear of churches. In addition to the sprinkling at the door, it was permitted that, "The people may carry some away in clean vessels so as to sprinkle their houses, fields, vineyards, and cattle." It was even recommended that the water be sprinkled over table food.[29]

During the fourth century there are various writings, "the authenticity of which is free from suspicion," which mention water sanctified either by a liturgical blessing or by the blessing of an individual of some holiness.[30] A number of these saintly men are named as having used blessed water to cure a number of ailments.

One of these Saints was THEODORE THE HOLY (d. 368), abbot of a community of holy recluses. The Saint worked a number of miracles, foretold things to come and worked other wonders. One of his miracles provides an early example of the use of blessed water as a sacramental for the healing of body and soul.

The event was recorded by a contemporary, St. Ammon, who tells that a man arrived at the monastery at Tabenna, asking St. Theodore to come and pray over his daughter who was gravely ill. Theodore was not able to go, but reminded the man that God could hear his prayers wherever they were offered. Disappointed, the man then produced a silver vessel of water and asked the Saint to at least invoke the name of God upon the water so that it might serve as medicine. Theodore prayed and made the Sign of the Cross over the water. On arriving home, the man found his daughter unconscious. Opening her clenched teeth, he poured some of the water down her throat. "And by virtue of the prayer of St. Theodore, the girl was saved and recovered her health."[31]

During the fifth and sixth centuries a special prayer was used for the blessing of oil and water during Mass. The prayer reads in part:

> We bless these creatures in the Name of Jesus Christ
> . . . we invoke upon this water and this oil the Name of
> Him who suffered . . . Grant unto these creatures the
> power to heal; may all fevers, every evil spirit, and all
> maladies be put to flight by him who either drinks these
> beverages or is anointed with them, and may they be a
> remedy in the Name of Jesus Christ, Thy only Son.[32]

ST. SAMSON (d. 565) gives us an early example of the healing power of holy water. One day he and several companions were sent to pull weeds in a wheat field. While they were occupied in this activity, a deadly serpent crept up to one of the companions and bit his leg. The death of the boy was said to be imminent, but the Saint poured oil into the wound and sprinkled the leg with holy water. The venom is said to have exuded drop by drop, thus preventing an excruciating death.[33]

Since it was permitted to bless vineyards and fields with holy water, this was done by ST. GUNTHIERN (sixth century) when worms were starting to eat the wheat in the fields of a distinguished personage. Worried that his vassals would suffer famine as a result, the landowner had applied to St. Gunthiern for a remedy. The Saint gave the messenger some holy water and instructed that it should be sprinkled over the fields. Immediately this was done. The worms disappeared as a result, and the crop was saved.[34]

ST. BEDE THE VENERABLE (d. 735) gives us another early example of the healing power of holy water in his *Ecclesiastical History of the English Nation*. The account features ST. CUTH-BERT (d. 687), a bishop who was traveling around his territory with fellow priests baptizing and administering the Sacrament of Confirmation. He at length came to the mansion of a certain earl whose wife lay dying. After expressions of hospitality, the earl

> besought him to consecrate some water to sprinkle on her . . . The man of God assented to his prayers, and having blessed the water which was brought to him, gave it to one of the priests, directing him to sprinkle it on the patient. He entered the bedroom in which she lay, as if dead, and sprinkled her and the bed, and poured some of the healing draught down her throat. Oh, wonderful and extraordinary circumstance! the holy water had scarcely touched the patient, who was wholly ignorant what was brought her, than she was so restored to health, both of mind and body, that being come to her senses she blessed the Lord and returned thanks to Him, that He thought her worthy to be visited and healed by such exalted guests.[35]

Another early example is mentioned in the life of ST. WILLI-
BROD (d. 8th century). A dreadful fever had infested the convent
of St. Irmina. Many of the nuns had died from it, and almost all
were affected by it.

St. Willibrod "was just at this crisis led by the hand of God to
visit this convent." When he arrived, St. Irmina implored him to lay
his hands on the sick that they might be restored to health. St.
Willibrod offered the Holy Sacrifice of the Mass and then sprinkled the sick with holy water, or gave it to them to drink. "And ere
that night the fever entirely abated, and all the sick were restored
to health."[36]

The benefits of using holy water as a curative were known to ST.
MALACHY (d. 1148), a native of Ireland who became the archbishop of Armagh.

Once when he was returning home after visiting the Pope, he
passed through Scotland, where King David "entreated him to heal
his son Henry, who lay dangerously ill." The Saint said to the sick
prince, "Be of good courage; you will not die this time." Then he
sprinkled him with holy water, and the next day Henry was perfectly recovered.[37]

In the thirteenth century we learn that ST. DOMINIC (d. 1221)
often used holy water for a number of reasons. We read that he was
once in the company of cardinals and nuns, who were conducting
business about the acquisition of a new convent, when they were
suddenly interrupted by a man who excitedly announced that "The
nephew of my lord Stephen has just fallen from his horse, and is
killed!" The young man's uncle,

> hearing him named, sank fainting on the breast of the
> blessed Dominic. They supported him; the blessed
> Dominic rose, and threw holy water on him; then, leav-
> ing him in the arms of the others, he ran to the spot
> where the body of the young man was lying, bruised and
> horribly mangled . . .

After celebrating Holy Mass, the Saint prayed by the body and
then commanded the young man to return to life, which he did.[38]

ST. VINCENT FERRER (d. 1419) was in Piedmont when the inhabitants of Montcallier complained to him that every year a tempest had ruined their vineyards. The Saint gave them some holy water and told them to sprinkle it on their vines. The effect is said to have been marvelous, "for when the tempest came, it did no harm whatever to the vines which had been sprinkled, whereas those vineyards which had not been sprinkled were ruined."[39]

We learn that ST. PAUL OF THE CROSS (d. 1775) had a relic of the Blessed Virgin (probably a medal or cross touched to a miraculous image). With this relic he is known to have blessed holy water and to have recited certain prayers in her honor. This water he gave to the sick for them to drink with devotion and confidence. Astonishing miraculous effects are said to have resulted. Many were instantaneously delivered from grave illnesses, and some, who were in a dying state, for whom the doctors could do no more, were delivered from death to life.[40]

Holy water, as we have seen, was very effective in curing ailments and restoring deathly ill people to health when it was used with faith and confidence, but holy water was known to the Saints for yet another purpose—to chase away demons.

As early as the seventh century ST. ACHARD (d. 687), then an abbot, would go through his abbey every night after all had retired to their cells and bless the dormitories with cross and holy water to ward off evil spirits.[41]

The efficacy of holy water was known to ST. TERESA OF AVILA (d. 1582), who used it on a number of occasions to dismiss demons. The Saint tells in her *Autobiography:*

> Once, when I was in an oratory, he (the devil) appeared on my left hand in an abominable form . . . I was very much afraid and made the Sign of the Cross as well as I could, whereupon he disappeared, but immediately returned again. This happened twice running and I did not know what to do. But there was some holy water there, so I flung some in the direction of the apparition, and it never came back.[42]

The Saint writes:

> From long experience I have learned that there is
> nothing like holy water to put devils to flight and pre-
> vent them from coming back again. They also flee from
> the Cross, but return; so holy water must have great
> virtue. For my own part, whenever I take it, my soul
> feels a particular and most notable consolation.

Once again the Saint writes that a devil was tormenting her:

> Then I sprinkled some in the direction of the place
> where the little demon was standing, and immediately he
> disappeared and all my troubles went, just as if someone
> had lifted them from me with his hand . . .

Another curious event took place after the Saint routed a demon:
two of her nuns entered her cell and "noticed a very bad smell, like
brimstone. I could not detect it myself, but it had remained there
long enough for them to have noticed it."[43]

ST. GERARD MAJELLA (d. 1755) also knew the effectiveness
of holy water, which he used to strengthen himself against the
assaults of demons who annoyed him on many occasions. After
their physical attacks, when the Saint was bruised all over with
blows, he used a few drops of holy water to instantly cure the
wounds.

The relics of the Saints were likewise the objects of his faith. He
even used the dust from the tomb of St. Teresa to cure the sick or
to prevent accidents.[44]

FR. PAUL OF MOLL (d. 1896), who was a visionary, mystic,
healer and is regarded as "The Wonder-Worker of the Nineteenth
Century," was displeased to see people entering church without
blessing themselves with holy water. To a gentleman who did not
stop to bless himself, the good priest said, "Take holy water; there
at least, the devil is not present."[45]

Holy water was used to bless the fields by ST. CHARBEL
MAKHLOUF (d. 1898) in the late nineteenth century when a

scourge of grasshoppers threatened the farm lands of his monastery in Lebanon. After the blessing, the insects departed.[46]

While ministering at Sacred Heart Friary in Yonkers, New York, VEN. SOLANUS CASEY (d. 1957) was often visited by people who consulted him about their problems or their sick relatives. His reputation as a holy priest was well known, especially three blocks from the monastery in a neighborhood of immigrant Italians who could not speak English. A little girl named Carmella Petrosino, a girl of the neighborhood who was about eight or nine years old, acted as interpreter for Fr. Solanus and would go with him from house to house, interpreting during Fr. Solanus' pastoral visits.

One day Mrs. Maria De Santo of the neighborhood was having a difficult time with a delivery. After the baby was born an infection set in, so that all concerned thought she might die. Little Carmella was sent to the monastery to ask Fr. Solanus to come and bless the mother. Carmella relates that she went "and told him that one of the ladies who just had a baby was going to die. So we started down the hill into the valley where we lived."

> As soon as Father came in, he asked for holy water. But they had no holy water. Fr. Solanus said, "Oh, poor, poor, poor." I ran over to our house and got some. When I came back he prayed over her, blessed her and from then on the woman got over her infection and lived a long time afterwards.[47]

The holy priest often used holy water in his blessings, with marvelous results. Fr. Solanus Casey, a native of Prescott, Wisconsin who died in Detroit, was declared Venerable in July of 1995.

THE SAINTS AND FIRE

Fire as an Early Indicator of Holiness

The future sanctity of ST. FRANCIS OF PAOLA (d. 1508) was indicated nine months before his birth when tongues of fire danced above the humble home of Giacomo and Vienna d'Alessio, a deeply religious couple who were childless after fifteen years of marriage. As the Saint's biographer relates,

> The neighbors, highly excited, called out the d'Alessios to see this strange phenomena. The d'Alessios were as puzzled as their neighbors. However, while they wondered at the dancing flame, they felt no fear. They saw it as a sign from God.[1]

The house in which the Saint was born was converted into a chapel during the Saint's lifetime. Known as Sanfrancischiello, the chapel was restored in 1940 and can be found in the district of Terravecchia. A miracle of another kind took place during World War II when the Sanfrancischiello miraculously survived destruction by bombing, even though all the other buildings in the area were destroyed.

Fires Defend the Faith

ST. DOMINIC (d. 1221) defended in a marvelous way the principles of our religion and the honor of Our Lord during the Albigensian heresy that flourished during the 12th and 13th centuries. This heresy, among other errors, denied the humanity of Christ. We are told that one day some of the heretics approached St. Dominic and proposed a challenge. Each side would put in writing the strongest defense of their cause; that of the Catholics would be the work of St. Dominic. Chosen as judges to decide the outcome were three persons whose sentiments were commonly known to favor the Albigensian view. After the arguments were heard, the three panel members refused to pronounce a decision. It was then that the heretics demanded a different form of trial—that of fire. Both books were to be committed to a fire so that God Himself would declare His choice. Bl. Jordan of Saxony, who succeeded St. Dominic in the administration of the order and who was the Saint's first biographer, writes:

> and the two volumes were cast therein; that of the heretics was immediately consumed to ashes; the other, which had been written by the blessed man of God, Dominic, not only remained unhurt, but was borne upward by the flames in the presence of the whole assembly. Again a second and a third time they threw it into the fire, and each time the same result clearly manifested which was the true faith, and the holiness of him who had written the book.[2]

This miracle is given, it is said, by every contemporaneous writer. It is also mentioned in the lessons for the Divine Office composed by Constantine Medici, Bishop of Orvieto, in 1254. Some years after the miracle, Charles le Bel, King of France, purchased the house where the event had taken place and converted it into a chapel under the patronage of St. Dominic. The large beam of wood on which the book had eventually fallen was preserved. Castiglio tells us in his account of the miracle that, "A few of the heretics were converted to the truth of our holy faith, but as to the rest, it produced no effect, this being the just reward of their great sins."[3]

In the life of ST. ANTHONY MARY CLARET (d. 1870) we read of an almost similar event with fire and a book. The Saint was for a time the Archbishop of Santiago, Cuba, and was the founder of an order known as the Claretian Fathers. He was also a prolific writer. One day in April, 1852, while a mission was being conducted in Balaguer, a missionary gave one of Fr. Claret's books entitled *Advice to Maidens* to a young servant girl who had been to Confession. Proud of her new treasure, especially since it was written by Fr. Claret, the girl returned home and showed her new possession to the master of the house, who immediately became infuriated. He snatched the book from her hands and replaced it with an obscene novel. The young girl reacted by brushing the novel aside with holy indignation. The master of the house reacted in a different way by throwing Fr. Claret's book into the fire, saying, "Thus I would do with the author, if I could." Much to their amazement, the live coals immediately burst into flames which spread into the room, burning the obscene novel, but protectively surrounding Fr. Claret's book, which remained unharmed. While the girl cried out that a miracle had taken place, the man fled from the house in terror. He sought out his friends and exclaimed, "Either my servant and the missionaries are demons, or they have a special protection of God." Unable to sleep that night because of the miracle, the man lost no time the next day in finding a priest to hear his Confession.[4]

Fire Defends a City

The Dominican BL. CESLAUS (d. 1242) founded convents and monasteries for Dominican religious in Prague and other parts of Bohemia. The house he founded in Breslau became his center of activities, and it was there in 1241 that the Tartars lay siege to the city. The friars prayed and fasted that the city would be spared, and when matters seemed darkest, a great miracle took place. Three years later St. Clare of Assisi would repel the Saracens by holding the Blessed Sacrament before them, but now Bl. Ceslaus would accomplish the same by holding before the Tartars the image of Christ crucified. Courageously mounting the ramparts with a crucifix in his hand, Bl. Ceslaus paused and held the crucifix before the enemy. Then, to the astonishment of all, "a great ball of fire descended from heaven and settled above him. Arrows of fire shot out from the heavenly weapon and the Tartars fled in terror, leaving the city unmolested."[5]

Saints and Heavenly Protection from Fire

ST. FRANCIS OF PAOLA (d. 1507), the founder of an order of friars known as the Minims, confronted fires on numerous occasions and took phenomenal control of them, demonstrating in this way his total confidence and reliance on God. When the new monastery was being built for his community, a furnace was constructed in which lime for mortar was to be prepared. When the furnace was completed a fire was started. It was then that workers noticed that some of the stones of the wall had shifted. With all speed they notified the Saint of the problem and expressed their fear that the furnace would collapse. The Saint assessed the situation, made the Sign of the Cross and, before the eyes of witnesses, entered the roaring flames. After a few moments he walked out completely unharmed by the fire. The furnace was repaired and is still standing beside the monastery on the outskirts of Paola, near the chapel of St. Mary of the Angels, which the Saint also built.

During the canonization hearings in 1519, eight different witnesses testified that they had seen the Saint enter the flames and withdraw totally unaffected by the fire.[6]

Another Saint who was protected from fire was ST. CATHERINE OF SIENA (d. 1380), whose life is told to us by her confessor, Bl. Raymond of Capua. As the daughter of a Sienese dyer of cloth, she at times helped in the shop, which contained many boiling cauldrons for the dyes. One day she was engaged in turning the spit when she fell into an ecstasy, as she often did. Lisa, her sister-in-law, saw this, replaced her at the spit and then later had to leave the room to do other chores, leaving Catherine still in ecstasy. When she returned to the shop area, she saw that the ecstatic Catherine had fallen over some live coals. Terrified that Catherine was severely burned, Lisa dragged her from the fire and discovered that neither Catherine's body nor her clothes were the least affected by the fire, although she must have been lying on the fire for several minutes.[7]

Another time Catherine was in the church of the Friar Preachers in Siena when she leaned her head against the lower part of a column on which a number of Saints were depicted. A votive candle located higher on the column unexpectedly fell on her head while she was in ecstasy. The candle continued to burn until all the wax was consumed and then went out, leaving the Saint and her veil uninjured, with no trace of wax or ash. This seems incredible, but Catherine's biographer, Bl. Raymond, reports that the incident was confirmed by credible witnesses including her companions Alexia, Francesca, and her sister-in-law, Lisa.[8]

We know about the incidents in which the sanctity of ST. FRANCIS OF ASSISI (d. 1226) tamed animals and birds. The Saint also tamed the heat of a fire when he was suffering from an infirmity of his eyes. The condition must have been severe, since he was persuaded to allow the services of a physician. When the doctor arrived he had with him a cauterizing iron and ordered it to be put in the fire. While waiting for it to become "red hot" the Saint spoke to his "brother the fire," asking that it would temper its heat so that "it would burn me gently."

After his prayer the doctor picked up the glowing iron. At that point "all the brothers, overcome by human weakness, fled." The Saint, for his own part, remained calm and gave himself willingly to the treatment. "The iron was plunged into the tender flesh with a hiss, and it was gradually drawn from the ear to the eyebrow in its cauterizing."

When notified that the treatment was completed the friars returned. Looking at them with a smile, the Saint remarked, "O faint-hearted and weak of heart, why did you flee? In truth I say to you, I did not feel either the heat of the fire or any pain in my flesh." Turning to the doctor, he said: "If my flesh is not sufficiently burned, burn it again."

The doctor, remembering how other patients had reacted to the cauterizing process, exclaimed: "I say to you brothers, I have seen wonderful things today."[9]

Fire and the Tomb

Fire is sometimes used by the Redeemer to signal the holiness of the deceased. Such was the case with BL. ANTONIO VICI OF STRONCONE (d. 1461), a humble Franciscan lay brother who advanced so rapidly in virtue he was assigned by his superiors to assist in the training of novices. In addition to this assignment, he helped the order by begging alms. He died at the age of eighty after spending sixty-eight years in the religious life and was buried in the common sepulchre beneath the flooring in the sanctuary of the Church of San Damiano.

A year minus one day after his death, a flame was seen burning brightly on the slab, a miracle that was accepted by St. James of the Marches as a sign from Heaven. An almost immediate exhumation was conducted which revealed the perfectly intact and sweetly perfumed body of the humble religious—a discovery that might not have been made had not the appearance of the flame alerted them.[10]

The Saints and Their Power over Fire

A medieval biographer tells of an incident in which holiness triumphed over destructive earthly forces in the life of BL. MARGARET OF CASTELLO (d. 1320), the dwarfed, blind and hunchbacked servant of God. The biographer explained that houses in Costello at that time were of wood, with roofs of wooden shingles or thatched straw. Built close together on narrow streets, they presented a fire hazard—especially in winter, when hearth fires were kept almost continually in operation against the Apennine cold. Because of the danger of fire leaping from one house to the other, a law was enacted that required every able-bodied man to respond at the very first indication of danger.

One wintry day the dreaded alarm was raised on the street of the Venturino home where Bl. Margaret had taken up residence. Men immediately responded. They dashed from the fountain and cisterns to the home in a desperate, but apparently hopeless effort. Fire was devouring the downstairs area and heading up timbers to the next level. Lady Gregoria, who was then returning home, expressed profound grief at the loss of her home, and then realized that Bl. Margaret was still upstairs. Margaret's name was shouted with a warning about the fire and a command to come down immediately, but Margaret stood at the top of the stairs in complete calm. She took off her mantle, rolled it up and threw it down with instructions to throw it into the fire. The medieval biographer reports that, "In the sight of the crowd of men who had rushed to the Venturino house to fight the blaze, when the cloak of Margaret was thrown into the flames, the raging fire was instantly extinguished."[11]

Not a cloak, but a relic similarly stopped a fire as recorded in a biography of ST. RITA OF CASCIA (d. 1457). This marvel did not take place during the lifetime of the Saint, but two centuries after her death. The fire took place in Narni on April 27, 1652, when the house belonging to Signora Clara Calderini caught fire. Because of the scarcity of water, all hope was abandoned that the house could be saved. But someone had a relic of St. Rita, a small piece of woolen cloth that had touched, not the body, but only the veil of the Saint. This small bit of woolen cloth was thrown into the flames with the immediate result that the fire was extinguished. This prodigy was witnessed by the officials of the city of Narni, who attested to the miracle in a document dated May 21 of the same year.[12]

BL. BONAVITA (d. 1375) was of humble birth and earned his livelihood as a blacksmith in the little Italian town of Lugo. We read: "Although his hands were black and sooty, he preserved his soul immaculately white and clean even from his youth. His life agreed with his name: *bona vita* meaning good life."

After joining the Third Order of St. Francis he advanced rapidly in virtue. He was generous to the poor and worked a number of miracles on their behalf, such as multiplying the food he was giving away and healing many sick persons by the Sign of the Cross. It was also by the Sign of the Cross that he once extinguished a fire in Lugo that had destroyed a number of homes and was continuing to spread. Bonavita was only thirty-seven years old when he died a most holy death.[13]

In addition to the heavenly protection given ST. FRANCIS OF PAOLA (d. 1507) in the fiery furnace as mentioned earlier, another miracle took place during the construction of a different monastery of the order when Bernardino Pugliano of Paterno set fire to a stand of trees and shrubs to clear his land. Suddenly a strong wind arose and whipped the flames, rapidly burning all the growth on Bernardino's property and threatening the monastery's adjoining property, where lumber for the new monastery was stacked. At that moment St. Francis of Paola was passing by and saw the danger threatening the lumber. Raising his hand he shouted, "Fire, in the name of Charity, burn what you are supposed to burn, but do not touch what is mine." Pugliano, who had stood nearby watching helplessly as the fire burned out of control, saw the flames quiet and smoulder out on the order of the Saint.[14]

An astounding miracle took place when St. Francis of Paola was dying, being then ninety-one years old. He had called together his brethren to give them final instructions and his last blessing. When he finished speaking the brazier that was used for the heating of the room suddenly burst into flames. The friars reacted by quickly moving away from the flaming heater, but the Saint got out of bed and walked over to the brazier and picked it up with his bare hands, saying to the astonished friars, "Be assured, my brothers, that it is not difficult for one who truly loves God to carry out what He wishes, which for me is holding in my hands this fire." While flames leapt around his hands and arms, some of the friars brought bricks to make a platform. The Saint then placed the brazier down and returned to bed, while the friars knelt down weeping and marvelling at what they had witnessed.[15]

TRIAL BY FIRE. The book in which St. Dominic defended the Faith is preserved, while the book favoring the Albigensian heresy is consumed by fire.

ST. FRANCIS OF PAOLA holds fire from a flaming brazier to show that "it is not difficult for one who truly loves God to carry out what He wishes."

—Part IV—

MARVELS OF EVERY SORT

Bl. Antonio Vici

St. Margaret of Cortona

St. Zita

Sts. Maurus, Benedict & Placidus

— 35 —

MARVELS OF EVERY SORT

The Holy Monograms

The first two letters of the name of Christ are represented in the Greek alphabet as X and P. Combined, one over the other, they form a monogram that is thought to have originated following a vision of the Emperor CONSTANTINE (d. 337), who was a pagan at the time of his vision.

Constantine was forced to claim his rightful position as Caesar and to defend his honor against a rival named Maxentius. With an army of between 25,000 and 100,000 men, he marched toward Rome to do battle against Maxentius, whose army numbered 200,000. Sometime during the march, Constantine saw in the sky a cross surrounded by a brilliant, fiery light. Inscribed on the cross were the Latin words, *In Hoc Signo Vinces*: "By this sign thou shalt conquer."

Deeply impressed with this vision, Constantine had the standards of his soldiers altered to bear not only a cross, but also the holy monogram. Strengthened by the vision and the numerous symbols of his Creator, he continued the march to meet an overwhelming number of enemy troops. The confrontation took place at the Milvian Bridge that spanned the Tiber River.

Maxentius and his many soldiers were soundly defeated, and in gratitude to the God of the Christians, Constantine issued the Edict of Milan, by which the persecution of Christians was stopped. He was later converted on his deathbed.[1]

Eleven hundred years later, another monogram became prominent, this time during the lifetime of ST. BERNARDINE OF SIENA (d. 1444). Known for his many travels and his brilliant sermons, he attracted crowds of people and it was among them that he, together with St. John Capistran, popularized the sacred monogram, IHS, that had originated much earlier. This symbol represents the first three Greek letters of the Holy Name of Jesus.

A popular sign of respect by which the devout greeted the clergy

527

at that time was the kissing of the hands that consecrated the Holy Species. In his humility, Bernardine resisted this display and devised a system to thwart it. He had a small, hand-held tablet made on which was painted the monogram, surrounded by rays. It was this tablet he offered for the usual kiss of respect.

While on a preaching visit to Bologna, where the people were given to games of chance, St. Bernardine persuaded the citizens to resist gambling and provided for them a public bonfire in which they threw their dice and cards. When a card manufacturer complained about his loss of trade, St. Bernardine persuaded him to manufacture tablets inscribed with the holy symbol, IHS. The demand for these cards was so great that he actually made more money than ever before.[2]

From Constantine to St. Bernardine and to the present day, the holy monograms remain popular symbols of the Holy Name of Jesus Christ.

Mystical Pellets

We have read in the chapter "Mystical Hearts" about the figures of Our Lord's Passion that were found in the heart of ST. CLARE OF MONTEFALCO (d. 1308). During the same examination of her body following her death, three pellets were found in the gall of the Saint. According to information from the shrine,

> These pellets, about the size of hazel nuts, were judged by theologians to be symbols of the Trinity, as it was found that any one of them was as heavy as the other two, while at other times any one of them equalled the weight of all three together. The pellets can be seen under circular crystals in a jeweled cross that is kept in the Church of the Holy Cross in Montefalco.[3]

Whether or not the three pellets still possess this remarkable property is unknown.

The Ship in the Shrine

A miraculous image of Our Lady is enshrined in the Mercedarian church which is located in the city of Cagliari on the island of Sardinia. Dangling on a string before the statue is a small ivory sailing ship which was given to Our Lady in 1592. The history of the ship is as follows. A pilgrim on his way to the Holy Land was forced to abandon his journey at Cagliari. He had with him a little ivory ship that was carved in one piece. He had intended to leave the ship at the Holy Sepulchre as an ex-voto in thanksgiving for a favor received, but offered it instead to Our Lady of Bonaria and had it hung from the ceiling on a string.

The shrine of the miraculous image was, and is still, located above and behind the high altar in a recess. Pilgrims are permitted to pray beside the statue and reach it by a narrow stairway. After pausing to offer their prayer they descend by a stairway on the opposite side. The little ship in the shrine is far removed from drafts and the air currents on the sea; nevertheless, it was noticed that, from time to time, the ship was aimed in a different direction. The mystery was solved when it was demonstrated that the little ship pointed in the direction of the wind on the high seas. Experiments were made to test the theory, which proved to be correct.

The unusual movements of the little ship became well known and proved to be of exceptional interest to seamen. Since that time sailors have offered dozens of other tiny ships and pictures to Our Lady in thanksgiving for safe passages and in petition for her heavenly protection.[4]

A Long-Distance Connection

The stigmatic, ST. CATHERINE DEI RICCI (d. 1590), had many mystical gifts, especially one that is rarely mentioned in the lives of the Saints. This gift consisted in the privilege of conversing frequently with St. Philip Neri while he was in Rome and she in her convent at Prato. Although they had exchanged a number of letters, the two Saints never met, except through their mystical visits. St. Philip Neri readily admitted that the conversations took place. Additionally, five reputable people swore they had witnessed some of the communications.[5]

Long-Distance Voices

ST. VINCENT FERRER (d. 1419) is mentioned elsewhere in this book as having had the gift of tongues. Butler reports that the native tongue of the Saint was Limousin and that he had learned only a little Latin and Hebrew, but "We have it on the authority of reliable writers that all his hearers, French, Greeks, Germans, Sardinians, Hungarians and Italians understood every word he spoke."

The Saint traveled a great deal preaching the word of God in many lands and often in open places. It is said, again on the word of reliable witnesses, that his voice could be heard at enormous distances—distances at which the normal voice could not possibly be heard.

During these travels, and while visiting Bologna, he asked to see the celebrated preacher, BL. PETER GEREMIA (d. 1452). St. Vincent Ferrer congratulated him on the work he was doing in saving souls, and urged him to continue his preaching which God had so wonderfully blessed. As a Dominican, Bl. Peter was known as one of the finest preachers of the order. He often spoke in public squares, just as St. Vincent did, because all the churches were too small to hold the crowds that flocked to hear him. Again, like St. Vincent Ferrer's, Bl. Peter's voice was carried to great distances, often as far as half a league—a league being, according to the country, between 2.4 and 4.6 miles.

These facts regarding Bl. Peter are given us by one of his brethren who lived with him in the same monastery and was witness to the marvel.

Multiplication of Another Sort

We have already examined the ways in which food and money were multiplied. We will now consider a phenomenon concerning the mysterious multiplication of books.

The Saint in this case is ST. PHILOMENA (d. Roman era). The miracle worked by her involves her biography, which is described as a short narrative of the principal events of her history, written by the priest Don Francisco di Lucia. The little booklets proved to be immensely popular. Finally realizing that he would like to have a number of copies for his private distribution, the author wrote to Naples, asking for some of the copies. He was sent 221 books, which he placed on a table in five little stacks. He covered four of the stacks, so as to protect them from dust.

For five or six months he continued to distribute booklets from the uncovered stack, without realizing that he was taking from the stack more little books than it originally had contained.

On returning to his room one evening, he unlocked the door and was shocked to see booklets scattered all over the floor. At first he thought that perhaps St. Philomena was not pleased with what he had written, but then the good priest began to investigate. He uncovered the four stacks of books and found that each contained forty-five books—the exact number he had originally arranged. The fifth stack, from which he had already taken so many hundreds, still numbered nineteen copies. He then checked his accounts and found that he had taken from the one uncovered stack some 500 copies. The booklets on the floor numbered seventy-two. A prodigious mystery! It would seem, however, that the Saint wanted more booklets distributed so that she would be better known. In this way she would be able to use her intercessory powers to help more of God's children on earth.[6]

Fr. O'Sullivan, who also wrote a biography of St. Philomena, declares:

> Never have I seen a sanctuary so full of wonders, so alive with the atmosphere of the supernatural, where one sees so palpably heavenly manifestations, as in Mugnano. I do not mean to claim greater things for it than for other sanctuaries, but, as the dear Little Saint's special prerogative seems to consist in her amazing power of miracles and in the extraordinary abundance of favors which she so generously dispenses to her clients, so her sanctuary is especially distinguished for the constant, visible and striking signs which the Almighty is pleased to work in it.[7]

Heavenly Loaves

Many miracles regarding the multiplication of food during a famine are attributed to ST. ZITA (d. 1278), the patroness of domestic workers. A miracle of a different kind took place one day when she spent more time in church than was her custom. When she realized that it was baking day and that she had much to do before the loaves of bread were prepared for baking, she hurried home. On entering the kitchen, she found loaves of miraculously prepared bread neatly placed in rows, ready for placement in the oven.

St. Zita served the same family for forty-eight years. When she died at the age of sixty, she was deeply mourned by all who had made her acquaintance.[8]

Another baker was ST. CATHERINE OF BOLOGNA (d. 1463), a

member of the Poor Clare Order who served her community for many years in that capacity. The Saint one day had just placed loaves of bread in the oven when the convent bell rang to alert the nuns that Br. Albert, the Franciscan provincial, was about to deliver a sermon. Before leaving the oven, Catherine made the Sign of the Cross and commended the loaves to the protection of God. She left the bakery and entered the chapel to hear a sermon that occupied exactly five hours of time. Afterwards, when Catherine returned to the bakery, she opened the oven. After five hours of baking, the loaves should have been burned to cinders, but instead, the bread was of a beautiful brown color, more beautiful than normal. It is recorded that after the Saint's death the oven emitted a wonderfully sweet perfume ten days before each of her feastdays and for several days after.[9]

Crosses upon the Chest

Dressed as a pilgrim in a coarse habit, ST. ROCH (d. circa 1327) traveled from his native Montpellier to nurse the sick during a plague in Italy. From there he went to many other countries, curing many, both human and animal, through his prayers and the Sign of the Cross. At Piacenza he was infected with a disease contracted from the sick he was tending, but rather than burden a hospital with his care, he retreated to the woods to die. There he was fed by a dog who brought him scraps of bread from his master's table. Finding that the dog routinely carried bread out of doors, his master, a man named Gothard, followed and discovered the Saint, whom he nursed to health and from whom he gained the Faith.

After returning to the city of Piacenza St. Roch nursed the sick for a time before returning to Montpellier, where a war was in progress. Undoubtedly his intention was to assist the wounded, but instead he was taken prisoner as a spy and spent the last five years of his life in miserable circumstances.

The Saint was well known for his sanctity and healing powers, but he apparently did not disclose his identity to his jailers and fellow prisoners, or perhaps they did not believe him, since his identity was only confirmed after his death when a cross-shaped birthmark was discovered on his chest.

The popularity of the Saint after his death grew rapidly, since as many miracles were worked then as were performed during his lifetime. He is accepted by the Franciscans as one of their tertiaries and is honored by them on August 17.[10]

In art St. Roch is readily identified by the dog that is always at his side.

Another, even more spectacular symbol is mentioned in the biographies of ST. JULIANA FALCONIERI (d. 1341). The founding of the religious order known as the Servants of Mary (Servite Order) is credited to St. Philip Benizi, who wrote their constitution, but St. Juliana is honored by all the women religious of the order as their foundress. She lived fifty-six years as a member of the order. On her deathbed an astonishing miracle took place that was properly witnessed and recorded.

Said to have impaired her health by her strict mortifications, she was unable to retain food and was not permitted to receive the Holy Eucharist because of this difficulty. When she believed that she would be denied the Eucharist before she died, she begged Fr. James de Campo Regio to bring the Holy Sacrament to her. When It arrived in her room, her face is said to have become angelic. She then asked that a veil be placed on her chest and that the Sacred Host be placed there as a final consolation. This was permitted, but:

> Scarcely had the Host touched this loving heart than it was lost to sight and never more was found. Then Juliana, when the Host had disappeared, with a tender and joyous face, as if she were rapt in ecstasy, died in the kiss of her Lord, to the amazement and admiration of those who were present—to wit, of Sr. Joanna, Sr. Mary, Sr. Elizabeth, Fr. James and others of the house.

A document still in existence testifies to the disappearance of the Host, but this was not the only miracle that took place. There was another that also merited widespread attention.

One of the witnesses, Sr. Joanna Soderini, succeeded the foundress in her office as superior general. In a biography of Sr. Joanna, Servite Father Nicholas Mati wrote, about the year 1384, that as the body of St. Juliana had been prepared for burial many years previous,

> She (Sr. Joanna) was the happy disciple who, sooner than Sr. Elizabeth or the others, discovered upon the breast of St. Juliana that astounding marvel of the figure

of Christ nailed to the Cross impressed upon her flesh within a circle like a Host.[11]

A cross, but one of a different kind, was mentioned even before the birth of ST. CAMILLUS DE LELLIS (d. 1614). The Saint's mother is said to have had a vision in which she saw a child with a red cross on his chest and a standard in his hand, leading other children who bore the same sign. This was fulfilled in a unique fashion some years later when St. Camillus founded the Order of Ministers of the Sick in 1586. After receiving papal approval for the order, the Saint asked permission to wear on the front of their black habits the symbol of a red cross.[12]

This symbol, indicating help to the sick and suffering, was therefore first used in the sixteenth century, two centuries before the Swiss businessman Henri Dunant first conceived the idea of an organization of volunteers—the Red Cross—to help in times of war and disasters. Representatives from fourteen countries met in Geneva in 1864 and adopted a treaty called the Geneva Convention. As a symbol of the organization, and in honor of the Swiss Henri Dunant, the flag of Switzerland was reversed from a white cross on a red field to a red cross on a white field.

Canonized in 1746, St. Camillus de Lellis was given a triple designation by Pope Leo XIII and Pope Pius XI, being named the patron of the sick, of nurses and of hospitals. Members of his order still wear a red cross on the front of their habits.[13]

The Color of Love

ST. THERESA MARGARET OF THE SACRED HEART (Anna Maria Redi) (d. 1770) was a Discalced Carmelite nun of the Florence monastery who displayed an unusual sign of her love for God. According to the monastery annals,

> So intense would the fire of her love of God become that her countenance would be inflamed, then change color, becoming almost crimson at first, then purplish, finally ash-pale like that of a corpse. Once when she was holding with another nun the kind of spiritual discourse that occasioned this phenomenon, she fell in a dead faint after the three changes of color.[14]

It is understood that the three color changes of the Saint were a common occurrence.

The Miraculous Sun

Never before or since has a mystic been favored as was BL. ANNA MARIA TAIGI (d. 1837), a wife and the mother of seven children amid poor and trying circumstances. Shortly after her marriage to temperamental Domenico Taigi, she was favored with the mystical sun which the Decree of Beatification called a "prodigy unique."

The Decree also states:

> Among other gifts the most remarkable was that for a space of forty-seven years she saw a kind of sun in whose light she described things at hand and things afar off, foresaw future events, scrutinized the secrets of hearts and the most hidden and most inward impulses.

She received the favor while walking along a little back street of the Sdrucciolo. It was then that

> Anna saw a luminous, miniature sun that maintained a position before her. Above the upper rays was a large crown of interwoven thorns with two lengthy thorns on either side curving downward so that they crossed each other under the solar disc, their points emerging on either side of the rays. In the center sat a beautiful woman with her face raised toward heaven. In this vision Anna Maria saw things of the natural, moral and divine order and could see present or future events anywhere in the world, as well as the state of grace of living individuals and the fate of those departed.[15]

Cardinal Pedicini, a frequent visitor to Anna Maria's home, in telling about the countless wonders that she saw in her miraculous sun was quick to state: "Nor let anyone think I am exaggerating, for, on the contrary, I find myself incapable of describing the wonders of which I was for thirty years the witness."[16]

Because of her sanctity and mystical gifts, Anna Maria was visited by countless humble folk as well as distinguished persons of the Church including Pope Leo XII, Pope Gregory XVI, Cardinal Fesh and several holy souls who were later declared Saints of the Church.

S.A.G.—St. Anthony Guide

Those who know the meaning of the initials "S.A.G." and why they became popular often mark them on envelopes, thereby placing the letters under the protection of ST. ANTHONY OF PADUA (d. 1231), whom they trust will get them safely to their proper destination. The origin of the practice is this: A Spanish merchant named Antonio Dante left Spain for South America in 1729 to establish a business in Lima, Peru. His wife, who remained in Spain, wrote a number of letters to him without receiving a reply. In great distress and with the utmost simplicity, she brought a letter with her to the Church of St. Francis at Oviedo. In the church was a large statue of St. Anthony, and it was in his outstretched hand that she placed a letter to her husband. Her prayer of confidence was: "St. Anthony, I pray thee, let this letter reach him and obtain for me a speedy reply."

The next day she returned to the church and saw that her letter was still there. Weeping in frustration that her letter had not been delivered, she attracted the attention of the Brother sacristan, who listened to her story. Afterward, he told her that he had tried to remove the letter but could not, and he asked the lady if she would try to remove it. This she did with ease. The letter was not the one placed there the day before, but a letter from her husband. Immediately, three hundred golden coins fell from the sleeve of the statue. A number of the friars were alerted to the scene and waited while the miraculous letter was opened. The letter was dated July 23, 1729 and read:

> My dear wife. For some time I have been expecting a letter from you, and been in great trouble at not hearing from you. At last your letter has come, and given me joy. It was a Father of the Order of St. Francis who brought it to me. You complain that I have left your letters unanswered. I assure you that when I received none I believed you to be dead. So you may imagine my happiness at the arrival of your last one. I answer by the same religious, and send you three hundred golden

crowns, which will suffice you for your support until my approaching return. In the hope of soon being with you, I pray God for you, and I commend myself to my dear patron St. Anthony, and ardently desire that you may continue to send me tidings of yourself. Your most affectionate, Antonio Dante.

The original letter, written in Spanish, is preserved at Oviedo.[17] In memory of this event, the practice of writing S.A.G. (St. Anthony Guide) on letters became widespread. Little stamps were also manufactured, and still are, which display a likeness of St. Anthony and the three letters. These stamps are affixed to letters placed under the Saint's protection.

The Medal of St. Benedict

One of the most powerful medals one can wear is the medal on which St. Benedict is depicted holding a cross in one hand, his book of rules in the other. The reverse has a cross on which are letters, and surrounding it, other letters which stand for prayers such as "May the Holy Cross Be my Light." Other letters represent words that seek the protection of Our Lord and St. Benedict against the devil.

The medal is highly indulgenced, and its history is rendered extraordinary by a profusion of miracles.

One example of its effectiveness is mentioned in the life of BL. MARY FORTUNATA VITI (d. 1922). One time in the Benedictine convent of which she was a member, the sisters were busy making wine and putting it into casks. Unknown to them, one of the casks was defective, its ribs being imperfectly fitted. As a result, as soon as the cask was filled, wine began pouring out. In vain they tried to seal the leaks until, in the midst of the confusion, Sr. Fortunata encouraged them to have confidence in God. Then, taking a medal of St. Benedict, she made the Sign of the Cross with it over the cask and cried out three times: "Power and love of God, have mercy on us!" Instantly the flow of wine stopped and the fissure in the cask closed.[18]

It is recommended that medals of St. Benedict be blessed by a Benedictine monk using the specially prescribed prayers. It is also suggested that the medals be worn, placed in automobiles and on the doors and windows of our homes. When using the medal for any pious purpose, the following prayer may be said:

> May the intercession of the Blessed Patriarch and
> Abbot Benedict render Thee, O Lord, merciful unto us;
> that what our own unworthiness cannot obtain we may
> receive through his powerful patronage. Through Christ
> our Lord.[19]

The Fire of St. Brigid

Many miracles are credited to ST. BRIGID OF KILDARE (d.
525), the foundress of several convents in her native Ireland. What
we relate here is not necessarily a miracle, but a tradition maintained by her convent of nuns. This is known as the fire of St.
Brigid, which was regarded as inextinguishable—not that it could
not be put out, but because the nuns were so anxious and punctual
in keeping it ablaze.

Six centuries after the death of St. Brigid, Giraldus Cambrensis
collected some traditions that were observed at Kildare. He wrote:

> . . . Whereas in the time of Brigid twenty nuns here
> served the Lord, she herself being the twentieth, there
> have been only nineteen from the time of her glorious
> departure . . . But as each nun in her turn tends the fire
> for one night, when the twentieth night comes, the last
> virgin having placed the wood ready, saith, "Brigid, tend
> that fire of thine, for this is thy night." And the fire
> being so left, in the morning they find it still alight and
> the fuel consumed in the usual way. That fire is sur-
> rounded by a circular hedge of bushes, within which no
> male enters, and if one should presume to enter as some
> rash men have attempted, he does not escape divine
> vengeance.[20]

No reports are given as to when the fire was eventually extinguished—or perhaps it is still burning?

Preservation from Fire

We read in the life of the great ST. DOMINIC (d. 1221) that he
arrived in the city of Segovia, where he intended to establish his
first foundation, and lodged for a time in the house of a poor

woman. While staying there the Saint laid aside a hairshirt in exchange for one of a coarser material. Apparently the woman tidied his room or did his laundry, since she secretly took possession of the cast-off as a relic of the man all were acclaiming to be a saint. Sometime later, after the Saint had apparently moved to other accommodations, the house caught fire. It is reported that everything was burned except the box that contained the precious relic. The miraculous preservation made it seem fitting to place it in a more suitable location, and it is said that it was long preserved among the relics at the monastery of Valladolid.[21]

Imagine the Joy

After the death of ST. ANTHONY OF PADUA (d. 1231), the miracles worked at his tomb were so "prodigious" that the Bishop of Padua petitioned the Vatican for his canonization. A judicial inquiry was instituted without delay, and by an exception regarded as unparalleled in history, Pope Gregory IX, on May 30, 1232, solemnly pronounced the decree of canonization, only eleven months after Anthony's death.

His mother and two sisters who survived him had the extraordinary privilege of witnessing the ceremony and joining in the festivities that followed the announcement.[22]

The mother of ST. MARIA GORETTI (d. 1902) enjoyed the same privilege.

Maria was, of course, the twelve-year-old girl who was brutally stabbed while protecting her virginity. She was canonized in 1950 by Pope Pius XII. Her mother, Assunta, had the joy of witnessing her daughter being raised to the honors of the altar and being proclaimed the model of purity.

Also attending the ceremony were Maria's four siblings, two brothers and two sisters. One of the Saint's sisters joined the Franciscan Missionaries and is known as Sr. Maria Alexandra. Her brother Angelo, who discovered the wounded Maria, lived for many years near Washington, New Jersey.

St. Maria Goretti was honored by a visit of Pope John Paul II in 1979 when he journeyed to Nettuno to visit the little Saint's relics. At that time he exhorted young people to look upon Maria as an example of purity to be emulated in our permissive society.[23]

A Wonderful Support

When the church of St. Maria in Vallicella was given to ST. PHILIP NERI (d. 1595) and his community, there were many debates whether or not it should be repaired or torn down, since it was half buried in the ground and in great need of restoration. The Saint finally decided to demolish it and build anew. Left standing was one corner that was to be a chapel for the Blessed Sacrament and an ancient image of the Madonna. Early one morning St. Philip ordered that the roof of this corner should be torn down at once, explaining that during the night he had seen the Madonna supporting it with her hand, when it would otherwise have fallen. When the workmen went to remove the roof "it was found that the principal beam had in fact come out of the wall, and was suspended without visible support in the air."[24]

Weighed in the Balance

At an early age BL. WILLIAM OF TOULOUSE (d. 1369) joined the Hermits of St. Augustine. After ordination he became a celebrated preacher, a director of souls and a great promotor of prayer for the Holy Souls in Purgatory. One day a wealthy woman visited William with a bag of gold, asking him to pray for her deceased relatives. William prayed fervently: "Eternal rest give to them, O Lord; and let perpetual light shine upon them. May they rest in peace." Apparently that was all he was going to offer, since the woman is reported to have been very disappointed and to have voiced the opinion that she expected more for the gold. The holy priest then suggested that she write down his prayer on a piece of paper and weigh it in a balance with her bag of gold. This she did. Needless to report, the scale with the prayer fell, while the bag of gold was at the highest point the scale permitted. Apparently it is not only the saintly person who says the prayer that makes it of great value, but the love and fervor with which it is said.[25]

Healing Oils

The oil that burns in lamps before certain images has been used by various Saints with beneficial results.

ST. THERESA MARGARET REDI (d. 1770) used oil that burned before Our Lady's shrine to anoint various sisters of her community, with the result that all felt better and some were cured instantly. BL. ANNA MARIA TAIGI (d. 1837) also used oil that burned before an image of the Blessed Mother to cure many afflictions. BL. GERARD CAGNOLI (d. 1345) performed many miracles of healing by anointing the sick with the oil that burned in a lamp before a little shrine of his patron, St. Louis. ST. CLELIA BARBIERI (d. 1870) worked wonders with the oil that burned before the portrait of St. Francis of Paola, the patron of her community. BL. ANDRÉ (d. 1937), of St. Joseph's Oratory on Mount Royal, routinely used oil that burned in the lamp before a statue of St. Joseph to cure many diseases and injuries. Likewise, the oil of the lamps that constantly burn before the tomb of St. Rita manifests healing properties when applied to afflicted areas. Finally, the oil of ST. PHILOMENA (d. Roman era) that is blessed with a relic of the Saint has also proved to be beneficial.

Poison Gas in the Thirteenth Century?

We read in the life of ST. HEDWIG (d. 1243) that her son, Duke Henry II of Poland, led his army against the Mongol Tartars in the year 1240.

The greater part of the battle was fought near Wahlstätt, a battle in which it was charged that the Tartars used a kind of poison gas, since "a thick and nauseating smoke, issuing from long copper tubes shaped like serpents, stupefied the Polish forces." Unfortunately, Henry was killed in the course of the battle. St. Hedwig is said to have been spiritually informed of his death three days before the news was brought to her.[26]

The Cross and the Bloody Stone

After Pentecost, ST. THOMAS THE APOSTLE (d. circa 72) is known to have traveled extensively in spreading the Faith, and to have eventually made his way to India. It is believed that he died eight miles outside Madras, near the shore of the Bay of Bengal, by being pierced by the sword of a pagan. Located on the spot of execution is a stone engraved with a cross that was seen to ooze blood on December 18, 1558, and to have continued on that day each year with various interruptions until the year 1704.

The phenomenon first took place during the offering of Holy Mass and lasted four hours. Diocesan officials certified that at the end of the bleedings the stone turned a glistening white before returning to its original black.[27]

The Relic and the Mysterious Heat

Twenty-four years after the death of ST. MARTIN DE PORRES (d. 1639), his remains were exhumed for placement in a more honorable tomb. Although his remains seemed to be incorrupt, and all agreed that he looked very lifelike since the skin was unchanged, the bones were easily disjointed. During this exhumation, the superior announced that the taking of relics was forbidden since the Church had not yet given permission for doing so. But before placing the disjointed members of the Saint's body in a new casket, one of the religious secretly removed a rib of the Saint and hid it under his habit. Immediately he detected an excessive heat on his chest where the bone had been placed. Fearful that his theft of the relic might be discovered, he endured the heat until he managed to reach his cell.

During the night, the strange heat radiating from the stolen relic increased to such an extent that the friar became stricken in conscience and rushed to the superior to confess—and to surrender the ill-gotten bone. Before doing so, he apparently felt there was no harm in retaining a small piece and detached a fragment for his personal veneration. But once again, the heat coming from the small portion of bone returned until he could no longer endure it or the mysterious trembling that afflicted him. Once again he approached Fr. Juan de Barbaran to surrender the last vestige of his theft. The biographer of Bl. Martin reports that afterward, the friar was entirely relieved. The biographer continues: "Thus Blessed Martin kindly, yet firmly, taught him the salutary lesson of obedience and respect for the Seventh Commandment of God."[28]

They Learned to Read and Write

BL. ANNE OF ST. BARTHOLOMEW (d. 1626) was a peasant girl, the daughter of poor village laborers, who entered the convent of St. Teresa of Avila as its first lay sister. Since few peasant children of the time had access to teachers or schools, we can understand that she had little or no education. William Thomas Walsh, in his biography of St. Teresa, reports that Anne learned "to write miraculously by merely copying La Madre's (St. Teresa's) letters."[29] Butler adds that "She had signed her own profession with a simple cross."[30] She later became St. Teresa's constant companion and her secretary. Butler tells that at this time "she now found herself miraculously able to write. It may be that the gift of letters was bestowed upon her with other wisdom when she was about to be faced with new responsibilities."[31]

St. Teresa of Avila died in the arms of Sr. Anne of St. Bartholomew, who wrote an account of the Saint's death and burial. Under holy obedience Bl. Anne wrote her own autobiography and founded houses of the order.

It seems strange to report that the great ST. CATHERINE OF SIENA (d. 1380), early in her religious life, was still illiterate. For a long time she had wished to read the breviary, but despite her eagerness to learn and the lessons given by Alessia Saracini, she was unreceptive. Finally the Saint seemed to sigh, "If my Lord wishes me to praise Him through the daily office, then one day I shall be able to read. And if not, I will content myself with saying 'Our Father' and 'Ave Maria,' as other unschooled women do."[32] Suddenly she could read, "and she and her friends were convinced that a miracle had occurred, that the Divine 'Novice Master' was responsible for the teaching that had enabled her to overcome her previous difficulties with the written word . . ."[33]

Friar Thomas of Siena confirmed this opinion in a deposition, in which he swore on oath that

> The Blessed Catherine learned to write miraculously. One day, on coming from mental prayer, she wrote to Etienne Maconi a letter which concluded thus: "You must know, my beloved son, that this is the first letter I ever wrote myself." Etienne Maconi certifies that she wrote many after, and that several pages of the book that she composed are written with her own hand.[34]

In a letter to her confessor, Bl. Raymond of Capua, St. Catherine explained:

> I wrote this letter myself, and the one that I already sent you. For God gave me the facility to write, so that when coming forth from ecstasy, I might discharge my heart; and as the Master who instructed the pupil shows him the model which he must copy, so He placed before my mental vision, the things that I should write you.[35]

St. Catherine of Siena was the second woman to be named a Doctor of the Church.

A Treasure Lost and Found

During his childhood, ST. LOUIS MARIE GRIGNON DE MONTFORT (d. 1716) gave every indication that he was destined for the priesthood.

Always devoted to Our Lady and the Rosary, Louis was sent after his ordination to serve as chaplain to a hospital, where he attempted to remedy mismanagement and quarreling. Sent away for his efforts, he gave missions and founded two religious congregations: the Missionary Society of Mary for men and the Daughters of Wisdom for women.

It is said that he was met with stubborn opposition in everything he tried to do because of Jansenism, which infected many of the clergy and even some of the bishops. He was even poisoned by his enemies, but while recuperating he turned the evil into good by writing *True Devotion to the Blessed Virgin*.[36] After writing the book he prophesied:

> I clearly foresee that raging beasts shall come in fury to tear with their diabolical teeth this little writing and him whom the Holy Ghost has made use of to write it— or at least to smother it in the darkness and silence of a coffer, that it may not appear. They shall even attack and persecute those who shall read it and carry it out in practice.

The prophecy was exactly realized, since his spiritual sons were persecuted by the Jansenists for their zeal in spreading the devotion. The manuscript was hidden from those who would care to destroy it and was for all purposes lost for well over a century. It was finally discovered in the year 1842, when it was found in a chest of old books by a Montfort priest.

The book has since been a spiritual treasure for the faithful and has been acclaimed by several Popes, including Pope John Paul II, who wrote: "The reading of this book was a decisive turning-point in my life . . . It is from Montfort that I have taken my motto: *'Totus tuus'* ('I am all Thine')."[37]

The Angelic Couriers

We read in the life of ST. GEMMA GALGANI (d. 1903) that she was so familiar with her Guardian Angel that she sometimes entrusted her letters to him for safe delivery. We read:

> One day, with the most charming simplicity, she prayed her director's angel to take the letter she had written to him. Not the least doubt she had as to the result. She did not like to be asking for stamps, living dependent on the charity of the Giannini family; though her recourse to the angel was not continual, yet not one of all the letters she thus committed to him was lost.[38]

The director at one time wanted to conduct a test and instructed Gemma to give the letters she wanted to send him by the Angel to Aunt Cecilia, who was told to lock them in a place unknown to Gemma. On June 11, 1901 Gemma gave a letter to Aunt Cecilia, who in turn gave it to Don Lorenzo Agrimonti (a priest living with the Giannini family). He locked it in a chest in his own room and put the key in his pocket. During the afternoon of the next day Gemma sensed that the Angel had passed with her letter and notified Don Lorenzo. The letter had, in fact, disappeared from its secret location and was received in due course by her confessor.

To prove the matter yet another time, the same experiment was undertaken—a letter of Gemma's to her confessor was handed over to Don Lorenzo. He secretly hid the envelope between two pictures, one of St. Gabriel and the other of St. Paul of the Cross. This took place on May 22, 1901. The next day Gemma announced that her Angel had taken away the letter, which proved to be true. It is no wonder that the confessor called them "angelic letters."[39]

Cross-shaped Manna

The confessor and biographer of St. Catherine of Siena, Bl. Raymond of Capua, was also one of the first biographers of ST. AGNES OF MONTEPULCIANO (d. 1317).

Since he served as confessor of the monastery in which the body of Agnes was conserved, he was able to study at length the documents in the archives relating to her. In these carefully kept papers he reports about a visit of St. Catherine of Siena to the shrine in the company of her two nieces and their mother, Lysa.

We read what took place after St. Catherine prayed there.

> The Saint exclaimed, "What, do you not observe the present that heaven sends us: Do not be ungrateful!" At these words, Lysa and the others lifted their eyes and saw a very fine and very white manna falling like heavenly dews and covering not only Agnes and Catherine, but also all the persons present, and with such abundance that Lysa filled her hands with it.[40]

This was not the first time manna had fallen. Described as being white, cross-shaped particles, it was known to have fallen frequently upon Agnes and upon her immediate area during her ecstasies. Bl. Raymond questioned the witnesses about this and was told that the occurrences took place as reported in archival papers. Bl. Raymond wrote:

> Nuns belonging to the convent have equally affirmed before me and before the friars who were with me, that thus the occurrences took place. Many are now dead; but myself and my brethren recall perfectly their depositions; further, Lysa collected the manna which fell, showed it frequently, and gave it to several persons.[41]

A Roman Martyr in the United States

When the Discalced Carmelite Nuns of Wheeling, West Virginia petitioned Rome for a major relic of a saint, they were given the remains of ST. PAULA, a martyr of Roman times. On the urn which contained the relics were Latin words which translate: "Body of Saint Paula M.N.P. From the cemetery of Callistus."

The relics were received in Wheeling with due respect and ceremony on May 8, 1921. On that day the relics were examined and authenticated before they were carried processionally to the shrine prepared for them in the sanctuary of the monastery church, where Vespers of a Virgin Martyr were chanted by eleven priests. The next day, Monday the 9th, an appropriate sermon was preached before the exposition and Benediction of the Blessed Sacrament. On Tuesday the 10th of May, with a large congregation in attendance, ceremonies were again conducted with twenty-three priests in attendance. The relics were then carried in procession through the nuns' enclosure for placement under the altar in the nuns' choir, where they remained until 1975. At that time the monastery was closed. The relics were then removed to the Discalced Carmelite Monastery in Elysburg, Pennsylvania.

No details of St. Paula's life or death are known to us except that she died in her early forties. This was discovered after episcopal permission was received for the urn to be opened. The age of the Saint was determined by the proper authorities based on the condition of a tooth.

The urn containing the remains is located within a beautiful wax figure of the Saint which is clothed in a scarlet robe. A cluster of lilies denoting purity is arranged in the bend of the left arm, while a golden palm of victory is gently touched by the right hand. Gracefully arranged within a gold lacquered brass and crystal reliquary, the Saint reclines far from her place of triumph.[42]

The Word "Chapel"

The story is familiar. During a frigid winter ST. MARTIN OF TOURS (d. circa 400), a soldier stationed at Amiens, met a beggar who was shrivering in the cold. Having nothing to give the poor man except his sword and clothes, he drew his sword, cut his cloak into two pieces and gave one piece to the beggar, who gratefully wrapped himself in it. The following night Martin, in his sleep, saw Jesus dressed in that half of the garment. He then heard Jesus say to the angels who accompanied Him, "Martin, yet a catechumen, has covered Me with this cloak." Martin's biographer, Sulpicius Severus, states that as a result of the vision, Martin "flew to be baptized."

St. Martin resigned from the army, became a priest, established monasteries, labored as a missionary and gained a reputation as a wonder-worker. He was eventually elevated to the bishopric of Tours.

The part of the cloak that he retained was placed as a relic in an oratory which gradually became known as the *cappella,* a diminutive form of *cappa,* or cloak. The word gradually came to be known in English as "chapel."[43]

Preserved Scapulars of Our Lady of Mount Carmel

ST. JOHN BOSCO (d. 1888) had a number of mystical gifts, including the gift of multiplying food, of reading thoughts and consciences, the knowledge of what was transpiring in institutes belonging to his community, and levitating during the offering of Holy Mass. He was a prolific writer and founded an orphanage for boys, a religious order now known as the Salesians of St. John Bosco and an order for women known as the Congregation of the Daughters of Mary, Help of Christians.

The Saint died with a reputation of great holiness after suffering for years from a variety of painful ailments. The room in which he died has been kept as it was at the time of his death. Here are found a number of articles the Saint used, and many relics. One of these is the Saint's Scapular of Our Lady of Mount Carmel that was found in perfect condition during the first exhumation of the Saint's remains. This was regarded as a miracle since all the other fabric items in the coffin had deteriorated in the usual way.[44]

ST. ALPHONSUS LIGUORI (d. 1787) founded the Redemptorist Order and was the recipient of a number of mystical favors including bilocation, visions, prophecy and the knowledge of distant happenings. He was elevated to the bishopric and served in that position for thirteen years before resigning. Greatly devoted to the Blessed Virgin, the Saint wore the Scapular of Our Lady of Mount Carmel during his lifetime and was buried with it. Forty years after his burial, his scapular was found marvelously incorrupt, although everything else in the tomb had turned to dust. Because of his labors for the Church, his sanctity and his 110 books and pamphlets that are of great spiritual and moral benefit, he is numbered among the Doctors of the Church.

Relics of Iron

After his ordination, ST. WULFRIC (d. 1154) looked about for a place where he could practice great penances and was offered a cell adjoining the church at Haselbury. One of his austerities was the wearing of heavy chain mail next to his skin. Because the chain mail was long and prevented him from performing his many penitential prostrations, he asked that it be shortened. We are assured by his contemporaries that the iron links were cut with an ordinary pair of scissors. One of these contemporaries was Henry, Archdeacon of Huntingdon who, in 1145, published his *Historia Anglorum*. In this work he mentions that the iron links were cut by the scissors as if they were so much linen. He also wrote that many people possessed fragments and regarded them as relics. The tomb of St. Wulfric was a popular place of pilgrimage in the Middle Ages.[45]

The Water Lamp

ST. CHARBEL MAKHLOUF (d. 1898) joined the Lebanese Maronite Order when he was twenty-three years old and was assigned to the Monastery of St. Maroun. Ordained in 1859, he spent sixteen years in the practice of monastic virtues. After that time he received permission to retire to a hermitage a little distance from the monastery. Here he spent the remaining twenty-three years of his life. He was especially devoted to the Holy Eucharist and was known by his confreres as having performed a number of miracles. It is also known that he recited his Divine Office by the light of a lamp that a brother had purposely filled with water instead of oil.[46]

After his death his body displayed certain phenomena which are recounted elsewhere in this book.

A Lightning Conversion

A handsome young man named Norbert, of illustrious birth, received in his youth a worldly education, being interested in success and pleasures. He was one day riding with a servant to a village of Westphalia when suddenly thunder boomed and lightning flashed above his head. Far from shelter and thoroughly frightened, he allowed his horse to gallop as fast as possible to reach safety when loud thunder again clapped above him and a flash of lightning knocked both horse and rider to the ground. Norbert is said to have remained on the ground for a whole hour, without motion, and almost without life. When he regained his strength and his senses, like St. Paul who was similarly converted, he cried out: "Lord, what wouldst Thou have me to do?" An interior voice responded: "Do good and fly from evil. Seek peace and employ all your strength to acquire it."

Completely converted from his worldly ways, he became both a deacon and a priest on Christmas Day in 1115. He then gave away his possessions, dressed in poor clothing and traveled about the Rhineland preaching against the laxity of the clergy and the vices of Christians. He founded the Premonstratensian Order, which grew rapidly, and labored with St. Bernard of Clairvaux in ending schism, in preaching and in spreading the Faith. He became the

Bishop of Magdeburg and is now known as ST. NORBERT (d. 1134). His feastday is celebrated worldwide on June 6.[47]

The Miracle of the Marble Altar

After a wealthy attorney received the cure of his body and soul through the intercession of ST. PHILOMENA (d. first century), he and his wife donated a large marble piece for an altar in the chapel of the Saint. They employed a marble cutter from Naples, Don Giovanni Cimafonte, who was known for his skill, to work on the altar and install it. While going about the work, the marble cutter discovered a long, jagged crack that threatened to break the marble in two. He was extremely worried that disaster would visit the altar which would result not only in the loss of the altar, but also the loss of his reputation as a skilled craftsman. He could do nothing else but attempt to repair the crack, but it only lengthened until only a fourth of the original slab remained intact. He then supported the slab with an iron brace underneath and fastened the marble as best he could, but the surface was not smooth. He then found it necessary to fill the crevice with a chalk preparation, but it darkened, making the crack even more noticeable.

Kneeling humbly before the relics of the little martyr, he prayed fervently for assistance. Rising from his prayer he returned to the altar and found it solid, with the dark chalk line blended so that it appeared to be a natural vein in the marble.

A number of people who had been aware of the difficulty and had formerly sympathized with Don Giovanni now rejoiced with him at the miracle worked by their little Saint. Many of these witnesses gave testimony about the wonder, and an inscription commemorating it was placed in the church. Today, visitors to the shrine at Mugnano can view the marble altar that still bears the marks of a miracle.[48]

Inanimate Objects Obey

In his biography of ST. BENEDICT (d. 543), St. Gregory the Great tells of the many marvels worked by St. Benedict, the Great Patriarch of the Western Monks. Many of the Saint's miracles and spiritual gifts are recounted in this volume, but here we have his ability to manage a very heavy object. There was, for instance, a huge stone that lay in the area where cells of a cloister were being built. When three men found it impossible to move it, and thinking that perhaps the devil was trying to impede their work, they presented the problem to St. Benedict, who first prayed, then blessed the stone and gently moved it aside as though it had no weight whatsoever.[49]

This event is similar to one worked by ST. FRANCIS OF PAOLA (d. 1507) during the building of a church and monastery for the order he founded. The first difficulty that arose was the removal of a huge boulder that lay in the middle of the proposed monastery area. When St. Francis noticed the inability of the workmen to move the stone, he told them to move aside. After kneeling by the stone he offered a prayer with his arms raised toward Heaven. The miracle then took place. The boulder is said to have raised itself out of the ground and was easily moved away by the workmen. The stone is still positioned where the workmen left it and can be seen by visitors to the monastery who marvel at the miracle worked by the fervent prayer of the Saint.[50]

It was not a heavy stone, but rather a huge chestnut tree that obeyed the gentle command of ST. GERARD MAJELLA (d. 1755). The event took place while the Saint was passing through Senerchia, where the townfolk were trying unsuccessfully to move from a mountain several large chestnut trees that were to be used in the erection of their parish church. Seeing their inability to move the trees despite the efforts of oxen, the Saint asked to be taken up the mountain where the felled trees challenged their removal. Tying a rope to one of the largest trees, the Saint ordered it in the name of the Most Holy Trinity to follow him. The astonished townfolk watched as the Saint drew it along easily to the place where the church was to be built. Inspired by the prodigy the workmen recommended their labors to God, and with little effort removed the other trees from the mountain.[51]

St. Thérèse and the Sky
After the death of ST. THÉRÈSE OF THE CHILD JESUS AND OF THE HOLY FACE (d. 1897), her sister Celine—in religion Sr. Genevieve of the Holy Face—wrote a memoir in which she detailed brief lessons, memories and spiritual advice given by her sainted sister. Years afterward, Celine recalled that immediately after Thérèse's death:

Submerged in grief, I fled from the infirmary and went outdoors. In my naïvete, I was really hoping to catch a glimpse of her in the heavens, but as it was raining, the sky was completely overcast. Leaning against the column of one of the cloisters I began to sob. If only the stars would come out, I thought to myself.

Almost immediately, the clouds dispersed and stars were soon studding the sky.[52]

Another sister of Thérèse, Pauline—in religion Reverend Mother Agnes of Jesus—dutifully kept notes of the last conversations of her saintly sister, which spanned the period from the beginning of her entrance into the infirmary to the time of her death. We will end this book as Mother Agnes ended her notes, with her sad and poetic remembrance:

Moreover, throughout the course of her sickness our little saint had affirmed that an unclouded sky should mark the moment of her going forth to God. And so it befell, for the day of September 30 had been overcast and rainy, but towards seven o'clock the clouds all dispersed with surprising rapidity, and soon from a perfectly clear sky the stars appeared, scintillating with the brilliancy that always follows rain.[53]

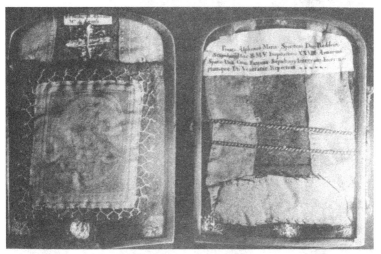

THE PRESERVED SCAPULARS of St. John Bosco (top) and of St. Alphonsus Liguori (front and back view), which were found preserved during the respective exhumations. (Lower picture from *Dear Bishop,* by John M. Haffert, AMI International Press.)

BL. ANNA MARIA TAIGI and the miraculous sun in which she could see past, present and future events, as well as the condition of souls.

—NOTES—

Chapter 1: Bilocation

1. Fr. D. F. Miller, C.SS.R. and Fr. L. X. Aubin, C.SS.R., *St. Alphonsus Liguori* (London: St. Alphonsus' Bookstore and Sands & Co. Publishers, 1940; Rockford, Illinois: TAN Books & Publishers, Inc., 1987), p. 194.
2. Ibid., pp. 270-271.
3. A Lay Brother of the Congregation of the Most Holy Redeemer, *The Life, Virtues and Miracles of St. Gerard Majella* (Boston: Mission Church, 1907), pp. 162-163.
4. Fr. Pius of the Name of Mary, *The Life of St. Paul of the Cross* (New York: P. O'Shea, 1924), pp. 121-122.
5. Rev. Angelo Pastrovicchi, O.M.C., *St. Joseph of Copertino* (St. Louis, Missouri: B. Herder Book Co., 1918; Rockford, Illinois: TAN, 1980), pp. 83-84.
6. J. K. Huysmans, *Saint Lydwine of Schiedam* (London: Kegan Paul, French, Trubner & Co., Ltd., 1923; Rockford, Illinois: TAN, 1979), p. 125.
7. J. C. Kearns, O.P., *The Life of Blessed Martin De Porres* (New York: P. J. Kenedy & Sons, 1937), pp. 118-120.
8. Ibid., p. 120.
9. Ibid., p. 121.
10. Ibid., pp. 121-122.
11. Joan Carroll Cruz, *The Incorruptibles* (Rockford, Illinois: TAN, 1977), p. 198.
12. James A. Carrico, *Life of Venerable Mary of Agreda—Author of the Mystical City of God: The Autobiography of the Virgin Mary* (San Bernardino, California: Crestline Book Company, 1959), pp. 45-50.
13. Gino J. Simi and Mario M. Segreti, *St. Francis of Paola, God's Miracle Worker Supreme* (Rockford, Illinois: TAN, 1977), p. 18.
14. Ibid., p. 45.
15. Rev. Alban Butler, *The Lives of the Saints* (New York: P. J. Kenedy & Sons, 1933), Vol. IV, p. 185.
16. Charles Warren Stoddard, *Saint Anthony, The Wonder Worker of Padua* (Notre Dame, Indiana: The Ave Maria, 1896; Rockford, Illinois: TAN, 1971), p. 56.
17. Marion A. Habig, O.F.M., *The Franciscan Book of Saints* (Chicago: Franciscan Herald Press, 1959), pp. 220-222.
18. Comte Paul Biver, Père Lamy (Dublin, Ireland: Clonmore and Reynolds, Limited, 1951; Rockford, Illinois: TAN, 1973), p. 180.
19. Edward Van Speybrouck, *The Very Rev. Fr. Paul of Moll* (Clyde, Missouri: Benedictine Convent, 1910; Rockford, Illinois: TAN, 1979), pp. 175-176.
20. Ibid., p. 240.
21. A. Auffray, S.D.B., *Saint John Bosco* (Tirupattur, South India: Salesian House, 1959), p. 219.
22. Ibid., p. 220.
23. C. Bernard Ruffin, *Padre Pio, The True Story* (Huntington, Indiana: Our Sunday Visitor, 1991), pp. 66-67.
24. Ibid., pp. 68-70.

Chapter 2: Levitation

1. St. Teresa of Avila, *The Life of Teresa of Jesus*, trans. by E. Allison Peers (Garden City, New York: Image Books, 1960), p. 191.
2. Ibid., pp. 190-191.
3. Ibid., p. 191.
4. Herbert Thurston, S.J., *The Physical Phenomena of Mysticism* (Chicago: Henry Regnery Co., 1951), p. 12.
5. Ibid., pp. 12-13.
6. Ibid., p. 13.
7. Ibid., pp. 22-23.
8. Lay Brother, op. cit., p. 81.

9. Ibid., p. 136.
10. Ibid.
11. Ibid., p. 137.
12. Miller and Aubin, op. cit., p. 148.
13. Van Speybrouck, op, cit., p. 154.
14. Ibid., pp. 156-157.
15. Fr. Juan Echevarria, *The Miracles of Saint Anthony Mary Claret* (Compton, California: Claretian Major Seminary, 1938; Rockford, Illinois: TAN, 1992), p. 177.
16. Kearns, op. cit., p. 25.
17. Ibid., pp. 91-92.
18. Ibid., pp. 92-93.
19. Ibid., p. 93.
20. Ibid., p. 95.
21. *A Lover of the Cross, St. Gemma Galgani* (Lucca, Italy: Monastero-Santuario di S. Gemma Galgani, Passioniste, 1940), p. 52.
22. Fr. Pius of the Name of Mary, op. cit., pp. 199-200.
23. Thurston., op. cit., p. 25.
24. Ibid., pp. 25-26.
25. Ibid., pp. 28-29.
26. Ibid., p. 29.
27. Ibid.
28. Ibid., p. 30.
29. Simi and Segreti, op. cit., p. 110.
30. Rev. E. Cobham Brewer, *A Dictionary of Miracles* (New York: Cassell & Company, Ltd., 1884), p. 215.
31. Ibid., p. 216.
32. Ibid., p. 217.
33. Ibid.
34. Ibid., p. 218.
35. Ibid.
36. Pastrovicchi, op. cit., p. 12.
37. Ibid., p. 23.
38. Ibid., p. 30.
39. Ibid., p. 32.
40. Ibid., pp. 33-34.
41. Ibid., pp. 34-35.
42. Ibid., pp. 35-36.
43. Thomas Merton, *What Are These Wounds?* (Milwaukee: The Bruce Publishing Company, 1950), p. 42.
44. Fr. William R. Bonniwell, O.P., *The Life of Blessed Margaret of Castello* (Rockford, Illinois: TAN, 1983), pp. 94-96.
45. Augusta Theodosia Drane, *The Life of St. Dominic* (New York and London: Burns & Oates, Ltd., 1919), p. 106.
46. Ibid., pp. 106-107.
47. V. J. Matthews, *St. Philip Neri, Apostle of Rome and Founder of the Congregation of the Oratory* (London: Burns Oates & Washbourne Ltd., 1934; Rockford, Illinois: TAN, 1984), pp. 104-105.
48. Raphael Brown, *The Little Flowers of St. Francis* (Garden City, New York: Image Books, 1958), p. 176.
49. Ibid., p. 181.
50. Butler, op. cit., 1937, Vol. VI, p. 147.
51. Butler, op. cit., 1932, Vol. III, p. 107.
52. Abbe Francis Trochu, *The Cure D'Ars: St. Jean Marie Baptiste Vianney* (London: Burns & Oates & Washbourne, 1927; Rockford, Illinois: TAN, 1977), pp. 542-543.
53. Bl. Raymond of Capua, *The Life of St. Catherine of Siena* (New York: P. J. Kenedy & Sons, 1960), p. 27.
54. Ibid., p. 174.
55. Ibid., p. 196.
56. Ibid., p. 175.
57. Mary Purcell, *The First Jesuit, St. Ignatius Loyola* (Chicago: Loyola University Press, 1981), p. 71.
58. Zsolt Aradi, *The Book of Miracles* (New York: Farrar, Straus and Cudahy, 1956), p. 178.
59. Habig, op. cit., pp. 633-634.
60. Cruz, *The Incorruptibles*, p. 132.
61. Fr. Joseph Sicardo, *St. Rita of Cascia* (Rockford, Illinois: TAN, 1990), p. 153.
62. Cruz, *The Incorruptibles*, p. 131.

Chapter 3: Odor of Sanctity

1. Herbert Thurston, S.J., *The Physical Phenomena of Mysticism* (Chicago: Henry Regnery Company, 1952), pp. 222-223.
2. Ildephonse Cardinal Schuster, O.S.B., *Saint Benedict and His Times* (London: B. Herder Book Company, 1951), p. 297.
3. Brewer, op. cit., p. 512.

4. Rev. Alban Butler, *The Lives of the Saints* (New York: P. J. Kenedy & Sons, 1937), Vol. VI, p. 316.
5. Brewer, op. cit., p. 511.
6. Butler, op. cit., 1933, Vol. IV, p. 151.
7. Huysmans, op. cit., p. 58.
8. Ibid., p. 104.
9. Ibid., p. 189.
10. Butler, op. cit., 1932, Vol. III, pp. 198-199.
11. Lady Georgiana Fullerton, *The Life of St. Frances of Rome* (New York: P. J. Kenedy & Sons, n.d.), p. 189.
12. Saint Teresa of Avila, *The Collected Works of St. Teresa of Avila,* trans. by Kieran Kavanaugh, O.C.D. and Otilio Rodriguez, O.C.D. (Washington, D. C.: Institute of Carmelite Studies, 1985), p. 262.
13. Msgr. Albert Farges, *Mystical Phenomena* (London: Burns, Oates & Washbourne, Ltd., 1926), p. 556.
14. Thurston, *The Physical Phenomena of Mysticism,* p. 228.
15. Pastrovicchi, op. cit., pp. 59-60.
16. Thurston, *Physical Phenomena of Mysticism,* pp. 229-230.
17. Ibid., p. 231.
18. Rev. Alban Butler, *The Lives of the Saints* (New York: P. J. Kenedy & Sons, 1938), Vol. XII, p. 188.
19. Ibid., p. 188.
20. Thurston, *The Physical Phenomena of Mysticism,* pp. 228-229.
21. Farges, op. cit., p. 556.
22. Lay Brother, op. cit., p. 201.
23. Ibid., p. 201.
24. Fr. Pius of the Name of Mary, op. cit., pp. 236-237.
25. Thurston, *The Physical Phenomena of Mysticism,* p. 230.
26. Fr. Juan Echevarria, C.M.F., *The Miracles of Saint Anthony Mary Claret, Archbishop and Founder* (Compton, California: Claretian Major Seminary, 1938; Rockford, Illinois: TAN, 1992), p. 106.
27. Thurston, *The Physical Phenomena of Mysticism,* p. 232.
28. Van Speybrouck, op. cit., p. 154.
29. Habig, op. cit., p. 312.
30. Ruffin, op. cit., 1991, p. 164.
31. Ibid., pp. 321-322.

Chapter 4: ODOR OF SIN

1. Frances Parkinson Keyes, *Three Ways of Love* (New York: Hawthorn Books, Inc., 1963), p. 239.
2. Blessed Raymond of Capua, op. cit., pp. 138-139.
3. Ibid., pp. 139-140.
4. Albert Bessieres, S.J., *Wife, Mother and Mystic* (London, England: Sands & Co., Ltd., 1952; Rockford, Illinois: TAN, 1970), p. 146.
5. Mons. Giuseppe Bardi, *St. Gemma Galgani* (Boston, Massachusetts: St. Paul Editions, 1961), p. 138.
6. Fr. Pius of the Name of Mary, op. cit., p. 237.
7. Pastrovicchi, op. cit., p. 59.
8. Ibid., p. 75.
9. Matthews, op. cit., p. 63.
10. Echevarria, op. cit., p. 225.
11. A. Auffray, S.D.B., *Saint John Bosco* (Tirupattur, South India: Salesian House, 1959), p. 244.

Chapter 5: MYSTICAL HEARTS

1. St. John of the Cross, *The Collected Works of St. John of the Cross,* trans. by Kieran Kavanaugh, O.C.D. and Otilio Rodriguez, O.C.D. (Washington, D. C.: Institute of Carmelite Studies, 1973), p. 598.
2. St. Teresa of Avila, op. cit., pp. 273-274.
3. Cruz, *The Incorruptibles,* p. 190.
4. Sister Agnes of Jesus, *Novissima Verba: The Last Conversations of St. Thérèse of the Child Jesus: May-September 1897* (London: Burns, Oates & Washbourne, Ltd., 1929), pp. 43-44.
5. *Soeur Thérèse of Lisieux, The Little Flower of Jesus* (Story of a Soul), T. N. Taylor, editor. (New York: P. J. Kenedy & Sons, 1912), p. 195.
6. C. Bernard Ruffin, *Padre Pio: The True Story* (Huntington, Indiana: Our Sunday Visitor, Inc., 1982), p. 152.
7. Ibid., p. 152.

8. Ibid.
9. *Sister Mary Martha Chambon, Religious of the Monastery of the Visitation, Chambery* (Montreal: The Companions of Jesus and Mary, 1986), p. 6.
10. Thurston, *Physical Phenomena of Mysticism*, p. 220.
11. Merton, op. cit., p. 127.
12. Cruz, *The Incorruptibles,* pp. 103-104.
13. Cruz, *Relics* (Huntington, Indiana: Our Sunday Visitor, Inc., 1984), p. 300.
14. Blessed Raymond of Capua, op. cit., p. 165.
15. Ibid., pp. 165-166.
16. Ibid., p. 166.
17. Ibid., p. 167.
18. Fullerton, op. cit., pp. 188-189.
19. Ibid., p. 189.
20. Sister Mary Jean Dorcy, O.P., *Saint Dominic's Family* (Dubuque, Iowa: The Priory Press, 1964; Rockford, Illinois: TAN, 1983), p. 286.
21. St. Margaret Mary Alacoque, *The Autobiography of St. Margaret Mary Alacoque* (Sisters of the Visitation, Roselands, Walmer, Kent, England, 1930; Rockford, Illinois: TAN, 1986), pp. 67-68.
22. Montague Summers, *The Physical Phenomena of Mysticism* (London: Rider and Company, 1950), p. 195.
23. Dorcy, op. cit., p. 131.
24. Lay Brother, op. cit., p. 138.
25. Pastrovicchi, op. cit., p. 118.
26. Matthews, op. cit., pp. 9-10.
27. Ibid., p. 111.
28. Cruz, *The Incorruptibles,* p. 211.
29. Fr. Pius of the Name of Mary, op. cit., pp. 197-198.
30. Cruz, *Relics,* pp. 251-252.
31. Ibid., p. 252.
32. Cruz, *The Incorruptibles,* p. 240.

Chapter 6: Miraculous Transport

1. Rev. Alban Butler, *The Lives of the Saints* (New York: P. J. Kenedy & Sons, 1936), Vol. X, pp. 54-55.
2. Ibid., p. 57.

3. Drane, *Life of St. Dominic,* p. 35.
4. Dorcy, op. cit., p. 57.
5. Butler, op. cit., 1933, Vol. VIII, p. 193.
6. Habig, op. cit., p. 732.
7. Stoddard, op. cit., pp. 95-96.
8. Butler, op. cit., 1926, Vol. I, pp. 42-43.
9. Biver, op. cit., p. 101.
10. Ibid., pp. 172-173.
11. Ibid., pp. 173-174.
12. Ibid., p. 174.
13. Albert Paul Schimberg, *Tall in Paradise: The Story of Saint Coletta of Corbie* (Francestown, New Hampshire: Marshall Jones Company, 1947), p. 67.
14. Butler, op. cit., 1937, Vol. VI, pp. 191-192.
15. Kearns, op. cit., pp. 124-125.
16. Ibid., pp. 125-126.
17. Ibid., p. 126.
18. Butler, op. cit., 1932, Vol. III, pp. 70-71.
19. Fr. Pius of the Name of Mary, op. cit., pp. 121-122.
20. Echevarria, op. cit., pp. 72-73.
21. Ibid., pp. 73-74.
22. Habig, op. cit., pp. 221-222.
23. Summers, op. cit., p. 68.
24. Butler, op. cit., 1934, Vol. IX, p. 53.
25. Lay Brother, op. cit., pp. 166-167.
26. Habig, op. cit., p. 496.
27. Simi and Segreti, op. cit., pp. 47-48.
28. Butler, op. cit., 1926, Vol. I, pp. 276-277.
29. Butler, op. cit., 1932, Vol. II, p. 280.
30. Dorcy, op. cit., p. 191.
31. Habig, op. cit., p. 819.

Chapter 7: Money Mysteriously Provided

1. Pope St. Gregory the Great, *The Dialogues* (Collegeville, Minnesota: The Liturgical Press, *n.d.*), pp. 57-58.
2. Dorcy, op. cit., pp. 59-60.
3. Huysmans, op. cit., pp. 159-160.
4. Fr. Joseph Sicardo, O.S.A., *St. Rita of Cascia, Saint of the Impossible* (Chicago: D. B. Hansen & Sons, 1916; Rockford, Illinois: TAN, 1990), p. 164.

5. Lay Brother, op. cit., p. 95.
6. Ibid., p. 66.
7. Butler, op. cit., 1926, Vol. I, p. 405.
8. Aradi, op. cit., p. 208.
9. Ibid., p. 203.
10. Trochu, op. cit., p. 386.
11. Van Speybrouck, op. cit., p. 211.
12. T. N. Taylor, op. cit., pp. 339-340.
13. Ibid., pp. 341-342.
14. Ibid., pp. 343-344.
15. Ibid., p. 338.
16. Blanche Morteveille, *The Rose Unpetaled* (Milwaukee, Wisconsin: The Bruce Publishing Company, 1942), p. 240.

Chapter 8: MULTIPLICATION OF FOOD

1. Butler, op. cit., May, 1936, pp. 195, 196.
2. Schuster, op. cit., p. 180.
3. Ibid., pp. 267-268.
4. Drane, *The Life of St. Dominic,* pp. 99-101.
5. Ibid., p. 143.
6. Ibid.
7. Raphael Brown, Translator, *The Little Flowers of St. Francis* (Garden City, New York: Image Books, 1958), pp. 84-85.
8. Thomas of Celano, *St. Francis of Assisi* (Chicago, Illinois: Franciscan Herald Press, 1988), p. 51.
9. Count De Montalembert, *The Life of Saint Elizabeth* (New York: P. J. Kenedy & Sons, 1886), p. 198.
10. Blessed Raymond of Capua, op. cit., pp. 268-269.
11. Ibid., p. 269.
12. Ibid., p. 270.
13. Ibid., pp. 272-273.
14. Keyes, op. cit., pp. 68-69.
15. Schimberg, op. cit., pp. 89-90.
16. Lay Brother, op. cit., pp. 95-96.
17. Ibid., pp. 170-171.
18. Simi and Segreti, op. cit., p. 44.
19. Ibid., p. 39.
20. Ibid.
21. Ibid., p. 47.
22. Ibid., pp. 102-103.
23. William Thomas Walsh, *Saint Teresa of Avila, A Biography* (Milwaukee: Bruce Publishing Company, 1943),

pp. 411-412.
24. Sister Mary Minima, *Seraph Among Angels—The Life of St. Mary Magdalene De'Pazzi,* trans. by Rev. Gabriel N. Pausback, O. Carm. (Chicago: The Carmelite Press, 1958), pp. 200-201.
25. Sister Mary Alphonsus, O.SS.R., *St. Rose of Lima: Patroness of the Americas* (St. Louis, Missouri: B. Herder Book Co., 1968; Rockford, Illinois: TAN, 1982), pp. 164-166.
26. Ibid., p. 166.
27. Albert S. Foley, S.J., *St. Regis, A Social Crusader* (Mobile, Alabama: Spring Hill College Press, 1961), pp. 134-135.
28. Ibid., pp. 135-136.
29. Trochu, op. cit., pp. 202-204.
30. Ibid., p. 204.
31. Thurston, *The Physical Phenomena of Mysticism,* pp. 386-387.
32. Ibid., pp. 387-388.
33. Butler, op. cit., 1933, Vol. IV, p. 304.
34. Butler, op. cit., 1937, Vol. VI, June, p. 85.
35. Ibid.
36. Aradi, op. cit., pp. 207-208.
37. Auffray, op. cit., p. 239.
38. Ibid., pp. 238-239.
39. Bessieres, op. cit., p. 123.
40. Butler, op. cit., 1933, August, p. 280.
41. Dorcy, op. cit., p. 191.
42. Ibid., pp. 194-195.
43. Fr. Pius of the Name of Mary, op. cit., p. 195.
44. Ibid., pp. 194-195.
45. Dorcy, op. cit., p. 242.
46. Sicardo, op. cit., p. 163.
47. Dorcy, op. cit., p. 196.

Chapter 9: MYSTICAL MARRIAGE AND HEAVENLY JEWELRY

1. St. Teresa of Avila, *The Interior Castle,* trans. by E. Allison Peers (Garden City, New York: Image Books, 1944), p. 119.
2. Ibid., p. 207.
3. *The Collected Works of St. John of the Cross,* op. cit., p. 619.
4. Ibid., p. 497.

5. Abbe Theodore Ratisbonne, *St. Bernard of Clairvaux: Oracle of the Twelfth Century* (New York: P. J. Kenedy & Sons, *n.d.*; Rockford, Illinois: TAN, 1991), p. 289.

6. P. Marie-Eugene, O.C.D., *I Am a Daughter of the Church* (Westminster, Maryland: Christian Classics, 1979), p. 543.

7. Butler, op. cit., Vol. II, 1932, pp. 191-192.

8. Ibid., p. 193.

9. Dorcy, *St. Dominic's Family*, p. 252.

10. Butler, op. cit., 1934, Vol. IX, p. 53.

11. Dorcy, op. cit., p. 252.

12. *The Life and Revelations of Saint Gertrude: Virgin and Abbess of the Order of St. Benedict* (Westminster, Maryland: The Newman Press, 1949), pp. 114-115.

13. Blessed Raymond of Capua, op. cit., pp. 99-100.

14. Mother Mary Francis, *Walled in Light: Saint Colette* (Chicago: Franciscan Herald Press, 1985), p. 160.

15. Aradi, op. cit., pp. 176-177.

16. Trochu, op. cit., pp. 544-545.

17. Cruz, *Relics*, p. 170.

18. Mother Mary Francis, op. cit., p. 233.

19. St. Teresa of Avila, op. cit., p. 270.

20. Sister Marie Helene Mohr, S.C., *Saint Philomena—Powerful With God* (Milwaukee: The Bruce Publishing Company, 1953; Rockford, Illinois: TAN, 1988), p. 9.

21. Ibid.

22. Fr. Paul O'Sullivan, *Saint Philomena—The Wonder-Worker* (Lisbon: Catholic Printing Press, 1954; Rockford, Illinois: TAN, 1993), p. 42.

Chapter 10:
MIRACULOUS PROTECTION

1. Butler, op. cit., 1935, Vol. XII, p. 270.

2. Matthews, op. cit., p. 3.

3. Leon Cristiani, *St. John of the Cross, Prince of Mystical Theology* (Garden City, New York: Doubleday & Company, Inc., 1962), pp. 5-6.

4. Ibid., p. 10.

5. Echevarria, op. cit., p. 17.

6. Fr. Patrick O'Connell, B.C., *The Life and Work of Mother Louise Margaret Claret De La Touche* (Ireland: Priests' Universal Union of the Friends of the Sacred Heart, 1950; Rockford, Illinois: TAN, 1987), p. 3.

Chapter 11: LIGHTS AND RAYS OF LOVE

1. *Exodus* 34:29-30 (NAB).

2. *Matt.* 17:2 (NAB).

3. Beda Venerabilis, *Bede's Ecclesiastical History of the English Nation* (New York: J. M. Dent & Sons, Ltd., 1958), pp. 119-120.

4. Ibid., pp. 175-176.

5. De Montalembert, op. cit., pp. 162-163.

6. Rev. Alban Butler, *Lives of the Saints,* Edited, Revised and Copiously Supplemented by Herbert Thurston, S.J. and Donald Attwater. (New York: P. J. Kenedy & Sons, 1933), August, p. 145.

7. Ibid., March, p. 28.

8. Blessed Raymond of Capua, p. 285.

9. Butler, op. cit., 1938, December, p. 32.

10. Fullerton, op. cit., p. 124.

11. Mother Mary Francis, op. cit., p. 155.

12. Schimberg, op. cit., p. 161.

13. Simi and Segreti, op. cit., p. 110.

14. Butler, op. cit., 1934, September, p. 277.

15. Butler, op. cit., 1936, May, p. 314.

16. Fr. Genelli, *The Life of St. Ignatius of Loyola* (New York: Benziger Brothers, 1917; Rockford, Illinois: TAN, 1988), p. 165.

17. Ibid., p. 68.

18. Butler, op. cit., 1933, November, pp. 166-167.

19. Thomas Dubay, S.M., *Fire Within* (San Francisco: Ignatius Press, 1989), p. 25.

20. Ibid., p. 18.

21. Fr. Bruno De J.M., O.C.D., *Three Mystics* (New York: Sheed & Ward, 1949), p. 85.

22. Butler, op. cit., 1933, April, pp. 53-54.

23. Aradi, op. cit., p. 174.
24. Ibid., p. 173.
25. Thurston, *The Physical Phenomena of Mysticism*, p. 165.
26. Butler, op. cit., 1936, May, p. 154.
27. John of St. Samson, O. Carm., *Aspiration and Contemplation*, trans. by Venard Poslusney, O. Carm. (New York: Alba House, 1975), p. 10.
28. Kearns, op. cit., p. 24.
29. Ibid., pp. 24-25.
30. Ibid., p. 96.
31. Pastrovicchi, op. cit., pp. 114-115.
32. Brewer, op. cit., pp. 216-217.
33. Fr. Paul O'Sullivan, O.P., *The Wonders of the Mass* (Lisbon, Portugal: Edicões do Corpo Santo, *circa* 1963; Rockford, Illinois: TAN, 1993), p. 18.
34. Lay Brother, op. cit., p. 140.
35. Fr. Pius of the Name of Mary, op. cit., p. 198.
36. Miller and Aubin, op. cit., pp. 25-26.
37. Ibid., p. 148.
38. Trochu, op. cit., pp. 530-531.
39. Echevarria, op. cit., p. 88.
40. Ibid., p. 177.
41. Ibid., p. 206.

Chapter 12: FIRE AND HEAT OF LOVE

1. Lay Brother, op. cit., p. 139.
2. St. Margaret Mary Alacoque, op. cit., pp. 69-70.
3. Ibid., p. 70.
4. Ibid., p. 95.
5. Lay Brother, op. cit., p. 139.
6. Ibid., p. 95.
7. Blessed Raymond of Capua, op. cit., pp. 172-173.
8. Sister Mary Minima, op. cit., p. 283.
9. Aradi, op., cit., p. 173.
10. Butler, op. cit., 1937, Vol. VI, p. 316.
11. Summers, op. cit., p. 71.
12. Bessieres, op. cit., p. 119.
13. Thurston, *The Physical Phenomena of Mysticism*, p. 209.
14. Ibid.
15. Matthews, op. cit., p. 9.

16. Thurston, *The Physical Phenomena of Mysticism*, pp. 210-211.
17. Ibid., p. 211.
18. Matthews, op. cit., p. 9.
19. Matthews, op. cit., p. 111.
20. Thurston, *The Physical Phenomena of Mysticism*, p. 211.
21. Fr. Pius of the Name of Mary, op. cit., pp. 197-198.
22. Thurston, *The Physical Phenomena of Mysticism*, p. 221.
23. Merton, op. cit., p. 115.
24. Ibid., p. 220.
25. Ibid., p. 221.
26. Joan Carroll Cruz, *Eucharistic Miracles* (Rockford, Illinois: TAN, 1987), p. 261.
27. Summers, op. cit., p. 71.
28. Brewer, op. cit., p. 217.
29. Gennaro Preziuso, "The Padre's Fevers," *The Voice of Padre Pio* (Our Lady of Grace Capuchin Friary, Italy), 24, No. 6, (1994), pp. 11-14.

Chapter 13: PROPHECY

1. Van Speybrouck, op. cit., pp. 318-319.
2. Cruz, *Relics*, p. 217.
3. Ratisbonne, op. cit., pp. 102-103.
4. Drane, *Life of St. Dominic*, p. 147.
5. Ibid., p. 147.
6. Stoddard, op. cit., p. 57.
7. Ibid., p. 57.
8. Habig, op. cit., pp. 270-272.
9. Bonniwell, op. cit., p. 77.
10. Fullerton, op. cit., p. 122.
11. Ibid., p. 122.
12. Mother Mary Francis, op. cit., pp. 232-233.
13. Schimberg, op. cit., p. 99.
14. Simi and Segreti, op. cit., pp. 121-122.
15. Ibid., pp. 122-123.
16. Sister Mary Minima, op. cit., pp. 108-109.
17. Kearns, op. cit., pp. 50-51.
18. Ibid., pp. 144-145.
19. Pastrovicchi, op. cit., pp. 79-80.
20. Lay Brother, op. cit., p. 146.
21. Ibid., p. 149.
22. Ibid., p. 148.

23. Ibid., pp. 148-149.
24. Fr. Pius of the Name of Mary, op. cit., pp. 163-165.
25. Ibid., pp. 238-239.
26. Ibid., p. 241.
27. Ibid., p. 242.
28. Bessieres, op. cit., p. 159.
29. Ibid., p. 160.
30. Ibid., p. 163.
31. Echevarria, op. cit., pp. 110-111.
32. Ibid., pp. 138-140.
33. Auffray, op. cit., p. 207.
34. Ibid., p. 208.
35. Ibid., pp. 211-212.
36. Ibid., p. 212.
37. John Clarke, O.C.D. (Translator), *St. Thérèse of Lisieux, Her Last Conversations* (Washington, D. C.: ICS Publications, 1977), p. 256.
38. Ibid., p. 190.
39. Ibid., p. 91.
40. Ibid., p.126.
41. Ibid., p. 263.
42. In the year 1910 the Carmel at Lisieux received a total of 9,741 letters. After the beatification the number of letters received numbered from 800 to 1,000 daily.
43. John Clarke, O.C.D. (Translator), *Story of a Soul, The Autobiography of St. Therese of Lisieux* (Washington, D. C.: ICS Publications, 1975), p. 287.
44. *A Lover of the Cross, St. Gemma Galgani,* op. cit., p. 78.
45. Alden Hatch, *The Miracle of the Mountain: The Story of Brother Andre and the Shrine on Mount Royal* (New York: Hawthorn Books, Inc., 1959), p. 118.
46. Ruffin, op. cit., 1991, p. 318.
47. Ibid., p. 343.

Chapter 14: INVISIBILITY

1. Simi and Segreti, op. cit., p. 128.
2. Ibid., pp. 128-129.
3. Ibid., pp. 130-131.
4. Aradi, op. cit., pp. 179-180.
5. Lay Brother, op. cit., pp. 168-169.
6. Kearns, op. cit., p. 123.
7. Van Speybrouck, op. cit., pp. 159-160.

Chapter 15: SAINTS WHO KNEW THE DATE OF THEIR DEATH

1. Van Speybrouck, op. cit., pp. 331-332.
2. Drane, *Life of St. Dominic,* pp. 207-211.
3. Habig., op. cit., p. 233.
4. Aradi, op. cit., p. 173.
5. Sister Mary Alphonsus, op. cit., pp. 292-303.
6. Kearns, op. cit., pp. 149-154.
7. Pastrovicchi, op. cit., pp. 112-117.
8. Lay Brother, op. cit., p. 150.
9. Ibid., pp. 200-205.

Chapter 16: THE STIGMATA

1. Kavanaugh, op. cit., p. 599.
2. Ibid., p. 599.
3. Brown, op. cit., p. 191.
4. Ibid., pp. 191-192.
5. Thomas of Celano, op. cit., pp. 84-86.
6. Brown, op. cit., p. 194.
7. Merton, op. cit., p. 127.
8. Ibid., p. 128.
9. Butler, op. cit., 1938, Vol. XI, p. 302.
10. Huysmans, op. cit., p. 94.
11. Ibid., p. 94.
12. Ibid., p. 104.
13. *The Catholic Encyclopedia* (New York: The Encyclopedia Press, Inc., 1912), Vol. XIV, p. 295.
14. Fullerton, op. cit., pp. 149-150.
15. Summers, op. cit., pp. 137-138.
16. Ibid., pp. 152-153.
17. Thurston, *The Physical Phenomena of Mysticism,* pp. 66-67.
18. Summers, op. cit., pp. 153-154.
19. Cruz, *The Incorruptibles,* p. 157.
20. *A Lover of the Cross: St. Gemma Galgani,* op. cit., pp. 42-43.
21. Bardi, op. cit., pp. 100-102.
22. Ruffin, op. cit., 1982, p. 70.
23. Ruffin, op. cit., 1991, pp. 151-152.
24. Ibid., pp. 154-155.
25. Ruffin, op. cit., 1982, p. 150.
26. Ibid., p. 303.
27. Butler, op. cit., 1926, Vol. I, p. 93.
28. Blessed Raymond of Capua, p. 175.
29. Ibid., pp. 176-178.

30. Sister Mary Minima, op. cit., pp. 274-281.
31. Butler, op. cit., 1936, Vol. X, p. 78.
32. Schimberg, op. cit., p. 158.
33. Butler, op. cit., 1932, Vol. III, p. 98.
34. *The Catholic Encyclopedia,* op. cit., 1912, pp. 294-295.

Chapter 17: GIFT OF TONGUES

1. St. Anthony of Padua was actually born in Lisbon, Portugal which at the time of the incident might have been a part of Spain.
2. Brown, op. cit., pp. 130-131.
3. Stoddard, op. cit., p. 41.
4. Fr. Pius of the Name of Mary, p. 121.
5. Drane, *Life of St. Dominic,* p. 153.
6. Cruz, *Relics,* p. 301.
7. Dorcy, op. cit., p. 317.
8. Kearns, op. cit., p. 122.
9. Butler, op. cit., 1933, August, p. 281.
10. Trochu, op. cit., pp. 529-530.
11. Ibid., p.154.
12. Ibid.
13. Habig, op. cit., p. 496.
14. Ruffin, op.c it., 1991, p. 313.

Chapter 18: MYSTICAL FASTS

1. Butler, op. cit., 1938, Vol. XI, p. 38.
2. Thurston, *The Physical Phenomena of Mysticism,* p. 344.
3. Merton, op. cit., p. 40.
4. Ibid., p. 42.
5. Ibid., pp. 42-43.
6. Blessed Raymond of Capua, p. 152.
7. Ibid., p. 153.
8. Ibid., p. 162.
9. Butler, op. cit., 1938, Vol. XI, p. 302.
10. Huysmans, op. cit., p. 76.
11. Ibid., pp. 75-78.
12. Butler, op. cit., 1933, Vol. III, p. 374.
13. Dorcy, op. cit., p. 234.
14. Thurston, *The Physical Phenomena of Mysticism,* p. 344.
15. Ibid., pp. 344-345.
16. *The Catholic Encyclopedia* (New York: The Encyclopedia Press, Inc., 1913), Vol. IX, p. 753.

17. Dorcy, op. cit., p. 365.
18. Sister Mary Alphonsus, op. cit., p. 239.
19. Trochu, op. cit., p. 527.
20. Ibid., pp. 527-528.
21. Bardi, op. cit., p. 151.
22. Andre Legault, C.S.C., *Brother Andre of the Congregation of the Holy Cross* (Montreal, Canada: Saint Joseph's Oratory), p. 12.
23. Alden Hatch, *The Miracle of the Mountain* (New York: Hawthorn Books, Inc., 1959), p. 62.
24. Ibid., p. 12.
25. Ibid., p. 151.
26. Ibid., pp. 167-168.
27. Legault, op. cit., p. 16.
28. Thurston, *The Physical Phenomena of Mysticism,* p. 362.

Chapter 19: MYSTICAL KNOWLEDGE

1. Blessed Raymond of Capua, pp. 251-253.
2. Ibid., pp. 254-255.
3. Huysmans, op. cit., pp. 104-105.
4. Butler, op. cit., 1936, Vol. X, pp. 220-221.
5. Andrea Sarra, *The Blessed Mary Fortunata Vita* (St. Benedict, Oregon: Benedictine Press, 1972), p. 52.
6. Butler, op. cit., 1933, Vol. IV, pp. 14-15.
7. Simi and Segreti, op. cit., p. 115.
8. Butler, 1933, Vol. IV, p. 14.
9. Matthews, op. cit., p. 64.
10. Ibid., p. 25.
11. Ibid., p. 63.
12. Kearns, op. cit., p. 49.
13. Ibid., pp. 124-125.
14. Ibid., p. 141.
15. Ibid., pp. 140-141.
16. Pastrovicchi, op. cit., p. 72.
17. Ibid., pp. 71-72.
18. Ibid., p. 73.
19. Ibid., p. 42.
20. Ibid., p. 75.
21. Thomas of Celano, op. cit., p. 45.
22. Butler, 1938, Vol. XII, pp. 160-161.
23. Lay Brother, op. cit., p. 154.
24. Ibid., p. 154.
25. Ibid., p. 151.

26. Ibid., p. 152.
27. Ibid., p. 153.
28. Fr. Pius of the Name of Mary, p. 243.
29. Ibid., pp. 244-245.
30. Ibid., p. 245.
31. Ibid., pp. 245-246.
32. Trochu, op. cit., p. 286.
33. Ibid., p. 282.
34. Ibid., p. 283.
35. Ibid., p. 285.
36. Ibid.
37. Ibid., pp. 284-285.
38. Echevarria, op. cit., p. 63.
39. Ibid., p. 142.
40. Auffray, op. cit., pp. 224.
41. Ibid., p. 222.
42. Ibid., p. 223.
43. Ibid., p. 216.
44. Butler, op. cit., 1936, Vol. V, p. 259.
45. Miller and Aubin, op. cit., p. 359.
46. Butler, 1937, Vol. VI, p. 315.
47. Rev. John S. Gaynor, Ph.D., DD., *The Life of St. Vincent Pallotti* (Clerkenwell, London: Pallottine Fathers, 1962), p. 53.
48. Hatch, op. cit., p. 107.
49. Ibid., pp. 107-108.
50. Ibid., p. 108.
51. Butler, 1936, Vol. X, p. 194.
52. Butler, 1934, Vol. IX, pp. 218-219.
53. Ruffin, op. cit., 1991, p. 255.
54. Ibid., p. 255.
55. Ibid., p. 317.
56. Ibid., p. 255
57. Dorcy, op. cit., p. 471.
58. Butler, op. cit., 1937, Vol. VI, p. 150.
59. Butler, op. cit., 1932, Vol. III, p. 71.

Chapter 20: THE INCORRUPTIBLES

1. Augusta Theodosia Drane, *The History of St. Catherine of Siena and Her Companions* (London: Longmans, Green and Co., 1899), Vol. II, p. 282.
2. This statement was furnished by the St. Catherine Cultural Center in Genoa, Italy.
3. Marcelle Auclair, *Teresa of Avila* (New York: Pantheon Books, Inc., 1953), p. 430.
4. Ibid., pp. 430-431.
5. Ibid., p. 434.
6. Most Rev. Cesare Orsenigo, *Life of St. Charles Borromeo* (St. Louis, Missouri: B. Herder Book Co., 1943), pp. 192-193.
7. Sister Mary Minima, op. cit., p. 348.
8. Cruz, *The Incorruptibles,* pp. 276-277.
9. Paul Daher, *A Miraculous Star in the East, Charbel Makhlouf* (Annaya-Djebeil, Lebanon: The Monastery of St. Maron, 1952), p. 25.
10. Theodosia Boresky, *Life of St. Josaphat, Martyr of the Union* (New York: Comet Press Books, 1955), p. 285.
11. James Brodrick, S.J., *Monumenta Xaveriana, ii. 897-898* (New York: The Wicklow Press, 1952), p. 527.
12. Cruz, *The Incorruptibles,* p. 173.
13. Broderick, op. cit., pp. 910-911.
14. Ibid., pp. 776-778.
15. Fr. Paschasius Heriz, O.C.D., *St. John of the Cross* (Washington, D. C.: College of Our Lady of Mount Carmel, 1919), pp. 203-204.
16. Ibid., p. 205.
17. L. A. de Porrentruy, *The Saint of the Eucharist,* trans. by O. Staniforth, O.F.M. Cap. (San Francisco: Press of Upton Bros. & Delzelle, Inc., 1905), p. 223.
18. Ibid., p. 223
19. Ibid., p. 232.
20. Martin P. Harney, S.J., *The Jesuits in History: The Society of Jesus Through Four Centuries* (New York: The America Press, 1941), pp. 272-273.
21. Cesare Moreschini, *The Life of Saint Andre Bobola of the Society of Jesus,* trans. by Louis J. Gallagher, S.J. and Paul V. Donovan, LL.D. (Boston: Bruce Humphries, Inc., 1939), pp. 203-204.
22. Ibid., p. 204.
23. Ibid., p. 205.

Chapter 21: BODIES TRANSFORMED, MOVED OR WEIGHTED AFTER DEATH

1. Butler, op. cit., 1932, March, p. 42.

2. Thomas of Celano, op. cit., pp. 101-102.
3. Ibid., p. 102.
4. Stoddard, op. cit., p. 90.
5. De Montalembert, op. cit., p. 343.
6. Dorcy, op. cit., p.162.
7. Huysmans, op. cit., p. 200.
8. Ibid., p. 200.
9. Fullerton, op. cit., p. 132.
10. Ibid., p. 133.
11. Mother Mary Francis, op. cit., pp. 243-244.
12. Ibid., p. 244.
13. Corcoran, op. cit., p. 146.
14. Sicardo, op. cit., pp. 131-132.
15. Butler, op. cit., 1932, March, p. 159.
16. Butler, op. cit., 1932, Feb., p. 44.
17. Newcomb, op. cit., p. 217.
18. Ibid., p. 219.
19. Ibid., pp. 219-220.
20. John Clarke, O.C.D., *St. Thérèse of Lisieux—Her Last Conversations* (Washington, D. C.: ICS Publications, Institute of Carmelite Studies, 1977), pp. 293-296.
21. Celine Martin, Sister Genevieve of the Holy Face, *A Memoir of My Sister Saint Thérèse* (New York: P. J. Kenedy & Sons, 1959), p. 244.
22. Clarke, *Story of A Soul, the Autobiography of St. Thérèse of Lisieux,* p. 271.
23. *A Novice of Saint Thérèse* (Allentown, Pennsylvania: Carmelite Nuns of the Ancient Observance, Carmel of the Little Flower, 1946), p. 43.
24. Butler, op. cit., February, 1932, pp. 247-248.
25. Brewer, op. cit., pp. 162-163.
26. Drane, *The Life of Saint Dominic,* p. 215.
27. Ibid., p. 216.
28. Bl. Raymond of Capua, op. cit., p. 240.
29. Ibid., p. 241.
30. Ibid., p. 242.
31. Willey DeSpens, *Saint Rita* (Garden City, New York: Hanover House, 1960), pp. 140-141.
32. Corcoran, op. cit., pp. 158-159.
33. *A Novice of Saint Thérèse,* op. cit., pp. 23-24.
34. Ibid., pp. 43-44.
35. Sister Mary Minima, op. cit., p. 322.
36. O'Sullivan, op. cit., p. 43.
37. Ibid., p. 36.
38. O'Sullivan, op. cit., p. 44.
39. Ibid., p. 45.
40. Mohr, op. cit., p. 38.
41. De Porrentruy, op. cit., pp. 216-217.

Chapter 22: Lights about the Bodies of Saints

1. Butler, op. cit., 1932, Vol. VII, p. 166.
2. Ibid., Vol. IV, pp. 295-296.
3. Sicardo, op. cit., p. 133.
4. Robert Sencourt, *Carmelite and Poet, A Framed Portrait of St. John of the Cross* (New York: The Macmillian Company, 1944), p. 210.
5. Cruz, *The Incorruptibles,* p. 199.
6. Lay Brother, op. cit., p. 251.
7. Cruz., *The Incorruptibles,* p. 295.

Chapter 23: Blood Miracles

1. Mohr, op. cit., pp. 8-9.
2. O'Sullivan, op. cit., p. 134.
3. Ibid., pp. 42-43.
4. Cruz, *Relics,* pp. 182-186.
5. Ibid., pp. 186-188.
6. Ibid., pp. 188-189.
7. Thurston, *Physical Phenomena of Mysticism,* op. cit., p. 283.
8. Cruz, *The Incorruptibles,* pp. 97-98.
9. Summers, op. cit., pp. 132-136.
10. Thurston, *The Physical Phenomena of Mysticism,* p. 289.
11. Ibid., p. 285.
12. Cruz, *The Incorruptibles,* p. 174.
13. Fr. Paschasius Heriz, O.C.D., *St. John of the Cross* (Washington, D.C.: College of Mount Carmel, 1919), pp. 203-206.
14. Cruz, *Relics,* pp. 153-154.
15. Butler, 1935, Vol. XI, pp. 112-113.
16. Rev. Herbert Thurston, S.J., *The Month,* January 1927, p. 47.
17. Butler, op. cit., 1938, Vol. XI, p. 113.
18. Butler, op. cit., 1932, Vol. VII, pp. 32-33.
19. Summers, op. cit., pp. 138-139.
20. Cruz, *The Incorruptibles,* pp. 233-234.

21. Thurston, *Physical Phenomena of Mysticism,* p. 291.
22. Dorcy, op. cit., p. 138.
23. Simi and Segreti, op. cit., pp. 111-113.
24. Robin Anderson, *Saint Pius V* (Rockford, Illinois: TAN, 1989), pp. 97-98.
25. Thurston, *The Month,* February 1927, pp. 123-126.
26. Ibid., p. 132.

Chapter 24: VOICES OF THE DEAD

1. Cruz, *The Incorruptibles,* pp. 99-101.
2. Ibid., p. 150.
3. Frances Parkinson Keyes, *The Third Mystic of Avila, The Self Revelation of Maria Vela* (New York: Farrar, Straus & Cudahy, 1960), p. 36.
4. James A. Carrico, *Life of Venerable Mary of Agreda* (San Bernardino, California: Crestline Book Company, 1959), p. 23.
5. Cruz, *Relics,* p. 274.
6. Taylor, ed., op. cit., p. 345.
7. Paolo Risso, *A Song of Love* (Casa Madre Suore Minime Dell' Addolorata, Le Budrie di Persiceto, 1989), p. 47.
8. Ibid., pp. 78-80.
9. Ibid., p. 104.
10. Caesare Zappulli, *The Power of Goodness—The Life of Blessed Clelia Barbieri* (Boston: Daughters of St. Paul, 1980), pp. 61-62.
11. Risso, op. cit., p. 108.
12. Zappulli, op. cit., p. 62.
13. Cruz, *The Incorruptibles,* p. 100.
14. Risso, op. cit., p. 126.

Chapter 25: DEATH WARNINGS AND OTHER SIGNALS FROM THE DEAD

1. O'Sullivan, op. cit., p. 70.
2. Mohr, op. cit., p. 68.
3. O'Sullivan, op. cit., p. 47.
4. Mohr, op. cit., pp. 67-68.
5. Cruz, *The Incorruptibles,* pp. 208-209.
6. Luciano Canonici, *Antonio Vici, Principe Conteso* (Edizione Porziuncolo, 1961), p. 160.

7. Cruz, *The Incorruptibles,* p. 110.
8. *The Catholic Encyclopedia* (New York: The Encyclopedia Press, Inc., 1913), Vol. II, p. 375.
9. Butler, op. cit., 1936, Vol. V, p. 305.
10. Dorcy, op. cit., p. 191.
11. Joseph L. Cassidy, *Mexico, Land of Mary's Wonders* (Paterson, New Jersey: St. Anthony Guild Press, 1958), pp. 104-109.

Chapter 26: MANNA

1. Cruz, *Relics,* pp. 192-194.
2. Ibid., p. 196.
3. Ibid.
4. Ibid., p. 197.
5. Ibid., pp. 200-201.
6. Lay Brother, op. cit., p. 228.
7. Ibid., p. 228.
8. Ibid., p. 257.
9. De Montalembert, op. cit., p. 377.
10. Herbert Thurston, S.J., *The Life of St. Hugh of Lincoln* (New York: Benziger Brothers, 1898), p. 580.
11. Ibid., p. 581.
12. St. Raymond of Capua, op. cit., p. 240.
13. Ibid., p. 242.
14. Ibid., p. 243.
15. Cruz, *The Incorruptibles,* p. 109.
16. Ibid., p. 110.
17. V. Sackville-West, *The Eagle and the Dove* (Garden City, New York: Doubleday, Doran and Company, Inc., 1944), p. 90.
18. De Porrentruy, op. cit., p. 212.
19. Cruz, *The Incorruptibles,* p. 206.
20. Butler, op. cit., 1938, Vol. XII, p. 311.
21. Sister Mary Minima, op. cit., p. 348.
22. Ibid., p. 326.
23. C. C. Martindale, S.J., *Life of St. Camillus* (London: Sheed & Ward, 1946), p. 154.
24. Cruz, *The Incorruptibles,* p. 222.
25. Boresky, op. cit., p. 279.
26. Cruz, *The Incorruptibles,* p. 236.
27. Ibid., p. 263.
28. Daher, op. cit., pp. 32-36.
29. Sister Marie Helene Mohr, op. cit., pp. 129-130.

Chapter 27: PERFUME FROM THE SAINTED BODIES OF THE DEAD

1. Thurston, *The Physical Phenomena of Mysticism,* p. 223.
2. Ibid.
3. Ibid.
4. Butler, op. cit., 1926, Vol. I, p. 19.
5. Thurston, *The Physical Phenomena of Mysticism,* p. 224.
6. Butler, op. cit., 1932, Vol. VII, p. 334.
7. Drane, *The Life of St. Dominic,* p. 143.
8. Ibid., pp. 214-215.
9. Ibid., p. 216.
10. Ibid.
11. Farges, op. cit., p. 556.
12. De Montalembert, op. cit., pp. 343-344.
13. Fullerton, op. cit., pp. 134-135.
14. Schimberg, op. cit., p. 169.
15. Ibid., p. 170.
16. Rev. M. J. Corcoran, O.S.A., *Our Own St. Rita—A Life of the Saint of the Impossible* (New York: Benziger Brothers, 1919), pp. 160-161.
17. Sicardo, op. cit., p. 174.
18. Canonici, op. cit., p. 155.
19. Cruz, *The Incorruptibles,* pp. 142-143.
20. Butler, op. cit., 1932, Vol. VII, p. 109.
21. Fullerton, op. cit., p. 157.
22. Cruz, *The Incorruptibles,* p. 169.
23. Ibid., p. 292.
24. Edward Healey Thompson, M.A., *St. Stanislaus Kostka of the Company of Jesus* (Philadelphia: Catholic Bookseller, 1876), pp. 280-281.
25. Marcelle Auclair, *Teresa of Avila* (New York: Pantheon Books, Inc.), pp. 430-431.
26. Ibid., p. 292.
27. Cruz, *The Incorruptibles,* p. 200.
28. Kearns, op. cit., p. 157.
29. Ibid., p. 165.
30. Cruz, *The Incorruptibles,* pp. 235-236.
31. Msgr. James F. Newcomb, P.A., *St. Theresa Margaret of the Sacred Heart of Jesus* (New York: Benziger Brothers, 1934), p. 220.
32. Ibid., p. 223.
33. Ibid., pp. 223-224.
34. Echevarria, op. cit., p. 279.
35. Habig, op. cit., p. 312.
36. Taylor, op. cit., p. 418.

Chapter 28: EARTH, SEA AND SKY

1. Miller and Aubin, op. cit., p. 307.
2. Butler, op. cit., 1935, Vol. I, pp. 404-405.
3. Dorcy, op. cit., p. 200.
4. Echevarria, op. cit., p. 174.
5. Butler, op. cit., 1936, Vol. X, p. 282.
6. Simi and Segreti, op. cit., pp. 125-126.
7. Butler, op. cit., 1932, Vol. III, pp. 381-382.
8. Pastrovicchi, op. cit., p. 41.
9. Drane, *The Life of St. Dominic,* p. 194.
10. Echevarria, op. cit., p. 81.
11. Butler, op. cit., 1936, Vol. V, p. 135.
12. Butler, op. cit., 1932, Vol. III, p. 312.

Chapter 29: RAIN, SNOW AND ICE

1. Butler, op. cit., 1936, Vol. X, p. 282.
2. Van Speybrouck, op. cit., pp. 327-329.
3. Butler, op. cit., 1926, Vol. III, p. 284.
4. Drane, *The Life of St. Dominic,* p. 147.
5. Auffray, op. cit., pp. 121-123.
6. Lay Brother, op. cit., p. 165.
7. Fr. Pius of the Name of Mary, op. cit., pp. 117-118.
8. *The Catholic Encyclopedia,* 1913, Vol. I, p. 557.
9. Ibid., p. 557.
10. Aradi, op. cit., p. 208.
11. Ratisbonne, op. cit., p. 68.
12. Cruz, *The Incorruptibles,* p. 213.
13. Thomas of Celano, op. cit., pp. 168-169.
14. Joan Carroll Cruz, *Miraculous Images of Our Lady* (Rockford, Illinois: TAN, 1993), pp. 137-141.
15. Butler, op. cit., 1935, Vol. V, p. 135.
16. *Story of a Soul, the Autobiography of St. Thérèse of Lisieux* (Washington, D.C.: Institute of Carmelite

Studies Publications, 1975), pp. 154-156.
17. Cruz, *Miraculous Images of Our Lady,* pp. 56-61.
18. Ibid., pp. 363-366.

Chapter 30: PLANTS, FRUIT AND FLOWERS

1. Butler, op. cit., 1937, Vol. VI, p. 60.
2. Brewer, op. cit., p. 395.
3. Taylor, ed., op. cit., p. 415.
4. Butler, op. cit., 1934, Vol. IX, p. 178.
5. Ibid., Vol. VI, p. 197.
6. Corcoran, op. cit., pp. 96-97.
7. Cruz, *The Incorruptibles,* p. 133.
8. Fr. Pius of the Name of Mary, op. cit., pp. 68-69.
9. Butler, op. cit., 1933, Vol. IV, p. 308.
10. Butler, op. cit., 1932, Vol. II, p. 211.
11. Butler, op. cit., 1926, Vol. I, p. 356.
12. Kearns, op. cit., pp. 115-116.
13. Ibid., p. 116.
14. Ibid.
15. Stoddard, op. cit., pp. 23-24.
16. Butler, op. cit., 1933, Vol. VIII, p. 37.
17. Dorcy, op. cit., pp. 210-211.
18. Pastrovicchi, op. cit., p. 107.
19. Butler, op. cit., 1937, Vol. VI, p. 85.
20. Ibid., p. 317.
21. Schuster, op. cit., p. 70.
22. Brewer, op. cit., p. 448.
23. Van Speybrouck, op. cit., p. 87.
24. De Montalembert, op. cit., p. 155.
25. Cruz, *The Incorruptibles,* p. 213.
26. Corcoran, op. cit., p. 141.
27. Ibid., p. 142.
28. Cruz, *Relics,* pp. 77-83.
29. Sister Mary Alphonsus, op. cit., p. 160.
30. Trochu, op. cit., p. 177.
31. Dorcy, op. cit., p. 162.

Chapter 31: BIRDS, BEES AND BUGS

1. Joseph S. Brusher, S.J., *Popes Through the Ages* (Princeton, New Jersey: D. Van Nostrand Company, Inc., 1959), p. 40.
2. Butler, 1935, Vol. I, p. 265.
3. Brewer, op. cit., p. 365.

4. Ibid., p. 366.
5. Van Speybrouck, op. cit., pp. 308-309.
6. Schuster, op. cit., p. 68.
7. The Venerable Bede, *Ecclesiastical History of the English Nation* (London: J. M. Dent & Sons, Ltd., 1910 & 1958), p. 314.
8. Ibid., pp. 314-315.
9. Butler, op. cit., 1934, Vol. IX, p. 24.
10. Cruz, *Miraculous Images of Our Lady,* pp. 426-428.
11. Butler, op. cit., 1932, Vol. III, p. 138.
12. Butler, 1932, Vol. VII, p. 397.
13. Cruz, *The Incorruptibles,* pp. 78-80.
14. Thomas of Celano, op. cit., pp. 53-54.
15. Butler, op. cit., 1936, Vol. X, p. 44.
16. Brown, op. cit., pp. 177-178.
17. De Montalembert, op. cit., pp. 344-345.
18. Ibid.
19. Dorcy, op. cit., p. 52.
20. Butler, op. cit., 1933, Vol. IV, p. 43.
21. Dorcy, op. cit., p. 127
22. Ibid., p. 221.
23. Sister Mary Alphonsus, op. cit., pp. 285-286.
24. Kearns, op. cit., p. 115.
25. Pastrovicchi, op. cit., pp. 67-68.
26. Ibid., p. 67.
27. Ibid., p. 66.
28. Lay Brother, op. cit., p. 165.
29. Echevarria, op. cit., p. 317.
30. Sr. Agnes of Jesus, op. cit., p. 193.
31. Rev. Gabriel Locher, O.S.B., *A Brief Biography of Sister Mary Fortunata Viti* (Clyde, Missouri: Benedictine Convent of Perpetual Adoration, 1940), pp. 136-137.
32. Rev. Joseph Cacella, *The White Doves of Peace* (New York: Vatican City Religious Book Company, Inc., 1949), p. 4.
33. Ibid., pp. 3-4.
34. John M. Haffert, *Russia Will Be Converted* (Washington, New Jersey: AMI International Press, 1950), p. 195.
35. Ibid., p. 193.
36. Servite and Cacella, op. cit., p. 9.
37. Ibid., pp. 8-9.
38. All information concerning the sec-

ond pilgrimage of Our Lady through Portugal and Spain was taken from *The White Doves of Peace* by Servite and Rev. Joseph Cacella.

39. Butler, op. cit., 1932, Vol. II, p. 199.
40. Ibid., Vol. IX, p. 69.
41. Cruz, *Secular Saints* (Rockford, Illinois: TAN, 1984), p. 284.
42. Cruz, *Relics,* p. 284.
43. Ibid., pp. 284-285.
44. Sicardo, op. cit., pp. 154-156.
45. Biver, op. cit., p. 103.
46. Michael H. Crosby, O.F.M. Cap., *Thank God Ahead of Time, The Life and Spirituality of Solanus Casey* (Chicago: Franciscan Herald Press, 1984), pp. 207-208.
47. Butler, op. cit., 1932, Vol. VII, p. 195.
48. Butler, op. cit., 1926, Vol. I, p. 114.
49. Habig, op. cit., p. 496.
50. Schuster, op. cit., p. 70.
51. Thomas of Celano, op. cit., pp. 274-275.
52. Butler, op. cit., 1934, Vol. IX, p. 309.
53. Brewer, op. cit., p. 362.
54. Ibid., p. 364.
55. Ratisbonne, op. cit., p. 83.
56. Walsh, op. cit., pp. 294-297.
57. Pastrovicchi, op. cit., p. 106.
58. Simi and Segreti, op. cit., pp. 43-44.
59. Cruz, *The Incorruptibles,* pp. 286-287.

Chapter 32: Animals, Reptiles and Creatures of the Sea

1. Butler, op. cit., 1935, Vol. II, pp. 48-49.
2. Butler, op. cit., 1933, Vol. IV, pp. 19-22.
3. Ibid., Vol. IV, p. 238.
4. Butler, op. cit., 1938, Vol. XI, pp. 307-308.
5. The Venerable Bede, op. cit., pp. 301-302.
6. Butler, op. cit., 1933, Vol. IV, p. 282.
7. Ibid., 1937, Vol. VI, pp. 200-201.
8. Brown, op. cit., pp. 86-91.
9. Thomas of Celano, op. cit., pp. 167-168.
10. Ibid., p. 55.
11. Ibid., pp. 320-321.
12. Stoddard, op. cit., p. 57.
13. Kearns, op. cit., p. 111.
14. Lay Brother, op. cit., p. 164.
15. Butler, op. cit., 1932, Vol. II, pp. 307-309.
16. Ibid., pp. 350-351.
17. Fr. Pius of the Name of Mary, op. cit., p. 202.
18. *St. Joseph Benedict Cottolengo* (The Mother House of the Cottolengo, Pinerolo, Turin, Italy, 1950), p. 25.
19. Butler, op. cit., 1936, Vol. V, p. 259.
20. Simi and Segreti, op. cit., p. 23.
21. Sister Mary Minima, op. cit., p. 226.
22. Pastrovicchi, op. cit., p. 54.
23. Ibid., p. 67.
24. Ibid.
25. Lancelot C. Sheppard, *Don Bosco* (Westminster, Maryland: The Newman Press, 1957), pp. 78-79.
26. Ibid., pp. 79-80.
27. Ibid., p. 80.
28. Ibid.
29. Ibid.
30. Drane, *The Life of St. Dominic,* p. 4.
31. Cruz, *The Incorruptibles,* p. 213.
32. Dorcy, op. cit., p. 209.
33. Brewer, op. cit., p. 115.
34. Ibid., p. 112.
35. Locher, op. cit., pp. 145-146.
36. Brewer, op. cit., p. 143.
37. Brown, op. cit., pp. 131-133.
38. Dorcy, op. cit., pp. 199-200.
39. Paul Van Dyke, *Ignatius Loyola, The Founder of the Jesuits* (New York: Charles Scribner's Sons, 1926), pp. 323-324.
40. Ibid., p. 329.

Chapter 33: Wells, Springs and Holy Water

1. Mary Sharp, *A Guide to the Churches of Rome* (New York: Chilton Books, 1966), pp. 178-179.
2. Sharp, op. cit., p. 161.
3. Ibid., pp. 177-178.
4. Omer Englebert, *The Lives of the Saints* (New York: Collier Books, 1964), pp. 55-56.
5. Butler, op. cit., 1932, Vol. VII, pp. 416-417.

6. The Venerable Bede, op. cit., p. 13.
7. Ibid., p. 13.
8. Donald Attwater, *The Penguin Dictionary of Saints* (Baltimore, Maryland: Penguin Books, 1966), p. 37.
9. Brewer, op. cit., p. 332.
10. Butler, op. cit., 1933, Vol. IV, p. 237.
11. Butler, op. cit., 1938, Vol. XII, pp. 69-70.
12. Pope St. Gregory the Great, op. cit., pp. 18-19.
13. Brewer, op. cit., p. 334.
14. Ibid., p. 333.
15. Bede, op. cit., p. 216.
16. Ibid., p. 312.
17. Brewer, op. cit., p. 335.
18. Ibid., p. 334.
19. Brown, op. cit., pp. 176-177.
20. Habig, op. cit., pp. 526-527.
21. Schimberg, op. cit., pp. 91-92.
22. Cruz, *The Incorruptibles,* p. 148.
23. Simi and Segreti, op. cit., p. 44.
24. Ibid., pp. 49-50.
25. Ibid., p. 130.
26. St. Teresa of Avila, op. cit., p. 167.
27. Zappulli, op. cit., p. 64.
28. Brewer, op. cit., p. 505.
29. *The Catholic Encyclopedia,* op. cit., Vol. VII, pp. 432-433.
30. Ibid., p. 433.
31. Butler, op. cit., 1935, Vol. XII, p. 267.
32. *The Catholic Encyclopedia,* op. cit., Vol. VII, p. 432.
33. Brewer, op. cit., p. 505.
34. Ibid.
35. Beda Venerabilis, op. cit., p. 327.
36. Brewer, op. cit., p. 505.
37. Butler, op. cit., 1938, Vol. XI, p. 36.
38. Drane, *The Life of Saint Dominic,* pp. 106-107.
39. Brewer, op. cit., p. 505.
40. Fr. Pius of the Name of Mary, op. cit., pp. 187-188.
41. Brewer, op. cit., p. 505.
42. *The Life of Teresa of Jesus,* trans. by E. Allison Peers (Garden City, New York: Image Books, 1944), p. 187.
43. Ibid., p. 289.
44. Lay Brother, op. cit., p. 58.
45. Van Speybrouck, op. cit., pp. 233-234.
46. Cruz, *Relics,* p. 187.
47. Crosby, op. cit., pp. 52-53.

Chapter 34: THE SAINTS AND FIRE

1. Simi and Segreti, op. cit., p. 15.
2. Drane, *The Life of Saint Dominic,* p. 16.
3. Ibid., pp. 16-17.
4. Echevarria, op. cit., pp. 249-250.
5. Dorcy, op. cit., p. 35.
6. Simi and Segreti, op. cit., pp. 28-29.
7. Blessed Raymond of Capua, op. cit., p. 114.
8. Ibid., pp. 114-115.
9. Thomas of Celano, op. cit., pp. 271-272.
10. Cruz, *The Incorruptibles,* p. 137.
11. Bonniwell, op. cit., pp. 87-89.
12. Sicardo, op. cit., p. 141.
13. Habig, op. cit., p. 804.
14. Simi and Segreti, op. cit., p. 57.
15. Ibid., pp. 185-186.

Chapter 35: MARVELS OF EVERY SORT

1. Joan Carroll Cruz, *Miraculous Images of Our Lord* (Rockford, Illinois: TAN, 1993), pp. 225-226.
2. Butler, op. cit., 1936, Vol. V, p. 248.
3. Cruz, *The Incorruptibles,* p. 104.
4. Cruz, *Miraculous Images of Our Lady,* pp. 169-170.
5. Cruz, *The Incorruptibles,* p. 198.
6. O'Sullivan, op. cit., p. 48-49.
7. Ibid., p. 49.
8. Butler, op. cit., 1933, Vol. IV, pp. 304-305.
9. Butler, op. cit., 1932, Vol. III, p. 156.
10. Butler, op. cit., 1933, Vol. VIII, pp. 190-191.
11. Butler, op. cit., 1937, Vol. VI, pp. 247-248.
12. Cruz, *The Incorruptibles,* pp. 220-222.
13. Ibid., p. 223.
14. Friar Stanislaus of St. Theresa, O.D.C., *St. Theresa Margaret of the Sacred Heart of Jesus* (New York: Benziger Brothers, 1934), p. 168.
15. Cruz, *Relics,* p. 210.
16. Bessieres, op. cit., p. 48.

17. Stoddard, op. cit., pp. 74-76.
18. Lay Sister of the Benedictine Convent, Italy, *A Brief Biography of Sister Mary Fortunata Viti* (Clyde, Missouri: Benedictine Convent of Perpetual Adoration, 1940), p. 146.
19. Right Rev. Dom Prosper Gueranger, O.S.B., *The Medal or Cross of St. Benedict* (1880; rpt. Albany, New York: Preserving Christian Publications, Inc., 1992), p. xviii.
20. Butler, op. cit., 1932, Vol. II, p. 13.
21. Drane, *The Life of St. Dominic,* pp. 146-147.
22. Stoddard, op. cit., p. 99.
23. Cruz, *Relics,* p. 277.
24. Matthews, op. cit., pp. 81-83.
25. Butler, op. cit., 1936, Vol. V, pp. 229-230.
26. Butler, Vol. X, p. 220.
27. John M. Haffert, *Soul Magazine* (Washington, New Jersey: Ave Maria Institute, 1978), Vol. 29, No. 4, p. 17.
28. Kearns, op. cit., pp. 164-166.
29. Walsh, op. cit., p. 559.
30. Butler, op.cit., 1937, Vol. VI, p. 101.
31. Ibid., p. 101.
32. Keyes, op. cit., p. 166.
33. Ibid., pp. 166-167.
34. Blessed Raymond of Capua, op. cit., pp. 335-336.
35. Ibid., pp. 336.
36. Dorcy, op. cit., pp. 474-475.
37. St. Louis Marie Grignon DeMontfort, *True Devotion to Mary* (Rockford, Illinois: TAN, 1985), pp. xii-xiii.
38. *A Lover of the Cross, St. Gemma Galgani,* op. cit., pp. 130-131.
39. Ibid., p. 131.
40. Cruz, *The Incorruptibles,* p. 108.
41. Ibid., p. 108.
42. From information supplied by the Discalced Carmelite Nuns of Elysburg, Pennsylvania.
43. Butler, op. cit., 1938, Vol. XI, p. 120.
44. Cruz, *Relics,* p. 262.
45. Butler, op. cit., 1932, Vol. II, pp. 288-289.
46. Cruz, *Relics,* p. 286.
47. Ratisbonne, op. cit., pp. 197-198.
48. Mohr, op. cit., pp. 43-44.
49. Van Speybrouck, op. cit., p. 313.
50. Simi and Segreti, op. cit., p. 25.
51. Lay Brother, op. cit., p. 166.
52. Martin, op. cit., p. 243.
53. Sister Agnes of Jesus, op. cit., p. 194.

— INDEX —

Achard, St. 514
Agnes of Montepulciano, St.
. . . . 30, 309, 317, 367, 444, 545
Agricolus, St. 437
Aloysius Gonzaga, St. 212
Alpais, Bl. 247
Alphonsus Liguori, St.
. . . 1, 23, 43, 169, 274, 399, 548
Alvarez of Cordova, Bl.
. . . . 100, 136, 356
Ammon the Great, St. 87
Andre, Bl. 203, 255, 541
Andrew Avellino, St. 335
Andrew Bobola, St. 295
Andrew the Apostle, St. 359
Angela of Foligna, Bl. . . . 255, 280
Angelo of Borgo Sepolcro, Bl. 395
Anna Maria Taigi, Bl.
. . . . 63, 135, 176, 197, 535, 540
Anne of Constantinople, St. . . 384
Anne of St. Bartholomew, Bl. . 542
Anthony Grassi, Bl. 267
Anthony Mary Claret, St. . . 24, 59,
. . . . 64, 96, 158, 171, 198,
. . . . 272, 400, 403, 447, 518
Anthony of Padua, St. 9, 90,
. . 188, 239, 258, 299, 408, 425,
. . . 477, 489, 493, 494, 536, 539
Anthony Vici of Stroncone, Bl.
. . . . 354, 388, 521, 526
Antony the Great, St. 500
Archangela Girlani, Bl. 423
Augustine Gazotich, Bl. 425
Bartholomew of Cerverio, Bl.
. . . . 425
Basolus, St. 473
Beatrice d'Este, Bl. 355, 371
Bede the Venerable, St. 512
Benedict Joseph Labré, St. 39
Benedict the Moor, St. . . 166, 396
Benedict XIV, Pope 49
Benedict, St. 50-51, 88, 104,
. . . . 117, 186, 210,
. . . . 419, 427, 435, 464,
. . . . 501, 526, 550
Benno, St. 475

Bentivoglia de Bonis, Bl. 90
Bernard of Clairvaux, St.
. . . . 143, 187, 409, 466
Bernard Scammacca, Bl.
. . . . 215, 307, 444
Bernardine of Siena, St. . 243, 527
Bernardino Realino, St.
. . . . 22, 166, 175, 335
Bertrand of Garriga, Bl. 459
Blaise, St. 472
Bonavita, Bl. 522
Boniface, St. 420
Bonizella Piccolomini, Bl. . . . 459
Botwid, St. 440
Brigid of Kildare, St. 538
Brigid, St. 318
Camillus de Lellis, St. . . . 372, 534
Catalina de Cardona. 53
Catalina de Cristo, Ven. 395
Catherine dei Ricci, St.
. . . . . 6, 54, 144, 166, 222, 529
Catherine Laboure, St. 215
Catherine of Bologna, St.
. . . . 303, 333, 388, 531
Catherine of Genoa, St. . . 252, 284
Catherine of Racconigi, Bl. . . . 97,
. . . . 147, 255
Catherine of Siena, St. . 38, 42, 62,
. . . . 73, 82, 121, 148, 155, 163,
. . . . 174, 232, 236, 248,
. . . . . . 259, 282, 283, 520, 543
Ceslaus, Bl. 519
Charbel Makhlouf, St. . . 287, 320,
. . . . 375, 468, 516, 549
Charles Borromeo, St. 285
Charles of Sezze, St. 71
Clara of Rimini, Bl. 30
Clare of Assisi, St. 162
Clare of Montefalco, St.
. . . . ii, 72, 331, 528
Claritus, Bl. 355
Clarus, St. 383
Clelia Barbieri, St. 347, 351,
. . . . 398, 509, 541
Clement I of Rome, St. 497
Clement Mary Hofbauer, St. . . 207

Colette, St. 93, 103, 123, 149,
. . . . 164, 191, 234,
. . . . 302, 386, 506
Conrad of Ascoli, Bl. 189
Conrad, St. 465
Constantine. 527
Cunegunda, Bl. 505
Cuthbert, St. . . 436, 474, 503, 512
Didacus of Alcala, St. 395
Dominic of Jesu Maria, Ven. . . . 27
Dominic, Bl. 318
Dominic, St. 34, 88, 118, 139,
. . 188, 211, 240, 245, 308, 384,
. . . 402, 485, 513, 517, 524, 538
Dominica A. Paradiso, Ven. 53, 74
Drogo, St. 8, 307
Elias 433, 470
Elizabeth of Hungary, St. 120
. . . . 162, 300, 365, 385,
. . . . 398, 428, 442
Elizabeth the Good, Bl. . . 221, 250
Ethelwald, St. 402
Eustochia Calafato, Bl. 343
Eustochia of Padua, Bl. 506
Eutychus, St. 487
Flora of Beaulieu, Bl. 36
Frances of Rome, St.
. . . . 122, 163, 190, 302, 385
Francesca Dal Serrone, Ven. . . . 180
Francis de Sales, St. . . 79, 81, 170
Francis of Assisi, St. 119, 217,
. . 238, 267, 299, 385, 410, 428,
. . . . 441, 464, 475, 505, 520
Francis of Camporosso, Bl. . . . 277
Francis of Paola, St. 8, 29, 98,
. . 102, 125, 164, 192, 206, 262,
. . . . 338, 341, 401, 468, 481,
. . . 507, 517, 519, 523, 524, 551
Francis of Posadas, St.
. . . . 30, 169, 181, 278
Francis Patrizzi, Bl. 215
Francis Regis, St. 128
Francis Solano, St. . . 98, 243, 464
Francis Xavier Bianchi, Bl.
. . . . 106, 399
Francis Xavier, St.
. . . . 10, 289, 333, 395, 491
Frediano, St. 404
Friard, St. 465
Fulco of Neuilly, Bl. 279
Fursey, St. 503
Gandulphus of Binasco, Bl.
. . . . 211, 443

Gaspar del Bufalo, St. . . . 106, 409
Gemma Galgani, St.
. . . . . 26, 63, 203, 227, 255, 545
Gerard Cagnoli, Bl. 541
Gerard Majella, St. 2, 18, 23,
. . . . . 58, 76, 97, 106, 115, 124,
. . 169, 174, 195, 207, 214, 258,
. . . . 267, 320, 363, 407, 447,
. . . . 478, 515, 551
Gerard of Monza, Bl. . . . 134, 426
Gerard of Villamagna, Bl. 215
Germaine Cousin, St.
. . . . 93, 334, 409, 429, 485
Gertrude the Great, St. 148
Gertrude Van Oosten, Bl. 231
Gervinus, St. 298
Godric, St. 274, 480
Gonsalvo of Amarante, Bl. . . . 105
Gregory Nazianzen, St. 383
Gregory, Bl. 318
Gunthiern, St. 512
Guthlac, St. 384
Hedwig, St. 261, 541
Henry Suso, Bl. 162
Heribert, St. 406
Herman, St. 52
Hilarion, St. 401, 405
Hugh of Lincoln, St. 366, 440
Hyacinth, St. 88, 101
Ida of Louvain, Bl. 52
Ignatius of Loyola, St.
. . . . 39, 165, 180, 185, 280
Isidore the Farmer, St. . . . 116, 504
James of Bevagna, Bl. . . . 215, 338
James of Bitetto, Bl. 423
James the Almsgiver, Bl. 424
James, St. 463
Jane (Joan) Scopelli, Bl. 389
Jane Frances de Chantal, St.
. . . . 80, 81
Jane of Signa, Bl. 101
Januarius, St. 324, 342
Jean Marie Baptiste Vianney, St.
. . . . 37, 107, 129, 150, 171,
. . . . 242, 254, 270, 431
Jeanne de Lestonnac, Bl. 304
Joan Marie of the Cross of
Rovereto, Ven. 55
John Baptist da Fabriano, Bl.
. . . . 52-53
John Bosco, St. 13, 65,
. . . . 134, 200, 258, 273, 280,
. . . . 407, 482, 547

John Cantius, St. 136
John Joseph of the Cross, St.
. . . . 30, 95, 279
John Liccio, Bl. 137
John Marie Baptiste Vianney, St.
(see Jean Marie Baptiste
Vianney, St.)
John of God, St. 389
John of Sahagun, St. 279
John of St. Facond, St. 31
John of St. Samson 167
John of the Cross, St. 47, 66,
. . . . 141, 157, 217, 292,
. . . . 319, 334, 391
John Ruysbroeck, Bl. 163
John the Dwarf, St. 421
Jordan of Pisa, Bl. 258
Josaphat, St. 337, 373
Joseph Benedict Cottolengo, St.
. . . . 107, 134, 480
Joseph of Cupertino, St. 3, 31,
. . . . 45, 48, 54, 64, 77,
. . . . . . 140, 168, 194, 213, 265,
. . . 398, 402, 426, 446, 467, 481
Joseph of Leonissa, St. 215
Juan Diego, Bl. 430
Julian, St. 497
Juliana Falconieri, St. 533
Julie Billiart, St. 374
Julitta, St. 498
Ladislaus, Bl. 403, 411
Lawrence, St. 329
Leufredus, St. 466
Louis Bertrand, St.
. . . . 166, 215, 242, 395
Louis Marie Grignon de Montfort,
St. 544
Lucy of Narni, Bl. 223, 389
Lutgarde of Aywieres, St.
. . . . 33, 71, 179, 220, 248
Lydwine of Schiedam, St.
. . . . 4, 52, 105,
. . . . 221, 250, 260, 301
Madeleine Sophie Barat, St.
. . . . 215, 286
Malachy, St. 513
Marcellinus, St. 329, 500
Margaret Mary Alacoque, St.
. . . . 75, 173
Margaret of Castello, Bl. . . . 33, 76
. . . . 190, 521
Margaret of Cortona, St.
. . . . 478, 526

Margaret of Metola (see Margaret
of Castello)
Margaret of Savoy, Bl. 485
Maria Goretti, St. 539
Maria of the Passion, Sr. 29
Maria Vela, Ven. 344
Maria Villani of Naples, Ven.
. . . . 21, 70, 179
Marianus, St. 473
Marie Celine of the Presentation,
Ven. 60, 394
Martin de Porres, St. . . . 4, 25, 93,
. . 167, 193, 208, 213, 242, 264,
. . . 392, 424, 446, 477, 495, 542
Martin of Tours, St. 547
Martinianus 497
Mary Anne de Paredes, Bl. 254
Mary Fortunata Viti, Bl.
. . . . 262, 450, 487, 537
Mary Frances of the Five Wounds
of Jesus, St. 59, 234
Mary Magdalene de' Pazzi, St.
. . . 83, 127, 175, 192, 233, 286,
. . . . 312, 371, 395, 481
Mary Martha Chambon, Sr. 70
Mary of Agreda, Ven.
. . . . 6, 17, 28, 282, 345
Mary of Egypt, St. 472
Mary of Jesus Crucified, Bl.
. . . . 29, 59
Mary of Oignies, Bl.
. . . . 51, 176, 247, 275
Mary of the Angels, Bl. 56
Matthia Nazzarei of Matelica, Bl.
. . . . 355, 368
Maura, St. 318
Meinrad, St. 438
Micaela Desmaisieres, St. 394
Michael of the Saints, St. 75
Modomnoc, St. 459
Mother Louise Margaret Claret
de la Touche 158
Mother Maria of Jesus, Ven.
. . . . 373, 392
Nazarius, St. 329
Nicholas of Tolentino, St.
. . . . 282, 329
Nicholas Palaea, Bl. 214, 443
Nicholas Von Flüe, St. 251
Nicholas, St. 360
Olav, St. 508
Osanna of Mantua, Bl. 226
Oswald, St. 160

Pacificus di San Severino, St.. 337
Pacomius, St. 243
Padre Pio 14, 60, 69, 85
. . . 181, 184, 204, 229, 244, 277
Paschal Baylon, St.
. . . . 293, 316, 353, 370, 395
Passitea Crogi, Ven.. . 28, 223, 337
Patricia, St. 282, 328
Patrick, St. 486
Paul of Moll, Fr. 12, 24, 60,
. . . . 108, 209, 427, 448, 515
Paul of the Cross, St. . . . 3, 27, 58,
. . . . 63, 78, 95, 137, 169,
. . . . 178, 196, 240, 269,
. . . . 408, 423, 480, 514
Paul, St. 497
Paul, The Bishop of Leon, St.. 488
Père Lamy 11, 91, 461
Peter, St. 329
Peter Geremia, Bl.. . 400, 490, 530
Peter of Alcantara, St.. 44, 97, 253
Peter of Gubbio, Bl. 343
Peter of Ravenna, St. 420
Peter of Tiferno, Bl. 138, 277
Peter Regalado, St. . . . 10, 97, 332
Pharaildis, St. 504
Philip Benizi, St. 135, 242
Philip Neri, St. 35, 64, 77,
. . . . . . 156, 164, 177, 263, 540
Philomena, St. 153, 313, 352,
. . . . 376, 381, 530, 541, 550
Pius V, Pope St. 279, 339
Polycarp, St. 50, 382
Processus 497
Raymond of Penafort, St. 99
Rita of Cascia, St. 40-41,
. . . . 105, 137, 222, 237,
. . . . 303, 310, 319, 386, 422,
. . . . 429, 432, 460, 471, 522
Robert Bellarmine, St. 167
Roch, St. 532
Rosa Maria Serio, Ven. 179
Rose of Lima, St.
. . . . 212, 254, 431, 445
Rose of Viterbo, St. 39
Sabas, St. 500
Samson, St. 435, 512
Scholastica, St. 405, 419
Sebastian Apparicio, Bl. 479

Serafina Di Dio, Ven. 181
Seraphin of Montegranaro, St. . 89
Servulus, St. 383
Severin, St. 395
Severinus, St. 463
Simeon Stylites, St. 383
Solanus Casey, Ven.. . . . . 462, 516
Stanislaus Kostka, St.
. . . . 165, 177, 390
Stephanie de Quinzanis, Bl.
. . . . 147, 214
Stephen, St. 329
Teresa of Avila, St.. 19, 46, 53, 67,
. . . 84, 126, 141, 143, 152, 165,
. . . 284, 369, 391, 466, 508, 514
Thecla of Moriana, St. 435
Theodore the Holy 511
Theresa Margaret Redi, St.. . . 304,
. . . . 393, 534, 540
Thérèse of Lisieux, St. (See
Thérèse of the Child Jesus and
of the Holy Face, St.)
Thérèse of the Child Jesus and of
the Holy Face, St. (The Little
Flower). 68, 108,
. . . . 201, 305, 346, 394
. . . . 412, 421, 450, 551
Thomas Becket, St. 156
Thomas Corsini, Bl. 426
Thomas of Aquinas, St. 36
Thomas of Cori, O.S.F., Bl. 28
Thomas of Villanova, St. 164
Thomas the Apostle, St. 541
Tychon, St. 422
Ursus, St. 502
Valery, St. 51
Veremundus, St. 439
Veronica Giuliani, St.
. . . . . . 57, 73, 86, 150, 224, 280
Villana De Botti, Bl. 301, 431
Vincent, St. 434
Vincent Ferrer, St.. . 241, 514, 529
Vincent Pallotti, St. 10, 275
Walburga, St. 362, 380, 381
William Firmatus, St. 474
William of Toulouse, Bl. 540
William, St. 513
Wulfric, St. 548
Zita, St. 133, 526, 531

—SELECTED BIBLIOGRAPHY—

Agnes of Jesus, Reverend Mother. *Novissima Verba*, "The Last Conversations of St. Thérèse of the Child Jesus." (May-September). London: Burns Oates & Washbourne, Ltd., 1929.

Alacoque, St. Margaret Mary. *The Autobiography of St. Margaret Mary Alacoque.* Sisters of the Visitation, Trans. 1930; rpt. Rockford, Ill.: TAN, 1986.

Anderson, Robin. *St. Pius V.* Rockford, Illinois: TAN Books and Publishers, Inc., 1989.

Angelini, Fr. Atanasio. *Life of Saint Rita of Cascia.* Terni, Italy: Poligrafico Alterocca, 1953.

Aradi, Zsolt. *The Book of Miracles.* New York: Farrar, Straus and Cudahy, 1956.

Attwater, Donald. *The Penguin Dictionary of Saints.* Baltimore, Maryland: Penguin Books, 1966.

Attwater, Donald. *The Avenel Dictionary of Saints.* New York: Avenel Books, 1977.

Auclair, Marcelle. *Teresa of Avila.* Garden City, New York: Image Books, 1953.

Auffray, S.D.B., Rev. A. *Saint John Bosco.* North Arcot, South India: Salesian House, Tirupattur, 1930.

Bardi, Mons. Giuseppe. *St. Gemma Galgani.* Boston: St. Paul Editions, 1961.

Battaglia, Eliseo. *Blessed Nuno, Carmelite.* Fatima, Portugal: The Carmelite Third Order Press, 1962.

Beda Venerabilis. *Bede's Ecclesiastical History of the English Nation.* New York: J. M. Dent & Sons. Ltd., 1958.

Bergergon, C.S.C., Rev. Henry-Paul. *Brother Andre, C.S.C.* New York: Benziger Brothers, 1938.

Bessieres, S.J., Albert. *Wife, Mother and Mystic.* 1952; rpt. Rockford, Illinois: TAN, 1970.

Biver, Comte Paul. *Père Lamy.* 1951; rpt. Rockford, Illinois: TAN, 1973.

Bonniwell, O.P., Fr. William R. *The Life of Blessed Margaret of Castello.* Rockford, Illinois: TAN, 1983.

Boresky, Theodosia. *Life of St. Josaphat, Martyr of the Union.* New York: Comet Press Books, 1955.

Brewer, E. Cobham. *A Dictionary of Miracles.* N.Y.: Cassell & Company, Ltd., 1884.

Brief Biography of Sister Mary Fortunata Viti, A. Rev. Gabriel Locher, O.S.B. and Rev. Stephen Radtke, Trans. Clyde, Missouri: Benedictine Convent of Perpetual Adoration, 1940.

Brodrick, S.J., James. *Saint Francis Xavier.* Garden City, New York: Image Books, 1957.

—*Monumenta Xaveriana.* New York: The Wicklow Press, 1952.

Brusher, S.J., Joseph S. *Popes Through the Ages.* Princeton, New Jersey: D. Van Nostrand Company, Inc., 1959.

Butler, Rev. Alban. *The Lives of the Saints.* Twelve-volume set. New York: P. J. Kenedy & Sons, 1932-1938.

Canonici, Luciano. *Antonio Vici, Principe Conteso.* Edizione Porziuncolo, 1961.

Carrico, James A. *The Life of Venerable Mary of Agreda.* Bernardino, California: Crestline Book Company, 1959.

Cassidy, Joseph L. *Mexico, Land of Mary's Wonders.* Paterson, New Jersey: St. Anthony Guild Press, 1958.

Catherine of Siena, St. *The Dialogue of the Seraphic Virgin Catherine of Siena.* Algar Thorold, Trans. 1907; rpt. Rockford, Illinois: TAN, 1974.

Catholic Encyclopedia. New York: The Encyclopedia Press, Inc., 1912.

Collett, Rev. M. *Life of St. Vincent of Paul, Founder.* Baltimore, Maryland: John Murphy & Co., 1850.

Corcoran, O.S.A., Rev. M. J. *Our Own St. Rita: A Life of the Saint of the Impossible.* New York: Benziger Brothers, 1919.

Coulson, John, Ed. *An Angelus Book of*

Saints. New York: Guild Press, 1957.

Cristiani, Leon. *St. John of the Cross: Prince of Mystical Theology*. Garden City, New York: Doubleday & Company, 1962.

Crosby, O.F.M. Cap., Michael H. *Thank God Ahead of Time: The Life and Spirituality of Solanus Casey*. Chicago: Franciscan Herald Press, 1984.

Cruz, Joan Carroll. *Eucharistic Miracles*. Rockford, Illinois: TAN, 1987.

—*The Incorruptibles*. Rockford, Illinois: TAN, 1977.

—*Miraculous Images of Our Lady*. Rockford, Illinois: TAN, 1993.

—*Relics*. Huntington, Indiana: Our Sunday Visitor, 1984.

Daher, Paul. *A Miraculous Star in the East: Charbel Makhlouf*. Annaya-Djebeil, Lebanon: The Monastery of St. Maron, 1952.

De Montalembert, Count. *The Life of Saint Elizabeth*. New York: P. J. Kenedy & Sons, 1886.

de Porrentruy, L. A. *The Saint of the Eucharist*. Translated by O. Staniforth, O.F.M. Cap. San Francisco: Press of Upton Brothers & Delzelle, Inc., 1905.

de Robeck, Nesta. *Saint Elizabeth of Hungary*. Milwaukee: The Bruce Publishing Company, 1954.

Dorcy, O.P., Sister Mary Jean. *Saint Dominic's Family*. 1964; rpt. Rockford, Illinois: TAN, 1983.

Drane, Augusta Theodosia. *The Life of St. Dominic*. London: Burns & Oates, Ltd., 1919.

Dubay, S.M., Thomas. *Fire Within*. San Francisco: Ignatius Press, 1989.

Ebon, Martin. *Saint Nicholas: Life and Legend*. New York: Harper & Row, 1975.

Echevarria, C.M.F., Father Juan. *The Miracles of St. Anthony Mary Claret*. Rockford, Illinois: TAN, 1992.

Engelbert, Omer. *The Lives of the Saints*. N.Y.: Collier Books, 1964.

Farges, Mgr. Albert. *Mystical Phenomena*. London: Burns, Oates & Washbourne, Ltd., 1926.

Finuncane, Ronald. C. *Miracles and Pilgrims*. Totowa, New Jersey: Rowan and Littlefield, 1977.

Foley, S.J., Albert S. *St. Regis: A Social Crusader*. Mobile, Alabama: Spring Hill College Press, 1961.

Fullerton, Lady Georgiana. *The Life of St. Frances of Rome*. New York: P. J. Kenedy & Sons.

Garrigou-LaGrange, O.P., The Rev. *The Three Ages of the Interior Life*. Volume Two. 1948; rpt. Rockford, Illinois: TAN, 1989.

Gaynor, Rev. John S. *The Life of St. Vincent Pallotti*. Clerkenwell, London: Pallottine Fathers, 1962.

Genelli, Father. *The Life of St. Ignatius Loyola*. 1917; rpt. Rockford, Illinois: TAN, 1988.

Giordani, Igino. *Catherine of Siena: Fire and Blood*. Milwaukee: The Bruce Publishing Company, 1959.

Gregory the Great, Pope St. *Life and Miracles of St. Benedict*. Book Two of the *Dialogues*. Collegeville, Minnesota: The Liturgical Press, n.d.

Gueranger, O.S.B., Right Rev. Dom Prosper. *The Medal or Cross of St. Benedict*. 1880; rpt. Albany, New York: Preserving Christian Publications, Inc., 1992.

Habig, O.F.M., Marion A. *The Franciscan Book of Saints*. Chicago: Franciscan Herald Press, 1959.

Haffert, John M. *Russia Will Be Converted*. Washington, New Jersey: AMI International Press, 1950.

Hanley, O.F.M., Boniface. *Brother Andre*. Montreal, Canada: St. Joseph's Oratory, 1979.

Harney, S.J., Martin P. *The Jesuits in History: The Society of Jesus Through Four Centuries*. New York: The America Press, 1941.

Hatch, Alden. *The Miracle of the Mountain*. New York: Hawthorn Books, Inc., 1959.

Heriz, O.C.D., Fr. Paschasius. *St. John of the Cross*. Washington, D. C.: College of Mount Carmel, 1919.

Hoever, Rev. Hugo H. *Saint Bernard of Clairvaux*. New York: Catholic Book Publishing Company, 1952.

Huysmans, J. K. *Saint Lydwine of*

Schiedam. 1923; rpt. Rockford, Illinois: TAN, 1979.

Jeremy, O.P., Sister Mary. *Scholars and Mystics.* Chicago: Henry Regnery Company, 1962.

John of St. Samson, O. Carm. *Prayer, Aspiration and Contemplation.* Translated by Venard Poslusney, O. Carm. New York: Alba House, 1975.

John of the Cross. St. *The Collected Works of St. John of the Cross.* Trans. by Kieran Kavanaugh, O.C.D. and Otilio Rodriguez, O.C.D. Washington, D. C.: Institute of Carmelite Studies, 1973.

Kearns, O.P., J.C. *The Life of Blessed Martin de Porres.* New York: P. J. Kenedy & Sons, 1937.

Keyes, Frances Parkinson. *Three Ways of Love.* New York: Hawthorn Books, Inc., 1963.

Lay Brother of the Congregation of the Most Holy Redeemer. *Life, Virtues and Miracles of St. Gerard Majella.* Boston: Mission Church, 1907.

Legault, C.S.C., Andre. *Brother Andre of the Congregation of the Holy Cross.* Montreal, Canada: Saint Joseph's Oratory.

Life and Revelations of Saint Gertrude, Virgin and Abbess of the Order of St. Benedict. 1862; reprinted at Westminster, Maryland: The Newman Press, 1949.

Little Flowers of St. Francis of Assisi, The. Raphael Brown, Trans. Garden City, N.Y.: Doubleday Image, 1958.

Lover of the Cross, A: St. Gemma Galgani. Lucca, Italy: Monastero-Santuario di S. Gemma Galgani Passioniste, 1940.

Loyola, St. Ignatius. *The Autobiography of St. Ignatius of Loyola.* Translated by Joseph F. O'Callaghan. New York: Harper and Row, Publishers, 1974.

Lozano, S.M.F., Juan Maria. *Mystic and Man of Action: Saint Anthony Mary Claret.* Chicago: Claretian Publications, 1977.

Macken, Rev. Thomas F. *The Canonisation of Saints.* Dublin, Ireland: M. H. Gill & Son, Ltd., 1910.

Marie-Eugene, O.C.D., P. *I Am A Daugh-*

ter of the Church. Westminster, Maryland: Christian Classics, Inc., 1979.

Martin, Celine. (Sister Genevieve of the Holy Face). *A Memoir of My Sister St. Thérèse.* New York: P. J. Kenedy & Sons, 1959.

Martindale, S.J., C.C. *Life of St. Camillus.* London: Sheed & Ward, 1946.

Mary Alphonsus, O.SS.R., Sister. *St. Rose of Lima.* 1968; rpt. Rockford, Illinois: TAN, 1982.

Mary Francis, Mother. *Walled in Light: St. Colette.* Chicago: Franciscan Herald Press, 1959.

Mary Minima, Sister. *Seraph Among Angels—The Life of St. Mary Magdalene De' Pazzi.* Chicago: The Carmelite Press, 1958.

Matthews, V. J. *St. Philip Neri.* 1934; rpt. Rockford, Illinois.: TAN, 1984.

Maynard, Theodore. *The Odyssey of Francis Xavier.* Westminster, Maryland: The Newman Press, 1950.

Merton, Thomas. *What Are These Wounds? The Life of a Cistercian Mystic, Saint Lutgarde of Aywieres.* Milwaukee: The Bruce Publishing Company, 1948.

Miller, C.SS.R., Fr. D. F. and Father L. X. Aubin, C.SS.R. *Saint Alphonsus Liguori.* 1940; rpt. Rockford, Illinois: TAN, 1987.

Mohr, S.C., Sister Marie Helene. *Saint Philomena: Powerful with God.* 1953; rpt. Rockford, Illinois: TAN, 1988.

Monden, S.J., Louis. *Signs and Wonders.* New York: Desclee Company, 1966.

Moreschini, Cesare. *The Life of Saint Andrew Bobola of the Society of Jesus, Martyr.* Translated by Louis J. Gallagher, S.J. and Paul V. Donovan. Boston: Bruce Humphries, Inc., 1939.

Morteveille, Blanche. *The Rose Unpetaled.* Milwaukee: The Bruce Publishing Company, 1942.

Newcomb, P. A., Msgr. James F. *St. Theresa Margaret of the Sacred Heart of Jesus.* New York: Benziger Brothers, 1934.

Novice of St. Therese, A. Allentown, Pennsylvania: Carmelite Nuns of the Ancient Observance, Carmel of the Little Flower, 1946.

O'Connell, B. C., Fr. Patrick. *The Life and Work of Mother Louise Margaret Claret de la Touche.* 1950; rpt. Rockford, Illinois: TAN, 1987.

Orsenigo, Most Rev. Cesare. *Life of St. Charles Borromeo.* St. Louis, Missouri: B. Herder Book Company, 1943.

O'Sullivan, O.P., Father Paul. *Saint Philomena The Wonder-Worker.* 1954; new ed. Rockford, Illinois: TAN, 1993.

—*The Wonders of the Mass.* 1963; new ed. Rockford, Illinois: TAN, 1993.

Parente, Pascal P. *The Mystical Life.* St. Louis: B. Herder Book Company, 1946.

Pastrovicchi, O.M.C., The Rev. Angelo. *St. Joseph of Copertino.* 1918; rpt. Rockford, Illinois: TAN, 1980.

Peers, E. Allison. *The Mystics of Spain.* London: George Allen & Urwin, Ltd., 1951.

Pius of the Name of Mary, Father. *The Life of Saint Paul of the Cross.* New York: P. O'Shea, 1924.

Preziuso, Gennaro. "The Padre's Fevers." *The Voice of Padre Pio* Magazine. San Giovanni Rotondo, FG, Italy. Vol. XXIV, No. 6, 1994.

Purcell, Mary. *The First Jesuit: St. Ignatius Loyola.* Chicago: Loyola University Press, 1981.

Ratisbonne, Abbe Theodore. *St. Bernard of Clairvaux.* N.d.; new ed. Rockford, Illinois: TAN, 1991.

Ravier, S.J., Andre. *Saint Colette De Corbie.* Poligny, France: Monastere de Sta. Claire, 1976.

Raymond of Capua, Blessed. *The Life of St. Catherine of Siena.* New York: P. J. Kenedy & Sons, 1960.

Risso, Paolo. *A Song of Love.* Le Budrie di Persiceto, Italy: Casa Madre Suore Minime Dell'Addolorata.

Ruffin, C. Bernard. *Padre Pio: The True Story.* Huntington, Indiana: Our Sunday Visitor, Inc., 1982.

—*Padre Pio: The True Story.* Revised and expanded. Huntington, Ind.: Our Sunday Visitor, Inc., 1991.

Sackville-West, V. *The Eagle and the Dove.* Garden City, New York: Doubleday, Doran and Company, Inc., 1944.

Saint Joseph Benedict Cottolengo. Turin, Italy: Cottolengo Printing School, 1950.

St. Thérèse of Lisieux: Her Last Conversations. John Clarke, O.C.D., Trans. Washington, D.C.: Institute of Carmelite Studies, 1977.

Sarra, Andrea. *The Blessed Mary Fortunata Vita.* St. Benedict, Oregon: Benedictine Press, 1972.

Schimberg, Albert Paul. *Tall in Paradise: The Story of Saint Coletta of Corbie.* Francestown, New Hampshire: Marshall Jones Company, 1947.

Schuster, O.S.B., His Eminence Ildephonse Cardinal. *Saint Benedict and His Times.* St. Louis, Missouri: B. Herder Book Company, 1947.

Sencourt, Robert. *Carmelite and Poet: A Framed Portrait of St. John of the Cross.* New York: The Macmillan Company, 1944.

Servite. *The White Doves of Peace.* Revised and edited by Rev. Joseph Cacella. New York: Vatican City Religious Book Company, Inc., 1949.

Sharp, Mary. *A Guide to the Churches of Rome.* New York: Chilton Books, 1966.

Sheppard, Lancelot C. *Don Bosco.* Westminster, Maryland: The Newman Press, 1957.

Sicardo, O.S.A., Fr. Joseph. *St. Rita of Cascia.* 1916; new ed. Rockford, Illinois: TAN, 1990.

Simi, Gino J. and Mario M. Segreti. *Saint Francis of Paola.* Rockford, Illinois: TAN, 1977.

Sister Mary Martha Chambon. Sisters of the Visitation, Trans. Montreal: Companions of Jesus and Mary, 1986.

Soeur Thérèse of Lisieux: The Little Flower of Jesus. T.N. Taylor, ed. New York: P. J. Kenedy & Sons, 1912.

Stanislaus of St. Theresa, O.C.D., Friar. *St. Theresa Margaret of the Sacred Heart of Jesus.* New York: Benziger Brothers, 1934.

Stoddard, Charles Warren. *Saint Anthony, The Wonder-Worker of Padua.* 1896; rpt. Rockford, Illinois:

TAN, 1971.

Tanquerey, The Very Rev. Adolphe. *The Spiritual Life: A Treatise on Ascetical and Mystical Theology.* Westminster, Maryland: The Newman Press, 1930.

Teresa of Avila, Saint. *The Collected Works of St. Teresa of Avila.* Volume Three. Translated by Kieran Kavanaugh, O.C.D. and Otilio Rodriguez, O.C.D. Washington, D. C.: Institute of Carmelite Studies, 1985.

—*The Life of Teresa of Jesus.* E. Allison Peers, Trans. Garden City, N.Y.: Image Books, 1960.

Teresa Margaret, D. C., Sister. *God Is Love—St. Teresa Margaret: Her Life.* Milwaukee, Wisconsin: Spiritual Life Press, 1964.

Thérèse of Lisieux. *Story of a Soul.* Washington, D. C.: ICS Publications, Institute of Carmelite Studies, 1975.

Thomas of Celano. *St. Francis of Assisi.* Chicago: Franciscan Herald Press, 1988.

Thompson, M. A., Edward Healey. *St. Stanislaus Kostka of the Company of Jesus.* Philadelphia: Peter F. Cunningham Catholic Bookseller, 1876.

Trochu, Abbe Francis. *The Curé D'Ars: St. Jean-Marie-Baptiste-Vianney.* 1927; rpt. Rockford, Illinois: TAN, 1977.

Thurston, S.J., Herbert. *Surprising Mystics.* Chicago: Henry Regnery Company, 1955.

—*The Physical Phenomena of Mysticism.* Chicago: Henry Regnery Company, 1952.

—*The Life of St. Hugh of Lincoln.* New York: Benziger Brothers, 1898.

Van Dyke, Paul. *Ignatius Loyola: The Founder of the Jesuits.* New York: Charles Scribner's Sons, 1926.

Van Speybrouck, Edward. *The Very Rev. Father Paul of Moll.* 1910; rpt. Rockford, Illinois: TAN, 1979.

Walsh, William Thomas. *Saint Teresa of Avila.* Milwaukee, Wisconsin: Bruce Publishing Company, 1943.

Woodward, Kenneth L. *Making Saints.* New York: Simon and Schuster, 1990.

Zimmerman, O.C.D., The Very Rev. Benedict. *The Life of St. Teresa of Jesus.* Westminster, Maryland: The Newman Press, 1948.

Zappuli, Caesare. *The Power of Goodness, The Life of Blessed Clelia Barbieri.* Boston: Daughters of St. Paul, 1980.

ABOUT THE AUTHOR

Joan Carroll Cruz is a native of New Orleans and was educated by the School Sisters of Notre Dame. She attended grade school, high school and college under their tutelage. About her teachers Mrs. Cruz says, "I am especially indebted to the sisters who taught me for five years at the boarding school at St. Mary of the Pines in Chatawa, Mississippi. I cannot thank them enough for their dedication, their fine example and their religious fervor, which made such an impression on me." Mrs. Cruz has been a tertiary in the Discalced Carmelite Secular Order (Third Order) for the past 28 years. She is married to Louis Cruz, who owns a swimming pool repair and maintenance business. They are the parents of five children.

Other books by Mrs. Cruz include *Miraculous Images of Our Lord, Miraculous Images of Our Lady, Prayers and Heavenly Promises, Secular Saints, The Incorruptibles* and *Eucharistic Miracles,* all published by TAN Books and Publishers, Inc.; *The Desires of Thy Heart,* a novel with a strong Catholic theme published in hardcover by Tandem Press in 1977 and in paperback by Signet with an initial printing of 600,000 copies; and *Relics,* published by Our Sunday Visitor, Inc. For her non-fiction books Mrs. Cruz depends heavily on information received from foreign shrines, churches, convents and monasteries. The material she receives requires the services of several translators. Mrs. Cruz is currently working on another book which also involves a great deal of research.

Spread the Faith with . . .

TAN·BOOKS

A Division of Saint Benedict Press, LLC

TAN books are powerful tools for evangelization. They lift the mind to God and change lives. Millions of readers have found in TAN books and booklets an effective way to teach and defend the Faith, soften hearts, and grow in prayer and holiness of life.

Throughout history the faithful have distributed Catholic literature and sacramentals to save souls. St. Francis de Sales passed out his own pamphlets to win back those who had abandoned the Faith. Countless others have distributed the Miraculous Medal to prompt conversions and inspire deeper devotion to God. Our customers use TAN books in that same spirit.

If you have been helped by this or another TAN title, share it with others. Become a TAN Missionary and share our life changing books and booklets with your family, friends and community. We'll help by providing special discounts for books and booklets purchased in quantity for purposes of evangelization. Write or call us for additional details.

TAN Books
Attn: TAN Missionaries Department
PO Box 410487
Charlotte, NC 28241

Toll-free (800) 437-5876
missionaries@TANBooks.com

TAN · BOOKS

TAN Books was founded in 1967 to preserve the spiritual, intellectual and liturgical traditions of the Catholic Church. At a critical moment in history TAN kept alive the great classics of the Faith and drew many to the Church. In 2008 TAN was acquired by Saint Benedict Press. Today TAN continues its mission to a new generation of readers.

From its earliest days TAN has published a range of booklets that teach and defend the Faith. Through partnerships with organizations, apostolates, and mission-minded individuals, well over 10 million TAN booklets have been distributed.

More recently, TAN has expanded its publishing with the launch of Catholic calendars and daily planners—as well as Bibles, fiction, and multimedia products through its sister imprints Catholic Courses (CatholicCourses.com) and Saint Benedict Press (SaintBenedictPress.com).

Today TAN publishes over 500 titles in the areas of theology, prayer, devotions, doctrine, Church history, and the lives of the saints. TAN books are published in multiple languages and found throughout the world in schools, parishes, bookstores and homes.

For a free catalog, visit us online at
TANBooks.com

Or call us toll-free at
(800) 437-5876

...tion can be obtained
...esting.com
...e USA
...508270121
...V00001B/17